☆

Interpretations of American History

PATTERNS AND PERSPECTIVES

VOLUME II: SINCE 1877

SIXTH EDITION

EDITED BY

Gerald N. Grob
George Athan Billias

THE FREE PRESS

New York London Toronto Sydney Tokyo Singapore

The Free Press
A Division of Simon & Schuster Inc.
1230 Avenue of the Americas
New York, N.Y. 10020

Printed in the United States of America

printing number
3 4 5 6 7 8 9 10

Library of Congress Cataloging-in-Publication Data

Interpretations of American history : patterns and perspectives /
  edited by Gerald N. Grob, George Athan Billias.—6th ed.
    p. cm.
  Includes indexes.
  Contents: v. 1. To 1877—v. 2. Since 1877.
  ISBN 0-02-912685-1 (v. 1):
  ISBN 0-02-912686-X (v. 2)
    1. United States—History. 2. United States—Historiography.
  I. Grob, Gerald N. II. Billias, George Athan.
  E178.6.I53 1992
  973–dc20   91-22263
                                                        CIP

For Joshua David Grob and Scott Athan Billias

CONTENTS

PREFACE TO THE SIXTH EDITION

We designed this two-volume book of readings to accompany American history survey courses. Reflecting our philosophy of teaching history, the choice of readings is based on four main assumptions. First, that the approach to history should be broadly conceptual and not narrowly factual. Second, that students should read both the most recent scholarship and older and more traditional interpretations. Third, that students should have available historiographical introductions to shed light on the readings. And lastly, that the readings themselves should be intellectually stimulating, rich in interpretation, and attractive in style.

To meet the challenge posed by our first assumption, we chose selections that are conceptual in character. In each case these selections represent an interpretation that illuminates a particular problem or period. Despite the different issues or eras presented, one theme emerges from all the selections: the view of American history is constantly changing.

Generally speaking, new interpretations appear for two reasons. First, the perspective of American historians of a given generation has been shaped in large measure by the sweep of events in the world outside the scholar's study. Scholars have tended to reflect in their writings, either explicitly or implicitly, the problems or predilections of the age in which they live. Each succeeding generation, therefore, has rewritten America's past, in part, to suit the felt needs of its own time. In our introductions we have sought to show how contemporary concerns of the age in which scholars wrote shaped their starting assumptions, gathering of evidence, and interpretation of events. From the 1960s to 1990, for example, the consciousness of many American historians was influenced by various social changes affecting racial minorities, women, ethnic groups, and social classes as well as by recent political, economic, and technological developments. It is not surprising, then, to find these same themes cropping up in the writings of recent scholars dealing with earlier periods of American history.

Secondly, the picture of America's past is constantly changing because of intellectual shifts within the historical profession itself. These changes have taken place inside the scholar's study, so to speak.

History, like most academic disciplines, has developed a built-in tendency toward self-generating change. When scholars sense they have reached the outermost limits in applying what has become an accepted interpretation, they do one of two things: they either introduce major revisions to correct the prevailing point of view, or they abandon it altogether and strike off in new directions. Some selections represent the writings of scholars seeking to revise existing interpretations. Other readings, however, reflect the work of a generation of younger scholars who wrote over the past three decades what has been called the "new history." The "new history" as will be shown in the text, differed from the "old," and superseded it.

To address ourselves to the third assumption and to answer the needs of students, we have written chapter-length introductions. These introductions will enable students to approach the selections with greater ease because they provide a historiographical background. In that historiography we have identified certain "schools" of historians, and in doing so have sometimes placed scholars within them in an admittedly arbitrary manner.

Finally, we sought historians who write with a distinctive literary flair. Much of the most exciting work in American history has been done by scholars who have a lively writing style and present their findings in spirited prose. Students will discover how stimulating history can be when they read in these pages the selections written by superb stylists like Perry Miller, Bernard Bailyn, Gordon S. Wood, Joyce Appleby, Arthur M. Schlesinger, Jr., John Hope Franklin, Gerda Lerner, Nathan I. Huggins, Eric Foner, and John A. Garraty, among others.

The preparation of a work of this kind becomes a cooperative enterprise. We are grateful to many who helped us in different ways during the quarter century this work has been in print.

First and foremost, we thank those scholars who granted permission to reprint the selections. Without their cooperation, the six editions we have prepared would not have been possible.

We also wish to thank fellow scholars who made helpful comments, suggestions, and criticisms in previous editions: my colleagues at Clark University, Paul Lucas and Daniel R. Borg; Ronald A. Petrin, Oklahoma State University; Milton M. Klein, professor emeritus, University of Tennessee; Francis G. Couvares, Amherst College; Ronald P. Formisano, University of Florida, Gainesville; Nancy Cott, Yale University; Peter S. Onuf, University of Virginia; the late Nathan I. Huggins of Harvard University; Robert Kolesar, John Carroll University; Sidney Hart, National Portrait Gallery; and Gordon Marshall, Library Company of Philadelphia.

Joyce Seltzer and the late Harry McConnell of The Free Press were helpful and encouraging editors over the years.

For this sixth edition we thank colleagues who read chapters in which they were experts and saved us from errors. At Clark University, Drew R. McCoy read the chapters on the Revolution, Constitution, and Federal Era; Jacqueline Goggin on Black History Since 1865; Sarah Deutsch and Deborah Gray on Women in History; and Douglas Little on the chapter on the 1980s. Colleagues at other institutions also contributed criticisms: Ronald A. Petrin, Milton M. Klein, Robert Kolesar, and Martin Ridge at the Huntington Library on the chapter on the 1980s; Barbara Lacey of St. Joseph College on Women in History; James Hoopes of Babson College on the Puritans; and Peter S. Onuf of the University of Virginia on the Introduction.

Members of the Clark community contributed greatly in preparing this sixth edition. Mary Hartman, Irene Walch, and Edward McDermott, reference librarians at the Robert Hutchings Goddard Library went beyond the bounds of professional duty in responding to calls for help. Susan Baughman, Librarian, kindly extended numerous courtesies. Rene Baril, once again, provided her accurate typing skills. Trudy Powers, secretary of the History Department, also assisted in many ways.

We owe a special debt of gratitude to our generous wives—Lila K. Grob and Margaret Rose Billias—whose love, cheerfulness, and moral support were so absolutely essential to this enterprise.

Last, but most importantly, we dedicate these volumes to our grandsons—Joshua David Grob and Scott Athan Billias—in the hope they will live in a better America, a more just society, and a safer world.

☆ 1 ☆

Introduction

"Every true history is contemporary history." Thus wrote Benedetto Croce, the great Italian philosopher and historian, over a half century ago. By his remark Croce meant that history—as distinguished from mere chronicle—was meaningful only to the degree it struck a responsive chord in the minds of contemporaries who saw mirrored in the past the problems and issues of the present.

Croce's remark has special relevance to the writing of American history. Every generation of American scholars has reinterpreted the past in terms of its own age. Why is this so? One compelling reason, no doubt, has been the constant tendency of scholars to reexamine the past in light of the prevailing ideas, assumptions, and problems of their own day. Every age has developed its own climate of opinion—or particular view of the world—which, in turn, has partially conditioned the way it looks upon its own past and present. Thus, each succeeding generation of Americans has rewritten the history of the country in such a way as to suit its own self-image. Although there were other reasons for this continual reinterpretation of American history, the changing climate of opinion more than any other single factor caused historians to recast periodically their view of the past.

Changing interpretations arose also from the changing nature of American historians and their approach to the discipline. The writing of history in America, broadly speaking, has gone through three distinct stages. In the first stage—the era of Puritan historians during the seventeenth century—historical writing was dominated by ministers and political leaders of the Puritan colonies who sought to express the religious justification for their New World settlements. The second stage—the period of the patrician historians—saw the best history being written by members of the patrician class from the early eighteenth century to the late nineteenth century. Patrician historians—often gentlemen of leisure with private incomes—normally had little

1

or no connection with the church or other formal institutions, as had the Puritan historians. They were stirred to write history by a strong sense of social responsibility that characterized the class from which they sprang, and by a personal conviction that each individual had a moral obligation to employ his best talents for the betterment of humankind. Their works, as a general rule, reflected the ideology and preconceptions of their class. Although they were amateur scholars for the most part, many patrician writers succeeded in reaching a high level of literary distinction and accuracy. The third stage—the period of the professional scholars—began during the 1870s and may properly be called "the age of the professional historians." These scholars qualified as professionals on several counts: they were specifically trained for their craft; they supported themselves by full-time careers of teaching, writing, and research at colleges and universities; and they looked to their professional group to set the standards of achievement by which historical studies were evaluated. Their work has been characterized by constant revisionism: they attempted to correct one another, to challenge traditional interpretations, and to approach old historical problems from new points of view.[1]

During each of these three stages of historical writing, the intellectual milieu in America was distinctly different. In the seventeenth century the best histories were written by Puritan ministers and magistrates who saw history as the working out of God's will. Theirs was a Christian interpretation of history—one in which events were seen as the unfolding of God's intention and design. Borrowing the concept of a Chosen People from the ancient Hebrews, they viewed the colonization of America in Biblical terms. They cast the Puritans in the same role as the Jews in the Old Testament—as a regenerate people who were destined to fulfill God's purpose. New England became for them New Canaan—the place God had set apart for man to achieve a better way of Christian living. Massachusetts, therefore, was more than simply another colony. In the words of John Winthrop, it was to be a "city upon a hill"—a model utopia to demonstrate to the rest of the world that the City of God could be established on earth along the lines set forth in the New Testament.

The major theme of most Puritan historians, whether they were ministers or lay leaders, was the same: to demonstrate God's special concern for His Chosen People in their efforts to build a New Canaan. New England's history served their purposes best because it was here that God's mercy could be seen more clearly than in any other part of the globe. To the Puritans, New England's history was one long record of the revelation of God's providence toward His people. Their disasters as well as their triumphs were seen only in relation to God, and

---

[1]John Higham *et al.*, *History* (Englewood Cliffs, N.J., 1965), pp. 3–5.

the setbacks they suffered were viewed as evidence of God's wrath and displeasure.

Of all the Puritan histories, William Bradford's *Of Plimouth Plantation* was, perhaps, the preeminent work of art. Written in the 1630s and 1640s while Bradford was governor of the colony, this book recounted the tale of the tiny band of Pilgrims who fled first to Holland and then to the New World. No other narrative captured so perfectly the deep feeling of religious faith of New England's early settlers. None illustrated better the Puritan ideal of a plain and simple literary style, or mastered so well the rhythms of Biblical prose. Yet like most Puritan literature it was written during the few spare moments that Bradford could find from his more important activities as a governor of a new community in the wilderness.

The patrician historians of the eighteenth century replaced the Puritan historians when the church ceased to be the intellectual center of American life. The Christian theory of history with its emphasis on supernatural causes increasingly gave way to a more secular interpretation based upon the concepts of human progress, reason, and material well-being. Influenced by European Enlightenment thinkers, American historians came to believe that humans, by use of their reason, could control their destiny and determine their own material and intellectual progress in the world.

The patrician historians were profoundly influenced also by ideas derived from the writings of Sir Isaac Newton. This seventeenth-century English scientist, by applying a rational, mathematical method, had arrived at certain truths, or "natural laws," concerning the physical universe. Newton's systematization of scientific thought led many men to conclude that the same mathematical-scientific method could be employed to formulate similar natural laws in other fields. In order to develop a theory of history in keeping with Newtonian thought, writers began to postulate certain natural laws in the field of history. Thus, patrician historians abandoned the Christian theory in which God determined the events for a view of the universe in which natural laws were the motivating forces in history.

This shift from a Christian interpretation of history to a more secular approach was reflected in the change of leaders among American historians. Minister-historians were increasingly replaced by members of the patrician class—political leaders, planter-aristocrats, merchants, lawyers, and doctors.[2] In the eighteenth century, for example, America's outstanding historians included Thomas Hutchinson, member of the Massachusetts merchant aristocracy and royal governor of that colony; William Smith of New York, doctor, landowner, and lieutenant governor of that colony; and Robert Beverley and William Byrd of Vir-

---

[2]Harvey Wish, *The American Historian* (New York, 1960), p. 25.

ginia, who were planter-aristocrats, large landowners, and officeholders. Most of these men possessed a classical education, a fine private
library, and the leisure time in which to write. With the growth of
private wealth and the opening up of new economic opportunities,
more members of the upper classes were in a position to take up the
writing of history as an avocation.[3]

The reaction against the Christian interpretation of history was
particularly evident in the writings of Thomas Jefferson. In his *Notes
on the State of Virginia*, first published in 1785, Jefferson stressed reason and natural law instead of divine providence as the basis for historical causation. Jefferson believed also that men were motivated by self-
interest, and he employed this concept as one means of analyzing the
course of historical events. As he wrote in his history of Virginia,
"Mankind soon learn to make interested uses of every right and power
which they possess, or may assume."

Jefferson's history showed the impact of yet another major influence—nationalism—which affected historical writing after 1776. As
author of the Declaration of Independence, Jefferson felt a fierce, patriotic pride in the free institutions that emerged from the Revolution.
He was convinced that America as a democratic nation was destined
to pave the way for a new era in world history. A whole new generation
of patrician historians sprang up after the Revolution, writing in a similar nationalistic vein—David Ramsay, Mercy Otis Warren, Jeremy
Belknap, and Jared Sparks. They likewise contrasted America's free institutions with what they considered to be Europe's corrupt and decadent institutions.

During the first three quarters of the nineteenth century, the writing of history continued to be dominated by patrician historians. The
influence of the romantic movement in the arts with its heightened
appreciation of the past, emphasis upon pictorial descriptions, and
stress upon the role of great men, caused history to be viewed increasingly as a branch of literature. Many outstanding literary figures—
Washington Irving, Francis Parkman, Richard Hildreth, William H.
Prescott, and John Lothrop Motley—wrote narrative histories about
America, other lands, and other times, in a romantic style calculated
to appeal to a wide reading public. Such authors were often part of
an Anglo-American literary culture, for many English historians were
writing in the same vein.

America's patrician historians, however, were not always content
to provide only a colorful narrative. Writing within a developmental
framework, they sought to reveal some of the underlying principles
which they believed lay behind the rational evolution of historical
events. For the most part, their writings reflected certain assumptions

[3]Higham, *History*, p. 3.

that were common to many historians on both sides of the Atlantic in the first half of the nineteenth century—the idea that history was essentially the story of liberty; that the record of the human race revealed a progressive advance toward greater human rights down through the ages; and that peoples of Anglo-Saxon origin had a special destiny to bring democracy to the rest of the world.

Many of these American historians, influenced by the pronounced nationalism of the period, used such broad assumptions within a chauvinistic framework. They felt a responsibility to help establish the national identity of the new United States. Thus, they employed history as a didactic tool to instruct their countrymen along patriotic lines and presented America's story in the best light possible. Running through their writings were three basic themes: the idea of progress—that the story of America was one of continuous progress onward and upward toward greatness; the idea of liberty—that American history, in essence, symbolized the trend toward greater liberty in world history; and the idea of mission—that the United States had a special destiny to serve as a model of a free people to the rest of humankind in leading the way to a more perfect life. The last theme, in effect, was nothing more than a restatement of the idea of mission first set forth by the Puritan historians.

George Bancroft, the most distinguished historian of the mid-nineteenth century, organized his history of the United States around these three themes. After studying in Germany in the 1820s, Bancroft returned to America determined to apply Teutonic ideas of history to the story of his own country. Bancroft believed in the progressive unfolding of all human history toward a future golden age in which all peoples would eventually achieve complete freedom and liberty. This march of all humankind toward a greater freedom was in accordance with a preordained plan conceived by God. One phase of God's master plan could be seen in the way that a superior Anglo-Saxon people developed a distinctive set of democratic institutions. The United States, according to Bancroft, represented the finest flowering of such democratic institutions. American democracy, then, was the fruition of God's plan, and the American people had a unique mission in history to spread democracy throughout the rest of the world. Such was the central theme of Bancroft's famous twelve-volume work, *History of the United States from the Discovery of the American Continent*, written between 1834 and 1882.

Francis Parkman, a patrician historian from New England, held many views similar to those of Bancroft. Writing about the intercolonial wars in his *France and England in North America*, Parkman portrayed the American colonists as democratic Anglo-Saxons of Protestant persuasion whose superior qualities enabled them to conquer authoritarian-minded French Catholics in Canada. But in many other ways the two writers were quite different. Parkman was more representative of the gentlemen-historians of the nineteenth century who, being drawn from the upper classes, usually reflected an aristocratic bias in their writings, advocated a conservative Whig philosophy, and were distrustful of the American masses. Bancroft, on the other hand, eulogized the common man and was a Jacksonian in politics; his history was distinctly democratic in outlook.

By the 1870s two profound changes began to influence the writing of American history. The first was the change in leadership from amateur patricians to professional historians. Until the last quarter of the nineteenth century, American history had been written almost exclusively by men who had received no special training as historians—except, of course, for a few individuals like Bancroft. From this point on, however, the writing of history was dominated by professionally trained scholars educated in the universities of America and Europe. Professionalization in the field was made possible by developments in higher education as graduate schools appeared in increasing numbers in America to train college history teachers. In the last three decades of the century, this trend proceeded at a rapid rate: the Johns Hopkins University, the first institution devoted to graduate study and research, began its activities in 1876; the American Historical Association was founded in 1884; and the *American Historical Review* made its appearance in 1895.

The advent of professional historians brought about a marked transformation in the field. No longer was historical writing to be vested mainly in the hands of amateurs—though it should be emphasized that many patrician historians had been superb stylists, creative scholars, and researchers who made judicious use of original sources. Nor would historians be drawn almost exclusively from the patrician class in the Northeast, particularly from New England. Professional scholars came from all walks of life, represented a much broader range of social interests than the patricians, and hailed from different geographic regions. Finally, instead of being free-lance writers, as many patricians had been, professionals made their living as teachings in colleges and universities.

The second major development affecting the writing of American history was the emergence of a new intellectual milieu that reflected the growing dominance of novel scientific ideas and concepts. Influenced by Darwinian biology and its findings in the natural sciences, historians began to think of history as a science rather than as a branch of literature. Why couldn't the historian deal with the facts of history in much the same way that the scientist did with elements in the laboratory? If there were certain laws of organic development in the scientific field, might there not be certain laws of historical development? What historian, wrote Henry Adams, with "an idea of scientific method can have helped dreaming of the immortality that would be achieved by the man who should successfully apply Darwin's method to the facts of human history?"[4]

The first generation of professional historians—who held sway from about 1870 to 1910—was best exemplified by two outstanding scholars, Henry Adams and Frederick Jackson Turner. Henry Adams, a descendant of the famous Adams family that contributed American presidents, statesmen, and diplomats, turned to history and literature as his avocation after his hopes for high political office were dashed. In 1870 he was invited to Harvard and became the first teacher to introduce a history seminar at that institution. Adams pioneered in training his students in the meticulous critical methods of German scholarship, and searched for a time for a scientific philosophy of history based on the findings in the field of physics. His nine-volume history of the United States during the administrations of Jefferson and Madison was destined to become one of the classics of American historical literature. Although he left Harvard after a few years, his career symbolized the transformation from patrician to professional historian and the changing intellectual climate from romanticism to a more scientific approach in the writing of American history.

While Henry Adams was attempting to assimilate history and physics, Frederick Jackson Turner—perhaps the most famous and influential representative of the scientific school of historians in the first generation of professional historians—was applying evolutionary modes of thought to explain American history. Born and reared in a frontier community in Wisconsin, Turner attended the University of Wisconsin, received his Ph.D. from the Johns Hopkins University, and then went on to a teaching career first at Wisconsin and later at Harvard. Like Adams, Turner believed that it was possible to make a science out of history; he attempted, therefore, to apply the ideas of Darwinian evolution to the writing of history. Turner emphasized the concept of evolutionary stages of development as successive frontier environments in America wrought changes in the character of the people and their institutions. As one frontier in America succeeded another, each more remote from Europe than its predecessor, a social evolutionary process was at work creating a democratic American individualist. The unique characteristics of the American people—their rugged individualism, egalitarianism, practicality, and materialistic outlook on life—all resulted from the evolutionary process of adapting to successive frontier environments. Turner's famous essay, "The Significance of the Frontier in American History," written in 1893, re-

---

[4]Henry Adams, "The Tendency of History," *Annual Report of the American Historical Association for the Year 1894* (Washington, D.C., 1895), p. 19.

mains a superb statement of one approach that was employed by the scientific school of historians.

Between 1910 and 1945 a second generation of professional scholars—the Progressive historians—came to maturity and helped to transform the discipline by introducing new ideas and methodologies. Many of them were influenced by the Progressive movement of the early 1900s—a period when the future of American democracy appeared to be threatened by new economic and social forces arising from the rapid industrialization of American society. Rejecting the views of the older and more conservative patrician historians, the Progressive scholars viewed history as an ideological weapon that might explain the present and perhaps help to control the future. In sympathy with the aims and objectives of the Progressive movement between 1900 and 1920, these scholars continued to write history from a Progressive point of view even after the decline of the Progressive movement following World War I.

Unlike the New England patrician historians of the nineteenth century, the Progressive scholars tended to hail more from the Midwest and South. These Progressives complained that in the past American history had been presented mainly as an extension of the history of New England. American civilization, they argued, was more than a transplanted English and European civilization that had spread out from New England; it had unique characteristics and a mission all its own. But while the Progressive historians were as nationalistic as the patrician school, their nationalism was different in nature. The patricians had conceived of nationalism as a stabilizing force, preserving order and thus assuring the continued ascendancy of the aristocratic element in American life. The Progressives, on the other hand, considered nationalism a dynamic force. To them the fulfillment of democracy meant a continued and protracted struggle against those individuals, classes, and groups who had barred the way to the achievement of a more democratic society in the past.

In changing the direction of American historical writing, Progressive scholars drew upon the reform tradition that had grown out of the effort to adjust American society to the new demands of an urban-centered and industrialized age. This tradition had originated in the 1890s and reached maturity in the early part of the twentieth century with the Progressive movement. Drawing upon various sources, the adherents of the Progressive movement rejected the idea of a closed system of classical economic thought which assumed that certain natural laws governed human society. Society, these reformers maintained, was open-ended and dynamic; its development was determined not by immutable laws, but by economic and social forces that grew out of the interaction between individuals and their environment.

Reacting against the older emphasis upon logic, abstraction, and deduction, these reformers sought a meaningful explanation of human society that could account for its peculiar development. Instead of focusing upon immutable laws, they began viewing society and individuals as products of an evolutionary developmental process. This process could be understood only by reference to the past. The function of the historian, then, was to explain how the present had come to be, and then to try and set guidelines for future developments. As a result of this approach, history and the other social sciences drew together, seeking to explain the realities of social life by emphasizing the interplay of economic, technological, social, psychological, and political forces.

History, according to its Progressive practitioners, was not an abstract discipline whose truths could only be contemplated. On the contrary, historians had important activist roles to play in the construction of a better world. By explaining the historical roots of contemporary problems, historians could provide the knowledge and understanding necessary to make changes which would bring further progress. Like the Enlightenment *philosophes,* historians could reveal prior mistakes and errors and thus liberate men from the chains of tyranny and oppression of the past. When fused with the social sciences history could become a powerful tool for reform. "The present has hitherto been the willing victim of the past," wrote James Harvey Robinson, one of the greatest exponents of Progressive history; but "the time has now come when it should turn on the past and exploit it in the interests of advance."[5]

Clearly, the sympathy of this school lay with change and not with the preservation of the status quo. Committed to the idea of progress, they saw themselves as contributing to a better and more humane world for the future. Consequently they rejected the apparent moral neutrality and supposed objectivity of the scientific school in favor of a liberal philosophy of reform. In so doing they rewrote much of American history, greatly widening its scope and changing its emphasis. Instead of focusing on narrow institutional studies of traditional political, diplomatic, and military history, they sought to delineate those determinant forces that underlay human institutions. In their hands American history became a picture of conflict—conflict between polarities of American life: aristocracy versus democracy; economic "haves" versus "have-nots"; politically overprivileged groups versus those underprivileged; and between geographical sections, as the East versus West. In short, the divisions were between those dedicated to democratic and egalitarian ideals and those committed to a static conservatism.

---

[5]James Harvey Robinson, "The New History," *The New History: Essays Illustrating the Modern Historical Outlook* (New York, 1912), p. 24.

Believers in inevitable progress, the Progressive historians assumed that America was continually moving on an upward path
toward an ideal social order. Not only was American society growing
in affluence, but in freedom, opportunity, and happiness as well. The
primary determinant of progress was the unending conflict between
the forces of liberalism and those of conservatism. Thus all periods in
American history could be divided into two clear and distinct phases:
periods of active reform and periods of conservative reaction. As
Arthur M. Schlesinger, Sr., wrote in 1939: "A period of concern for the
rights of the few has been followed by one of concern for the wrongs
of the many."[6]

Turner, a transitional figure between the scientific and Progressive
historians, with Charles A. Beard and Vernon L. Parrington, best presented the Progressive point of view. After his epochal essay on the
frontier in 1893—an essay that emphasized unity rather than conflict—Turner's interest turned elsewhere, particularly to the idea of
sectional conflict. From the late 1890s until his death in 1932, he elaborated and refined his sectional conflict hypothesis. Turner and his students attempted to understand not only how a section came into being,
but also the dynamics of conflict that pitted the East against West,
North against South, labor against capital, and the many against the
few. Under Turner's guiding hand American scholars wrote a series of
brilliant monographs as well as broad interpretive studies that emphasized the class and sectional divisions in American society. Although
a few favored the conservative side, the overwhelming majority of historians made clear their preference for democratic liberalism and progress.

While Turner was developing and elaborating his sectional approach, Charles A. Beard was applying the hypothesis of an overt class
conflict to the study of American institutions. His *An Economic Interpretation of the Constitution*, written in 1913, was perhaps the most
influential historical work of the twentieth century. Beard attempted
to demonstrate that the Constitution, far from representing a judicious
combination of wisdom and idealism, was actually the product of a
small group of propertied individuals who were intent upon establishing a strong central government capable of protecting their interests
against the encroachments of the American masses. In a series of
books climaxed by *The Rise of American Civilization* in 1927, Beard
argued that American history demonstrated the validity of the class
conflict hypothesis between "haves" and "have-nots." Time and again,
he showed the paramount role that economic factors played in determining human behavior. Fusing his ardent faith in progress with a

---

[6]Arthur M. Schlesinger, Sr., "Tides of American Politics," *Yale Review* 29 (December 1939):220.

qualified economic determinism, Beard made clear that his sympathies lay with the forces of democracy as opposed to those of reaction
and privilege.

The culmination of the Progressive interpretation came with the
publication of Vernon L. Parrington's *Main Currents in American
Thought*. Using literature as his vehicle, Parrington portrayed American history in clear and unmistakable terms. The two central protagonists of Parrington's work were Jefferson and Hamilton. Jefferson stood
for a decentralized agrarian democracy that drew its support from the
great masses of people. Hamilton, on the other hand, represented a
privileged and aristocratic minority seeking to maintain its dominant
position. American history, according to Parrington, had witnessed a
continual struggle between the liberal Jeffersonian tradition and the
conservative Hamiltonian one. Underlying Parrington's approach was
one major assumption that had also governed the thought of Turner
and Beard: that ideology was determined by the materialistic forces in
history. Like Turner and Beard, Parrington clearly preferred the forces
of reform and democracy, but there were times when he was much less
certain of their eventual triumph than his two intellectual compan-
ions.

The Progressive point of view generally dominated the field of
American historical scholarship down to the end of World War II.
Class and sectional conflict, Progressive historians implied, was a
guarantor of progress. Even during those eras in American history
when the forces of reaction triumphed—as in the post-Civil War period—their victory was only temporary; ultimately the forces of progress and good regrouped and thereby gained the initiative once again.
Such an approach, of course, led to broad and sweeping interpretive
syntheses of American history, for the basic framework or structure
was clear and simple, and the faith of historians in the ultimate triumph of good over evil remained unquestioned.

Beginning in the 1930s, however, some American scholars began
to question the idea of progress that was implicit in this view. The rise
of Nazism in the 1930s and 1940s, and the menace of communism in
the 1950s and 1960s, led to a questioning of older assumptions and
generalities. How, some asked, could one subscribe to the optimistic
tenets of liberalism after the horrors of Auschwitz, Buchenwald, Hiroshima, Nagasaki, and the threat of modern totalitarianism? Indeed,
had not American historians, through their own optimistic view of
history and their faith in progress, failed to prepare the American
people for the challenges and trials that they would face during the
middle of the twentieth century? Parrington himself had recognized as
early as 1929 that the Progressive faith was under attack by those who
did not subscribe to its basic tenets. "Liberals whose hair is growing
thin and the lines of whose figures are no longer what they were," he

wrote, "are likely to find themselves today in the unhappy predicament of being treated as mourners at their own funerals. When they
pluck up heart to assert that they are not yet authentic corpses, but
living men with brains in their heads, they are pretty certain to be
gently chided and led back to the comfortable armchair that befits se-
nility. Their counsel is smiled at as the chatter of a belated post-
Victorian generation that knew not Freud, and if they must go abroad
they are bidden take the air in the garden where other old-fashioned
plants—mostly of the family *Democratici*—are still preserved."[7]

Following the end of World War II, a third generation of professional historians appeared on the scene to challenge the Progressive
point of view. They were sometimes called neoconservatives because
they seemed to hark back to the conservative historical position that
had prevailed prior to Turner and Beard. Their rise was partly a result
of pressures—both external and internal—upon the historical profession in the postwar era.

External pressures resulting from changing political conditions in
the world at large brought about a major change in the mood of many
Americans. Some neoconservative historians reflected, either consciously or unconsciously, an outlook that prevailed in the United
States as the nation assumed the sober responsibility of defending the
world against the threat of communism. During the Cold War era,
when the country felt its security endangered from abroad, these
scholars wanted, perhaps, to present an image to the rest of the world
of an America that had been strong and united throughout most of its
history. Hence, the neoconservative scholars pictured American history in terms of consensus rather than conflict.

Internal pressures within the profession itself likewise brought
changes. Particular points of view expressed in any academic discipline
seem to have an inner dynamism of their own. After subscribing to a
given interpretation for a time, scholars often sense that they have
pushed an idea to its outermost limits and can go no farther without
risking major distortion. A reaction inevitably sets in, and revisionists
began working in a different direction. Such was the case of the Progressive interpretation of history. Having written about American history from the standpoint of conflict and discontinuity, scholars now
began to approach the same subject from an opposite point of view—
that of consensus and continuity.

One way this new group of scholars differed from the Progressives
was in their inherent conservatism. Progressive historians had had a
deep belief in the idea of progress. Neoconservative historians, on the

---

[7]Vernon L. Parrington, *Main Currents in American Thought*, 3 vols. (New York,
1927–1930), 3:401.

other hand, often rejected progress as an article of faith. Skeptical of the alleged beneficial results of rapid social change, they stressed instead the thesis of historical continuity.

Given their emphasis on continuity the neoconservatives were less prone to a periodized view of American history. Progressive scholars had seen American history in terms of class or sectional conflicts marked by clearly defined turning points—the Revolution, the Constitution, the Jeffersonian era, the Jacksonian period, the Civil War, and so forth. These periods represented breaks, or discontinuities, from what had gone on before. For the Progressives, American history was divided into two distinct phases that followed one another in a cyclical pattern: periods of reform or revolution when the popular and democratic forces in society gained the upper hand and forced social changes, and periods of reaction and counterrevolution, when vested interests resisted such changes. For the neoconservative scholars, however, the enduring and unifying themes in history were much more significant. To them the continuity of common principles in American culture, the stability and longevity of institutions, and the persistence of certain traits and traditions in the American national character represented the most powerful forces in history.

Consensus, as well as continuity, was a characteristic theme of the neoconservative historians. Unlike the Progressives, who wrote about the past in terms of polarities—class conflicts between rich and poor, sectional divisions between North and South or East and West, and ideological differences between liberals and conservatives—the neoconservatives abandoned the conflict interpretation of history and favored instead one that viewed American society as stable and homogeneous. The cement that bound American society together throughout most of its history was a widespread acceptance of certain principles and beliefs. Americans, despite their differences, had always agreed on the following propositions: the right of all persons in society to own private property; the theory that the power of government should always be limited; the concept that men possessed certain natural rights that could not be taken from them by government; and the idea of some form of natural law.

One of the foremost neoconservative historians writing in the 1950s was Louis Hartz. In *The Liberal Tradition in America*, Hartz took issue with those Progressive historians who had viewed the American Revolution as a radical movement that fundamentally transformed American society. America had come into being after the age of feudalism, Hartz claimed, and this condition had profoundly shaped its development. Lacking a feudal past, the country did not have to contend with the established feudal structure that characterized the *ancien régime* in Europe—a titled aristocracy, national church, national army, and the like. Hence, America was "born free" and did not require a radical social revolution to become a liberal society—it was one already. What emerged in America, according to Hartz, was a unique society characterized by a consensus upon a single tradition of thought—the liberal tradition. The absence of a feudal heritage enabled the liberal-bourgeois ideas embodied in the political principles derived from John Locke to flourish in America almost unchallenged. "The ironic flaw in American liberalism," wrote Hartz, "lies in the fact that we have never had a conservative tradition."[8]

What, then, of the "conservatives" in American history about whom the Progressive scholars had written? When viewed within the context of comparative history, Hartz said, American conservatives had much more in common with their fellow American liberals than with their European counterparts. Many of the presumed differences between so-called American conservatives and liberals was in the nature of shadowboxing rather than actual fighting, he concluded, because both groups agreed on a common body of liberal political principles. The Federalists, for example, were not aristocrats but whiggish liberals who misunderstood their society—they misread the Jeffersonian Democrats as being "radicals" rather than recognizing them as fellow liberals. What was true of the Federalists and Jeffersonians held for the other political confrontations in American history; if measured in terms of a spectrum of thought that included European ideologies, the American conflicts took place within the confines of a Lockean consensus.

Daniel J. Boorstin, another major neoconservative historian, also offered a grand theory which pictured American history in terms of continuity and consensus. Boorstin, like Hartz, stressed the uniqueness of American society, but he attributed this development to other causes. A neo-Turnerian, Boorstin postulated an environmental explanation of the American national character. To him the frontier experience was the source of America's conservatism.

In two books written in the 1950s—*The Genius of American Politics* and *The Americans: The Colonial Experience*—Boorstin denied the significance of European influences and ideas upon American life. Boorstin's premise was that the Americans were not an "idea-centered" people. From the very beginning Americans had abandoned European political theories, European blueprints for utopian societies, and European concepts of class distinctions. Americans concerned themselves instead with concrete situations and the practical problems experienced by their frontier communities. Thus they developed little knack for theorizing or any deep interest in theories as such. The "genius of American politics" lay in its emphasis on pragmatic mat-

---

[8]Louis Hartz, *The Liberal Tradition in America* (New York, 1955), p. 57.

ters—its very distrust of theories that had led to radical political changes and deep divisions within European societies.[9]

The American way of life which evolved during the colonial period, wrote Boorstin, set the pattern for the nation's later development. That pattern placed a premium on solutions to practical problems, adaptations to changing circumstances, and improvisations based upon pragmatic considerations. Lacking a learned class or professional traditions, the colonists were forced to create their own ways of doing things in the areas of education, law, medicine, science, diplomacy, and warfare. During this process the "doer" dominated over the "thinker" and the generalist over the specialist. Over the course of time this nontheoretical approach developed into a distinctive American life-style—one characterized by a naive practicality that enabled Americans to unite in a stable way of life and to become a homogeneous society made up of undifferentiated men sharing the same values.

The "cult of the 'American Consensus,'" as one scholar called it, made the nation's past appear tame and placid; it was no longer a history marked by extreme group conflicts or rigid class distinctions.[10] The heroes in America's past—Jefferson, Lincoln, Wilson, and Franklin D. Roosevelt—became less heroic because there occurred no head-on clash between individuals on the basis of ideology since all Americans shared the same middle-class Lockean values. Conversely, the old villains—Hamilton, Rockefeller, and Carnegie—became less evil and were portrayed as constructive figures who contributed much to their country. The achievements of the business community in particular were glorified. Without the material achievements of American entrepreneurs, according to some scholars, the United States could not have withstood the challenges to democracy during World War I and World War II. The underdogs in American history—the reformers, radicals, and working class—were presented as being less idealistic and more egocentric as neoconservative scholars sought to demonstrate that the ideology of these elements in society was no less narrow and self-centered than that of other elements. The "cult" of the neoconservatives continued into the 1960s—though "cult" was perhaps too strong a term, and implied a unanimity rarely found in the historical profession.

Besides Boorstin and Hartz, other neoconservative scholars published specialized studies which revised the Progressive point of view

---

[9]Daniel J. Boorstin, *The Genius of American Politics* (Chicago, 1953), and *The Americans: The Colonial Experience* (New York, 1958). Boorstin further elaborated on his views in two more volumes: *The Americans: the National Experience* (New York, 1965), and *The Americans: The Democratic Experience* (New York, 1973).

[10]John Higham, "The Cult of the 'American Consensus': Homogenizing Our History," *Commentary* 27 (February 1959): 93–100.

in virtually every period of American history. The neoconservative trend, marked by a new respect for tradition and a de-emphasis on class conflict, brought many changes in American historiography: the revival of a sympathetic approach to the Puritans; the treatment of the American Revolution as a conservative movement of less significance; the conclusion that the Constitution was a document faithfully reflecting a middle-class consensus; the favorable, if not uncritical, attitude toward the founding fathers of the new republic; the diminution of the traditional ideological differences between Hamiltonianism and Jeffersonianism; the consensus interpretation of the Jacksonian era; the enhanced reputation of America's business tycoons; a renewed appreciation of such controversial political leaders as Theodore Roosevelt; the inclination to play down the more radical aspects of the Progressive and New Deal periods; the predisposition to support the correctness of America's recent foreign policy; and the tendency to view American society as being satisfied, unified, and stable throughout most of the nation's history. Implicit in the neoconservative approach was a fear of extremism, a yearning to prove that national unity had almost always existed, and a longing for the security and way of life America presumably had enjoyed before becoming a superpower and leader of the free world.

During the decades of the 1960s and 1970s the assumptions and conclusions of the neoconservative historians were rudely overturned by two major developments. First, the mood of the American people shifted markedly as the seemingly placid decade of the 1950s was succeeded by tumultuous events in America's foreign and domestic affairs. Second, within the historical profession itself a reaction to the neoconservative point of view led to the rise of many revisionist interpretations. The result was a pronounced fragmentation in the field of American historiography.

The prevailing mood among the American people shifted dramatically in the 1960s and 1970s because of a series of shattering events on the domestic scene. Gone were the complacency, national self-confidence, optimism, and moral composure that seemed to have characterized the 1950s. Many historians were stirred by the great social upheavals that undermined previously held assumptions. A marked trend toward racial divisions within American society appeared with the newfound militancy among blacks during the civil rights movement. The resulting hostility to integration among many whites showed that American society was hardly as homogeneous as had been previously believed. At the same time, an increased tendency toward violence during the urban riots in the 1960s indicated that Americans were not always committed to the idea of peaceful compromise. President Kennedy's assassination in 1963 followed by that of Martin Luther King and Robert Kennedy revealed that the United States was as vulnerable to political terrorism as other societies. There was also a renewed awareness of poverty with the economic downturn in the 1970s, and some scholars began voicing doubts about the supposed social mobility within American society, the virtues of technological change, and the benefits of economic growth.

The appearance of numerous social-protest movements during those two decades also made many American historians more conscious of the importance of minority groups in the nation's past. Having witnessed protest movements by the blacks, the poor, and the women's liberation movement, some scholars took a greater interest in black history, women's history, and in protest groups like the Populists and IWW. Generally speaking, historians became more sympathetic to the role of the underdog in American history.

Changes in America's foreign affairs during these decades similarly had a profound effect on the writing of history. The Vietnam War, above all, divided the American people. Students participated in large-scale antiwar demonstrations, and college campuses were transformed into centers of political protest and activism. Many intellectuals grew disenchanted with the government's military policy and became increasingly suspicious of the political establishment in general. The Vietnam War also exposed the dangers of what one historian termed "the imperial presidency." President Nixon and the Watergate scandal revealed further the threat posed to constitutional government by this concept of the presidency. As some historians grew more critical of America's foreign policy, they began to question the credibility of the government both in the present and past.

During the course of the 1960s and 1970s scholars were affected also by sweeping intellectual changes within the historical profession itself. Some began by challenging the traditional approach to history—one that assumed the discipline was separate and self-contained. Acting on the premise that the other social sciences—psychology, sociology, anthropology, and political science—could contribute to the study of history, they turned more to an interdisciplinary approach. In doing so, these historians applied concepts, laws, and models from other social sciences in order to understand the conduct of individuals and social groups in the past. This interdisciplinary approach could hardly be called new for it had been employed during the first half of the twentieth century. Still, there was a strong tendency among scholars to apply social science techniques during these two decades.

A second major development was the use of new methodological approaches to the study of history. Some historians began relying more on quantative techniques in their efforts to derive scientifically measurable historical data to document their studies. Other scholars turned to a comparative history approach—comparing entire societies or segments of societies—to illuminate the American past. Quantitative and comparative history were but two of a number of methodological approaches which were employed with greater frequency in the 1960s and 1970s.

It was within this general context that there arose a significant challenge to the neoconservative historians in the 1960s from a group of younger radical scholars known as the New Left. Like the older Progressives, these historians sought to fuse historical scholarship with political activism, and might be called neo-Progressives. Unlike the neoconservatives who emphasized consensus, continuity, and stability, the New Left saw social and economic conflict as the major theme in American history. Of all historians, the individuals identified with the New Left were the most disenchanted with the course of events in recent American history. As a result they presented a radical critique of American society and took a more jaundiced view of the American past.

These scholars reinterpreted American history along more radical lines and insisted that their colleagues pay far greater attention to the lower classes and minority groups of all kinds. Members of the New Left were exceedingly critical in particular of those neoconservative scholars who tended to celebrate the virtues and achievements of the American people. Because the neoconservatives had excluded conflict in their interpretation, the New Left argued, the American people were unprepared to cope with the social upheavals that occurred in the 1960s. These younger historians declared that the resort to violence by social groups to achieve their goals was a theme that had deep roots in the American past. The New Left historians sought to create a "usable past"—a history that would account for the country's social problems, such as racism, militarism, economic exploitation, and imperialism, and would serve as the basis for reforming American society. American history had too often been written from "the top down"—that is, from the point of view of elites and the articulate like Washington, Lincoln, and Franklin D. Roosevelt. History, they argued, should be written "from the bottom up," a perspective which would reflect the concerns of the common people, the inarticulate masses, and nonelites. Viewing history in this way, scholars would discover the radicalism inherent in the American past.

In their treatment of America's foreign policy, for example, the New Left developed a much more critical interpretation than previous historians. America from its beginnings, they argued, had been an aggressive, expansionist, and imperialist nation. It expanded first at the expense of the Indians, and then later at the expense of its weaker neighbors like Mexico. The United States turned subsequently to an overseas imperialist foreign policy based on its need for foreign markets, raw materials, and investment opportunities, This expansionist foreign policy had global ramifications, the New Left claimed. America had played a major role in precipitating two world wars and was primarily responsible for bringing about the Cold War. The Vietnam War, according to the New Left, was simply a logical extension of America's aggressive and expansionist foreign policy.

The New Left view of American history never attained the importance of cohesion of either the Progressive or the neoconservative interpretation. One reason was that few Americans were prepared to accept either the analyses or the solutions proposed by these radical historians. Another was that the American withdrawal from Vietnam and the economic downturn of the 1970s brought a halt to most radical protest movements. Although New Left scholarship failed to develop the potential many had expected of it, some of its insights and concerns were absorbed by nonradical historians seeking to break out of the mold and limitations of the neoconservative approach of the 1950s.

A more significant challenge to both the older school of Progressive historians and the neoconservatives came from the "new social historians," who transformed the writing of American history between the 1960s and the 1990s. Generally speaking, the main focus of these scholars was on the American social structure and the changes this structure underwent over the course of time. The "new social historians" claimed they differed from more traditional historians in four ways: their approach to history; their subject matter, the nature of their evidence; and the methodologies and philosophies of history they employed.[11]

The "new social historians" claimed that their approach to history was more analytical. Traditional historians, they argued, had written descriptive, narrative history in narrow terms, and depicted historical events in isolation from broad conceptual considerations. The "new social historians" declared that social, political, and economic events were inevitably related to changes in America's social structure, and that such events could be traced back to that structure in an analytical way.

Regarding the subject matter treated, the "new social historians" charged that traditional historians had focused on political events, diplomacy, revolutions, and wars. The new scholars insisted that they studied a much broader spectrum of human affairs. Thus, they focused more on social groups rather than individuals, on the masses rather than on elites, and on ordinary folk rather than prominent people. They were interested in exploring the consciousness and actions of various groups—women, races, workers, ethnics, immigrants, and na-

---

[11]The term "new social historians" was used to distinguish these scholars from an older generation of social historians—scholars who wrote descriptive and narrative history dealing with the manners and lifestyle of the common people that was sometimes termed "pots and pans history."

tional minorities. They concentrated more on the activities of ordinary people and sought to present events "from the bottom up." By doing so, they could view the masses not as inarticulate and impotent with no control over events and constantly at the whim of impersonal forces, but rather as actors in their own right building a culture or sub-cultures, creating strategies of survival, and influencing events as much as they were influenced by them.

The "new social historians" argued also that the traditional historians had made generalizations based on vague and fuzzy evidence. Historical evidence, they said, should be more precise and approached in a scientific manner. Numerical evaluations expressed in such vague terms as "some," "few," and "many," were unacceptable. Such evidence where possible should be set forth in quantitatively verifiable terms to provide greater precision. Moreover, evidence of this sort should be employed to test in a systematic way broad conceptual hypotheses about human behavior advanced by other social science disciplines.

The "new social historians" focused more on material matters. They were interested more in material considerations such as geography, demography, economics, and technology, and somewhat less in ideology. Institutions concerned with the socialization of individuals—the family, schools, factories, prisons and asylums—were also apt to draw their attention. Their greatest interest, perhaps, was in the processes affecting social change—sexism, racism, classism—and in social and geographical mobility. A more materialistic approach, they declared, would lead to a richer synthesis of American history.

The "new social historians" also applied new methodologies in their studies. To reconstruct meaningful patterns of behavior about the so-called inarticulate masses, they borrowed methods from the other social and behavioral sciences—psychology, sociology, and anthropology. At the same time they resorted to different methodological techniques, including model-building and the use of paradigms, and also were prone to analyze large data sets and to use computers.

Finally, some "new social historians" raised anew the question of epistemology: How do historians know what they know? There was disagreement about how objective historians could be; whether objectivity was possible at all; what the relationship between historians and their subject matter should be; and what interpretive strategies should be employed in research.[12]

Several important influences affected the rise of the "new social history" in America. First, French scholars since the 1930s had been moving away from narrow political and institutional studies, and

---

[12]With regard to the issue of objectivity, see Peter Novick, *That Noble Dream* (Cambridge, 1988).

raised new questions or resorted to novel methodologies. The most significant outlet for the work of these European scholars was the *Annales*, a French journal. The aim of this distinguished publication was to break down traditional disciplinary barriers and to create a new and more unified approach to understanding the totality of human experience. Under the editorship of Lucien Febvre and Marc Bloch, the *Annales* became the leading journal in creating the new field of social history. Continuing such innovative studies after World War II, the *Annales* increasingly served scholars who used quantitative techniques or multidisciplinary approaches. Slowly but surely, the influence of this French scholarship made itself felt in England and the United States.

A second influence on history was work in the behavioral and social sciences on history after World War II. Behavioral and social science methodologies were applied increasingly in other fields to attack certain contemporary social problems. Such issues included race relations, sexism, family problems, child-rearing, patterns of social and geographical mobility, crime, and the improvement of educational and employment opportunities. American historians inevitably began to examine the historical roots of such problems and to study them with the aid of insights derived from other disciplines.

A third influence came from the powerful protest movements that swept through American society during the troubled decades of the 1960s through the 1980s. Scholars shifted their focus to the history of social groups that heretofore had been largely "invisible" in American history—women, blacks, Indians and the poor, among many others. By becoming visible in the public eye, such social groups became more visible to historians. Scholars responded by writing history that was directly relevant to the expressed needs for these social movements. Thus, the women's liberation movement stimulated interest in women's history and the civil rights movement spurred black history.

The fourth and final major influence on the "new social historians" was the use of new quantification techniques and computers. These methods permitted the "new social historians" to analyze historical evidence from previously unusable sources. Before the advent of computers, scholars found it almost impossible to analyze massive amounts of data. Historians, for example, had been unable to make much of manuscript census schedules that formed the basis for published federal and state censuses. These census schedules, which furnished information about individuals, families, and households in the past, had remained untouched because of problems encountered in reducing the mass of discrete information to usable data. Computers made it possible to collect and manipulate these data, while new quantitative techniques enabled researchers to analyze the information in more meaningful ways. New quantification techniques that made use of computers also made it possible to pose and answer historical questions in new and different ways.

Although the "new social historians" were loosely united in their efforts to examine the American social structure, they did not constitute a coherent coalition of scholars. They were fragmented instead into separate groups and divided along different lines in terms of subject matter. As Thomas Bender pointed out, the groups were assumed to be autonomous, and there was no organizing synthesis to show how the various parts might be related to some whole.[13]

The "new social history" was only one part of a totality that came to be called "the new history." American history as a whole was splintered into different specialties: the "new political history," "new economic history," "new intellectual history," "new women's history," "new labor history," and "new urban history," among others. Some disciplines, like the "new women's history," in turn, split into subfields like "family history." This bewildering array of specialties and subdisciplines was identified under the general broad heading of the "new history."

The "old history," by way of contrast, differed somewhat from the "new history." It was concerned with politics—administration, regimes, and legislation—diplomacy and foreign policy, wars, revolutions, and intellectual movements in a more traditional way. Its method was usually narrative in form. Its cast of characters often hailed from elite groups—presidents, politicians, and important leaders in public life. It was sometimes described as elitist history written "from the top down." It tended to place greater emphasis on the role of individuals in history rather than on the workings of impersonal forces. And it often stressed more the idealist rather than the materialist approach to history.

The "new history" began initially as a revolt against the "old." But as is so often the case, what started as rebellion ended up as orthodoxy. Within the historical profession, the "new history" soon triumphed over the "old." The "old history," once at the center of the profession, was relegated to the periphery.

Despite the differences, the "old" and "new" histories did not constitute mutually exclusive categories. Some eminent senior historians writing so-called "old history" used methodologies and approaches usually associated with "new history." By the same token, some enterprising younger scholars simply applied new methodologies to old and more traditional topics. Nevertheless, the degree of emphasis and in-

---

[13]Thomas Bender, "Wholes and Parts: The Need for Synthesis in American History," *Journal of American History* 73 (June 1986):127.

tent was sufficiently different to justify making the distinction between "old" and "new" history.[14]

An example of how the "old history" was transformed to the
"new" could be seen in intellectual history. Older intellectual historians, like Perry Miller, had been interested in ideas, but ideas largely
disembodied from their social and economic origins. The "new intellectual historians" took a different approach. Many of them employed
a new concept of ideology advanced by Clifford Geertz, a cultural anthropologist. Geertz insisted upon viewing ideology in a new way, as
a cultural system—a set of symbols, values, and beliefs that enabled
members of a society to give meaning and find order in their political
and social lives. Ideology, in Geertz's terms, reflected the way of life of
an entire society, not just the status and thought of a particular group.
Puritanism, for example, was viewed in such terms by recent scholars
like Kenneth Lockridge, who published a study of society in Dedham,
Massachusetts. The "republican synthesis" postulated by J.G.A. Po-
cock, discussed later in this volume, was also in this mode. Eugene
Genovese's work on the plantation ideology in the slave South, however, cited the Italian theorist Gramsci. These new approaches to ideology changed the older tradition by insisting more on the primacy of
the social structure when dealing with ideas.[15]

Another example of the "new intellectual history" was what one
historian termed the "emerging organizational synthesis." This hypothesis presupposed the triumph of a new bureaucratic ideology
based on the needs and values of large-scale management in the American economy. In some accounts this ideology arose as an inevitable
response to the modernization and centralization of American society
in the nineteenth century. It provided a framework of belief appropriate for living in a mature industrial state where business, labor, and
government were all organized on a national scale. Its practitioners
were scholars such as Robert Wiebe, Alfred Chandler, Louis Galambos,
and Samuel P. Hays. These scholars emphasized that the behavior of
individuals might be better understood when seen within such an organizational context.[16]

But the dominance of the "new history" did not eliminate older
and more traditional approaches that were continued. First, as previously mentioned, the old Progressive tradition was carried on after
World War II by a group of scholars down as the neo-Progressives.
These historians, who included among them the populist-oriented

---

[14]Much of this discussion is drawn from Gertrude Himmelfarb, *The New History
and the Old* (New York, 1987).

[15]Daniel J. Singal, "Beyond Consensus: Richard Hofstadter and American Historiography," *American Historical Review* 89 (October 1986):998–1001.

[16]*Ibid.*, 1001.

New Left, continued to interpret American history in ways similar to those of their Progressive predecessors.

A second development—comparative history—likewise represented an extension of an older tradition that was continued. Comparative historians usually studied the histories of two or more countries in search of similarities and differences in national experiences. Their approach was often transnational in character; this goal was to shed light on the origins and destiny of the modern world. At other times they compared ideas and concepts like democracy, nationalism, and imperialism to discover what effects these concepts had and whether they operated the same or differently within diverse historical settings.

A third development—the Marxist or neo-Marxist tradition—was also continued among some American historians. Many of them were influenced by the writings of two English radical historians—Eric Hobsbawm and Edward P. Thompson. But the collapse of communist ideology worldwide during the 1980s decade dealt a severe setback to this tradition.

The result of all this intermingling of "new" and "old" history led to intellectual confusion, particularly when dealing with subjects and methodologies. Some approached the discipline of history differently in terms of subject matter and studied a major specialty such as the "new economic history" or "new political history." Others studied an older subfield (community studies), or new subfields (women's or black history). Scholars resorted also to different new methodologies, including quantitative techniques and linguistic theories to tackle historical problems. Such eclecticism led to the charge that history had become so fragmented as to be incoherent as a separate discipline. History, it was said, was "a discipline in crisis."

What is the status of American history, and just where does the field stand at the beginning of the 1990s? Fragmentation is its hallmark; any unifying or synthesizing theme is lacking. There is a diversity and disparity of both subjects and methods. Part of the problem arises from the intense specialization within the field. The "new social history" in particular has given rise to a loose coalition of scholars in subdisciplines or subfields analyzing a variety of discrete problems rather than a community of scholars, a community which can agree on what is worth investigating and how the results of research should be evaluated.

First, there is fragmentation in the subjects studied. Greater specialization, to be sure, has opened up new areas of research, led to new methodologies, and produced more sophisticated interpretations. But at the same time, overspecialization posed difficulties for scholars seeking to maintain some coherence within the discipline as a whole.

Secondly, fragmentation arises from the application of new and different methodologies. Quantification is a case in point. The issue was not over quantification as a technique; it raised instead a profound epistemological question regarding the meaning of reality itself. On one side were the materialists, who sought to prove their theories by statistical exactness, replicable precision, and generalized knowledge. On the other were historians seeking to restore the role of the individual in history, or to discover meaning through an intuitive personal study of *mentalités*—that is, the study of popular beliefs, customs, sentiments and modes of behavior within society.[17]

Another cause of fragmentation was the presence of two other broad competing sets of historians in certain areas—those committed to radical change, and those who believed in the use of concepts and methods drawn from the social and behavioral sciences. They overlapped and often could be identified with the groups of scholars already discussed. At issue between them were two competing paradigms of historical understanding. The radicals—social democrats of different persuasions—were highly critical of American society and skeptical of its presumed liberalism. They distrusted also the use of computers. They saw them as conservative instruments created by what they called America's ruling class. Those drawn toward the social sciences, on the other hand, relied more heavily on statistical methods, serial data, and computer analysis. What was significant in separating these two groups were four main issues: the character of American society regarding its liberalism or conservatism; the source and scope of theories of history to be applied; the proper methods of evaluating data and drawing conclusions; and the role that moral judgments should play in the writing of history.[18] When writing on a given subject, the two groups often came to opposite conclusions because of divergent starting assumptions.

The attempts by certain scholars to turn history more in the direction of social sciences likewise led to greater fragmentation. Traditional-minded scholars successfully resisted such efforts for the most part. Many rejected these moves on the grounds that a dangerous reductivism was inherent in the social science approach.

The process of fragmentation was exacerbated, moreover, by the tendency of historians to apply methodologies borrowed from the other behavioral sciences. Social theories from other disciplines—psychology, sociology, and increasingly of late, anthropology—often enabled historians to develop new insights. At the same time, however, these methodologies were derived from certain behavioral sciences that were themselves in intellectual disarray. Thus, fragmentation in

---

[17]Robert Swierenga, "Historians and Computers: Has the Love Affair Gone Sour?" *O.A.H. Newsletter* (November 1984).

[18]Robert Berkhofer, "Two Histories: Competing Paradigms for Interpreting the American Past," *O.A.H. Newsletter* (May 1982).

the other disciplines sometimes compounded the problems historians were encountering in their own profession.

The result of all this fragmentation led to a loss of direction and any sense of coherence. As John Higham has argued, somewhere in the late 1960s the ruling paradigms of homogeneity and consensus were replaced by the paradigms of fragmentation and heterogeneity. He described historians, perhaps too harshly, as a field of solitary gophers, each digging its own hole.[19]

Despite the diversity and confusion within the historical profession, there were some signs that suggested a more fruitful reconceptualization may be in the offing. One was the greater emphasis the "new social history" placed on various so-called minority groups—women, blacks, Indians and immigrants—and less stress laid on more elite groups—mostly whites, males, and prominent persons. This change of focus brought about a better balance in American history; it incorporated into the story social groups that had been neglected before. It also emphasized the ties, values, and experiences of family, sisterhood, fraternity, and sense of community that bound together these subordinate social groups and gave them a sense of group consciousness. What needs to be explored now is a new agenda: the relationship of these groups to public life and to society as a whole.[20]

A second sign has been the call for a return to narrative history voiced by two leading historians in America—Bernard Bailyn and Lawrence Stone—among others. Both called on scholars to emphasize more narrative effects, readability, and human interest aspects in their writings. Such a narrative approach would arouse and hold reader interest and recapture the wider audience once held.[21]

A third sign might be seen in Carl Degler's presidential address to the American Historical Association in 1987, when he called upon historians to rediscover our national unity and national identity. This could be done, he suggested, by using as a framework the following broad question: "What does it mean to be an American, that is, a citizen of the United States?" By framing this question, Degler hoped to integrate traditional emphases with findings in the "new history."[22]

To return, then, to the main issue: What is the status of American history?[23] The finest answer is that with fragmentation has come re-

---

[19]John Higham cited in Lawrence W. Levine, "The Unpredictable Past: Reflections on Recent American Historiography," *American Historical Review* 94 (June 1989):672.

[20]Thomas Bender, "Making History Whole Again," *New York Times Book Review,* (October 6 1985).

[21]Bernard Bailyn, "The Challenge of Modern Historiography," *American Historical Review* 87 (February 1982):1–24; and Lawrence Stone, *The Past and the Present* (Boston, 1981).

[22]Carl N. Degler, "In Pursuit of the American Dream," *American Historical Review,* 92 (February 1987):1–2.

[23]A recent development in historiography worth mentioning, perhaps, was the notion of the "end of history" suggested by Francis Fukuyama, a State Department policy

form. Scholars instead of worrying about the "crisis" in the discipline should take some solace in how far they have come. At the end of the nineteenth and beginning of the twentieth centuries, scholars were writing a narrowly conceived history. This history was conceptualized mostly as the history of liberty on an onward and upward course, its concern was mainly with high politics, wars, and diplomacy, and its actors were mostly white, males, and prominent persons. Since the end of World War II, however, scholars have broadened the field both in terms of subjects and methodologies. They have been more creative, perhaps, than at any other time in American history. This exciting change, to be sure, was achieved at some cost—the loss of hegemony, diminution of the narrative form, and decline in a wide reading public. But as Joan W. Scott has observed, history has always been a changing field, and she concluded that "those who expect moments of change to be comfortable and free of conflict have not learned their history."[24]

A second answer is the possible effect that the collapse of socialist and communist movements throughout the world in the 1980s will have upon American scholars. The shattering events of the revolutions in Europe in 1989 and the break-up of the Soviet empire in 1990 will, no doubt, affect the views of American scholars. We have seen that American historians in the past have been influenced by their writings by developments taking place outside their library studies; we may safely assume that in this instance history will repeat itself.

In conclusion, it may be said that two provocative questions will continue to pose challenges to American historians in future years: Who has the right to write about whom in American history? Is it possible to write a history of our country which is convincing, or at least plausible, to us all?

---

planner. In the summer of 1989, he proclaimed that America and the world at large had arrived at a different crucial point in time that had never been achieved before—namely, the end of history. Fukuyama argued that the two challenges to Western liberalism—fascism and communism—had been defeated, and therefore the ultimate triumph or millennium was near at hand in the form of the universal homogeneous liberal state. The West had essentially achieved the classless society Karl Marx had envisioned, the modern America was the very model of such a society. The other two potential obstacles to the "end of history" were religion and nationalism, but these were troublesome only in the Third World and trouble spots in Europe like Northern Ireland. Thus, the Western world—and the United States in particular—had nothing to fear from communism, socialism, nationalism, racism, or religious fundamentalism, and history would end as the consciousness of Western liberalism ultimately spread and remade the material world in its own image.

This post-historicism had little to recommend it, and is not to be taken seriously. The United States, with its homeless roaming the streets, was hardly the picture of a model classless society. Fukuyama overlooked the fervent nationalism America itself reflects. He disregarded the racism and sexism still prevalent in advanced Western society, including the United States. Moreover, he greatly underestimated the power of religious fundamentalism—for example, in Islamic countries—which motivated many parts of the world.

[24]Joan W. Scott, "History in Crisis: The Other Side of the Story," *American Historical Review*, 94 (February 1989):692.

☆ 2 ☆

The American Businessman

INDUSTRIAL INNOVATOR OR ROBBER BARON?

For many students of American history, the problems of war and peace appear to be the dominant ones in the years from 1850 to 1877. Yet during this same period the country was undergoing an industrial and urban transformation that inevitably resulted in profound changes in the structure of American society. Few individuals or institutions remained unaffected by the forces at work, and the nation as a whole was destined to experience fundamental changes which enabled it to emerge as a leading world power by the close of the nineteenth century. "The old nations of the earth, "Andrew Carnegie observed in 1886 with considerable pride, "creep on at a snail's pace; the Republic thunders past with the rush of the express. The United States, [in] the growth of a single century, has already reached the foremost rank among nations, and is destined soon to outdistance all others in the race. In population, in wealth, in annual savings, and in public credit; in freedom from debt, in agriculture, and in manufactures, America already leads the civilized world."[1] Industrial growth and the accumulation of wealth, Carnegie suggested, would lay the cornerstone of a better America: Ultimately, material progress would lead to spiritual and intellectual progress.

Although this new burst of industrialism gave the United States one of the highest standards of living in the world, it was not always greeted with unrestrained enthusiasm. To some the new industrialism was destroying the very traits that had given American immunity from class strife, internal divisions, and rivalries that had long plagued Europe. Others feared the greed and ugliness that accompanied the industrial transformation. Walt Whitman, in "Democratic Vistas," summed up the opposition: "The depravity of the business classes of our coun-

---

[1] Andrew Carnegie, *Triumphant Democracy* (New York, 1886), p. 1.

28

try is not less than has been supposed but infinitely greater. The official services of America, national, state, and municipal, in all their branches and departments, except the judiciary, are saturated in corruption, bribery, falsehood, mal-administration; and the judiciary is tainted. The great cities reek with respectable as much as non-respectable robbery and scoundrelism. . . . In business (this all-devouring modern word, business), the one sole object is, by any means, pecuniary gain. . . . [M]oney-making is our sole magician's serpent, remaining today sole master in the field. . . . I say that our New World democracy, however great a success in uplifting the masses out of their sloughs, in materialistic development, products, and in a certain highly deceptive superficial popular intellectuality, is, so far, an almost complete failure in its social aspects, and in really grand religious, moral, literary, and esthetic results."[2] In short, America was adversely affected by the material forces at work.

The differences between the views of Carnegie and Whitman were by no means atypical; Americans have always been ambivalent in their attitudes toward material affluence. While emphasizing the virtues of acquisitiveness, individualism, and competition, they have been unable to throw off the influence of their religious heritage and the sense that the nation as a whole has a mission. At times this dual heritage has created an internal conflict because attempts to harmonize American materialism and idealism have not always succeeded. Some Americans have dealt with this conflict by proclaiming that material well-being is a prerequisite of spiritual and intellectual achievement; others have criticized a system that emphasizes material values at the expense of other values; still others have insisted that America's abundance was proof of its superior moral character.

This ambivalent attitude toward our heritage has exercised a profound impact on the writing of American history. Historians, on the whole, have also displayed divided attitudes when studying the rise of industry and its implications for American society. Nowhere can this dichotomy of thought be better seen than in the changing image of such great entrepreneurs as Rockefeller and Carnegie. To many historians these captains of industry represented more than the rise of industrialism; they symbolized some of the basic characteristics of modern American culture.

The first attempts to evaluate the achievements of these industrial giants occurred at the beginning of the twentieth century. Many of the early studies took their cue from the writings of Henry Demarest Lloyd. A journalist and a scholar, Lloyd, until his death in 1903, played a significant part in reform movements that developed out of the social and economic unrest of that era. Critical of laissez-faire corporate mo-

---

[2]Walt Whitman, "Democratic Vistas," in *Prose Works 1892*, Floyd Stovall, ed., 2 vols. (New York, 1963–1964), 2:370.

nopoly he insisted that the American people were confronted with a choice between reform or revolution. Public ownership of monopolies and an increased role for government were absolutely necessary, according to Lloyd, if the American people were to avoid the fratricidal class struggles that had wracked other nations in the Western world.

In 1894 Lloyd spelled out his case in *Wealth Against Commonwealth*, a book that anticipated the writings of later muckrakers and Progressive journalists and also set the stage for much of the controversy among historians over the captains of industry. The book ostensibly was a study of the Standard Oil Company and the techniques used by John D. Rockefeller to gain a virtual monopoly over the petroleum industry. Actually *Wealth Against Commonwealth* was an indictment of the entire capitalistic system as it then existed. Businessmen, wrote Lloyd, paid lip service to the ideal of competition, but their true purpose was to achieve monopoly. If the captains of industry continued to have their way, the result would probably be a violent and bloody class struggle. There was little time to act, declared Lloyd, for the nation was already faced with "misery, plagues, hatreds, [and] national enervation."[3]

While Lloyd's principal purpose was to issue a call for national regeneration, he had drawn an unfavorable yet influential portrait of the typical industrial tycoon to make his point. His stereotype of the American businessman was in many respects similar to the one held by other American reformers, including the Populists, as well as many Progressives. Much of the debate over reform in the years from 1900 to 1917, indeed, centered about the unbridled power and selfishness of the captains of industry—a group, many claimed, who were motivated only by a desire to amass great wealth regardless of the cost to the American people. The specific political issues of the Progressive era—monopolies, trusts, federal regulation—were all based upon the proposition that Americans could no longer afford to permit these autocratic barons to shape the nation's destiny.

Many of the studies dealing with the American businessman written prior to World War I were done not only by historians, but by social scientists and, to a lesser extent, socialists seeking to prove that the system of capitalism was identified with social and individual selfishness and egoism. Among the social scientists were economists and sociologists such as Thorstein Veblen and E. A. Ross, who implicitly denounced the predatory, profit-seeking, amoral businessman for refusing to recognize the pressing needs of society. In the latter category were Gustavus Myers and Algie Simons, who portrayed businessmen as malefactors of wealth and looked forward to their eventual extinc-

---

[3]Henry Demarest Lloyd, *Wealth Against Commonwealth* (New York, 1894), p. 517.

tion as the historical process reached its inevitable destiny in the emergence of a socialist utopia.

While the interpretation of the businessman as robber baron was being etched in the public's imagination, historians, under the influence of the New History, were themselves beginning to inquire into the economic realities of capitalism in order to buttress their own predilection for democracy and reform. But not until the 1920s—a decade that was notable for the debunking activities of a small group of intellectuals—did historians turn their full attention to the study of the rise of American industry. With the publication in 1927 of Charles and Mary Beard's *Rise of American Civilization* and the first volume of Vernon L. Parrington's monumental *Main Currents in American Thought*, the scene was set for a radical reevaluation of the role of the businessman in American history.

Although the Beards refrained from any direct or outward condemnation of the industrial tycoon in their panoramic study of American civilization, their description suggested the analogy of a medieval baron—an individual who was despotic and autocratic within his own sphere. The story of American industry, they wrote, is "the story of aggressive men, akin in spirit to military captains of the past, working their way up from the ranks, exploiting natural resources without restraining, waging economic war on one another, entering into combinations, making immense fortunes, and then, like successful feudal chieftains or medieval merchants, branching out as patrons of learning, divinity and charity. Here is a chronicle of highly irregular and sometimes lawless methods, ruthless competition, menacing intrigues, and pitiless destruction of rivals."[4]

Parrington, on the other hand, was much clearer and far less ambiguous in his description of postwar industrial developments. Writing within a Jeffersonian agrarian framework, which stressed individualistic values, he sought to defend his particular vision of liberalism. In Parrington's eyes the predatory and materialistic tycoon of industry represented the greatest threat to those humane and democratic values that had made America great. Businessmen had created the America of the present, with "its standardized life, its machine culture, its mass-psychology—an America to which Jefferson and Jackson and Lincoln would be strangers." These giants of industry, Parrington wrote in colorful and emotion-laden terms, "were primitive souls, ruthless, predatory, capable; single-minded men; rogues and rascals often, but never feeble, never hindered by petty scruple, never given to puling or whining—the raw materials of a race of capitalistic buccaneers."[5]

---

[4]Charles and Mary Beard, *The Rise of American Civilization*, 2 vols. (New York, 1927), 2:177.

[5]Vernon L. Parrington, *Main Currents in American Thought*, 3 vols. (New York, 1927–1930), 3:12 and 26.

The debunking atmosphere of the 1920s and depression years of the 1930s provided a favorable climate of opinion for the growing idea of the businessman as a robber baron. For decades the business community had taken great pains to convince the American people that the nation's greatness rested on the achievements of ambitious and energetic entrepreneurs. A. C. Bedford, a tycoon in the oil industry, made this point very clear in 1925. In his eyes work was even of more importance than love, learning, religion, or patriotism. "I have come to the conclusion," he wrote, "that industry is the fundamental basis of civilization. The high office of civilization is to train men to productive efforts."[6] Other business leaders during the 1920s echoed Bedford's observations; if anything they were even more ecstatic in extolling the contributions of business to American civilization. With the exception of a dissenting minority of reformers, many Americans agreed with President Coolidge's dictum that "The business of America is business."

Having taken credit for the apparent prosperity of the 1920s the business community, ironically enough, was forced to accept responsibility for the catastrophic depression of the 1930s. The capitalist free enterprise system, which supposedly accounted for the greatness of America, seemingly failed in 1929. Millions who sought work were unable to find jobs; bankruptcies increased at an astounding rate; and many Americans even faced a real threat of starvation. Indeed, the United States appeared to be on the threshold of disaster. For once the business community found that the time-honored cliché that wealth was the product of ambition, talent, and drive, no longer held true. Capitalism and free enterprise perhaps had come to the end of the road, many argued, and new approaches were required if the needs of a modern, complex industrial society in America were to be satisfied.

Given these conditions it was not surprising that much of the historical scholarship of the 1930s took an antibusiness turn. Beard and Parrington had anticipated this development; their writings during the late 1920s echoed some of the critical literature of this era. Sinclair Lewis's unforgettable portrait of Babbitt, while not wholly intended to debunk businessmen, contributed to a stereotype already widely held. The massive attack on the image of the American businessman, however, came in the Great Depression. During the 1930s the robber baron idea came to full bloom.

In presenting a highly unfavorable portrait of the industrial tycoon most writers in this tradition were implicitly attacking an economic system that they thought had failed to live up to its promises and ex-

---

[6]Quoted in James W. Prothro, *The Dollar Decade: Business Ideas in the 1920's* (Baton Rouge, 1954), p. 67.

pectations. Oddly enough many—though not all—of the critical studies during the 1930s were written by nonacademic figures who were critical of capitalism rather than by academic historians. Thus Lewis Corey, a socialist, in his *The House of Morgan* (1930), detailed the techniques whereby a major banking and investment concern exercised near dictatorial control over corporations having assets well in excess of twenty billion dollars. His lesson was not lost upon his readers. It was Corey's purpose to marshal as much evidence as possible to demonstrate the evil, selfish, and corrupting nature of industrial and finance capitalism. Other historical and literary writers, attracted by Marxian ideas, lent support to the growing body of critical studies of the American economic system.

The book that did the most to fix in American historical scholarship the enduring stereotype of the late nineteenth-century industrialist, however, was Matthew Josephson's brilliantly written *The Robber Barons: The Great American Capitalists 1861–1901*, which appeared in 1934. Fittingly enough, Josephson dedicated his book to Charles and Mary Beard, who themselves had interpreted American history in terms of a struggle between haves and have-nots, debtors and creditors, agrarians and industrialists, workers and capitalists. Josephson set the tone of his work in his introduction. "This book," he began, "attempts the history of a small class of men who arose at the time of our Civil War and suddenly swept into power. . . . These men more or less knowingly played the leading roles in an age of industrial revolution. . . . Under their hands the renovation of our economic life proceeded relentlessly: large-scale production replaced the scattered, decentralized mode of production, industrial enterprises became more concentrated, more 'efficient' technically, and essentially 'cooperative,' where they had been purely individualistic and lamentably wasteful. But all this revolutionizing effort is branded with the motive of private gain on the part of the new captains of industry. To organize and exploit the resources of a nation upon a gigantic scale, to regiment its farmers and workers into harmonious corps of producers, and to do this only in the name of an uncontrolled appetite for private profit—here surely is the great inherent contradiction whence so much disaster, outrage, and misery has flowed." Josephson conceded that the robber barons had many imposing achievements to their credit. On the other hand the debits far outweighed the credits. Ultimately, he concluded, the "extremes of management and stupidity would make themselves felt. . . . The alternations of prosperity and poverty would be more violent and mercurial, speculation and breakdown each more excessive; while the inherent contradictions within the society pressed with increasing intolerable force against the bonds of the old order." The implications of Josephson's ideas were obvious. The unfavorable portrait of the busi-

nessman has in muted form persisted as a theme in American historical writing.[7]

At the same time the robber baron concept was reaching maturity
another school of thought was emerging. Although it is difficult to give
this school a particular name, the designation "business history" is
not wholly inaccurate. The foundation of business history had already
been laid by the 1930s. As a result of the work of Norman S. B. Gras
and others at the Harvard Graduate School of Business Administration
as well as the publication of a number of sympathetic biographies of
individual business leaders, some historians and economists began to
depart from the unfavorable stereotype of the American industrialist.
Business history, however, was not merely a reevaluation of the contributions of industrialists; it represented a radically new approach to the
study of American economic history. Indeed, business historians by
the 1950s—because of their differences with other academic historians—had created their own professional organization, developed a
new vocabulary and research techniques, published their own journal,
and in some cases had even founded new departments within the university separate from regular history departments.

Generally speaking business historians insisted that the careers of
industrial leaders were far more complex than earlier scholars had realized. Business leaders were not predatory money seekers. Indeed, in
many cases they were talented individuals whose creative contributions to the economy—and to American society as a whole—were very
great. Allan Nevins, who published a major revisionist biography of
John D. Rockefeller in 1940, argued that much of the blame heaped on
this man was unwarranted. It was true, Nevins conceded, that Rockefeller used methods that were of dubious moral character. On the other
hand the kind of monopoly control attained by Standard Oil was a natural response to the anarchical cutthroat competition of the period and
reflected the trend in all industrial nations toward consolidation. To
Nevins Rockefeller was not a robber baron; he was a great innovator
who imposed upon American industry "a more rational and efficient
pattern." Rockefeller's objective was not merely the accumulation of
wealth; he and others like him were motivated by "competitive
achievement, self-expression, and the imposition of their wills on a
given environment."[8]

Thirteen years later Nevins pushed this thesis even further when

---

[7]Matthew Josephson, *The Robber Barons: The Great American Capitalists 1861–
1901* (New York, 1934), pp. vii–viii, 453; H. Wayne Morgan, ed., *The Gilded Age* (rev.
ed.: Syracuse, 1970). For a discussion of the robber baron theme see Hal Bridges, "The
Robber Baron Concept in America History," *Business History Review* 32 (Spring
1958):1–13.

[8]Allan Nevins, *John D. Rockefeller: The Heroic Age of American Enterprise,* 2 vols.
(New York, 1940), 2:707–714.

he published a second biography of Rockefeller. He was, Nevins force-fully argued, an "innovator, thinker, planner, bold entrepreneur." Tak-ing a confused and disorganized industry, Rockefeller organized it with completeness, efficiency, and constructive talent; in his philanthropy he set a model for all to follow. Had it not been for men like him—men who helped to create within a brief span of time great and power-ful industrial units in steel, oil, textiles, chemicals, electricity, and au-tomotive vehicles—"the free world might have lost the First World War and most certainly would have lost the Second."[9]

The points that Nevins made about Rockefeller were not funda-mentally different from those made by other students of business his-tory. The great nineteenth-century entrepreneurs, business historians emphasized, actually played a vital role in making the United States the greatest industrial power in the world and giving its people the highest standard of living. Far from being immoral, unethical, or evil individuals—although sometimes their methods involved question-able tactics—these industrial statesmen stepped into a disorganized, unstructured, anarchic economy, restored order and rationality, created giant organizations that were in a position to exploit fully the great natural resources of the nation, and took full advantage of the potentialities of the American economy.

Like students in the robber baron tradition of American historiog-raphy, business historians began with certain underlying assumptions that undoubtedly influenced the way in which they approached their subject. It is quite clear that they rejected the hostile critique of Pro-gressive historians who believed that the social and economic costs of late-nineteenth-century industrialization could have been far lower and less painful and degrading to the mass of Americans, and that the result need not have been a dangerous centralization of economic power that ostensibly threatened freedom and democracy. On the con-trary business historians tended to eulogize rather than to disparage the American economic system. Did not the growth and development of the large corporation, they maintained, give the American people the highest standard of living in the world and make possible the vic-tory against totalitarianism? Was not America's industrial capacity re-sponsible for the strength of a large part of the free world in the strug-gle with communism? To put it another way these historians concluded that the large corporation, despite its monopolistic and oli-gopolistic position, was far more of an asset than a liability, Unlike Progressive historians who defined the problem in terms of a tension

---

[9]Allan Nevins, *Study in Power: John D. Rockefeller, Industrialist and Philanthro-pist*, 2 vols. (New York, 1953), 1:viii–ix; 2:436. For a direct confrontation of views see the enlightening article, "Should American History Be Rewritten? A Debate Between Allan Nevins and Matthew Josephson," *Saturday Review* 37 (February 6, 1954):7–10 and 44–49.

between democracy and the menace of the concentration of economic power in the hands of a few, business historians minimized the threat of such dangers and opposed efforts to employ historical analysis as an ideological anticorporation weapon.

Perhaps the most sophisticated example of recent developments in business history is the work of Alfred D. Chandler, Jr. Unlike Nevins, Chandler was essentially disinterested in the biographical approach that sought to vindicate the career of an individual against his detractors. He was more concerned in the process whereby new forms, methods, and structures came into being in the late nineteenth and twentieth centuries. In a major work issued in 1962 Chandler identified four stages in the development of large industrial enterprises. First came a period of expansion and the accumulation of resources. During the second period these resources were "rationalized." In the third phase the organization expanded its operations to include new products in order to ensure the most efficient use of existing resources. In the fourth and final phase new structures were created to promote effective use of resources in order to meet immediate and long-range demands. Borrowing heavily from work in the social sciences Chandler saw large corporations as complex economic, political, and social systems with common administrative problems. He insisted, moreover, that most large firms went through similar stages of development. "Strategic growth," he noted, "resulted from an awareness of the opportunities and needs—created by changing population, income, and technology— to employ existing or expanding resources more profitably. A new strategy required a new or at least refashioned structure if the enlarged enterprise was to be operated efficiently."[10] The result was the large, decentralized, multidivisional corporation.

Less interested in the moral dimensions of industrial entrepreneurship, Chandler attempted to analyze the forces that led businessmen to develop new products, new markets, and new sources of raw materials. By 1900, he pointed out, these industrial leaders had created the modern corporation, which integrated the functions of purchasing, manufacturing, marketing, and finance. Each of the major processes was managed by a separate department, and all were coordinated and controlled by a central office. Such a complex organization was a response to the emergence of the urban market that followed the creation of a national transportation system. Minimizing the role of technological innovation Chandler concluded that entrepreneurs like Rockefeller and others were successful because they accurately analyzed the economic situation and responded in a creative manner.

---

[10]Alfred D. Chandler, Jr., *Strategy and Structure: Chapters in the History of the Industrial Enterprise* (Cambridge, Mass., 1962), p. 15. A revised edition of this work appeared in 1990.

Their contributions, he suggested, played an important role in the dramatic growth of the economy and the creation of an affluent society.[11] The first selection in this chapter is an article by Chandler on the role of business in American society.

In a subsequent Pulitzer Prize–winning book, *The Visible Hand*, Chandler analyzed the manner in which the development of large-scale vertically organized corporations altered the American economy between the Civil War and the depression of the 1930s. He once again reiterated the crucial role of management and business executives in guiding these changes, and suggested that Adam Smith's concept of the market as the decisive element in the economy was no longer applicable to the present. Nevertheless *The Visible Hand* also paid tribute to the crucial role of technology. Indeed, Chandler argued that modern business first appeared, grew, and flourished in industries characterized by new and advancing technology and by expanding markets.[12]

Business historians have also dealt with the role of individuals in modern economic development. Harold C. Livesay, for example, noted that the rise of bureaucratic structures did not stifle the creative and innovative processes that are the hallmark of capitalism and free enterprise. Bureaucracy, he concluded, did not necessarily obliterate the entrepreneurial spirit nor did it blur (as Joseph Schumpeter suggested) the differences between mature capitalist and socialist systems. Some individuals make institutions; in this sense human beings are not helpless captives of impersonal social and economic systems and structures. In a recent study of the Morgans, Vincent and Rose Carosso emphasized the importance attributed to character and personal ties that characterized the House of Morgan as well as its innate conservatism.[13]

Business historians tended to see the large corporation as essentially an economic organization. Other scholars, however, were less concerned with understanding the corporation in structural and functional terms; they were more concerned with the political aspects of business and the threat to democratic institutions posed by such huge conglomerations. This concern took two different forms in the 1950s and 1960s. The first was a sophisticated body of scholarship that exam-

---

[11]Alfred D. Chandler, Jr., "The Beginnings of 'Big Business' in American Industry," *Business History Review* 33 (Spring 1959):1–31.

[12]Alfred D. Chandler, Jr., *The Visible Hand: The Managerial Revolution in American Business* (Cambridge, Mass., 1977). For a brief and clear summary of the findings of business historians see Glenn Porter, *The Rise of Big Business, 1860–1910* (New York, 1973).

[13]Harold C. Livesay, "Entrepreneurial Persistence Through the Bureaucratic Age," *Business History Review* 51 (Winter 1977):415–443; Vincent and Rose Carosso, *The Morgans: Private International Bankers, 1854–1913* (Cambridge, 1987).

ined business in a critical vein, though not with a view that sought the end of capitalism and the establishment of a socialist society. Typical of this approach was the work of Carl Kaysen, an economist who also served for a time as the director of the Institute for Advanced Study in Princeton, New Jersey. Kaysen noted the overwhelmingly disproportionate importance of large corporations in the economy. Because of their size these large units were less influenced by changes in economic activity and exercised considerable power over their smaller suppliers and customers. Their investment decisions and research activities, moreover, had important implications for society. The bigger market power that absolute and relative size gave to the large corporation also resulted in political and social as well as economic power. Kaysen noted that American society possessed three alternate ways of controlling business power: the promotion of competitive markets, control by agencies external to business, and institutionalization within the firm of responsibility for the exercise of power. Traditionally the United States relied on the first in the form of antitrust activities, although far more could have been done along this line. Kaysen's conclusions were equivocal, for he felt that effective control of business power remained an unfinished task.[14]

Scholars like Kaysen were essentially in a reform tradition; they sought to eliminate imperfections in American society rather than overthrow it. By the early 1960s, however, a small but growing number of scholars in a variety of disciplines were coming to the conclusion that American society was fundamentally immoral and that a radical change in its structure was required. This point of view was best expressed by historians associated with the New Left. War, poverty, racism, they argued, were direct outgrowths of American capitalism. If this were so then only the abolition of capitalism could make possible the establishment of a just and peaceful society. This belief, of course, led to a rejection of those scholars who had defended business as well as those who were critical of it but did not seek its destruction.

One of the first monographs embodying a New Left approach was Gabriel Kolko's *The Triumph of Conservatism: A Reinterpretation of American History, 1900–1916*, which appeared in 1963. Kolko argued that the distinctive feature of American society—what he designated as political capitalism—dated only from the first two decades of the twentieth century. Rejecting the belief that large-scale business enterprise was inevitable, Kolko maintained that competition was actually increasing at the turn of the century. Even the merger movement and the capitalization of new combinations on an unprecedented scale failed to stem the tide of competitive growth. Corporate leaders, there-

---

[14]Carl Kaysen, "The Corporation: How Much Power? What Scope?," in *The Corporation in Modern Society*, Edward S. Mason, ed. (Cambridge, Mass., 1959), Chapter 5.

fore, turned to government to control competition and to prevent the possibility of a formal political democracy that might lead to a redistribution of wealth. The result was a synthesis of business and government, with the former emerging as the dominant element. In contrast to Chandler, Kolko believed that large-scale units turned to government regulation precisely because of their inefficiency. The lack of a viable alternative to political capitalism at that time made its victory a certainty, for neither the Populists nor the socialists (who themselves accepted the necessity of centralization) understood that the Progressive movement—far from being antibusiness—was actually a movement that defined the general welfare in terms of the well-being of business.[15]

Kolko's controversial thesis did not persuade other scholars, many of whom rejected his radical ideological assumptions and questioned his conclusions. Shortly after Kolko published his study of railroad regulation in 1965, Edward A. Purcell, Jr., criticized his thesis that businessmen favored government regulation because they feared competition and desired to forge a government-business coalition in which they would be the dominant partner. In an examination of the attitudes of businessmen during the passage of the Interstate Commerce Act of 1887 Purcell came to a quite different conclusion. Rejecting the idea that the actions of businessmen grew out of a particular ideology, he insisted that entrepreneurs and managers were more interested in solving particular problems than they were in adhering to any coherent body of thought. Hence some favored regulation while others opposed it. In general, Purcell concluded, diverse economic groups who felt threatened by the new national economy and rate discrimination turned to the federal government in the hope of protecting their interests. Political control of the economy was not their ultimate goal; they simply wanted to protect their own interests.[16]

More recently the history of American business and the history of technology have drawn closer, if only because of the intimate relationship between industrial growth and technology. Even Alfred D. Chandler—whose work dealt largely with the origins and development of business organizations—gave technology a more important place. In

---

[15]In addition to *The Triumph of Conservation: A Reinterpretation of American History, 1900–1916* (New York, 1963), see Kolko's *Railroads and Regulation 1877–1916* (Princeton, 1965) for an illustrative case study of his interpretation.

[16]Edward A. Purcell, Jr., "Ideas and Interests: Businessmen and the Interstate Commerce Act," *Journal of American History* 54 (December 1967):561–578. See also Albro Martin, "The Troubled Subject of Railroad Regulation in the Gilded Age—A Reappraisal," *ibid.* 61 (September 1974):339–371; and *Enterprise Denied: Origins of the Decline of American Railroads 1897–1917* (New York, 1971); and Thomas K. McGraw, "Regulation in America: A Review Article," *Business History Review*, 49 (Summer 1975):159–183; and Thomas K. McGraw, ed., *Regulation in Perspective: Historical Essays* (Cambridge, Mass., 1981).

focusing on technology historians have raised new and difficult issues. What is responsible for technological innovations? How has technology shaped or been shaped by the social and economic organization of modern society?

Business historians, of course, tended to see technology as a positive force in its own right.[17] Others have come to very different conclusions. David F. Noble, for example, argued that machines and technology are never by themselves "the decisive forces of production." At every point technology was mediated by "social power and domination, by institutional fantasies of progress, and by the contradictions rooted in the technological projects themselves and the social relations of production." In *America by Design* Noble attempted to demonstrate how engineering failed to develop an independent point of view, and thus came to serve the needs of corporate capitalism. In a subsequent work he specifically rejected the allegation that technology was an independent variable. Implicit in his work was a political point: that the social relations of production rather than technological determinism were crucial, and only a movement from below could liberate the mass of workers from an economic system that degraded rather than enhanced their lives. Noble's work is a recent restatement of an older antibusiness tradition from the perspective of the modern political left.[18]

More recently James Livingston has emphasized the flaws in traditional interpretations of the triumph of big business. To be sure, administrative responses to market integration as well as technological innovation played a role in altering social relations. Yet Livingston suggested that neither structural nor technological forces were decisive. Employing quasi-Marxian categories and borrowing from the "new social history" and the "new economic history," he insisted that the victory of corporate capitalism was neither inevitable nor easy. The working class, for example, was capable of logical collective action and winning many of its struggles against big business in the decades before 1900; its members were neither powerless nor irrational. During these same years prices, profits, per capita output, and labor productivity growth were declining; the determination of prices remained with the demand side. Hence efforts to reduce wages, regulate output, and increase profits led to bitter and acrimonious conflict, and big business

---

[17]For a discussion of this point see Louis Galombos, "Technology, Political Economy, and Professionalization: Central Themes of the Organizational Synthesis," *Business History Review* 57 (Winter 1983):472–478.

[18]David F. Noble, *America by Design: Science, Technology, and the Rise of Corporate Capitalism* (New York, 1977); "Social Choice in Machine Design: The Case of Automatically Controlled Machine Tools, and a Challenge for Labor," *Politics & Society* 8, Nos. 3–4 (1978):313–347; and *Forces of Production: A Social History of Industrial Automation* (New York, 1984).

found itself in a precarious position and unable to impose its hegemony. Its "solution" included three elements: weakening if not eliminating individual entrepreneurs; forging a novel and asymmetrical relationship that shifted control of the labor process from workers to employers; and creating a new class of corporate capitalists. The rise of corporate capitalism, then, represented an economic solution to a social stalemate. Livingston's analysis of social and economic change in late nineteenth-century America is reprinted as the second selection in this chapter.

In assessing businessmen and the rise of corporate capitalism in the late nineteenth century it is important to understood that differing interpretations often reflect diverging viewpoints regarding the nature of economic development and the impact of technological innovation. Ironically enough, adherents of the robber baron and New Left school implicitly (and sometimes explicitly) extol the virtues of a competitive economy when they criticize the monopolistic objectives of most entrepreneurial and financial leaders. Business historians, on the other hand, tend to argue that the movement toward consolidation arose out of a cutthroat and disorganized economy whose productive potential could never have been realized without the large, decentralized, multidivisional corporation. Still others see the problem within a far more complex framework involving a fundamental shift in class relations.

Which of these viewpoints is justified? Was consolidation a necessary prerequisite for the emergence of a complex industrial economy? Is bigness synonymous with efficiency? Was technology a beneficent or a destructive force? Did the rise of corporate capitalism reflect a fundamental shift in class and social relations? On all these issues opposing schools of thought give very different answers. The upholders of the robber baron and New Left approach insist that the monopolistic control that often accompanies large productive units frequently reflects the inability of these units to meet the challenges of smaller competitors who do not have high overhead and fixed costs. Thus consolidation actually reflects inefficiency rather than efficiency. Some of these historians, moreover, argue that the movement toward consolidation was the result of bureaucratic business reorganizations rather than an effort to increase efficiency. Similarly, a specific use of technology ensured the dominance of capitalism. Most business historians, on the other hand, reject this interpretation. They tend to correlate consolidation with order and efficiency; the most innovative entrepreneurs are those who combined a profit motive with an interest in productive efficiency. Technology, which is both shaped by and shapes the economic environment, is generally considered a positive force by most business historians.

In the final analysis any interpretation of the careers and accomplishments of American industrialists and the role of the large corporation will depend in part on the starting assumptions and values of the scholars making a particular judgment. Despite claims of objectivity it is difficult, if not impossible, for historians to divest themselves of beliefs and standards that influence their analysis of this problem. In some ways an evaluation of business and businessmen is even more controversial than other problems in American history. For underlying such an evaluation is the larger issue of the quality and meaning of the American experience. To some historians the significance of America is directly related to its productive capacity. America, they maintained, has demonstrated to the world that it is possible to create an affluent society within a democratic capitalist framework. Thus the American economy—a creation of industrial pioneers and bold entrepreneurs—should be given credit. Similarly technology, although not without risks, has been a positive force. Other historians, however, pursue quite different lines of thought. The social costs of industrialism, they maintain, could have been far lower had it not been for the greed and quest for power by businessmen. By placing a premium on acquisitive and amoral values and by creating an economic system characterized by gross inequality, they insist, these entrepreneurs and their large corporations contributed to a narrow materialistic spirit. Political capitalism, they allege, was responsible for the wars, racism, and poverty that characterized much of the twentieth century. The use of technology for business purposes also tended to dehumanize rather than enrich the lives of millions of Americans. Any judgment on the role of business, then, often becomes a judgment on the nature and quality of American civilization itself.

Alfred D. Chandler, Jr.

ALFRED D. CHANDLER, JR. (1918-   ) *is Straus Professor of Business History at the Harvard Graduate School of Business Administration. He is the author of a number of books in American business history, including* Henry Varnum Poor *(1956),* Strategy and Structure *(1969), and the Pulitzer Prize-winning* The Visible Hand *(1977).*

For a paper on the historical role of business in America to provide a solid foundation for discussions of the present and future, it must examine a number of questions: Who were the American businessmen? How did they come to go into business? How were they trained? How broad was their outlook? And, of even more importance, what did they do? How did they carry out the basic economic functions of production, distribution, transportation, and finance? How was the work of these businessmen coordinated so that the American economic system operated as an integrated whole? Finally, how did these men and the system within which they worked adapt to fundamental changes in population, to the opening of new lands, resources, and markets, and to technological developments that transformed markets, sources of supply, and means of production and distribution? The answers to these questions, as limited as they may be, should help to make more understandable the present activities and future capabilities of American business.

The Colonial Merchant

The merchant dominated the simple rural economy of the colonial period. By the eighteenth century he considered himself and was considered by others to be a businessman. His economic functions differentiated him from the farmers who produced crops and the artisans who made goods. Although the farmers and artisans occasionally carried on business transactions, they spent most of their time working on the land or in the shop. The merchant, on the other hand, spent nearly all his time in handling transactions involved in carrying goods

Alfred D. Chandler, Jr., "The Role of Business in the United States: A Historical Survey," *Daedalus* 98 (Winter 1969):23–40. Reprinted by permission of *Daedalus*, Journal of the American Academy of Arts and Science, Boston, Mass.

through the process of production and distribution, including their transportation and finance.

The colonial merchant was an all-purpose, non-specialized man of business. He was a wholesaler and a retailer, an importer and an exporter. In association with other merchants he built and owned the ships that carried goods to and from his town. He financed and insured the transportation and distribution of these goods. At the same time, he provided the funds needed by the planter and the artisan to finance the production of crops and goods. The merchant, operating on local, inter-regional, and international levels, adapted the economy to the relatively small population and technological changes of the day and to shifts in supply and demand resulting from international tensions.

These men of business tended to recruit their successors from their own family and kinship group. Family loyalties were important, indeed essential, in carrying on business in distant areas during a period when communication between ports was so slow and uncertain. Able young clerks or sea captains might be brought into the family firm, but sons and sons-in-law were preferred. Trading internationally as well as locally, the merchants acquired broader horizons than the farmer, artisan, and day laborer. Only a few of the great landowners and leading lawyers knew the larger world. It was the colonial merchants who, allied with lawyers from the seaport towns and with the Virginia planters, encouraged the Revolution, brought about the ratification of the Constitution, and then set up the new government in the last decade of the eighteenth century.

The Rise of the Wholesaler, 1800–1850

During the first half of the nineteenth century, although the American economy remained primarily agrarian and commercial, it grew vigorously. The scope of the economy expanded as the nation moved westward into the rich Mississippi Valley, and as increasing migration from Europe still further enlarged its population. Even more important to American economic expansion were the technological innovations that occurred in manufacturing in Great Britain. Without the new machines of the Industrial Revolution, the westward movement in the United States and the migration to its shores would have been slower. These innovations reshaped the British textile industry, creating a new demand for cotton from the United States. Before the invention of the water frame, the spinning jenny, the mule, and then the power loom, cotton had never been grown commercially in the United States, but by 1800 it had become the country's major export. The new plantations in turn provided markets for food grown on the smaller farms in both the Northwest and Southwest. The growth of eastern commercial cities and the development of the textile industry in New England and the middle states enlarged that market still further. The titanic struggle between Great Britain and Napoleon obscured the significance of these economic developments, but shortly after 1815 the economy's new orientation became clear.

The merchants who continued to act as economic integrators had the largest hand in building this new high-volume, regionally specialized, agarian-commercial system. The merchants of Philadelphia, Baltimore, and New York took over the task of exporting cotton, lumber, and foodstuffs and of importing textiles, hardware, drugs, and other goods from Great Britain and the Continent. Those in the southern coastal and river ports played the same role in exporting cotton and importing finished goods to and from the eastern entrepôts; those in the growing western towns sent out local crops and brought in manufactured goods in a similar way. At first the western trade went via rivers of the Mississippi Valley and New Orleans. Later it began to be transported east and west through the Erie Canal and along the Great Lakes. To meet the needs of the expanding trade, the merchants, particularly those of the larger eastern cities, developed new forms of commercial banking to finance the movement of crops, set up packet lines on "the Atlantic Shuttle" between New York and Liverpool to speed the movement of news and imports, founded specialized insurance companies, and helped to organize and finance the new canals and turnpikes that improved transportation between them and their customers.

These innovations enabled the merchants to handle still more business, and the high-volume trade in turn forced the merchants to alter their functions and, indeed, their whole way of life. They began to specialize, becoming primarily wholesalers or retailers, importers or exporters. They came to concentrate on a single line of goods—dry goods, wet goods, hardware, iron, drugs, groceries or cotton, wheat or produce. Some became specialists in banking and insurance and spent their time acting as managers for these new financial corporations.

Of the new specialists, the wholesalers played the most influential role, taking the place of the colonial merchants as the primary integrators and adaptors of the economy. More than the farmers or the retailers, the wholesalers were responsible for directing the flow of cotton, corn, wheat, and lumber from the West to the East and to Europe. More than the manufacturers, they handled the marketing of finished goods that went from eastern and European industrial centers to the southern and western states.

Moreover, the wholesalers financed the long-term growth of the economy. Enthusiastic promoters of canals, turnpikes, and then railroads, they provided most of the local capital for these undertakings. They pressured the state and municipal legislatures and councils (on which they or their legally trained associates often sat) to issue bonds or to guarantee bonds of private corporations building transportation enterprises. At times they even persuaded the state to build and operate transport facilities.

The wholesalers also encouraged the adoption of the new technology in manufacturing. In Boston, the Appletons, the Jacksons, and the Cabots financed the new textile mills of Lowell and Lawrence. In New York, the Phelps and the Dodges started the brass industry in the Connecticut Valley, while in Philadelphia and Baltimore wholesalers like Nathan Trotter and Enoch Pratt financed the growing Pennsylvania iron industry. They not only raised the funds for plants and machinery, but also supplied a large amount of the cash and credit that the new manufacturers needed as working capital to pay for supplies and labor.

Although the wholesalers made important contributions to early-nineteenth-century economic life, they played a less dominant role in the economy than had the colonial merchant of the eighteenth century. The economic system had become too complex—involving too many units of production, distribution, transportation, and finance—for one group to supervise local, inter-regional, and international flows. Nonetheless, the wholesalers had more influence in setting prices, managing the flow of goods, and determining the amount and direction of investment than had other groups—the farmers, manufacturers, retailers, and bankers.

As the economy expanded, the recruitment of businessmen became more open than it had been in the colonial period. At the same time, the outlook of even the most broad-gauged businessmen grew narrower. Family and family ties became less essential, although they could still be a useful source of capital. Businessmen began to place more value on personal qualities, such as aggressiveness, drive, and self-reliance. Nor did one need any lengthy training or education to set up a shop as a wholesaler. Because of their increasing functional specialization, this new breed of wholesalers rarely had the international outlook of the colonial merchants. Not surprisingly, they and the lawyers and politicians who represented them saw their needs in sectional rather than national terms—as did so many Americans in the years immediately prior to the Civil War.

The Rise of the Manufacturer Before 1900

By mid-century the American agrarian and commercial economy had begun to be transformed into the most productive industrial system in the world. The migration of Americans into cities became more significant in this transformation than the final settling of the western frontier. Immigration from Europe reached new heights, with most of the new arrivals staying in the cities of the East and the old Northwest. By 1900, therefore, the rate of growth of the rural areas had leveled off. From then on, the nation's population growth would come almost wholly in its cities.

The second half of the nineteenth century was a time of great technological change—the age of steam and iron, the factory and the railroad. The steam railroad and the steamship came quickly to dominate transportation. In 1849 the United States had only six thousand miles of railroad and even fewer miles of canals, but by 1884 its railroad corporations operated 202,000 miles of track, or 43 per cent of the total mileage in the world. In 1850 the factory—with its power-driven machinery and its permanent working force—was a rarity outside the textile and iron industries, but by 1880 the Bureau of the Census reported that 80 per cent of the three million workers in mechanized industry labored in factories. And nearly all these new plants were powered by steam rather than by water.

America's factories made a vital contribution to the nation's economic growth. By 1894 the value of the output of American industry equalled that of the combined output of the United Kingdom, France, and Germany. In the next twenty years American production tripled, and by the outbreak of World War I the United States was producing more than a third of the world's industrial goods.

As manufacturing expanded, the wholesaler continued for many years to play a significant role in the economy. The period up to 1873 was one of increasing demand and rising prices. The manufacturers, concentrating on building or expanding their new factories, were more than happy to have the wholesalers supply then with their raw and semifinished materials and to market their finished goods. In addition, wholesalers continued to provide manufacturers with capital for building plants, purchasing equipment and supplies, and paying wages.

After the recession of 1873, however, the manufacturers began to replace the wholesaler as the man who had the most to say about coordinating the flow of goods through the economy and about adapting the economy to population and technological changes. The shift came for three reasons. First, the existing wholesale network of hundreds of thousands of small firms had difficulty in handling efficiently the growing output of the factories. Secondly, the manufacturer no longer needed the wholesaler as a source of capital. After a generation of production, he was able to finance plant and equipment out of retained profits. Moreover, until 1850 the commercial banking system had been almost wholly involved in financing the movement of agricultural products, but about mid-century it began to provide working capital for the industrialist. Commercial banks also began to provide funds for plant and equipment, particularly to new manufacturing enterprises.

The third and most pervasive reason why the manufacturer came

to a position of dominance resulted from the nature of factory production itself. This much more efficient form of manufacturing so swiftly
increased the output of goods that supply soon outran demand. From
the mid-1870's to the mid-1890's, prices fell sharply. Moreover, the
large investment required to build a factory made it costly to shut
down and even more expensive to move into other forms of business
activity. As prices fell, the manufacturers organized to control prices
and the flow of goods within their industries. If the wholesalers would
and could help them in achieving such control, the manufacturers welcomed their cooperation. If not, they did it themselves. In most cases,
the industrialist came to play a larger role than the wholesalers in integrating the economy.

The wholesaler was pushed aside in transportation before he was
in manufacturing. Railroad construction costs were high, and after
1849 when railroad expansion began on a large scale, the local merchants simply could not supply the necessary capital. Modern Wall
Street came into being during the 1850's to meet the need for funds.
By 1860 the investment banker had replaced the wholesaler as the primary supplier of funds to American railroads.

In the 1850's and 1860's the railroads also captured many of the
merchant's functions. They took over freight forwarding in large
towns and eliminated the merchant by handling through traffic in
many commercial centers along the main routes west and south. Indeed, during the 1860's the railroads had absorbed most of the fast
freight and express companies developed earlier by the wholesalers in
order to use the new rail transportation. By the 1870's the coordination
of the flow of most inter-regional transportation in the United States
had come under the direction of the traffic departments of a few large
railroads.

The first manufacturers to move into the wholesalers' domain
were those who found that the wholesaler could not meet their special
needs. These were of two types. The makers of new technologically
complex and relatively expensive durable products quickly realized
that wholesalers were unable to handle the initial demonstration to
the consumer, provide consumer credit, or ensure the repair and servic-
ing of the products sold. Thus manufacturers of agricultural imple-
ments, sewing machines, typewriters, cash registers, carriages, bicy-
cles, or, most important of all, electrical machinery and equipment
created national and even international marketing organizations well
before the turn of the century. So did the second type, the processors
of perishable goods requiring refrigeration, quick transportation, and
careful storage for their distribution—fresh meat, beer, bananas, and
cigarettes.

Once the pioneers of both types of enterprises—the McCormicks,
the Remingtons, George Westinghouse and Charles Coffin, the Swifts

and Armours, the Pabsts and Schlitzes, Andrew Preston and James B. Duke—had created their widespread distribution networks, they began again to eliminate the wholesaler by doing their own purchasing. They could not run the risk of stopping complex fabricating or assembling processes because they lacked critical parts or materials. Some integrated backwards even further, doing their own purchasing by building or buying factories to manufacture parts, controlling their own iron, steel, or lumber, or obtaining their own refrigerated cars and ships.

The manufacturers who produced standard commodities that might be distributed easily through the existing wholesaler network were slower to move into wholesaling. Even though the pioneering firms were demonstrating the economies resulting from a combination of mass production and mass distribution, most manufacturers had to be pushed rather than enticed into a strategy of vertical integration. They did so only after they failed to meet the oppressive pressure of falling prices by the more obvious methods of price control through trade associations, cartels, and other loose combinations.

The railroads pioneered in developing ways to control prices in the face of excess capacity and heavy fixed costs. During the 1870's, the railroads formed regional associations, of which the Eastern Trunk Line Association was the most powerful. By the 1880's, however, the railroad presidents and traffic managers admitted defeat. The associations could only be effective if their rulings were enforced in courts of law, but their pleas for legalized pooling went unheard. Indeed, the Interstate Commerce Act of 1887 specifically declared pooling illegal. As a result, the American railroad network became consolidated into large "self-sustaining," centrally managed regional systems. By 1900 most of American land transportation was handled by about twenty-five great systems informally allied in six groupings.

Where the railroads had hoped for legalized pooling, the manufacturers sought other ways of obtaining firmer legal control over the factories in their industries. They began personally to purchase stock in one another's companies. After 1882 when the Standard Oil Company devised the trust as a way of acquiring legal control of an industry, companies began to adopt that device. The holding company quickly superseded the trust as a more effective and inexpensive way of controlling price and production after 1889, when New Jersey passed a general incorporation law that permitted one company to hold stock in many others. The Supreme Court's interpretations of the Sherman Antitrust Act (1890) encouraged further consolidation in manufacturing. Court decisions discouraged loose combinations of manufacturers (or railroads) in any form, but (at least until 1911) appeared to permit consolidation of competing firms through a holding company if that company came to administer its activities under a single centralized management.

In many cases these new consolidations embarked on a strategy of vertical integration. Where the railroads formed "self-sustaining" systems to assure control of traffic over primary commercial routes, the manufacturers attempted to assure the uninterrupted flow of goods into and out of their production and processing plants. John D. Rockefeller and his associates at Standard Oil were the first of the combinations to adopt this strategy. The Standard Oil Trust had been formed after associations in the petroleum industry had proven to be, in Rockefeller's words, "ropes of sand." Legal control of the industry was followed by administrative consolidation of its refineries under a single centralized management. In the mid-1880's, the trust began to build its own distribution network of tank farms and wholesaling offices. Finally, after enlarging its buying organization, it moved in the late-1880's into the taking of crude oil out of the ground.

The examples of Standard Oil, the Swifts, the McCormicks, and others who had by-passed the wholesaler, the rulings of the Supreme Court, the memories of twenty years of declining prices resulted between 1898 and 1902 in the greatest merger movement in American history. Combinations, usually in the form of holding companies, occurred in nearly all major American industries. Holding companies then were often transformed into operating companies. After manufacturing facilities were centralized under a single management, the new consolidated enterprise integrated forwards and backwards.

At the same time, retailers who began to appreciate the potential of mass markets and economies of scale also moved to eliminate the wholesalers—although they did so in a more restricted way than the manufacturers. The mail order houses (Sears, Roebuck and Montgomery Ward), which turned to the rural markets, and the department and chain stores, which looked to the growing cities, began to buy directly from the manufacturers. By the turn of the century, some large retailers had even bought into manufacturing firms. As a result, wholesalers' decisions were of less significance to the operation of the economy than they had been fifty years earlier. Far more important were the decisions of the manufacturers who had combined, consolidated, and integrated their operations and the few giant retailers who had adopted somewhat the same strategy.

As manufacturers replaced wholesalers as key coordinators in the national economy, they became the popular symbol of American business enterprise. The industrialists and the railroad leaders were indeed the reality as well as the symbol of business power in the Gilded Age. The recruitment of this new dominant business group remained open, at least for a generation. As had been true earlier for the wholesaler, aggressiveness, drive, and access to capital or credit were prerequisites for success. Lineage or specialized learning were less important, but some technological knowledge was an advantage. Although the manufacturers' horizons were more national and less regional than the wholesalers', they came to view the national scene from the perspective of their particular industry. They and their representatives in Washington tended to take positions on the major issues of the day—tariff, currency, immigration, and the regulation of business—from an industrial rather than a sectional or regional viewpoint.

It was not long, however, before the needs of the manufacturers and their response to these needs altered the recruitment and training of the nation's most powerful businessmen. The increasingly high investment required for large-scale production made the entry of new men and firms more difficult. The emergence of the vertically integrated enterprise limited opportunities still further. By 1900 it was becoming easier to rise to positions of business influence by moving through the new centralized managements than by starting a business enterprise of one's own. This pattern was already clear in the railroads, the nation's first modern business bureaucracies.

The Dominance of the Manager Since 1900

Although the twentieth century was to become the age of the manager, the growing significance of the manager's role in the operation of the American economy was not immediately apparent. Until the 1920's manufacturers and their assistants concentrated on rounding out their integrated enterprises, creating the internal structures and methods necessary to operate these business empires, and employing the managers necessary to staff them.

At first, external conditions did not seriously challenge the new enterprises. Population trends continued, and heavy migration from abroad sustained urban growth until the outbreak of World War I. During the war, migration from the rural areas to the cities increased. At the same time, impressive technological innovations, particularly those involved with the generating of power by electricity and the internal combustion engine created new industries and helped transform older ones. The continuing growth of the city, the expansion of the whole electrical sector, and the coming of the automobile and auxiliary industries made the first decades of the twentieth century ones of increasing demand and rapid economic growth.

The initial task of the men who fashioned the first integrated giants at the beginning of this century was to build internal organizational structures that would assure the efficient coordination of the flow of goods through their enterprises and permit the rational allocation of the financial, human, and technological resources at their command. First came the formation of functional departments—sales, production, purchasing, finance, engineering, and research and development. At the same time, central offices were organized, usually in the form of an executive committee consisting of the heads of the functional departments. These offices supervised, appraised, and coordinated the work of the departments and planned long-term expenditures.

By the late-1920's the pioneer organization-builders at du Pont, General Motors, General Electric, Standard Oil of New Jersey, and Sears, Roebuck had developed new and sophisticated techniques to perform the vital coordinating and adaptive activities. They based both long- and short-term coordination and planning on a forecast of market conditions. On the basis of annual forecasts, revised monthly and adjusted every ten days, the companies set production schedules, purchases of supplies and semifinished products, employment and wage rolls, working capital requirements, and prices. Prices were determined by costs, which in turn closely reflected estimated volume of output. The annual forecasts took into consideration estimates of national income, the business cycle, seasonal fluctuations, and the company's normal share of the market. Long-term allocations were based on still broader estimates of demand. After 1920, the managers of many large corporations began to include in these allocations the funds and personnel needed to develop new products and processes through technological innovation. From that time on, the integrated firm began to diversify. The Depression and World War II helped to spread these methods, so that by mid-century most of the key industries in the United States were dominated by a few giant firms administered in much the same way.

Their managers considered themselves leaders in the business community and were so considered by others. Yet their differed greatly from the older types of dominant businessmen—the merchants, the wholesalers, and the manufacturers. They were not owners; they held only a tiny portion of their company's stock; they neither founded the enterprise nor were born into it; and most of them had worked their way up the new bureaucratic ladders.

Even to get on a ladder they were expected to have attended college. Studies of business executives in large corporations show that by 1950 the large majority had been to college—an advantage that was shared by few Americans of their age group. Like most of those who did receive higher education, these managers came primarily from white Anglo-Saxon Protestant stock. Once the college man with his WASP background started up the managerial ladder, he usually remained in one industry and more often than not in a single company. That company became his career, his way of life.

As he rose up the ranks, his horizon broadened to national and international levels. Where his firm diversified, his interests and concerns spread over several industries. Indeed, in some ways his perspectives were wider in the 1950's than those of most Americans; nevertheless, because of his specialized training, he had little opportunity to become aware of the values, ideas, ambitions, and goals of other groups of Americans. He had even fewer direct contacts with farmers, workers, and other types of businessmen than had the wholesaler and the manufacturer.

The dominance of the large integrated enterprise did not, of course, mean the disappearance of the older types of businessmen. Small business remained a basis and essential part of the American economy. The small non-integrated manufacturer, the wholesaler, and retailer have all continued to be active throughout the twentieth century. The number of small businesses has continued to grow with the rapid expansion of the service industries (such as laundries and dry cleaners, service and repair shops not directly tied to the large firm); with the spread of real-estate dealers, insurance agencies, and stock brokerage firms; and with the continuing expansion of the building and construction industries. Throughout the century small businessmen have greatly outnumbered the managers of big business. The former were, therefore, often more politically powerful, particularly in the local politics, than the latter. Economically, however, the managers of the large integrated and often diversified enterprises remained the dominant decision-makers in the urban, industrial, and technologically sophisticated economy of the twentieth century. Their critically significant position has been repeatedly and properly pointed out by economists ever since Adolf A. Berle and Gardner C. Means wrote the first analysis of the role and functions of the modern corporation in 1932.

In many ways, the managers were more of an elite than the earlier businessmen had been. Even though this elite was based on performance rather than birth and played a critically constructive role in building and operating the world's most productive economy, its existence seemed to violate basic American democratic values. At the same time, its control of the central sector of the American economy challenged powerful economic concepts about the efficacy of a free market. After 1930, the managers came to share some of their economic power with others, particularly the federal government. Nevertheless, they were forced to do so *not* because of ideological reasons, but because they failed by themselves to assure the coordination and growth of the economy, the basic activities they had undertaken after 1900.

Until the Depression, the government had played a minimal part in the management of the American economy. The merchants had used the government to assist in financing internal improvements that they found too costly or risky to undertake themselves, and the manufacturers had called upon the government to protect them from foreign competition. Small businessmen—wholesalers and retailers—had joined farmers and workers to use the government to regulate the large corporation, but such regulation did not deter the growth of big business nor significantly alter the activities of the managers. Before the Depression, the government had developed few means to influence consciously the over-all performance of the American economy, the major exception being the creation of a central banking system in 1913.

The Depression clearly demonstrated that the corporation managers alone were unable to provide the coordination and adaptation necessary to sustain a complex, highly differentiated, mass-production, mass-distribution economy. The coming of the Depression itself reflected population and technological developments. Legislation in the 1920's cut immigration from abroad to a tiny flow. After World War I, migration from country to city slowed. Meanwhile, new industries, particularly the electric and automobile industries, reached the limit of demand for their output permitted by the existing size and distribution of the national income. At the same time, improved machinery as well as the more efficient management of production and distribution meant that in still other industries potential supply was becoming greater than existing demand. By the mid-1920's prices had begun to decline. Only the existence of credit helped maintain the economy's momentum until 1929.

Corporate giants, like General Motors, General Electric, and du Pont, fully realized that the demand was leveling off in the 1920's, but they could do little more than maintain production at the existing rate or even cut back a bit. When the 1929 crash dried up credit and reduced demand, they could only roll with the punch. As demand fell, they cut production, laid off men, and canceled orders for supplies and materials. Such actions further reduced purchasing power and demand and led to more cuts in production and more layoffs. The downward pressure continued relentlessly. In less than four years, the national income was slashed in half. The forecasts at General Motors and General Electric for 1932 indicated that, at best, the firms would operate at about 25 per cent capacity.

The only institution capable of stopping this economic descent appeared to be the federal government. During the 1930's it undertook this role, but with great reluctance. Until the recession of 1937, Franklin D. Roosevelt and his Secretary of the Treasury still expected to balance the budget and to bring the end to government intervention in the economy. Roosevelt and his Cabinet considered large-scale government spending and employment only temporary. When Roosevelt decided in 1936 that the Depression was over despite high unemployment, he sharply reduced government expenditures. National income, production, and demand immediately plummeted in 1937. The nation then began to understand more clearly the relationship between government spending and the level of economic activity, although acceptance of the government's role in maintaining economic growth and stability was a decade away.

World War II taught other lessons. The government spent far more than the most enthusiastic New Dealer had ever proposed. Most of the output of these expenditures was destroyed or left on the battlefields of Europe and Asia. But the resulting increased demand sent the nation into a period of prosperity the like of which had never before been seen. Moreover, the supplying of huge armies and navies fighting the most massive war of all time required a tight, centralized control of the national economy. This effort brought corporate managers to Washington to carry out one of the most complex pieces of economic planning in history. That experience lessened the ideological fears over the government's role in stabilizing the economy. This new attitude, embodied in legislation by the Employment Act of 1946, continued to be endorsed by Eisenhower's Republican Administration in the 1950's.

The federal government is now committed to ensuring the revival of investment and demand if, and only if, private enterprise is unable to maintain full employment. In 1949 and again in 1953, 1957, and 1960, the government carried out this role by adjusting its monetary and fiscal policies, building roads, and shifting defense contracts. The continuing Cold War made the task relatively easy by assuring the government ample funds. The new role has been defined so that it meets the needs of the corporate managers. The federal government takes action only if the managers are unable to maintain a high level of aggregate demand; it has not replaced the managers as the major coordinators in the economy, but acts only as a coordinator of last resort.

The Depression helped bring the federal government into the economy in another way. During the late-nineteenth and twentieth centuries, workers, farmers, and (to some extent) retailers, wholesalers, and other small businessmen had formed organizations to help them share in making the economic decisions that most intimately affected their well-being. During the 1930's, when the managers were having difficulties in maintaining economic stability, these numerically larger and more politically influential groups were able to get the federal and state governments to support their claims. Through government intervention many workers acquired a say in determining policies in wages, hours, working rules, promotions, and layoffs; farmers gained control over the prices of several basic commodities; and retailers and wholesalers increased their voice in the pricing of certain goods they sold. Nevertheless, the Wagner Act, the Agricultural Adjustment Acts, the Robinson-Patman Act, and the "fair trading" laws did not seriously infringe on the manager's ability to determine current output and to allocate resources for present and future economic activities.

The growth of organized labor during the twentieth century indicates much about the economic power of the large corporation, for this politically powerful group has been able to impress its will on the decisions of corporate managers only in a limited way. Until the Depression, labor unions had little success in organizing key industries dominated by large, managerially operated enterprises. Even during its first major period of growth at the turn of the century, the American Federation of Labor was not successful in the manufacturing industries. From the start, organized labor's strength lay in mining, transportation, and the building and construction trades. In the manufacturing sector, the Federation's gains came not in factory but small-shop industries, such as cigar, garment, hat, and stove-making and ship-building. During the first quarter of the twentieth century, organized labor acquired its members in those industries where skilled workers achieved their goals by bargaining with many small employers. (The railroads were the exception.) The geographically oriented operating structure developed by the American Federation of Labor unions was admirably suited to this purpose.

Precisely because the craft union had grown up in industries where the factory and the large integrated enterprise had never been dominant, the American Federation of Labor found itself in the 1930's unable to organize, even with strong government support, the mass-production, mass-distribution industries so basic to the operation of the modern economy. To unionize these industries required the creation of a structure to parallel the structure of the large integrated enterprise and a program that appealed to semiskilled rather than skilled workers. The AF of L failed to meet this challenge. Only after "a civil war" within the ranks of labor and the creation of a new national labor organization, the CIO, did the automobile, iron and steel, nonferrous metal, rubber, electrical machinery, and other key industries become fully unionized.

During the great organizing drives of the late-1930's and immediately after World War II, union leaders rarely, if ever, sought to gain more than a voice in the determination of wages and hours, working rules, and hiring as well as promotion and layoff policies. Even when they asked (unsuccessfully) for an opportunity "to look at the company's books," union spokesmen did so primarily with the hope of assuring themselves that they were obtaining what they considered a fair share of the income generated by the firm. The critical issue over which management and labor fought in the years immediately following World War II was whether the managers or the union would control the hiring of workers. The unions almost never asked to take part in decisions about output, pricing, or resources allocation. With the passage of the Taft-Hartley Act of 1947, the managers obtained a control over hiring which has never been seriously challenged. Nor have any further inroads into "management's prerogatives" been seriously proposed.

Since 1950, business managers have continued to make the decisions that most vitally affect the coordination of the economy and the pace of its growth. They have also continued to have a major say in how the economy adapts to external forces generated by population movements and technological change.

Population movements in the 1960's present a different challenge than they did before the 1930's. Migration from abroad has remained only a trickle and that from the country to the city has continued to drop. The move to the suburbs, the most significant post-Depression development, has expanded the urban sprawl and undermined the viability of the central city. The resulting problems are, however, more political and social than economic. Whether government officials are better trained than corporate managers to handle these new problems is open to question. If the business managers fail to meet these new challenges, the government will obviously have to do so.

Meanwhile, technological change has maintained a revolutionary pace. Through their concentration on research and development of new products and new methods of production and distribution, corporate managers have been trained to handle the processes and procedures of technological innovation. The large corporation had so "internalized" the process of innovation that this type of change is no longer simply an outside force to which businessmen and others in the economy adjust. Here the expertise of the business manager covers a broader field than that of governmental or military managers. In most of the costly government programs involving a complex technology, the development and production of new products have been turned over to the large corporations through the contracting process. The federal government does, however, supply the largest share of funds for research and development. Thus, even though the business manager continues to play a critical part in adapting the economy to technological change, government officials are in a position to determine the direction and the areas in which research and development will be concentrated.

This brief history of the role of business in the operation of the American economy suggests several tentative conclusions. From the beginning, it seems, businessmen have run the American economy. They can take the credit and the blame for many of its achievements and failures. They, more than [any] other group in the economy, have managed the production, transportation, and distribution of goods and services. No other group—farmers, blue-collar workers, or white-collar workers—has ever had much to do with the over-all coordination of the economic system or its adaptation to basic changes in population and technology.

Over the two centuries, however, the businessman who ran the economy has changed radically. Dominance has passed from the merchant to the wholesaler, from the wholesaler to the manufacturer, and from the manufacturer to the manager. In the last generation, businessmen have had to share their authority with others, largely with the federal government. Even so, the government's peace-time role still remains essentially a supplementary one, as coordinator of last resort and as a supplier of funds for technological innovation.

In the past, businessmen have devoted their energies to economic affairs, giving far less attention to cultural, social, or even political matters. Precisely because they have created an enormously productive economy and the most affluent society in the world, the non-economic challenges are now becoming more critical than the economic ones. There is little in the recruitment, training, and experience of the present business leaders—the corporate managers—to prepare them for handling the difficult new problems, but unless they do learn to cope with this new situation, they may lose their dominant position in the economy. As was not true of the merchant, wholesaler, or manufacturer, the corporate managers could be replaced by men who are not businessmen. To suggest how and in what way the managers will respond to the current challenges is, fortunately, not the task of the historian. Such analyses are properly left to social scientists and businessmen.

James Livingston

JAMES LIVINGSTON (1949–   ) *is associate professor of history at Rutgers University. He is the author of* Origins of the Federal Reserve System: Money, Class, and Corporate Capitalism, 1890–1913 *(1986).*

Until recently, historians writing about the late nineteenth-century United States cast their story as if the hopelessly outclassed "people" inevitably lost whatever battle they happened to be fighting against "big business" or the larger but no less irresistible forces of market integration and technological innovation. Richard Hofstadter, Samuel Hays, and Irwin Unger, for example, differed with Fred Shannon, John Hicks, and Matthew Josephson on the sources and rationality of the majority's resistance to modernity in the form of corporate capitalism, but all assumed that the outcome was never in doubt, indeed, that another outcome would have been somehow unnatural. Over the last fifteen to twenty years, new historiographical approaches have so deeply undermined this consensus that to retrieve its substance would require exhumation, not resuscitation.

James Livingston, "The Social Analysis of Economic History and Theory: Conjectures on Late Nineteenth-Century American Development," *American Historical Review* 92 (February 1987):69–97. Reprinted with the permission of the American Historical Association and James Livingston.

The most important of these approaches are the new labor history and the new economic history. The new labor historians have demonstrated that the working class was perfectly capable of rational collective action, of winning its battles against big business, and of making history in its own right. Meanwhile, a few of the new economic historians have suggested that the late nineteenth century could not have been altogether pleasant for big business because prices, profits, per capita output, and labor productivity growth declined alarmingly from 1870 to 1896. The silence that has settled on the border between these two fields is particularly unfortunate, since both sides evidently agree that, in the late nineteenth century, big business simply did not have the political, economic, or cultural authority customarily ascribed to it.

This unacknowledged agreement between the new labor and new economic historians emerges at a moment when departures in political and cultural history lend powerful support to their revisionist theses. It is probably fair to say that from the remains of the old consensus a new one is already emerging, one which suggests that the late nineteenth century may best be characterized in terms of political, economic, and cultural stalemate. In any case, the recent literature shows that capitalists could not and did not make their social power legitimate or authoritative in any sphere of life until the last decade of the century.

This inadvertent consensus may be taken as an invitation to rewrite the history of the United States in the late nineteenth century. It suggests at the very least that the relation between market power, political power, and cultural authority was anything but linear between 1870 and 1900. But this insight raises a methodological problem that must be addressed before we accept the invitation to rewrite a part of U.S. history: how do we propose, describe, and test a historical relation between the political and economic events we can quantify and the social or cultural phenomena we cannot? To put it another way, how can we integrate the new economic and the new labor history?

One promising solution is to be found in economic theory, the discipline that, as Robert Fogel has suggested, is the source of the new economic history. Over the last twenty-five years, the lack of an adequate theory of distribution consistent with the principle of marginal productivity has driven many economists toward the post-Keynesian model that emerged from the Cambridge debate on neoclassical capital theory, from 1954 to 1970. The most striking and significant finding of this unfinished model—it is more a critique of neoclassical economics than a theory in its own right—reveals that, since no such thing as a "quantity of capital" can exist apart from a given rate of profit, one cannot deduce rates of profit and other elements of income distribution from that quantity, no matter how it is measured. Instead, econo-

mists must posit a real wage and a "rate of exploitation" of labor and
then proceed to estimate incomes as if capital is a continuum of ownership, not a quantity of goods whose measurable value is determined
by its prospective yield. It follows that the distribution of income depends fundamentally on the balance of social power between the active factors of production (capital and labor), and not, as neoclassical
theory holds, on the marginal productivity of capital goods. At a higher
level of argument, it also follows that economic events are explicable
only by reference to the social relations within which they appear—by
reference, that is, to historically specific contexts of production and
exchange.

The new economic history in the late 1960s rose on theoretical
foundations that had been found inadequate to bear any appreciable
load of quantitative data and measurement. It is only now, in the aftermath of the Cambridge debate, that we can see that the social and
cultural context of economic change is not what the new economic
historians have assumed it to be—an "exogenous factor" that can
safely be ignored in building quantitative models of economic behavior
and growth. We can see instead that Karl Marx, Thorstein Veblen, and
Joseph Schumpeter were not so very wrong to claim that economic
change and progress have social and cultural causes and to analyze economic history and theory on that assumption. If these new historiographical tendencies represent an invitation to rewrite U.S. history of
the late nineteenth century, the post-Keynesian critique of neoclassical theory provides a good reason to accept the invitation: a rationale
for an attempt to reintegrate the economic and the social dimensions
of that history.

This attempt begins with three hypotheses. First, the relative but
significant retardation of growth rates after 1870 was the economic
consequence of a social stalemate. Second, renewed economic growth
after 1896 was but one aspect of a broader shift in the balance of social
power and cultural authority. Third, the American version of the mar-
ginalist revolution in economic theory was part of a larger, pragmatic
effort to grasp economic retardation as a problem of distribution—a
social problem—and thus to describe the conditions under which capital could be defined as a factor of production and a legitimate claimant
to a share of national income. Together, these hypotheses constitute
an argument about the emergence of corporate capitalism that may be
read as an alternative to both the new economic history and the so-
called organizational synthesis; they suggest that the innovation we
know as the modern corporate system was an economic solution to a
stubborn social impasse, not merely an administrative response to
market integration or technological imperatives. . . .

If we can judge from the work of the new labor historians, this
acceleration is precisely what capitalists could not accomplish in the

late nineteenth century. Until the mid-to-late 1890s, skilled workers were able to enforce social norms that sanctioned their control of machine production. Before then, the extent of the division of labor and the pace of mechanization in the factory were largely determined, it seems, not by management's new rules of efficiency and reasonable profitability, but by work rules first enacted spontaneously by skilled trades, then codified in union contracts, and ultimately enforced by strikes. The official historian of the Carnegie Homestead Works complained, for example, that, until the skilled workers' union was destroyed by a lockout in 1892, the "method of apportioning the work, of regulating the turns, of altering the machinery, in short, every detail of working the great plant, was subject to the interference of some busybody representing the Amalgamated Association." Extraordinary as it might sound, this complaint was neither unfounded nor confined to the steel industry.

John Frey, an experienced iron molder and a leading labor journalist, ascribed the considerable power exercised by skilled workers at the point of production to the indivisibility of mental and manual labor that workers maintained, first as an unspoken cultural tradition and, then, more consciously, through union work-rules: "It is this unique *possession* of craft knowledge and craft skill on the part of a body of wage workers, that is, their *possession* of these things and the employers' ignorance of them, that has enabled the workers to organize and force better terms from the employers." But, as Frey recognized, the mechanization of industrial production threatened to remedy the ignorance of employers because it entailed a "separation of craft knowledge from craft skill"—that is, it promised to reconstitute and systematize in specialized machines the "scattered craft knowledge" of skilled workers, leaving them with only their "manual skill and dexterity" to sell in the labor market. "The machinery instead of the man is the brains," as a young machinist explained the result to a Senate committee in 1883.

It was this fundamental division of mental and manual labor, not machine production or "industrialism" as such, that skilled workers and their allies fought with remarkable tenacity in the 1880s and 1890s. There are three ways to measure their success. First, wages were not reduced to the extent that managers wanted or sought between 1886 and 1894, largely because longer hours could not be imposed on workers. Second, the gross surplus available to manufacturers—the share of revenue from value added that industrial capitalists could retain after covering wages—declined noticeably over the same years. Third, the growth of productivity virtually ceased until 1895–96. But skilled workers were successful in these terms because they did not have to rely on the resources they could bring to bear at the point of production. They did not ignore or misuse their ultimate weapon, the

TABLE 1
Issues in Strikes, 1881–1905

	Strikes over Working Conditions* Including Hours Excluding Wages	Strikes over Working Conditions Excluding Union Recognition
1881–85	30.6%	22.8%
1886–90	51.1%	37.1%
1891–95	49.7%	34.3%
1896–1900	50.2%	34.3%
1901–1905	60.7%	31.6%

*working conditions = hours, union recognition and rules, employment of
certain persons, method and time of payment, work
rules, discipline, etc.

SOURCE: Adapted from P. K. Edwards, *Strikes in the United States, 1881–1974* (New
York, 1981), Table 4.3 at p. 92.

strike—in fact, they struck more often when the battle over control of
the workplace intensified in the late 1880s and 1890s. (See Tables 1
and 2.) Even so, skilled workers could not have been as effective as
they were if their identification with and access to the sources of political power and cultural authority had not protected and enlarged the
social meaning of their strikes. For example, external forces of "law
and order" were usually neutralized during the strikes of the 1880s,
since many local officeholders, editors, and shopkeepers supported
striking workers (skilled and unskilled) against the large employers.
This solidarity was possible partly because the market power of large
capital had not yet been acknowledged as a permanent or legitimate
dimension of American society. This situation made strikebreaking

TABLE 2
Strikes and Their Resolution, 1881–1905

	Number		Percent by Labor		
Years	Strikes	Establishments	Won	Compromised	Lost
1881–85	2,491	12,443	56.1	8.7	35.2
1886–89	4,849	27,270	44.2	13.1	42.8
1890–93	6,153	27,635	43.7	9.8	46.5
1894–97	4,668	29,123	53.0	15.1	31.9
1898–1901	7,556	35,282	54.4	15.0	30.6
1902–05	11,040	52,990	38.5	19.1	42.4

SOURCES: *Twenty-First Annual Report of the U.S. Commissioner of Labor: Strikes and
Lockouts, 1881–1905* (Washington, D.C., 1906), 15; Edwards, *Strikes*, Table 2.6 at p. 42.

and union-busting more difficult and, to that degree, upheld skilled workers' claims at the point of production.

In the 1880s and, to a lesser extent, the 1890s, skilled workers were able to enforce, in contracts and by strikes, those social norms that presumed and sanctioned their control of machine production. In short, they won the battle against "systematic management." They lost the war, of course, as both the new and old labor historians have demonstrated. But the number, pattern, and resolution of strikes in the 1880s and early 1890s suggest that, by and large, skilled workers were successfully meeting the challenges of employers to effective control of machine production and were thus enforcing the disparity between productivity and real wages that transferred income from capital to labor. Skilled workers, by maintaining their control of machine production, may also have slowed the rate of "technological convergence"—the rate at which new metal-working techniques are exported from machine tool industries and adapted to wider uses in the capital good sector—and thus may have prevented the kind of cost reductions, improved capital efficiency, and increased productivity that technological innovation in this sense often promotes. From either standpoint, late nineteenth-century economic retardation derived from a fundamental social stalemate. . . .

Before we take up this approach, however, it should be noted that, in the late nineteenth century, the discussion of the "social question" normally implied or simply meant discussion of the "labor problem." The assumption that industrialization in the United States was producing a permanent working class and a class society according to the European model informed almost every contemporary analysis of economic development, regardless of the analyst's political sympathies. By the last decade of the century, equating the social question and the economic question had become typical. For capitalists as well as Populists, the reorganization or redefinition of the market economy became the only basis of social stability, progress, and justice.

From the standpoint of the capitalists, coming to terms with the labor problem meant solving the problem of overproduction. As long as the determination of prices was left to the demand side, profits could be raised or reinstated only by cutting wages and breaking unions. Bitter class conflict appeared to be the inevitable result. In any case, wage cuts and lockouts did not always succeed in their purpose; at least, they had not between 1884 and 1892. The vice-chairman of the Chicago Conference on Trusts explained the dilemma this way: "A large part of the friction that has existed between capital and labor, causing strikes, lockouts and riots, was the result, in part, of overproduction. The product was unloaded at a loss, the owners tried to recompense themselves by cutting the wages of their workmen." Carroll D. Wright analyzed the problem in similar terms: "If there are more goods in the market than there is any demand for, and goods must be

made at a loss, and there is no advantage in the purchase of raw material, labor is the only elastic feature in the [cost of the] product."
Arthur T. Lyman, the treasurer of the Lowell Manufacturing Company,
was more succinct: "When profits disappear wages must fall."

Business leaders and influential interpreters of economic development had the same answer to the problem of overproduction: "combination," a corporate consolidation of control over investment and production. They proposed to narrow the social basis of investment
decisions by centralizing claims to productive assets through the legal
device of corporations. For example, Jeremiah Jenks noted that the
"waste of competition . . . which comes from the inability of adapting
one's plants and output to the needs of the market . . . can be partly
saved by combination of many manufacturing establishments in one
industry under one management." On this, the economists and the
capitalists were practically unanimous. If prices could be stabilized at
a level that allowed reasonable profits, because supply was adjusted to
demand—if overproduction was to this extent abolished—then capitalists would not have to treat wages as the crucial variable in calculating
the difference between costs and prices that equaled profits. Thus, resorting to class war would not represent the best alternative to operating at a loss. This corporate alternative presupposed a social agenda;
for, if it were to succeed, the small or marginal entrepreneurs would
have to be effectively disciplined or simply purged from the economic
organism: they would have to give up their once-commanding role in
resource allocation if overproduction were not to be resurrected from
the supply side. William Jennings Bryan's "broader class of businessmen" became an endangered species by the mid-1890s. "They are the
ones who have been caught between the upper and the nether mill
stones," as James J. Hill of the Great Northern Railway put it, "they
are the middlemen, and the small competitor who was unable to meet
the larger concern in the open market."

The social agenda announced in this corporate alternative to overproduction necessarily included more than an elimination of small-
scale entrepreneurs. Control of supply under corporate auspices meant
consolidating ownership of the separate companies and dispersed
plants that had competed with each other for sales and profit within
limited markets. It also meant establishing or consolidating managerial control at the point of production, where skilled workers held
sway. In the view of the corporate innovators, bringing an end to "ruinous competition" was senseless unless the plants that remained in operation after a merger or reorganization could be made more efficient
and productive. If wage rates were not flexible (as indeed they were
not), the condition of greater efficiency and productivity was the further mechanization of the labor process. Charles R. Flint, a founder of
the U.S. Rubber Company and perhaps the most outspoken promoter
of corporate consolidation, explained how this condition could be met

only within the new institutional framework of the corporate system: "The American workingman to-day earns higher wages than are paid in any other country. This condition has been made possible . . . because the American workingman produces more, and he produces more because he has been supplied with the most perfect system of labor-saving machinery on earth. To supply this machinery, large capital is necessary. The individual manufacturer, standing alone, is not in a position to perfect his machinery in the same measure as the consolidated enterprise."

In these terms, the most important of the "economies of scale" to be realized by the large corporations was their capacity to finance greater investment in fixed capital while reducing the ratio of fixed costs to the value of total output. Of the "various economies" residing in the large scale of the corporations, Flint and his peers emphasized above all else that "centralized manufacture permits the largest use of special machinery." The corporation thus constituted a means to the end of mechanizing, and controlling, the labor process. Skilled workers and capitalists agreed that technological innovation at the point of production was a preeminently social process that would determine whether employers or employees controlled the labor process. A survey of production methods in industry by the U.S. Commissioner of Labor in 1898 found, for example, that cutting leather parts for shoes and boots could be (and was) done by hand in about half the time it took by machine. The apparent anomaly bothered the commissioner enough to query one respondent. "When called to the attention of the manufacturer he stated that the time was correct, and that a smart cutter unhampered by 'union rules' could perform the work in the time specified." The point of installing the cutting machinery was, then, to shift control of output from labor to capital, even though, as the commissioner's report noted, the "greatest efficiency is obtained under the primitive method."

Labor unions had a role in the corporate dispensation, but they could not be allowed to exercise any meaningful control of machine production. If unions limited the use of new labor-saving machinery to preserve the indissolubility of craft skill and craft knowledge, the "economies of scale" promised in the mechanization of production could not be realized. This threat held special significance when corporate leaders contemplated the development of foreign markets, a field of enterprise in which the large corporations were indispensable. For example, Frank Vanderlip, the vice-president of New York's National City Bank, declared in 1903 that "controlling the world's industrial markets" was almost certainly the destiny of the United States. "The only serious obstacle in the way of that," he noted, "will be our labor organizations." Unions that sought to increase wages were perfectly acceptable. If they sought any role in determining rates of output, however, as they were accustomed to doing in the late nineteenth century, they would undermine American competitiveness in world markets: "We are surrounded by conditions that will permit us to pay two or three times as much wages as our foreign competitors and still meet successfully their competition, but we cannot, in addition to that handicap, of high wages, permit the workers to limit production and hope for a successful outcome in a world contest."

The corporate innovators were ultimately able to abolish any formal control of output by skilled or unionized workers; they succeeded where the entrepreneurs had failed. The builders and promoters of the corporations explained the difference in social terms. Their new creations provided the "means to industrial managers to combat unfair demands on the part of labor organizations," as Vanderlip stated, "for they are better united and able to meet organization with organization." The great industrial combinations were, then, both cause and effect of a new social order, because the concentration of capitalists as well as capital was a natural result of the corporate movement. John E. Searles, a director of the American Sugar Refining Company from its founding in 1891, described the process this way: "Perhaps the greatest of all benefits in the centralization is the concentration of technical knowledge and ability of the people connected with the business. . . . When the Trust was organized, these gentlemen were brought together and this technical knowledge and skill was concentrated and utilized for the common good." James B. Dill, a lawyer who drafted the New Jersey statute of 1889 under which four out of five corporations were chartered during the merger wave of 1898–1903, took a broader view: "Industrial combinations are producing a new class of financiers, a new order of corporate men."

According to its proponents, the corporate alternative to overproduction and class war established or entailed a social agenda that included at least three items. These were, first, the demise of those small, freely competing entrepreneurs who constituted the nineteenth-century version of a middle class; second, the creation of a new relation between workers and the mechanical conditions of work, through which control of the labor process could be shifted to employers and the growth of labor productivity could be guaranteed; third, the emergence of a new class of capitalists, a "new order of corporation men." In each case, the corporation represented the institutional means to the kind of social change that would allow economic recovery. Insofar as it destroyed the social basis of overproduction—a surplus of entrepreneurs—the corporation gave capitalists the opportunity and the resources to deal with the labor problem as a social question at the point of production.

☆ 3 ☆

Women in History

MAINSTREAM
OR MINORITY?

American women, astonishing as it sounds, have been "invisible" in the historical literature throughout most of American history. To be sure, there were sometimes quick glimpses in the past of a few famous women in the pages of history books—heroines like Amelia Earhart, authors such as Harriet Beecher Stowe, and reformers like Jane Addams. But by and large one was given the impression that American men had given birth to themselves, and were nurtured and raised by their fellow males. "From reading history in textbooks one would think half our population made only a negligible contribution to history," complained Arthur Schlesinger, Sr., the eminent Harvard historian, in 1922. With the rise of the women's liberation movement in the 1960s, however, there came a dramatic change. Women's groups suddenly became visible to the public eye, and when that happened they became visible to scholars. Since the 1960s there has been a veritable explosion in women's studies and books on the role of women in American culture.

One issue has dogged women's studies, however. There has been a kind of identity crisis regarding the subject as a whole. Was the study of women in history part of the mainstream of American history? Or was women's history to be treated as "minority history"—a history separated and unconnected from "men's history"? Should the findings in women's studies be related to trends in traditional American history? Or should women in history be treated as a subgroup—even though they have comprised half of the American population? Was women's history a subfield of social history? Or was the experience of women so different because of their sex that they should be considered in a completely different category?

The tradition of neglecting women in history was a reflection of the way in which historical writing developed down through the ages.

For centuries kings and generals provided the main focus for most historians. In the nineteenth century politicians and businessmen, as they advanced to hold more power, came into greater historical prominence. Women, with the exception of a few queens here and there, had traditionally been excluded from the seats of power and were rarely mentioned in history books as a result.

With the development of American social history in the first half of the twentieth century, however, groups previously ignored by historians—working people, racial and ethnic minorities, and women—were scrutinized more carefully by scholars. But the history of women was still restricted to their struggles for suffrage or for more legal rights because that seemed to be the only part of the story worth telling. Only in the past three decades have scholars begun to give this important subject the attention it deserves. For this reason women's history in American is still in its infancy.

The development of the field of women's history has been hampered, moreover, by two interrelated factors: the lack of any general conceptual scheme to show the direction in which social changes were moving; and the lack of agreement on assumptions regarding the field as a whole. Despite these persistent problems historians have managed to make some scholarly contributions on the subject.

In chronological terms historical writings about women in America may be broken down roughly into four stages. First, there was the formative stage—1607–1900—during which initial steps were taken to write works and to collect materials for a more systematic study of the role of women in society. Second, the Progressive stage of historiography—1900 to the end of World War II—when many but not all of the writings were produced or influenced by Progressive historians. Third, the preparatory period—the mid-1940s to 1960—when a number of fine scholarly works were written, but during which women's studies remained a subfield of American history. Finally, the contemporary period—1960 to the present—when women's studies came into its own as a major field and witnessed an outpouring of books on the subject.

During the formative stage in the seventeenth and eighteenth centuries almost nothing was written about women and women's history. Lacking the right to vote and absent from the seats of power, women were not considered an important force in history. Anne Bradstreet wrote some significant poetry in the seventeenth century, Mercy Otis Warren produced the best contemporary history of the American Revolution, and Abigail Adams penned important letters showing she exercised great political influence over her husband, John. But little or no notice was taken of these women and their contributions. During these first two centuries women remained invisible in history books.

Throughout the nineteenth century this lack of visibility continued despite the efforts of female authors writing about members of their own sex. These writers, like most of their male counterparts, were amateur historians. Their writings were celebratory in nature and they were uncritical in their selection and use of sources.

During the nineteenth century, however, certain feminists showed a keen sense of history by keeping records of activities in which women were engaged. National, regional, and local women's organizations compiled accounts of their doings. Personal correspondence, newspaper clippings, and souvenirs were saved and stored. These sources form the core of the two greatest collections for women's history in America—one at the Elizabeth and Arthur Schlesinger Library at Radcliffe College, and the other the Sophia Smith Collection at Smith College. Such sources provided valuable materials for later generations of historians.

Throughout the nineteenth century most of the writing about women conformed to the "great women" theory of history, just as much of mainstream American history concentrated on "great men." To demonstrate that women were making significant contributions to American life, female authors singled out women leaders and wrote biographies, or else important women produced their autobiographies. Most leaders were involved in public life either as reformers, suffragettes, or authors, and were not representative at all of the great mass of ordinary women. The lives of ordinary women remained untold in the American histories being published for the most part.

Elizabeth Cady Stanton wrote what was surely the most famous women's document of the nineteenth century when she framed the Declaration of Sentiments for the women's rights convention held in Seneca Falls, New York, in 1848. She deliberately shaped the document to echo the language in the Declaration of Independence—though within a different context. "We hold these truths to be self-evident: that all men and women are created equal," she wrote. In a brilliant paraphrase she suggested that the male sex dominated women in the same way George III had oppressed the colonists. It was a masterful propaganda stroke and fired the imagination of those present. Stanton, along with Susan B. Anthony, a colleague in the woman's suffrage movement, helped to compile the first three volumes of the *History of Woman Suffrage* and published them from 1881 to 1886. Two years later Stanton produced her memoirs, *Eighty Years or More*, which defined her particular brand of feminism and proclaimed it to be the dominant one for her era.

Susan B. Anthony, Stanton's close friend and collaborator, was equally anxious to spread her ideas through her writings. She not only contributed a fourth volume to the *History of Woman Suffrage*, but used her personal funds to buy up most of the first edition and presented the volumes to colleges and universities. In 1908 a three-

volume work entitled *Life and Work of Susan B. Anthony* was produced by Ida Husted Harper, an editor who had worked on the wom-
en's suffrage series.

Stanton and Anthony identified themselves with a particular
brand of feminism, one that was shaped by a special set of circumstances and carried with it certain assumptions. By background they
were both middle class, educated, and white. They may be seen as the
first generation of equal-rights feminists—women who came to their
sweeping assessment of the subordination of women through their participation in the reform movements for abolitionism and temperance.
Their demand for equality sprang from their frustration in seeking
moral reforms that could not be realized without legislative and judicial change. Their inability to bring about such change led them to
search for a constituency or group that might support such reforms—
the first such constituency being black, the second the working-class
movement, and the final one middle-class women who were interested
mainly in gaining the right to vote.

While groping their way to this final constituency both women
were radicalized by a series of events. First, by the rejection of the
women's cause by black men and by fellow white male reformers. Second, by their hostile encounters with members of the trade union
movement. And finally, by their contacts and brief alignment with
Victoria Woodhull—an American editor who supported such controversial issues as women's suffrage, free love, and socialism. These developments led Stanton and Anthony to adopt a conspiracy theory in
their account of the women's suffrage movement. They attributed the
delays in securing the vote to two groups: male politicians, who were
fearful of the women's vote; and to the liquor interest, which worried
lest enfranchised women might impose prohibition.[1]

A different brand of feminism was espoused by Frances Willard,
showing that the Stanton-Anthony conspiracy theory was not necessarily sound. Willard's attitudes were shaped by a different set of circumstances. Coming from a poor family and an isolated rural background in New York State, Willard differed from most nineteenth-
century reformers who were drawn from the middle class and hailed
from urban areas. She discovered her constituency with relative ease
among Methodist women in the West. Willard, who had a genius for
organization, helped to mobilize these women around a movement for
temperance reform. Her own experiences and those of other leaders
in the Women's Christian Temperance Union were described in two
books—her autobiography, *Glimpses of Fifty Years*, published in 1889,

---

[1]The foregoing analysis was drawn largely from Jill K. Conway's excellent bibliography, *The Female Experience in Eighteenth- and Nineteenth-Century America* (New
York, 1982), p. 199.

and her *Portraits and Biographies of Prominent American Women,* written with a colleague and issued twelve years later.

Willard's writings showed that her attitudes and those of her compatriots were at some variance with the ideas of Stanton and Anthony, the equal-rights feminists. Willard's interests extended to a number of different reforms including suffrage, women's dress, and labor reform—though her main focus remained on temperance. She stressed the religious roots and motivation of her movement and its effect in preserving the women's sphere in the home. Willard's brand of feminism, therefore, was interested less in raising women to an equal status with men and more in simply enhancing the authority of women.

The writings by and on these nineteenth-century women were representative of an entire genre that dealt with other important female figures. Some were eulogistic biographies of women involved in reform movements: Dorothea Dix, who was interested in the care of the insane; Lucretia Mott, the Quaker abolitionist; and the Grimke sisters, who were involved in both abolitionism and the women's rights movement. Others dealt with leading literary figures, such as Harriet Beecher Stowe and Margaret Fuller. Catharine Beecher, on the other hand, made her national reputation by writing a housekeeping manual in which she portrayed domestic life as the very foundation of a stable democracy.[2]

There was relatively little writing or attention paid, however, to working-class women. Lucy Larcom, a factory textile worker in Lowell, Massachusetts, left a classic autobiography. *A New England Girlhood,* published in 1889, telling of her experiences. In her book Larcom described firsthand the boardinghouse system, the attempts to organize mill workers, and the creation of a local female culture. Daniel D. Addison five years later wrote the story of Larcom's life and published a collection of her letters.[3]

Carroll Wright, the first United States Commissioner of Labor, meanwhile, was compiling invaluable information on the conditions of women's employment in his *Industrial Evolution of the United States,* issued in 1895. Although there were great masses of ordinary women in the society undergoing different experiences—immigrant women; women from different ethnic, racial, and religious groups; and

---

[2]Francis Tiffany, *Life of Dorothea Lynde Dix* (Boston, 1982); Anna Hallowell, ed., *James and Lucretia Mott* (Boston, 1884); Catherine H. Birney, *The Grimke Sisters* (Boston, 1885); Theodore Weld, *In Memory: Angelina Grimke Weld* (Boston, 1880); Charles E. Stowe, *Harriet Beecher Stowe* (Boston, 1890); Annie Fields, *Life and Letters of Harriet Beecher Stowe* (Boston, 1898); Thomas W. Higginson, *Margaret Fuller Ossoli* (Boston, 1884); Julia Ward Howe, *Margaret Fuller* (Boston, 1890); and Catharine Beecher, *A Treatise on Domestic Economy* (Boston, 1841).

[3]Daniel D. Addison, *Lucy Larcom* (Boston, 1894).

women suffering the rigors of the frontier—for the most part, they escaped the attention of historians until 1900.

During the second stage of writing on women's history—1900 to the mid-1940s—much but not all of the writing reflected the work or influence of four major Progressive historians—Mary R. Beard, Charles A. Beard, Arthur M. Schlesinger, Sr., and Frederick Jackson Turner. The Progressive historians, generally speaking, dominated the field of American history from the turn of the century down to the end of World War II. Stressing class and sectional conflict as major interpretive themes they rewrote the outlines of American history as a whole. When it came to writing women's history they stressed these same themes, and emphasized social and economic factors as the most important forces operating in history. The Progressive historians tended also to take a more materialistic approach in explaining the workings of history. Besides such attitudes these scholars were professionally trained historians and introduced a more scholarly and conceptual approach in the writing of women's history.

During the first four and a half decades of the twentieth century, moreover, conditions changed the climate of opinion regarding the status of women. Writers in the seventeenth and eighteenth centuries had viewed the women's sphere as being confined to domestic affairs and being divinely ordained. Throughout most of the nineteenth century writers felt that the woman's place was in the home. But in the first half of the twentieth century a different spirit was abroad in the land. In economic terms women entered industry in massive numbers—especially during World War I and World War II. Politically women received the vote in 1920 and became a force to be reckoned with at the polls. Socially, in these decades, a more liberated woman emerged in the form of the flapper—an archetype who became a symbol for greater sexual and social freedom. These changes helped to set the stage for a different approach in the writing of women's history.

Mary R. Beard, for example, developed an important theory of women's history in her *Woman as Force in History*, a remarkable, wide-ranging book. Written at the very end of the Progressive stage of historiography—in 1946—this work advanced a broad conceptual approach for giving women a more prominent place in history. Mary Beard's main argument was that the endless subjugation women had had to endure throughout world history had caused them to misunderstand their strength in the past. Women had internalized this myth of secondary status and had built this analysis into their view of themselves. By stressing only the obstacles to their fulfillment as persons rather than their strengths, women had been prevented from understanding the potential power they had held down through the ages.

Mary Beard went on to propose an outline of world history—one that would describe the contributions women had made to world civilization in their roles as rulers, queens, teachers, abbesses, and builders of institutions. She was concerned primarily with the role and effect of women operating in the public world rather than in the domestic sphere. Because she believed in the inevitability of democratic progress she conceptualized the reconstruction of women's history in which their role as a civilizing force would be stressed. She had great faith, moreover, that the women of her day were about to cast off their chains and to emerge as leaders in the progress of civilization.[4]

During the Great Depression of the 1930s Mary Beard wrote two books that laid the groundwork for her major work of the following decade. In 1931 she published *On Understanding Women*. In 1933 she wrote *America through Women's Eyes* to show how differently American history looked when seen from a female point of view.

Mary Beard also coauthored a two-volume work with Charles Beard, *The Rise of American Civilization*, in 1927—one of the most influential college textbooks of its time. The Beards insisted upon the importance of public life, in part because of their focus on power as a major motivating force in history. For this reason they viewed women's roles as crucial and presented a whole range of women's contributions in the field of politics, economics, and religion. Through their efforts the Beards succeeded in moving women's history somewhat closer to the mainstream of American history.

Arthur Schlesinger, Sr., another Progressive historian, was also a prime mover in the attempts to bring women's studies nearer to the mainstream. In his *New Viewpoints of American History*, published in 1922, Schlesinger protested that most standard textbooks left women out of their treatment of American history. They therefore gave the impression that women had not made any worthwhile contributions to American history. "Before accepting the truth of this assumption," Schlesinger went on, "the facts of our history need to be raked over from a new point of view." Schlesinger then added, "It should not be forgotten that all great historians have been men and were likely therefore to be more influenced by a sex interpretation of history all the more potent because [it was] unconscious."[5] In *The Rise of the American City*, published in 1933, Schlesinger devoted an entire chapter to women's history. He sought to place women's history in the mainstream rather than have it treated as a kind of minority history. Despite his challenge and the example he set Schlesinger's call went largely unheeded by his academic colleagues.

---

[4]Ann D. Gordon, Mari Jo Buhle, and Nancy Schrom, "Women in Society," *Radical America* 5 (1971):4–5.

[5]Arthur M. Schlesinger, Sr., *New Viewpoints in American History* (New York, 1922), p. 126.

Although Frederick Jackson Turner did not deal directly with women's studies his influence could be seen in several major books published during the Progressive stage. One was Arthur W. Calhoun's *Social History of the American Family*, a three-volume work published from 1917 to 1919. For decades this work remained the classic study of the American family. Calhoun's discussion of courting customs, marriage, and the family within the various sections of the country was clearly derived from Turner. Although Calhoun's statistics about early marriages in colonial times, fertility rates, and family size were found by present-day historians to be inaccurate, it was a pioneering work in its time in terms of the questions it raised.

Turner's influence was also evident in the work of Richard B. Morris whose *Studies in the History of American Law*, published in 1930, employed a Turnerian approach to demonstrate how frontier conditions in the colonies brought about changes in British law. Morris showed how American courts stretched the letter and spirit of British law to allow women greater latitude in marriage contracts, property holding, and property settlements. In his *Government and Labor in Early America*, published in 1946, Morris also integrated valuable information regarding the status of women in colonial times.

Throughout the Progressive stage there were a number of important works by other historians showing the significant contributions that women made to economic and social life in colonial days. Elizabeth Dexter in *Colonial Women of Affairs*, published in 1924, ransacked newspapers and business directories to reconstruct the working lives of women in colonial times, and revealed a wide range of female skills and occupations. In *Women in Eighteenth-Century America*, issued in 1935, Mary Benson contributed a pioneering work on the subject. Julia Cherry Spruill's *Women's Life and Work in the Southern Colonies*, which appeared in 1938, was another scholarly work covering women during the colonial period.

One of the major works to appear stressing the influence of ideas in marriage and the family in colonial New England was Edmund Morgan's *Puritan Family*, published in 1944. Morgan's book provided a sensitive portrait of how Puritanism defined a woman's rights within marriage as well as her relations with her husband. His work was a superb synthesis and demonstrated how intellectual history, religious history, and women's history could be integrated.

As America matured and women began moving out of the home and into the factory other scholars focused on the impact of industrialization on women's lives. The work of Helen Sumner was of the utmost importance in this regard. She edited, along with John Commons and others, the fifth and sixth volumes of *Documentary History of American Industrial Society*, an eleven-volume work issued in 1910. Sumner also produced a major study entitled "Women in Industry in the United States," which was later incorporated into the nineteen-volume *Report on the Condition of Women and Child Wage Earners in the United States,* issued in 1910.

In another important economic study, *Women in Industry,* which also appeared in 1910, Edith Abbott surveyed the working conditions of women in certain industries—textiles, printing, and cigar-making. The position of women in these businesses, Abbott concluded, was undermined by the steady process of mechanization. Abbott pointed out, moreover, the increasing disparity that took place between men's and women's wages in jobs within these industries.

From the turn of the century to the end of World War II—the period labeled the Progressive stage of historiography—women's history had made considerable progress. Some outstanding scholars had contributed important works and had begun promoting the cause of women's history. Despite the advances made, however, the field still lay outside the accepted confines of the discipline as a whole. Women were still "invisible" whenever scholars discussed the most important forces or groups shaping American history.

The preparatory period from the mid-1940s to 1960 witnessed the appearance of two works, one in France and the other in the United States, which set the stage for the contemporary period to come. Simone de Beauvoir's *The Second Sex,* written by France's outstanding philosopher intellectual, was a wide-ranging work of stunning brilliance. De Beauvoir postulated a grand synthesis of all previous feminist arguments, and described women's subordinate position and status in all known societies in Western culture. Although Beauvoir's monumental book failed to exercise a decisive influence on feminist thinkers when it first appeared in America in translation in 1953, it had a great impact in subsequent years.

De Beauvoir argued that in every known society persons were assigned specific roles and indoctrinated to perform to certain expectations established within their respective societies. For women this process invariably meant socialization to a value system that imposed upon them greater restrictions regarding their range of choices than those imposed upon men. This meant that women had been socialized to fit into institutions created, shaped, and controlled by men. The definitions of selfhood and fulfillment by women as a result always remained subordinate to patriarchal concepts. In this sense women everywhere have always been "the second sex," and relegated to a position comparable to that of racial minorities. De Beauvoir's book helped to radicalize the thought of many American feminist theorists of the 1960s.

The most important book written in America during the preparatory period was Eleanor Flexner's *Century of Struggle,* published in

1959. Her work covered the women's rights movement from 1820 to 1920, when the fight for the right to vote was finally successful. Flexner's book was no narrow history of the women's rights movement. It provided a synthesis of women's history by setting the subject within the broad context of the labor movement and other reform movements. The questions Flexner raised, her meticulous research, and her carefully couched conclusion that after a century of agitation for their rights women had made only relatively modest gains, prepared the way for the next generation of historians of women.

The impact of Flexner's pioneering effort was not immediately apparent, however. At the start of the contemporary period beginning in the 1960s, David Potter, the distinguished American historian, was still calling attention to the invisibility of women in American history. He challenged the generally held assumption that historical events in America applied equally to both men and women. Pointing to the Turner thesis Potter commented that in almost all the accounts that thesis was shown to apply to men alone. The city, ,not the countryside, was the "frontier" that provided the greatest opportunities for women, Potter argued.[6]

The contemporary period in the writing of women's history from 1960 to 1990 may, from a quantitative viewpoint, be divided roughly in half. This breakdown resulted from changes taking place throughout the historical profession: women's history gradually became the subject of serious study in graduate schools; women entered the profession in increasing numbers and began publishing; and courses in women's history became part of the regular college curriculum attracting more potential scholars. From 1960 to the mid-1970s, however, the growth was relatively slow and modest. The number of books in the field were few; courses on the graduate level almost nonexistent, with only four historians defining themselves as specialists in women's history; and scholars writing were self-trained and numbered more men than women.

The real takeoff point in the field occurred during the five-year period 1975–1980 when 36 books were published, three-quarters of them by women. The authors were young, had emerged out of the women's movement of the 1960s, and by and large were still trained by male mentors. Scholarship on the subject exploded during the decade of the 1980s; by 1986 over 1000 scholars were working in the field in the United States. Between 1981 and 1987, 40 books were published. Many of them were by younger women, taught by female mentors and trained thoroughly in women's history. Journals were founded to pub-

---

[6]David Potter, "National Character," in *American History and Social Sciences*, Edward Saveth, ed. (New York, 1964), p. 427.

lish and promote research, including *Signs, Feminist Studies, Women's Studies Quarterly,* and *Journal of Women's History.* The contemporary period may be said to mark the coming of age of women's history, and it gave rise to what was called the "new women's history."[7]

Such changes were the result, in part, of developments taking place outside the scholar's study, so to speak. The decade of the 1960s witnessed a series of momentous developments that signaled the day of a new feminism was at hand. The publication of Betty Friedan's best-selling *Feminine Mystique* in 1963 provided evidence that modern feminism had emerged as an important topic in the public mind. In that same year a government commission appointed by President Kennedy published a report documenting the widespread discrimination against women when seeking employment, educational opportunities, or political advancement. In 1964 Congress added the word *sex* in the Civil Rights Act, thereby prohibiting discrimination against women seeking employment. The founding of the National Organization for Women (NOW) under the presidency of Betty Friedan in 1966, and the appearance of radical women's groups proclaimed the existence of a new mass movement—the women's liberation movement. All this newfound interest about women's issues had the effect of raising the consciousness of scholars writing about women's history, attracting women to the historical profession, and raising a whole host of new questions about women in America's past.

At the same time changes were taking place within the historical profession—inside the scholars' study—which also affected the writing of women's history. Among these were the rise of the "new social historians," the resurgence in black history, and the activism of the New Left which all occurred at about the same time as the women's movement. The "new social historians" were profoundly influenced by the *Annales* school of French historians, as noted previously. They tended to focus more on the lives of ordinary people, resorted to new sources such as wills, deeds, and tax lists to re-create the universe of the inarticulate, adopted the approaches of other social sciences, emphasized demography and multidisciplinary methods, and used new computer and quantification techniques. The "new social historians" had emphasized also such social categories as race, class, age, and family status. Scholars of the "new women's history," in turn, adopted many of the methods of the "new social historians," but went one step farther: they utilized yet another most important variable—sex or gender differentiation.

---

[7]Gerda Lerner, "Priorities and Challenges in Women's History Research," *Perspectives* (April 1988):17–20. In the discussion of the "new women's history," it should be noted that studies about black women are omitted for the most part, and dealt with in the chapter "Black History Since 1865."

By using sex as a category of analysis, however, the "new women's history" went well beyond the "new social historians." Urban historians, for example, had paid no special attention to women, even though urban populations as they developed in America usually had more women than men. Religious studies rarely noted that among American Protestant converts and followers the figures were heavily skewed toward women. Histories of social reform movements, such as abolitionism or progressivism, generally failed to acknowledge sufficiently the role of women. The studies of class mobility based on tax and census lists of the occupation under "household heads" usually overlooked women's economic contributions, and thus presented faulty conclusions regarding family wealth levels. In short, American scholars had produced a rather one-sided picture of events by viewing much of American history in male-centered terms.[8]

The addition of sex as a category of analysis, however, did not resolve all problems—including the issue of mainstream or minority. Some female historians felt that simply adding the activities of women to the traditional story of American history did not go far enough. Their criticism was that such an approach resembled an "add-and-stir" recipe, in putting in one more ingredient. The explanatory power of women's history was such, they argued, that it should bring about a complete re-conceptualization of all American history. Instead of using the traditional approach to our history, which is still mired in the male mode, when categorizing, ordering, and analyzing events, the entire corpus of American history should be restructured, they claimed.[9]

The "new women's history" sought to restore the visibility of women in American history by three means: different perspectives, various theories, and new methodologies. In terms of perspectives, women historians often adopted either a liberal, Marxist, or radical feminist point of view. Liberal feminists influenced mainly by the women's liberation movement took up issues raised by that movement, such as gaining equal rights for women, but they did so within the context of a liberal capitalistic system. Marxist feminists, on the other hand, emphasized that under the capitalistic system job segregation in the modern labor market along sexist lines was the result of certain underlying structural conditions, for example, the organization of domestic work performed by women within the household. They went farther, moreover, than the usual Marxist emphasis on class struggle and the fight for control over the means of production: they added a new dimension of analysis by insisting that control over the processes of human reproduction were as important as changes in

---

[8]Nancy Cott and Elizabeth Pleck, *A Heritage of Her Own* (New York, 1979), p. 16.

[9]Gerda Lerner, "Reconceptualizing Differences Among Women," *Journal of Women's History*, 1, No. 3 (Winter 1990):106–122.

modes of production of goods and services. Socialist feminists disagreed with Marxist feminists, on the one hand, and liberal feminists on the other. Although they agreed with Marxist feminists about the sexual division of labor as a conceptual tool of analysis, socialist feminists emphasized more the psychological as well as physical differences between men and women. They sought to show how the ideology of gender shaped the sexual division of labor. Finally, radical feminists, although recognizing the role of capitalism in the subordination of women, considered the major problem to be that of patriarchy, that is, men's age-old control of women within the family. Radical feminist views on three issues—the oppression of women, women's economic dependence on men within the family, and definitions of the female sex role—all stemming from the concept of patriarchy, profoundly influenced the writing of women's history.

Some women historians relied heavily upon various theorists to develop their perspectives. Marxist feminists relied on the writings of Marx and Engels, both of whom emphasized the sexual division of labor and its relationship to the development of capitalism. Many feminist scholars found the writings of the French philosopher and historian, Michel Foucault, especially useful. His emphasis on rupture and discontinuity which undermined the traditional approaches some scholars took toward truth, his insistence on the relationship between power and knowledge, and his stress of the "discourse" of sexuality, changed the way many feminist historians approached their research. Jacques Lacan also proved to be a fruitful source of inspiration because of his emphasis on the significance of language and use of symbolic representation in the development of sexual identity. Scholars employing an anthropological approach to history often resorted to the work of Clifford Geertz and his way of viewing ideology as a cultural system. No single theorist proved dominant, however, and a healthy eclecticism prevailed within the field in this regard.

In an effort to fill existing gaps in women's history, women scholars, some of them feminists and some not, sought also to develop a distinctive methodology that would place women in American history in a more meaningful way. Such historians focused initially on the status and consciousness of white middle-class women. In doing so, they implicitly assumed that their findings represented the experience of American women as a whole. This effort to achieve some notion of a universal female past proved to be somewhat counterproductive in the end. By the 1980s, because of certain political developments, changes in feminist goals, and shifts in ideas, scholars began stressing more the differences among women based on race, class, and ethnicity, rather than any kind of universalism.

The single most important organizing principle used by historians to reconceptualize the role of women in the nineteenth century was the practice and ideology of domesticity, i.e., the idea that women's proper place was in the home. This notion had been highlighted in Friedan's book, *Feminine Mystique*, which concluded that in the American culture of the 1950s women were confined to a separate sphere of domestic life in which they were presumed to seek fulfill-ment and self-identity in the feminine roles they played within the family and home. Friedan's insight soon led women historians to seek the roots of domesticity in American history.[10]

Women historians developed a hypothesis called the "cult of do-mesticity" to explain the status of some women during the 1820s and 1830s in terms of two spheres. The women's sphere was located in the home—an ordered and harmonious sphere—where as wives and mothers they were to dispense love and moral guidance to their hus-bands and children. The men's sphere was the business world—disor-derly and competitive—into which men went forth as breadwinners to provide for the family's security. The changing economic scene during the Jacksonian era that resulted in the transition from a rural-artisan and family-centered economy to an increasingly industrialized and ur-banized one presumably helped to bring about a greater separation of the two spheres.[11]

This separation made the distinction between the respective sex roles more rigid. Within the "cult of domesticity", an ideology which historians identified mainly with white middle-class women, the tradi-tional family was pictured as consisting of mother, father, and children grouped together within a private household. The family's influence reached outward, affecting the status of church and state in society, as

---

[10]Friedan went on to observe that there was a mystique about feminine fulfillment in America during the 1950s—a mystique about how women were *supposed* to act and feel when they were sexually defined as women. After analyzing the lifestyle of educated middle-class housewives pursuing this so-called mystique with its emphasis on domes-ticity, conformity, and consumerism, she concluded most of them found their lives empty, boring, and unsatisfying. Her book raised the consciousness of millions of women and helped to launch the women's liberation movement. Betty Friedan, *Femi-nine Mystique* (New York, 1963), *passim.*

[11]The concept of a "cult of domesticity" grew out of the article by Barbara Welter, "The Cult of True Womanhood, 1820–1860," *American Quarterly* 18 (Summer 1966):151–174; Aileen Kraditor introduced the phrase in her important readings book, *Up from the Pedestal* (Chicago, 1968). For emphasis on the Jacksonian era and class as an analytical category, see Gerda Lerner, "The Lady and the Mill Girl: Changes in the Status of Women in the Age of Jackson," *MidContinent American Studies Journal* 10 (Spring 1969):5–15. For a brilliant exposition of how the notion of separate spheres influ-enced the writing of women's history from the mid-1960s through much of the 1980s, see Linda Kerber, "Separate Spheres, Female Worlds, Woman's Place: The Rhetoric of Women's History," *Journal of American History* 75 (June 1988):9–39. The separate spheres framework during the Progressive era was restated in Paula Baker's incisive arti-cle, "The Domestication of Politics: Women and American Political Society, 1790–1820," *American Historical Review,* 89 (June 1984):620–647. Baker noted that until the Progressive period American political culture remained separate from the domestic cul-ture.

well as inward, helping to shape the character of the individuals involved. Great importance was placed upon women's roles as wives, mothers, and managers of households. The ideology both observed and prescribed accepted behavior for women: they were to be both pure and submissive.

While such idealization placed women up on a pedestal, the "cult of domesticity" at the same time kept women down and in a subordinate role in real life. Women were subordinate to men both within marriage and in society at large. In schools, churches, and the workplace, they were rarely treated as equals. When it came to politics, they were virtually impotent. Women, once married, had almost no legal existence separate from their husbands. They could not sue, write contracts, or execute wills on their own. Their persons, estates, and wages were considered the property of their husbands. Divorce was theoretically possible, but given the social attitudes and constraints of the time, relatively rare. Although women had no right to vote, they were still subject to the laws of the land.

But as Nancy Cott pointed out in her classic study of New England women, *Bonds of Womanhood* (1977), the 1830s decade presented a paradox. At the same time women were being held down, the period proved to be an important turning point as far as their economic involvement, public participation, and social visibility were concerned. During that decade women entered the industrial labor force in large numbers for the first time. Middle-class women likewise took up their one important political weapon—the petition—to demand legislation enabling wives to retain rights over their property and earnings. Moreover, they entered into a variety of reform movements either to pursue goals in their own self-interest (women's rights) or to improve society at large (abolitionism). Cott claimed that the nineteenth-century feminist political movement had grown out of the separation of spheres and was shaped by that phenomenon.

Some radical feminist historians like Carroll Smith-Rosenberg, however, argued for a different interpretation. In a pathbreaking essay published in 1975, Smith-Rosenberg claimed that instead of being oppressed within their separate sphere by men, women in the nineteenth century had in fact created an autonomous women's culture. They developed a "sisterhood" based on female friendships and widespread support networks that empowered women. The existence of this sisterhood heightened their sense of a distinctive women's culture, and led women to participate in various reform movements.[12]

What was involved in Smith-Rosenberg's view was essentially a

---

[12]Carroll Smith-Rosenberg, "The Female World of Love and Ritual: Relations Between Women in Nineteenth-Century America," *Signs* 1 (Autumn 1975):1–29; and elaborated upon in her *Disorderly Conduct* (New York, 1985), pp. 28, 41.

separatist approach to women's history. She insisted that there existed a separate nineteenth-century female world, one in which women's values were so distinctly different from those of men that the two could not be assimilated. The women's sphere was a world filled with female love and rituals so secret that men did not understand them from the day they were born until they died. Implicit in this separatist feminist interpretation was the idea that women's history was not and should not be a part of American mainstream history.[13]

But Smith-Rosenberg's view that men and women occupied separate spheres of emotion and behavior was undermined by works like Ellen K. Rothman's study of courtship in America from the 1770s to the 1920s. In her book *Hands and Hearts* (1984), Rothman found evidence suggesting that in their courtship patterns men and women shared many values in common regarding acceptable sexual behavior. More evidence along these lines could be found in Karen Lystra's *Searching the Heart* (1989), a study of nineteenth-century love letters showing that similar views of romantic love encouraged men and women to seek reciprocal understanding.

The broad question regarding the status of women in society during different periods of American history was destined to spark a controversy that absorbed women historians for some time. What was involved was the issue of whether women were better off during colonial days than their descendants in nineteenth-century America, on the one hand, and their counterparts in England on the other. Older works claimed that conditions for American women were more favorable in colonial times for several reasons. The number of women was small during the early days of settlement, and work by all hands, male and female, was desperately needed simply for survival. Distinctions between sex roles could not be tolerated under such circumstances, the argument ran. Women engaged in whatever occupations they wished, and encountered few legal or social restraints if they sought work outside the home. Moreover, the high sex ratio of men over women, especially in the Southern colonies, presumably gave women a better bargaining position in the marriage market. Children were viewed as assets because they became part of the labor force on family farms. Women, as a result, were highly prized by men and by society at large both for their work and childbearing. Colonial women, it was argued also, were better off than their English counterparts. English common law, which restricted women's independence, was never fully enforced in the American colonies, or else it was circumvented.

This hypothesis of a "golden age" for women in colonial times was fully developed by the mid-1940s and subsequently was incorporated into the scholarship on women's studies in the 1960s and 1970s. The

---

[13]Peter Novick, *That Noble Dream* (Cambridge, 1988), pp. 500–501.

interpretation was often employed to contrast the condition of women in the nineteenth century and to demonstrate that a decline in women's status had taken place. In short, the "golden age" hypothesis held that the position of American women had declined between the seventeenth and nineteenth centuries. What was at stake were two questions: What periodization should be employed in any analysis of women's history? And what changes had the position of women undergone—had it improved, declined, or remained unchanged? By implication the "golden age" thesis placed women closer to the mainstream of American history; it assumed that distinctions between men and women in the colonial era had been relatively negligible.[14]

Mary Beth Norton, in an important article published in 1984, took issue with this interpretation. She concluded that there was no such "golden age" in the colonial period, and that during the revolutionary era, in particular, changes took place that increased women's autonomy. There was increased political participation in public affairs, growing access to education, and an introduction to the language of individual rights that women quickly interpreted in feminist terms. These changes in women's roles occurred without conscious intent, Norton concluded, and were caused by trends taking place within society as a whole. So great were these changes, Norton claimed, that the country embarked upon a public dialogue on the subject of women and what their proper role in society should be.[15]

Linda Kerber's *Women of the Republic*, published in 1980, offered a somewhat similar assessment of the impact of the Revolution upon women's status, though on different grounds. Kerber contended that even if political theory appeared less radical and more conservative when seen against the conscious refusal of constitution-makers to recognize women's presence in the republic, some gains had been made. Women were offered the role of "republican motherhood," had increased access to education, and adopted the language of individual rights to their own circumstances. The republic, it was believed, could only be sustained by a virtuous people, and the important task of rai-

---

[14]The following works presented the "golden age" interpretation: Elizabeth Dexter, *Colonial Women of Affairs* (Boston, 1925); Richard B. Morris, *Studies in the History of American Law* (New York, 1930); Herbert Moller, "Sex Composition and Correlated Culture Patterns of Colonial America," *William and Mary Quarterly* 3d. ser. 2 (April 1945):113–153; Mary R. Beard, *Woman as Force in History* (New York, 1946); and Roger Thompson, *Stuart England and America* (London 1974).

[15]Mary Beth Norton, "The Evolution of White Women's Experience in Early America," *American Historical Review* 89 (June 1984):593–619. For a regional breakdown of a discussion of women's roles, see: Laurel Ulrich, *Good Wives* (New York, 1982); Lois Green Carr and Lorena Walsh, "The Planter's Wife: Experiences of White Women in Seventeenth-Century Maryland," *William and Mary Quarterly*, 3d ser. 34 (October 1977):542–571; and Michael Zuckerman, ed., *Friends and Neighbors* (Philadelphia, 1982), *passim*.

sing such citizens was to be left to republican mothers.[16] Thus, while women gained greater prestige, that prestige was narrowly defined within a sex-specific role appropriate to their gender.

Historiographical controversies like that regarding the so-called golden age for women in the colonial period made it clear that the business of measuring women's status at any given time was a complex problem. Too often such an approach took men as the measure of what women have achieved in history rather than viewing their achievements within their own terms. Women were not affected in the same way as men by many historical events. It was obvious, too, that the story of women's status could not be written in linear terms. Neither a history that postulated a straight-line decline nor a progressive development that showed women's status improving in an onward and upward direction would prove satisfactory. Suzanne Lebsock's fine study *Free Women of Petersburg* (1984) provided an interesting discussion of this problem.[17]

While many women in the nineteenth century seemed to be concerned with enlarging their separate sphere, others like Susan B. Anthony and Elizabeth Cady Stanton were seeking to dismantle the boundaries of that separate sphere so that women might relate to men on more equal terms in the social, economic, and political arenas. They became involved in the reform movements to seek the vote for women as well as in the abolition and temperance movements. The biographies written about such women worthies in the 1880s and 1890s were eulogistic and celebratory. But in the "new women's history," works by Ellen C. DuBois in *Feminism and Suffrage* (1978), Kathryn K. Sklar's *Catharine Beecher* (1973), and Gerda Lerner's *The Grimke Sisters of South Carolina* (1967), the activities of these women reformers were treated analytically and realistically.

One excellent study about women reformers in the nineteenth century was Nancy A. Hewitt's *Women's Activism and Social Change* (1984). The author examined various women's secular voluntary associations involved in temperance, suffrage, antislavery, and philanthropic activities in Rochester, New York, for a period of fifty years. Members of these organizations were all white, Protestant, and middle-class women, constituting about 10 percent of the city's population. Her analysis broke the members down into three categories: the "benevolents," "perfectionists," and "ultraists." Benevolents were wealthy women from pioneer elite families who set up the earliest

---

[16]See Mary Beth Norton's article and her book, *Liberty's Daughters* (Boston, 1980), and Linda Kerber, *Women of the Republic* (Chapel Hill, 1980). See also Joan Hoff-Wilson, "The Illusion of Change: Women and the Revolution," in *The American Revolution*, Alfred Young, ed. (DeKalb, Ill., 1976).

[17]Suzanne Lebsock, *Free Women of Petersburg* (New York, 1984), pp. xiii–xx.

social welfare institutions; they encountered relatively little societal opposition despite their departure from usual domestic activities. The perfectionists were composed of prosperous evangelicals who were motivated by the religious revivals in the region. At first they sought to battle sin in the rapidly growing commercialized city, but when opposed they retreated to try and save those who might become potential sinners. The ultraists, or agrarian Quakers, proved to be the most radical of all in terms of their ideology and bold techniques. They openly defied prevailing traditions and insisted upon having a voice in making social policies. Hewitt analyzed the positive achievements of these groups, as well as showing the interaction and differences among the three.

The status of women was obviously conditioned by their role as wives and mothers, and as a result of the subfield of family history made its appearance. As part of the "new social history," family history concerned itself with the role of women in marriage, the family, and parenting over time. Many scholars in this field suggested that there had been an increased emphasis on love as a prerequisite to marriage beginning in the period after the 1750s. Prior to that time, it was said, marriages were more in the nature of economic alliances arranged mainly by parents. After the 1750s there seemed to be a greater emphasis on the notion of marriage as a romantic union. For both men and women the goal of marriage appeared to be the pursuit of happiness rather than the pursuit of property. Family historians consequently focused on those factors that shaped the family: courtship customs, fertility rates, childbearing practices, demographic patterns that indicated the sex ratio between men and women within a given area, social organization within the household, and the concept of the family life cycle.

The work of family historians in America was shaped to a large degree by the studies of foreign scholars—the *Annales* school in France and the work of Philippe Aries and Louis Henry in particular; the findings of Peter Laslett in England; and the research of English-born Lawrence Stone who came to America. *Centuries of Childhood*, Aries's pathbreaking work published in 1962, profoundly changed the view of the family in past times. In it he advanced the hypothesis that the modern concept of childhood in European culture began as late as the seventeenth century. The notion of childhood as a separate stage of development, therefore, appears to have been a relatively recent phenomenon. Laslett's work made a crucial distinction between the household and family, showing that in preindustrial England people living under one roof were not always members of the family. Stone, on the other hand, dealt with English attitudes about family, sex, and marriage from the 1500s to the 1800s. He thereby provided a context for subsequent American developments in his *The Family, Sex and Marriage in England, 1500 to 1800*, published in 1977.

Philip Greven in America led the way with his intensive analysis of colonial families living within the single community of Andover, Massachusetts. In *Four Generations*, which appeared in 1970, Greven introduced the concept of a family life cycle. Greven found that there was a distinct relationship between landholding patterns and demographic trends in Andover. Landholding patterns often led to the development of what he termed a "modified extended family." His findings revised the idea of a nuclear family in colonial America pictured in the earlier work by Bernard Bailyn, *Education in the Forming of an American Society* (1960). Bailyn had postulated a rapid erosion of parental authority within the presumed nuclear family in colonial America because the frontier and other economic opportunities pulled children away from the home. Greven discovered instead that in the modified extended family, family members although not gathered in a single household, often lived nearby. This situation developed because fathers in the first generation, while still living, refused to relinquish their lands to their sons and continued to maintain parental control. Only in the third and fourth generations when the local lands were taken up did sons begin to move away from Andover. Greven pointed out, moreover, that it was important to build the picture of the family with systematic comparisons drawn from one generation to the next. Then, and only then, could one see the life cycle through which the family moved over time.[18]

The concept of a family life cycle was broadened by Tamara Hareven. She undertook studies of individual families over time as opposed to scholars who assumed that a single point in time based on a particular census or tax record would supply researchers with an accurate picture of family patterns. Working with nineteenth-century records, Hareven showed that the same families exhibited quite different household patterns over time. Boarders and lodgers, for example, were taken in at some stages of the family cycle of those residing in nineteenth-century industrial cities but absent in other situations. Thus the patterns of family life cycle were not simple expressions of biological time affecting such matters as fertility and aging. They were also family social patterns that varied according to an internal logic of

---

[18]See also Philip Greven, *The Protestant Temperament* (New York, 1977), in which the author resorted to an intellectual history approach to produce a major reinterpretation of child-rearing practices in early America. His paradigm was based on three distinct personality types or temperaments—the evangelical, moderate, and genteel—all derived from child-rearing practices within Protestant families. Greven's earlier work was criticized because it purported to discuss the family yet totally ignored women. For a woman-centered study of colonial families, see Laurel Ulrich's fine study, *Good Wives* and her prize-winning *A Midwife's Tale* (New York, 1990).

their own. Historians of the individual life cycle, such as Erik Erikson, had shown that life stages such as childhood and adolescence were socially as well as biologically defined. Hareven suggested that the same might be true for the family life cycle.[19]

Demographic studies likewise changed the picture of the attitudes and knowledge we have of the American family. We now know there was a steady decline in white fertility rates from 7.04 births in 1800 to 3.56 births in 1900. The growth of population for the country as a whole, therefore, was the result of immigration. From this demographic data historians inferred certain assumptions regarding sexual behavior in the nineteenth century. There was evidence that the native-born appeared to be limiting family size by some means. According to Daniel Scott Smith, a historical demographer, wives influenced the decision to control fertility in the nineteenth century by insisting upon abstinence from intercourse at times. But other historians claimed that married, middle-class white women may have been using contraceptives or resorting to abortion.[20]

Family history was affected not only by analytical tools like the concept of family life cycle; it was influenced also by major factors that influenced the course of American history as a whole—race, ethnicity, class considerations, urbanization, and regionalism.

In terms of race, black families obviously had different experiences than white families, especially when living under slavery. Herbert Gutman in *Black Family in Slavery and Freedom, 1750–1925,* examined the role of black women and men and concluded that Afro-Americans managed to create a stable and successful family structure even under slave conditions. The black family not only survived the transition to freedom but continued in the northern urban ghetto, at least until 1925 when Gutman's study ended. Black family patterns during slavery were also discussed in Eugene Genovese's *The World the Slaveholders Made,* published in 1969, and his *Roll, Jordan, Roll,* published in 1974. Problems encountered by black families since the Civil War were treated in Robert Staples's edited work, *Black Family*

---

[19]John Modell and Tamara K. Hareven, "Urbanization and the Malleable Household: Boarding and Lodging in Nineteenth-Century Families," *Journal of Marriage and the Family* 35 (August 1973):467–479. The concept of family life cycle applies to population-wide processes such as reproductivity, mortality, and property transfers. The term "life course" is now supplanting "cycle" for individuals and families. See Tamara K. Hareven, "The History of the Family and the Complexity of Social Change," *American Historical Review* 96 (February 1991):95–124, which is the most recent and best historiographical essay on family history.

[20]Daniel Scott Smith, "Family Limitation, Sexual Control, and Domestic Feminism in Victorian America," in *Clio's Consciousness Raised,* Mary Hartman and Lois Banner, eds. (New York, 1974):119–136. For the use of contraceptives or abortion, see Carl Degler, *At Odds* (New York, 1980):Chaps. 8–10, and James C. Mohr, *Abortion in America* (New York, 1978).

(1991), the collection of essays edited by Sharon Harley and Rosalyn Terborg-Penn, *Afro-American Women* (1978), and certain articles in *Unequal Sisters* (1990) edited by Ellen C. DuBois and Vicki L. Ruiz. The latter work also contained essays dealing with Asian, Chicano, and Native American families.[21] Other groups undoubtedly had different experiences from those of white middle-class families upon whom historians focused primarily, and scholars have only recently begun to investigate this area.

Ethnicity was equally important in studying family history because immigrant families arriving in America invariably underwent different experiences from those of "native stock" families. Immigration was an ongoing phenomenon, and the acculturation of foreign-born families was a continuous process throughout American history. Family patterns obviously differed from one ethnic group to another: in some the women ventured out of their homes to work, and in others they did not; in some a high premium was placed on marriage within the ethnic group, and in others the insistence on such unions disappeared rather quickly; in some childbearing practices lingered for generations, while in others such practices were Americanized in short order.

Studies of ethnic families became a rapidly growing subfield. Older works such as Arthur W. Calhoun's *A Social History of the American Family from Colonial Times to the Present* (1917–1919) and Sophonisba Breckenridge's *The Family and the State* (1913) were superseded. A more recent work was edited by Charles H. Mindel and Robert W. Havenstein entitled *Ethnic Families in America* (1976), as was Maxine Seller's *Immigrant Women* (1981), an edited collection which described rather than analyzed the anecdotal accounts of different immigrant women and their families. Hasia Diner's *Erin's Daughters in America* (1983) was a thoughtful study of immigrant Irish women both married and single in the nineteenth century, and contained much information about families as well as the hostile reaction of the Irish-American community to the emerging women's movement of the time. One of the best books on the subject was Judith E. Smith's comparative study of Italian and Jewish immigrants and their families in Providence, Rhode Island, from the turn of the century to World War II entitled *Family Connections* (1985). Smith analyzed the patterns of immigrant family life and pictured skillfully and imaginatively the interplay between the changing economic structure of that city and the internal dynamics of the immigrant cultures involved.

---

[21]Franklin E. Frazier's older study, *The Negro Family in the United States* (Chicago, 1939), which postulated a black matriarchy theory, occasioned considerable controversy. Gerda Lerner brought together documents bearing upon black women and black families in *Black Women in White America* (New York, 1972).

Class was as significant a variable as ethnicity in studying family history. With the emphasis that the "new social historians" were placing on the heretofore inarticulate groups in American society, scholars began paying more attention to working-class family life. One book that successfully combined a number of variables—class, ethnicity, sex, age, and generational change—to analyze the relationship between family life and industrialized labor was Tamara K. Hareven's *Family Time and Industrial Time*, published in 1982.

Hareven's work was revisionist in nature and sought to demolish the myth that industrialization destroyed traditional family ties. Studying the relationship between a textile company and its employees in a single New England community during the half-century prior to the 1930s, Hareven concluded that the family as a cooperative unit did not decline. Despite the rise of specialization and the advent of new machinery in factories, families continued to perform useful functions and individual decisions were made within the context of family needs. Families recruited their kinfolk, instructed them in work routines, and allowed workers to cover for one another when breaks from industrial routines were needed. French Canadians were the dominant ethnic group in the company, and Canadian-born women were more likely to work than married women from eastern Europe. Women's work usually stopped not so much because of marriage but at a stage of motherhood, so there was, indeed, some correlation between family time and factory time. Family patterns changed over generations, but immigrant households tended to rely to a greater extent on the income of working children than did native-born workers who were better off. Hareven discovered, moreover, there was a developing sense of working-class consciousness in this labor force. Worker reactions on a collective basis were not uncommon. This showed that these later generations of industrial workers were less submissive than earlier workers operating in preindustrial regions.

Another class-oriented analysis of family history was Linda Gordon's *Woman's Body, Woman's Right* (1976), which was written along Marxist feminist lines and dealt with the history of the birth control movement in America. The movement, Gordon concluded, passed through three distinct stages prior to the revival of feminism in the 1960s. First, there was a "voluntary mother" phase during the 1870s when contraception was linked to the defense of women's presumed superior place within the traditional family on moral grounds. Second, came the "birth control" phase in the decade between 1910 and 1920 when the movement became radical and revolutionary as it attacked establishment positions on sex, politics, class, and economics. Finally, there occurred the "Planned Parenthood" phase after 1920 when conservative forces dominated the movement. Planned Parenthood, according to Gordon, proceeded to impose bourgeois values and norms on others. Gordon accused Planned Parenthood of seeking two goals: to preserve and strengthen the prevailing view of the success of American capitalism; and to limit the growth of minorities, the poor, and the populations of third world countries. The polemical tone of the work, however, detracted from its significant insights.

Gordon was interested also in the problem of violence within the family, along with other scholars. She published *Heroes of Their Own Lives* in 1988, which constituted a feminist critique of child abuse, incest, and wife beating in Boston from the late nineteenth century to 1960. A pioneering work, the book broke new ground in the history of family violence, the social work profession, and origins of the welfare state. Elizabeth Pleck produced a much broader study on the same subject in the same year entitled *Domestic Tyranny*. Her work was a comprehensive survey of social policies against family violence and was divided into three reform eras during which statutory and institutional remedies were implemented. In the first period, 1640 to 1680, the Puritans passed laws against wife beating and, in general terms, against child abuse. During the second stage, 1874 to 1890, steps were taken to establish private societies to protect physically-abused women and children. The third era, from 1962 through the 1970s, saw reformers (a coalition of feminists, social workers, physicians and pediatricians) working to pass federal and stage legislation. In the years between these reforms, reports of violence between family members were generally met with apathy, disinterest, or derision, according to Pleck.

The writing of family history posed another problem for researchers who had to cope with the existence of differing regional traditions of family. According to William Taylor's *Cavalier and Yankee* (1961), there were contrasting attitudes toward family life and women in the North and South during the antebellum period. These separate traditions arose from an emerging sense of regional and cultural identities. In the popular imagination a woman in the North, especially in Yankee New England, presented an image of a bourgeois, hardworking, and utilitarian individual. The role of the woman in the South, on the other hand, was seen as a lady of aristocratic leisure, decorative in function, and projecting a sense of utter helplessness. Although these two images changed over time and suggested various concepts of domesticity, female roles within the two regions seemed to differ quite markedly.[22]

The foregoing discussion of family history as a subfield of the "new social history" shows that many scholars were becoming increasingly aware of one thing: women could hardly be studied in complete isolation from men. As a separate sex, women are often most closely tied

---

[22]For the image of Southern white middle- and upper-class women from 1830 to 1930, see Ann Firor Scott, *The Southern Lady* (Chicago, 1970).

to members of the male sex by marriage, physical association, kinship connections, and common interests in raising children. There was, to be sure, a long-established history of female bonding, affinity, and close association with other women, but this tradition has had to contend with the other stronger structural ties women have to men.[23]

One of the most important studies to appear during the contemporary period was Carl Degler's *At Odds*, published in 1980. Its aim was to integrate the two fields—women's studies and family history. The thesis of Degler's book was summed up in his title: women and the family were "at odds" with one another because the family acted as an inhibitor to women's personal plans. The modern companionate family that arose in the 1830s and continued to the present day, created a newfound status for women within society. At the same time this newfound status, combined with declining fertility in the nineteenth century, led to an opening of more opportunities for women outside the family in careers, education, and other activities. The emergence of the modern family made it possible for women not only to think of themselves as individuals, but to pursue individualistic activities separate from their family life. Degler suggested, then, that women, in creating the modern family, had built both a prison and a path to freedom for themselves.

With the coming of the modern family women achieved a higher status, according to Degler: first as wives, because their husbands loved and depended upon them; and then as mothers, because American culture began to view children and child-rearing in a more positive light. At the same time, however, women were brought into conflict with the family because the family unit depended for its very existence upon women's subordination. When women began demanding more autonomy through feminist causes like suffrage, their drive for individual rights ran up against the demands imposed upon them by their families.

The national women's organizations that developed in the nineteenth century, said Degler, gained their effectiveness precisely because of the widely accepted view of women's purity. Since women were considered the moral guardians of both home and society, for example, they could work with impunity on a reform to destroy "demon rum." Suffrage, on the other hand, was a truly radical demand because the right to vote was a right based on women's individuality rather than on their family status. For this and other reasons suffrage took a long time to achieve, simply because it challenged women's subordination within the family.

---

[23]For a fine bibliography on family history as well as women's history in general, but one which ends in the early 1980s, see Jill K. Conway, *et al.*, *Female Experience in Eighteenth and Nineteenth-Century America*.

Like other scholars Degler dealt with domesticity and feminism within the same context. He successfully challenged the older myth that the Victorians had been responsible for surrounding sex with a conspiracy of silence. He showed that Victorian sexual attitudes were the creation, at least in part, of women themselves. One aspect of this growing female autonomy was the desire of women for fewer children. Women influenced the decision to control fertility, and Degler provided evidence that married middle-class white women probably used contraception, and abortion, as well as abstinence from sex to do so. Thus Degler suggested that women were not necessarily victims of the transformation of family life; they themselves had played a central role in bringing about the changes that took place.

Bringing his study up to the present, Degler looked at the historical pattern of women's work. Despite changes in the number of working wives and despite the lifting of discriminatory employment practices, he argued, women, for the most part, still hold low-paying, dead-end jobs. Women continued to do so, Degler concluded, because they thought of themselves as secondary workers and unselfishly oriented their jobs around their family life. Men, on the other hand, did not think along such lines.

There were many scholars who argued against Degler's approach of integrating family history and women's history. Linda Gordon, for example, in *Heroes of Their Own Lives* took the position that scholars conceptualizing the family as a unit were guilty of creating a historical construct that was misleading. Such an approach overlooked the social reality that families were composed of individuals each of whom had his or her agenda and that there were struggles within the family over power, resources, and goals. Too often in studying the family, she concluded, scholars saw the father as representing the views of the unit as a whole, thereby rendering other family members invisible. This criticism involving the concept of patriarchy had considerable merit, and raised questions about whether family history and women's history should be integrated in the future.[24]

Despite the superb work done in women's history and family history, there was some dissatisfaction during the decade of the 1980s among several leading female scholars because research in the field had been too narrowly defined. There was increasing recognition that the notion of a universal female past was too narrowly construed; those writing the "new women's history" in spite of their many brilliant insights, had failed to account enough for the differences among women and the diversity of their experiences. Too often the scholarship explicitly or implicitly had been rooted in the experiences of

[24]Linda Gordon, *Heroes of Their Own Lives* (New York, 1988), p. vi.

white, middle-class women living in the Northeast or New England, and generalizations made were based on that model. Study after study appeared in the 1980s showing that women differed from this model by region, race, class, and ethnic affiliation. When it came to gender roles, it was increasingly realized that women not only differed from men, but differed among themselves on critical issues.

The great diversity in women's experiences was beautifully illustrated in Sarah J. Deutsch's excellent study, *No Separate Refuge* (1987), which resorted to anthropology as well as history. Regionally, the book focused on the Southwest; racially on Chicanas or Hispanic women; culturally on Spanish-speaking and English-speaking populations; in class differentiation on poor Mexican migrants and well-to-do Anglo employers; and in gender terms, on the dynamic interaction between and among men and women of both cultures. Deutsch traced the experiences of Chicanas from their communal Mexican villages to multi-ethnic coal mining camps in Colorado and ultimately to Anglo cities, as they passed through successive cultural and physical frontiers. The Chicanas had some autonomy and social standing in their native rural villages, based on individual crops they raised on small garden plots, but their status was altered as they moved through different environments and were reduced ultimately to lesser roles as minority workers hired for low-paying jobs in Anglo industries. Deutsch's book demonstrated that many variables impinged on the lives of Chicanas—space (in the form of the differing rural and urban environments), ethnicity, culture, class, and gender. In doing so, she not only revealed a much richer interpretation of women's history, but revised Frederick Jackson Turner's male-oriented frontier thesis in the process.[25]

Nancy Cott, a liberal feminist, in her penetrating revisionist interpretation of the early twentieth-century women's movement entitled *The Grounding of Modern Feminism* (1987), also emphasized the diversity among women rather than their shared concerns. Unlike the so-called woman movement of the nineteenth century, modern feminism was forced to grapple with the paradoxes reflected in the complexities of twentieth-century life. Feminists wanted unity among women, but recognized women's diversity. They wanted equality with men, but also emphasized differences from them. They hoped for gender consciousness, but hoped also to eliminate gender-determined roles. Although women's organizations flourished in the 1920s, the feminist movement because of these paradoxes achieved only limited success. By focusing on intra-group conflict, Cott not only brought to bear some self-criticism on the "new women's history," but corrected

---

[25]For an older work that stressed class and regionalism in women's history, see Margaret Hagood, *Mothers of the South* (Chapel Hill, 1939), which was reissued in 1977.

earlier views on why women failed to make better use of the political rights for which they fought so vigorously.[26]

Elizabeth Fox-Genovese, a socialist feminist, presented a different perspective in her *Within the Plantation Household* (1988). Her book presented a controversial analysis of the relationship between white and black women in the plantation households in the antebellum South, and was based on diaries, family papers, and writings of ex-slaves. Reacting against what she called the "New Englandization" of women's history, Fox-Genovese wrote from a socialist feminist point of view. Wives of slaveholders, she concluded, were acutely conscious of their social status, took the slavery system for granted, and in terms of gender roles accepted the male dominance prevalent in the South. White mistresses, despite certain ties of affection and intimacy with some of their black female slaves, appeared to be even more racist than their husbands. Slave women for their part not only performed typical female chores, but on some plantations did "men's" work as well. Like enslaved black males, they lived in a world where no independently guaranteed institutions could mediate between their basic relations of gender and the power of the master.[27]

Christine Stansell also challenged the simplistic approach of the Northeast model by insisting on the variations in women's experience by class in her *City of Women* (1986). She argued that the world of working-class women was not the same as that of middle-class women nor even of working-class men in the city of New York in the antebellum period. Using geography as a mode of social analysis, Stansell reconstructed the city to show how New York represented a working-class female city within a city. This city of women had its own political economy, patterns of socializing, and uses of streets which varied by class and gender, and was far more complex than the male-centered urban histories had pictured previously.

Other scholars produced studies of working women which also stressed class as an important variable on a national level rather than confining themselves to New England. Alice Kessler-Harris in *Out to Work* (1982), writing from a socialist-feminist perspective, produced an historical overview showing that women workers organized and took militant action in the workplace despite the neglect and hostility of labor union leaders. At the same time, she noted, women workers always faced a tension between the competing demands in their domestic role within the home and their place in the labor force. Women

---

[26]For an earlier view of the women's suffrage movement in the early twentieth century, see William O'Neill, *Everyone Was Brave* (Chicago, 1969).

[27]For other works written from a feminist and socialist or Marxist perspective, see Deborah Gray White, *Ar'n't I a Woman?* (New York, 1985); Jacqueline Jones, *Labor of Love, Labor of Sorrow* (New York, 1985); Bell Hooks, *Ain't I A Woman?* (Boston, 1981); and Catherine Clinton, *The Plantation Mistress* (New York, 1981).

invariably chose to place a higher priority on their domestic roles as wives and mothers; this decision inevitably resulted in males getting the better-paying, skilled and supervisory positions. Ruth Milkman in *Gender at Work* (1987) likewise took up the question of why women were segregated on the job into the poorly paid and low status occupations. She argued that occupational sex-typing was deeply rooted in industrial structures which could only be understood in historical terms. The sexual division of labor within a given industry or labor market was inevitably shaped by the economic, political and social forces operating at the historical moment the labor process was first being crystallized. The fate of the struggles women workers faced, Milkman concluded, was always inextricably bound up with issues of class.

These signs of dissatisfaction with a universal female past brought forth a chorus of calls for reconceptualizing "new women's history."[28] Joan W. Scott in *Gender and the Politics of History* (1988) following Foucault and some of the post-structuralist literary scholars felt that gender (as a primary way of signifying relationships of power) could be used as a category of analysis, not only for a direct study of the social interaction between women and men, but to gain a better understanding of power, politics, and state policy and other matters. Mary H. Blewett broke new ground in her study of the relationship of women and men workers in the New England shoe industry from the 1780s to about 1910. She demonstrated how gender analysis could provide a conceptual tool for revising the traditional categories of labor history in her *Men, Women, and Work* (1988). Peggy Pascoe in *Relations of Rescue* (1990) provided a different model by showing how two different gender systems in conflict—one idealized in China and the other in nineteenth century America—of Chinese immigrant women in San Francisco helped to shape one possible alternative for a distinctive Chinese-American culture.

One of the most difficult problems to research in terms of gender was the issue of women's sexuality. Historians focused mainly on two broad subjects—women's sexual ideology and their sexual behavior—but because of the privacy of sexual practices answers to questions were hard to come by. What scholars sought to discover was how the decline in fertility during the nineteenth century was related to women's sexual appetites. In theory nineteenth-century marriage and sex manuals advocated male self-control and female passionlessness. But what was the practice? Were women passionless? Carl Degler in an article published in 1974 based in part on a survey of a small number of white, middle-class married women showed that they exhibited sexual

---

[28]Joan W. Scott, in Margaret R. Higgonet *et al.*, *Behind the Lines* (New York, 1987), p. 22.

desires and that a significant number experienced orgasm. Other scholars, like Linda Gordon, suggested that women indeed might have experienced an aversion to sex because they dreaded pregnancy and childbirth as well as being influenced by the social proscriptions on female passion. Nancy Cott explored the cultural sources of the ideal of female passionlessness in the literature of the late eighteenth and nineteenth centuries. Along different lines, Estelle Freedman and John D'Emilio published the best history of sexuality in America, *Intimate Matters* in 1988.[29]

Carroll Smith-Rosenberg in her book of essays entitled *Disorderly Conduct* (1985) discussed the subject of female sexuality from several different perspectives. In one article she presented the view of nineteenth-century male doctors regarding women from the time of puberty to menopause. Analyzing the use to which these views were put, she concluded that this was one way by which society took cognizance of the importance of women's sexuality, and, at the same time, tried to confine that sexuality solely to reproductive purposes. In another article she examined some of the tensions arising from women's roles in the nineteenth century, and demonstrated how such conflicts manifested themselves in some form of hysteria in certain cases. According to Smith-Rosenberg, hysteria was a form of individual expression or protest against the conditions of frustration or repression resulting from proscribed feminine roles. In a third article she drew attention to the close female bonding of young women that often took place, and noted that such intense female relationships often had to contend and compete with romantic ties to men. Finally, in a fourth article, she dealt with the way in which emerging social pressures imposed heavier responsibilities for sexual attractiveness on women during the decade of the 1830s. This response, as Smith-Rosenberg saw it, was related to unrecognized tensions that arose from stressful changes taking place during the turbulent Jacksonian period.

In response to the many calls for reconceptualization, certain scholars set out to explore ways of arriving at some new synthesis of women's history. Ellen C. DuBois and Vicki L. Ruiz edited their readings book whose aim was to move toward a broad new, approach. Noting that earlier historians had focused too much on the notion of a universal female past, they suggested instead a multicultural approach: one that would present greater diversity in analyzing the social relations among men and women as well as between women of differing races, classes, and cultures. Such a multicultural approach would

---

[29]Carl Degler, "What Ought to be and What Was: Women's Sexuality in America in the Nineteenth Century," *American Historical Review* 79 (December 1974):1467–1490; Linda Gordon, *Woman's Body, Woman's Right: A Social History of Birth Control in America*, pp. 105–106 and Nancy Cott, "Passionlessness: An Interpretation of Victorian Sexual Ideology, 1790–1850," *Signs* 4 (Winter 1978):219–236.

cut across races and classes of women, represent diverse cultures, and recognize that different groups of women were unequal in terms of the power they possessed. Some scholars, such as Sarah Deutsch and Peggy Pascoe, for example, had already moved in that direction. The first reading in this chapter is from the introduction of the DuBois and Ruiz volume.

The second selection is from a searching essay by Gerda Lerner, one of the preeminent leaders in the field who suggested a more far-reaching and ambitious synthesis. She proposed the creation of a new holistic history: one in which men and women would "in the various aspects of their lives, interact in various ways, reflecting the differences among them." Such interaction would take cognizance of the system of patriarchal dominance in America that had generated the power for the race, class, and gender oppression existing within the country. In effect, women's history instead of fitting into or being added onto United States history would become the means for restructuring and revolutionizing traditional American history.

This brief historiographical survey touches only lightly upon certain methodologies, theories, and themes presented in the voluminous literature in women's history—one of the most vibrant, exciting, and rapidly growing fields in all of American history. But it has failed to answer the question posed at the beginning of the chapter: Was women's history to be part of the mainstream of traditional American history? Or was it to become, as Gerda Lerner suggested, a means by which all of American history might be restructured and revolutionized? Was the American past gender-determined? Can there be a separate history of American men and women—under a separatist rather than an integrated approach? One thing is certain: with the writing of women's history in the past three decades, women in American history will never be as invisible as they once were.

Ellen C. DuBois
and Vicki L. Ruiz

ELLEN C. DUBOIS (1947–   ) *is professor of history at the University of California, Los Angeles. She is the author of numerous articles and books, including* Feminism and Suffrage *(1978) and* Feminist Scholarship *(1985).* VICKI L. RUIZ *is associate professor of history at the University of California, Davis. She has written* Cannery Women, Cannery Lives *(1987) and edited* Women on the U.S.-Mexico Border *(1987).*

Well into its second decade, the field of women's history stands at a crossroads. Growing demands for the recognition of "difference"— the diversity of women's experiences—can no longer be satisfied by token excursions into the histories of minority women, lesbians, and the working class. The journey into women's history itself has to be remapped. From many quarters comes the call for a more complex approach to women's experiences, one that explores not only the conflicts between women and men but also the conflicts among women; not only the bonds among women but also the bonds between women and men. Only such a multifaceted perspective will be sufficient "to illuminate the interconnections among the various systems of power that shape women's lives."

In *Unequal Sisters* we seek to address such issues in the context of American women's history. In particular, this anthology highlights scholarship on women of color, from which we draw more than half of our articles. In addition, other selections explore "difference" with respect to class and sexual preference. The dynamics of race and gender, however, are the pivotal point of this collection.

Most of the early work in U.S. women's history paid little attention to race and assumed instead a universal women's experience, defined in contrast to "man's" history. While a stark focus on the difference between the male and female past helped to legitimize women's history, the past it explored usually was only that of middle-class white women. In this uniracial model, the universal man of American history was replaced with the universal woman.

For instance, much nineteenth-century women's history scholar-

---

ship rests on the assumption that women's lives were lived in a separate domestic "sphere," on which basis they were able to claim a kind
of social power distinct from that of men. This concept grew out of
the historical experience of white, leisured women. And despite historians' earnest efforts to include less privileged women—notably female
slaves and immigrant wives—the narrative line of women's history
could not help but marginalize them. These other histories came
across either as exotic or deviant, providing no clue to the larger history of American womanhood. In this uniracial model, race and gender
cannot be brought into the same theoretical field. White women appear "raceless," their historical experiences determined solely by gender. By contrast, the distinct historical experiences of women of color,
to the degree they are acknowledged, are credited solely to race. The
uniracial framework leads women's historians, eager to expand their
range, right into the trap of "women-and-minorities," a formula that
accentuates rather than remedies the invisibility of women and color.

While the notion of a universal female past focuses on power relations between men and women, scholarship has begun to appear that
explores power relations *between women*—of different races, classes,
and cultures. Slaveowner and slave, mistress and maid, reformer and
immigrant, social worker and client are some of the many relationships of inequality that run through American women's history. When
focused on questions of race, we term this sort of approach "biracial."
Scholarship in this biracial mode benefits from a paradigm for examining power, not only between men and women but also within women's
history itself. This biracial approach shatters the notion of a universal
sisterhood. Simply stated, it permits feminist historians to discard celebration for confrontation, and allows them to explore the dynamics
through which women have oppressed other women.

While the biracial approach has effectively broken through the notion of a universal female experience, it has its limits. The framework
itself leads the historian to focus her examination on the relation between a powerful group, almost always white women, and minority
women, the varieties of whose experiences are too often obscured. In
other words, the historical emphasis is on white power, and women of
color have to compete for the role of "other." The historical testimo-
nies of women of color thus tend to be compacted into a single voice.
The biracial framework has helped create a situation in which the demand for a greater understanding of race can be reduced to a black-and-
white analysis—literally and figuratively.

Much as the uniracial framework in women's history is closely
associated with the Northeast, the biracial model has its own regional
bias and seems best to describe the Southeast. For the possibilities of
a richer palate for painting women's history, we turn to "the West."
Western women's historians are taking the lead in moving beyond bi-
racialism, if only because the historical experiences of the region re-

quire a multifaceted approach. Given the confluence of many cultures and races in this region—Native American, Mexican, Asian, Black, and Anglo—grappling with race at all requires a framework that has more than two positions. Nor is white history always center stage. Even the term "the West" only reflects one of several historical perspectives; the Anglo "West" is also the Mexican "North," the Native American "homeland," and the Asian "East." Nor are the possibilities for such an approach limited to one region. Even in areas that seem racially homogeneous or in which the struggle between two races understandably preoccupies historians, there are other people and positions to consider.

To describe this third framework, the one we seek to elaborate in *Unequal Sisters*, we use the term "multicultural." We chose the term "multicultural" over "multiracial" because we seek to focus on the interplay of many races and cultures, because we acknowledge that not all white women's histories can be categorized under one label, and because we seek to suggest that the term "race" needs to be theorized rather than assumed. As a framework for women's history, a multicultural approach poses a variety of challenges to scholarship. Many groups of women, rarely explored or incorporated into women's history, await further study. There are distinctions to note, comparisons to be made, among different groups of women, with respect to family life, forms of work, definitions of womanhood, sources of power, bonds among women. The various forms of white domination must be examined for their impact on women's history: the dispossession of Mexican land after 1848; the genocide and relocation of Native Americans; the legal exclusion of Asian Americans. Even slavery takes on multiple meanings for women's history through a multicultural lens. Finally, a multicultural approach to women's history invites the study of cultural contact and transformation, so important in understanding the development of family patterns, childrearing practices, sexuality, and other cultural arenas crucial to women's history concerns.

In U.S. history, race has coincided closely with class. The segmentation of people of color in lower-echelon industrial, service, and agricultural jobs has served to blunt their opportunities for economic mobility. The multicultural framework allows for an analysis that takes class into account, not as a separate variable, but as an intertwined component of both race and gender. The history of women cannot be studied without considering both race and class. Similarly, working-class culture cannot really be understood without reference to gender and race. Many of the essays in this volume provide insight into the structural and ideological components of class, as it interplays with race and gender in the formation of women's consciousness.

At the risk of overreaching, it does seem that a multicultural approach, one in which many pasts can be explored simultaneously, may be the only way to organize a genuinely national, a truly inclusive, history of women. As Jacquelyn Dowd Hall has written, women's history must develop "a historical practice that turns on partiality, that is self-conscious about perspective, that releases multiple voices rather than competing orthodoxies, and that, above all, nurtures an 'internally differing but united political community.'" To allow for overlapping narratives and to recognize multiple forms of power, this is both an old populist dream and a postmodern challenge.

Such a kaleidoscopic approach undoubtedly runs the risk of fragmentation. But in moving beyond the notion of women's history as a monolith, coherence need not be abandoned. "We should not have to choose between a common legacy and cultural diversity, especially in a nation where diversity is a legacy," writes James Quay, director of the California Council of the Humanities. We hope, in this volume and in the future scholarship it may encourage, to contribute to a reconceptualization of American women's history, as a series of dialectical relations among and across races and classes of women, representing diverse cultures and unequal power. Rather than segregate and group our selections by race, therefore, we have tried to integrate them with a synthetic sweep of women's history, to begin to identify some unifying themes of women in the past at the same time as we allow for diversity.

While it is too soon to develop a fully coherent new framework, the articles in this anthology begin to challenge long-standing generalizations about women's history and to suggest rich new possibilities for understanding women's complex pasts. We offer the following observations as notes toward a new synthesis.

Family: What is "the family" and what is its place in women's history? A multicultural perspective helps us to see how much "home" as distinct from "household" is an ideological concept in women's history. For middle-class women, the type of authority that historians have dubbed "domestic feminism" is rooted in class and racial distinctions as much as in the difference of gender; working-class women, women of color, were necessary to middle-class women's claims of social authority, whether as charitable objects or as domestic servants. Indeed, as the work of Linda Gordon, Christine Stansell, and Martha May demonstrates, for many women, the creation and maintenance of "family life" has been as much a site for class conflict as for gender definition.

Nor does the private/public dichotomy that underlies scholarship of "women's sphere" hold up very well from a multicultural perspective. Even for middle-class women, to whom the concept of separate spheres most directly applies, the separation of community and family has never been complete. Although focusing on different causes and time periods, Paula Baker and Amy Swerdlow explore how, and with what consequences, middle-class women cloaked their political activ-

ism in the garb of domesticity. More profoundly, the inextricable nature of family life and wage work in the histories of immigrant wives
and women of color explores the false oppositions at the heart of the
public/private dichotomy. As members of a "family wage economy,"
they worked as an extension of their familial responsibilities, pooling
their resources to put food on the table. And, as evident in Deena J.
González's article, family networks and community ties provided
strength and nourishment, even resources for resistance, in the work
lives of women of color.

Work: As a multicultural perspective erodes the distinction between "work" and "home," we can expect "work" to play a larger role
in the overall syntheses of women's history. Evelyn Nakano Glenn's
pioneering research on Asian Americans is a harbinger of the attention
that domestic labor, paid and unpaid, will receive as women of color
emerge from the shadows of women's history. The history of domestic
service demonstrates the centrality of this class relationship between
mistress and maid, with all its inequality and deception, to the development and movement of notions of "womanhood" across cultures
and classes.

Scholarship such as that of Joan M. Jensen and Deborah Gray
White reminds us that industrialized wage work is only one of many
systems of labor organization important in women's history; others
include slavery, subsistence agriculture, personal service, and debt pe-
onage. With respect to wage labor, the particular feminist perspective
that argues that work means liberation has little relevance to women
who have historically worked in the lowest, least mobile sectors of
the labor force, where the notion of work as "opportunity" has little
meaning. Indeed, when women of color move "from margin to center"
in women's history, we can begin to see how the rise of wage labor
among women in general represents not so much a personal choice as
a historical necessity.

Once in the labor force, women have tried to exert some control
over their work lives. They created shop-floor cultures, which could
either reinforce or challenge the prerogatives of management. As Vicki
L. Ruiz and Meredith Tax demonstrate, their "workplace struggles"
include not only classic union battles (in which, by the way, they become more prominent in the modern period) but also the creation of
informal networks and day-to-day resistance.

Politics: On the one hand, research has begun to reveal that the
conventional aspects of women's politics are not quite as homogeneous as they once seemed. The scholarship of Ellen Carol DuBois,
Alma M. Garcia, and Judy Yung shows that working-class women and
women of color have their own histories of activism in women's movements, such as birth control and suffrage, despite efforts to read them
out. Complex relations between races and classes shaped the course of

these movements and should be incorporated into our evaluation of them. As George J. Sanchez and Robert A. Trennert demonstrate, the history of the welfare state looks considerably less benign when, in evaluating women's role, we recognize that women were clients as well as agents.

On the other hand, women have long histories of leadership in the organization of their own communities, in which their activism is conjoined with, not counter to, that of men. It is this history that has led Elsa Barkley Brown to endorse Alice Walker's neologism "womanism" over the older term "feminism" to capture the full political history of women of color. Like the line between home and work, the distinction between daily life and politics, already eroded by prior work in women's history, may become even more problematic in multicultural scholarship.

Sexuality: Presumptions of a universal female experience are especially problematic in the realm of sexuality because it is so politically and culturally contextualized. In the nineteenth century, assertions of women's "passionlessness" were never as all encompassing as they seemed. Rayna Green and others explore how, in order to highlight the purity of white women, women of color were associated with the unspeakable "dark side" of women's sexual nature. This duality of good and bad women, of virgin and whore, was rooted in political conquest and imperialism, chattel slavery and the cash nexus. Unconsciously expressing these associations, progressive-era reformers settled on the term "white slavery" to describe the procurement of women into prostitution. The adjective "white" was necessary to signify sexual slavery because the assumption was that women of color were lascivious by nature.

The multicultural framework also highlights the various ways women have fought against the stereotyping and control of their sexuality. Darlene Clark Hine courageously explains how African American women resisted: tainted with the brush of promiscuity, they created a "culture of dissemblance . . . that created the appearance of openness and disclosure but actually shielded the truth of their inner lives and selves from their oppressors." Her work also suggests that once the full extent of rape and sexual violence is acknowledged, the silence about other aspects of the history of women's sexuality may begin to be broached. In quite different ways, Hazel V. Carby, Jessie M. Rodrique, Kathy Peiss, and Jacquelyn Dowd Hall portray women reaching for the right to express their own sexuality.

Sexuality moreover cannot be approached solely within the boundaries of male/female relations. As Elizabeth Lapovsky Kennedy and Madeline D. Davis demonstrate, lesbians have struggled to create their own identities and to build their own communities in the midst of the most hostile environments. Carving a sense of sexual self amid such oppression was a courageous act of preservation, both personally and politically.

Women's relationships: Lesbianism is one aspect of a larger world of women's relationships with other women. As Kathryn Kish Sklar stresses, the theme of women's relationships is one of the most basic ways that women's history has reordered historical inquiry. The multi-cultural investigation of the networks women have created by and for themselves has taken many forms. Deborah Gray White on slave women, Virginia Sanchez Korrol on Puerto Rican nuns, and Valerie Matsumoto on Japanese Americans in the internment camps, all demonstrate the rich networks women formed to support one another and share resources. Indeed, the fewer material resources a group of women has, the more communal their history may turn out to be.

On the other hand, a multicultural perspective raises basic questions about the women's networks outside of and between homogeneous groups. As numerous articles in this anthology demonstrate—by Nancy A. Hewitt, Linda Gordon, Peggy Pascoe, Christine Stansell, Evelyn Nakano Glenn—women's relations across class and cultural divides look considerably less harmonious when seen from the bottom up than from the top down. The "bonds of womanhood" looked different to Italian-American welfare clients than to their social workers. It is hoped that the exploration of these female antagonisms may enrich the conceptualization of women's relationships to include conflict as well as concert.

History's purposes: History is unavoidably political, and our research reflects our politics. Alice Kessler-Harris writes, "For many of us, history is about exploring the nature of social change." In her article, she demonstrates that the obliteration of racial and class differences among women has had serious consequences for the generalizations made about women's history and the purposes to which those generalizations have been put. As historians we must attend more carefully to the uses made of our scholarship. We cherish the hope that what we do as historians has relevance and indeed applicability to issues women face today. In other words, we look to the past to recover insights into the present and future.

Gerda Lerner

GERDA LERNER (1920–   ) *is Robinson-Edwards Professor of History at the University of Wisconsin at Madison. She is the author of many articles and books, including* The Grimke Sisters from South Carolina *(1971),* The Majority Finds Its Past *(1979), and* The Creation of Patriarchy *(1986).*

The development of women's history in the past twenty years has not only helped to bring new subject matter to history, but has forced us to deal with the concepts and values underlying the organization of historical studies and of all intellectual fields. It has forced us to question not only why certain content was previously omitted, ignored, and trivialized, but also to consider who decides what is to be included. In short, we have begun first to question and then to challenge the conceptual framework for the organization of traditional knowledge. We challenge it because of its omissions: it leaves out the experiences, activities, and ideas of half or more of humankind. We challenge it because it is elitist: it leaves out not only all women, but most men, those of non-white races, those of various ethnicities, and, until quite recently, those of lower classes. In so doing, it defines all the groups omitted as less significant than the groups included. Patently, this is untrue and therefore it is unacceptable. We challenge it because what traditional history teaches us denies our own experience of reality. We live in a world in which nothing happens without the active participation of men and women and yet we are constantly being told of a past world in which men are parts which add up to a whole. This is indeed a conceptual advance, but it is insufficient as a model of reality because it ignores power, dominance, hegemony. It assumes that the process of doing justice to "differences" is additive—leave the whole concept intact and add the infinite variety in which humankind appears in society and history.

If one ignores "differences" one distorts reality. If one ignores the power relations built on differences one reinforces them in the interest of those holding power. I would like to propose a different conceptual model for dealing with "differences."

When men discovered how to turn "difference" into dominance they laid the ideological foundation for all systems of hierarchy, in-

Gerda Lerner, "Reconceptualizing Differences Among Women," *Journal of Women's History,* 1 (Winter 1990):106–118.

equality, and exploitation. They found a way of justifying such systems and of keeping them functioning with the cooperation of the dominated. This "invention of hierarchy" can be traced and defined historically: it occurs everywhere in the world under similar circumstances, although not at the same time. It occurs when the development of militarism due to the technological innovations of the Bronze Age coincides with the economic shifts occasioned by the agricultural revolution. Small groups of men, usually military leaders, usurp power in their domain, usually following some conquest of foreigners, and consolidate such power by ideological and institutional means. These means always rest upon the discovery that "difference" can justify dominance. For Western civilization, these events occur in the Ancient Near East in the third and second millennium B.C. and take the form of state formation.

States formed through the consolidation of early military conquests by tribal chiefs or kings become legitimized by the creation of myths of origin, which confer divine or semi-divine power upon their rulers, and by the formation of laws, which set up rules increasing hierarchy and regulating dominance. Everywhere, the first step toward turning "difference into dominance" is the institution of patriarchal privileges of men over women.

A small group of men dominate resources and allocate them to the women they have acquired as sexual property and to their children, to other less powerful men, and to a newly-created underclass of slaves. The texture of power relationships thus created balances privileges and obligations for each group in such a way as to make the whole arrangement acceptable and to continue it in the interest of the dominant male group. Women and their children, in an age of rampant militarism and constant warfare and in an age of high infant and maternal mortality, needed protection in order for the tribes as a whole to survive. Such reasoning led women in the first place to accept and cooperate with the "patriarchal bargain"—in exchange for their sexual and reproductive services to one man, they will be guaranteed protection and resources for themselves and their children. Slavery, which develops at a time when men first acquire sufficient resources to keep captives alive instead of killing them, initially starts with a similar bargain. Slave women and later men accept that bargain the moment they accept the gift of their life after military conquest in exchange for their enslavement.

It is no accident that everywhere the first slaves known are women of foreign tribes. Often such tribes are racially and visibly different from their conquerors, which makes it easier for the conquerors to designate them permanently as an underclass. But where such racial differences do not exist, it is possible to create them by "marking" the slaves—with a brand, a peculiar way of cutting the hair, a special way of dressing or other means. Always, what is accentuated is "difference." The slave is different from the master and because he is different he can be designated as inferior. Because he or more likely she is designated as inferior she can be exploited, commodified, and designated as in some way sub-human. The institutionalization of militarism as a way of life presupposes hierarchical thinking—some people who dominate have the right to dominate because they are superior; the dominated must accept bring dominated because they are inferior.

How can one tell who is to be dominant and who is to be dominated? By force, first of all—the victors dominate; the conquered are dominated. But rule by force alone is untenable in the long run. Even the fiercest warriors could not long enslave other warriors unless they had several conquerors watching each conquered warrior day and night. Dominance is only possible if it can be justified and accepted both by the dominant and the dominated and by the large majority of people who are neither. And, historically, what makes dominance acceptable, is putting a negative mark on difference. This group or that group is different from us; they are our "Other". And because they are our "Other" we can rule them. It is upon such ideological foundations that class dominance was made acceptable even to people who did not directly benefit from it. At the time of the formation of the archaic states non-slaveholding men accepted the bargain of being dominated and exploited in regard to resources by more powerful men of their own group because they were simultaneously offered the chance to dominate and control the resources of others, the "different" others, namely the women and children of their own class. Even to men who did not themselves hold slaves, the existence of an underclass raises their own sense of status and made them accept their own relative inequality as a fair arrangement.

Once the system of dominance and hierarchy is institutionalized in custom, law, and practice, it is seen as natural and just and people no longer question it, unless historical circumstances change very dramatically. For the dominated, the benefits the original bargain conferred upon them are lost, once slavery becomes hereditary—it is then simply exploitation based on arbitrary power.

What I have briefly outlined here is a pattern of development which took many hundreds of years to consolidate. What is important is that this analysis shows, in its simplest and rudimentary form, the connectedness of various forms of difference-turned-into-dominance. It shows that sex, class, and race dominance are interrelated and inseparable, from the start. The difference between men and women was the first, most easily notable difference and therefore dominance by men could first be acted out on that terrain. But class and race dominance (in the form of the enslavement of conquered foreign people) developed almost immediately upon this first human "discovery" of how to use power so as to benefit people unequally. The function of all designations of "otherness" or deviance is to keep hierarchy in place for the benefit of the dominant. I am not here trying to set up priorities of oppression. Which system of oppression came first and which second is insignificant, if we understand that we are dealing with one, inseparable system with different manifestations.

But we do need richer, more complex, and more relational definitions of terms with which we usually work, such as "class" and "race." In Marxist terms "Class" is defined, as a group "who play the same part in the mechanism of production" or, alternatively, "men's relationship to the means of production". The Weberian definition is "people who have life chances in common, as determined by their power to dispose of goods and skills for the sake of income." No matter what the definition, class has been so defined that women are subsumed under the category "men." Males and females are considered as belonging to the same class, without definite distinctions between them. But "class" never describes a single set of locations, relations, and experiences. "Class" is generic, that is it is expressed and institutionalized in terms that are *always different* for men and women. For men, "class" describes their relationship to the means of production and their power over resources and women and children. For women, "class" describes their relationship to the means of production *as mediated* through the man to whom they render sexual and reproductive services and/or the man on whom they are dependent in their family of origin. In the case of women who enjoy economic independence, "class" still describes not only their relationship to the means of production, but their control (or lack thereof) over their reproductive capacity and their sexuality.

The concept "race" will similarly have to be expanded and redefined. The definition of "race" as a mark of difference and, thereby, inferiority antedates the formation of Western civilization, as I have shown. From its inception, "race" as a defining term was created genderically, that is it was applied in a different way to men and women. Men of oppressed races were primarily exploited as workers; women were *always* exploited as workers, as providers of sexual services, and as reproducers. Dominant elites, once they had institutionalized slavery, acquired the unpaid labor of enslaved men and women, but they also acquired the sexual and reproductive services of slave women as a commodity. That is, the children of slave women became an actual commodity to be worked, sold, and traded; the unrewarded sexual services of slave women to their master enhanced the master's status among his peers, as in the form of harems; slave women's sexual services were and could be commodified in the form of prostitution.

The binary gendered opposition (male/female) which is so firmly rooted in our culture and cultural product as well as in our language and thought, makes it difficult for us to see the complexity of other structural relationships in society. We have thought of classifications such as "class" and "race" as being vertical boxes into which to sort people in history, but it has been difficult for us to conceptualize the overlapping boundaries of the two concepts. When we think not in terms which compare two separate oppressive systems which may show some overlap, but in terms of one system with several, fully integrated aspects which depend for their existence one upon the other, a truer relationship can be visualized. We can then discuss not "priorities" of oppression or primacies (is a black woman more oppressed because of her sex or of her race?) but we can show the inter-relatedness of both aspects of oppression and their interdependency. Once we do that, a richer description, more closely related to actual relationships, can be drawn.

The system of male dominance over resources and women, called patriarchy, depends for its existence on creating categories of "deviants" or "others." Such groups, variously constituted in different times and places, are always defined as being "different" from the hegemonic group and assumed to be inferior. It is upon this assumption of the inferiority of presumed "deviant" groups that hierarchy is instituted and maintained. Hierarchy is institutionalized in the state and its laws, in military, economic, educational, and religious institutions, in ideology and the hegemonic cultural product created by the dominant elite. The system which has historically appeared in different forms, such as ancient slavery, feudalism, capitalism, industrialism, depends, for its continuance on its ability to split the dominated majority into various groups and to mystify the process by which this is done. The function of various forms of oppression, which are usually treated as separate and distinct, but which in fact are aspects of the same system, is to accomplish this division by offering different groups of the oppressed various advantages over other groups and thus pit them one against the other. Racism, anti-Semitism, various forms of ethnic prejudice, sexism, classism, and homophobia are all means to this end. If we see these various forms of creating "deviance" and "other-ness" as aspects of one and the same system of dominance, we can demystify the process by which the system constructs a reality which constantly sustains and reinforces it.

Let me illustrate this by a concrete example. In the antebellum South lower-class white males, whose long-range economic interests were actually opposed to the economic interests of the planter class, derived psychological and status benefits from racism. They had control over the sexuality and reproduction of women of their own class and enjoyed sexual privileges over Black women. This combination of sexual and status privileges made them cooperative with the planter's hegemonic system, despite the fact that they were deprived of educational opportunities, had limited access to political power and had to subordinate their economic interest to that of the planters.

White and Black women of all classes in the antebellum South were also denied political and legal rights and access to education. Although neither group controlled their sexuality nor their reproduction, the differences between them were substantial. White women, regardless of class, owed sexual and reproductive services to the men to whom they were married. Black women, in addition to the labor extracted from them, owed sexual and reproductive services to their white masters and to the Black men their white masters had selected for them. Since the white master of Black women could as well be a white woman, it is clear that racism was for Black women and men the decisive factor which structured them into society and controlled their lives. Conversely, white women could offset whatever economic and social disadvantages they suffered by sexism by the racist advantages they had over both Black men and women. Practically speaking, this meant that white women benefited from racism economically, insofar as they owned slaves; that they could relieve themselves of child-rearing (and at times even childbearing) responsibilities by using the enforced services of their female slaves; that they were relieved of doing unpaid domestic labor by using slave labor. In addition white men and women of all classes derived a sense of higher status from the racist system which decisively affected their consciousness.

Another way of saying this is that dominant elite, white, upper-class men benefit from all aspects of their dominance—economic and educational privilege, sexual and reproductive control, and higher status. Women of their own class benefit sufficiently from racist and economic privilege so as tó mask for them the disadvantages and discrimination they experience because of sexism. Whites of the lower classes benefit sufficiently from racism and (in the case of males) from sexism so that they support the system, even in face of obvious economic and political disadvantages. For those dominated and oppressed by racism, classism, and sexism, all aspects of the oppressive system work to make their emancipation more difficult.

The fact that in the case of antebellum slavery the dominant elite understood the importance of all aspects of the oppressive system to the continuance of their privileges is shown in the increasing severity with which laws against educating slaves were enforced in that period and in the continuous existence of unequal laws in regard to sexual crimes. From the middle of the eighteenth century on, sexual crimes of Black men against white women were punished by death, while sexual crimes of white men against Black women were not only not considered crimes but were considered white male rights. The denial to African-American men not only of sexual privilege over women of their own race, but of their ability to protect women of their families from the attacks of white men was a further means of dehumanizing them, defining them as "other" and forcing them to accept lower-status self-definitions. Racism never succeeded in actually making Black men internalize such self-definitions; yet dominant whites never gave up the attempt to impose them on slaves and later on freedmen.

That Black men were well aware of the intended effect of this strategy can be seen in the Reconstruction period when they first claimed male privilege over their women as a symbol of their "manhood." Black women were to render domestic and nurturant services to their own families only (a goal many Black women understandably supported); Black men were to be breadwinners; Black men were to be able to protect their women from sexual assault by whites. One of the marks of the failure of Reconstruction and of the continuing existence of the racist system was precisely that these goals were not realizable in the nineteenth-century South.

The importance of sexism as a means of enforcing racism can also be seen in the way racist double standards were used in the post-Civil War period to keep freedmen and later all southern Blacks in subordinate status despite the end of slavery. The rise of violence against Black males and the sharp increase in lynchings, always excused as being "in defense of white womanhood," served to intimidate the free Black community in the post-Reconstruction period and again at the turn of the century, when Blacks in the South were virtually disfranchised. It was African-American women in their clubs, and especially Ida B. Wells, who first uncovered the workings of this sexist-racist double standard and who exposed the falsity of the charge that white women needed protection from Black men. Similarly, the history of the U.S. trade union movement abounds with evidence of the ways employers were able to exploit ethnic and racial differences among their work force in order to retard or prevent unionization, sometimes for decades. Racially or ethnically defined status privileges often induced white workers to act against their best economic self-interest, as did lower-class whites in the antebellum South.

The inter-relatedness of distinctions based on race, class, ethnicity, and sex is not so clearly demonstrable in contemporary industrial society as it is in the society of the antebellum South. Gender-relations have undergone considerable change, and some of the more obvious male sexual privileges have altered under the impact of women's political struggle and economic changes. Men no longer have property rights in women and children; women have, at least on a formal level, equal access to education and are entitled to equality of political representation, even if they do not actually enjoy it in practice. Large numbers of women, except for the poor, now have access to economic resources directly, that is, not mediated through a man, although this does not hold for married women who are full-time homemakers. The control of women's reproductive resources is no longer exerted by individual men but instead by male-dominated institutions such as the courts, the state, the churches, and the medical professional establishment.

Still, in contemporary USA, white males of elite groups continue to control the major corporations, the legal and political establishment, the news media, the academic establishment (despite some inroads made by women), the trade union movement, the churches. The economic dependency of women (and, with it, the basic inequality in access to and control of resources) continues. It is secured through the definition of heterosexuality as the norm; through gender-indoctrination; the continued existence of women's unpaid domestic labor and child-rearing services; the gender-based wage discrimination against women and their concentration in low-paid, temporary, or dead-end service jobs. Male dominance and privilege is further expressed through the definition of professionalism to fit the male model and through the denial to women of professional career patterns suited to their life cycles. It also is manifested in sexual harassment on the job as a means of keeping women out of better jobs. Male control of women's sexuality and reproduction is now exerted through the politicization of issues of reproductive choice, the continuing growth of the pornography establishment and the sex industry, and of prostitution, which, as it has been for millennia, is predominantly an occupation of lower-class women. The ever growing phenomenon of violence against women and children is another distorted and perverted form of male dominance.

All whites derive tangible benefits from racism, but such benefits vary by class and sex so that upper-class males benefit more from racism than do lower-class people of both sexes and upper-class women. Racism, by splitting people from one another, helps to prevent alliances of lower-class people which might effectively challenge the system. Racism gives the illusion of superiority to lower-class whites, which convinces them to support the dominant elites, often against their true economic interests.

The benefits to upper- and middle-class women of the race/class system are so tangible that it is easy for them to overlook and disregard its oppressive aspects, even to themselves. The gains made by women over a century of struggle have benefited upper-class women disproportionally. This group has control over its own property; it reaps the economic benefits of racism and classism and shares them with upper-class men. Women of this group share, even if on a lower level, the benefits of education and of opportunities for professional careers. Class and race privileges allow such women to fulfill their domestic and child-rearing services by substituting another woman for themselves. Their economic independence allows them to define sexual relations in their own interest and to secure divorces without great economic loss. In short, it is their class privilege which helps them offset any disadvantages arising from their subordinate status as women.

The women less privileged economically are more vulnerable since they are in a worse bargaining position. For many middle- and lower-class women, gaining some economic independence by working means assuming the burden of a double working day. Such women are usually not in a position to support themselves and their children in case of divorce, which means they are unable to bargain for better conditions within their marriages or to make other choices. This is the large group of women of whom it can be said that they are "one man away from poverty." This is also the group of white women most committed against feminism since their security and economic opportunities seem to them entirely to rest on the maintenance of their marriages and the good will of the men with whom they are affiliated. Such women have a direct economic investment in maintaining their "respectability" against people of other races or ethnicities or against the most dangerous "other"—non-respectable women. Black women of this economic group do not necessarily expect Black men to support them and their children; thus, their attitude toward a feminism of their own definition is more positive than that of white women of the same economic class.

In modern industrial society, the majority of the poor are women and children. The "feminization of poverty" is the modern expression of the multifaceted system of patriarchal dominance. Women become poor because they are abandoned by men; because they are oppressed by being in a lower class or a nonwhite race; because they are members of a "deviant" group (lesbians, drug users, handicapped, "immoral," single mothers) or because they are old. Modern society has created new adaptations for the old definitions of "Otherness," but the function of defining "Otherness" as deviance has not changed. It helps to raise the status of dominant males to define themselves against despised outgroups; such raised status perceptions secure the collaboration of middle- and lower-class people in the system that robs them of equity and justice.

Historians who understand the inter-relatedness of the various aspects of the system of patriarchal dominance are in a better position to interpret the history of women than are those who continue to regard class, race, and gender dominance as separate though intersecting and overlapping systems. The intellectual construct of separate systems inevitably marginalizes the subordination of women.

Race, class, and gender oppression are inseparable; they construct, reinforce, and support one another. The form which class first took historically was genderic and racist. The form racism first took was genderic and classist. The form the state first took was patriarchal. These are the starting points for re-conceptualization.

Above all, historians and teachers must consciously attempt to step outside of the vertical boxes of patriarchal thinking. We are not going to have an integrated history by being additive, nor by structuring a history of "upstairs and downstairs," "private and public", "production and reproduction." We will need to re-think the ways we organize what we teach in order to do justice to "differences" by making them central to our thinking. Just what does that mean concretely?

It means first of all, as I have shown in my example of antebellum history, that we should always vary our generalizations by creating an interactive contextual model which considers the ways in which factors of race, class, ethnicity, and sex are expressed in regard to men and women of the groups under discussion. It means also that we must use new strategies to organize the content of our teaching so as to make these issues visible.

If we teach a U.S. survey following a traditional textbook, the text will barely mention women. If we then simply "add" women, we have improved on this outline but not by much. The women we have added will either be women much like the men we talk about or they will look inferior by comparison with the men. To make women central to our conceptual framework, we must assume that what they do and think is equally important with what the men do and think. If we make such an assumption, we will ask about every unit we teach: what were the women doing while the men were doing what we are teaching? and, going an analytical step further, how did the women interpret what they were doing? This immediately changes the whole unit: we are now talking not only of a world populated by male actors and evaluated according to male standards, but we are talking of a world populated by male and female actors and evaluated by male and female standards.

Now let us see what happens when we make "difference" central to our analysis. We can, of course, be additive, and I would guess that in most cases people who want to do justice to the varieties of ethnic and racial experiences are now teaching in that way: it was like this for European immigrants to the colonies, and it was like that for Native Americans, and like that for African Americans—the old salad bowl approach. But what if we told the story of settlement not from the moment Columbus "discovered America," a statement and organization which immediately tells the students that what happened on American soil before that time was insignificant and that the arrival of this particular group of Spaniards is of more significance than earlier arrivals or the lives and activities of native peoples? We might start, instead, with the earliest records of Native Americans on this continent, with the way they lived and thought and acted, with their social organization—which was, in many cases, not patriarchal—with their religions, their economies, their values. We might then talk about the various groups of invaders consecutively, and we would be giving students a totally different perspective on the significance of the arrival of the little Spanish flotilla, which made its discovery only because of a navigational error. Following such an approach—which, by the way, already exists in some texts—we might then tell the story of the various decisive events in U.S. history with an equally even-handed view. We would want to present not only different points of view—in each case drawing as much as possible on primary sources of the relevant groups—but we would want to represent accurately the power relations existing between the various groups as they interacted in the same place and time. Some teachers have already experimented with organizing women's history survey courses by starting with Native American women and then moving, not from East to West, as traditional historiography does, but from West to East. Since settlement in the West actually antedates the development of English settlement in the East, this method has distinct advantages. It also builds a comparative approach into the very structure of the course.

All re-conceptualization must start with a new conceptual framework. We must have our goal firmly in mind and approach our task by finding new analytic questions. If we do this, the integration of new materials will not have to come at the expense of omitting something else of importance. Rather, the question will arise: why is this important and not that? It is not an easy task, and it will challenge the best of our collective minds and energies. But it is a worthwhile enterprise from every point of view. What we are trying to do is to create a holistic history in which men and women, in the various aspects of their lives, interact in various ways, reflecting the differences among them. The textured richness of such a reconstruction of the past depends on our ability to embrace difference, hear many languages, and see interdependencies rather than separation. Learning from female language and modes of perception, we will need to be relational, existential, and aware of our own involvement even as we use the male mode to categorize, order, and analyze. The point is that the two modes always have been coexisting and complementary. We must adapt our own craft to that reality by ourselves becoming conscious and accepting of it.

☆ 4 ☆

Black History Since 1865

REPRESENTATIVE OR RACIST?

Historical writings by scholars dealing with black history from the Civil War to the present—the era of the freed blacks—reflect a distinct ambiguity. Most writings were by white historians who claimed to represent the entire profession and said they were treating these subjects with scholarly objectivity, honesty, and fairness. On the other hand one could see in some of these same writings evidence of racial bias either in the positions taken, attitudes adopted, or subjects addressed. White historians for a long time simply assumed that black writers could not be objective about subjects like black Reconstruction or on most matters dealing with race. Such a biased attitude reflected the racial prejudice that has existed in America as a whole; American society, its claims and laws to the contrary notwithstanding, remains a race-conscious society.

As long as the United States continues to be race-conscious this prejudice will continue to influence historical writings about blacks. One historian in the late 1950s, for example, described the historiography of the Reconstruction era as "dark and bloody." As Afro-Americans receive more attention in historical writings in the future, that ground will probably be seen as even darker and bloodier.[1]

This persistence in racial bias among American scholars during the past century and a quarter has warped our understanding of the Civil War and Reconstruction eras for one thing. Two illustrations leap to mind which reveal the racial bias of white scholars—a bias often un-

---

[1]Bernard Weisberger, "The Dark and Bloody Ground of Reconstruction Historiography," *Journal of Southern History* 25 (1959):427–447.

conscious in its manifestations. First, they have done relatively little research on the careers and accomplishments of those black politicians and black officials who served with distinction during the Reconstruction era, 1865 to 1877. Second, for a long time those phases of black Reconstruction taken up by scholars were treated unfairly because the historians were either prejudiced white Southerners or outright white supremacists.

Despite the fact that both black and white historians have been writing about post-Civil War black history for the past century and a quarter, the field is still in its infancy. This generalization holds true because almost every phase of black history has been shrouded in myths and misconceptions. One of the most persistent and pernicious of these myths was that the blacks were a passive people. Blacks were often cast in the role of victims; they were always acted upon and incapable of acting for themselves. They were viewed, moreover, as a people and a race whose fate was determined solely by their relationship with the white race. Such an approach led inevitably to a number of studies on white attitudes and actions toward blacks.

It has only been in recent years that scholars have finally begun to delve into the historical records for independent ideas and activities by the blacks. Only with the introduction of the "new social history," moreover, have scholars resisted the temptation to present black history as nothing more than a series of biographical sketches of black leaders—such men as Booker T. Washington, W. E. B. Du Bois, Marcus Garvey, and Martin Luther King, Jr. The shift to writing about black history in different terms—in terms of a changing black social structure, sister institutions separate from those of whites, and values of the black community as a whole—is a relatively recent phenomenon and barely a quarter of a century old.

There were other reasons why scholars were slow to write meaningfully on black history. Black history was invariably viewed in tragic terms; it went contrary to the optimistic outlook usually adopted by most scholars writing before the end of World War II. When writing immigrant history, for example, historians typically traced the arrival of some ethnic group to the New World, depicted its struggles for existence, and then showed how the group was ultimately assimilated into American society to become virtually indistinguishable from earlier immigrant groups. Black history hardly fitted such a pattern. The circumstances of immigration were different: the movement to America was involuntary not voluntary; there was continuing conflict between the two races; and black history did not end on a theme of assimilation. Black history was tragic in its outlook because blacks have yet to be fully accepted into American life; their status in American society remains uncertain.

Black history also did not fit the pattern of most American history written before World War II, which was oriented around success as a theme. Most past scholars emphasized success; they tended to neglect those groups in American history who had failed in some lost cause, such as the Loyalists or the Antifederalists. Even where certain social movements failed to achieve their goals—the Populists, for example—historians often ended on a triumphant note anyway. They usually concluded their discussion with the observation that Populist principles eventually had been incorporated into the Democratic and Republican party platforms. But black history presented a problem: it was difficult to fit its tragic outcome within this typical pattern of progress and success. Because black history could neither be ignored nor readily incorporated into the mainstream, it has been presented in ways that ranged through a whole spectrum of thought—from blatant racism at one end to rather objective representation at the other.

With these distinctions in mind it is possible to break down the writing of black history since 1865 into roughly four different periods. First there was the period of paternalism—1865 to the late 1920s—when many of the standard authorities were patronizing or patently racist in their writings. The second was the period of transition—1920s to 1950s—when the attitude of scholars toward blacks began to change and racist writings were no longer the generally accepted mode. The third was the period of maturation—the 1950s and 1960s—when liberal white scholars first began writing black history on a large scale and became more acutely aware of the racist attitudes of the earlier eras. The fourth was the period of accommodation—the 1970s to the present—during which scholars have become more sensitive about the existence of a separate black subculture—a subculture with its own values, institutions, and attitudes. This did not mean that scholars had reached a millennium; it meant only that historians were writing with fewer myths and misconceptions in mind.

Around 1900 two major works in the period of paternalism set forth a point of view on Reconstruction that persisted for more than two decades. James Ford Rhodes, a Northern businessman who lacked professional training but had a great love of history, published his multivolume *History of the United States from the Compromise of 1850* covering the years between 1865 and 1877. John W. Burgess, a college professor in the field of political science, ex-Confederate, and former slaveholder, released his *Reconstruction and the Constitution* in 1902. These two interpretations laid the groundwork for what came to be called the Dunning school of Reconstruction historiography.

Professor William A. Dunning, who taught at Columbia University, published his rigorous study, *Reconstruction, Political and Economic,* in 1907. Dunning's graduate students proceeded to flesh out his interpretation with a series of state studies. Reconstruction, according to Dunning, was the lowest point in the South's long history. A coalition of carpetbaggers (opportunistic Northerners who moved to the South) and scalawags (turncoat white Southern Republicans) supported by federal troops presided over the prostrate South. Under their rule the most corrupt, expensive, and inefficient state governments in the history of the South held sway. Taxes and public debts soared and fraud was rampant. The real villains of the period were the recently freed blacks, concluded Dunning. Ignorant and uneducated, unprepared for freedom, the former slaves wrought havoc on the region. They refused to work, stole from the public coffers, insulted their former masters, and abused white women. The South, unrepresented in Congress and occupied by Northern military troops, was exploited in every way by rapacious Yankees and Republicans who gave the illiterate blacks free rein.

Popular historians spiced up the Dunning school interpretation with insulting racist remarks. One of the best-selling books on the subject was by Claude Bowers, entitled *The Tragic Era*, which came out in 1929. Bowers, who later served as ambassador to Spain for Franklin D. Roosevelt, described black politicians as "the type seldom seen outside the Congo." "Little above the intellectual level of the mules they drove," Bowers went on, they ran South Carolina with "chuckles and guffaws, the noisy crackling of peanuts and raucous voices. . . ." "Asleep in their chairs, eating peanuts and soaked in whiskey, quarreling, fighting, pursuing one another with murderous intent," they turned Louisiana's Senate into a "monkey-house" and proposed amendments "too obscene to print." Bowers concluded that "the Southern people literally were put to the torture. . . ."[2]

The documentation Bowers employed points up some of the methodological problems that plagued the writing of black history at the time. One of Bowers's most enthusiastically-cited sources was James S. Pike's *The Prostrate State: South Carolina under Negro Government*, published in 1874. Pike, according to his biographer, had a "pronounced racial antipathy toward the Negro." Another Bowers source was *Reconstruction in South Carolina* by John S. Reynolds, issued in 1905. According to W. E. B. Du Bois, the great black scholar, the works of Pike and Reynolds were "openly and blatantly propaganda," and that Bowers's book itself "was absolutely devoid of historical judgment or sociological knowledge."[3]

Many of the other standard secondary sources on the period were similarly paternalistic or racist. The primary sources available at that time often contributed to this racial bias. Since slaves had been forbid-

---

[2]Claude Bowers, *The Tragic Era* (New York, 1929), pp. vi, 353, 358, 362, and 364.

[3]Robert F. Durden, *James Shepherd Pike* (Durham, N.C., 1957), p. viii; and W. E. B. Du Bois, *Black Reconstruction* (New York, 1935), pp. 720–721.

den to read or write, records of their early years of freedom were sparse. White men often became self-appointed spokesmen for both races, thereby obscuring the viewpoint of the blacks completely. Records of black officials were sometimes deliberately destroyed. The archives of the black Florida superintendent of education who helped to establish the public school system in that state, for example, disappeared once his white successors took office. The state of Alabama tried to obliterate the printed records of black Reconstruction altogether. Libraries and public archives meanwhile were reluctant to gather any documents that were related to the black history of the Reconstruction era.

The Dunning interpretation remained dominant for over two decades. It was openly racist, and any hope of reaching a balanced and more objective point of view was out of the question. Despite the protests of W. E. B. Du Bois and a handful of white historians, the Dunning position prevailed throughout the profession.

The Progressive school of historians who dealt with the whole span of American history and not simply with the Reconstruction era did little to help the cause of black history. This school, while not explicitly racist, served to minimize the significance of blacks in American history. Because of its focus on the impersonal forces operating in history—economic in the case of Beard and environmental in the case of Turner—the Progressive school de-emphasized the role of individuals both black and white. Beard made capitalism and the triumph of Northern industrialism over the South's cotton kingdom the thesis in the two-volume 1927 work entitled *The Rise of American Civilization.* He argued that Northern financiers and industrialists had maneuvered the country into the war, and the South out of and back into the Union, in a successful attempt to wrest control of the national economy from the cotton planters. This interpretation had the effect of reducing black abolitionists, black soldiers, and black politicians (as well as whites for that matter) to mere pawns operating within the context of a gigantic capitalist conspiracy. Frederick Jackson Turner, in his famous essay on "The Significance of the Frontier," written in 1893, concluded that once American history was viewed in the correct light slavery would be seen merely as an "incident" and not an important institution with tragic consequences.

What the Progressives did was to shift the focus of attention away from the blacks. Since the turn of the century the majority of scholars—racists and nonracists alike—had assumed that the blacks had been a crucial factor in the coming of the Civil War and the shaping of Reconstruction. Most historians had accepted the notion that Afro-Americans, both acting and acted upon, had largely dominated the national scene from 1861 to 1877. Progressives like Beard and Turner, however, shifted the perspective away from the blacks. Beard claimed that slavery was in no real sense the central issue of the Civil

War. By diminishing the role played by individuals and their ideas—
both blacks and whites—and emphasizing instead other deterministic
elements which shaped history, the Progressives make blacks less visible.

From the late 1920s to the 1950s—the period of transition—
scholars began to view the developments during the Reconstruction
era and the role of blacks differently from the Dunning school. The so-
called revisionists—an anti-Dunning school—restudied the Reconstruction era and concluded it was not as bad as previously pictured.
Influenced in part by the Progressive school they challenged certain
findings of the Dunningites. The revisionists refused to view Reconstruction as a kind of morality play—one that depicted the history of
the period as a struggle between the forces of good and evil, whites and
blacks, Democrats and Radical Republicans.[4]

Although the revisionists accepted many of the findings of the
Dunning school, they started from different premises and assumptions. Consequently they arrived at different conclusions. Quite often
revisionists did so after examining the very same data the Dunningites
had used. The revisionists, for one thing, viewed the blacks and their
role during Reconstruction in a much more favorable light. They denied that the worst features of Reconstruction had arisen from black
domination of Southern political offices. In no single state in the South
had the blacks controlled both houses of the legislature, the revisionists pointed out. There were no black governors elected and only one
black state supreme court justice was appointed. On the national level
only two blacks were elected to the Senate, and barely fifteen to the
House of Representatives. On the basis of such findings the charge of
the Dunningites that blacks were responsible for the presumed excesses of Reconstruction governments could hardly be substantiated.
The so-called black Reconstruction, it appeared, was not so "black"
after all.

The accusation that blacks had been inefficient and unintelligent
in government administration in the states where they played a most
active political role was also shown to be false. Vernon L. Wharton, in
a path-breaking study of the Mississippi state government during the
postwar period, *The Negro in Mississippi, 1865–1890*, published in
1947, found little difference on the county level within certain agencies when either blacks or whites were in office. As state governments
went, that of Mississippi between 1870 and 1876, when a coalition of

---

[4]Gerald N. Grob, "Reconstruction: An American Morality Play," In *American History: Retrospect and Prospect*, George Athan Billias and Gerald N. Grob, eds. (New York,
1971), pp. 191–231.

black and white Republicans was in control, was not a bad one, Wharton concluded.

Finally the revisionists disagreed with the idea that the Radical governments had been unusually expensive or corrupt. Although expenses went up sharply in the postwar period, it was not always the result of inefficiency or theft, they said. Wartime destruction required the use of public funds to rebuild cities and devastated areas. Even more important was the fact that the South was forced for the first time to provide certain public services for its black slaves–turned–citizens. Schools were erected, hospitals built, and mental institutions established. Such facilities had not existed before the Civil War, and the rise in spending during the Reconstruction era could be accounted for, in large part, by these new social services.

The revisionists revealed as well a greater sensitivity and awareness of the racist attitudes and prejudices of past historians. Francis Simkins, a Southern scholar and leading exponent of the revisionist school, commented on this point in an important article written in 1939. Earlier historians had given a distorted picture of Reconstruction, Simkins said, because they began with the basic premise that blacks were racially inferior. Their approach, as a result, was based on ignorance, and their conclusions were warped by their prejudices. Only by abandoning these biases, Simkins concluded, could scholars hope to arrive at a more accurate understanding of the past.[5]

Black scholars made the same point. W. E. B. Du Bois, a Harvard-trained historian and sociologist, thorough-going professional, and the outstanding black scholar of his day, took issue with the writings of the Dunning school. Proud of his race, Du Bois presented an impressive defense of the activities of blacks during Reconstruction in his massive 1935 study entitled *Black Reconstruction*. Du Bois, who had become a Marxist by this time, advanced the rather dubious thesis that the freed blacks had shown considerable class-consciousness during the Reconstruction years.

Carter Woodson, another pioneering black historian, was also sharply critical of the Dunning school. An influential scholar and propagandist for the study of the black past, Woodson founded the *Journal of Negro History*. In the fourth edition of his important book, *The Negro in Our History*, published in 1927, Woodson took racist white historians to task for their prejudices.

Throughout the period of transition the search for primary sources of black history also grew more intense. During the depression of the 1930s the W.P.A. and other federal agencies made a more concentrated

---

[5]Francis B. Simkins, "New Viewpoints of Southern Reconstruction," *Journal of Southern History* 5 (1939):49–61. See also the classic article by Howard K. Beale, "On Rewriting Reconstruction History," *American Historical Review* 45 (1939–1940):807–27.

effort to compile and research records for such materials. These steps were taken with the knowledge that better black history could be produced if primary sources written by Afro-Americans themselves were available.

Between the 1920s and 1950 the single most significant event that improved the status of blacks within American society was World War II. Confronted with the blatant racism of Nazi Germany toward the Jews, Americans finally were brought face-to-face with the racism against blacks in their own society. How could scholars in a society fighting Nazi racism support overt racism against blacks at home? World War II, then, proved to be a most important turning point for American historians in making them aware of the detrimental effects of racism on scholarly inquiry. This change in the climate of opinion was reflected by a marked shift away from the racist perspective during the period of transition.

A second development in this same period was the work of anthropologists and psychologists who undermined the intellectual respectability of racist ideas. Anthropologist Franz Boas showed that physical types within the human species were not fixed and unalterable. Social psychologists looked again at the evidence on the distribution of high and low levels of intelligence and rejected the notion that some races were superior and others inferior.

The intellectual underpinnings for this more liberal outlook could be seen in the writings of Swedish scholar Gunnar Myrdal, who was commissioned to write a work on American race relations. Myrdal produced a classic on the conditions of blacks in America entitled *An American Dilemma*, which appeared in 1944. He based his study on an explicitly liberal premise. Myrdal assumed that the problem of race relations presented a moral dilemma to most Americans. They deeply believed, on the one hand, in the American moral creed of liberty and justice for all. On the other hand most Americans were painfully aware that they and their society had fallen far short of such ideals. Hence most white Americans were forced to live with the enduring moral dilemma that there was a great gap between their stated ideals and their day-to-day existence.

Despite the move toward a less racist stance among historians during and after World War II, there was by no means unanimity within the profession. As late as 1947—at the very end of the period of transition—E. Merton Coulter, a distinguished Southern scholar, published a patently racist study entitled *The South During Reconstruction*. The work appeared, moreover, in the "History of the South" series—a series whose aim was to present the latest and best scholarship written about the region.

The climate of opinion about blacks changed even more dramatically during the period of maturation—the decades of the 1950s and 1960s. With the 1954 Supreme Court decision of *Brown et al.* v. *Board of Education in Topeka* the segregation of black and white children in public schools was ruled illegal. This ruling, calling for equal and integrated schools for blacks, helped to set off the greatest civil rights movement in American history. Liberal white public opinion in the North began to move slowly toward a more racially egalitarian viewpoint. Martin Luther King, Jr., and other black leaders, meanwhile, were demonstrating that nonviolent direct action could succeed in bringing about change in parts of the South.

The dynamics of international power politics likewise contributed to the domestic changes already in progress. Soviet propaganda about racism in America was part of the intellectual offensive in the Cold War; it embarrassed Americans and caused many of them to reassess their position on this issue. The rise of newly emerging African nations in the 1950s and 1960s, moreover, gave some American blacks a more confident self-image at home. Pan-Africanism provided a newfound sense of pride.

All these developments gave rise to what was called a "black revolution in expectations." Blacks no longer felt they had to put up with the humiliation of second-class citizenship—segregated schools, disenfranchisement, and discrimination in employment practices. Such humiliations, though not as great as in the past, seemed more intolerable than ever before. This increasing impatience and dissatisfaction led to a mounting crescendo of nonviolent direct action in the late 1950s in the form of student sit-ins and massive protest marches. In the mid-1960s, however, the tension exploded in mass race riots in many major American cities. There were a series of such race riots after Martin Luther King, Jr., the revered black leader, was assassinated in 1968. These changes in the world outside the scholar's study spurred white historians to take up the study of black history more than ever before.

At the same time changes within the historical profession itself caused scholars to look at black history anew. There was a profound change in perspective among historians, and a shift toward analyzing the totality of human social experience. Influenced in part by the French *Annales* school, in part by the populist-oriented concerns of the 1960s, and in part by the impact of emerging behavioral science methodologies—such as computer quantification techniques—scholars began writing the "new social history." Scholars realized that the discipline of history had to encompass more than a compilation of facts about the lives, thoughts, and perceptions of political and intellectual leaders—the elites in American society. To comprehend more fully the total sum of human experience many "new social historians" felt compelled to study the lives, habits, customs, and practices of all persons, the common and everyday folk as well as the learned and the great. It was within this context that more white scholars proceeded to take up the study of black history.

One other change affected the writing of history in the 1950s and 1960s, and that was the political activism of some younger scholars. Certain young historians, such as the New Left, either became participants in or were close observers of the civil rights movement during these two decades. The failure of American society to allow significant changes in the lives of most blacks—especially those living in Northern urban ghettoes and the black belt regions of the lower South—demonstrated to these scholars how deeply racism was entrenched in American society. Some historians were radicalized as a result. They regarded racism not as some anomaly—as was implied when slavery was termed the "peculiar institution"—but rather as a phenomenon functional in American society from its very start. Such radical historians did not perceive American society as a pluralistic "melting pot" and the blacks as simply another immigrant group: the blacks had been brought unwillingly to the New World, they pointed out, and for most blacks the melting pot never melted.[6]

Such developments gave rise to a new school of Reconstruction historiography in the 1950s called the "neorevisionists." These scholars tended to stress moral rather than economic considerations in their interpretation of the Reconstruction era. The differences between the revisionists and the neorevisionists were often slight; the neorevisionists, in fact, frequently relied on the findings of the revisionists to reach their conclusions. For this reason it is difficult to distinguish or label clearly certain historians as belonging to one group or another. The major difference between the two groups was this: the neorevisionists rejected the revisionist approach which interpreted the Reconstruction era basically from an economic point of view.

Another major distinction between the two groups was that the neorevisionists placed a heavy emphasis on race as a moral issue. Kenneth Stampp, a major neorevisionist, published, in 1965, *The Era of Reconstruction*—a work that stressed such a moral perspective. Stampp argued there was one central question during the Reconstruction period: What was to be the place of the recently freed slaves within American society as a whole and especially within Southern society? President Andrew Johnson and his followers believed in the innate inferiority of blacks on racial grounds. They were opposed, therefore, to any program based upon egalitarian assumptions. The

---

[6]During the period of maturation there were also some Marxist historians writing on blacks in the Reconstruction era. See Herbert Aptheker, ed., *Documentary History of the Negro People in the United States* (New York, 1951), which has many documents on the activities of black leaders during the 1860s; and Philip S. Foner, *The Life and Writings of Frederick Douglass*, 4 vols. (New York, 1950–1955), especially volumes 3 and 4.

Radical Republicans, on the other hand, took seriously the ideals of equality, natural rights, and democracy. Many of the Radical Republicans, in fact, had been associated with the abolitionist movement before the war, and carried over their ideas and attitudes to the Reconstruction era. Stampp recognized that many Radical Republicans also had some self-interest in supporting blacks: they hoped that the freed blacks would join the Republican party out of gratitude for what it had done for them. But to claim that the Radicals had solely selfish motives, Stampp said, was to do them in injustice and to present a distorted picture of the postwar era.

The Radical Republicans, according to Stampp, failed to achieve their aims. Most Americans at the time harbored racial prejudices—either consciously or unconciously—and were unwilling to accept blacks as equals. By the 1870s the North was weary and anxious to abandon the blacks and their fate to Southern whites for three reasons. First, there was a deep desire to return to normal relations between the two regions. Second, Northern industrialists were eager to invest in Southern plants. And third, there was a growing conviction that the cause of the blacks was no longer worth the trouble it was creating within the country.

But the heroic struggle of the Radicals was not in vain, Stampp said. The Radical state governments passed certain laws that protected the rights of blacks. More important, on the national level, the Radicals succeeded in framing the Fourteenth and Fifteenth amendments. "[I]t was worth a few years of radical reconstruction to give the American Negro the ultimate promise of equal civil and political rights," Stampp concluded.[7]

The single most important scholar writing during the period of maturation was the liberal white historian C. Vann Woodward. In his *Strange Career of Jim Crow*, published in 1955, Woodward argued that the system of segregation established by the infamous Jim Crow laws did not commence right after the Civil War. Instead these laws were primarily the result of the intensified hostility aroused among Southern whites during the late nineteenth and early twentieth centuries.

The Civil Rights Act of 1875 and similar legislation had had an effect, Woodward claimed, and the period from the end of Reconstruction in 1877 to the 1890s was marked by a rough equality in law and practice between the races. Woodward concluded that segregation though in evidence was not so harsh and rigid during this interim period. The Jim Crow laws really resulted from the politics of the 1890s. When the Populist threat of a new coalition between black and white farmers under the leadership of white agrarian radicals arose, Southern white conservatives reacted violently. They feared possible racial

---

[7]Kenneth Stampp, *The Era of Reconstruction, 1865–1877* (New York, 1966), p. 215.

amalgamation or the renewal of another era of black rule. To put down this Populist threat, blacks were terrorized by lynchings, disenfranchised at the polls, and segregated socially in public life in the 1890s and thereafter. Woodward's study constituted a historiographical landmark, and its appearance was timely because national attention was being focused on the civil rights movement following the Supreme Court decision of 1954.

Woodward's work soon became the center of a historiographical controversy. Other scholars had located the genesis of the Jim Crow system elsewhere in terms of space and time. Leon Litwack's 1961 study, *North of Slavery*, provided examples of widespread racial discrimination in the antebellum North, showing that racism was a national and not simply a Southern problem. Richard Wade in his *Slavery in the Cities*, published in 1964, found that Jim Crow practices had originated in Southern cities before the Civil War in response to the growing urban black population. Joel Williamson's *After Slavery*, which appeared in 1965, dated the origins of Jim Crow within a specific time period. Williamson furnished evidence that in South Carolina whites tried to expand the system of segregation only after slavery had been destroyed. When Woodward published a revised third edition of his *Strange Career of Jim Crow* in 1974, he acknowledged the validity of the arguments of Wade and Williamson, but held nevertheless quite closely to his original thesis.[8]

Black scholars meanwhile were also busy making major contributions to black history during the 1950s and 1960s. Prior to this time black history had been largely the domain of black scholars from black colleges and universities who published in such learned periodicals as the *Journal of Negro History*. A survey of the articles in this journal prior to the period of maturation reveals the surprising degree to which black scholars had anticipated the work done later by white scholars. The work of black scholars on matters dealing with race was generally confined to this journal because they encountered obstacles when they attempted to publish their findings in the standard historical periodicals.

John Hope Franklin, the most distinguished black scholar writing during this period, made several important contributions at this time and subsequently. Many of Franklin's writings dealt with the era be-

---

[8]C. Vann Woodward, *Strange Career of Jim Crow* (New York, 1974), Chapter 1; August Meier and Elliott Rudwick, in "A Strange Chapter in the Career of Jim Crow," in *The Making of Black America*, Meier and Rudwick, eds. (New York, 1969), II:14–19, believe there is some validity to all three positions of Woodward, Wade, and Williamson.

Woodward, resorting to the use of such ideas as "social distance" and "physical distance" derived from the fields of sociology and comparative history, stressed that such concepts should be applied in any future study of race relations and Jim Crow laws in America; see his chapter in *American Counterpoint* (Boston, 1971), pp. 234–260.

fore 1865: these included *The Militant South,* issued in 1956; *The Emancipation Proclamation,* which appeared in 1963; and parts of his textbook, *From Slavery to Freedom,* first published in 1947 and revised periodically over the next three decades. But Franklin's *Reconstruction: After the Civil War,* which came out in 1961, took up the time period covered in this chapter. Franklin's book not only revised the Dunning interpretation, but also undertook to make some overall generalizations regarding the Reconstruction era. He presented conclusive evidence that Radical Reconstruction was neither overwhelmingly "black" nor wholly inept. Although Franklin agreed that some black legislators were corrupt, he argued corruption was a nationwide problem and not confined to the South alone. Franklin ended his volume with a harsh indictment of the failure by the country to carry through its wartime promises of racial justice for blacks.

Benjamin Quarles, another black historian, in his *Negro in the Civil War,* published in 1953, revised sharply the role of blacks during that conflict. He demonstrated and documented the contributions blacks had made to the Union cause. His *Lincoln and the Negro,* in 1962, covered that important subject. Quarles's *Black Abolitionists,* which appeared in 1969, however, dealt with the prewar as well as postwar periods. This book revealed that the tensions that arose between black and white abolitionists before the war resulted from the race prejudices of the whites. White abolitionists had a totally unrealistic view of what the rights of freed blacks ought to be. In the Reconstruction era these enduring tensions caused a split between the two groups, driving the black abolitionists to resort to their own devices and to pursue their own goals.

Charles Wesley, another black historian, reflected in an article published in 1964 the major problem facing many black historians at that time. In his piece Wesley argued for the instrumentalist use of history—that is, to use black history not to inquire but to instruct. Using Jewish history as his example Wesley claimed that the knowledge and awareness of their past triumphs had enabled Jews to achieve great things in the face of hopeless odds, and to instill group pride in the current generation. Blacks, Wesley argued, should employ their past in the same way: to use black history as a tool for building black pride rather than to inquire after the truth in an objective way.[9]

The problem became a pressing one for scholars—both black and white—in the 1950s and 1960s as the civil rights movement burst upon the scene. There was a tendency among some historians to apply a compensatory principle and to applaud the achievements of blacks in history in an uncritical way. Sometimes such scholars were overre-

---

[9]Charles H. Wesley, "Creating and Maintaining an Historical Tradition," *Journal of Negro History* 49 (1964):13–33.

acting to the neglect black history had suffered in the past. They sought to make amends, therefore, by blowing out of proportion the historical importance of black leaders, black groups, and the black people as a whole. At other times such scholars were white historians motivated by a sense of guilt about race prejudice in America; they wrote in a mood of contrition as though they might expatiate their guilt. In some ways this approach resembled the kind of celebratory history written earlier about certain immigrant groups, which had stressed their achievements in an overly laudatory manner. Scholars writing in this vein about blacks presented black history as though it were a succession of individuals like Benjamin Banneker, the brilliant mathematician and astronomer; George Washington Carver, the chemist; Jackie Robinson, the baseball player; and Martin Luther King, Jr.

This approach so troubled C. Vann Woodward, a liberal with profound sympathy for blacks, that he wrote an article in 1969 and protested that this tendency was unprofessional. Black history written by whites in the past, he noted, had been characterized by two approaches: the "invisible man solution," and the "moral-neutrality approach." The "invisible man solution" portrayed American history without any blacks because they failed to fit the image of America as a country of ideal democratic fulfillment. The "moral-neutrality approach" was characterized by Beard and Turner. They recognized the existence of blacks but then ignored the moral problems raised by their presence or else diminished such problems by writing about them with morally neutral explanations in mind. Neither approach was satisfactory any more, said Woodward. Nor for that matter was the mythmaking and filiopietism in which black and white scholars had indulged when motivated by the impulse for compensatory exaggeration.

Woodward called for a revision of black history—one that would on one hand honestly credit the achievements of blacks when warranted, and, on the other, recount the painful and tragic relations between the two races. One possible solution, Woodward suggested, was to deal with black history in terms of irony and humor. "Anything so full of tears as the black experience, and anything so full of the absurd as the relations between the races in America, cannot be wholly devoid of existential humor," he observed.[10]

During the 1960s as well, there were writings on black history by blacks who were not scholars, strictly speaking, but who reflected nevertheless the wide spectrum of black thought of the day. Martin Luther King, Jr., the brilliant black leader, expressed his credo in *Strength to Love*, published in 1963. King believed in the idea of nonviolence both as a tactic and a philosophy—as a means and an end. As a tactic nonviolence could so stir the conscience of an opponent, he be-

---

[10]C. Vann Woodward, "Clio with Soul," *Journal of American History* 56 (1969):19.

lieved, that reconciliation could finally become a reality. Adopting the course of nonviolent resistance implied that the resister had to love his enemy. On a philosophical level King declared that nonviolent resistance was the key to building a new world. Down through history man had met violence with violence and hate with hate. King believed that only nonviolence and love could break this vicious cycle of revenge and retaliation. His hope was that blacks, through the use of nonviolent resistance, could help bring about a new day. Before King could finish his work he was tragically assassinated.[11]

By the mid-1960s the civil rights movement had hit its peak and black people were being attracted to black leaders other than King. One of the most dynamic was Malcolm X, whose *Autobiography of Malcolm X* appeared in 1966. His book provided some important and realistic insights into twentieth-century black America. Although born Malcolm Little he identified himself as Malcolm X to symbolize with his number that he had been robbed of his name and heritage by whites. His ancestors had been taken forcibly from Africa by whites, he noted, making it impossible for him to locate his roots or to trace his history. Coming from the ghetto, Malcolm X could appeal to ghetto residents in a way that King, whose origins were middle class, could not. Joining the Black Muslim movement—an antiwhite separatist group dedicated to the Islamic religion—Malcolm X emerged as a charismatic leader. In 1964 he broke with the Black Muslims, however, and after a trip to Africa planned to start a secular black nationalist movement of his own. Toward the end of his life Malcolm X qualified his black racism as a result of his travels in Africa. Formerly his hatred toward whites was such that he had referred to them as "devils." But after his visit to Africa, he began to preach reconciliation between the two races. In 1965 he was gunned down before he had an opportunity to formulate his new philosophy.

In the summer of 1966 the slogan "Black Power" burst upon the public consciousness and reverberated across the country. Stokely Carmichael, a young black leader, employed this motto to question the worth of nonviolence as a tactic and the value of integration as a goal. Carmichael attacked the idea of building a coalition between a group that was economically secure—middle-class white liberals—and one that was insecure—poor blacks. Carmichael also challenged the concept of integration, claiming that it would result in the continuance of white supremacy. Both societies—black and white—should build the kind of communities they wanted, he said, and integration instead of being a one-way street should be reciprocal. In *Black Power: The Poli-*

---

[11]The tactic of nonviolent resistance among American blacks was first used in the summer of 1942 by members of CORE (the Congress of Racial Equality). See August Meier and Elliott Rudwick, *CORE* (New York, 1973), pp. 1–23

tics of Liberation, written with Charles Hamilton in 1968, Carmichael stressed that America's existing political structure would have to be changed if racism was to be overcome.

The thinking of other blacks, both in the past and present, became a focus of major concern for historians during the 1960s. The ideas of contemporary blacks during the period of racial violence were expressed in H. Rap Brown's *Die, Nigger, Die,* published in 1969; Eldridge Cleaver's *Soul on Ice,* in 1968; and Claude Brown's autobiography *Manchild in the Promised Land,* which came out in 1965. But there were also more scholarly books published. Harold Cruse's provocative *Crisis of the Negro Intellectual,* in 1967, was critical of most leading black figures of the twentieth century. August Meier, on the other hand, produced *Negro Thought in America, 1880–1915* in 1963—an outstanding analysis of black thought and life during those years.

This all-too-brief account of books on black history written in the period of maturation hardly touches the mountain of literature on the subject that appeared during these two decades. Historiographical controversies raged over numerous topics in the field—the extent to which Southern blacks had participated in the Populist party and the degree of their equality in this political involvement; the contrast between the leadership of Booker T. Washington and W. E. B. Du Bois; the attitude of the labor movement toward blacks in different periods; Marcus Garvey's back-to-Africa movement; the New Deal and its policies toward blacks; the participation of blacks in World War II; the civil rights movement and the conflicting ideas of its leaders; and the precise role of the black power movement. This explosion of articles, monographs, and books demonstrated that the subject of black history had become at last a matter of vital concern to scholars.

But as millennial expectations waned in the late 1960s many black scholars objected to what was going on in the field of black history. They protested that by segregating so-called black topics from the rest of American history the historical profession was, in effect, indulging in racism under a different guise. This charge that black history still reflected elements of racism showed that black scholars saw many of the works produced as prejudiced and biased.

The proliferation of works on black history during the so-called period of accommodation since 1970 was even more impressive than in the past. There were numerous reasons for this dramatic change: black history was more generally accepted by the American historical profession as a legitimate and respected field of study; "new social historians" became more aware of the existence of a separate black community with a distinct set of values of its own; and, most important of all, a large new generation of black scholars emerged—"perhaps the

best-trained group of historians of Afro-America that had ever appeared," according to one senior black scholar.[12] This new generation
of younger scholars was destined to mark a new departure in the field
of black history.

During the 1970s and 1980s, the "new social historians," many of
them black scholars, studied the migration of blacks after the Civil
War. They discovered a much more complex picture than the generalizations based on the so-called Great Migration, the movement to industrial cities in the North during World War I. First of all, right after
the Civil War more freed slaves poured into the cities of the South
than those of the North. During the late 1870s, moreover, Nell Painter
showed in *The Exodusters*, published in 1977, that the main thrust of
black migration was westward to states like Kansas. By the 1890s
blacks were continuing to leave the rural South and moved to both
northern and southern cities. They were pushed by poverty and the
destruction wrought by the boll weevil plague, and pulled by the bright
promise of a living wage in industrial urban areas. World War I brought
this mass movement which ranks as one of the greatest internal migra-
tions of peoples in all of American history to a climax. Florette Henri,
in her *Black Migration*, published in 1975, argued that this movement
during the years 1900 to 1920 opened up a newfound sense of black
identity in two ways. One was the literal separatist path epitomized
by Marcus Garvey and his back-to-Africa movement in the 1920s. The
other was metaphorical: the return to racial pride in African cultural
and heritage symbolized by the artistic movement known as the Harlem Renaissance. Allen Ballard's *One More Day's Journey*, published
in 1984, continued this focus on the phenomenon of black migration.

Other scholars, including many "new social historians," became
interested in the black urban experience and the process of ghettoization. This historiographical trend may be said to have started in the
1960s (though there were earlier scattered studies), and was spurred by
the civil rights movement and ghetto riots during that decade. Two
pathbreaking studies in the 1960s on the rise of black ghettoes—Gil-
bert Osofsky's *Harlem: The Making of A Ghetto, Negro New York,
1890–1930* and Allan Spear's *Black Chicago: The Making of a Negro
Ghetto, 1890–1920*—led the way. Stephan Thernstrom, a well-known
"new social historian," provided a trenchant analysis of the workings
of black communities. In his *The Other Bostonians*, published in 1973,
Thernstrom devoted one chapter to Boston blacks. He viewed the
blacks from two perspectives: the effect that the community had upon
them; and the effect they had upon Boston. Boston, to be sure, was not

---

[12]Peter Novick, *That Noble Dream* (New York, 1988), pp. 489–491; John Hope
Franklin, "On the Evolution of Scholarship in Afro-American History," in Darlene Clark
Hine, *The State of Afro-American History* (Baton Rouge, 1986), p. 18.

a typical Northern metropolis; it attracted less than its share of blacks during the Great Migration. Nevertheless, Thernstrom came to some interesting conclusions in his study.

Like incoming immigrants from southern and eastern Europe during the first three decades of the twentieth century, Thernstrom discovered, Boston blacks tended to cluster in ghettoes. But he argued against the "last-of-the-immigrants" theory advanced by other scholars—writers who compared the experiences of Boston blacks with those of the European newcomers. There was some upward social mobility experienced by first- and second-generation immigrants, he noted, especially after they had resided in the city for some time. But for first- and second-generation blacks arriving from the South, a lengthy stay in the city made little difference in their social mobility; they stayed stuck in low-paying, low-skilled jobs. His conclusion was obvious: racism prevented blacks from making much progress.[13]

By the two decades of the 1970s and 1980s, there was an outpouring of studies dealing with the black urban experience in specific cities. David Katzman, Elizabeth Pleck, Kenneth Kusmer, and Thomas Cox examined Detroit, Boston, Cleveland, and Topeka, respectively, for the period between the Civil War and the early twentieth century. August Meier and Elliott Rudwick, who published jointly a number of significant works on black history, produced a book that focused on blacks in Detroit and the rise of the United Auto Workers Union. Studies on such northern cities as Chicago, Philadelphia, and Milwaukee were accompanied by pioneering studies on southern cities like New Orleans and Savannah.[14] Some earlier studies on this subject had tended to view black urbanization as a "pathological process," one which witnessed the presumed breakdown of the black community as a direct result of class and racial discrimination, but the newer works called for dropping this pejorative approach of pathology and its implied racial bias.

The important issue of black segregation in cities also came under study during the same two decades by both white and black scholars

---

[13]For a work on Pittsburgh from 1900 to 1960 which takes issue with some of Thernstrom's findings about Boston blacks, see John Bodnar, Roger Simon, and Michael Weber, *Lives of Their Own* (Urbana, 1982).

[14]The literature on the subject is voluminous, and this list is by no means complete: David Katzman, *Before the Ghetto* (Urbana, 1973); Elizabeth Pleck, *Black Migration and Poverty* (New York, 1979); Kenneth Kusmer, *A Ghetto Takes Shape* (Urbana, 1976); Thomas Cox, *Blacks in Topeka, Kansas, 1865–1915* (Baton Rouge, 1982); August Meier and Elliott Rudwick, *Black Detroit and the Rise of the UAW* (New York, 1979); Arnold Hirsch, *Making the Second Ghetto* (Cambridge, 1983); Theodore Hershberg, ed., *Philadelphia: Work, Space, Family and Group Experience in the Nineteenth Century* (New York, 1981); William Trotter, Jr., *Black Milwaukee* (Urbana, 1983); John Blassingame, *Black New Orleans, 1860–1880* (Chicago, 1972); and Robert Perdue, *The Negro in Savannah, 1865–1900* (New York, 1973).

influenced by the "new social history." It became increasingly evident that earlier post-hole studies which concentrated on residential patterns in single cities probably were misleading in explaining the development of black ghettoes. The nature of the nineteenth-century city inhibited the growth of such ghettoes in many instances. Both black and immigrant populations tended to be more dispersed for many reasons: the absence of adequate transportation systems; rapid growth in urban areas; mixed models of land use; and decentralized patterns in work and residence. In the North and to a lesser degree in the South, segregation levels were therefore low. But by the eve of the Great Migration, many major industrial areas in the North witnessed the beginnings of the modern black ghetto.[15] Kenneth Kusmer, who studied this phenomenon, concluded that broad generalizations were difficult to arrive at—though prior to World War I the level of segregation was highest in the most fully developed industrial cities in the North and the lowest in the major gulf ports in the South—and that differences in long-term structural forces (size, region, and historical period) resulted in different patterns of ghettoization in northern and southern cities in the twentieth century.[16] Such differences shattered the picture of "tragic sameness" which often led to negative conclusions in the study of black urban history and overlooked the positive ways in which blacks had responded to an urban environment.

Migration to the North plunged most blacks into the midst of an industrial world for which they were ill-prepared because of their rural background in the South. Manufacturers faced a labor shortage during World War I when the supply of cheap immigrant labor was cut off and this situation created job opportunities for blacks. The numbers accepted in factories were few, however, because of race discrimination. It was white workers more than employers who raised objections to hiring blacks. The record of the organized labor movement was largely negative in this regard right up to the Great Depression. Scholars were slow to write about the black worker, as they were about so many areas of black life, and studies on this subject during the decades from the 1920s to the 1950s were few and far between.

But in the 1970s and 1980s, some of the "new labor historians" took a renewed interest in labor history in general and in the black worker in particular. Leading the way was the gifted historian Herbert Gutman, whose articles in the 1960s and writings on such laborers in *Work, Culture, and Society in Industrializing America*, published in 1976, broke new ground by presenting a series of case studies covering

---

[15]James Oliver Horton, "Comment," in Hine, ed., *The State of Afro-American History*, pp. 130–131.

[16]Kenneth Kusmer, "The Black Urban Experience in American History," in Hine, ed., *The State of Afro-American History*, pp. 108–111.

black workers at different places in different historical periods. Milton Cantor edited a book of collected essays by various scholars entitled *Black Labor in America* in 1970. William H. Harris, a black historian, published *The Harder We Run* in 1982, a study of black workers since the Civil War, and a monograph in 1977 on the *Brotherhood of Sleeping Car Porters*, the largest and most influential black union. Philip Foner, a radical historian, produced in 1974 a survey of black labor history from colonial times to the 1970s. Herbert Hill, on the other hand, showed the difficulties black workers encountered in coping with barriers in the American legal system.[17]

The subject of the black family also came under close scrutiny at the same time. Herbert Gutman's magnum opus *Black Family in Slavery and Freedom, 1750–1925*, published in 1976, emerged as the most insightful study on the subject. Gutman was stirred to write in reaction to the 1965 government report, *The Case for National Action on the Negro Family*, prepared by Daniel P. Moynihan, then secretary of labor. Moynihan had pointed with alarm to what he called the dangerous "pathology" of the black family in urban ghettoes, and he underscored the widespread illegitimacy and high number of female-headed households that existed. He endorsed the idea that the weaknesses of the black family could be traced back to the slave experience. Many slave owners had neither fostered Christian marriages among slave couples nor hesitated to separate couples at slave auctions. The result was that marriage and the family had little meaning for blacks, according to Moynihan. The slave household had developed into a female-headed family where no father was present. This pattern persisted into the twentieth century, Moynihan postulated, and was the major cause for the numerous welfare cases in black ghettoes.

Gutman, using the analytical tools of demography developed by the "new social historians," presented an altogether different picture. He concluded on the basis of case studies of certain plantations that Afro-Americans did manage to establish remarkably stable and long-lived marriages despite the debilitating slave system. Strong family ties existed, black fathers were present to help raise and discipline children, and the black family adapted and was not simply the victim of white oppression. Presented in the manner of a lawyer's brief, Gutman's study sought to show that the black family tradition was strong

---

[17]William H. Harris, *Keeping the Faith* (Urbana, 1977); Philip Foner, *Organized Labor and the Black Worker, 1619–1973* (New York, 1974); Herbert Hill, *Black Labor and the American Legal System* (Washington, 1977).

Generally speaking, black workers have been ignored as part of American labor history for two reasons. First, the focus of American labor history was on unions and unionized workers whose past was marred by racism. Second, labor historians tended to concentrate on industrialized labor, an area from which blacks were largely barred before World War II.

enough to survive the migration from the rural South to the urban North in the post-Civil War era. Elizabeth Pleck's *Black Migration and Poverty, Boston, 1865–1900,* a case study of the move of blacks to Boston published in 1979, supported Gutman's findings.

Black women began to attract attention of more scholars as the women's liberation movement and the rise of the "new social historians" took place more or less simultaneously in the 1960s. American society in the late nineteenth century moved toward what has been characterized as "biracial dualism." Black leaders in the late nineteenth century sought to win political, economic, and educational rights against whites who assumed black subordination reflected some kind of Darwinian natural order. But black women in the 1890s through their families, churches, and voluntary associations began a national campaign to mobilize their forces to achieve sexual as well as black racial equality. They were anxious most of all to alter the negative sexual image and alleged immorality of all black women.[18] This movement and other matters were dealt with in two edited works. Gerda Lerner, *Black Women in White America* (1973) treated some of theoretical implications involved in considering the matter of race and gender. Bert Lowenberg and Ruth Bogin, *Black Women in Nineteenth-Century American Life* (1976) also had important essays dealing with this subject during the century.

The best synthesis of the history of black working women in America was Jacqueline Jones's *Labor of Love, Labor of Sorrow* (1985) which covered the topic from the days of slavery to the present. Her thesis was that black women inhabited a unique subculture, and experienced historical events differently from black men or white women. After slavery the work of many black women was mainly devoted to two worlds: that of their families and communities, where they often earned respect and honor; and that of the paid labor force where they were forced because of race discrimination into despised, low-paying jobs as domestics. White employers tended to view as detrimental to their interests the responsibilities black mothers had for their families. There was constant tension, therefore, between these two conflicting interests which defined the lives and work experience of black women in a unique way. Jones portrays black women employed in menial positions not only as victims of discrimination but also as agents for social change. They defended their own and their families' rights, defined the cultural goals of their communities, and tried to mediate the relations between Afro-American and white culture.

Dolores E. Janiewski, a labor historian, in her book, *Sisterhood De-*

---

[18]Darlene Clark Hine, "Lifting the Veil, Shattering the Silence: Black Women's History in Slavery and Freedom," in Hine, ed., *The State of Afro-American History,* pp. 234–237.

nied (1985) showed that it was possible at times, however, for black and white workers, both women and men, to come together and to transcend racial and gender antagonisms. In the 1930s in Durham, North Carolina, workers in the textile and tobacco industries cooperated to stage and win massive strikes. Such cooperation was short-lived. Janiewski concluded that for the most part old inequalities persisted, and splits along racial lines proved to be more significant than any other decisive antagonisms.

Since the field of black women's history was relatively new and still in the formative stage, much work was done in the form of articles. A sixteen-volume work edited mainly by Darlene Clark Hine called *Black Women in American History*, published in 1990, brought together many of the most important articles in one source. Another important collection giving the historical perspective of black women was that edited by Sharon Harley and Rosalyn Terborg-Penn entitled *The Afro-American Women* (1978).

Black female historians in both the books and articles they wrote were often divided in the perspective they took. Many wrote within a liberal capitalist framework, insisting that racism and sexism were more important than capitalism in determining the status of black women in American society. But others took a different point of view. Angela Y. Davis, adopting a Marxist approach in a historically-oriented theoretical overview insisted that class and race were mainly responsible for the oppression of black women in her *Women, Race and Class* (1981). She argued that black women would not be liberated until after the capitalist system had been destroyed.

Bell Hooks, writing from both a leftist and feminist point of view, however, stressed sexism more than class and racism. Her primary purpose in *Ain't I A Woman* (1981) was to establish that sexism determined the social status and experience of black women. Her argument was as much against black men as with some white women. But in *Talking Back* (1989), Hooks appeared to be moving toward a position that was more accommodating to white feminists. The political developments in the 1980s, including the collapse of socialism and communist movements throughout the world greatly complicated the problems of black feminist historians writing from the position of the extreme left.

Prior to the emergence of the modern welfare state in America, black women had had to rely on their own efforts to provide settlement houses, educational institutions, and health care activities. They created sister institutions that reflected the same spirit of voluntarism that characterized the efforts of white women in the twentieth century. The work of two outstanding black women in this regard—Ida Wells Barnett and Mary McLeod Bethune—is treated in John Hope Franklin and August Meier, eds., *Black Leaders in the Twentieth*

Century (1982). Cynthia Neverdon-Morton's study, *Afro-American Women of the South and the Advancement of the Race, 1895–1925* (1989) concentrated on five major cities and described the social service activities of middle-class black club women.

One important case study for a single state was Darlene Clark Hine, *When the Truth Is Told* (1981) which took up the story of the community activities of black women in Indiana from the 1870s to the 1950s. Although scholars examined black women leaders and their formal institutions, the informal activities of local black women of the lower classes have yet to be treated adequately. It may well be that when the history of black working women's culture is written it will produce different findings.

Class as well as gender was an important variable in the study of black history. But there appeared to be a reluctance on the part of scholars to introduce class distinctions among blacks lest it undermine the major theme of racial oppression and imply it was less severe. Class was de-emphasized for another reason: to downplay the idea of intraracial conflict for fear of revealing evidence of racial disunity. One pioneering work that did study the effects of class and color stratification in politics was Thomas Holt's superb *Black Over White*, published in 1977.[19]

Regionalism was another factor increasingly taken into account in the writing of black history. Regional differences among blacks during the Reconstruction era were revealed as blacks from the North and South came into contact in greater numbers. Although the majority of black people in the mid-nineteenth century had southern roots, blacks born and raised in the South differed culturally from those in the North, and such differences became increasingly evident. Certain themes regarding sectional differences among Afro-Americans were explored in the volume edited by Morgan Kouser and James M. McPherson, *Region, Race, and Reconstruction*, published in 1982. In a later period during the Great Migration, tensions were evident between northern black families and southern migrants in such cities as Detroit, Cleveland, and Topeka.

The Great Migration to the urban North stirred black intellectuals and artists to a new sense of self-confidence and racial consciousness. During the 1920s decade, many of them—poets, novelists, musicians, sculptors, historians, and sociologists—became involved in a movement called the Harlem Renaissance. Black artists took great pride in their African ancestry and deliberately cultivated a form of Pan-African cultural nationalism. Their works were sometimes an outlet for the

---

[19]See Armstead Robinson, "The Difference Freedom Made: The Emancipation of Afro-Americans," and Nell Painter, "Comment," in Hine, *The State of Afro-American History*, pp. 51–79 and 80–83.

frustration blacks experienced in the post-World War I era as unemployment and racial violence dashed their hopes for equality in white America. These artistic endeavors gained the respect of the New York community at large and at the same time strengthened the cultural hopes and traditions of the blacks themselves. But in producing such works, black artists confronted two dangers. First, they ran the risk of appealing, either consciously or unconsciously, to the conventional concepts of standards of excellence as defined by the white middle class. Second, some artists in their works tended to reinforce or make reference to certain stereotyped white notions of black life. Nathan I. Huggins in *Harlem Renaissance,* published in 1971, presented the finest scholarly treatment of this fascinating movement.

Older black scholars continued to remain active during the so-called period of accommodation. John Hope Franklin, the country's foremost black historian in the eyes of many, had a career that symbolized the changes taking place within the profession. During the two decades after the publication of his classic *From Slavery to Freedom* in 1947, Franklin gradually won acceptance as the leading black scholar within the profession. After teaching twenty years in black universities, he became the first black historian to receive a regular faculty position at a white institution. In the 1970s he was elected president of three leading professional organizations—the Southern Historical Association, Organization of American Historians, and American Historical Association.[20]

Franklin in his scholarly writings kept insisting he was not a black historian, but a "historian of the South" who happened to the black. His position was that black history should not be a separate field but viewed within the broader context of American history, and that black historians should be integrated into the mainstream of the profession. As the fury of the blacks exploded into violence during the 1960s and many new young black historians of the 1970s and 1980s disagreed with the aim of integration, Franklin's position came under attack.

Some idea of Franklin's views could be seen in his *Racial Equality,* published in 1976. His lectures in this book traced the course of race relations in the United States and focused on three epochs: the American Revolution, the Reconstruction era, and the twentieth century. In the revolutionary period, the founding fathers were not really committed to equality as generally believed because they failed to change the status of blacks within the new nation. Franklin's picture of Recon-

---

[20]Among Franklin's other works were: *The Militant South* (Cambridge, 1956); *Reconstruction After the Civil War* (Chicago, 1961); *Emancipation Proclamation* (Garden City, New York, 1963); *A Southern Odyssey* (Baton Rouge, 1976); *Racial Equality in America* (Chicago, 1976); and *George Washington Williams* (Chicago, 1985).

struction was equally gloomy. Congress was no better prepared to extend equality to blacks, Franklin concluded, than it was to guarantee their freedom. The reconstruction era was marked by some half-hearted steps taken to introduce only a semblance of racial equality.

In the twentieth century, Franklin conceded, the concept of equality became more meaningful to the American people. The prime concern of policymakers, however, was to create distinctions between those who were regarded as equals and those who were not, i.e., blacks. He acknowledged that whites played a significant role in the civil rights movement and that the government had assumed more responsibility for promoting equality. But at the same time, Franklin concluded, there was no real American heritage of liberalism upon which blacks could rely. Although past generations had often promoted racial justice, American society as a whole had yet to extend true equality of treatment and opportunity to blacks. Franklin's bleak view that racism was still strongly entrenched in American society provided a stout argument against those white scholars who claimed their writings were representative and not race-conscious, and that the recent advances made by blacks were evidence that America's liberal tradition had triumphed after all.

When Franklin was elected president of the American Historical Association in 1980, he used his presidential address to protest the shortcomings of the profession in dealing with certain aspects of black history. He pointed out that one of the more popular college textbooks written in the 1960s and still in use in 1980—Thomas Bailey's *American Pageant*—contained racist remarks. Franklin complained, moreover, that few major studies tried to synthesize or generalize about the history of blacks from emancipation to the present day, to say nothing about the important Reconstruction period. Noting that scholars tended to focus more on the slavery era than the subsequent period of freedom, Franklin protested: "Whatever the reason [for this emphasis], the result has been to leave the major thrust of the Reconstruction story not nearly far enough from where it was in 1929 when Claude Bowers published *The Tragic Era*."[21] As an integrated professional, Franklin called for assimilating black history more into the mainstream of American history. Part of his presidential address is included as the first section in this chapter.

The rise of a new generation of younger black historians in the 1970s and 1980s created a controversy which showed that the perspective among black scholars themselves on American history was as yet unresolved. Some of these scholars were products of the Black Studies programs founded in over 500 colleges and universities in the early

---

[21]John Hope Franklin, "Mirror for Americans: A Century of Reconstruction History," *American Historical Review* 85 (1980):12.

1970s. Trained in graduate schools from every part of the country, they differed from earlier generations of Afro-American historians who had come out of only three or four major universities in the East and Midwest. In many instances they were trained increasingly by black mentors with whom they did not always agree. Taken as a group, their appearance marked a major development in the writing of American history from a black perspective.

With greater numbers of black scholars involved in writing and research, the whole field of Afro-American history was subjected to scrutiny and many problems and periods were reinterpreted. Using some of the newer methodologies and approaches, they moved the field to a higher level of achievement. The works of such scholars as John Blassingame, Barbara Fields, Thomas Holt, Darlene Hine, Wilson Moses, Nell Painter, and Armstead Robinson, among others, made major contributions which broadened considerably the outlook on black history. Some of these scholars agreed with Franklin about assimilating black history into the mainstream and integrating black scholars into the profession, while others did not.

Fragmentation among black scholars was reflected also by older Afro-American historians who changed their minds. Nathan Huggins, who held a chair at Harvard and served as director of the W.E.B. DuBois Institute for Afro-American Studies, had been an integrated professional. His work on the Harlem Renaissance cited earlier, his speeches against substituting myth for history, and his call for maintaining objectivity in black scholarship in the 1960s and 1970s had identified him as one who believed in assimilating black history and American history. But when he published his book *Black Odyssey* in 1979, his position was quite different. "We blacks writing Afro-American history, no matter how much distance we like to maintain, are drawn to 'tell the story of our people' in epic scale." His book, in other words, was written by a black for blacks.[22] The second selection in this chapter is from an article by Huggins.

Further evidence of fragmentation among black scholars was the work of Vincent Harding who had always distanced himself somewhat from the overwhelming white historical profession. In all his writings, Harding was highly skeptical of the claims of white scholars regarding their presumed objectivity. To Harding the major theme in the history of black Americans was that of continual resistance. In his 1981 magnum opus, *There Is a River*, Harding's central metaphor became the river of resistance relentlessly flowing through the black struggle for freedom. Harding's slaves were always on the verge of rebellion moti-

---

[22]Nathan I. Huggins, "Integrating Afro-American History into American History," in Hine, *The State of Afro-American History*, p. 164; and Peter Novick, *That Noble Dream*, p. 491.

vated both by religious messianism and revolutionary black nationalism. Needless to say, orthodox white historians did not view slaves in
the same light.[23]

Students of history are left, therefore, to ponder the following questions. Does black history written by American scholars, either white
or black, represent a true picture of events that took place? Or is there
an inherent racial bias in these writings in terms of the questions
posed, the emphasis given, and the values stressed? Should black history be integrated into American history as some scholars insisted? Or
should it be written as a separatist epic by blacks for black people? Is
it possible for white historians to write black history as Woodward
claimed? Or are the attitude, values, and mind sets of whites and
blacks so different as to make any attempt at objectivity impossible?
If one decides to rely upon black historians, should it be John Hope
Franklin or his critics? One thing is certain: the questions of whether
black history is representative or racist will remain a highly debatable
issue in the 1990s.

----

[23]Novick, *That Noble Dream*, p. 490.

John Hope Franklin

JOHN HOPE FRANKLIN (1915–   ) *is James Duke Professor Emeritus of History at Duke University. He has written widely in Afro-American history, and his books include* The Free Negro in North Carolina 1790–1860 *(1943),* The Militant South 1800–1861 *(1956),* Reconstruction After the Civil War *(1961),* The Emancipation Proclamation *(1963), and* From Slavery to Freedom *(5th ed., 1980).*

Perhaps no human experience is more searing or more likely to have a long-range adverse effect on the participants than violent conflict among peoples of the same national, racial, or ethnic group. During the conflict itself the stresses and strains brought on by confrontations ranging from name-calling to pitched battles move people to the brink of mutual destruction. The resulting human casualties as well as the physical destruction serve to exacerbate the situation to such a degree that reconciliation becomes virtually impossible. The warring participants, meanwhile, have done irreparable damage to their common heritage and to their shared government and territory through excessive claims and counterclaims designed to make their opponents' position appear both untenable and ludicrous.

Situations such as these have occurred throughout history; they are merely the most extreme and most tragic of numerous kinds of conflicts that beset mankind. As civil conflicts—among brothers, compatriots, coreligionists, and the like—they present a special problem not only in the prosecution of the conflict itself but in the peculiar problems related to reconciliation once the conflict has been resolved. One can well imagine, for example, the utter bitterness and sense of alienation that both sides felt in the conflict that marked the struggle for power between the death in 1493 of Sonni Ali, the ruler of the Songhay empire, and the succession of Askia Muhammad some months later. The struggle was not only between the legitimate heir and an army commander but also between the traditional religion and the relatively new, aggressive religion of Islam, a struggle in which the military man and his new religion emerged victorious.

Historians have learned a great deal about these events, although they are wrapped in the obscurity and, indeed, the evasive strategies

John Hope Franklin, "Mirror for Americans: A Century of Reconstruction History," *American Historical Review* 85 (February 1980):1–14. Reprinted with the permission of the American Historical Association and John Hope Franklin.

of the late Middle Ages. Despite the bitterness of the participants in the struggle and the dissipating competition of scholars in the field, we have learned much more about the internal conflicts of the Songhay empire of West Africa and about the details of Askia Muhammad's program of reconstruction than we could possibly have anticipated—either because the keepers of the records were under his influence or because any uncomplimentary accounts simply did not survive. Interestingly enough, however, the accounts by travelers of the energetic and long-range programs of reconstruction coincide with those that the royal scribes provided.

Another example of tragic internal conflict is the English Civil War of the seventeenth century. The struggle between Charles I and those who supported a radical Puritan oligarchy led not only to a bloody conflict that culminated in the execution of the king but also to bizarre manifestations of acrimony that ranged from denouncing royalism in principle to defacing icons in the churches. Not until the death of Oliver Cromwell and the collapse of the Protectorate were peace and order finally achieved under Charles II, whose principal policies were doubtless motivated by his desire to survive. The king's role in the reconstruction of England was limited; indeed, the philosophical debates concerning, as well as the programs for, the new society projected by the Protectorate had a more significant impact on England's future than the restoration of the Stuarts had.

Thanks to every generation of scholars that has worked on the English Civil War and its aftermath, we have had a succession of illuminations without an inordinate amount of heat. Granted, efforts to understand the conflict have not always been characterized by cool objectivity and generous concessions. But, because historians have been more concerned with understanding the sources than with prejudging the events with or without the sources, we are in their debt for a closer approximation to the truth than would otherwise have been the case.

I daresay that both the Africanists concerned with Songhay and the students of the English Civil War will scoff at these general statements, which they may regard as a simplistic view of the struggles that they have studied so intensely. I am in no position to argue with them. The point remains that, whether one views the internal conflicts of the people of Songhay in the fifteenth century, the English in the seventeenth century, or the Americans in the nineteenth century, the conflict itself was marked by incomparable bitterness and extensive bloodshed. The aftermath, moreover, was marked by continuous disputation over the merits of the respective cases initially as well as over the conduct of the two sides in the ensuing years. These continuing disputations, it should be added, tell as much about the times in which they occurred as about the period with which they are concerned. And, before I do violence either to the facts themselves or to the views of those who have studied these events, I shall seek to establish my claim in the more familiar environment of the aftermath of the Civil War in the United States.

In terms of the trauma and the sheer chaos of the time, the aftermath of the American Civil War has few equals in history. After four years of conflict the burden of attempting to achieve a semblance of calm and equanimity was almost unbearable. The revolution in the status of four million slaves involved an incredible readjustment not only for them *and* their former owners but also for all others who had some understanding of the far-reaching implications of emancipation. The crisis in leadership occasioned by the assassination of the president added nothing but more confusion to a political situation that was already thoroughly confused. And, as in all similar conflicts, the end of hostilities did not confer a monopoly of moral rectitude on one side or the other. The ensuing years were characterized by a continuing dispute over whose side was right as well as over how the victors should treat the vanquished. In the post-Reconstruction years a continuing argument raged, not merely over how the victors did treat the vanquished but over what actually happened during that tragic era.

If every generation rewrites its history, as various observers have often claimed, then it may be said that every generation since 1870 has written the history of the Reconstruction era. And what historians have written tells as much about their own generation as about the Reconstruction period itself. Even before the era was over, would-be historians, taking advantage of their own observations or those of their contemporaries, began to speak with authority about the period.

James S. Pike, the Maine journalist, wrote an account of misrule in South Carolina, appropriately called *The Prostrate State,* and painted a lurid picture of the conduct of Negro legislators and the general lack of decorum in the management of public affairs. Written so close to the period and first published as a series of newspaper pieces, *The Prostrate State* should perhaps not be classified as history at all. But for many years the book was regarded as authoritative—contemporary history at its best. Thanks to Robert Franklin Durden, we now know that Pike did not really attempt to tell what he saw or even what happened in South Carolina during Reconstruction. By picking and choosing from his notes those events and incidents that supported his argument, he sought to place responsibility for the failure of Reconstruction on the Grant administration and on the freedmen whom he despised with equal passion.

A generation later historians such as William Archibald Dunning and those who studied with him began to dominate the field. Dunning was faithfully described by one of his students as "the first to make scientific and scholarly investigation of the period of Reconstruction."

Despite this evaluation, he was an unequivocal as the most rabid opponent of Reconstruction in placing upon Scalawags, Negroes, and
Northern radicals the responsibility for making the unworthy and unsuccessful attempt to reorder society and politics in the South. His
"scientific and scholarly" investigations led him to conclude that at
the close of Reconstruction the planters were ruined and the freedmen
were living from hand to mouth—whites on the poor lands and "thrift-
less blacks on the fertile lands." No economic, geographic, or demographic data were offered to support this sweeping generalization.

Dunning's students were more ardent than he, if such were possible, in pressing their case against Radical Republicans and their black
and white colleagues. Negroes and Scalawags, they claimed, had set
the South on a course of social degradation, misgovernment, and corruption. This tragic state of affairs could be changed only by the intervention of gallant men who would put principle above everything else
and who, by economic pressure, social intimidation, and downright
violence, would deliver the South from Negro rule. Between 1900 and
1914 these students produced state studies and institutional monographs that gave more information than one would want about the
complexion, appearance, and wearing apparel of the participants and
much less than one would need about problems of postwar adjustment, social legislation, or institutional development.

Perhaps the most important impact of such writings was the influence they wielded on authors of textbooks, popular histories, and fiction. James Ford Rhodes, whose general history of the United States
was widely read by contemporaries, was as pointed as any of Dunning's students in his strictures on Reconstruction: "The scheme of
Reconstruction," he said, "pandered to ignorant negroes, the knavish
white natives, and the vulturous adventurers who flocked from the
North. . . ." Thomas Dixon, a contemporary writer of fiction, took the
findings of Rhodes's and Dunning's students and made the most of
them in his trilogy on Civil War and Reconstruction. In *The Clans-
man*, published in 1905, he sensationalized and vulgarized the worst
aspects of the Reconstruction story, thus beginning a lore about the
period that was dramatized in *Birth of a Nation*, the 1915 film based
on the trilogy, and popularized in 1929 by Claude Bowers in *The Tragic
Era.*

Toward the end of its most productive period the Dunning school
no longer held a monopoly on the treatment of the Reconstruction era.
In 1910 W. E. B. Du Bois published an essay in the *American Historical
Review* entitled, significantly, "Reconstruction and Its Benefits." Du
Bois dissented from the prevailing view by suggesting that something
good came out of Reconstruction, such as educational opportunities
for freedmen, the constitutional protection of the rights of all citizens,
and the beginning of political activity on the part of the freedmen. In

an article published at the turn of the century, he had already hinted "that Reconstruction had a beneficial side," but the later article was a clear and unequivocal presentation of his case.

Du Bois was not the only dissenter to what had already become the traditional view of Reconstruction. In 1913 a Mississippi Negro, John R. Lynch, former speaker of the Mississippi House of Representatives and former member of Congress, published a work on Reconstruction that differed significantly from the version that Mississippi whites had accepted. Some years later he argued that a great deal of what Rhodes had written about Reconstruction was "absolutely groundless." He further insisted that Rhodes's account of Reconstruction was not only inaccurate and unreliable but was "the most one-sided, biased, partisan, and prejudiced historical work" that he had ever read. A few years later Alrutheus A. Taylor published studies of the Negro in South Carolina, Virginia, and Tennessee, setting forth the general position that blacks during Reconstruction were not the ignorant dupes of unprincipled white men, that they were certainly not the corrupt crowd they had been made out to be, and that their political influence was quite limited.

The most extensive and, indeed, the most angry expression of dissent from the well-established view of Reconstruction was made in 1935 by W. E. B. Du Bois in his *Black Reconstruction*. "The treatment of the period of Reconstruction reflects," he noted, "small credit upon American historians as scientists." Then he recalled for his readers the statement on Reconstruction that he wrote in an article that the *Encyclopaedia Britannica* had refused to print. In that article he had said, "White historians have ascribed the faults and failures of Reconstruction to Negro ignorance and corruption. But the Negro insists that it was Negro loyalty and the Negro vote alone that restored the South to the Union, established the new democracy, both for white and black, and instituted the public schools." The *American Historical Review* did no better than the *Encyclopaedia Britannica*, since no review of *Black Reconstruction*, the first major scholarly work on Reconstruction since World War I, appeared in the pages of the *Review*. The work was based largely on printed public documents and secondary literature because, the author admitted, he lacked the resources to engage in a full-scale examination of the primary materials and because Du Bois thought of his task as the exposure of the logic, argument, and conclusions of those whose histories of Reconstruction had become a part of the period's orthodoxy. For this task he did not need to delve deeply into the original sources.

From that point on, works on Reconstruction represented a wide spectrum of interpretation. Paul Herman Buck's *Road to Reunion* shifted the emphasis to reconciliation, while works by Horace Mann Bond and Vernon L. Wharton began the program of fundamental and

drastic revision. No sooner was revisionism launched, however, then
E. Merton Coulter insisted that "no amount of revision can write away
the grievous mistakes made in this abnormal period of American history." He then declared that he had not attempted to do so, and with
that he subscribed to virtually all of the views that had been set forth
by the students of Dunning. And he added a few observations of his
own, such as "education soon lost its novelty for most of the Negroes";
they would "spend their last piece of money for a drink of whisky";
and, being "by nature highly emotional and excitable . . . , they carried
their religious exercises to extreme lengths."

By mid-century, then, there was a remarkable mixture of views of
Reconstruction by historians of similar training but of differing backgrounds, interests, and commitments. Some were unwilling to challenge the traditional views of Reconstruction. And, although their
language was generally polite and professional, their assumptions regarding the roles of blacks, the nature of the Reconstruction governments in the South, and the need for quick—even violent—counterac-
tion were fairly transparent. The remarkable influence of the
traditional view of Reconstruction is nowhere more evident than in a
work published in 1962 under the title *Texas under the Carpetbaggers.*
The author did not identify the carpetbaggers, except to point out that
the governor during the period was born in Florida and migrated to
Texas in 1848 and that the person elected to the United States Senate
had been born in Alabama and had been in Texas since 1830. If Texas
was ever under the carpetbaggers, the reader is left to speculate about
who the carpetbaggers were! Meanwhile, in the 1960s one of the most
widely used college textbooks regaled its readers about the "simple-
minded" freedmen who "insolently jostled the whites off the side-
walks into the gutter"; the enfranchisement of the former slaves set
the stage for "stark tragedy," the historian continued, and this was
soon followed by "enthroned ignorance," which led inevitably to "a
carnival of corruption and misrule." Such descriptions reveal more
about the author's talent for colorful writing than about his commitment to sobriety and accuracy.

Yet an increasing number of historians began to reject the traditional view and to argue the other side or, at least, to insist that there
was another side. Some took another look at the states and rewrote
their Reconstruction history. In the new version of Reconstruction in
Louisiana the author pointed out that "the extravagance and corruption for which Louisiana Reconstruction is noted did not begin in
1868," for the convention of 1864 "was not too different from conventions and legislatures which came later." Others looked at the condition of the former slaves during the early days of emancipation and
discovered that blacks faced freedom much more responsibly and successfully than had hitherto been described. Indeed, one student of the

problem asserted that "Reconstruction was for the Negroes of South Carolina a period of unequaled progress." Still others examined institutions ranging from the family to the Freedmen's Savings Bank and reached conclusions that were new or partly new to our understanding of Reconstruction history. Finally, there were the syntheses that undertook, unfortunately all too briefly, to make some overall revisionist generalizations about Reconstruction.

Up to this point my observations have served merely as a reminder of what has been happening to Reconstruction history over the last century. I have not intended to provide an exhaustive review of the literature. There have already been extensive treatments of the subject, and there will doubtless be more. Reconstruction history has been argued over and fought over since the period itself ended. Historians have constantly disagreed not only about what significance to attach to certain events and how to interpret them but also (and almost as much) about the actual events themselves. Some events are as obscure and some facts are apparently as unverifiable as if they dated from several millennia ago. Several factors have contributed to this state of affairs. One factor, of course, is the legacy of bitterness left behind by the internal conflict. This has caused the adversaries—and their descendants—to attempt to place the blame on each other (an understandable consequence of a struggle of this nature). Another factor is that the issues have been delineated in such a way that the merits in the case have tended to be all on one side. A final factor has been the natural inclination of historians to pay attention only to those phases or aspects of the period that give weight to the argument presented. This inclination may involve the omission of any consideration of the first two years of Reconstruction in order to make a strong case against, for example, the Radicals. Perhaps such an approach has merit in a court of law or in some other forum, but as an approach to historical study its validity is open to the most serious question.

Perhaps an even more important explanation for the difficulty in getting a true picture of Reconstruction is that those who have worked in the field have been greatly influenced by the events and problems of the period in which they were writing. That first generation of students to study the postbellum years "scientifically" conducted its research and did its writing in an atmosphere that made the conclusions regarding Reconstruction foregone. Different conclusions were inconceivable. Writing in 1905 Walter L. Fleming referred to James T. Rapier, a Negro member of the Alabama constitutional convention of 1867, as "Rapier of Canada." He then quoted Rapier as saying that the manner in which "colored gentlemen and ladies were treated in America was beyond his comprehension."

Born in Alabama in 1837, Rapier, like many of his white contemporaries, went North for an education. The difference was that instead of stopping in the northern part of the United States, as, for example, William L. Yancey did, Rapier went on to Canada. Rapier's contemporaries did not regard him as a Canadian; and, if some were not precisely clear about where he was born (as was the *Alabama State Journal*, which referred to his birthplace as Montgomery rather than Florence), they did not misplace him altogether. In 1905 Fleming made Rapier a Canadian because it suited his purposes to have a bold, aggressive, "impertinent" Negro in Alabama Reconstruction come from some non-Southern, contaminating environment like Canada. But it did not suit his purposes to call Yancey, who was a graduate of Williams College, a "Massachusetts Man." Fleming described Yancey as, simply, the "leader of the States Rights men."

Aside from his Columbia professors, Fleming's assistance came largely from Alabamians: Thomas M. Owen of the Department of Archives and History, G. W. Duncan of Auburn, W. W. Screws of the Montgomery *Advertiser*, and John W. Du Bose, Yancey's biographer and author of *Alabama's Tragic Decade*. At the time that Fleming sought their advice regarding his Reconstruction story, these men were reaping the first fruits of disfranchisement, which had occurred in Alabama in 1901. Screw's *Advertiser* had been a vigorous advocate of disfranchisement, while Du Bose's *Yancey*, published a decade earlier, could well have been a campaign document to make permanent the redemption of Alabama from "Negro-carpetbagger-Scalawag rule." It is inconceivable that such men would have assisted a young scholar who had any plans except to write an account of the Reconstruction era that would support their views. In any case they could not have been more pleased had they written Fleming's work for him.

But the "scientific" historians might well have been less pleased if they had not been caught up in the same pressures of the contemporary scene that beset Fleming. They, like Fleming, should have been able to see that some of the people that Fleming called "carpetbaggers" had lived in Alabama for years and were, therefore, entitled to at least as much presumption of assimilation in moving from some other state to Alabama decades before the war as the Irish were in moving from their native land to some community in the United States. Gustavus Horton, a Massachusetts "carpetbagger" and chairman of the constitutional convention's Committee on Education in 1867, was a cotton broker in Mobile and had lived there since 1835. Elisha Wolsey Peck, the convention's candidate for chief justice in 1867, moved to Alabama from New York in 1825. A few month's sojourn in Illinois in 1867 convinced Peck that the only real home he could ever want was Alabama. Charles Mayes Cabot, a member of the constitutional convention of 1865 as well as of the one of 1867, had come to Alabama from his native Vermont as a young man. He prospected in the West in 1849 but was back in Wetumka in the merchandising business by 1852.

Whether they had lived in Alabama for decades before the Civil War or had settled there after the war, these "carpetbaggers" were apparently not to be regarded as models for Northern investors or settlers in the early years of the twentieth century. Twentieth-century investors from the North were welcome provided they accepted the established arrangements in race relations and the like. Fleming served his Alabama friends well by ridiculing carpetbaggers, even if in the process he had to distort and misrepresent.

In his study of North Carolina Reconstruction published in 1914, Joseph G. de Roulhac Hamilton came as close as any of his fellow historians to reflecting the interests and concerns of his own time. After openly bewailing the enfranchisement of the freedmen, the sinister work of the "mongrel" convention and legislatures, and the abundance of corruption, Hamilton concluded that Reconstruction was a crime that is "to-day generally recognized by all who care to look the facts squarely in the face." But for Reconstruction, he insisted, "the State would to-day, so far as one can estimate human probabilities, be solidly Republican. This was clearly evident in 1865, when the attempted restoration of President Johnson put public affairs in the hands of former Whigs who then had no thought of joining in politics their old opponents, the Democrats." Hamilton argued that in his own time some men who regularly voted the Democratic ticket would not call themselves "Democrats." In an effort to appeal to a solid Negro vote, the Republicans had lost the opportunity to bring into their fold large numbers of former Whigs and some disaffected Democrats. In the long run the Republicans gained little, for the Negroes, who largely proved to be "lacking in political capacity and knowledge, were driven, intimidated, bought, and sold, the playthings of politicians, until finally their so-called right to vote became the sore spot of the body politic." In his account of Reconstruction, which placed the blame on the Republican-Negro coalition for destroying the two-party system in North Carolina, Hamilton gave a warning to his white contemporaries to steer clear of any connection with blacks whose votes could be bought and sold if the franchise were again extended to them.

And the matter was not only theoretical. In 1914, while Hamilton was writing about North Carolina Reconstruction, Negro Americans were challenging the several methods by which whites had disfranchised them, and Hamilton was sensitive to the implications of the challenge. He reminded his readers that, after the constitutional amendment of 1900 restricting the suffrage by an educational qualification and a "grandfather clause," the Democrats elected their state ticket. His eye was focused to a remarkable degree on the current political and social scene. "The negro has largely ceased to be a political question," he commented, "and there is in the State to-day as a consequence more political freedom than at any time since Reconstruction." The lesson was painfully clear to him, as he hoped it would be to his readers: the successful resistance to the challenges that Negroes were making to undo the arrangements by which they had been disfranchised would remove any fears that whites might have of a repetition of the "crime" of Reconstruction. Segregation statutes, the white Democratic primary, discrimination in educational opportunities, and, if necessary, violence were additional assurances that there would be no return to Reconstruction.

Unfortunately, the persistence of the dispute over what actually happened during Reconstruction and the use of Reconstruction fact and fiction to serve the needs of writers and their contemporaries have made getting at the truth about the so-called Tragic Era virtually impossible. Not only has this situation deprived the last three generations of an accurate assessment of the period but it has also unhappily strengthened the hand of those who argue that scientific history can be as subjective, as partisan, and as lacking in discrimination as any other kind of history. A century after the close of Reconstruction, we are utterly uninformed about numerous aspects of the period. Almost forty years ago Howard K. Beale, writing in the *American Historical Review*, called for a treatment of the Reconstruction era that would not be marred by bitter sectional feelings, personal vendettas, or racial animosities. In the four decades since that piece was written, there have been some historians who have heeded Beale's call. It would, indeed, be quite remarkable if historians of today were not sensitive to some of the strictures Beale made against those who kept alive the hoary myths about Reconstruction and if scholars of today's generation did not attempt to look at the period without the restricting influences of sectional or racial bias. And yet, since the publication of Beale's piece, several major works have appeared that are aggressively hostile to any new view of Reconstruction. Nor has Beale's call been heeded to the extent that it should have been.

If histories do indeed reflect the problems and concerns of their authors' own times, numerous major works on Reconstruction should have appeared in recent years. After all, since the close of World War II this nation has been caught up in a reassessment of the place of Negroes in American society, and some have even called this period the "Second Reconstruction." Central to the reassessment has been a continuing discussion of the right of blacks to participate in the political process, to enjoy equal protection of the laws, and to be free of discrimination in education, employment, housing, and the like. Yet among the recent writing on Reconstruction few major works seek to synthesize and to generalize over the whole range of the freedmen's experience, to say nothing of the problem of Reconstruction as a whole. Only a limited number of monographic works deal with, for example, Reconstruction in the states, the regional experiences of freedmen, the freedmen confronting their new status, aspects of educational, religious, or institutional development, or phases of economic adjustment.

In recent years historians have focused much more on the period of slavery than on the period of freedom. Some historians have been most enthusiastic about the capacity of slaves to establish and maintain institutions while in bondage, to function effectively in an economic system as a kind of upwardly mobile group of junior partners, and to make the transition to freedom with a minimum of trauma. One may wonder why, at this particular juncture in the nation's history, slavery has attracted so much interest and why, in all of the recent and current discussions of racial equality, Reconstruction has attracted so little. Not even the litigation of *Brown* v. *The Board of Education*, which touched off a full-dress discussion of one of the three Reconstruction Amendments a full year before the decision was handed down in 1954, stimulated any considerable production of Reconstruction scholarship. Does this pattern suggest that historians have thought that the key to understanding the place of Afro-Americans in American life is to be found in the slave experience and not in the struggles for adjustment in the early years of freedom? Or does it merely mean that historians find the study of slavery more exotic or more tragic and therefore more attractive than the later period of freedom? Whatever the reason, the result has been to leave the major thrust of the Reconstruction story not nearly far enough from where it was in 1929, when Claude Bowers published *The Tragic Era*.

That result is all the more unfortunate in view of what we already know and what is gradually and painfully becoming known about the period following the Civil War. With all of the exhortations by Howard Beale, Bernard Weisberger, and others about the need for more Reconstruction studies, the major works with a grand sweep and a bold interpretation have yet to be written. Recent works by Michael Perman and Leon F. Litwack, which provide a fresh view respectively of political problems in the entire South and of the emergence of the freedman throughout the South, are indications of what can and should be done in the field. And, even if the battle for revision is being won among the professionals writing the monographs (if not among the professionals writing the textbooks), it is important to make certain that the zeal for revision does not become a substitute for truth and accuracy and does not result in the production of works that are closer to political tracts than to histories.

Although it is not possible to speak with certainty about the extent to which the Reconstruction history written in our time reveals the urgent matters with which we are regularly concerned, we must take care not to permit those matters to influence or shape our view of an earlier period. That is what entrapped earlier generations of Reconstruction historians who used the period they studied to shape attitudes toward problems they confronted. As we look at the opportunities for new synthesis and new interpretations, we would do well to follow Thomas J. Pressly's admonition not to seek confirmation of our views of Reconstruction in the events of our own day. This caveat is not to deny the possibility of a usable past, for to do so would go against our heritage and cut ourselves off from human experience. At the same time it proscribes the validity of reading into the past the experiences of the historian in order to shape the past as he or she wishes it to be shaped.

The desire of some historians to use the Reconstruction era to bolster their case in their own political arena or on some other ground important to their own well-being is a major reason for our not having a better general account of what actually occurred during Reconstruction. To illustrate this point, we are still without a satisfactory history of the role of the Republican Party in the South during Reconstruction. If we had such a history, we would, perhaps, modify our view of that party's role in the postbellum South. We already know, for example, that the factional fights within the party were quite divisive. The bitter fight between two factions of Republicans in South Carolina in 1872 is merely one case in point. On that occasion the nominating convention split in two and each faction proceeded to nominate its own slate of officers. Only the absence of any opposition party assured a Republican victory in the autumn elections. In some instances blacks and whites competed for the party's nomination to public office, thus indicating quite clearly the task facing a Negro Republican who aspired to public office. That is the task that John R. Lynch faced when he ran for Congress in 1872 and defeated the white incumbent, L. W. Pearce, who was regarded even by Lynch as "a creditable and satisfactory representative." And it was not out of the question for white Republicans to work for and vote for white Democrats in order to make certain that Negro Republican candidates for office would be defeated. So little is known of the history of the Republican Party in the South because the presumption has generally been that Lincoln's party was, on its very face, hostile to Southern mores generally and anxious to have Negroes embarrass white Southerners. Indeed, had historians been inclined to examine with greater care the history of the Republican Party in the South, they would have discovered even more grist for the Democratic Party mill.

Thus, studying works on Reconstruction that have been written over the last century can provide a fairly clear notion of the problems confronting the periods in which the historians lived but not always as clear a picture of Reconstruction itself. The state of historical studies and the level of sophistication in the methods of research are much too advanced for us to be content with anything less than the high level of performance found in works on other periods of United States history. There is no reason why the facts of Reconstruction should be the subject of greater dispute than those arising out of Askia Muhammad's rule in Songhay or Cromwell's rule in Britain. But we are still doing the spade-work; we are still writing narrowly focused monographs on the history of Reconstruction. We need to know more about education than Henry L. Swint, Horace Mann Bond, and Robert Morris have told us. Surely there is more to economic development than we can learn from the works by Irwin Unger, George R. Woolfolk, Robert P. Sharkey, and Carl Osthaus. And race, looming large in the Reconstruction era, as is usually the case in other periods of American history, is so pervasive and so critical that the matter should not be left to Herbert G. Gutman, Howard Rabinowitz, John H. and La Wanda Cox, Thomas Holt, and a few others.

Recent scholarship on the Reconstruction era leaves the impression that we may be reaching the point, after a century of effort, where we can handle the problems inherent in writing about an internal struggle without losing ourselves in the fire and brimstone of the Civil War and its aftermath. Perhaps we have reached the point in coping with the problems about us when we no longer need to shape Reconstruction history to suit our current needs. If either or both of these considerations is true, we are fortunate, for each augurs well for the future of Reconstruction history. It would indeed be a happy day if we could view the era of Reconstruction without either attempting to use the events of that era to support some current policy or seeking analogies that are at best strained and provide little in the way of an understanding of that era or our own.

"Not since Reconstruction" is a phrase that is frequently seen and heard. Its principal purpose is to draw an analogy or a contrast. Since it usually neither defines Reconstruction nor makes clear whether it is a signpost of progress or retrogression, searching for some other way of relating that period to our own may be wise, if not necessary. In the search for the real meaning of Reconstruction, phrases like "not since Reconstruction" provide no clue to understanding the period. Worse still, they becloud the relationship between that day and this. To guard against the alluring pitfalls of such phrases and to assure ourselves and others that we are serious about the postbellum South, we would do well to cease using Reconstruction as a mirror of ourselves and begin studying it because it very much needs studying. In such a process Reconstruction will doubtless have much to teach all of us.

Nathan I. Huggins

NATHAN I. HUGGINS (1927–1989) *was professor of Afro-American history at Harvard University. He was the author of numerous articles and books, including* Harlem Renaissance *(1971),* Black Odyssey *(1977), and* Slave and Citizen *(1980).*

Afro-American history and American history are not only essential to one another. They share a common historical fate. Both the American nation and the Afro-American people are creations of the New World. Both were ruptured from tradition. History for both, therefore, has been problematic. Tradition is a legitimizing phenomenon. All peoples and all nations want to tie themselves to an ancient past (ideally, preliterate and mythic). The traditions are often related to place or to migration where antiquity alone would explain the *naturalness* and *rightness* of the present. Medieval political leaders like to relate themselves (often as illicit offspring) to the myths of Homer and Virgil. The modern state of Israel rests its territorial claims and its foreign policy on the Old Testament. Certainly, a nation born of revolution in a "New World" and a people snatched from the web of their tradition would face a similar problem of finding their legitimacy in history.

The Founding Fathers were conscious that the actual history could not be the rationale on which their new nation could rest. They wanted to found their roots in a classical and honored past, while they were deliberately severing themselves from the one tradition that gave them place and reason. Afro-Americans, too, are new, a new people brought into being as a consequence of American history, a new people for whom after several generations in America it was impossible to trace back to any tradition beyond the American experience itself. This newness of people and nation has caused in both a problematic relationship with tradition.

Consider the generation of the so-called Founding Fathers. Here was a nation which they themselves had established, deliberately breaking from their immediate connections with the past. At the same time, nevertheless, they tried heroically to place themselves in a real, identifiable, classical tradition—one which could explain their pres-

---

ent, more so than their past. America, the land and its native peoples, of course, had its own past, but it was not one the Anglo-American newcomers could honor (nor would that indigenous past honor them). America was not Britain or France or Italy or Greece, where the earth itself yielded up evidence that its contemporary generation belonged to something extending back beyond recorded time.

In America there were no ruins (except for Indian mounds) to be dug up, no statues as in Greece, the Holy Land, or Italy; no arches as in Rome; no Coliseum, none of that sort of thing. Yet, at the same time, this generation of new Americans went about identifying and naming their cities Rome and Troy and Athens and Syracuse and Ithaca and Utica and Alexandria and Augusta, names that clearly associated the present with an ancient past. And they did not simply choose place names, but they called on tradition to name the very institutions of their newly established polity. They might have called themselves a *commonwealth*, but they turned to the Roman *res publica* for *republic*. For their new leader, they thought of titles such as "His Mightiness," "His Highness," "Protector," "Regent," or "Serenity"; they chose "President" from *praesidens*. When they established themselves a legislature, it was not a "parliament," but a "congress," from *congressus*. Through it all, one sees this deliberate effort to establish a legitimacy with an ancient and glorious past.

As a further illustration, take the symbolism on the dollar bill. The great seal of the United States bears an eagle which, except for being an American bald eagle, suggests the eagle of the Roman legions. Both the olive branch and the sheaf of arrows it clasps—emblems of peace and war—have classical connotations and were not common symbols in this country before the Revolution. Then, the Latin phrase, *E pluribus unum*. On the obverse side, above the truncated pyramid, above the triangle in glory with the eye of God, one reads: *annuit coeptis*— he has favored our beginnings. Below the pyramid is *Novus ordo seclorum*—a new order of the ages. And at the base of the pyramid, in Roman numerals for greater dignity and authority, is MDCCLXXVI, which is when the new order of ages began. The Founding Fathers wanted to imbue 1776 with ancient virtue.

In these pretenses the Founding Fathers were . . . no different from all peoples who through myth and symbol attached themselves to a grand tradition from which they gain legitimacy and meaning. It was the rupture from their immediate and natural tradition (the final achievement of which was the American Revolution), the need to establish new birthright claims, that made their deliberate and self-conscious link with the classical past necessary.

Africans who were brought to America suffered a similar rupture from their immediate and natural tradition. They, too, were to become a new people, but it would not be easy to find a satisfactory linkage with any past known to them. The ancient European tradition was impossible, and the developing American myth of a providentially designed free society of democratic institutions did not accord with the black experience. For many, Christianity made possible the identification with the Children of Israel of the Old Testament.

But Afro-Americans lacked a specific and direct tie to Africa; we were alienated from, yet elemental to, the New World. Dissatisfied with our own history of slavery and oppression, we have desired to leap over the Afro-American experience altogether, to place ourselves in a tradition which is not immediately ours but certain to give us a sense of grandeur and legitimacy. Such mythologizing is not what we professional historians mean by historical study, but it is a deep human and social need which insinuates itself into our scholarship and criticism.

Even we professionals want history to give us legitimacy as a people or as a nation, and this is true whether we are Afro-Americans thinking of ourselves as a people or Americans thinking of ourselves as a nation. That is why the dominant Anglo-Saxon story of American history, that is to say the Bancroftian myth, persisted so long and with such strength in our historiography. The black and nonwhite experiences never comported well with the central myth—thus the tendency to deal with such groups as anomalous or egregious. That is why Afro-Americans have from the nineteenth century wanted to use the same history of America to demonstrate that we were here "before the Mayflower," that we were part of a developing nation and its history, and thus use American history to establish our birthright.

Consider the Sally Hemmings story, the power of it, its persistence. The evidence is circumstantial; we will never establish a *truth* all will accept. Certainly, we will never get Thomas Jefferson or Sally Hemmings to testify to the facts. There are those people, custodians of the Jefferson legacy, who have a clear stake in protecting not only his historical reputation but his progeny from the taint of race mixture. Similarly, there are those—I venture to say most black people— who *know* the rumors are essentially true despite gaps and problems with the evidence. Why is it so important? Sally Hemmings was certainly not the first or the only black woman so used. Why the fuss? Is it not Sally Hemmings, but Thomas Jefferson who makes the difference. He was a Founding Father of the nation, and, the rumor had it, he sired children by a slave woman. In the overall effect of that story, it does not matter whether or not it was *actually* true. It is *symbolically* true. The story, like so many legitimizing myths, symbolically ties a people (through Sally Hemmings) to the founding of the nation. It is ironic, too, because of the illicit means of establishing legitimacy. That, too, is common in such birthright myths.

Alex Haley's *Roots,* to point to another example, for all of its many historical problems, captured the American imagination—white and black—like no recent work of history has. It accomplished two important things: (I) It evidenced the direct and specific connections between an Afro-American and a traditional Old World culture. It authenticated the Afro-American experience by means of an oral tradition, similar to the Old Testament and the *Iliad*. It authenticated an individual black man, a family, a family enlarged into the Afro-American people. (2) It integrated itself into the dominant Bancroftian myth of providential destiny of America, the American people and nation. The story ends with that onward, upward, progressive vision so characteristic of the American faith. Through *Roots*, black people could be mythically integrated into the American Dream. It does not matter whether or not Haley *actually* traced his family back to a West African village. Whatever the truth, the story will continue to stand as emotionally and symbolically true.

In 1971, I was inclined to dismiss myth as not the proper work of historians. Although I still believe that professional historians have a responsibility not to pander to primal emotional needs and fantasies, I have come to appreciate better how the mythic can suggest itself into the most scholarly work. We blacks writing Afro-American history, no matter how much distance we like to maintain, are drawn to "tell the story of our people" in epic scale.

Vincent Harding's *There Is a River* and my own *Black Odyssey* are works driven by such need. There are many differences between these two works: differences in scale, in vision, in sense of history. Yet the similarities are noteworthy: their literary character, the use of literary devices to insinuate oneself and one's ideas into the experience of both the subject and the reader. Both attempt to include the reader into the *we* of the history. These are not *they* and *me* books. *We* and *our* are the dominant (though often implied) pronouns: we as reader, we as writer, we as Africans, we as Afro-Americans, we as slaves.

They are similar in another way: each has a dominant theme making the book cohere. That theme is explicit and relentless in Harding's work. In my own it is implicit, but nonetheless deliberate and obvious. Harding tells the history of black Americans as a story of resistance, with the "river" of resistance being the central metaphor. For my part, I make the slave experience one of transcendence of tyranny. The themes are not only narrative devices, they are instruments of historical selection and interpretation. The strokes are broad, antithesis muted or denied. In short, both works are attempts at epic.

In the attempt, however, both authors illustrate the problematic character of an Afro-American epic written in the late twentieth century. For, as one is asked to focus on the theme of resistance, the power of the oppressor necessarily remains dominant. As one is invited to celebrate the victory of the slave's humanity over the tyranny of his condition, one is drawn to the unmoved and immovable tyrant. It only reminds us (for those who need reminding) of the paradoxical character of the Afro-American experience. There is no way out of it. History "from the bottom up" as important as that is, will not turn the world upside down. Our reading of Harding or Huggins serves finally to convince us that the "river" and the "transcendence"—the oppression and tyranny that spawn them—have gone one, will continue to go on, far into the future. It is, perhaps, this problem that prompted August Meier to characterize *There Is a River as* "pessimistic."

In a more general sense, these remarks suggest the central problem of the narrative (as well as the epic) for American history. . . . The modern American epic will have to discover the theme or metaphor that can bring all of the parts together in a common American story. Such a theme is latent in the American imagination. I think of the central idea in Martin Luther King, Jr.'s "I Have a Dream," as a force for unity, a river different from Harding's. It is surely more compelling and enduring than Booker T. Washington's metaphor of the hand and the fingers. As a practical matter, however, no such epic theme can work without the factual and experiential basis on which to make it credible. So far, such optimistic themes work better as dreams of future possibility and as America's unrealized calling than as history.

Black Americans, like the American nation itself, will be forever searching into the past to provide a sense of legitimacy and historical purpose, forever bound and frustrated in the effort. I do not suggest this is something they ought not to do, but that it must be done again and again, never with satisfaction. In this regard, black Americans who work in this field are different from their white colleagues. It is *their* history, and in a deep, personal and emotional way they will never be able to escape their personal identification with it however much scholarly distance is achieved. That is fair enough and no different from other historians with what they consider *their* history.

I mean this to be neither a validating nor an invalidating idea regarding black or white historians working in the field. It is merely to state the obvious. I hope we have moved beyond the view, pervasive within the profession before the 1960s, that a black historian's judgment about slavery, etc., had to be discounted as naturally biased, while whites had no ax to grind, and the equally foolish idea of the 1960s and 1970s that white historians could not write or comment on the black experience. I mean only to point to the dual character of history. We need to know how and why we use history: to serve both our needs of personal and group identity as well as for the more "scientific" and humanistic purposes of historical analysis. We should know the differences and not confound them.

Most of what we read as Afro-American history is really not so cosmic as all of this. Rather, it is quite limited, particular, and precise.

Most do not address large, ideational issues. Most, I am forced to say, are rather parochial. It has been an "archaeological" work, digging and opening new ground. It brings to our attention particulars, data that is new to us. These shards, in themselves, are not starting discoveries, but they constitute a new history as far as Americans are concerned. We now have a number of monographs that have made genuine contributions.

So you get studies of blacks in Kentucky, blacks in Illinois, blacks in Indiana, or wherever. The history gets repeated again and again; we need the reiteration, each with its particular or special angle or twist. We need to know the sameness to discover in it what is unique. Sometimes the angle of vision is only slightly shifted: now it is "black men," now it is "black women." We take old, much-studied issues and institutions and reconsider them with blacks in mind. We look at individual lives, often by means of oral histories and interviews, to bring into our consciousness ranges of human experience previously remote or inaccessible to us. It is all extremely important work, and the production of the past decade has been impressive.

The danger, however, is that we see this work as the end and purpose of Afro-American history—creating a narrow specialty over which we establish a proprietary interest, squeezing our concerns to the point of historical insignificance. It is a danger because the American academic professions encourage such mindless territoriality, and because many are fearful to venture beyond their carefully cultivated certitudes.

We ought, rather, to see this work as the building blocks of a new synthesis, a new American history. Would that the work should raise such fundamental questions of American society as to provoke discourse among American historians to change the history they write. We are able now to say, as we were not fifteen years ago, that blacks (black leaders, the black experience, etc.) is *included* in the textbooks. That is not enough.

Recently, I was asked to review a manuscript for a college textbook in American history. It seemed all right; it omitted no notable group; it made no mistakes; it covered all the bases. It was, nevertheless, a poor history. The authors had a chapter on mid-nineteenth-century reform. William Lloyd Garrison and the abolitionists were there. Frederick Douglass was not. He was in another chapter, the one on blacks. Surely we must know that what actually happened in that historical moment was a consequence of the interaction between Douglass and Garrison. It cannot be told as a story of *black history* and *white history*. It must be told as one. While that idea is simple enough—a truism indeed—too few of us accept the radical implications of it. We do not put it into our thinking, our writing, our courses. That idea, nevertheless, is a key to any new, successful narrative of American history.

It may be that the Afro-American story remains too discordant with progressive assumptions to be comfortably incorporated into the American story, Alex Haley notwithstanding. Dominant, national narratives, after all, are *selected* from a matrix of historical experience. What is chosen, and how it is put together, tells us how a people would like to perceive themselves—their future as well as their past. As Americans, we have liked the succession of events to move in ever-ascending stages, each today better than all yesterdays. Surely there were problems, but there were reforms and resolutions. Things worked out. All national histories are not so optimistic and progressive as our own. Some are characteristically ironic, some cyclical, some fatalistic.

Except for Alex Haley's *Roots*, I know of no treatment of the Afro-American story that shares the dominant optimism and faith in progress, certainly not one written in the late twentieth century. The Afro-American story has more been told in terms of failed hopes, frustrated and ambiguous victories, dreams deferred. In contrast to the dominant American story, it is most often characterized as tragic. It may well be that the new American narrative, when it is written, will resonate to a more experienced, a wiser, nation. We might, then, see as if for the first time, the elemental truth in the black American experience; rather than being an anomaly, it is central to the story. That would result in a new American history, indeed.

We need not wait for such grand, synthetic efforts; there is much to be done. Old questions in American history demand new answers from the angle of vision of Afro-American history. Old topics seem different from that perspective: the city, economic development, citizenship, federalism, majority rule, and so on. On the scale of dissertation and monograph, with a new vision there is new history to be written if historians and teachers are willing to be genuinely challenging. Moreover, historians of the Afro-American experience must reach beyond ethnic history by choosing topics having historical significance beyond narrow bounds of race, by developing the implications of their work for the general history, and by raising through their work general questions, provoking discourse among historians and contributing to the new American history.

☆ 5 ☆

American Imperialism

ALTRUISM OR AGGRESSION?

During the last quarter of the nineteenth century, the United States emerged as a world power. Its industrial and agricultural productivity, large size, growing population, and modern navy gave it a prominence that could not be ignored. The acquisition of an overseas empire added to America's stature. In 1898 and 1899 the United States suddenly acquired the Hawaiian Islands and gained control over Puerto Rico, the Philippines, and part of the Samoan archipelago. Within a year and a half American had become a dominant power in both the Caribbean and the Pacific.

Curiously enough many Americans were ambivalent about their country's new role. Some feared that America's democratic institutions were incompatible with an overseas empire and the large military establishment that would be required to sustain it. Others rejected the concept of empire because they opposed bringing under the American flag groups they regarded as racial or social inferiors. Some Americans, on the other hand, favored the entry of the United States into world affairs either because of a crusading zeal to spread American institutions or a desire to find new economic markets. Although the United States entered the twentieth century as a world power, its people remained divided over the wisdom or desirability of pursuing their new destiny.

These divisions among the public over foreign policy had their counterpart among diplomatic historians. Just as Americans debated the wisdom of particular policies, so historians disagreed about interpretations of past events. The historical debate, in reality, was not confined simply to an analysis of the past; implicit in many interpretations of diplomatic history was a vision of what America ought to be. To argue that the United States traditionally was a champion of freedom and democracy was to take a position on certain contemporary policies toward the nondemocratic world. Similarly the argument that America was an imperialistic nation bent on imposing its economic

163

and military power on the rest of the world had implications for contemporary foreign and domestic policy issues.

The historical literature dealing with the decade of the 1890s,
which culiminated in the Spanish-American War, is a case in point.
Charles and Mary Beard, whose *Rise of American Civilization* symbolized the Progressive school of American historiography, implied that
economic issues led President William McKinley to ask for a declaration of war. The Spanish government, after all, had practically acceded
to his demands. McKinley, the Beards insisted, revised Cleveland's policy of neutrality, presumably because of the threat to American investments in and trade with Cuba. In the final analysis war grew out of a
desire to protect America's economic interests in that region. The ensuing acquisition of overseas territory provided further proof of the
Beards' charge that the nation's business community played an important role in determining the country's foreign policy. Although the
Beardian thesis was presented in somewhat qualified form, it clearly
implied the primacy of economic forces.[1]

Relatively few scholars, however, followed the Beards' interpretation. To Samuel Flagg Bemis, whose synthesis of American diplomatic
history appeared in 1936, the acquisition of an overseas empire represented a "great aberration." Before the war, Bemis noted, "there had
not been the slightest demand for the acquisition of the Philippine Islands." A military victory, however, fanned imperialist sentiment.
McKinley proved unable to resist jingoist sentiment, and he instructed
his peace commission to demand the Philippine Islands, a demand that
demonstrated "adolescent irresponsibility." McKinley's decision, concluded Bemis, was largely unplanned, and was not in accord with the
traditional American aversion to imperialism.[2]

At the same time Bemis's influential textbook appeared Julius W.
Pratt published his *Expansionists of 1898.* Also rejecting an economic
interpretation of war causation, Pratt suggested instead that intellectual and emotional factors were responsible for the new expansionism.
The emergence of social Darwinism, with its emphasis on competition
and survival of the fittest, provided some people with an intellectual
justification for expanding America's sphere of influence. Many argued
that nations, like individuals, were engaged in a remorseless test of
their fitness to survive. The criterion of success was dominion over
others; failure to expand, on the other hand, meant stagnation and decline. Other expansionist-minded individuals were affected by religious and humanitarian concerns; they wished to bring American civil-

---

[1] Charles A. Beard and Mary R. Beard, *The Rise of American Civilization,* 2 vols.
(New York, 1927), 2:369–382.

[2] Samuel Flagg Bemis, *A Diplomatic History of the United States* (4th ed., New
York, 1955), pp. 463–475.

ization and morality to less advanced peoples. Still others accepted the doctrines developed by Captain Alfred Thayer Mahan, who saw growing American sea power as the key to the nation's greatness. Sea power, however, required overseas naval bases. Pratt, interestingly enough, noted that the business community, which was still recovering from the depression that began in 1893, opposed intervention in Cuba for fear that it might block the road to economic recovery. With Admiral Dewey's dramatic victory in the Philippines, American businessmen became converted to the expansionist cause by the alluring prospect of dominating the potentially large Chinese market. These same businessmen now found it easy to apply the same rationale in the Caribbean and supported expansion in that area. The reasons why the United States went to war, therefore, were quite different from the reasons that led its government to acquire an overseas empire. Indeed, Pratt concluded, American imperialism consisted of a blend of religious, humanitarian, and economic components.[3]

These early historians agreed, at least in part, that foreign policy was to a significant extent determined by domestic considerations. There were significant differences, nevertheless, between their approaches. To the Beards the business community, with its emphasis on profits, pushed the nation into war. Bemis, on the other hand, saw the results of war as a repudiation of the traditional anti-imperialist sentiment of Americans. To Pratt a variety of influences—domestic and foreign—came into play, although no one in particular exercised the decisive role. In general two approaches ultimately came to dominate the writing of American diplomatic history. Those in the Beard tradition would interpret America's foreign policy primarily in terms of domestic considerations. A second tradition would emphasize, in addition, the importance of actions taken by foreign governments. Although the two approaches would on occasion come together in the work of an individual scholar, more often than not they would remain separate and distinct.

After the publication of Pratt's work in 1936 scholarly interest in American imperialism and the Spanish-American War tended to flag. Between the 1930s and 1950s diplomatic historians were primarily interested in illuminating the causes and consequences of the First and Second World Wars. But in 1959 William Appleman Williams published his influential book *The Tragedy of American Diplomacy*, which had a profound impact on the writing of all diplomatic history. This book, indeed, became the starting point for the work of many revisionist and New Left historians, who believed that America's for-

---

[3]Julius W. Pratt, *Expansionists of 1898* (Baltimore, 1936), and *America's Colonial Experiment: How the United States Gained, Governed, and in Part Gave Away a Colonial Empire* (New York, 1950).

eign policies were dominated by the narrow economic interests of a small elite.

The Williams thesis, briefly stated, rested on the premise that foreign policy was a function of the structure and organization of American society. During the depression of the 1880s and 1890s the business community had concluded that foreign markets were indispensable for America's well-being. These markets would help to avoid any internal problems that might arise from economic stagnation resulting from America's tendency to produce more goods than its people consumed. The result was a fundamental shift in the nation's foreign policy. Policymakers adopted what became known as the Open Door policy—an open door "through which America's preponderant economic strength would enter and dominate all underdeveloped areas of the world. . . . [T]he Open Door Policy was in fact a brilliant strategic stroke which led to the gradual extension of American economic and political power throughout the world."[4] Indeed, most of American diplomacy in the twentieth century, Williams insisted, was directed toward the goal of assuring the nation's economic supremacy on a global scale. Pursuit of this goal led to involvement in two world wars, the Korean and Vietnam conflicts, and the Cold War that had pitted the Soviet Union and the United States against each other. In other words Williams posited a continuity in American foreign policy from the late nineteenth century to the present.

The origins of modern American foreign policy, Williams argued, could be traced back to the economic crisis of the 1890s. During that decade a new national consensus was reached. Americans no longer debated whether or not an expansionist policy should be pursued but rather what form expansion should take. This expansionist policy was based on the conviction that American diplomacy and prosperity went hand in hand and required access to world markets. Any restrictions on the flow of American goods and capital would lead to a depression and social unrest. Support for economic expansion, therefore, played a crucial role in precipitating the Spanish-American War and in the subsequent debate over the desirability of acquiring overseas possessions.

In 1963 Walter LaFeber published a prize-winning volume on American expansionism from 1860 to 1898 that lent strong support to the Williams thesis. The Civil War, LaFeber noted, marked an important dividing line in America's expansionist policies. Before 1860 expansionism was confined to the American continent; it reflected the desire of an agrarian society to find new and fertile lands. Post–Civil

---

[4]William Appleman Williams, *The Tragedy of American Diplomacy* (2d rev. and enl. ed., New York, 1972), pp. 45–46. See also Williams's *The Roots of the Modern American Empire* (New York, 1969).

War expansionism, on the other hand, was motivated by the belief that foreign markets were vital to America's well-being. By the 1890s the American business community and policymakers had concluded that additional foreign markets "would solve the economic, social, and political problems created by the industrial revolution." Given Europe's imperialist penetration in many regions of the world Americans also concluded that their country needed strategic bases if they were to compete successfully. The diplomacy of the 1890s and the Spanish-American War grew out of these concerns. Indeed, LaFeber insisted that the debate between the imperialists and anti-imperialists during this decade was a limited one; they differed over the tactical means that the United States should use in order to attain its objectives. "By 1899," concluded LaFeber, "the United States had forged a new empire. American policy makers and business men had created it amid much debate and with conscious purpose. The empire progressed from a continental base in 1861 to assured pre-eminence in the Western Hemisphere in 1895. Three years later it was rescued from a growing economic and political dilemma by the declaration of war against Spain. During and after this conflict the empire moved past Hawaii into the Philippines, and, with the issuance of the Open-Door Notes, enunciated its principles in Asia."[5]

Since the 1960s many scholars have continued to follow the Williams interpretation of American diplomatic history. In 1967 Thomas McCormick published a book that traced the growing interest of Americans in the 1890s in the potentially large China market. Four years later Milton Plesur analyzed the origins of the "large policy" of the 1890s, which he located in the years between 1865 and 1890. The new diplomacy, he concluded, "was rationalized on the basis of racial and moral superiority, a sense of national mission, strategic considerations, enhancement of national prestige, and aversion to a worldwide imperialism from which we were excluded economically. Though originally not seeking territory for ourselves, we could not allow other powers to jeopardize what we thought were our legitimate interests." In a similar vein Ernest N. Paolino emphasized the degree to which William H. Seward had laid the foundations for an expansionist policy during the 1860s.[6]

The Williams-LaFeber interpretation of the origins of modern

---

[5]Walter LaFeber; The New Empire: An Interpretation of American Expansionism 1860–1898 (Ithaca, 1963), pp. 412–417.

[6]Thomas McCormick, China Market: America's Quest for Informal Empire 1893–1901 (Chicago, 1967): Milton Plesur, America's Outward Thrust: Approaches to Foreign Affairs, 1865–1890 (DeKalb, Ill., 1971), pp. 235–236; Ernest N. Paolino, The Foundations of American Empire: William Henry Seward and U.S. Foreign Policy (Ithaca, 1973). See also Charles S. Campbell, The Transformation of American Foreign Relations 1865–1900 (New York, 1976).

America's foreign policy had a powerful appeal during the 1960s and 1970s, particularly as disillusionment with American society grew during the Vietnam conflict. The argument that the nation's diplomacy was based less on altruism, idealism, and anti-imperialism and more on a desire to safeguard an international order that made possible America's economic supremacy, of course, had important implications for contemporary concerns. The Cold War, for example, rather than resting on a moral foundation that pitted freedom against communism, was seen as a product of America's continued insistence on structuring a world order along lines that preserved its liberal capitalist hegemony. Thus American foreign policy, which grew out of domestic institutions and developments, was allegedly responsible in large measure for initiating and perpetuating the Cold War and causing the Vietnam conflict.[7] Williams's work spawned a whole school of historians who proceeded to write revisionist accounts of the history of American foreign policy.

Walter LaFeber—undoubtedly the most articulate scholar associated with the Williams school—continued to emphasize the imperialist basis of American diplomacy. In 1983 he authored a history of United States relations with Central America since the nineteenth century. Almost from the beginning of the American republic, policymakers had been motivated by a desire to strengthen capitalist interests in this region and thus had forged a diplomatic policy aimed at dominating and exploiting Central Americans. The result, according to LaFeber, was the degradation of the indigenous masses in this region and the maintenance in power of right-wing dictatorial regimes. The turbulence of this region in the 1980s, he concluded, was directly attributable to the desire of Americans to create an informal imperialist empire.[8]

The Williams thesis, however, did not gain universal acceptance in historical circles. Not all scholars, for example, agreed with this portrait of American society. Others were critical of a viewpoint that emphasized the importance of domestic factors in the determination of foreign policy and belittled or ignored actions by other nations. In their eyes diplomatic policies were also influenced by the external actions and reactions of foreign governments. A more balanced approach, they argued, called for an understanding of the behavior of other governments, which, in turn, implied a multinational approach to diplomacy and multiarchival research. Rejecting the idea of American om-

---

[7]See Walter LaFeber, *America, Russia, and the Cold War 1945–1966* (New York, 1967); Lloyd C. Gardner, "American Foreign Policy 1900–1921: A Second Look at the Realist Critique of American Diplomacy," in *Towards a New Past: Dissenting Essays in American History*, Barton J. Bernstein, ed. (New York, 1968), pp. 202–231; David Healy, *U.S. Expansionism: The Imperialist Urge in the 1890s* (Madison, Wis., 1970).

[8]Walter LaFeber, *Inevitable Revolutions: The United States in Central America* (New York, 1983).

nipotence in world affairs they stressed other than economic factors and attempted to demonstrate that the purposefulness attributed to American policymakers was not justified by a critical examination of the sources.

Typical of this approach was Ernest R. May's *Imperial Democracy: The Emergence of America as a Great Power*, published in 1961. May argued that in the 1890s the United States had not sought to play a new role in world affairs. On the contrary diplomatic problems concerning Hawaii, China, Venezuela, and Cuba had almost intruded upon the domestic issues in which most statesmen and political leaders were primarily interested. "Some nations," May observed, "achieve greatness; the United States had greatness thrust upon it."

President McKinley, for example, rather than being the harbinger of imperialism, was portrayed as a leader who was trying to keep his nation out of war and at the same time to resolve the Cuban dilemma that had inflamed public opinion. His initiatives were ultimately doomed to failure, for Spain would neither grant Cuba autonomy nor suppress the rebellion. McKinley then gave Spain an ultimatum, which included American mediation in the event Spain and the Cubans could not reach some arrangement (a mediation that in all likelihood would have meant Cuban independence). To the Spanish government such an ultimatum was unacceptable. McKinley then faced a crucial choice. He could embark upon a war that he did not want or could defy public opinion and accept some compromise. The latter course might have led to the unseating of the Republican party if not the overthrow of constitutional government. "When public opinion reached the point of hysteria, he succumbed," said May.

Did McKinley accept the decision for war because of a need for foreign markets and strategic bases as Williams argued? Most assuredly not, insisted May. "Neither the President nor the public had any aim beyond war itself. The nation was in a state of upset. Until recently its people had been largely Protestant and English; its economy predominantly rural and agricultural. . . . Now, however, the country was industrialized and urbanized. Catholics were numerous and increasing. People of older stock found themselves no longer economically or even socially superior to members of immigrant groups or to others. . . . The panic of 1893 made this new condition even more visible by depressing agricultural prices, rents, investment income, professional fees, and white-collar salaries. . . . In some irrational way, all these influences and anxieties translated themselves into concern for suffering Cuba. For the people as for the government, war with monarchical Catholic, Latin Spain had no purpose except to relieve emotion."[9]

---

[9] Ernest R. May, *Imperial Democracy: The Emergence of America as a Great Power* (New York, 1961), pp. 268–270.

In a certain sense May's thesis was anticipated a decade earlier by Richard Hofstadter. In 1952 Hofstadter published an article that rejected an economic explanation of American diplomacy in the 1890s and suggested instead that the hysteria and jingoism of this decade grew out of the anxieties occasioned by social and economic change. Indeed, shortly thereafter Hofstadter proposed a comparable explanation of the roots of McCarthyism. Although sympathetic to liberalism Hofstadter's work in the 1940s and 1950s contributed to the emerging rejection of the basic tenets of the Progressive school of American historiography. In his eyes modern American liberalism reflected less a concern for the welfare of the masses of Americans and more the inner feelings of select middle-class groups alienated from their society because of economic and technological change and a consequent decline in their social status. Foreign policy, implied Hofstadter, mirrored these irrational and noneconomic influences.[10]

In 1969 May published a second work in which he used concepts drawn from the social sciences in order to present a fuller portrait of the diplomacy of those years. In that work May examined the structure and role of public opinion in order to illuminate how the United States briefly became imperialistic in outlook and then even more quickly turned away from overseas expansion. After analyzing public opinion in terms of various categories involving elites with different interests and concerns, May argued that the anticolonialist consensus was briefly broken in 1898 and 1899, which resulted in the transfer of leadership to a wider circle. The outcome was a new consensus that accepted the desirability of acquiring foreign possessions and owed much of its inspiration to European, and especially British, opinion. Shortly thereafter the more traditional anticolonial view prevailed, especially after the difficulties faced by the British during the Boer War in South Africa and the growth of an anti-imperialist movement in Britain. May concluded by insisting that the imperialist-anti-imperialist debate could not be understood solely in terms of what Americans said or did, for they were members of a much broader Atlantic civilization.[11]

Another attack on the Williams school came from James A. Field, Jr. Much of the literature on American imperialism, Field charged, was a version of the Whig theory of history. Beginning with perceptions of American immorality in the twentieth century Williams and his followers had interpreted the past with "the same perceptions of false continuities and imputations of sin." The historical literature dealing

---

[10]Richard Hofstadter, "Manifest Destiny and the Philippines," in *America in Crisis: Fourteen Crucial Episodes in American History*, Daniel Aaron, ed. (New York, 1952), pp. 173–200.

[11]Ernest R. May, "American Imperialism: A Reinterpretation," *Perspectives in American History* 1 (1967):123–283; also published as *American Imperialism: A Speculative Essay* (New York, 1968).

with the 1890s suffered from a number of failings: the adoption of a strictly rational explanation of events and a rejection of chance; the use of overly broad terms to describe complex situations; a treatment of diplomacy that was excessively ethnocentric; and a discussion that ignored "time, distance, costs, or technological feasibility."

Rejecting explanations of American imperialism based on the application of Darwinian theory, the psychic crisis of imperialism, the new navy, and the importance of the Pacific highway to Asia, Field proposed a new hypothesis. The new American navy that came into existence in the late nineteenth century was a defensive answer to European developments; "its deployment reflected a shrunken perimeter." The search for bases was a response to the strategic problems of the proposed canal linking the Atlantic and Pacific oceans. The ideologists of that period, moreover, were of negligible importance. "What Americans, whether travellers or missionaries or businessmen, wanted of the outer world was the freedom to pursue happiness, to do their thing, to operate insofar as possible unhindered by arbitrary power or obsolete ideas. Proud of their own self-determined independence, they were sympathetic to similar desires on the part of Samoan chiefs, Korean kings, Egyptian khedives, Armenian Christians, Brazilians, Venezuelans, and Chinese. Most of all, because they were nearest and most visible and noisiest, it was the Cubans who engaged this sympathy." Indeed, Field suggested that the rapid deployment of the American navy headed by Admiral Dewey in the Pacific was largely a result of the rapidity of communication made possible by new cables linking nations and continents. Dewey's victory in turn focused public attention on the Far East; only then did an avalanche of publicity descend upon the American people. "Imperialism," according to Field, "was the product of Dewey's victory." Field's criticisms drew a sharp rejoinder from both LaFeber and Robert Beisner (another diplomatic historian and author of several works on late-nineteenth century American foreign policy). The debate between these three scholars appears as the selection for this chapter.[12]

The discussion over the origins and nature of American "imperialism," of course, involved an evaluation of its consequences as well. To historians critical of the role America in world affairs in the twentieth century these consequences were largely negative. Williams, for example, argued that American foreign policy to a considerable degree rested on "a posture of moral and ideological superiority." Its leaders believed that underdeveloped nations had to be changed in order for the United States to harvest the fruits of expansionism. The goals of

---

[12]For a somewhat different rejection of the Williams school, see Richard E. Welch, Jr., *Response to Imperialism: The United States and the Philippine-American War, 1899–1902* (Chapel Hill, 1979).

foreign policy (as compared with changing tactics) were to maintain markets for industrial exports, to control access to raw materials, and the right to take part in the economic life of other nations by establishing factories and other enterprises. Economic imperialism, in turn, led to efforts to establish political hegemony. Cuba, Williams noted, was a case in point. The United States "dominated the economic life of the island by controlling, directly or indirectly, the sugar industry, and by overtly and covertly preventing any dynamic modification of the island's one-crop economy. It defined clear and narrow limits on the island's political system. It tolerated the use of torture and terror, of fraud and farce, by Cuba's rulers. But it intervened with economic and diplomatic pressure and with force of arms when Cubans threatened to transgress the economic and political restrictions established by American leaders."[13]

In many respects the Williams-LaFeber approach implies a more general interpretation of the nature of American society. As a matter of fact Thomas J. McCormick, a historian whose sympathies lie with both, has advanced a series of propositions that in his eyes deserve testing. American capitalism, McCormick suggests, has always been concerned with expanding production. Given its bias against income distribution it has turned to marketplace expansionism overseas. Given the corporatist nature of American society it followed naturally that elite leaders of corporatist syndicates were also the prime makers of foreign policy. Eventually organized labor and the farm bloc were brought in as junior partners. The result was the rationalization of corporate capitalism on the domestic scene, and the expansion of efforts to create a greater global corporatism in the more recent period.[14]

Just as the Williams-LaFeber interpretation of the origins of the Spanish-American War came under criticism, so, too, did their view of twentieth-century American imperialism. Paul A. Varg, for example, argued that a careful examination of the specific actions of the United States in world affairs precluded any simple or facile generalizations about imperialism or America's world power status. China was *not* of major importance to American policy officials. Even the dominant role of the United States in the Caribbean was never pursued solely for economic considerations; strong opposition to any American intervention in that area arose during each crisis. In Varg's view few American leaders pursued foreign policy concerns out of a conviction that the nation's welfare was dependent upon developments in other parts of the world. Although the United States did become a world power it

---

[13]Williams, *Tragedy of American Diplomacy,* pp. 2 and 59.

[14]Thomas J. McCormick, "Drift or Mastery? A Corporate Synthesis for American Diplomatic History," *Reviews in American History* 4 (December 1982):318–330.

was not because of any master plan designed to control the destiny of other nations.[15]

The claim that American imperialism necessarily had a harmful impact on foreign nations was also challenged indirectly by Stanley Lebergott. Lebergott pointed to the relative insignificance of American foreign investment in Latin America from 1890 to 1929, and denied as well that it worked to the detriment of either workers or landowners in the nations that were affected. Indeed, American foreign investments increased the income of workers and peasants by expanding the need for labor; land values in many Latin American nations increased in value because of the opening of American markets to native products. Lebergott conceded that American business enterprise sometimes destroyed the vested interests of native business groups and their monopoly profits, and also created new entrepreneurial groups. The heart of the ensuing anti-imperialist contest, he concluded, was not between America and Latin America, but between two capitalist groups, one native and the other foreign, each fighting over the spoils of progress.[16]

The debate among historians about the nature of late-nineteenth- and early-twentieth-century American diplomacy in part reflected visions not only of what American society was, but what it ought to have been. Charles A. Beard, writing within the Progressive school tradition, tended to emphasize the role of economic factors. In the late 1940s he spelled out more precisely his belief that domestic reform and involvement in world rivalries were incompatible and benefited relatively small groups of affluent elites. Samuel Flagg Bemis, on the other hand, wrote within an older patriotic tradition that emphasized the anti-imperialist nature of the American people and their desire to avoid foreign adventures; hence he characterized the Spanish-American War as a "great aberration" and a war productive of no good. William Appleman Williams, a critic of American capitalism whose views became influential during the 1960s and 1970s, saw diplomacy as an extension of the need of American capitalism to dominate the world in an economic sense. The two world wars, the Korean and Vietnam conflicts, and the Cold War, he and his followers charged, were all products of internal flaws in American society; only by radical change could these flaws be eradicated. Recent critiques of the Wil-

---

[15]Paul A. Varg, "The United States as a World Power, 1900–1917: Myth or Reality?," in *Twentieth-Century American Foreign Policy*, John Braeman, Robert H. Bremner, and David Brody, eds. (Columbus, Ohio, 1971), and *The Making of a Myth: The United States and China, 1897–1912* (East Lansing, Mich., 1968). For other examples of work in this tradition see Howard K. Beale, *Theodore Roosevelt and the Rise of America to World Power* (Baltimore, 1956), and Raymond A. Esthus, *Theodore Roosevelt and the International Rivalries* (Waltham, Mass. 1970).

[16]Stanley Lebergott, "The Returns to U.S. Imperialism, 1890–1929," *Journal of Economic History* 40 (June 1980):229–249.

liams approach were in part a reaction to his harsh criticisms of American society and in part a denial of American omnipotence. Events in other nations, as Ernest R. May noted, played a role in shaping American foreign policy, and a knowledge of the domestic determinants of policy, although indispensable, was insufficient by itself.

As long as Americans continue to discuss and fight over the proper role of their nation in world affairs, the events of the 1890s and early part of the twentieth century will continue to hold the interest of historians. In studying the origins and consequences of the Spanish-American War scholars in all probability will continue to raise many of the same questions asked by their predecessors for over three quarters of a century. Did the United States go to war to resolve basic contradictions within its economic and social systems? Was the acquisition of an overseas empire a cause or a consequence of war? To what degree did moral, religious, and humanitarian sentiments play a role in the diplomacy of the 1890s? To what extent was American foreign policy a response to the diplomacy of other nations and events beyond its control? Did the United States in fact abandon its interests in empire after 1900, or did it create a new form of colonialism through the use of its economic power? Above all, did the United States become a world power because its leaders consciously recognized the importance of other regions to the nation's well-being, or did it simply stumble into its new status without a clear grasp of the underlying issues? Americans will struggle with these and other questions as long as they continue to debate foreign policy issues and the role America has and should play as a world power.

James A. Field, Jr.

JAMES A. FIELD, JR. (1916–   ) *is professor of history at Swarth-more College. He has written a number of works in diplomatic history, including* Japanese at Leyte Gulf *(1947) and* America and the Mediterranean World 1776–1882 *(1969).*

A few months ago the mail brought a copy of a new textbook on American diplomatic history. Feeling some obligation to the publisher, I gave it the standard check and read through the chapter on the 1880s and 1890s—"The New American Spirit." Like so many such chapters, it failed the test. Disappointed again, I crossed the hall to ask a learned colleague what he thought was predictably the worst chapter in any general history of American foreign relations. "The worst?" he asked, and then answered without a pause, "The one on the end of the nineteenth century."

This "worst chapter" may be summarized somewhat as follows:

The publication of Charles Darwin's Origin of Species *gave rise to some new American mutations called John Fiske, Josiah Strong, Alfred T. Mahan, and Brooks Adams. Unlike their ancestors, they were all racists and wanted battleships and naval bases. At the same time the American churches, desirous of saving souls, demanded political control of "native peoples." In the closing years of the century American farmers began to ship more wheat and cattle to "Europe and other places." Standard Oil and other companies were investing overseas. An "avalanche" of books, articles, editorials, and speeches consequently descended upon the American people, sending it into the "psychic crisis" of the 1890s and turning the country to "populism and jingoism." The result of all of this was the arrival of a Samoan chief in search of a treaty, a riot in a Valparaiso saloon, a revolution in Hawaii, and a naval development program that bore fruit in a new secret weapon, a twenty-inch gun, which was test-fired in the direction of Whitehall in 1895. The "logical outcome" of this new spirit (described in the next chapter) was "The War with Spain" and the annexation of the Philippines as part of a policy of "insular imperialism" aimed at the markets of China.*

James A. Field, Jr., "American Imperialism: The Worst Chapter in Almost Any Book," with comments by Walter LaFeber and Robert L. Beisner, *American Historical Review* 83 (June 1978):644–683. (The original footnotes have been reduced in number and magnitude with the permission of the author.) Reprinted by permission of James A. Field, Jr., Walter LaFeber, and Robert L. Beisner.

This curious narrative, which in mildly variant forms appears to have gained wide acceptance, represents the product of some fifty years of historical construction by a number of architects and builders. Surprisingly, the foundations still reflect the handiwork of Julius W. Pratt (although John A. Hobson and Charles A. Beard have crept back into the cellar); the eclectic superstructure derives from the efforts of, among others, Richard Hofstadter, William A. Williams, Walter La-Feber, and Thomas J. McCormick. Although the mansion was origi-nally designed to house the 1880s and 1890s, the carpenters in recent years have added wings that extend backward in time to provide lodg-ing for William H. Seward and forward to house Vietnam. The result of this architectural agglomeration is an inverted Whig interpretation of history, differing from its predecessor primarily in that now the chil-dren of darkness triumph over the children of light. But there remains the same insistence on seeing the past through the prism of the pres-ent, the same perceptions of false continuities and imputations of sin, and the same tendentious impact on generalization and abridgment. Works of this genre have a certain utility, no doubt, for classroom dis-cussion of how and how not to write history, but they also raise serious questions. How should we grapple with this segment of our past? How escape the conventional formulations so uncritically and tediously passed from article to article, book to book, and text to text?

Much of the literature on the 1890s suffers from a number of com-mon failings. First, the approach is too rational. Chance (or the unex-pected), which plays so important a part in the life of the individual, seems unacceptable in the life of the nation: these authors simply will not remember the *Maine.* Events must have their antecedent phil-osophers and strategists and must also, apparently, flow logically from previous intentions. Since the United States did entangle itself in Asia in 1898, these requirements have led to a backward approach to his-tory and to the transformation of a record of almost total lack of accomplishment—in the search for naval bases, in Hawaiian an-nexation, in the construction of Chinese railroads, and in reviving the merchant marine, reforming the consular service, or revising the tariff—into evidence of an overwhelming wave of imperialism. Sec-ond, the picture is too unitary. The use of such terms as "America," "American," and "United States" to describe both public and private doings imposes a deceptive solidity upon a very mixed bag of phenom-ena, confuses the governmental and private sectors, underplays the many overseas Americans who showed small interest in government support and none in territorial expansion, and obscures regional vari-ation. Mapping late-nineteenth-century American activity abroad pro-duces a whole variety of overlays—economic, strategic, cultural, phil-anthropic, entrepreneurial—that are by no means geographically coincident. Third, the treatment is excessively ethnocentric. Everything that happens is attributed to the purposeful action of the United States, and the philosophers and strategists must all be American. But while the America of the 1890s possessed a large and influential package of skills and resources, both its strengths and its aims were limited. Indeed, with the recent history of the big influence of small allies available to reinforce that of the Cuban junta and the Hawaiian Annexation Club, it could perhaps be argued that the United States has been as much or more the used as it has the user, and that much of its involvement in the outer world has come in response to Macedonian cries.[1] Fourth, the discussion takes small account of time, distance, costs, or technological feasibility. Words do duty for things and presumed intentions for actual capabilities. Finally, the wrong questions are often asked. In the case of Hawaii, for example, the interesting problem is surely not why it was annexed in 1898, but rather why so "natural" a development was so long delayed. The answer is that ruling circles in the United States did not much want to annex Hawaii, unless, perhaps, to pre-empt annexation by others; contrariwise, influential folk in the islands ardently desired to annex the United States but, with only a small and feeble country at their disposal, had to wait for special circumstances before they could manage it.

Moving from the general to the particular, a brief look at various aspects of the treatments of "American imperialism"—ideological, bureaucratic, semantic, geographical, and technological—may help to separate what is useful from what is not. The presumed necessity for events to follow logically from what preceded, the importance scholars give to words, and the happy fact that quotations to support almost any argument can be rummaged out of the grabbag of the past have led many historians to fall in love with ideology. Hence, the chapters on "The New American Spirit" and, hence, the emphasis on Darwin and on something called "Social Darwinism." From the *Origin of Species*, it is suggested, came a mental climate that spawned oppressive capitalists at home and promoters of oppressive imperialism abroad. But there are problems here. The kind of activist government required for imperial ventures appears to have had small appeal for capitalists, and few seem to have busied themselves in the cause. The standard ideologists who are alleged to have infected the American people with the disease of Darwinist expansionism were few in number and of doubtful leverage, and the standard quotations from their works are selective and unrepresentative. One should not, it would seem, quote Fiske, Strong, Mahan, Adams, and the rest without having read their works.

Strong's main concerns in the 1880s, for instance, were clearly fo-

---

[1] Acts 16:9–24. The modern reader of this text, observing how Paul became aware of the cry out of Macedonia and what befell him when he answered it, will sense ambiguities which seem to have eluded our missionary-minded forefathers.

cused on the country's internal problems. As a high-minded Social Gospeller he worried mightily about Mormonism, Catholicism, drink, and tobacco; and his single chapter on the outer world appears to have been designed to emphasize what was at stake at home. There was, in any case, nothing new in 1885 about his ideas on the triumph of Anglo-Saxondom, Christianity, and civil liberty that would postulate "a new American spirit"; similar sentiments had been voiced in the 1840s by Hollis Read, another missionary author.[2] Fiske's general attitude was strongly antimilitary, and his recipe for the world's future, far from being one of conquest, was essentially that of world federalism, another old American idea with roots reaching back to the eighteenth century.[3]

With Mahan the case is somewhat different: invariably invoked, he is seldom quoted, doubtless because his thought was focused on hemispheric defense—"America is our sphere"—and helpful quotations about transpacific expansion are hard to find.[4] It may, indeed, be

---

[2]Josiah Strong, *Our Country*, Jurgen Herbst ed. (Cambridge, Mass., 1963); Dorothea R. Muller, "Josiah Strong and American Nationalism," *JAH*, 53 (1968):487–503; Frederick Merk, *Manifest Destiny and Mission in American History* (New York, 1963), pp. 239–246; and Hollis Read, *The Hand of God in History* (Hartford, 1849). Strong's much-quoted vision of the Anglo-Saxons of North America pressing down upon the southern continent appears to have been merely the conventional wisdom of the day: projecting the historic growth rates of the English- and Spanish-speaking populations of the New World into the twentieth century, the *Britannica* had recently foreseen for the latter a future confined to the hill country, like the Welsh. *Encyclopaedia Britannica*, 9th ed., 1:716–717.

[3]John Fiske, *American Political Ideas Viewed from the Standpoint of Universal History* (New York, 1885), pp. 101–152; Merk, *Manifest Destiny*, p. 239; and Milton Berman, *John Fiske: The Evolution of a Popularizer* (Cambridge, Mass., 1961), 138–140. For some early expressions of the federal idea, see the sources cited in James A. Field, Jr., *America and the Mediterranean World* (Princeton, 1969), pp. 13–15 and 23–24.

[4]Robert Seager II and Doris D. Maguire, eds., *Letters and Papers of Alfred Thayer Mahan* (hereafter Mahan, *Letters and Papers*), 3 vols. (Annapolis, 1975), 2:443, *passim*; and Alfred T. Mahan, *The Interest of America in Sea Power* (Boston, 1897); pp. 261, and 265, and *The Problem of Asia* (Boston, 1900), pp. 7–8. This hemispheric emphasis was lasting: Mahan's war college lectures of the late 1880s, only slightly revised for later publication, focus on isthmus and Caribbean, and consider the Hawaiian Islands in reference to the West Coast. Mahan, *Naval Strategy* (Boston, 1911), *passim*. But historians have not scrupled to invent what they have failed to discover, and one may marvel at the words that have been put into the captain's mouth. Philip S. Foner has stated that in an article in *Harper's Monthly* in October 1897, Mahan called for "expansion of American economic activity in Latin America and Asia," urged aggressive moves into the markets of the Far East, and saw "a clear connection between the Caribbean and the vast market of China . . . , the coaling and cable station system in the Ladrones and Samoa, the Philippines . . ."; "Why the United States Went to War with Spain in 1898," *Science and Society* 32 (1968):57–58. This simply is not true. Mahan's article, "Strategic Features of the Gulf of Mexico and the Caribbean Sea," discussed what the title promised and nothing more; reprinted in Mahan, *Interest of America in Sea Power*, pp. 271–314. For perhaps the best extended discussion of Mahan's influence, see William E. Livezey, *Mahan on Sea Power* (Norman, Okla., 1947). But see, *per contra*, Peter Karsten, "The Nature of 'Influence': Roosevelt, Mahan, and the Concept of Sea Power," *American Quarterly* 23 (1971):585–600. And, for negative evidence, see John D. Long, *The New*

time for a collective rereading of Mahan's pre-1898 writings, although how many will wish to work at length through what Admiral Castex described as a style "particulièrement abstraite et soporifique" is open to question. But such an exercise would find little "imperialism." The feeling that the United States should begin to look outward, "righteously but not with feeble scrupulosity," is matched by the finding that it was disinclined to do so: if, in fact, imperialism was spreading "like wildfire," Mahan did not know it. There is little stress on the expansion of the merchant marine and no concern for projection of power outside the hemisphere. Sea control, it is clearly stated, will never again be as important as during the eighteenth-century wars for empire. Emphasis is given the "aggressive restlessness" of the Europeans, as evidenced in overseas competition, and its implications for the Monroe Doctrine; the danger of possible collision with Britain, Spain, or Germany is raised; some concern is evinced about the awakening Orient. If there is a focus, it is on the strategic importance of the isthmus, and on the consequent need for protective offshore bases and a smallish but efficient navy, competent to defend against the detachments a European power might send against the United States. But the general effect is cloudy, and certainly no clear "imperialistic" plan emerges: reviewing *The Interest of America in Sea Power*, the British army officer George Sydenham Clarke, a great admirer of *The Influence of Sea Power upon History*, found it "extremely difficult to extract a definite meaning from his pages."[5]

It seems possible that one reason for the perdurability of these authors in treatments of this period is their use of the terms "Anglo-Saxon" and "race," in the context of what the twentieth century has done to words like these. But in 1885 there was nothing either very novel or very naughty in this usage. The term "Anglo-Saxon" as an umbrella word for British and Americans was some forty years old. The word "race," as any dictionary will show, can be used in either a biological or a cultural sense, and few contemporaries would have thought that references to the "French race," the "Spanish race," or the "Anglo-Saxon" or "English-speaking" race had anything to do with the vexed question of whether the biological races of mankind numbered five as suggested by Johann Blumenbach, eleven as argued by Charles Pickering, or four as proposed by Thomas Huxley. If talk of the achievements of the "Anglo-Saxon race" seems nowadays a little

---

American Navy (New York, 1903), and Harry Thurston Peck, *Twenty Years of the Republic, 1885–1905* (New York, 1906).

[5]Mahan, *Influence of Sea Power, passim, Interest of America in Sea Power, passim*, and *Letters and Papers, passim*; James A. Field, Jr., "Alfred Thayer Mahan Speaks for Himself," *Naval War College Review* 29 (1976):47–60; and George Sydenham Clarke, "Captain Mahan's Counsels to the United States," *Nineteenth Century* 43 (1898):292–300.

out of style, they could hardly have been overlooked in the 1880s. In extent of imperial sway no country equalled Great Britain, and in territorial growth none the United States. The Industrial Revolution, commenced in England, had leapt the Atlantic to produce a still greater economic expansion. On the scales of civil liberty and representative democracy none could match the British and Americans. Nor had any other societies deployed so many missionaries and mechanics to carry the gift of salvation, whether by conversion or modernization, to those who dwelt in darkness.

On the question of the "Anglo-Saxon race," these authors—though often confusing in their usage—were anything but racist in the anthropological sense. "I use the term," Strong wrote, "somewhat broadly to include all English-speaking peoples." In his approval of the "commingling of races" that was taking place in America, he was at one with the American editor of the *Riverside Natural History* who, in this same *annus mirabilis* of 1885, argued the superiority of mixed stocks, with Darwin and with Mahan (who was very clear on the mixed origins of both British and Americans and who came to include the Japanese within the "European family"). Even Brooks Adams, who fussed a good deal about the international Jewish banking community, thought the survival of civilizations dependent upon the infusion of "barbarian blood."[6]

Since contemporaries, like later historians, may well have read selectively, one should perhaps test the assertions that these authors were influential. Josiah Strong's *Our Country* sold a good many copies over the years, but the book got short shrift from the establishment press and no one has yet named a policymaker influenced by Strong's ideas. John Fiske's histories decorated everyone's library shelves, but *American Political Ideas*, which contained his piece on "'Manifest Destiny,'" was not one of his fastest sellers, and the allegation that he delivered this chapter as a speech to a receptive president and cabinet rests on a misreading of the evidence. Brooks Adams published noth-

---

[6]Strong, *Our Country*, pp. xxi, 202, and 210–211; John S. Kingsley, ed., *The Riverside Natural History* (Boston, 1885), 6:471–472; Charles Darwin, *The Descent of Man* (New York, 1888), p. 142; Mahan, *Problem of Asia*, pp. 147–148 and 193; Brooks Adams, *The Law of Civilization and Decay* (New York, 1898), pp. xi, 362–365, and 383; and Arthur Beringause, *Brooks Adams* (New York, 1955), pp. 119, 132, 141–142, and 178–179. Howard Mumford Jones has some sensible comments on nineteenth-century Anglo-Saxonism (as does Mr. Dooley, whom he quotes); Jones, *The Age of Energy* (New York, 1973), pp. 200–211. On the "racism" of Theodore Roosevelt, see Howard K. Beale, *Theodore Roosevelt and the Rise of America to World Power* (Baltimore, 1956), pp. 26–34. The rhetoric of Fiske and Strong is not our rhetoric, no doubt, but toploftiness is not imperialism. Given the world of the 1880s, there seems nothing very tendentious in their formulations. The basic idea, indeed, would shortly prove persuasive to Frenchmen; see Edmond Demolins, *A quoi tient la superiorité des Anglo-Saxons* (Paris, 1897).

ing on American foreign policy until the summer of 1898.[7] Captain Mahan no doubt deserves some credit for the increased popularity of navies and the arguments for battleships, but his principal effort to influence policy misfired badly: throughout his life he remained convinced that his annexationist article on Hawaii had brought about his transfer by the Cleveland administration from writing and lecturing at the Naval War College to a greatly undesired tour of sea duty.

If the claimed impact of the so-called "imperialist" tracts on either the American people or important figures in government tends to dissolve on inspection, one would still presume that the publicists themselves, if they were in fact concerned with empire, would have turned excitedly to work as the Cuban crisis deepened. Alas, the picture is far otherwise. In the spring of 1898 John Fiske, preoccupied with the preparation of lectures on science and religion, was distressed by the possibility of war.[8] Josiah Strong, like the good reformer he was, was busy founding the League for Social Service. Brooks Adams left Washington for his home in Quincy in August 1897, sailed for Europe in September, and did not return until spring; early in 1898, as war seemed imminent, he wrote his brother Henry, "I am in despair to have this silly business forced on us, where we can gain neither glory nor profit."[9] Ten weeks after the navy had begun a precautionary rede-

---

[7]For a list of his writings, see Thornton Anderson, *Brooks Adams, Conscientious Conservative* (Ithaca, 1951), pp. 229–231. Foner has stated that Adams's *Law of Civilization and Decay* argued the health of imperialism and "advocated American control of the Western hemisphere and economic dominance of Asia"; "Why the United States Went to War," p. 45. It does not. The book starts with the ancient world and ends with nineteenth-century Britain; its subject is "the origin, rise and despotism of the gold-bug"; the United States is barely mentioned. See, in default of the work itself, Anderson, *Brooks Adams*, pp. 50–72; Beringause, *Brooks Adams*, 117–128; and Ernest Samuels, *Henry Adams, The Major Phase* (Cambridge, Mass., 1964), pp. 127–130.

[8]Clarke, *John Fiske*, 2:472–473; and Berman, *Fiske*, pp. 251–252. In December 1897 Fiske wrote an historical introduction for a book by his son-in-law on the Cuban insurrection. Although Anglo-Saxon attitudes pervaded the discussion of the "absolute despotism" of the Spanish Empire and the "Satanic" Inquisition, a strong sympathy for the Cuban cause led to the argument that "for the sake of Cuba's best interests, it is to be hoped that she will win her independence without receiving from any quarter, and especially from the United States, any such favors as might hereafter put her in a position of tutelage. . . ." Grover Flint, *Marching with Gomez* (Boston, 1898), pp. xv and xxvii.

[9]Beringause, *Brooks Adams*, pp. 161–162; and Frederic Cople Jaher, *Doubters and Dissenters* (New York, 1964), p. 173. In these circumstances the elevation of Brooks Adams, whose expansionist efforts were unknown to the generation of Julius W. Pratt, to the rank of principal pre-1898 imperialist, is surely one of the most remarkable developments in recent historical writing. William A. Williams has described him as "something of the chairman of an informal policy-planning staff for the executive department in the years from 1896 to 1908," and Walter LaFeber has stated that Adams, along with Mahan, "exerted more direct influence on policymakers than did any of the other intellectuals," and that "throughout 1897 and early 1898 Adams" saw great opportunities in the coming war with Spain, entertained such important people as Cushman Davis, Lodge, and Mahan at dinners in Washington, and was hailed as a prophet by leading figures of the McKinley administration. Williams, "The Frontier Thesis and American Foreign Policy," *Pacific Historical Review* 24 (1955):387; Williams, *America in a Chang-*

ployment, six weeks after the publication of the De Lôme letter, five weeks after the sinking of the *Maine,* and four weeks after the *Oregon* had been started east, the secretary of the navy appointed Captain Mahan the United States representative at a Florentine celebration in honor of Vespucci and Toscanelli, and on March 26, 1898, America's best-known strategic thinker sailed for Naples. Theodore Roosevelt's old racist teacher, John W. Burgess, prostrated by the events of 1898, turned out to be antiwar, anti-imperialist, and anti-Roosevelt. The greatest of the Social Darwinists, William Graham Sumner, thought the upshot of the war disastrous—*The Conquest of the United States by Spain.*

Yet, whatever the facts about these much-quoted intellectuals, it might still be possible that the 1890s were years of burgeoning sentiment for imperialism and concern for the China market. If so, one would suppose this could be documented by a bureaucratic analysis and by lists of people who really mattered—presidents, secretaries of state or navy, senior military officers, Wall Street giants—who were energetic in the cause. The task has not been easy, notwithstanding the recent boom for Benjamin Harrison and his secretary of the navy, Benjamin F. Tracy, and their very ineffective efforts to gain a naval base on Hispaniola.[10] Faced with a foot-dragging Senate, and lacking both suitable movers and shakers and evidence in party platforms and presidential messages, the convention has been to fall back on Fiske and Strong, on the Omaha *Bee,* on the social thought of Harry Thurston Peck, and on the improbable (or at least highly irrational) desire of farmers for a China market to absorb the surplus. In place of identifiably influential persons or pressure groups, there has developed a usage which suggests the virtue of semantic analysis. Persuasion is attempted by incantation: by the use of reiterated statements that "the imperialists" did this and "the imperialists" did that, that "imperialism spread like wildfire," and that under the prodding of the remarkably faceless "imperialists" the American people went island-grabbing.[11] What generally escapes notice is that, when the anti-imperi-

---

ing World (New York, 1978), p. 38; and LaFeber, *The New Empire,* pp. 80 and 84–85. Foner has added that Henry Adams "worked actively in Washington in favor of intervention in Cuba"; "Why the United States Went to War," p. 45. But Henry was abroad from April 1897 to November 1898 and learned of the loss of the *Maine* while boating on the Nile; Samuels, *Henry Adams,* pp. 185 and 589.

[10]Walter R. Herrick, *The American Naval Revolution* (Baton Rouge, 1966), and B. F. Cooling, *Benjamin Franklin Tracy: Father of the Modern American Fighting Navy* (Hamden, Conn., 1973). For a useful list of influential individuals who did not want war in 1898, see Wayne S. Cole, *An Interpretive History of American Foreign Relations* (Homewood, Ill., 1968), pp. 268–269.

[11]See, for example, Herrick, *Naval Revolution,* pp. 24, 60, 69, 84–87, 90, 103–107, 196, and 220. On the "imperialism" of one of the few identified "imperialists," Henry Cabot Lodge, see John A. S. Grenville and George B. Young, *Politics, Strategy, and American Diplomacy* (New Haven, 1966), pp. 201–238. In general this literature appears to

alists come on stage, there is no problem at all in producing a formidable roster of distinguished citizens—Carl Schurz, E. L. Godkin, William Vaughan Moody, David Starr Jordan, Andrew Carnegie (who briefly thought of personally purchasing and liberating the Philippines but who, regrettably for the exceptionalism of American history, failed to act on this impulse), Mark Twain, William Jennings Bryan—the list goes on and on.[12]

With semantic analysis, in addition to the question of the unidentified "imperialists," other problems appear. It may be proper to speak figuratively of a unitary "American people" after the sinking of the *Maine*, but, given the politics of 1892 and 1896, earlier unqualified use of the phrase seems questionable. A similar problem of precision arises in relation to that naughty minority of "Americans in Hawaii" who were busily conspiring for annexation. For one thing not all were: the most strongly nativist prime minister of the latter years of the Hawaiian kingdom, Walter M. Gibson, had grown up in New York and New Jersey, and the biggest sugar grower, Claus Spreckels, came to oppose annexation. For another, some of these "Americans" had been born and raised in the islands. Is nationality inalienable? Was Albert Gallatin always a Swiss and Andrew Carnegie always a Scot? Was Spreckels a German or an American or a Hawaiian? Despite the obvious goodheartedness of those who inveigh against the Hawaiian annexationists as against the apostles of Anglo-Saxonism, their own usage seems curiously racist.

Another context in which it is useful to remember that words are not things, and to look through the word to the phenomenon for which it stands, is in discussion of navies and naval bases. The creation of the new American navy in the last two decades of the century was an event of undoubted importance, which might, at first glance, seem to provide bureaucratic evidence for an expansionist policy. But navies can be designed for various purposes: there is no necessary connection

---

depend heavily upon code-words ("imperialism," "new empire," "commercial empire," "hegemony," "commercial hegemony of the world," etc.) whose effects seem more emotive than heuristic. For an attractively written example, see Ernest N. Paolino, *The Foundations of American Empire: William Henry Seward and U.S. Foreign Policy* (Ithaca, 1973). Paolino has argued that plans for the rationalization of the world's coinage and the stringing of the international telegraph were intended to bring about (but how?) American "world commercial hegemony"; see, in particular, pages 6, 14, and 25. LaFeber's extensive repetition of the title phrase—*New Empire*—appears to have persuaded many that the concept existed in its own right long before Brooks Adams published his own book with that title in 1902.

[12]For a representative treatment, see the chapter on "Empire Beyond the Seas" in John M. Blum *et al.*, *The National Experience* (3d ed, New York, 1973), pp. 491–506. The terms "imperialist," "imperialists", and "imperialism" appear twenty-one times and eight pre-1898 "imperialists" are named (Strong, Burgess, Fiske, and Mahan constitute half of the contingent); the corresponding terms "anti-imperialist," "anti-imperialists," and "anti-imperialism" are used four times and nineteen individuals are identified.

between naval building and commercial expansion or colonization, and battleships do not equate with empire.[13] The military characteristics of a naval force—the capabilities designed into it—should give some indication of its intended missions; and the reiterated statements of the secretaries to the effect that the New Navy was purely defensive, intended only "as a police force for the preservation of order and never for aggression," are substantiated by the instrument that they created.

Given the limitations of American industry, reinforced as they were by American naval tradition, the first phase of naval revival perforce involved the construction of that "fleet of swift cruisers to prey on the enemy's commerce" desired by Mahan. Here the remoteness of the United States from important European trade routes and from such centers of interest as the River Plate, Valparaiso, and Honolulu strongly affected ship characteristics and by 1890 had brought about the design of cruisers of remarkable coal capacity and endurance. Such ships would seem to have been ideally suited for distant ventures; but, once domestic sources of armor and of castings for gun barrels became available, the emphasis switched to the completion of heavily armed monitors for harbor defense and to construction of "sea-going coastline battleships," restricted in range by congressional enactment and in draft by the hydrography of gulf ports, to contest the control of North American waters. Still further expression of these defensive concerns developed during the 1890s in the authorization of a score of short-range torpedo boats and in the recommendation of 1897—based on the argument that "the traditional policy of our Navy has been a defensive one"—that future units of this type be designed to use the new oil fuel available only at home.[14]

In the early years of the building program the emphasis on commerce raiding and defense of home waters had left the ancient mission of maintaining a presence on such distant stations as the China coast and the River Plate to the wooden ships of the Old Navy. But, as these decayed beyond repair or were washed or blown ashore, replacements

---

[13]Leaving aside the European great powers, eight nations (Argentina, Brazil, Chile, China, Denmark, Greece, Spain, Turkey) had acquired battleships by 1893, while the United States still had none. At least on paper China and Spain were clearly superior in cruiser strength as well. None of these countries showed much sign of expansionist or imperialist policy. *Report of the Secretary of the Navy, 1893.*

[14]On commerce raiders, see Mahan, *Letters and Papers,* 1:593. Mahan emphasized the importance of defense against blockade and bombardment; *Influence of Sea Power,* pp. 83–87. So did Theodore Roosevelt in his review of the book; *Atlantic,* October 1890. Shortly after completion of his term as secretary, Hilary A. Herbert noted that battleship design had been predicated on the assumption of employment close to home, pressed the need for torpedo boats, emphasized the vulnerability of coastal cities and coastal shipping, and pointed to the possibility of collision with Great Britain, with Spain over Cuba, or with Japan over the Hawaiian Islands; "A Plea for the Navy," *Forum* 24 (1897):1–15.

became necessary. Over a period of ten years, beginning in 1885, authorization was secured for a number of new gunboats for this service; and, since coaling stations in these far-off regions existed neither in fact nor in contemplation, the specifications for four of the class of 1895 called for "full sail power." Finally, it may be noted, the New Navy was not, as seems sometimes assumed, the product of a presumably expansionist Republican Party: by 1896 the two Cleveland administrations had gained authorization for half again as much tonnage as had those of Arthur and Harrison.[15]

Related to the naval building question is "the search for bases." Unquestionably, the coming of steam raised serious problems of range and endurance for the world's navies, but solutions to the coal problem varied as widely as the intended employment of the forces to be coaled. A rented site for a coal pile at Yokohama, Honolulu, or Pago Pago was one thing; a defended position like Gibraltar, Aden, or Hong Kong was quite another. When considering the meaning of such terms as "base" and "coaling station," it is well to be as precise as possible, and precision in chronology is also desirable. One should not, for example, use the "magnificent naval base at Pearl Harbor" as evidence of vigorous transpacific expansionism twenty years before anyone dredged the mouth of the Pearl River.[16] And, if the search for bases is to be taken as an index of outward-looking aspiration, it may be well to recognize that the real proliferation of overseas naval facilities came in the 1840s and 1850s, in the period of maritime greatness, when the United States had resident navy agents or naval storekeepers in London, Marseilles, Spezia, Porto Praya, Buenos Aires, St. Thomas, Rio de Janeiro, Lima, Valparaiso, Honolulu, Macao, and Shanghai.[17] Once again, perhaps, the wrong questions are at issue. Is not more to be learned about established national policy by asking not what proposals were made for the

---

[15]*Report of the Secretary of the Navy, 1891, 1895, 1896.* For a convenient listing of naval units with dimensions, armament, coal capacity, and dates of authorization and commissioning, see the *Report* for 1897. It seems hardly necessary to debate the proposition that so costly, continuing, and bipartisan a creation as the New Navy was the product of the status anxiety of junior officers; see Lloyd C. Gardner, Walter F. LaFeber, and Thomas J. McCormick, *Creation of the American Empire* (Chicago, 1973), pp. 206–207.

[16]LaFeber, *The New Empire*, p. 141, *passim.* Herrick has American ships (and even Captain Togo in HIJMS *Naniwa*) entering Pearl Harbor in the years before the War with Spain; *American Naval Revolution*, pp. 105, 168, 199–200, and 221. But the limiting depth at the mouth of the Pearl River was two fathoms, the House rejected an appropriation for dredging in 1897, funds did not become available until 1908, and the first major ship entered only in 1911. See Willis E. Snowbarger, "The Development of Pearl Harbor" (Ph.D. dissertation, University of California, Berkeley, 1950).

[17]Equally, one should not automatically equate the "New Navy" of the 1890s with a big navy: the total personnel strength of 1897 (11,985) was only 7 percent greater than that of 1845 (11,189), although the U.S. population had more than tripled. Bureau of the Census, *Historical Statistics of the United States, Colonial Time to 1957* (Washington, 1960), pp. 7 and 736–737.

acquisition of coaling stations in the Caribbean or elsewhere, but rather why so little came of them? Why were the possibilities dangled at various times by Portuguese, Danes, Liberians, Peruvians, and Koreans not accepted? Why was so little done before the War with Spain to turn such available sites as Pearl Harbor and Pago Pago to strategic advantage? Why, indeed, was Pacific base development so slow after 1898?

Allied to the semantic question is the cartographic one: just as words are not things, a map is not the country it represents. In the late nineteenth century, the map was the same color from sea to shining sea, but the United States was, as it had always been, an Atlantic nation: on a Mercator world it belong functionally at the left and not in the center. The frontier may have shaped the American character, but, whatever the history of the West Coast fur trade and of the California clippers, the United States remained an eastward-facing country. Despite the recorded aspirations of Pacific railway promoters and the later assertions of historians, the Far East was not a farther West. Aspiration was less substantial than geographic and economic reality.

For this assertion some evidence may be adduced. The *Empress of China* and a number of other American merchantmen had reached Canton by way of the Cape of Good Hope before Robert Gray arrived in the *Columbia* from the West Coast. American naval ships operated in the Indian Ocean long before the first one entered the Pacific. The sequence of commercial treaty negotiations with nonwestern societies proceeded eastward, from the Barbary powers to Turkey and thence to Muscat and Siam. Edmund Roberts went out by way of the Cape of Good Hope, and so did Caleb Cushing and Matthew C. Perry and Robert W. Shufeldt. The missionary effort indubitably had profound impact in Hawaii, but its first target had been India and its greatest efforts, until late in the century, were devoted to India and the Near East.[18] The big export-import trade was Atlantic in orientation, the product of the eastern concentration of population, wealth, and industry and of the receptivity of European markets to the torrent of agricultural exports that developed in the 1880s. Tenuously connected by rail with the eastern metropolis, the mountain and Pacific states contained in 1890 less than 5 percent of the nation's population. Of the 5 percent of total exports that emanated from the Pacific coast, a considerable portion consisted of grain bound eastward to Europe. Strategically, the same was true: Europe, the traditional enemy, lay to the eastward, and European island bases watched the eastern seaboard; in the 1880s, with memories of the French in Mexico still green, the subdivision of Africa

---

[18]James A. Field, Jr., "Near East Notes and Far East Queries," in *The Missionary Enterprise in China and America*, John K. Fairbank, ed., (Cambridge, Mass., 1974), pp. 25–26 and 31–38.

drew fresh attention to European capabilities, while the British occupation of Egypt and the presence of Ferdinand De Lesseps in Panama emphasized what attractive nuisances isthmuses could become. The existence of a perceived threat to the Atlantic coastline was evident in the Endicott Board's report on fortifications, the design and deployment of the New Navy, and to concern for Caribbean base facilities.[19]

In the Pacific and eastern Asia, by contrast, the position of the United States was marginal. Captain David Porter's early inspired admission of the inhabitants of Nukahiva to the "great American family" had been permitted to lapse, as had Perry's initiatives regarding Port Lloyd and Formosa. Against the annexation of archipelagos commenced by the French in 1842, the British in 1874, the Japanese in 1876, and the Germans in 1884, the United States could show only uninhabited and undredged Midway, some claims to guano islands, paper base rights at an unusable Pearl Harbor, and a share in the tripartite administration of Samoa. In China, it is true, the 1880s saw the missionary movement enter a period of remarkable growth, but in commercial matters the American position was weakening. China trade as a percentage of total foreign commerce had been declining since the 1840s, as trade with Europe grew and as Forbeses and Delanos, reacting to the lack of Asiatic investment opportunity, shifted their assets and energies from the treaty ports to western railroads. In commercial and political geography, moreover, the United States had suffered a considerable setback with the opening of the Suez Canal. Prior to 1869, when the route to the Far East was by way of the Cape of Good Hope, New York and Liverpool had been roughly equidistant from China, but now the Europeans were closer by the length of the Atlantic crossing. Although this situation provided southern textile exporters and their representatives in Congress with strong arguments for an isthmian canal, such a facility would be long in coming. For the balance of the nineteenth century European pressures on the Far East grew steadily, but until the Battle of Manila Bay American pressures did not.

The Atlantic orientation of the United States was quite naturally reflected in the distribution of American-owned merchant shipping, whether of domestic or foreign registry. Of the former there was of course not much, and the postwar failure to restore the country's maritime greatness went far to justify Mahan's pessimism about "The United States Looking Outward," and his original choice of title for

---

[19]For concern about European economic and political ambitions in the Western Hemisphere, see David M. Pletcher, *The Awkward Years: American Foreign Relations under Garfield and Arthur* (Columbia, Mo., 1962), pp. 129–134, *passim*. As early as 1880 Mahan had predicted that the prospect of an isthmian canal would require "a very large Navy . . . [or] we may as well shut up about the Monroe doctrine at once"; *Letters and Papers*, 1:482. Ten years later he pinned his hopes for "the motive, if any there be, which will give the United States a navy" upon the isthmus; *Influence of Sea Power*, p. 88.

his article of 1890s, "The United States Asleep." In the Atlantic, nevertheless, efforts at subsidized shipping lines had brought modest results in the establishment of continuous scheduled services with gulf and Caribbean ports and intermittent service with Brazil. "Whitewashed" iron and steel steamship tonnage—American-owned but under foreign registry—was also concentrated in the Atlantic. On the West Coast success was more limited. There, in 1865, the Pacific Mail Steamship Line had been granted a subsidy for monthly service to the Far East. The company's ships, which originally sailed via Hawaii, were soon shifted to the shorter and more economical northern route, with the result that in 1867 the North Pacific Transportation Company received a subsidy for a one-ship service between San Francisco and Honolulu. Such exiguous connections with the islands and the Orient seemed all the traffic would justify. Both lines found greater profit and employed more ships on coastal runs between Panama, Mazatlan, San Francisco, and Puget Sound.[20]

If, indeed, an expanding merchant marine is seen as an index of imperialistic tendencies, these were far less evident in the United States than elsewhere in the Pacific basin. In the Hawaiian Kingdom, of such small interest to American shipping interests, a period of insular expansionism brought the founding in 1881 of J.D. Spreckels's Oceanic Line, connecting Honolulu with San Francisco and reaching southwest to the Antipodes. The completion of the Canadian Pacific Railroad in 1885 was quickly followed by the establishment of subsidized steamship service between Vancouver and Hong Kong. But the truly important developments in Pacific shipping were those of the "insular imperialists" of Japan. In 1890 the 94,000-ton total of Japanese steam tonnage was less than half that which the United States employed in international trade, but with the commencement of state subsidies in that year the Japanese merchant marine entered a period of explosive growth. By 1896 service had been established with China, the East Indies, Australia, San Francisco, and Seattle, and by 1900 the 543,000 tons of Japanese-flag steam tonnage totalled more than half again that of the United States. The contrast between this achievement and the difficulties that beset the McKinley administration in finding ships to carry troops to the Philippines (as indeed the contrast in end-of-the-century transpacific population movements) may serve as an indication of which Pacific power was outward-looking.

The United States Navy in the 1890s was equally an East Coast Atlantic-oriented institution. In the outward-looking antebellum days,

---

[20]The superior attractions of the North Atlantic were strikingly demonstrated, even after the War with Spain had brought presumed Pacific opportunity, in the creation by J. P. Morgan of the International Mercantile Marine Co., the world's largest privately owned fleet, which in 1902 controlled 136 ships totalling more than a million gross tons, all in the Atlantic.

when American merchant shipping covered the globe, the navy had maintained six overseas cruising stations—Mediterranean, Pacific, West Indies, South Atlantic, East Indies, and African—to which the bulk of its active units was assigned. With the end of the Civil War this traditional practice was resumed, "irreflectively," as Mahan later wrote, and by 1872 the Asiatic Squadron, successor to the old East Indies Squadron, had been brought up to a strength of eleven ships, more than a quarter of the total deployed on distant stations. But this return to the ancient ways—also reflected in the concern of Secretary of State William M. Evarts and Secretary of the Navy Richard W. Thompson for foreign markets, in naval interest in the Amazon and Congo basins, Zanzibar, and Korea, and in Secretary of the Navy William E. Chandler's call of 1883 for coaling stations everywhere—ended with the 1880s. The last years of the century witnessed an initial compartmentalization of the world in terms of naval power as the rivalries of the industrialized nations, the range limitations that accompanied the shift to steam, and the logistical and material requirements of modern warships brought a retirement of the world's navies upon their home bases.

This development, most strikingly epitomized in the Royal Navy's redeployment of 1904–05, had become apparent in the distribution of the United States fleet well before the War with Spain. With the shift to coal and the focus on the European threat, talk of markets and bases gave way in the reports of the secretaries to emphasis on foreign building programs and concern for the safety of the hemisphere. Since the coming of steam had given a new predictability to the movements of ships and squadrons, there also followed the first efforts at rational war planning. At the infant Naval War College the focus was on "what is necessary for a state of war," and early sessions concentrated on the study of Atlantic trade routes in preparation for efficient commerce raiding. In 1890 Captain Mahan was called to Washington to draw up contingency plans for hostilities with Great Britain or Spain; the possibility of a German takeover of Dutch possessions in the Western Hemisphere also excited concern. Starting in 1894, as the new battleships began to come into commission, the war college's annual problems focused on the defense of the Atlantic Coast, its lectures and war games emphasized the strategic geography of gulf and Caribbean, and its studies international law dealt with such matters as the defense of the Hawaiian Kingdom against foreign aggression and the maintenance of the neutrality of an isthmian canal.[21]

---

[21]The *Reports of the Secretary of the Navy* in the years from 1877 to 1887 stressed trade expansion, overseas bases, and the problem of the merchant marine; after 1889 the emphasis shifted to the defense of coastal cities. Mahan, *Letters and Papers*, 1:444; for his 1890 "Contingency Plan of Operations in Case of War with Great Britain" and his comments on a plan of 1895 (after the first battleships had been commissioned), see

Together with the new technology, these concerns governed the deployment of the New Navy. Despite the continuing problems of the China coast, the west coast of Latin America, the Bering Sea seal fisheries, Samoa, and Hawaii, the new steel ships were assigned in the first instance to the North Atlantic Squadron. The first modern warship to serve on the West Coast, the small cruiser *Charleston,* joined the Pacific Squadron only in the 1890s, and the show of force that followed the Chilean crisis was provided by units drawn from the Atlantic. Not until 1892, by which time eight protected cruisers had been commissioned, did the first new ship, the 900-ton gunboat *Petrel,* join the Asiatic Squadron. By 1897 the North Atlantic Squadron contained by far the largest concentration of available force. Compared with four first- and second-rates in the eastern Pacific and two in the Asiatic Squadron, the North Atlantic had ten; and, since these included five of the six battleships and both armored cruisers, the disproportion in fighting strength was far greater than the mere number of ships suggests.

The limited forces assigned to the Pacific and Asiatic Squadrons hardly seem indicative of a forward policy. Such a policy, in any event, would not have been easy. The coming of steam had made the geography of coal and of coaling stations a question of prime strategic interest. The developed coal mines of the United States were in the East, and hopes of Alaskan coal deposits to ease the West Coast naval problem had not been fulfilled. Indeed, throughout the Pacific basin the supply of coal was effectively a British monopoly. The needs of the Hawaiian islands had traditionally been filled by sailing ships from England, and the important new regional sources, Vancouver Island and New South Wales, were also British. American base facilities to mitigate the magnificent distances of the Pacific were lacking, and few seemed to care. The capabilities of West Coast navy yards were limited; the Hawaiian request for annexation had been rejected; and Pearl Harbor and Pago Pago remained undeveloped. The Asiatic Squadron was, in fact, an eastward projection of an Atlantic-facing country, and one greatly attenuated by distance. For materiel it depended on the New York Navy Yard, and its units traditionally proceeded to their duty stations by way of the Mediterranean and Suez, a passage extraordinarily vulnerable to European interference. With the German seizure of Tsingtao in 1897, the Asiatic Squadron became the only naval force in the Far East without a local base of its own. The consequences of being so far out at the end of the line can be seen in Dewey's coal and

---

ibid., 3:559–576, 2:425–428; and for his assessment of the German threat, see *ibid.,* 2:27, 37–38, and *Interest of America in Sea Power,* pp. 15 and 294–295. For visual evidence of the central strategic concerns, see the painting by Rufus Zogbaum, which shows the war college class of 1894 gaming the defense of an East Coast harbor (apparently Narragansett Bay) before a large wall chart of the Gulf and Caribbean; *Harper's Weekly,* 39 (1895):149.

ammunition problems and in the fact that when war came he not only had to destroy a fleet but also had to capture a harbor. These problems had been visible long before the war; they were reflected in the limited nature of the force that was maintained in Asiatic waters for the protection of American interests. In 1898 the Asiatic Squadron was outgunned by British, Russian, German, and Japanese forces in the area. Against a dozen major Japanese units, the United States boasted two— hardly an armament with which to go adventuring so far from home.

But where does all this leave us? If we rule out the conventional wisdom about Darwin, the psychic crisis of imperialism, the New Navy, and the Pacific highway to Asia, what remains? What was, in fact, the nature of American relations with the outer world between the end of Reconstruction and the War with Spain?

Generally, it may be said, these relations were far more individual than governmental. As the wounds of war healed, an extraordinarily energetic society deployed its representatives abroad in a wide variety of roles: explorers, tourists, art collectors, philanthropists, missionaries, synarchists, railroad promoters, and mining engineers. Although much of this activity was sufficiently traditional, its scale and impact were increasing as a result of the remarkable economic development of these years, itself evidenced externally in three important and interconnected ways: the growth of North Atlantic trade and the progressive integration of the North Atlantic economic community; the spillover of American enterprise into Canada, Mexico, and the Caribbean; and the beginnings of direct investment abroad. From these developments, Asia (especially China) was largely excluded: except for the skills of synarchists—half-missionary and half-mercenary in motivation—and the export of Christian truth, it was primarily a source of imports, not a market, and only the missionary effort grew significantly in the years before 1898.[22]

But, it may be objected, there were all those naval and diplomatic incidents of the 1880s and 1890s. Did these not constitute the preseason warm-up for imperialism and the projection of national power? Here two points may be noted. First, most of these incidents, like the greater part of the naval modernization program, took place in the administrations of the anti-imperialistic Cleveland, the same president

---

[22]For useful information on overseas activities in the 1880s, see Milton Plesur, *America's Outward Thrust* (DeKalb, Ill., 1971). Also see Merle Curti and Kendall Birr, *Prelude to Point Four* (Madison, Wis., 1954); and Mira Wilkins, *The Emergence of Multinational Enterprise* (Cambridge, Mass., 1970). For a valuable and much neglected regional treatment, see J. Fred Rippy, *Latin America and the Industrial Age* (New York, 1944). On synarchy, see John K. Fairbank, "Synarchy under the Treaties," in his *Chinese Thought and Institutions* (Chicago 1957), pp. 204–231; and James A. Field, Jr., "Transnationalism and the New Tribe," *International Organization* 25 (1971):353–372. On the growth of missions, see Field, "Near East Notes," pp. 34–38.

who resisted the treaty provision for base rights at Pearl Harbor, refused to participate in the Berlin agreement on the Congo, withdrew
the Hawaiian treaty of annexation, and declined to intervene in China
or in Turkey on behalf of the Armenians. The Harrison administration
did, it is true, conclude the Samoan treaty of 1889, mount an unsuccessful search for Caribbean bases, and support Hawaiian efforts at annexation; but its liveliest accomplishment was to preside over the consequences of the riot in the True Blue Saloon, and few have suggested
that the United States contemplated the annexation of Chile. By contrast, the first Cleveland administration handled the first years of the
Samoan fuss and carried out the Panama landings of 1885; the second
managed the Brazilian intervention, the Corinto business, and the Venezuela boundary affair. Second, since most American naval inter-
ventions occurred in the Western Hemisphere and involved a real or
presumed European presence, it would seem reasonable to see them as
reflecting the same Monroeist (and Mahanist) strategy that governed
the design and deployment of the New Navy. The importance of the
Brazil trade, which greatly exceeded that with China, may be conceded, but Valparaiso, Corinto, and Caracas were hardly regions of any
very impressive "new empire" economic interest at the time.

All this having been said, it is nevertheless still possible to find a
persuasive linkage among economic activity, accelerating diplomacy,
and naval demonstrations. To do this one must move again beyond
economics and ideology to the generally neglected area of technological capabilities and consider, along with the consequences of steam
propulsion, the revolution in communications that occurred with the
coming of ocean cables. As these progressively joined together the already existing regional telegraph nets, those in the Western world who
possessed the requisite skills and inclinations found it possible to administer modernity, public or private, at previously unheard-of distances. Without this development, it seems proper to suggest, the
world would not have witnessed the late-nineteenth-century growth
of multinational enterprise, the particular kind of reactive and competitive European imperialism that marked the 1880s and 1890s, or the
rash of international crises of the closing years of the century.

Despite the traditional prominence of the name of Cyrus Field, this
wiring of the world was, like so much of nineteenth-century history,
primarily a British accomplishment. The principal inventions were
British, gutta percha for cable insulation was a British imperial monopoly, in techniques of cable manufacture the British were far in the lead,
and only in Britain was investment capital available on the required
scale. Logically enough, then, the progress of long-range communications reflected the image of the world held by those looking outward
from London. The Dover-Calais cable of 1851 was soon followed by
other links to Europe. The Crimean War brought the extension of the

overland telegraph, first to Balaclava and then to Constantinople. In 1865 Bombay and the Indian telegraph system was connected with that of Europe. In 1866 the Atlantic cable joined the European and North American telegraph nets. In 1870 an all-British cable route to India was opened, and in the next year Japan and the China coast were tied in, both landline across Siberia and by cable via India, Singapore, and Saigon.

By the early 1870s, then, much of the world had been linked. When everything was working well, a telegram could be sent (albeit by way of London and at great expense) from San Francisco to Tokyo. But there were as yet no connections with interior China, with Africa south of Egypt, or with Latin America south of the Caribbean; and no cable yet spanned the Pacific. Not unnaturally, given their predominance in communications technology and international trade, it was the British who took the first great steps to link up the southern continents, with cables from Portugal to Brazil in 1874, and down the East African coast to Durban in 1879. But, while the British were progressively tying together what seemed important to them, one American looking outward from New York was connecting up the Western Hemisphere. So now, if we need an "imperialist," or at least an individual who worked purposefully and effectively with Wall Street backing to increase his countrymen's capabilities abroad, we can have one. He is curiously absent from books on the "new empire," but he did exist. His name was James A. Scrymser.

Scrymser, in 1865, organized the International Ocean Telegraph Company. Two years later, armed with franchises from Congress and Spain and with support from Secretary of State William H. Seward, he entered the Caribbean with a line from Florida to Havana. But further accomplishments in this area were frustrated by British competition and corporate infighting and there followed a change in aim. In 1878–79 Scrymser established, with financial backing from J. P. Morgan and other leaders of the New York financial community, the Mexican Telegraph Company and the Central and South American Telegraph Company and directed his efforts southward toward the west coast of South America. Mexico City was linked with Galveston in March 1881; by October 1882, the line had reached Lima with stops at various Central American way stations; in 1883 a Brazilian connection was established; in 1890 the cable was extended to Valparaiso, and in the next year the purchase of a trans-Andean telegraph line gave access to Argentina. The result of Scrymser's work was to make possible rapid communication between the United States and South America without having to route messages through London and Lisbon and with consequent greater speed, greater security, and diminished cost.[23]

---

[23]The attractiveness of Scrymser's venture as compared to contemporary Chinese promotional schemes, may be seen in the ease with which he gained financial backing

Since the British were a nation of shopkeepers and the business of America was business, the purpose of the international cable net was to facilitate the work of the world and its geography reflected existing economic interest. But, as duplicate cables were laid on major routes, word-saving business codes were developed, and costs went down, the new technology took on its own creative role. With their lines eastward to Hong Kong and Shanghai, and across the South Atlantic to Brazil, the British enhanced their regional economic positions. In the Western Hemisphere the pattern of the American economic spillover largely replicated that of the telecommunications network. Increasingly, the successors of William Wheelwright and Henry Meiggs found themselves under the control of the home office—as was soon shown by the transfer of control of the Grace enterprises from Lima to New York in the 1880s and the appearance of two Grace brothers as members of Scrymser's board of directors. In the transatlantic context, where earlier attempts by American manufacturers to establish plants in Great Britain had failed, the years after 1866 brought routine success; as London became more and more the hub of world cable communications, firms such as Singer and Eastman Kodak increasingly entrusted the administration of Eastern Hemisphere business to their British branches.

In the Pacific the story was very different: there another history of nonaccomplishment further emphasized the marginal nature of American interest. The Collins overland telegraph project had been killed off by the Atlantic cable. In 1870 Admiral David D. Porter urged a Pacific cable, a recommendation repeated by the Congress in 1873 and subsequently by Presidents Grant, Hayes, Cleveland, and Harrison, but to no avail. In Australia interest began to be evident in 1877 and in Canada soon after; in 1894 British imperial concern brought an abortive attempt to annex Necker Island in the Hawaiian chain as a relay station for a cable between Vancouver and the Antipodes. But, despite these signs of British interest and though the Hawaiians granted franchises in 1891 and 1895, though the navy made a hydrographic survey for a Hawaiian cable in 1891–92, though the Hawaiian commissioners urged action in 1893, and though Scrymser organized a Pacific Cable Company in 1896, nothing was done. By 1898 there were twelve active North Atlantic cables, nine of them duplex, and Scrymser had doubled up his South American lines five years before, but no action had yet been taken to span the Pacific.

Although economic interests had shaped the ocean cable network,

---

and in his weighty board of directors, which included, in addition to J. P. Morgan, such worthies as John E. Alexandre (steamships), William R. and Michael P. Grace (South American trade and finance), Henry L. Higginson (banking), Charles Lanier (banking, railroads), and Richard W. Thompson (secretary of the navy, French Panama Canal Company).

the blessings of rapid communications transcended the economic sphere. Capabilities are often as determining as intentions—as Mahan once observed," 'Can,' as well as 'will,' plays a large part in the decisions of life"—and the capability that now existed could be employed in various ways. The new speed of communication, combined with technological advances in printing and papermaking, gave rise to a revolution in journalism and ushered in the great age of the war correspondent, a profession in which such Americans as Januarius Aloysius MacGahan and Richard Harding Davis early attained high place. In countries afflicted with high literacy rates there developed an attentive audience for latter nineteenth-century theatrics—the Crimea, the Nile quest, the Bulgarian Horrors, the Armenian massacres, the sinking of the *Maine*—whose response in times of crisis constituted a new burden for their governments. Compared to the consequences of modern technology and universal education, the contributions of Charles Darwin to jingoism appear small.

There were also more direct consequences for the foreign offices of the world. When information previously transmitted in intermittent chunks could move in a steady flow, and when dispatches that once took weeks or months in transit could now arrive in hours, a wholly new tempo of diplomatic activity developed. The apparent virtue of the quick response, as a means of increasing pressure on the French to withdraw from Mexico, led Seward to run up an enormous cable bill. In the *Virginius* affair of 1873, Scrymser's line to Havana and the preexisting connections by way of London with Madrid and Mediterranean ports gave Hamilton Fish the country's first experience in "crisis management" and permitted the speedy recall of the European Squadron. From this time on the lives of secretaries of state would never be quite the same, and March 7, 1867, the date of appointment of the department's first telegrapher, may perhaps be taken as the date of origin of the "new paradigm" of diplomacy that developed as the century wore on.[24]

A final important consequence of the extension of ocean cables was the increased speed of naval movements. The revolution in propulsion that had imposed upon navies new base requirements and new limitations of range had also enabled them to steam upwind and in calm. Now, as consuls and ministers could cable for help and govern-

---

[24]Compared to same or next-day delivery by cable, late-nineteenth-century surface mail transit time for State Department dispatches was on the order of ten days to three weeks for Western Europe, three to four weeks for Russia, a month to six weeks for Argentina, Brazil, and Chile, and upwards of six weeks for East Asia. Department of State, Instructions and Despatches, *passim*. Seward's dispatch of November 23, 1866, which cost $13,000 and took two days to decipher, was the wonder of the Parisian diplomatic corps. Fish had made brief use of the cable in the Cuban incident of 1869; in the *Virginius* affair its employment was central.

ments could cable orders, a wholly new speed of response developed. In 1861 the European Squadron did not reach New York until two and a half months after the firing on Fort Sumter. When summoned back in 1873 at the time of the *Virginius* crisis, it was home in five weeks; and from this time to the Boxer Rebellion a series of unprecedentedly quick arrivals of outside military forces hastened the course of history. The strategic significance of the submarine telegraph was early appreciated: by the late 1870s the Admiralty had cable communication with all important British overseas naval stations; in 1890, in his contingency plan for war with Britain, Captain Mahan called for an immediate cutting of the Halifax-Bermuda cable.[25] The importance of Scrymser's contribution to American capabilities in these matters can be seen in a comparison of the dilatory course of surface-mail diplomacy and the freedom of local initiative that marked the Samoan and Hawaiian questions with the rapid reaction to events in Panama, Chile, Brazil, and Nicaragua and the degree of central control maintained over these demonstrations.

The responses of the United States government to these events in Latin America were, one may say, defensive in nature, comporting with the fears expressed by Secretary of the Navy Tracy of "the aggressive policy of foreign nations" and of the political threat posed by "the establishment of complete commercial supremacy by a European power in any state in the Western Hemisphere." They were part of intended American policy in a way in which the island conquests of 1898 were not. But when events in Cuba wrenched American policy into a new path, the new technology proved of governing importance in the conduct of what an accomplished army officer subsequently described as a war of "coal and cables." Starting in January 1898, cabled despatches were employed to accomplish a preliminary redeployment of the navy. Cable connections with the Far East (by way of London) carried the orders to Dewey to concentrate his force, keep full of coal, and proceed against the Philippines. A new cable from Hong Kong to Manila forewarned Admiral Montojo and permitted him to gather his ships in shoal water, but no cable yet reached Guam, where the garrison was taken by surprise.[26]

---

[25]Field, *Mediterranean World*, pp. 305 and 333–334; and Arthur Hezlet, *The Electron and Seapower* (London, 1975), p. 9. The first instance of continuous governmental control of a distant operation was the bombardment of Alexandria in 1882, when a British cable ship grappled the line from Malta and set up in business offshore. Even more than the fuel question, the problems of communications technology tend to be slighted by naval historians: the anatomists of sea power concentrate on bone and muscle to the neglect of the alimentary and nervous systems.

[26]George O. Squier, "The Influence of Submarine Cables upon Military and Naval Supremacy," *U.S. Naval Institute Proceedings* 26 (1900):599; French E. Chadwick, *The Relations of the United States and Spain: The Spanish-American War*, 2 vols. (New York, 1911), 1:3–5. Tribolet, *Electrical Communications*, pp. 155 and 245.

Energetically carrying out his orders, Dewey dispensed with the Spanish squadron and captured the harbor he had to have. In the American press the cabled reports of the battle produced a victory so famous that the politicians could hardly disown it, while the fact, made possible by these same cables' annihilation of distance, that Manila Bay preceded the Cuban landings by six weeks and the Battle of Santiago by two months, worked powerfully to focus public attention on the Far East. Now, at last, an "avalanche" of speeches, editorials, articles, and books did descend upon the American people. "Imperialism," we may say, was the product of Dewey's victory.[27]

It should be emphasized, however, that results had little to do with intentions. Faced with the problem of how to employ the Asiatic Squadron in the event of war with Spain, the naval planners had given no automatic priority to the Philippines. Among the possibilities considered in the year before the outbreak of hostilities was the withdrawal of these units westward to join in an attack on the Canaries. Even after Manila became the settled objective, the aim was merely to gain leverage to pry Spain out of Cuba and to acquire security for the payment of an indemnity. The role reversal that found the Spanish giving up the islands and the United States doing the paying had occurred to none: in the words of the distinguished naval officer who wrote the history of the war, "Perhaps none were more surprised to find a great archipelago at their command than were the gentlemen composing the administration in Washington."[28]

Lamenting the "Great Aberration," Samuel Flagg Bemis once echoed McKinley's observation that, if only "old Dewey" had sailed along home after the battle, it would have saved much subsequent complication. It is in many ways an appealing thought, but to have done so would have been to abandon a war that had barely begun and to forego that "inducement" to Spain to leave Cuba that had been the

---

[27]Richard W. Leopold, *The Growth of American Foreign Policy* (New York, 1962), pp. 150–152 and 180–183; and Walter Millis, *The Martial Spirit* (Boston, 1931), pp. 174–177 and 195–199. Since naval officers are often grouped with the "imperialists," it may be worth noting that Dewey never recommended retention of the Philippines. A practical man, he wondered why, if colonies were indeed desired, the United States did not look to such handy locations as Mexico or Central America.

[28]Grenville and Young, *Politics, Strategy, and Diplomacy*, pp. 267–296; Chadwick, *Spanish-American War*, 1:90–91, 154, 208; 2:472–473. Mahan later wrote that the aim of the war had been "to enforce the departure" of Spain from Cuba, commented on the surprising fact that trouble in Cuba had led onward to Asia, noted that the expansionist vision had never reached beyond Hawaii, observed that the Philippines had never previously risen above his "mental horizon," and attributed the outcome to the will of God. "The War on the Sea and Its Lessons, I: How the Motive of the War Gave Direction to its Earlier Movements," *McClure's Magazine* 12 (1898):110–118, *Problem of Asia*, pp. 7 and 11, and *Letters and Papers*, 2:566, 579–580, 619. To the financial writer Charles A. Conant it seemed that traditional issues had suddenly been "tinged with a strange, new light by the flash of Dewey's guns in the Bay of Manila"; *The United States in the Orient* (Boston, 1900), p. 226.

object of the move against the Philippines. Yet, while departure was unthinkable, to remain was impossible without support from home. As Dewey swung around the anchor in Manila Bay, his ammunition depleted, his communications dependent upon British goodwill, and with an hourly diminishing coal supply, McKinley ordered forth a collier, a cruiser, two monitors, and some army troops.[29] This effort at reinforcement underlined once again the marginal American position in the Pacific. The eastward transfer of army forces for the campaign in Cuba had reduced the strength of the Department of California to 25 officers and 418 men and had stripped the Pacific Coast of arms and ammunition. The *Oregon* had been sent east and the cruiser *Charleston*, laid up at Mare Island, had yet to be reactivated. To obtain the twenty merchant ships required for the summer's troop movements, it proved necessary to threaten seizure of some and to transfer others from the Atlantic and from foreign flags. The logistics of the transpacific effort depended upon the enthusiastic unneutrality of the Hawaiian Republic. But, once the troops did reach the Philippines, they stayed; and the problems of administering so distant a dependency brought forth the single preplanned insular annexation of the period, as Wake Island was taken as a landing station for the now-imperative American Pacific cable.

Returning finally to the "worst chapter," we may conclude that much of it is wrong and most of it irrelevant to "imperialism" and the events of 1898.[30] The New Navy was a defensive answer to European

---

[29]Dewey's victory gave rise to novel and difficult problems in the areas of coal and communications. Since the Spanish refused him use of the Manila-Hong Kong cable, his telegraphic dispatches to Washington had first to travel by ship to Hong Kong. The need to fuel *McCulloch* for the round trip (since coal for warlike use was contraband and only on condition of immediately heading homeward could any of his ships have coaled in neutral ports) was in part responsible for the delayed transmission of his action report. Prior to 1898 the British had worried about the vulnerability of their worldwide cable system; since transmission by a neutral of belligerent dispatches raised serious problems of international law, the Americans (and doubtless others) had worried about British control of the world cable network. Learning of Dewey's isolation, Scrymser at once offered to lay a new cable between Hong Kong and Manila with financing by J. P. Morgan, but the proposal was refused by London. The British at Hong Kong did, however, accept Dewey's dispatches under the fiction that the traffic was nonmilitary; it is interesting to speculate on his position had they refused to bend the rules. The five-day minimum reply time imposed by the need to communicate by ship with the Asiatic mainland complicated dealings with Aguinaldo and von Diederichs and made the situation in Manila Bay (as in Samoa and Hawaii) one where central control was diminished and events tended to take charge.

[30]It sometimes seems as difficult to discover the "very heart of contemporary revisionism" as it is to elucidate the message of Mahan. If it is that after 1898 American policymakers sought to preserve a "long-term option" in China, one can hardly argue: that is what sensible policymakers try to do. But if, regarding the War with Spain, the "central question" turns on the contention that the acquisition of the Philippines was "the product of a conscious, pragmatic effort to provide . . . integrated, protectible trade routes across the Pacific," the policy seems irrational, the argument dubious, and the evidence lacking. Thomas J. McCormick, "American Expansion in China," *AHR* 75

developments; its deployment reflected a shrunken rather than an enlarged strategic perimeter. The "search for bases" was a response to the strategic problems of isthmus, Caribbean, and eastern Pacific. Neither missionary work nor burgeoning exports nor the beginnings of foreign investment called for the extension of political control. The ideologists, so selectively quoted by posterity, were of negligible importance. What Americans, whether travellers or missionaries or businessmen, wanted of the outer world was the freedom to pursue happiness, to do their thing, to operate insofar as possible unhindered by arbitrary power or obsolete ideas. Proud of their own self-determined independence, they were sympathetic to similar desires on the part of Samoan chiefs, Korean kings, Egyptian khedives, Armenian Christians, Brazilians, Venezuelans, and Chinese. Most of all, because they were nearest and most visible and noisiest, it was the Cubans who engaged this sympathy.

Such traditional aims and attitudes had little to do with any "new American spirit," or with Asiatic markets, or with "insular imperialism." The western Pacific acquisitions, which opened a new era of American history, were in one sense the product of the new technological developments; in another, they can be seen as historical "accidents." If the British had kept the Philippines after the Seven Years' War, the War with Spain would have been confined to the Atlantic. If the Filipinos had been happy under Spanish rule (or if the Asiatic Squadron had been sent against the Canaries), this rule might well have continued. If Spain had either pacified or given up Cuba, there would have been no war; perhaps, indeed, war might have been averted had the *Maine* not been sent to Havana.[31] If this was indeed the case (and unless a conspiracy theory is at once developed on the basis of

---

(1970):1394–1396. What is an "integrated" trade route? Why across the Pacific? The American import-export community was in the East, and the China trade was an Atlantic trade. The route westward from New York was shorter, and faster for passengers (like Commodore Dewey, going out to his new command) and mail. But for freight it involved 3,000 miles of high-cost railroad carriage followed by the transit of an ocean where shipping was scarce and coal much more expensive than on the Atlantic-Suez route. As to whether this route was "protectible," the question is, against whom? Nobody ever solved the problem of the defense of the Philippines. In the early years they seemed vulnerable to German attack; as late as 1911 Mahan conceded to Japan the capability of bagging the Philippines, Guam, and Hawaii and landing on the West Coast before the battle fleet could reach the scene of action. For an interesting visual aid, which may have encouraged latter-day geopolitical misconception, see the schematic map of "Geography and American Sea Power, 1898–1922," in Harold and Margaret Sprout, *Toward a New Order of Sea Power* (Princeton, 1940), p. 22 (reprinted in E. M. Earle, ed., *Makers of Modern Strategy* [Princeton, 1943], p. 428). "Sea Power" appears in the form of enormous arrows projecting from the East and West Coasts, from the isthmus, and from the Hawaiian Islands, with those in the Pacific much the largest. Yet for most of the period in question the entrance to Pearl Harbor was not dredged, the Panama Canal was not completed, and the battle fleet was in the Atlantic.

[31] "Apparently as the result of an accident in Havana Harbor, the path of destiny has been opened for use in the East"; Conant, *United States in the Orient*, p. 63.

Lodge's prediction of "an explosion any day in Cuba"), the identity of the ship sent is perhaps the ultimate historical accident. A sunken *Texas*, say, would have contributed little to the torchlight parades of chanting patriots.

If there had been no war, the process of the "Americanization of the world," which so commended itself to the British reformer and journalist W. T. Stead (and which so exasperated other Englishmen), would no doubt have continued.[32] American heiresses would have continued to marry British milords; missionaries and student volunteers would have persisted in their work for China; engineers, promoters, and salesmen would have pressed on with their activities; multinational corporations would have continued to expand; Carnegie libraries would have gone on proliferating throughout the English-speaking world. But in political terms the outward thrust would, in all probability, have conformed to the relaxed anticipations of "Jingo Jim" Blaine, the strategic parameters of the "imperialistic" Mahan, and the proposals of the Republican platform of 1896: a suitable measure of control over the impending isthmian canal, over protective Caribbean naval bases, and over the Hawaiian islands. In the circumstances of the time, such a defensive policy seems quite reasonable.

Walter LaFeber

WALTER LAFEBER (1933–   ) *is professor of history at Cornell University. He is the author of a number of books dealing with American diplomatic history, including* The New Empire: An Interpretation of American Expansionism 1860–1898 *(1963),* America, Russia, and the Cold War 1945–1966 *(4th ed., 1980), and* Inevitable Revolutions: The United States in Central America *(1983).*

The 1890s—the decade that inaugurated modern America and particularly modern American foreign policy—continues to fascinate many American historians. James A. Field, Jr., however, believes these years to be the "worst chapter" in American diplomatic historiography. He ascribes the problem in part to historians who cling to certain conventional wisdom which, upon examination, should no longer be either conventional or considered wise. The long misplaced emphasis

---

[32]W. T. Stead, *The Americanization of the World; or, The Trend of the Twentieth Century* (New York, 1902).

on Social Darwinism is certainly an example of such mistaken conventional wisdom. Thomas McCormick, Paul Holbo, and, in unpublished work, Robert Dawidoff pointed out long ago that Social Darwinism was more a rationale for, than a cause of, American expansionism. Other historians have also previously argued Field's point that, when Josiah Strong discussed foreign policy, he wanted to stress "what was at stake at home." Indeed, these historians have argued that almost every American policymaker or public spokesman who discusses foreign policy emphasizes what is at stake at home.

Although the correction of such details is important, Field dismisses the more critical issue of how men and women of the 1890s conceptualized problems in foreign policy and developed (if they were lucky) solutions. In the process Field even attacks many recent historians who have tried to place the 1890s in this broader framework. In important respects, the first section of this essay is misleading, for the later emphasis on cable communication, while adding an important dimension to our knowledge of late-nineteenth-century expansionism, builds on the work and the approaches of, among others, Ernest Paolino, Charles Vevier, Harold Schonberger, and David Pletcher. This is all to the good. The story of how this communication network developed complements much of what we already know and makes it that much easier for us to think in broad terms about the importance of the 1890s.

The essay, however, ultimately fails to reconceptualize the foreign policies of the 1890s. One reason, the less important, is specific: at the critical point—1898—Field is forced to drop his thesis and instead emphasize "accidents" in history. This escape hatch is familiar. In Samuel Flagg Bemis's seminal text on American diplomatic history, written forty years ago, the grand story of American expansion rolls along until the narrative encounters 1898. Bemis could handle the next thirteen years only by calling them an "aberration." Such an explanation does not suffice, for it neither explains the particular events nor develops a framework that allows us to understand the era's importance in the totality of American history. The "aberration" is not dealt with adequately because any attempt to claim that the explosion that sank the *Maine* in February 1898 propelled the United States into war and that the explosion was one of those "accidents" of history begs the central question of why the *Maine* was in Havana harbor in the first place. The answer lies in President McKinley's decision to send it there to protect American lives and property after riots in mid-January indicated that Spanish reforms were not cooling the Cuban revolution and that Spain was losing control. Sending the *Maine* can thus be understood as making an important change in the president's previous policy of watchful waiting, and it anticipates his demands in the final ultimatum that Spain accept an American presence to mediate an end to the revolution. The February explosion may have been accidental, not Spanish-inspired, but there was nothing accidental about the causes or the consequences of the *Maine's* visit.

This particular problem is part of the larger problem, confronted by most historians of the era. How do the events before 1898 relate to events after 1898? Field sees little relationship. He argues, for example, that United States officials must not have been concerned about Asia before 1898 since so few warships were stationed in the Pacific. When they did consider the area, the officials viewed it as an eastern rather than a western problem. With few exceptions, however, the essay's examples of Americans traveling east to reach Asia are chosen from the years before 1846, that is, before the United States controlled the West Coast. By the 1890s, Seward had talked of traveling to Asia via the Aleutians, Grover Cleveland had called Hawaii (not the Cape of Good Hope) the stepping-stone to Asia, and Theodore Roosevelt was about to proclaim the "Pacific era" of American history.

The question is not how many warships, or cables, were in the Pacific. Neither naval officers nor cable owners made basic foreign policy decisions between 1890 and 1901—or after. (Field notes that James A. Scrymser is "curiously absent from books on the 'New Empire.'" There is nothing curious about it. A number of people are absent from my own account of the "new empire," most of them more important than Scrymser. In weak moments I fear such people may even number in the tens.) The absence of warships did not mean that political figures and business groups were not interested in the Pacific. From the mid-1890s until at least 1906, Alfred Thayer Mahan, for example, increasingly viewed the Pacific as an arena of great importance to the United States. He included Hawaii in this arena, since it is in the Pacific and several thousand miles from the West Coast. In his biography of Mahan, William E. Livezey has suggested that the officer's "program of action" can be summarized as "dominance in the Caribbean, equality and cooperation in the Pacific," and "interested abstention" from strictly European rivalries on the Continent. By 1910, however, Livezey has noted that Japan's rise forced Mahan to plot a retreat from the Pacific. Field emphasizes the later withdrawal but not the advance between the 1890s and 1906. Brooks Adams remains important for the same reasons. As Arthur F. Beringause has pointed out, Adams, Roosevelt, and Henry Cabot Lodge met in Henry Adams's house to plot strategy in 1897, and by the end of that year they reached a consensus on policy. And Thomas J. McCormick has argued that Roosevelt carried that consensus to McKinley.

To restate, the question is not how many battleships or cables were in the Pacific before 1898, but why McKinley and his advisers were able to move so rapidly into the Pacific after Dewey's victory at Manila Bay. Historians have now proven beyond doubt that the policymakers in 1898, like President Cleveland and Secretary of State Bayard before them, understood not only that American interests were developing in Asia but also that they were responsible for defending those interests. Such an argument hardly means that Latin America was unimportant; it was indeed primary in Washington's foreign policy priorities. Field's emphasis on South and Central America thus fits in well with the work of many historians who have noted the significance of the Venezuelan and Cuban crises during the 1890s. Those historians, however, have not argued that Washington officials were incapable of thinking about Latin America and Asia at the same time.

Since the term "new empire" did not appear until 1902, Field cannot understand how my own work has "persuaded many that the concept existed in its own right" before 1902. That puzzlement pinpoints the central problem in the essay. If, the essay asks, the cable system and battleship deployment indicated little interest in Pacific affairs before 1898, why did the United States control a "new empire" by 1900?

The result was no more accidental than McKinley sending the *Maine* to Havana. The course of an earlier empire provides a helpful analogy. By 450 B.C. the Athenians, who had once belonged to a "league," had slowly developed and expanded their own control until they transformed that alliance into their own empire. The result was not termed an empire until after 450 B.C., but the concept and the methods of empire preceded that date. As Russell Meiggs has written, even while Athens and its allies called their relationship a league or alliance, "the tools of empire had already been forged." In the same respect, the term "new empire" was perhaps not known until 1902, but the tools of empire were forged throughout the 1890s. The cable system was one of those tools, but it was hardly the entire toolbox. Others have also identified those tools, and it is inexcusable to say of their work that "much of it is wrong and most of it irrelevant to 'imperialism' and the events of 1898," especially since Field builds on the work of these historians but cannot explain some of the events these historians have succeeded in explaining.

The essay helps to paint our composite picture of the 1890s, but it is unable to finish the job, for in the end it cannot explain the policies of 1898 to 1901. It confuses cables with messages. An explanation of the foreign policies of the 1890s lies less with the communications network than with what officials were saying over the network, and this problem is not considered in the essay. In the 1890s, the media was not yet the message.

Field thus tells us why McKinley should not have annexed the Philippines and made the United States a major Pacific power, but to discover why the president did accomplish those objectives we must return to the work of McCormick, Charles S. Campbell, Jr., William Appleman Williams, Sylvester K. Stevens (who explains the importance if not "magnificence" of Pearl Harbor by the late 1880s), Paul Varg, Ernest May, H. Wayne Morgan, Marilyn Blatt Young, and others. For they have told us how the "tools of empire" that were forged in the 1890s constructed the new foreign policy edifice of 1898 and after. And few, if any of them, have to resort to Social Darwinism as an explanation. Whether or not we agree with their individual interpretations, their work forces us to conceptualize the era as a whole and to reconsider its roots and its significance for our time.

If the 1890s is the "worst chapter" in American diplomatic historiography, and I do not believe it is, the fault does not belong to those who have replaced "aberration" and "accident" with more useful, coherent, and defensible approaches to understanding the decade. Nor did those scholars believe it necessary to build an eye-catching structure on the historical landscape by attempting to reduce the already existing structures to rubble.

Robert L. Beisner

ROBERT L. BEISNER (1936–   ) *is professor of history at the American University. He has written several books in American diplomatic history, including* Twelve Against Empire *(1968) and* From the Old Diplomacy to the New 1865–1900 *(1975).*

James A. Field, Jr.'s effort to restructure the long-standing debate about "American imperialism" especially interests me because of my own recent attempt at the same task. As we all know, scholarly disputes often end in impasse. One scholar argues that unicorns are handsome; another contends that they are ugly; their disciples elaborate the cases pro and con without, however, either changing the terms of argument or resolving the dispute. What we usually need at such times are new questions and an alteration in terms of debate—perhaps suggested by someone who does not care whether unicorns are handsome or ugly, but who is instead fascinated by their relationship to griffins. Some kind of radical perspective is essential to shoving an old debate in a new direction. Otherwise, the ancient dispute is likely to persist tediously, fueled by students trying to make their mark with a conspicuous entrance into the established debate, by scholars focusing on "false dichotomous questions," or by historians simply miring themselves in the deadening sludge of old questions.

Something of this sort has occurred in the study of late-nineteenth-century American imperialism. The debate about its chronology and its underlying impulses and motives has persisted at least since the publication of Julius W. Pratt's *Expansionists of 1898* in 1936. It took on new but not *different* life with the publication of William A. Williams's *The Tragedy of American Diplomacy* (1959) and Walter LaFeber's *The New Empire: An Interpretation of American Expansion, 1860–1898* (1963). In all the years since Pratt's work, historians have been wrangling over such false dichotomous questions as

1898:   Aberration or Culmination?

The Spanish-American War: Popular Crusade or Drive for Markets?

McKinley: Chocolate Eclair or Clever Statesman?

Specifically, the debate, which actually encompasses some disparate and distinct interpretative problems, has been dominated by five main issues: (1) the "continuity" issue—that is, whether the events of the late 1890s represented an abrupt departure from the past or the logical product of earlier developments and trends; (2) the "realism" issue—that is, whether the United States sallied off to war in 1898 for emotional and idealistic reasons or fought to achieve "realistic" objectives; (3) the "economic" issue—that is, whether American imperialism was the result of a drive to expand foreign export markets or the consequence of ideological, security, and other motives; (4) the "semantic" issue—that is, whether the phenomena of the 1890s should be called "imperialism," "expansionism," or something else; and (5) the "deliberateness" issue—that is, wherther the key events by which we define American imperialism were the result of bungling, emotionalism, and "accident" or the consequences of forethought and deliberate calculation. The current state of the traditional debate is codified, so to speak, in Charles S. Campbell's *The Transformation of American Foreign Relations, 1865–1900* (1976), which is a thorough and excellent book but one that in no way tries to transform the terms of debate.

Clearly, the time has come for a new departure in the study of American imperialism, and it is in this light that I have approached James Field's essay, particularly since his title suggests that his purpose is to rewrite "The Worst Chapter in Almost Any Book." Has he merely offered new fuel to the old debate? Or has he redefined the debate itself? Has he produced a provocative new argument for the beauty of the unicorn? Or has he introduced us to a fabulous new field grazed also by griffins? Field states his first general criticisms of past interpretations with an élan that suggests we are to witness new ground being broken. I heartily concur the presentism, moralism, and a proclivity to see false continuities have had a "tendentious" impact on general views of U.S. foreign relations from 1865 to 1898, though I boggle at the casualness with which he suggests that historians, through an act of will, can avoid "seeing the past through the prism of the present. . . ." I also agree that most interpretations of American imperialism are too "rational," too "unitary," too "ethnocentric," too oblivious of the "environment," and too dependent on asking the wrong questions. Most of the critical parts of his essay—most notably his devastating assault on those attributing great influence to Social Darwinists and other intellectuals—are persuasive. But they do not take us anywhere new. His criticisms of past work in themselves neither define nor clearly point the way toward a novel conception of the historical problem of "American imperialism."

Field's contribution is not, then, his critique but his own new descriptive material. Briefly recapitulated, Field says that

1. The advent of steam propulsion bound modern navies to coal deposits and stations and impelled the United States Navy to abandon far-flung patrols for the security of its own home bases. Thus, the "New Navy" of the 1890s, however enlarged and modernized, was tied even closer to home and to defensive positions than it had been in the 1880s.

2. Instead of feeling a constant tug westward toward Asia, American exporters, shippers, diplomatic policymakers, and navalists were actually eastward-oriented throughout the era of the "new empire." When Americans "looked outward" for personal contacts or for economic opportunities abroad and when they hunted for potential threats to national security, they looked across the Atlantic, as they always had.

3. The rapid development of a vast network of telegraphic cables had linked Washington and New York to the rest of the world by 1898 but not yet by a direct route across the Pacific to Asia. The cable network can be seen reflected in America's Atlantic orientation and emphasis on hemispheric defense. The cables stimulated business activity abroad, accelerated the pace of diplomacy, shaped maritime strategy, and were eventually crucial in abruptly entangling the United States in the politics of East Asia in 1898.

Still, Field's general purpose is not clear. Is this new new material the foundation for a "best chapter" on American imperialism? It may be, but this is certainly not self-evident. Reduced to its essentials—however persuasive and however fascinating—it does not *explain* the historical phenomenon of American imperialism. Instead, by marshalling mostly new evidence, Field has simply produced a set of unfamiliar inferences (descriptive statements) we can make about the past. Thus, just as his spirited destruction of the old saw that intellectuals somehow brought about American imperialism boils down in part to the descriptive statement that "intellectuals neither advocated imperialist policies nor had access to foreign policymakers as much as former historians have maintained," so his new material finally comes down to the following historical inferences:

1. Naval developments in the 1890s betoken a defensive and hemispheric rather than an offensive and imperialist stance.

2. The United States looked eastward rather than westward, and its activities conformed with this point of view.

3. Although generally ignored by historians, the development of an international network of telegraphic cables, which did not include a link across the Pacific between the United States and East Asia, was quite important in this period.

What can bring these new descriptions of the past together into a new explanation of American imperialism or, at least, an argument that would alter the old terms of debate? Though at times Field comes tantalizingly close, he nonetheless fails to propose a general theory that can connect his new knowledge about diplomacy with an explanation of why things happened as they did. Implicitly, at least, he seems to favor some kind of materialistic theory of history. Underlying all of his novel "theses" are the development of two new technologies—steam propulsion and international cables—and new patterns of maritime and diplomatic traffic. Some of his direct statements seem to echo a hidden theoretical commitment: other historians have "words do duty for things and presumed intentions for actual capabilities"; "just as words are not things, a map is not the country it represents"; "aspiration was less substantial than geographic and economic reality"; "capabilities are often as determining as intentions"; "the anatomists of sea power concentrate on bone and muscle to the neglect of the alimentary and nervous systems"; and "results had little to do with intentions." One should especially note his remark that we "must move . . . beyond economics and ideology to the . . . area of technological capabilities. . . ."

Is Field suggesting a materialist (or perhaps behavioralist or environmentalist) theory of history to explain American imperialism? Unfortunately, we do not know, because Field never closes with the issue. And that reluctance to come to grips with theory mars other parts of his essay, especially considering its ambitious objectives. In the absence of an explicit theory discounting the relevance of ideas, sentiments, and rhetoric, for instance, I find his treatment of them wholly unsatisfactory. I am not referring here to his contention that certain intellectuals either did not think what has been attributed to them or did not possess the influence attributed to them (a contention I believe Field convincingly supports). I have in mind, rather, his almost total neglect of ideas. Yes, it would certainly appear that the development of cables was quite important in the acceleration of diplomacy. But which men chose to use those cables, to what purpose, and why? Cables alone cannot dictate the goals of diplomacy any more than computers can determine the policies of industry. Certainly, the availability of a new technological capability might influence the decisions of those responsible for making policy. But how are we going to understand why they chose to do one thing rather than another with the technology unless we determine what they thought, believed, and were concerned about? The U.S. government could choose or not choose to build modern steam-propelled warships. It could send Dewey's squadron to East Asia or somewhere else. Technology cannot account for the decisions that were made, only that certain kinds of decisions could be made.

Field's analysis seems based on what Lionel Trilling has described as the "liberal" sense of reality, which is seen as "hard, resistant, unformed, impenetrable, and unpleasant." Such a perspective caused historians like Charles A. Beard to assume that they could not "really" explain what motivated the Founding Fathers unless they could point to something concrete like land deeds or stock certificates. Given his criticism of the economic approach to American diplomatic history, one would think that Field might apply Trilling's observation to those who find export statistics at the bottom of American imperialism. Nonetheless, his own essay relies exclusively on such "hard" data as steam boilers, coal bins, shipping routes, and telegraphic cables. But we do not know whether he really believes in such a materialist sense of reality because Field has chosen not to grapple with theory directly. This becomes painfully obvious at the end of his essay when, alarmingly, he suddenly states that Americans wanted "the freedom to do their thing, to operate insofar as possible unhindered by arbitrary power or obsolete ideas," that they were "proud of their own self-determined independence," and "sympathetic to similar desires" elsewhere. What is this if not a purely intellectual explanation and, as well, unitary, ethnocentric, and undocumented?

This disinclination to deal directly with the theoretical bases of his arguments and assumptions also partially accounts for some of the highly dubious causal statements in the essay. Can historians of American imperialism rest content with the statement that Commodore Dewey "had to" destroy the Spanish fleet and seize Manila harbor as "a consequence" of "being so far out at the end of the [eastward-directed coal and ammunition] line"? Did new communications technology combined with literate publics lead to an "attentive audience" for war correspondents and thus to emotion-induced "times of crisis"? Why was the audience interested in war correspondents rather than architectural news? Was the U.S. government really so helplessly impressionable? "'Imperialism,' we may say," Field concludes, "was the product of Dewey's victory." Even allowing for hyperbole or deliberate oversimplification, this statement represents a crude definition of imperialism, a nonchalant dismissal of abundant evidence suggesting other conclusions, as well as a simplistic notion of causality. Even worse are the "arguments" about the "accidental" character of American imperialism that riddle Field's next-to-last paragraph, arguments that do violence to the subtle philosophical and theoretical problems involved in the concept of "historical accident." One could equally well argue that the American Revolution was an accident in that it would not have occurred "if the [colonists] had been happy under [British] rule rule" or that there would have been no Cold War if Stalin had been converted to capitalism.

Field asks, "But where does all this leave us?" About where we were before, I'm afraid. Some of the old debaters should be out hunting for a white flag to wave, perhaps, and much of Field's new material is suggestive. But its importance depends on what is made of it. It might be possible to argue, for instance, that accelerated diplomacy, in part a product of telegraphic cables, in turn helped to persuade American policymakers in the 1890s that they were performing in a new and more dangerous era than before. The Atlantic-orientation thesis— which needs to be supplemented with social and cultural evidence to become fully convincing—does not necessarily entail Field's conclusion that the American drive toward Asia was weak. I would argue instead the America's preoccupation with Hawaii, China, the Philippines, and Korea, despite the nation's traditional and still-intact Atlantic orientation, graphically demonstrates the strength of the "new paradigm" in American diplomacy that arose in the 1890s. Policymakers' decisions do not depend alone on the circumstances of the so-called real world (for example, cables and ships cross the Atlantic but not the Pacific) nor on what retrospective commentators think they should have done (for example, the general consensus today that the United States greatly exaggerated the importance of East Asia eighty years ago). They also depend on the lenses through which those policymakers "see" the real world, lenses tinted by altering circumstances and shifting perspectives. And the evidence remains convincing that American statesmen at the end of the nineteenth century believed profoundly that the international stakes in Asia were high. It was to Asia, not to Europe, that the United States sent warships and occupation troops; it was in Asia where the United States adamantly retained control of territory, even in the face of armed insurrection; and it was in Asia where the United States joined other great powers in disciplining the Chinese Boxers. How extraordinary, considering that the cables, dollars, and freighters were all spanning the Atlantic instead of the Pacific!

Thus, Field's essay has neither given us a persuasive new explanation of "American imperialism" nor substantially altered the terms of the now-wearisome debate. Although he is clearly uncomfortable with the present terms of debate, he does not manage to redefine them. An overriding ambiguity permeates his essay. It is never clear whether his purpose is to argue that American imperialism was an accident or that America was not imperialist at all (it was never a unicorn at all, but a griffin). He nudges the debate in a new direction, to be sure, but he does not succeed in shoving the debate aside. It appears that, when the mail next brings "a copy of a new textbook on American diplomatic history," there, smack on the first page of its "worst chapter," will be that same old picture of a unicorn, a little more elaborately depicted but the same creature we all know. Is the hope for a new debate a mere chimera?

Reply
by James A. Field, Jr.

Rarely, I am sure, has so argumentative an essay been so politely received by critics who hold other views. And if what is not disputed can be assumed to be conceded (a perhaps somewhat optimistic assumption, given the commentators' limitations of space), I can hardly feel disappointed. But since there seems as yet no complete marriage of minds and since some of the arguments appear to slide past each other (as often in such exchanges), we should perhaps continue the discussion a little longer.

We may perhaps begin with specifics. I think that some of the authors on whom Walter LaFeber suggests I build might better be cited as representatives of the "on to China for economic hegemony" school of which he is distinguished an exemplar. I quite agree that the dispatch of the *Maine* to Havana marked an escalation of pressure in the Cuban question; but since she presumably was neither sent to be sunk nor dispatched as a first step toward the Philippines, I do not see that her sailing made the Asiatic "New Empire" any the more probable. I thought the early examples of eastward-sailing Americans worth noting in view of prevalent assumptions that the term " 'Far East' . . . hinders the understanding of American expansion [since] the United States has more often considered this area as the Far West" and that the *Empress of China* and Commodore Perry somehow support this conclusion. The Athenian analogy seems to me more curious than enlightening: can it really be said that in 1897 American influence in Hawaii, the Philippines, and China (or, indeed, in Latin America) approximated Athenian control of Ionia in the decade before 450 B.C., that the Americans had already made off with the Delian treasury, or that the United States possessed "instruments of empire" like those described by Russell Meiggs? On the other hand, the underlying argument that facts are more important than labels seems to me central: as Robert Beisner has elsewhere observed, "Behavior, not occasional rhetoric, is the crucial test."

At this point I think I should confess my sneaking admiration for the "new empire" school's concern with the interests and influence of nongovernmental groups, assuming it can be properly articulated and focused. But if we employ it without preconceptions, I doubt we will find pre-1898 pressures for transpacific expansion, or even much pressure for the annexation of Hawaii. Theodore Roosevelt, at least, feared in the spring of 1898 that McKinley was incapable of dealing at once with Cuba and Hawaii, and that the president would let the islands slip away. Writing in 1900, Mahan noted of the expansionists that "their vision reached not past Hawaii, which also, as touching the United States, they regarded from the point of view of defense rather than as a stepping-stone." Thomas A. Bailey concluded that with no war there would have been no annexation, in which view he echoed Mahan: "To Dewey's victory, apparently, is due that we annexed Hawaii."

LaFeber refers twice to the "tools of empire" forged in the 1890s, to which I feel constrained to reply, what tools were these? Not the navy in the Pacific, certainly, and not Pacific merchant shipping (unless the words of Seward and Cleveland are still expected to do duty for real tonnage), and surely not a well-run consular service or a group of lively and energetic business men in hot pursuit of the China market. He observes that historians have "proven beyond doubt" that it was because McKinley and his advisers (which advisers?), like their predecessors (Cleveland?), understood the problem of Asia so well that they could "move so rapidly into the Pacific." The argument is hardly supported by the Philippine reinforcement, an exercise in improvisation if ever there was one, in which the first troops did not sail until three and a half weeks and the monitors (not, perhaps, the best type of ship for this assignment) until six and a half and eight and a half weeks after Manila Bay. If Camara had gone the route, the race promised to be a very tight one, and the slowness of this movement "into the Pacific" was the one thing Mahan later thought culpable in the work of the Naval War Board. Problems such as these seem to me illustrative of the kind of cement that is employed to hold the "worst chapter" together: mutually supporting references ("beyond doubt") and a usage of assertion and verbal prestidigitation which imposes false geographic unities (interest in the eastern Pacific becomes interest in "the Pacific," a far larger area) and confuses words with things ("tools of empire" with ships, prompt orders with delayed ship movements).

This question of "new empire" behavior as against "new empire" rhetoric leads us back to James A. Scrymser. I said "books" and did not mean to single out LaFeber, and of course we all leave some things out. But the surprising fact is that *everybody* leaves Scrymser out, along with his energetic fellow-laborers in southern vineyards. Given all the talk of the American China Development Company, it is instructive to compare the sketches in the *Dictionary of America Biography* of Scrymser, Henry Meiggs (a great-uncle, by the way, of Russell Meiggs, who thus enjoys both inherited and acquired qualifications as an historian of informal empire), Charles J. Harrah, William R. Grace, and Minor W. Keith, with the notice given them in *The New Empire*, or in Milton Plesur's *American Outward Thrust* (1971), or indeed in almost any book that comes to mind. This same problem of geographical displacement applies to missionary as well as business enterprise: we still get works that suggest that China was the only American mission field, yet as late as 1900 the four major missionary boards were spending half again as much money and supporting about half again as many workers in India, Burma, and Ceylon (hardly areas of American "imperial" activity) as they were in China.

It also applies within major regions: Beisner affirms America's "preoccupation" with Hawaii, China, the Philippines, and Korea (but at what dates?), yet makes no mention of Japan. But from 1895 to 1898 trade with Japan exceeded that with China, in 1898 in a proportion of three to two; the Japanese were buying such modern commodities as fertilizer and locomotives and electrical equipment; American missionaries in Japan were busy doing good and founding schools and colleges; and throughout the latter part of the century numerous individuals (in addition to the curious LeGendre) like Raphael Pumpelly, Horace Capron and William S. Clark, Ernest Fenollosa, David Murray, and Henry W. Grinnell were (I am sorry to have to say it again) in and out of Japan doing their things. This neglect of Japan is widespread in the literature. Why this geographical discrimination among outward thrusters? Or why the functional discrimination that concentrates on Denby and Wilson in China to the neglect of W. A. P. Martin, Philo McGiffin, and W. Pethick?

I am puzzled as to how to answer accusations of materialism and "almost total neglect of ideas," the more so, as I am simultaneously reproached for the use of "purely intellectual explanation." Certainly, I believe capabilities to be important. My critics are, of course, quite right in observing that the message on the cable is what starts things moving. Equally, however, if there is no cable to carry the message, Dewey will not get underway, and, if he has no coal, he cannot. I must confess to a slightly bruised *amour propre* in that Beisner did not find, in the continuous information flow made possible by cable communications, the explanation of the shift from "incidents" to "policy" in the "new paradigm" diplomacy which he propounded but never accounted for. In any case, I do not see how material matters and ideas can be divorced. Artifacts embody previous thought. Cables do not lay themselves, nor do freighters choose their own destinations, and the location of cables and shipping lines surely reflected contemporary views of what was important and what profitable.

On the question of accident in history, I can only feel that Beisner fails to understand me. Of course there are subtle and complex problems here, but in a one-paragraph treatment I would not think it necessary to explore them at length (any more than I would think it necessary at this date to heap up evidence to show America's social and cultural orientation toward Europe). The problem, it appears to me, is to get our minds out of the traditional boxes and to let them consider alternative possibilities (as those who were then running things surely had to do). So let me make one more attempt. As things were at the time, it was surely not too far-fetched to have hoped (as Cleveland and McKinley apparently did) that Spain might somehow manage to resolve the Cuban question on its own. If that had happened, would Beisner think we would have seen American troops fighting their way up to Peking in 1900? Or to take a fresh example: what if on that moonless night Dewey's navigator had piled the squadron up on the rocks while attempting to enter Manila Bay? Here, at last, we can profitably employ the Athenian analogy: if the commodore and his crews had suffered the fate of Nicias, what would the next decade have brought with regard to American policy in China?

To LaFeber's feeling that none should attack those who try to place the 1890s in a larger framework, and that it is "inexcusable" to say that much of their work is wrong or irrelevant, I would merely observe that I do not attack either the individuals or the effort, but merely the conclusions, and that criticism is one of the conventions of the profession. Beisner chides me for not having reformulated the entire argument and provided the entire answer. I think he asks too much of a single article. In any case he asks more than I undertook to do, which was to question some things that seemed to me wrong—although widely accepted—and to suggest some new ideas for consideration. The best chapter, like the "worst chapter" (if it is, in fact, the "worst chapter"), will surely turn out to be the product of collaborative effort.

It must be clear by now that much of my concern is with the monochromatic straight-line interpretation of the history of American foreign relations, which implies (in its most vulgarized textbook versions) that when Daniel Boone headed for Kentucky and Huck Finn lit out for the territory they were merely the advance guard of a relentless westward advance that, in due course, would cross the Pacific to end in the Cambodian incursion; and with the one-size-fits-all interpretation, which suggests that if only we repeat, like John Randolph's whippoor-will, "empire, empire, empire," everything from Jefferson to Nixon will be explained. The past is surely more interesting and diverse than this. So in conclusion I may perhaps be permitted to suggest "what is to be done," or at least a few things that I would like to see done, or not done.

It is true that I do not define "American imperialism" (nor do most writers on the period) nor, indeed, so far as I am aware does Beisner, although he uses the term liberally in both his critique and his book. In fact, I tried very hard not to use the word outside of quotation marks or paraphrase. I think it undesirable to begin with an assumption of an undefined "American imperialism": better describe the attitudes, the aims, the capabilities, and the events, and then see what they add up to. The question of "influence" is both important and difficult, but I doubt that snippets from the writings of historians and clergymen should be claimed as influential if they cannot be shown to be; here Karsten's observations on the influence of Mahan seem to me suscepti-ble of wider application. As to Brooks Adams, I have to confess feelings of despair: I thought he was dead, but clearly he will not lie down, and it may turn out that he is immortal. Nevertheless, I must report that I find no evidence in the pages in Arthur Beringause's biography cited by LaFeber of Adams plotting strategy with Roosevelt and Lodge, nor have I been able to discover in Thomas McCormick's study of the China Market any reference to Roosevelt's carrying the good word from Adams to McKinley. In this context it may be worth noting that Roosevelt's prewar correspondence provides unflattering judgments on the quality of Adams's thought.

I think more attention should be given to negative evidence of the sort that Holmes understood but that the unimaginative Inspector Gregory did not ("Silver Blaze"): if the dog does not bark in the night, if presidents will not urge, if the senate will not consent, if congress will not dredge, if capitalists will not invest, if the navy will not de-ploy, the facts seem to me at least as important for an understanding of "American policy" as the pleas of enthusiasts. I think chronology important: what happens second can hardly cause what happens first (even though it may help to explicate it), and the current literature is far too rich in the use of post-Manila bay quotations to define prewar aspirations. My critics speak of Mahan's views "from the mid-1890s until at least 1906," of the "decade of the 1890s," and of the "whole decade." Such chronological conflation seems particularly dangerous in periods like this. One may no doubt generalize about the years before 1898, and again regarding some period beginning in the summer of that year. But it appears to me that there is an important intervening break in which (to conflate Conant and Mahan) an accident at Havana and the flash of Dewey's guns first brought the Philippines above the mental horizon. I may not be able to persuade everybody, but I remain myself persuaded that unanticipated events can bring unanticipated results and that the *Maine* and Manila Bay (like Fort Sumter and Pearl Harbor) led to attitudes and consequences that could hardly have been foreseen.

One last thought on periodization as opposed to the straight-line view of history. Is it not possible that Seward's spread-eagle oratory, the "irreflective" re-establishment of the antebellum squadrons, the commercial concerns of Shufeldt and Evarts, and Chandler's call for lots of naval bases represent less a first step toward the Asian involvement of 1898 than the last manifestations of attitudes formed during the great age of sail and of the world-wide merchant marine and commerce-protecting navy? And that beginning in the late 1880s the new age of steam and of the navies of industrialism was finding its appropriate expression in concern for the defense of East Coast and Caribbean, in Mahan's emphasis on battleships and concentration of force, and in his growing realization that, although sea power may originally have derived from commerce, the missions of some modern navies (like the Russian and American) were primarily political?

My hope in this article has been to raise some questions and arguments, substantive and procedural, for consideration by the trade. If my colleagues (or at least those who are interested) will read it, and decide what they think persuasive and what not, then perhaps we can get back to the drawing boards and try to find out what the years preceding 1898 were all about, leaving the labeling until later. If this can be done the rubble question will solve itself: to the extent that they were founded upon rock, the pre-existing structures will presumably survive any winds that I or anyone else can blow against them; to the extent that they were built on sand, they may not, and perhaps should not.

☆6☆

The Progressive Movement

LIBERAL OR CONSERVATIVE?

The rise of American industry in the decades following the Civil War was a development whose impact can hardly be exaggerated. It involved more than a shift from a commercial and agrarian economy to an urban and industrial one; indeed, it effected fundamental changes in the nature and quality of American society. The far-reaching technological and industrial innovations forced Americans to reexamine their traditional values and beliefs, many of which seemed obsolete, if not irrelevant, to the problems of a new age.

Traditionally Americans were accustomed to think in terms of individualistic values. The rise of industry itself was often rationalized in the ideology of the self-made man who claimed he attained success by virtue of his own talents, drive, and ambition. By the end of the nineteenth century, however, it was becoming more difficult to conceive of industrial progress solely in terms of the achievements of a few creative individuals. The growth of a national transportation and communications system, which led to the rise of a national market, had stimulated the formation of large industrial units. This organizational revolution, to use Kenneth Boulding's convenient phrase,[1] was to have profound implications. Americans at the turn of the twentieth century found that their nation was being increasingly dominated by large corporations whose establishment resulted in the partial curtailment, if not abolition, of competition—a development that collided sharply with the ideology of individualism and freedom.

The position of the individual within the nation's increasingly industrialized society became a major source of concern for many Americans. If America's greatness was related to individual achievement, what would happen as freedom and social mobility were more and more circumscribed by giant corporations with their impersonal and

---

[1]Kenneth E. Boulding, *The Organizational Revolution: A Study in the Ethics of Economic Organization* (New York, 1953).

216

machinelike qualities? Did not the emphasis of corporations on efficient production and material objectives distort the human qualities
that had been responsible for America's rise to greatness? Was not the
growing disparity between rich corporations and poor workingmen creating a situation akin to that existing in many European countries
where there was open class strife? These and similar questions led
many Americans to advocate reforms that would restore dignity to the
individual and give meaning to his life.

The forces of reform gradually gathered momentum in the last
quarter of the nineteenth century. Although critics of American society could not agree upon a specific diagnosis, let alone remedial measures, they were united in a common conviction that some changes
would have to be made if the United States was to survive with its
historic values intact. The solutions presented were often diffuse.
Many were all-embracing panaceas that called for the preservation of
a competitive and individualistic society, but, at the same time, did
not sacrifice the affluence associated with technological progress.
Henry George, for example, gained international fame by presenting
his single tax scheme in 1879 in his book *Progress and Poverty,* while
Edward Bellamy, in his utopian novel *Looking Backward* (1886), argued that only the nationalization of all the means of production and
distribution would solve most of America's major problems. In a similar vein, many Protestant clergymen who were disturbed by the cleav-
ages in American society offered their own answers in what came to
be known as the Social Gospel. These religious critics argued that an
immoral society was incompatible with the ideals of moral men. Society, therefore, would have to be remade in the form of a Christian socialist commonwealth, thereby offering individuals an opportunity to
lead moral lives. Others including the Populists, socialists, advocates
of civil service reform, and academic critics also contributed to the
swelling chorus of reform.

Between 1900 and 1917 these uncoordinated efforts at reform were
institutionalized in what came to be known as the Progressive movement. Pluralistic rather than unitary, the Progressive movement was
actually a series of movements operating at the local, state, and national levels of government and society. The movement consisted of a
loose coalition of reformers who sought a variety of goals: political
reforms such as the initiative, referendum, recall, and the destruction
of urban political machines and corruption; economic reforms such as
the regulation of public utilities and the curtailment of corporate
power; and social reforms such as the Americanization of the immigrant, the amelioration of the lot of the urban poor, and regulation of
child and woman labor as well as many others. Among the symbolic
leaders of the movement were two presidents, Theodore Roosevelt and
Woodrow Wilson. These two men not only revived the moral author-

ity and leadership-potential inherent in the presidency, but they supported the enactment of a series of laws embodying major social reforms.

Until the period after World War II there was relatively little controversy among historians about the nature and character of the Progressive movement. Most American historians were writing within the tradition of the Progressive school. Consequently they interpreted these reform movements and reformers within a liberal framework. In their eyes the reformers in the movement had been challenging the dominant position of the business and privileged classes. The reformers' goals had been clear and simple: to restore government to the people; to abolish special privilege and ensure equal opportunity for all; and to enact a series of laws embodying principles of social justice. These reformers, Progressive historians emphasized, were not anticapitalist; they had not advocated the abolition of private property nor sought the establishment of a socialist society. On the contrary they had taken seriously the American dream; their fundamental goal had been a democratic and humane society based on egalitarian ideals and social compassion. The real enemies of society were the businessmen, dishonest politicians, and "special interests," all of whom posed a serious threat to the realization of American democracy.

Such an approach put progressivism squarely within the American liberal tradition and on the side of the "people" as opposed to the forces of wealth, self-interest, and special privilege. Vernon L. Parrington, one of the best-known Progressive historians, saw progressivism as a "democratic renaissance"—a movement of the masses against a "plutocracy" that had been corrupting the very fabric of American society since the Civil War. Thus the movement concerned itself not only with political democracy but with economic democracy as well. To Parrington progressivism was a broad-based movement that included members of the middle class, journalists, and scholars—men, in other words, whose consciences had been aroused by the "cesspools that were poisoning the national household," and who had set for themselves the task of reawakening the American people.[2]

Implicit in this point of view was the conviction that the course of American history had been characterized by a continuous struggle between liberalism and conservatism, democracy and aristocracy, and equal opportunity and special privilege. Most historians writing in the Progressive tradition believed that reformers, regardless of their specific goals or the eras in which they appeared, were cast in the same mold because they invariably supported the "people" against their enemies. Such was the position of John D. Hicks, an outstanding Ameri-

---

[2]Vernon L. Parrington, *Main Currents in American Thought*, 3 vols. (New York, 1927–1930), 3:406.

can historian whose textbooks in American history were used by tens of thousands of high school and college students between the 1930s and 1960s. Hicks in 1931 published *The Populist Revolt*, the first major account of populism based on wide research in the original sources. To Hicks the Populists carried the banner of reform in the 1890s and represented a first organized protest of the masses against the encroachments of a monopolistic plutocracy. Although the Populist movement ultimately failed, it was victorious in the long run, Hicks held, because much of its program was taken over by later reformers and enacted into law during the first two decades of the twentieth century. To a large extent his thesis rested on the assumption that American reform efforts drew much of their inspiration from the Jeffersonian agrarian tradition which had survived intact among the nation's farmers and rural population.[3]

Not all historians were as friendly and well-disposed toward populism and progressivism as was Hicks. Those historians writing within a socialist and Marxian tradition, for example, were highly critical of progressivism because of its superficial nature and its refusal to adopt more radical solutions to meet the basic needs of American society. To John Chamberlain, a young Marxist who in 1932 published a devastating critique of American reform, the Progressive movement was an abysmal failure. Its adherents, claimed Chamberlain, were motivated by an escapist desire to return to a golden past where honesty and virtue had dominated over egoism and evil.[4]

Oddly enough many of the detractors of the achievements of the reform movement from 1890 to 1917 were, like Chamberlain, within the Progressive school of history in that they accepted the idea that class conflict had been the major determinant of progress and social change in America. Many of them, particularly during the depression of the 1930s, condemned the Progressive reforms as being piecemeal and superficial in nature. The failure of the Progressive generation, these critics emphasized, had led to the reaction of the 1920s, which in turn had resulted in the disastrous depression of the 1930s. Disillusionment with the Progressive movement, however, did not necessarily imply disillusion with the efficacy of reform or with the aspirations and ideals of the liberal tradition in America. Even those intellectuals who flirted with Marxism during the depression did so out of their conviction that America could still be redeemed from the hands of its enemies.

Beginning in the 1940s and continuing in the 1950s and 1960s the mood of American historians began to change. The increasing homoge-

---

[3]John D. Hicks, *The Populist Revolt: A History of the Farmers' Alliance and the People's Party* (Minneapolis, 1931).

[4]John Chamberlain, *Farewell to Reform* (New York, 1932).

neity of American society began to dissolve the sectional, class, and ethnic groupings that had been employed by the Progressive school of history. No longer did historians have to vindicate the claims of the West against the East, the South against the rest of the nation, or to establish conclusively the contributions of the Puritans, the immigrants, the working class, or the businessmen. Such narrow loyalties appeared parochial in a milieu where national similarities seemed to be more significant than group differences.

The change in mood, however, was due to far more fundamental factors than a mere shift in the class and ethnic backgrounds of historians. Much more basic was the change in attitude and outlook that accompanied the revolutionary changes in the world since the 1940s. To scholars writing after 1940 the Progressive ideology appeared much too facile and simplified. Like many philosophers and theologians they began to criticize Progressive historians for underestimating man's propensities for evil and for overestimating his capacity for good. In brief, these critics argued that the interpretation of the Progressive school of history rested on an unrealistic evaluation of human nature. The result, they concluded, was that Americans had been unprepared for the dilemmas and challenges that they faced in the Great Depression of the 1930s and the worldwide conflict of the 1940s because of their tendency to view history in terms of a simple morality play where good always triumphed over evil.

The challenge to democracy by communism since World War II gave rise to a new group of scholars—the neoconservative historians—who were critical of the Progressive school and who embarked upon their own reevaluation of America's past. Writing from a conservative point of view these historians stressed the basic goodness of American society and the consensus that has characterized the American people throughout most of their history. Thus these scholars insisted that American history could not be written in terms of a struggle between democracy and aristocracy or the people against the special interests. On the contrary they tended to stress the unity and homogeneity of America's past, the stability of basic institutions, and the existence of a monistic national character. While they did not deny that conflicts and struggles between sections, classes, and special interest groups have occurred, the neoconservative historians insisted that such struggles were always fought within a liberal framework and that the protagonists were never really in disagreement over fundamentals. Moreover, these scholars were also much less certain about the value of desirability of social change. Having witnessed the effects of revolutionary movements in other parts of the world the neoconservatives questioned whether conflict and change would necessarily lead to a better society.

The result of this changed outlook was a sharp shift in the way historians interpreted the Progressive movement. The Progressive school of history had looked upon the Progressive era as but one phase in the continuing struggle against special privilege and business. The newer neoconservative school, in rejecting the older view, now began to ask new and different questions. If progressivism was not in the Jeffersonian liberal tradition, in what tradition could it be placed? If Progressives were not necessarily moral individuals fighting on behalf of the masses, who were they and what did they stand for? If they did not democratize and reform America by their efforts, just what did they accomplish? Such were the questions raised by historians who rejected the older Progressive view.

The attack on the Progressive school interpretation was led by Richard Hofstadter, the distinguished Columbia University historian. Oddly enough Hofstadter was writing within the Progressive tradition and as a liberal partisan. Yet he could not find very many constructive achievements to attribute to the American liberal tradition. Indeed, he found the liberal ideology to be narrow and deficient in many respects. In a number of brilliant books Hofstadter attempted to expose, by historical analysis, the shortcomings, inadequacies, and failures of American liberalism.

In 1948 Hofstadter published *The American Political Tradition and the Men Who Made It*. In this book he attempted to delineate the basic characteristics of the American political tradition by studying the careers of nearly a dozen presidents and political leaders, including Andrew Jackson, John C. Calhoun, Abraham Lincoln, Theodore Roosevelt, Woodrow Wilson, and Franklin Delano Roosevelt. Hofstadter's thesis was that the liberal tradition had failed because it was based upon the idea of a return to an ideology that emphasized acquisitive and individualistic values. Thus the Populists and Progressives had similar deficiencies; neither had faced up to the fundamental problems of an industrialized and corporate America. Even Franklin Delano Roosevelt, who did not share the nostalgia common to the Progressive tradition, was a pragmatist whose attraction lay in the force of his personality rather than in any consistent ideology or philosophy.

Seven years later Hofstadter spelled out his case in even greater detail in *The Age of Reform: From Bryan to F.D.R.* The Populists, he argued, were unsophisticated and simplistic reformers. Rather than approaching the farm problem within a broad national and international context they placed the blame for their difficulties upon elements of American society which were alien to them—Easterners, Wall Street bankers, Jews, and foreigners. Associated with populism, therefore, was a combination of attitudes made up of a curious blend of racism, nativism, and provincialism—attitudes that helped to explain the fears of agricultural and rural America that later manifested themselves in national paranoic scares. "The Populists," Hofstadter emphasized "looked backward with longing to the lost agrarian Eden, to the republican America of the early years of the nineteenth century in which there were few millionaires and, as they saw it, no beggars, when the laborer had excellent prospects and the farmer had abundance, when statesmen still responded to the mood of the people and there was no such thing as the money power. What they meant—though they did not express themselves in such terms—was that they would like to restore the conditions prevailing before the development of industrialism and the commercialization of agriculture."[5]

Nor were the Progressives, according to Hofstadter, very much more sophisticated. Traditionally progressivism had been viewed by historians as a liberal reform movement aimed at readjusting American institutions to the imperatives of a new industrial age. To Hofstadter, on the other hand, progressivism was something quite different. Borrowing heavily from the work of behavioral scientists he argued that progressivism was related to other influences, notably status anxiety. Playing down the role of economic factors in individual and group motivation, Hofstadter maintained that to a large extent American political conflicts reflected the drive of different ethnic and religious groups for a secure status in society. By the latter third of the nineteenth century a number of groups—clergymen, lawyers, professors, older Anglo-Saxon Protestant families—were finding themselves displaced from the seats of power and their traditional positions of leadership by a dangerous plutocracy and new political machines under the control of alien elements. The response of this displaced elite was a moral crusade to restore older Protestant and individualistic values—the Progressive movement. This crusade was based on the simple idea that only men of character—the "right sort of people"—should rule. Few Progressive leaders, including Theodore Roosevelt and Woodrow Wilson, were realistic in their appraisals of and solutions to America's problems. "In the attempts of the Populists and Progressives to hold on to some of the values of agrarian life, to save personal entrepreneurship and individual opportunity and the character type they engendered, and to maintain a homogeneous Yankee civilization," Hofstadter wrote, "I have found much that was retrograde and delusive, a little that was vicious, and a good deal that was comic."[6] Blinded by their moral absolutism and their righteous convictions, the Progressives were unable to foresee that much of their ideology was narrow and undemocratic and would prepare the groundwork for a later reaction that would threaten the very fabric of American liberty.

The implications of Hofstadter's interpretation were indeed strik-

[5]Richard Hofstadter, *The Age of Reform: From Bryan to F.D.R.* (New York, 1955), p. 62.

[6]*Ibid.*, p. 11.

ing. In brief, his line of thought led to the conclusion that American liberalism was not a liberal movement, but a movement by fairly well-to-do middle-class groups alienated from their society because of technological and industrial changes. There is no doubt that Hofstadter himself was writing from the left of the political spectrum, but it is clear also that he felt strongly that the United States never had had a viable and constructive liberal tradition. Implicit in his views, therefore, was the assumption that American history occurred within an illiberal or conservative mold, that a genuine struggle between classes—as portrayed by the Progressive historians—had never taken place.

Hofstadter's general interpretation of progressivism rested to a large degree upon the research of others particularly the work of George E. Mowry. Author of a number of important books on Theodore Roosevelt and the Progressive movement, Mowry was one of the first historians to see progressivism as a movement by a particular class aimed at reasserting its declining position of leadership. Motivated by an intense faith in individualistic values these groups opposed the rapid concentration of power in the hands of large corporate entities and the consequent emergence of an impersonal society. The Progressives, Mowry concluded, sought to recapture and reaffirm the older individualistic values, but they attempted to do so without undertaking any fundamental economic reforms or altering to any great extent the structure of American society.[7]

While the specific formulations of the Mowry-Hofstadter thesis have not been universally accepted,[8] most recent historians seem to agree that the older interpretation of progressivism as a struggle between the people and special interests is oversimplified, if not erroneous. Thus Louis Hartz, in his fascinating book *The Liberal Tradition in America: An Interpretation of American Political Thought Since the Revolution* (1955), argued that because America never had a feudal tradition it did not experience the struggles between conservatives, reactionaries, liberals, and Marxians that characterized the history of most European countries. On the contrary the United States had a

---

[7]George E. Mowry, "The California Progressive and His Rationale: A Study in Middle Class Politics," *Mississippi Valley Historical Review* 36 (September 1949):239–250.

[8]A number of historians have pointed to what they regard as a methodological flaw in the Mowry-Hofstadter analysis. To argue—as Mowry and Hofstadter have done—that the Progressives were a cohesive group requires that they show that the anti-Progressives represented a quite different social and economic group. One recent historian who did a study of the anti-Progressives in one state found that their social and economic and ideological characteristics were almost identical with those of the Progressives. See Richard B. Sherman, "The Status Revolution and Massachusetts Progressive Leadership," *Political Science Quarterly* 78 (March 1963):59–65; and Jerome M. Clubb and Howard W. Allen, "Collective Biography and the Progressive Movement: The 'Status Revolution' Revisited," *Social Science History* 4 (1977):518–534.

three-century-long tradition of consensus, wherein all Americans subscribed to the Lockean tenets of individualism, private property, natural rights, and popular sovereignty. The differences between Americans, Hartz maintained, have been over means rather than ends. Thus
Americans never had a conservative tradition in the European and Bur-
kean sense of the term because American liberalism, by virtue of its
continuity, was a conservative tradition. To view American history in
terms of class struggle, said Hartz, was to misunderstand the basic
agreements that united all Americans.

As a result of the rise of the neoconservative school of historians
the Progressive movement had begun to be interpreted in a new and
different light. Some of these scholars, for example, neatly reversed the
Progressive school approach. Instead of seeing early-twentieth-century
progressivism as a liberal movement, they argued that it was essentially conservative in nature—a characteristic that was a source of
strength rather than of weakness. Thus the historical stature of Theodore Roosevelt rose as historians such as John M. Blum saw him as a
conservative though responsible president who was flexible enough to
deal with the major issues of the day in a constructive yet practical
manner. Conversely the reputation of Woodrow Wilson among some
historians tended to decline because of his righteous moralism. Wilson's New Freedom, they wrote, was unrealistic because of its worship
of a bygone age where all individuals had equal opportunity in the economic sphere. His foreign policies also turned out to be dismal failures
because they rested on an exclusively moral foundation that omitted
any appreciation of the national interest or the realities of international affairs.[9]

Conversely the reputation of many American reformers suffered
as a result of the writings of neoconservative historians. Rather than
writing about their contributions and achievements historians have
shown the shortcomings and failures of various reform leaders. They
have exposed the personal and selfish factors that supposedly motivated the behavior of reformers and implicitly determined their unrealistic approach to contemporary problems. Above all, such historians
scored the reformers for accepting an optimistic moralism based on
their faith in progress. According to neoconservative scholars Progressive reformers tragically misunderstood man's propensity for evil. As
a result they failed to prepare Americans for the inevitable reaction
that followed their failure to establish a democratic utopia at home
and a peaceful international community of nations abroad in the first
two decades of the twentieth century.

---

[9]John M. Blum, *The Republican Roosevelt* (Cambridge, Mass., 1954). For a critical,
but by no means unsympathetic, interpretation of Wilson see Arthur S. Link, *Woodrow
Wilson and the Progressive Era 1910–1917* (New York, 1954).

At the same time that neoconservative scholars were attempting to undermine the Progressive school emphasis on reform and class conflict, other historians were in the process of developing an entirely new synthesis to explain American history since the late nineteenth century. Influenced by work in the social and behavioral sciences they began to apply organizational theory to historical study. Building on the impressive contributions of Max Weber and others, organizational historians saw American society as being increasingly dominated by hierarchical and bureaucratic structures, which were accompanied by a sharp acceleration in the process of professionalization. Associated with these developments was a corresponding shift in the nation's value system. Through the mid-nineteenth century individualistic values remained dominant; after that time they were replaced by an orientation that stressed ideals of efficiency, order, rationality, and systematic control.[10]

The organizational model—as we have already seen—had been employed by business historians such as Alfred D. Chandler, Jr., to explain the emergence of large corporations. But such a model was also capable of being applied in a far more inclusive manner. A number of historians, for example, advanced the thesis that progressivism represented largely an attempt to govern society in accordance with the new ideals of scientific management and efficiency. The conservation movement, to take one concrete illustration, was not—as historians of the Progressive school had maintained—a struggle by the American people and their champions against special interests and large corporate enterprises bent on depriving the nation of its natural resources and despoiling the landscape. On the contrary the conservation movement, according to Samuel P. Hays, was a movement of scientists and planners interested in "rational planning to promote efficient development and use of all natural resources." Frequently large corporations—which were profoundly influenced by the ideals of scientific management— were ardent supporters of conservationist policies because of their interest in long-range resource planning. Conversely small farmers, small cattlemen, homesteaders, and other groups that Progressive historians equated with the democratic masses often opposed conservation because it conflicted with their hopes of becoming rich quickly. "The broader significance of the conservation movement," Hays concluded, "stemmed from the role it played in the transformation of a decentralized, nontechnical, loosely organized society, where waste and inefficiency ran rampant, into a highly organized, technical, and

---

[10]For a penetrating discussion of this problem see Louis Galambos, "The Emerging Organizational Synthesis in Modern American History," *Business History Review* 44 (Autumn 1970):279–290, as well as his follow-up analysis, "Technology, Political Economy, and Professionalism: Central Themes of the Organizational Synthesis," *ibid.* 57 (Winter 1983):471–493.

centrally planned and directed social organization which could meet a complex world with efficiency and purpose."[11] Implicit in this approach was the assumption that conservation had little or nothing to do with the liberal-conservative categories of the Progressive school of historiography.

In a similar vein Hays argued that support for reform in municipal government came from business and professional groups. These groups felt that the welfare of the city could best be served if decision-making were centralized in their hands. In this way city governments would be run in a rational and businesslike manner. Hays's article appears as the first selection in this chapter.

In stressing the role of the "expert" and the ideals of scientific management as basic to an understanding of the Progressive era, organizational historians also reinterpreted other aspects of early-twentieth-century American history. Many of the Progressive reforms, they stressed, were directed not at making the government more democratic and responsive to the wishes of the American people, but to making it and the economy more efficient. The movement for federal regulation of business was not, as the Progressive school of historians had argued, motivated by fear or hatred of large corporate enterprise. Its goal, according to these newer historians, was the elimination of senseless and destructive competition in the economic system by making business and government partners in the effort to eliminate the ups and downs of the business cycle. Progressivism, therefore, reflected the desire of various professional groups to substitute planning for competition, to raise the "expert" to a position of paramount importance, and to end the inherent defects of democratic government by making government conform to the ideals of efficiency and rational planning.

The decline of the older view of the Progressive era was also evidenced in the changing historical interpretation of business and businessmen. For a good part of the twentieth century the liberal assumptions of most historians led them to portray the business community not only as monolithic in character but as being made up of men who were grasping, selfish, and narrow in their outlook. In recent scholarship, on the other hand, the businessman has been studied within a quite different framework. Business historians found in the careers of great entrepreneurs a creative and constructive leadership that brought into being America's phenomenal industrial capacity. Similarly a number of recent scholars have denied that the business community was necessarily reactionary or that all businessmen shared a common ide-

---

[11]Samuel P. Hays, *Conservation and the Gospel of Efficiency: The Progressive Conservation Movement, 1890–1920* (Cambridge, Mass., 1959), pp. 2 and 265. See also *American Political History as Social Analysis: Essays by Samuel P. Hays* (Knoxville, 1980).

ology. Instead they attempted to demonstrate that businessmen divided into various groups with conflicting ideas and that many of the Progressive reforms of the early twentieth century were actually introduced, supported, and endorsed by businessmen. In a study of the relationship between businessmen and the Progressive movement, for example, Robert H. Wiebe found a complex situation. Businessmen, he noted, rarely tried to improve the lot of low-income groups; they fought against unions and social insurance legislation; and while desiring to purify democracy they opposed its extension. Economic regulation, on the other hand, aroused a quite different response, for "at least one segment of the business community supported each major program for federal control. In this area businessmen exercised their greatest influence on reform and laid their claim as progressives."[12]

In *Businessmen and Reform* (1962) Wiebe had referred to the Progressive era as an "age of organization." Businessmen, he averred, turned to organization as a means of survival in an impersonal and changing world. Five years later, in a major work, Wiebe carried his analysis much further and provided one of the first attempts to synthesize American history around an organizational core. For much of the nineteenth century American society was composed of autonomous and semiautonomous "island communities." The United States was a nation more in name than in fact, for most individuals resided in relatively small, personal centers, each of which managed its affairs independently of other communities. By the 1880s, however, these communities no longer functioned in their traditional manner, for technological and economic forces had undermined their cohesiveness and caused "dislocation and bewilderment." The result, according to Wiebe, was a "search for order." Some attempted to restore the local community to a position of significance; others turned to agrarian reform; still others joined moral crusades in the belief that a return to traditional values would solve many problems. Ultimately most Progressives turned to organization to bring a new order and equilibrium to American society. In such diverse fields as law, medicine, economics, administration, social work, architecture, business, labor, and agriculture—to cite only a few examples—a new middle class appeared, tied together by their conviction that their expertise and occupational cohesiveness provided the means of ordering a fragmented society. "The heart of progressivism," wrote Wiebe, "was the ambition of the new middle class to fulfill its destiny through bureaucratic means."[13] Slowly but surely America was brought "to the edge of something as yet indefinable. In a general sense the nation had found its direction

---

[12]Robert H. Wiebe, *Businessmen and Reform: A Study of the Progressive Movement* (Cambridge, Mass., 1962), p. 212.

[13]Robert H. Wiebe, *The Search for Order 1877–1920* (New York, 1967), p. 166.

early in the twentieth century. The society that so many in the nineties had thought would either disintegrate or polarize had emerged tough and plural; and by 1920 the realignments, the reorientations of the Progressive era, had been translated into a complex of arrangements nothing short of a revolution could destroy."[14]

Curiously enough neoconservative, consensus, and organizational interpretations of the Progressive movement that grew in influence in the 1950s and 1960s were also echoed by New Left historians. Disillusioned by the continued existence of war, poverty, and racism, New Left scholars tended to write about the shortcomings and failures of American reform, a point of view that grew out of their own belief that only radical changes in the framework and structure of American society would solve these problems. Consequently the New Left interpretation of early-twentieth-century progressivism was written within a partial consensus framework (although those individuals writing within this radical tradition clearly rejected the consensus on which this movement was based) and an awareness of the importance of organizations in twentieth-century America.

To New Left historians the Progressive movement was anything but a reform movement. In one of the most significant studies of early-twentieth-century American history Gabriel Kolko argued that both major political parties shared a common ideology and set of values. This ideology—what Kolko called political capitalism—sought the elimination of a growing competition in the economy. Political capitalism, he noted, "redirected the radical potential of mass grievances and aspirations"; rather than federal regulation *of* business the norm became federal regulation *for* business. Between 1900 and 1916 a unique synthesis of economics and politics occurred. Progressivism, argued Kolko,

> *was initially a movement for the political rationalization of business and industrial conditions, a movement that operated on the assumption that the general welfare of the community could be best served by satisfying the concrete needs of business. But the regulation itself was invariably controlled by leaders of the regulated industry, and directed toward ends they deemed acceptable or desirable. In part this came about because the regulatory movements were usually initiated by the dominant businesses to be regulated, but it also resulted from the nearly universal belief among political leaders in the basic justice of private property relations as they essentially existed, a belief that set the ultimate limits on the leaders' possible actions.*

Since neither populism nor the Socialist party developed a specific diagnosis of existing social dynamics and relationships, Americans had

---

[14]*Ibid.*, pp. 301–302.

no viable alternatives, for the two major political parties became the means through which business domination was institutionalized. "The Progressive Era," concluded Kolko, "was characterized by a paucity of alternatives to the status quo, a vacuum that permitted political capitalism to direct the growth of individualism in America, to shape its politics, to determine the ground rules for American civilization in the twentieth century, and to set the stage for what was to follow."[15]

The reaction against the liberal interpretation of the Progressive movement, however, has not been shared by all historians. While admitting that older historians may have been wrong in their emphasis on a class conflict of the people versus the special interests, some scholars continue to see progressivism as an attempt to deal effectively with many social and economic problems that grew out of industrialism and the resulting concentration of power in the hands of a few individuals and groups. J. Joseph Huthmacher, for example, explicitly rejected the Mowry-Hofstadter idea that progressivism was a middle-class movement dominated by a system of values espoused by rural-Yankee-Protestant groups. On the contrary Huthmacher maintained that progressivism was much more broadly based, and that lower-class groups played an important role in the movement. Implicitly rejecting the neoconservative thesis Huthmacher argued that progressivism was an attempt to cope with the complex dilemmas of an urban-industrial society. Although he clearly rejected the Jeffersonian agrarian interpretation of progressivism his point of view was essentially a modification and elaboration of the Progressive school that saw the reform movement of 1900–1920 as a continuing phase in the perennial struggle of liberalism versus conservatism.[16]

Nor was Huthmacher alone in reasserting a version of the older interpretation of progressivism. John C. Burnham, for example, pointed to the voluntaristic flavor of progressivism and its effort to merge Protestant moral values with the hard facts of scientific and technological change. Indeed, Burnham insisted that moral commitment and immediacy lay at the heart of this movement, which left behind a number of specific achievements. Similarly John D. Buenker pointed to the broad-based nature of progressivism that included middle- and lower-class elements.[17]

---

[15]Gabriel Kolko, *The Triumph of Conservatism: A Reinterpretation of American History, 1900–1916* (New York, 1963), pp. 2–3, 285, and 303. See also James Weinstein, *The Corporate Ideal in the Liberal State, 1900–1918* (Boston, 1968).

[16]J. Joseph Huthmacher, "Urban Liberalism and the Age of Reform," *Mississippi Valley Historical Review* 44 (September 1962):231–241.

[17]John D. Buenker, John C. Burnham, and Robert M. Crunden, *Progressivism* (Cambridge, Mass., 1977). This volume is composed of three separate essays by three historians. Although there are important differences among them the degree of similarity is also striking. See also John D. Buenker, *Urban Liberalism and Progressive Reform* (New York, 1973).

Increasingly the Mowry-Hofstadter thesis that status tensions and insecurity were central to the origins of progressivism came under attack as well. Using the state of Wisconsin as a case study David P. Thelen could find no correlation between an individual's social characteristics and his political affiliation and ideology. Rejecting the sociological and psychological interpretation that progressivism was rooted in social tensions, he argued instead that its roots went back into the nineteenth century. The depression of the 1890s was of particular importance for it dramatized the failures of industrialism and gave rise to a search for alternatives. Out of this search came a broad consensus on a series of reform programs that cut across class lines. All groups could unite on the urgent necessity for tax reform and the need to control "corporate arrogance." "When the progressive characteristically spoke of reform as a fight of 'the people' or the 'public interest' against the 'selfish interests,' he was speaking quite literally of his political coalition because the important fact about progressivism, at least in Wisconsin, was the degree of cooperation between previously discrete social groups now united under the banner of the 'public interest' . . . Both conceptually and empirically it would seem safer and more productive to view reformers first as reformers and only secondarily as men who were trying to relieve class and status anxieties."[18]

Most interpretations of progressivism rested on studies of midwestern and eastern states. In a significant analysis of Alabama during the Progressive era, on the other hand, Sheldon Hackney found that many of the standard generalizations were open to question. He noted, for example, that there was little continuity between populism and progressivism in Alabama; following the demise of their party Populists either voted Republican or else withdrew from politics. Holding a social philosophy that viewed society in static terms they clearly preferred a minimal rather than an activist government; they were "primitive rebels." Nor were Progressives motivated by status anxiety or committed to producer values; they saw society in dynamic terms and insisted that economic opportunity could come about only through greater economic growth stimulated in part by positive governmental action. Unlike their forebears, Progressives were earnestly interested in changing southern society and bringing it into the modern industrial era. Indeed, Hackney found that Alabama progressivism resembled more the eastern, urban Roosevelt brand than the western, rural Bryan variety.

But progressivism, as Hackney observed, also had sharp implications for the status of black Americans in Alabama. During the years

---

[18]David P. Thelen, "Social Tensions and the Origins of Progressivism," *Journal of American History* 56 (September 1969):323–341, and *The New Citizenship: Origins of Progressivism in Wisconsin, 1885–1900* (Columbia, Mo., 1972).

from 1890 to 1910 the pattern of race relations in that state was highly fluid; inconsistency was its primary characteristic. One manifestation of this uncertainty was the high frequency of lynchings. Stability came to Alabama only when the Constitutional Convention of 1901 in effect eliminated black citizens from political participation. Curiously enough the movement for disfranchisement was led by opponents of reform. Their success helped Progressives create a new coalition from the purged electorate that owed little to Populist antecedents. Progressivism in Alabama, therefore, rested on the institutionalization of legal and political inequality. Hackney's book raised significant questions about the nature of progressivism and gave little support to either liberal, conservative, or radical schools of historical interpretation.[19]

Oddly enough virtually all historians, whether they are in the older Progressive or the newer neoconservative, organizational, or New Left traditions, seem to be in agreement on at least one major point; namely, that progressivism was an urban rather than a rural-centered movement. Once again historians seem to have been reflecting their milieu. In the past many of the major historians had come out of an environment dominated by rural and agrarian values; their attitude toward cities was partly conditioned by the prevailing view that American democracy was the creation of a rural agrarian society. Within the past two or three decades, however, the majority of historians have tended to come from a society and regions of the country much more concerned with the problems of urban life. They do not share the anti-urban attitudes held by many of their predecessors. As a result these historians have written about the contributions to American history of cities and growing urban areas.

More recently historians interested in progressivism once again turned their attention to the analysis of politics and political parties at the turn of the century. Most scholars had accepted the view that progressivism was a pluralistic, not a unitary, movement. No historian, however had provided a persuasive explanation as to why so many groups committed to social, economic, and political changes appeared simultaneously on both the state and national level. It was precisely on this point that the work of Walter Dean Burnham, a political scientist, became relevant to historians. Burnham had identified a major shift in American politics at this time: namely, a weakening of party loyalty accompanied by a massive decline in voting. The decline of party, in turn, magnified the significance of pressure groups of all kinds.[20]

---

[19]Sheldon Hackney, *Populism to Progressivism in Alabama* (Princeton, 1969).

[20]Walter Dean Burnham, "The Changing Shape of the American Political Universe," *American Political Science Review* 59 (March 1965):7–28, and *Critical Elections and the Mainsprings of American Politics* (New York, 1970), *passim*.

The problem for historians was to explain why the pull of parties had declined and what significance this development had upon American society. In dealing with this problem the stage was set for a shift in the interpretations of progressivism. In his book on New York State politics in the Progressive era Richard L. McCormick had shown how the hold of party bosses had been undermined by the attacks of reformers and antiparty crusaders, and how new issues had arisen that were incapable of being resolved by the traditional party technique of distributing favors as widely as possible. In a subsequent article McCormick pointed to the remarkable transformation that occurred between 1904 and 1908. The regulatory authority of government at this time increased in precisely the same period that voter turnout declined, ticket-splitting increased, and organized pressure groups gained power at the expense of party. In discovering that business corrupted politics during this era Americans created a demand for the regulatory and administrative state, thus facilitating the activities of organizationally minded individuals from business and the professions determined to complete a political transformation. Although not in fundamental disagreement with organizational historians such as Hays, McCormick insisted on the relevancy of ideas and perceptions that often shaped the outcome of events in unpredictable ways.[21] McCormick's article on the discovery that business corrupted politics appears as the second selection in this chapter.

As Daniel Rodgers has recently observed, historians no longer attempt to describe the Progressive era within a static ideological framework. Indeed, the roots of the Progressive distrust of arbitrary and unregulated power had diverse and even conflicting sources. But if Progressives lacked a systematic and coherent intellectual system they did possess tools that were sufficiently powerful to make an impact. In Rodgers's eyes, therefore, progressivism can only be understood in terms of dynamic and changing social and political structures. "To acknowledge that these are the questions that matter and to abandon the hunt for the *essence* of the noise and tumult of that era may not be . . . to lose the whole," he concluded. "It may be to find it."[22]

As the historiography of the Progressive movement shows, it is difficult to evaluate the specific contributions of the movement without dealing with certain moral values that inevitably influence the historical judgments of scholars studying the subject. To the Progressive school of historical scholarship progressivism was one of the first ef-

---

[21]Richard L. McCormick, *From Realignment to Reform: Political Change in New York State, 1893–1910* (Ithaca, 1981), and "The Discovery that Business Corrupts Politics: A Reappraisal of the Origins of Progressivism," *American Historical Review 86* (April 1981):247–274.

[22]Daniel T. Rodgers, "In Search of Progressivism," *Reviews in American History 10* (December 1982):113–132.

forts to adjust American values to an urban, industrialized society. The concentration of economic power was thwarting the workings of American democratic institutions as well as corrupting the moral fiber of its citizens. Since they agreed with the goals of reformers who were attempting to ameliorate this situation, the writings of the Progressive school of historians on the movement tended to be a favorable one. More recent scholars, on the other hand, operated within quite a different value structure. Business and other nonconservative historians, precisely because they emphasized the constructive achievements of American business, did not see much good in a movement which they believed was based on superficial knowledge, amateurism, and demagoguery. Because these historians were more complacent, even proud, of the accomplishments of American society they saw less need for radical reforms in America's past history. Hence they either emphasized the conservative nature of progressivism or else pointed to its lack of realism or its optimistic illusions in order to show why the movement failed. Similarly New Left scholars were equally hostile in their analysis of progressivism; they saw the movement as one dedicated to the control of government by business, giving it a reactionary rather than a reform character. Some historians who identified themselves with the liberal tradition also argued that American liberalism fell far short of enacting truly meaningful reforms during the Progressive era. Thus it was possible for neoconservative, liberal, and radical scholars to be critical of the Progressive movement from their respective viewpoints. And even organizational historians evidenced considerable ambivalence; they were not at all certain that a society based on bureaucratic values and structures was necessarily good.

The problem of evaluating the nature of the Progressive movement, therefore, is by no means easy or simple. Despite considerable research on this important era of American history the divisions among historians are not necessarily disappearing. On the contrary these divisions are in some respects growing sharper because of differences among historians pertaining to the nature and meaning of the American liberal tradition. In the final analysis, when historians are assessing progressivism, they are assessing also the ability of Americans to adapt themselves to new problems in any given era.

Aside from the ideological and philosophical conflicts among historians, there are several major questions and problems that must be dealt with in evaluating the Progressive movement. Was there a relationship between the Progressive movement and earlier as well as later reform movements, including populism and the New Deal? Who were the Progressives and what did they represent? Similarly what groups opposed progressivism and why did they do so? Were the reforms that were enacted between 1900 and 1917 constructive? What impact, if any, did they have upon American life? What significance did progress-

ivism have for black Americans and other minority groups? Why did
the Progressive movement come to an end as an organized movement,
or did it, indeed, come to an end at all?

These are only a few of the questions that historians have dealt
with in an effort to understand the development of American society
during the first two decades of the twentieth century. It is difficult, if
not impossible, to avoid addressing oneself to these issues because of
the bearing they have upon the larger question of understanding the
nature of the American experience.

Samuel P. Hays

SAMUEL P. HAYS (1921–   ) *is professor of history at the University of Pittsburgh. He has written widely in American social and political history; his books include* The Response to Industrialism 1885–1914 *(1957),* Conservation and the Gospel of Efficiency *(1959), and* American Political History as Social Analysis *(1980).*

In order to achieve a more complete understanding of social change in the Progressive Era, historians must now undertake a deeper analysis of the practices of economic, political, and social groups. Political ideology alone is no longer satisfactory evidence to describe social patterns because generalizations based upon it, which tend to divide political groups into the moral and the immoral, the rational and the irrational, the efficient and the inefficient, do not square with political practice. Behind this contemporary rhetoric concerning the nature of reform lay patterns of political behavior which were at variance with it. Since an extensive gap separated ideology and practice, we can no longer take the former as an accurate description of the latter, but must reconstruct social behavior from other types of evidence.

Reform in urban government provides one of the most striking examples of this problem of analysis. The demand for change in municipal affairs, whether in terms of overall reform, such as the commission and city-manager plans, or of more piecemeal modifications, such as the development of citywide school boards, deeply involved reform ideology. Reformers loudly proclaimed a new structure of municipal government as more moral, more rational, and more efficient and, because it was so, self-evidently more desirable. But precisely because of this emphasis, there seemed to be no need to analyze the political forces behind change. Because the goals of reform were good, its causes were obvious; rather than being the product of particular people and particular ideas in particular situations, they were deeply imbedded in the universal impulses and truths of "progress." Consequently, historians have rarely tried to determine precisely who the municipal reformers were or what they did, but instead have relied on reform ideology as an accurate description of reform practice.

The reform ideology which became the basis of historical analysis

---

Samuel P. Hays, "The Politics of Reform in Municipal Government in the Progressive Era," *Pacific Northwest Quarterly* 55 (October 1964):157–169. Reprinted by permission of the *Pacific Northwest Quarterly*.

is well known. It appears in classic form in Lincoln Steffens' *Shame of the Cities*. The urban political struggle of the Progressive Era, so the argument goes, involved a conflict between public impulses for "good government" against a corrupt alliance of "machine politicians" and "special interests."

During the rapid urbanization of the late nineteenth century, the latter had been free to aggrandize themselves, especially through franchise grants, at the expense of the public. Their power lay primarily in their ability to manipulate the political process, by bribery and corruption, for their own ends. Against such arrangements there gradually arose a public protest, a demand by the public for honest government, for officials who would act for the public rather than for themselves. To accomplish their goals, reformers sought basic modifications in the political system, both in the structure of government and in the manner of selecting public officials. These changes, successful in city after city, enabled the "public interest" to triumph.

Recently, George Mowry, Alfred Chandler, Jr., and Richard Hofstadter have modified this analysis by emphasizing the fact that the impulse for reform did not come from the working class. This might have been suspected from the rather strained efforts of National Municipal League writers in the "Era of Reform" to go out of their way to demonstrate working-class support for commission and city-manager governments. We now know that they clutched at straws, and often erroneously, in order to prove to themselves as well as to the public that municipal reform was a mass movement.

The Mowry-Chandler-Hofstadter writings have further modified older views by asserting that reform in general and municipal reform in particular sprang from a distinctively middle-class movement. This has now become the prevailing view. Its popularity is surprising not only because it is based upon faulty logic and extremely limited evidence, but also because it, too, emphasizes the analysis of ideology rather than practice and fails to contribute much to the understanding of who distinctively were involved in reform and why.

Ostensibly, the "middle-class" theory of reform is based upon a new type of behavioral evidence, the collective biography, in studies by Mowry of California Progressive party leaders, by Chandler of a nationwide group of that party's leading figures, and by Hofstadter of four professions—ministers, lawyers, teachers, editors. These studies demonstrate the middle-class nature of reform, but they fail to determine if reformers were distinctively middle-class, specifically if they differed from their opponents. One study of 300 political leaders in the state of Iowa, for example, discovered that Progressive-party, Old Guard, and Cummins Republicans were all substantially alike, the Progressives differing only in that they were slightly younger than the others and had less political experience. If its opponents were also middle-class, then one cannot describe Progressive reform as a phenomenon whose special nature can be explained in terms of middle-class characteristics. One cannot explain the distinctive behavior of people in terms of characteristics which are not distinctive to them.

Hofstadter's evidence concerning professional men fails in yet another way to determine the peculiar characteristics of reformers, for he describes ministers, lawyers, teachers, and editors without determining who within these professions became reformers and who did not. Two analytical distinctions might be made. Ministers involved in municipal reform, it appears, came not from all segments of religion, but peculiarly from upper-class churches. They enjoyed the highest prestige and salaries in the religious community and had no reason to feel a loss of "status," as Hofstadter argues. Their role in reform arose from the class character of their religious organizations rather than from the mere fact of their occupation as ministers. Professional men involved in reform (many of whom—engineers, architects, and doctors—Hofstadter did not examine at all) seem to have come especially from the more advanced segments of their professions, from those who sought to apply their specialized knowledge to a wider range of public affairs. Their role in reform is related not to their attempt to defend earlier patterns of culture, but to the working out of the inner dynamics of professionalization in modern society.

The weakness of the "middle-class" theory of reform stems from the fact that it rests primarily upon ideological evidence, not on a thorough-going description of political practice. Although the studies of Mowry, Chandler, and Hofstadter ostensibly derive from behavioral evidence, they actually derive largely from the extensive expressions of middle-ground ideological position, of the reformers' own descriptions of their contemporary society, and of their expressed fears of both the lower and the upper classes, of the fright of being ground between the millstones of labor and capital.

Such evidence, though it accurately portrays what people thought, does not accurately describe what they did. The great majority of Americans look upon themselves as "middle-class" and subscribe to a middle-ground ideology, even though in practice they belong to a great variety of distinct social classes. Such ideologies are not rationalizations or deliberate attempts to deceive. They are natural phenomena of human behavior. But the historian should be especially sensitive to their role so that he will not take evidence of political ideology as an accurate representation of political practice.

In the following account I will summarize evidence in both secondary and primary works concerning the political practices in which municipal reformers were involved. Such an analysis logically can be broken down into three parts, each one corresponding to a step in the traditional argument. First, what was the source of reform? Did it lie in the general public rather than in particular groups? Was it middle-class, working-class, or perhaps of other composition? Second, what was the reform target of attack? Were reformers primarily interested in ousting the corrupt individual, the political or business leader who made private arrangements at the expense of the public, or were they interested in something else? Third, what political innovations did reformers bring about? Did they seek to expand popular participation in the governmental process?

There is now sufficient evidence to determine the validity of these specific elements of the more general argument. Some of it has been available for several decades; some has appeared more recently; some is presented here for the first time. All of it adds up to the conclusion that reform in municipal government involved a political development far different from what we have assumed in the past.

Available evidence indicates that the source of support for reform in municipal government did not come from the lower or middle classes, but from the upper class. The leading business groups in each city and professional men closely allied with them initiated and dominated municipal movements. Leonard White, in his study of the city manager published in 1927, wrote:

> *The opposition to bad government usually comes to a head in the local chamber of commerce. Business men finally acquire the conviction that the growth of their city is being seriously impaired by the failures of city officials to perform their duties efficiently. Looking about for a remedy, they are captivated by the resemblance of the city-manager plan to their corporate form of business organization.*

In the 1930s White directed a number of studies of the origin of city-manager government. The resulting reports invariably begin with such statements as, "the Chamber of Commerce spearheaded the movement," or commission government in this city was a "businessmen's government." Of thirty-two cases of city-manager government in Oklahoma examined by Jewell C. Phillips, twenty-nine were initiated either by chambers of commerce or by community committees dominated by businessmen. More recently James Weinstein has presented almost irrefutable evidence that the business community, represented largely by chambers of commerce, was the overwhelming force behind both commission and city-manager movements.

Dominant elements of the business community played a prominent role in another crucial aspect of municipal reform: the Municipal Research Bureau movement. Especially in the larger cities, where they had less success in shaping the structure of government, reformers established centers to conduct research in municipal affairs as a springboard for influence.

The first such organization, the Bureau of Municipal Research of

New York City, was founded in 1906; it was financed largely through the efforts of Andrew Carnegie and John D. Rockefeller. An investment banker provided the crucial support in Philadelphia, where a Bureau was founded in 1908. A group of wealthy Chicagoans in 1910 established the Bureau of Public Efficiency, a research agency. John H. Patterson of the National Cash Register Company, the leading figure in Dayton municipal reform, financed the Dayton Bureau, founded in 1912. And George Eastman was the driving force behind both the Bureau of Municipal Research and city-manager government in Rochester. In smaller cities data about city government were collected by interested individuals in a more informal way or by chambers of commerce, but in larger cities the task required special support, and prominent businessmen supplied it.

The character of municipal reform is demonstrated more precisely by a brief examination of the movements in Des Moines and Pittsburgh. The Des Moines Commercial Club inaugurated and carefully controlled the drive for the commission form of government. In January 1906 the club held a so-called "mass meeting" of business and professional men to secure an enabling act from the state legislature. P. C. Kenyon, president of the club, selected a Committee of 300, composed principally of business and professional men, to draw up a specific proposal. After the legislature approved their plan, the same committee managed the campaign which persuaded the electorate to accept the commission form of government by a narrow margin in June 1907.

In this election the lower-income wards of the city opposed the change, the upper-income wards supported it strongly, and the middle-income wards were more evenly divided. In order to control the new government, the Committee of 300, now expanded to 530, sought to determine the nomination and election of the five new commissioners, and to this end they selected an avowedly businessman's slate. Their plans backfired when the voters swept into office a slate of anti-commission candidates who now controlled the new commission government.

Proponents of the commission form of government in Des Moines spoke frequently in the name of "the people." But their more explicit statements emphasized their intent that the new plan be a "business system" of government, run by businessmen. The slate of candidates for commissioner endorsed by advocates of the plan was known as the "businessman's ticket." J. W. Hill, president of the committees of 300 and 530, bluntly declared: "The professional politician must be ousted and in his place capable business men chosen to conduct the affairs of the city." I. M. Earle, general counsel of the Bankers' Life Association and a prominent figure in the movement, put the point more precisely: "When the plan was adopted it was the intention to get businessmen to run it."

Although reformers used the ideology of popular government, they in no sense meant that all segments of society should be involved equally in municipal decision-making. They meant that their concept of the city's welfare would be best achieved if the business community controlled city government. As one businessman told a labor audience, the businessman's slate represented labor "better than you do yourself."

The composition of the municipal reform movement in Pittsburgh demonstrates its upper-class and professional as well as its business sources. Here the two principal reform organizations were the Civic Club and the Voters' League. The 745 members of these two organizations came primarily from the upper class. Sixty-five percent appeared in upper-class directories which contained the names of only 2 percent of the city's families. Furthermore, many who were not listed in these directories lived in upper-class areas. These reformers, it should be stressed, comprised not an old but a new upper class. Few came from earlier industrial and mercantile families. Most of them had risen to social position from wealth created after 1870 in the iron, steel, electrical equipment, and other industries, and they lived in the newer rather than the older fashionable areas.

Almost half (48 percent) of the reformers were professional men: doctors, lawyers, ministers, directors of libraries and museums, engineers, architects, private and public school teachers, and college professors. Some of these belonged to the upper class as well, especially the lawyers, ministers, and private school teachers. But for the most part their interest in reform stemmed from the inherent dynamics of their professions rather than from their class connections. They came from the more advanced segments of their organizations, from those in the forefront of the acquisition and application of knowledge. They were not the older professional men, seeking to preserve the past against change; they were in the vanguard of professional life, actively seeking to apply expertise more widely to public affairs.

Pittsburgh reformers included a large segment of businessmen; 52 percent were bankers and corporation officials or their wives. Among them were the presidents of fourteen large banks and officials of Westinghouse, Pittsburgh Plate Glass, U.S. Steel and its component parts (such as Carnegie Steel, American Bridge, and National Tube), Jones and Laughlin, lesser steel companies (such as Crucible, Pittsburgh, Superior, Lockhart, and H. K. Porter), the H. J. Heinz Company, and the Pittsburgh Coal Company, as well as officials of the Pennsylvania Railroad and the Pittsburgh and Lake Erie. These men were not small businessmen; they directed the most powerful banking and industrial organizations of the city. They represented not the old business community, but industries which had developed and grown primarily within the past fifty years and which had come to dominate the city's economic life.

These business, professional, and upper-class groups who dominated municipal reform movements were all involved in the rationalization and systematization of modern life; they wished a form of government which would be more consistent with the objectives inherent in those developments. The most important single feature of their perspective was the rapid expansion of the geographical scope of affairs which they wished to influence and manipulate, a scope which was no longer limited and narrow, no longer within the confines of pedestrian communities, but was now broad and citywide, covering the whole range of activities of the metropolitan area.

The migration of the upper class from central to outlying areas created a geographical distance between its residential communities and its economic institutions. To protect the latter required involvement both in local ward affairs and in the larger city government as well. Moreover, upper-class cultural institutions, such as museums, libraries, and symphony orchestras, required an active interest in the larger, municipal context from which these institutions drew much of their clientele.

Professional groups, broadening the scope of affairs which they sought to study, measure, or manipulate, also sought to influence the public health, the educational system, or the physical arrangements of the entire city. Their concerns were limitless, not bounded by geography, but as expansive as the professional imagination. Finally, the new industrial community greatly broadened its perspective in governmental affairs because of its new recognition of the way in which factors throughout the city affected business growth. The increasing size and scope of industry, the greater stake in more varied and geographically dispersed facets of city life, the effect of floods on many business concerns, the need to promote traffic flows to and from work for both blue-collar and managerial employees—all contributed to this larger interest. The geographically larger private perspectives of upper-class, professional, and business groups gave rise to a geographically larger public perspective.

These reformers were dissatisfied with existing systems of municipal government. They did not oppose corruption per se—although there was plenty of that. They objected to the structure of government which enabled local and particularistic interests to dominate. Prior to the reforms of the Progressive Era, city government consisted primarily of confederations of local wards, each of which was represented on the city's legislative body. Each ward frequently had its own elementary schools and ward-elected school boards which administered them.

These particularistic interests were the focus of a decentralized political life. City councilmen were local leaders. They spoke for their local areas, the economic interests of their inhabitants, their residential concerns, their educational, recreational, and religious interests— i.e., for those aspects of community life which mattered most to those they represented. They rolled logs in the city council to provide streets, sewers, and other public works for their local areas. They defended the community's cultural practices, its distinctive languages or national customs, its liberal attitude toward liquor, and its saloons and dance halls which served as centers of community life. One observer described this process of representation in Seattle:

> The residents of the hill-tops and the suburbs may not fully appreciate the faithfulness of certain downtown ward councilmen to the interests of their constituents. . . . The people of a state would rise in arms against a senator or representative in Congress who deliberately misrepresented their wishes and imperilled their interests, though he might plead a higher regard for national good. Yet people in other parts of the city seem to forget that under the old system the ward elected councilmen with the idea of procuring service of special benefit to that ward.

In short, pre-reform officials spoke for their constituencies, inevitably their own wards which had elected them, rather than for other sections or groups of the city.

The ward system of government especially gave representation in city affairs to lower- and middle-class groups. Most elected ward officials were from these groups, and they, in turn, constituted the major opposition to reforms in municipal government. In Pittsburgh, for example, immediately prior to the changes in both the city council and the school board in 1911 in which citywide representation replaced ward representation, only 24 percent of the 387 members of those bodies represented the same managerial, professional, and banker occupations which dominated the membership of the Civic Club and the Voters' League. The great majority (67 percent) were small businessmen— grocers, saloonkeepers, livery-stable proprietors, owners of small hotels, druggists—white-collar workers such as clerks and bookkeepers, and skilled and unskilled workmen.

This decentralized system of urban growth and the institutions which arose from it reformers now opposed. Social, professional, and economic life had not only developed in the local wards in a small community context, but had also on a larger scale become highly integrated and organized, giving rise to a superstructure of social organization which lay far above that of ward life and which was sharply divorced from it in both personal contacts and perspective.

By the late nineteenth century, those involved in these larger institutions found that the decentralized system of political life limited their larger objectives. The movement for reform in municipal government, therefore, constituted an attempt by upper-class, advanced professional, and large-business groups to take formal political power from the previously dominant lower- and middle-class elements so that they might advance their own conceptions of desirable public policy. These two groups came from entirely different urban worlds, and the political system fashioned by one was no longer acceptable to the other.

Lower- and middle-class groups not only dominated the pre-reform governments but vigorously opposed reform. It is significant that none of the occupational groups among them, for example, small businessmen or white-collar workers, skilled or unskilled artisans, had important representation in reform organizations thus far examined. The case studies of city-manager government undertaken in the 1930s under the direction of Leonard White detailed in city after city the particular opposition of labor. In their analysis of Jackson, Michigan, the authors of these studies wrote:

> The Square Deal, *oldest Labor paper in the state, has been consistently against manager government, perhaps largely because labor has felt that with a decentralized government elected on a ward basis it was more likely to have some voice to receive its share of privileges.*

In Janesville, Wisconsin, the small shopkeepers and workingmen on the west and south sides, heavily Catholic and often Irish, opposed the commission plan in 1911 and in 1912 and the city-manager plan when adopted in 1923. "In Dallas there is hardly a trace of class consciousness in the Marxian sense," one investigator declared, "yet in city elections the division has been to a great extent along class lines." The commission and city-manager elections were no exceptions. To these authors it seemed a logical reaction, rather than an embarrassing fact that had to be swept away, that workingmen should have opposed municipal reform.

In Des Moines working-class representatives, who in previous years might have been council members, were conspicuously absent from the "businessman's slate." Workingmen acceptable to reformers could not be found. A workingman's slate of candidates, therefore, appeared to challenge the reform slate. Organized labor, and especially the mineworkers, took the lead; one of their number, Wesley Ash, a deputy sheriff and union member, made "an astonishing run" in the primary, coming in second among a field of more than twenty candidates. In fact, the strength of anticommission candidates in the primary so alarmed reformers that they frantically sought to appease labor.

The day before the final election they modified their platform to pledge both an eight-hour day and an "American standard of wages."

They attempted to persuade the voters that their slate consisted of men who represented labor because they had "begun at the bottom of the ladder and made a good climb toward success by their own unaided efforts." But their tactics failed. In the election on March 30, 1908, voters swept into office the entire "opposition" slate. The business and professional community had succeeded in changing the form of government, but not in securing its control. A cartoon in the leading reform newspaper illustrated their disappointment; John Q. Public sat dejectedly and muttered, "Aw, What's the Use?"

The most visible opposition to reform and the most readily available target of reform attack was the so-called "machine," for through the "machine" many different ward communities as well as lower- and middle-income groups joined effectively to influence the central city government. Their private occupational and social life did not naturally involve these groups in larger citywide activities in the same way as the upper class was involved; hence they lacked access to privately organized economic and social power on which they could construct political power. The "machine" filled this organizational gap.

Yet it should never be forgotten that the social and economic institutions in the wards themselves provided the "machine's" sustaining support and gave it larger significance. When reformers attacked the "machine" as the most visible institutional element of the ward system, they attacked the entire ward form of political organization and the political power of lower- and middle-income groups which lay behind it.

Reformers often gave the impression that they opposed merely the corrupt politician and his "machine." But in a more fundamental way they looked upon the deficiencies of pre-reform political leaders in terms not of their personal shortcomings, but of the limitations inherent in their occupational, institutional, and class positions. In 1911 the Voters' League of Pittsburgh wrote in its pamphlet analyzing the qualifications of candidates that "a man's occupation ought to give a strong indication of his qualifications for membership on a school board." Certain occupations inherently disqualified a man from serving:

> *Employment as ordinary laborer in the lowest class of mill work would naturally lead to the conclusion that such men did not have sufficient education or business training to act as school directors. ... Objection might also be made to small shopkeepers, clerks, workmen at many trades, who by lack of educational advantages and business training, could not, no matter how honest, be expected to administer properly the affairs of an educational system, requiring special knowledge, and where millions are spent each year.*

These, of course, were precisely the groups which did dominate Pittsburgh government prior to reform. The League deplored the fact that school boards contained only a small number of "men prominent throughout the city in business life . . . in professional occupations . . . holding positions as managers, secretaries, auditors, superintendents and foremen" and exhorted these classes to participate more actively as candidates for office.

Reformers, therefore, wished not simply to replace bad men with good; they proposed to change the occupational and class origins of decision-makers. Toward this end they sought innovations in the formal machinery of government which would concentrate political power by sharply centralizing the processes of decision-making rather than distribute it through more popular participation in public affairs. According to the liberal view of the Progressive Era, the major political innovations of reform involved the equalization of political power through the primary, the direct election of public officials, and the initiative, referendum, and recall. These measures played a large role in the political ideology of the time and were frequently incorporated into new municipal charters. But they provided at best only an occasional and often incidental process of decision-making. Far more important in continuous, sustained, day-to-day processes of government were those innovations which centralized decision-making in the hands of fewer and fewer people.

The systematization of municipal government took place on both the executive and the legislative levels. The strong-mayor and city-manager types became the most widely used examples of the former. In the first decade of the twentieth century, the commission plan had considerable appeal, but its distribution of administrative responsibility among five people gave rise to a demand for a form with more centralized executive power; consequently, the city-manager or the commission-manager variant often replaced it.

A far more pervasive and significant change, however, lay in the centralization of the system of representation, the shift from ward to citywide election of councils and school boards. Governing bodies so selected, reformers argued, would give less attention to local and particularistic matters and more to affairs of citywide scope. This shift, an invariable feature of both commission and city-manager plans, was often adopted by itself. In Pittsburgh, for example, the new charter of 1911 provided as the major innovation that a council of twenty-seven, each member elected from a separate ward, be replaced by a council of nine, each elected by the city as a whole.

Cities displayed wide variations in this innovation. Some regrouped wards into larger units but kept the principle of areas of representation smaller than the entire city. Some combined a majority of councilmen elected by wards with additional ones elected at large. All such innovations, however, constituted steps toward the centralization of the system of representation.

Liberal historians have not appreciated the extent to which municipal reform in the Progressive Era involved a debate over the system of representation. The ward form of representation was universally condemned on the grounds that it gave too much influence to the separate units and not enough attention to the larger problems of the city. Harry A. Toulmin, whose book *The City Manager* was published by the National Municipal League, stated the case:

> *The spirit of sectionalism had dominated the political life of every city. Ward pitted against ward, alderman against alderman, and legislation only effected by "log-rolling" extravagant measures into operation, mulcting the city, but gratifying the greed of constituents, has too long stung the conscience of decent citizenship. This constant treaty-making of factionalism has been no less than a curse. The city-manager plan proposes the commendable thing of abolishing wards. The plan is not unique in this for it has been common to many forms of commission government. . . .*

Such a system should be supplanted, the argument usually went with citywide representation in which elected officials could consider the city "as a unit." "The new officers are elected," wrote Toulmin, "each to represent all the people. Their duties are so defined that they must administer the corporate business in its entirety, not as a hodge-podge of associated localities."

Behind the debate over the method of representation, however, lay a debate over who should be represented, over whose views of public policy should prevail. Many reform leaders often explicitly, if not implicitly, expressed fear that lower- and middle-income groups had too much influence in decision-making. One Galveston leader, for example, complained about the movement for initiative, referendum, and recall:

> *We have in our city a very large number of negroes employed on the docks; we also have a very large number of unskilled white laborers; this city also has more barrooms, according to its population, than any other city in Texas. Under these circumstances it would be extremely difficult to maintain a satisfactory city government where all ordinances must be submitted back to the voters of the city for their ratification and approval.*

At the National Municipal League convention of 1907, Rear Admiral F. E. Chadwick (USN Ret.), a leader in the Newport, Rhode Island, movement for municipal reform, spoke to this question even more directly:

> *Our present system has excluded in large degree the representation of those who have the city's well-being most at heart. It has brought,*

in municipalies . . . a government established by the least educated, the least interested class of citizens.

It stands to reason that a man paying $5,000 taxes in a town is more interested in the well-being and development of his town than the man who pays no taxes. . . . It equally stands to reason that the man of the $5,000 tax should be assured a representation in the committee which lays the tax and spends the money which he contributes. . . . Shall we be truly democratic and give the property owner a fair show or shall we develop a tyranny of ignorance which shall crush him.

Municipal reformers thus debated frequently the question of who should be represented as well as the question of what method of representation should be employed.

That these two questions were intimately connected was revealed in other reform proposals for representation, proposals which were rarely taken seriously. One suggestion was that a class system of representation be substituted for ward representation. For example, in 1908 one of the prominent candidates for commissioner in Des Moines proposed that the city council be composed of representatives of five classes: educational and ministerial organizations, manufacturers and jobbers, public utility corporations, retail merchants including liquor men, and the Des Moines Trades and Labor Assembly. Such a system would have greatly reduced the influence in the council of both middle- and lower-class groups. The proposal revealed the basic problem confronting business and professional leaders: how to reduce the influence in government of the majority of voters among middle- and lower-income groups.

A growing imbalance between population and representation sharpened the desire of reformers to change from ward to citywide elections. Despite shifts in population within most cities, neither ward district lines nor the apportionment of city council and school board seats changed frequently. Consequently, older areas of the city, with wards that were small in geographical size and held declining populations (usually lower- and middle-class in composition), continued to be overrepresented, and newer upper-class areas, where population was growing, became increasingly underrepresented. This intensified the reformers' conviction that the structure of government must be changed to give them the voice they needed to make their views on public policy prevail.

It is not insignificant that in some cities (by no means a majority) municipal reform came about outside of the urban electoral process. The original commission government in Galveston was appointed rather than elected. "The failure of previous attempts to secure an efficient city government through the local electorate made the business men of Galveston willing to put the conduct of the city's affairs in the hands of a commission dominated by state-appointed officials." Only in 1903 did the courts force Galveston to elect the members of the commission, an innovation which one writer described as "an abandonment of the commission idea," and which led to the decline of the influence of the business community in the commission government.

In 1911 Pittsburgh voters were not permitted to approve either the new city charter or the new school board plan, both of which provided for citywide representation; they were a result of state legislative enactment. The governor appointed the first members of the new city council, but thereafter they were elected. The judges of the court of common pleas, however, and not the voters, selected members of the new school board.

The composition of the new city council and new school board in Pittsburgh, both of which were inaugurated in 1911, revealed the degree to which the shift from ward to citywide representation produced a change in group representation. Members of the upper class, the advanced professional men, and the large business groups dominated both. Of the fifteen members of the Pittsburgh Board of Education appointed in 1911 and the nine members of the new city council, none were small businessmen or white-collar workers. Each body contained only one person who could remotely be classified as a blue-collar worker; each of these men filled a position specifically but unofficially designed as reserved for a "representative of labor," and each was an official of the Amalgamated Association of Iron, Steel, and Tin Workers. Six of the nine members of the new city council were prominent businessmen, and all six were listed in upper-class directories. Two others were doctors closely associated with the upper class in both professional and social life. The fifteen members of the Board of Education included ten businessmen with citywide interests, one doctor associated with the upper class, and three women previously active in upper-class public welfare.

Lower- and middle-class elements felt that the new city governments did not represent them. The studies carried out under the direction of Leonard White contain numerous expressions of the way in which the change in the structure of government produced not only a change in the geographical scope of representation, but also in the groups represented. "It is not the policies of the manager or the council they oppose," one researcher declared, "as much as the lack of representation for their economic level and social groups." And another wrote:

> There had been nothing unapproachable about the old ward aldermen. Every voter had a neighbor on the common council who was interested in serving him. The new councilmen, however, made an unfavorable impression on the less well-to-do voters. . . . Election at large made a change that, however desirable in other ways, left the

voters in the poorer wards with a feeling that they had been deprived
of their share of political importance.

The success of the drive for centralization of administration and representation varied with the size of the city. In the smaller cities, business, professional, and elite groups could easily exercise a dominant influence. Their close ties readily enabled them to shape informal political power which they could transform into formal political power. After the mid-1890s the widespread organization of chambers of commerce provided a base for political action to reform municipal government, resulting in a host of small-city commission and city-manager innovations. In the larger, more heterogeneous cities, whose subcommittees were more dispersed, such communitywide action was extremely difficult. Few commission or city-manager proposals materialized here. Mayors became stronger, and steps were taken toward centralization of representation, but the ward system or some modified version usually persisted. Reformers in large cities often had to rest content with their Municipal Research Bureaus, through which they could exert political influence from outside the municipal government.

A central element in the analysis of municipal reform in the Progressive Era is governmental corruption. Should it be understood in moral or political terms? Was it a product of evil men or of particular sociopolitical circumstances? Reform historians have adopted the former view. Selfish and evil men arose to take advantage of a political arrangement whereby unsystematic government offered many opportunities for personal gain at public expense. The system thrived until the "better elements," "men of intelligence and civic responsibility," or "right-thinking people" ousted the culprits and fashioned a political force which produced decisions in the "public interest." In this scheme of things, corruption in public affairs grew out of individual personal failings and a deficient governmental structure which could not hold those predispositions in check, rather than from the peculiar nature of social forces. The contestants involved were morally defined: evil men who must be driven from power, and good men who must be activated politically to secure control of municipal affairs.

Public corruption, however, involves political even more than moral considerations. It arises more out of the particular distribution of political power than of personal morality. For corruption is a device to exercise control and influence outside the legal channels of decision-making when those channels are not readily responsive. Most generally, corruption stems from an inconsistency between control of the instruments of formal governmental power and the exercise of informal influence in the community. If powerful groups are denied access to formal power in legitimate ways, they seek access through procedures which the community considers illegitimate. Corrupt government, therefore, does not reflect the genius of evil men, but rather the lack of acceptable means for those who exercise power in the private community to wield the same influence in governmental affairs. It can be understood in the Progressive Era not simply by the preponderance of evil men over good, but by the peculiar nature of the distribution of political power.

The political corruption of the "Era of Reform" arose from the inaccessibility of municipal government to those who were rising in power and influence. Municipal government in the United States developed in the nineteenth century within a context of universal manhood suffrage which decentralized political control. Because all men, whatever their economic, social, or cultural conditions, could vote, leaders who reflected a wide variety of community interests and who represented the views of people of every circumstance arose to guide and direct municipal affairs. Since the majority of urban voters were workingmen or immigrants, the views of those groups carried great and often decisive weight in governmental affairs. Thus, as Herbert Gutman has shown, during strikes in the 1870s city officials were usually friendly to workingmen and refused to use police power to protect strikebreakers.

Ward representation on city councils was an integral part of grass-roots influence, for it enabled diverse urban communities, invariably identified with particular geographical areas of the city, to express their views more clearly through councilmen peculiarly receptive to their concerns. There was a direct, reciprocal flow of power between wards and the center of city affairs in which voters felt a relatively close connection with public matters and city leaders gave special attention to their needs.

Within this political system the community's business leaders grew in influence and power as industrialism advanced, only to find that their economic position did not readily admit them to the formal machinery of government. Thus, during strikes, they had to rely on either their own private police, Pinkertons, or the state militia to enforce their use of strikebreakers. They frequently found that city officials did not accept their views of what was best for the city and what direction municipal policies should take. They had developed a common outlook, closely related to their economic activities, that the city's economic expansion should become the prime concern of municipal government, and yet they found that this view had to compete with even more influential views of public policy. They found that political tendencies which arose from universal manhood suffrage and ward representation were not always friendly to their political conceptions and goals and had produced a political system over which they had little control, despite the fact that their economic ventures were the core of the city's prosperity and the hope for future urban growth.

Under such circumstances, businessmen sought other methods of influencing municipal affairs. They did not restrict themselves to the channels of popular election and representation, but frequently applied direct influence—if not verbal persuasion, then bribery and corruption. Thereby arose the graft which Lincoln Steffens recounted in his *Shame of the Cities*. Utilities were only the largest of those business groups and individuals who requested special favors, and the franchises they sought were only the most sensational of the prizes, which included such items as favorable tax assessments and rates, the vacating of streets wanted for factory expansion, or permission to operate amid anti-liquor and other laws regulating personal behavior. The relationships between business and formal government became a maze of accommodations, a set of political arrangements which grew up because effective power had few legitimate means of accomplishing its ends.

Steffens and subsequent liberal historians, however, misread the significance of these arrangements, emphasizing their personal rather than their more fundamental institutional elements. To them corruption involved personal arrangements between powerful business leaders and powerful "machine" politicians. Just as they did not fully appreciate the significance of the search for political influence by the rising business community as a whole, so they did not see fully the role of the "ward politician." They stressed the argument that the political leader manipulated voters to his own personal ends, that he used constituents rather than reflected their views.

A different approach is now taking root, namely, that the urban political organization was an integral part of community life, expressing its needs and its goals. As Oscar Handlin has said, for example, the "machine" not only fulfilled specific wants, but provided one of the few avenues to success and public recognition available to the immigrant. The political leader's arrangements with businessmen, therefore, were not simply personal agreements between conniving individuals; they were far-reaching accommodations between powerful sets of institutions in industrial America.

These accommodations, however, proved to be burdensome and unsatisfactory to the business community and to the upper third of socioeconomic groups in general. They were expensive; they were wasteful; they were uncertain. Toward the end of the nineteenth century, therefore, business and professional men sought more direct control over municipal government in order to exercise political influence more effectively. They realized their goals in the early twentieth century in the new commission and city-manager forms of government and in the shift from ward to citywide representation.

These innovations did not always accomplish the objectives that the business community desired because other forces could and often did adjust to the change in governmental structure and reestablish their influence. But businessmen hoped that reform would enable them to increase their political power, and most frequently it did. In most cases the innovations which were introduced between 1901, when Galveston adopted a commission form of government, and the Great Depression, and especially the city-manager form which reached a height of popularity in the mid-1920s, served as vehicles whereby business and professional leaders moved directly into the inner circles of government, brought into one political system their own power and the formal machinery of government, and dominated municipal affairs for two decades.

Municipal reform in the early twentieth century involves a paradox: the ideology of an extension of political control and the practice of its concentration. While reformers maintained that their movement rested on a wave of popular demands, called their gatherings of business and professional leaders "mass meetings," described their reforms as "part of a worldwide trend toward popular government," and proclaimed an ideology of a popular upheaval against a selfish few, they were in practice shaping the structure of municipal government so that political power would no longer be broadly distributed, but would in fact be more centralized in the hands of a relatively small segment of the population. The paradox became even sharper when new city charters included provisions for the initiative, referendum, and recall. How does the historian cope with this paradox? Does it represent deliberate deception or simply political strategy? Or does it reflect a phenomenon which should be understood rather than explained away?

The expansion of popular involvement in decision-making was frequently a political tactic, not a political system to be established permanently, but a device to secure immediate political victory. The prohibitionist advocacy of the referendum, one of the most extensive sources of support for such a measure, came from the belief that the referendum would provide the opportunity to outlaw liquor more rapidly. The Anti-Saloon League, therefore, urged local option. But the League was not consistent. Towns which were wet, when faced with a countrywide local-option decision to outlaw liquor, demanded town or township local option to reinstate it. The League objected to this as not the proper application of the referendum idea.

Again, "Progressive" reformers often espoused the direct primary when fighting for nominations for their candidates within the party, but once in control they often became cool to it because it might result in their own defeat. By the same token, many municipal reformers attached the initiative, referendum, and recall to municipal charters often as a device to appease voters who opposed the centralization of representation and executive authority. But, by requiring a high percentage of voters to sign petitions—often 25 to 30 percent—these innovations could be (and were) rendered relatively harmless.

More fundamentally, however, the distinction between ideology and practice in municipal reform arose from the different roles which each played. The ideology of democratization of decision-making was negative rather than positive; it served as an instrument of attack against the existing political system rather than as a guide to alternative action. Those who wished to destroy the "machine" and to eliminate party competition in local government widely utilized the theory that these political instruments thwarted public impulses, and thereby shaped the tone of their attack.

But there is little evidence that the ideology represented a faith in a purely democratic system of decision-making or that reformers actually wished, in practice, to substitute direct democracy as a continuing system of sustained decision-making in place of the old. It was used to destroy the political institutions of the lower and middle classes and the political power which those institutions gave rise to, rather than to provide a clear-cut guide for alternative action.

The guide to alternative action lay in the model of the business enterprise. In describing new conditions which they wished to create, reformers drew on the analogy of the "efficient business enterprise," criticizing current practices with the argument that "no business could conduct its affairs that way and remain in business," and calling upon business practices as the guides to improvement. As one student remarked:

> The folklore of the business elite came by gradual transition to be the symbols of governmental reformers. Efficiency, system, orderliness, budgets, economy, saving, were all injected into the efforts of reformers who sought to remodel municipal government in terms of the great impersonality of corporate enterprise.

Clinton Rodgers Woodruff of the National Municipal League explained that the commission form was "a simple, direct, businesslike way of administering the business affairs of the city . . . an application to city administration of that type of business organization which has been so common and so successful in the field of commerce and industry." The centralization of decision-making which developed in the business corporation was now applied in municipal reform.

The model of the efficient business enterprise, then, rather than the New England town meeting, provided the positive inspiration for the municipal reformer. In giving concrete shape to this model in the strong-mayor, commission, and city-manager plans, reformers engaged in the elaboration of the processes of rationalization and systematization inherent in modern science and technology. For in many areas of society, industrialization brought a gradual shift upward in the location of decision-making and the geographical extension of the scope of the area affected by decisions.

Experts in business, in government, and in the professions measured, studied, analyzed, and manipulated ever wider realms of human life, and devices which they used to control such affairs constituted the most fundamental and far-reaching innovations in decision-making in modern America, whether in formal government or in the informal exercise of power in private life. Reformers in the Progressive Era played a major role in shaping this new system. While they expressed an ideology of restoring a previous order, they in fact helped to bring forth a system drastically new.

The drama of reform lay in the competition for supremacy between two systems of decision-making. One system, based upon ward representation and growing out of the practices and ideas of representative government, involved wide latitude for the expression of grassroots impulses and their involvement in the political process. The other grew out of the rationalization of life which came with science and technology, in which decisions arose from expert analysis and flowed from fewer and smaller centers outward to the rest of society. Those who espoused the former looked with fear upon the loss of influence which the latter involved, and those who espoused the latter looked only with disdain upon the wastefulness and inefficiency of the former.

The Progressive Era witnessed rapid strides toward a more centralized system and a relative decline for a more decentralized system. This development constituted an accommodation of forces outside the business community to the political trends within business and professional life rather than vice versa. It involved a tendency for the decision-making processes inherent in science and technology to prevail over those inherent in representative government.

Reformers in the Progressive Era and liberal historians since then misread the nature of the movement to change municipal government because they concentrated upon dramatic and sensational episodes and ignored the analysis of more fundamental political structure, of the persistent relationships of influence and power which grew out of the community's social, ideological, economic, and cultural activities. The reconstruction of these patterns of human relationships and of the changes in them is the historian's most crucial task, for they constitute the central context of historical development. History consists not of erratic and spasmodic fluctuations, of a series of random thoughts and actions, but of patterns of activity and change in which people hold thoughts and actions in common and in which there are close connections between sequences of events. These contexts give rise to a structure of human relationships which pervade all areas of life; for the political historians the most important of these is the structure of the distribution of power and influence.

The structure of political relationships, however, cannot be adequately understood if we concentrate on evidence concerning ideology rather than practice. For it is becoming increasingly clear that ideological evidence is no safe guide to the understanding of practice, that what people thought and said about their society is not necessarily an accurate representation of what they did. The current task of the historians of the Progressive Era is to stop taking the reformers' own description of political practice at its face value and to utilize a wide variety of new types of evidence to reconstruct political practice in its own terms. This is not to argue that ideology is either important or unimportant. It is merely to state that ideological evidence is not appropriate to the discovery of the nature of political practice.

Only by maintaining this clear distinction can the historian successfully investigate the structure of political life in the Progressive Era. And only then can he begin to cope with the most fundamental problem of all: the relationship between political ideology and political practice. For each of these facets of political life must be understood in its own terms, through its own historical record. Each involves a distinct set of historical phenomena. The relationship between them for the Progressive Era is not now clear; it has not been investigated. But it cannot be explored until the conceptual distinction is made clear and evidence tapped which is pertinent to each. Because the nature of political practice has so long been distorted by the use of ideological evidence, the most pressing task is its investigation through new types of evidence appropriate to it. The reconstruction of the movement for municipal reform can constitute a major step toward the goal.

Richard L. McCormick

RICHARD L. McCORMICK (1947–   ) *is professor of history at Rutgers University. He has written about American politics in the nineteenth and twentieth centuries and his books include* From Realignment to Reform: Political Change in New York State, 1893–1910 *(1981) and* The Party Period and Public Policy: American Politics from the Age of Jackson to the Progressive Era *(1986).*

Richard L. McCormick, "The Discovery that Business Corrupts Politics: A Reappraisal of the Origins of Progressivism," *American Historical Review* 86 (April 1981):247–274. Reprinted with the permission of Richard L. McCormick.

Shortly after 1900, American politics and government experienced a decisive and rather rapid transformation that affected both the patterns of popular political involvement and the nature and functions of government itself. To be sure, the changes were not revolutionary, but, considering how relatively undevelopmental the political system of the United States has been, they are of considerable historical importance. The basic features of this political transformation can be easily described, but its causes and significance are somewhat more difficult to grasp.

One important category of change involved the manner and methods of popular participation in politics. For most of the nineteenth century, high rates of partisan voting—based on complex sectional, cultural, and communal influences—formed the American people's main means of political expression and involvement. Only in exceptional circumstances did most individuals or groups rely on nonelectoral methods of influencing the government. Indeed, almost no such means existed within the normal bounds of politics. After 1900, this structure of political participation changed. Voter turnout fell, and even among those electors who remained active, pure and simple partisanship became less pervasive. At approximately the same time, interest-group organizations of all sorts successfully forged permanent, nonelectoral means of influencing the government and its agencies. Only recently have historians begun to explore with care what caused these changes in the patterns of political participation and to delineate the redistribution of power that they entailed.

American governance, too, went through a fundamental transition in the early 1900s. Wiebe has accurately described it as the emergence of "a government broadly and continuously involved in society's operations." Both the institutions of government and the content of policy reflected the change. Where the legislature had been the dominant branch of government at every level, lawmakers now saw their power curtailed by an enlarged executive and, even more, by the creation of an essentially new branch of government composed of administrative boards and agencies. Where nineteenth-century policy had generally focused on distinct groups and locales (most characteristically through the distribution of resources and privileges to enterprising individuals and corporations), the government now began to take explicit account of clashing interests and to assume the responsibility for mitigating their conflicts through regulation, administration, and planning. In 1900, government did very little in the way of recognizing and adjusting group differences. Fifteen years later, innumerable policies committed officials to that formal purpose and provided the bureaucratic structures for achieving it.

Most political historians consider these changes to be the products of long-term social and economic developments. Accordingly, they have devoted much of their attention to tracing the interconnecting paths leading from industrialization, urbanization, and immigration to the political and governmental responses. Some of the general trends have been firmly documented in scholarship: the organization of functional groups whose needs the established political parties could not meet; the creation of new demands for government policies to make life bearable in crowded cities, where huge industries were located, and the determination of certain cultural and economic groups to curtail the political power of people they considered threatening. All of these developments, along with others, occurred over a period of decades— now speeded, now slowed by depression, migration, prosperity, fortune, and the talents of individual men and women.

Yet, given the long-term forces involved, it is notable how suddenly the main elements of the new political order went into place. The first fifteen years of the twentieth century witnessed most of the changes; more precisely, the brief period from 1904 to 1908 saw a remarkably compressed political transformation. During these years the regulatory revolution peaked; new and powerful agencies of government came into being everywhere. At the same time, voter turnout declined, ticket-splitting increased, and organized social, economic, and reform-minded groups began to exercise power more systematically than ever before. An understanding of how the new polity crystallized so rapidly can be obtained by exploring, first, the latent threat to the old system represented by fears of "corruption"; then, the pressures for political change that had built up by about 1904; and, finally, the way in which the old fears abruptly took on new meaning and inspired a resolution of the crisis. . . .

The evidence concerning these disclosures is familiar to students of progressivism, but its meaning has not been fully explored. The period 1904–08 comprised the muckraking years, not only in national magazines but also in local newspapers and legislative halls across the country. During 1905 and 1906 in particular, a remarkable number of cities and states experienced wrenching moments of discovery that led directly to significant political changes. Usually, a scandal, an investigation, an intraparty battle, or a particularly divisive election campaign exposed an illicit alliance of politics and business and made corruption apparent to the community, affecting party rhetoric, popular expectations, electoral behavior, and government policies.

Just before it exploded in city and state affairs, business corruption of politics had already emerged as a leading theme of the new magazine journalism created by the muckrakers. Their primary contribution was to give a national audience the first systematic accounts of how modern American society operated. In so doing, journalists like Steffens, Baker, Russell, and Phillips created insights and pioneered ways of describing social and political relationships that crucially affected how people saw things in their home towns and states. Since so many of the muckrakers' articles identified the widespread tendency for privilege-seeking businessmen to bribe legislators, conspire with party leaders, and control nominations, an awareness of such corruption soon entered local politics. Indeed, many of the muckraking articles concerned particular locales—including Steffens's early series on the cities (1902–03); his subsequent exposures of Missouri, Illinois, Wisconsin, Rhode Island, New Jersey, and Ohio (1904–05); Rudolph Blankenburg's articles on Pennsylvania (1905); and C. P. Connolly's treatment of Montana (1906). All of these accounts featured descriptions of politico-business corruption, as did many of the contemporaneous exposures of individual industries, such as oil, railroads, and meat-packing. Almost immediately after this literature began to flourish, citizens across the country discovered local examples of the same corrupt behavior that Steffens and the others had described elsewhere.

In New York, the occasion was the 1905 legislative investigation of the life insurance industry. One by one, insurance executives and Republican politicians took the witness stand and were compelled to bare the details of their corrupt relations. The companies received legislative protection, and the Republicans got bribes and campaign funds. In California, the graft trials of San Francisco city officials, beginning in 1906, threw light on the illicit cooperation between businessmen and public officials. Boss Abraham Ruef had delivered special privileges to public utility corporations in return for fees, of which he kept some and used the rest to bribe members of the city's Board of Supervisors. San Francisco's awakening revitalized reform elsewhere in California, and the next year insurgent Republicans formally organized to combat their party's alliance with the Southern Pacific Railroad. In Vermont, the railroad commissioners charged the 1906 legislature with yielding "supinely to the unfortunate influence of railroad representatives." Then the legislature investigated and found that the commissioners themselves were corrupt!

Other states, in all parts of the country, experienced their own versions of these events during 1905 and 1906. In South Dakota, as in a number of Midwestern states, hostility to railroad influence in politics—by means of free passes and a statewide network of paid henchmen—was the issue around which insurgent Republicans coalesced against the regular machine. Some of those who joined the opposition did so purely from expediency; but their charges of corruption excited the popular imagination, and they captured the state in 1906 with pledges of electoral reform and business regulation. Farther west Denver's major utilities, including the Denver Tramway Company and the Denver Gas and Electric Company, applied for new franchises in 1906, and these applications went before the voters at the spring elections. When the franchises all narrowly carried, opponents of the companies produced evidence that the Democratic and Republican Parties had obtained fraudulent votes for the utilities. The case made its way through the courts during the next several months, and, although they ultimately lost, Colorado's nascent progressives derived an immense boost from the well-publicized judicial battle. As a result, the focus of reform shifted to the state. Dissidents in the Republican Party organized to demand direct primary nominations and a judiciary untainted by corporate influence. These questions dominated Colorado's three-way gubernatorial election that fall.

To the south, in Alabama, Georgia, and Mississippi, similar accusations of politico-business corruption were heard that same year, only in a different regional accent. In Alabama, Braxton Bragg Comer rode the issue from his position on the state's railroad commission to the governorship. His "main theme," according to Sheldon Hackney, "was that the railroads had for years deprived the people of Alabama of their right to rule their own state and that the time had come to free the people from alien and arbitrary rule." Mississippi voters heard similar rhetoric from Governor James K. Vardaman in his unsuccessful campaign against John Sharp Williams for a seat in the U.S. Senate. Georgia's Tom Watson conjured up some inane but effective imagery to illustrate how Vardaman's opponent would serve the business interests: "If the Hon. John Sharp Williams should win out in the fight with Governor Vardaman, the corporations would have just one more doodle-bug in the United States Senate. Every time that a Railroad lobbyist stopped over the hole and called 'Doodle, Doodle, Doodle'—soft and slow—the sand at the little end of the funnel would be seen to stir, and then the little head of J. Sharp would pop up." In Watson's own state, Hoke Smith trumpeted the issue, too, in 1905 and 1906. . . .

State party platforms provide further evidence of the awakening to politico-business corruption. In Iowa, to take a Midwestern state, charges of corporation influence in politics were almost entirely confined to the minor parties during the years from 1900 to 1904. Prohibitionists believed that the liquor industry brought political corruption, while socialists felt that the powers of government belonged to the capitalists. For their part, the Democrats and Republicans saw little of this—until 1906, when both major parties gushed in opposition to what the Republicans now called "the domination of corporate influences in public affairs." The Democrats agreed: "We favor the complete elimination of railway and other public service corporations from the politics of the state." In Missouri, a different but parallel pattern emerges from the platforms. There, what had been a subordinate theme of the Democratic Party (and minor parties) in 1900 and 1902 became of central importance to both parties in 1904 and 1906. The Democrats now called "the eradication of bribery" the "paramount issue" in the state and declared opposition to campaign contributions "by great corporations and by those interested in special industries enjoying special privileges under the law." In New Hampshire, where nothing had been said of politico-business corruption in 1900 and 1904, both major parties wrote platforms in 1906 that attacked the issuance of free transportation passes and the prevalence of corrupt legislative lobbies. Party platforms in other states also suggest how suddenly major-party politicians discovered that business corrupted politics.

The annual messages of the state governors from 1902 to 1908 point to the same pattern. In the first three years, the chief executives almost never mentioned the influence of business in politics. Albert Cummins of Iowa was exceptional; as early as 1902 he declared, "Corporations have, and ought to have, many privileges, but among them is not the privilege to sit in political conventions or occupy seats in legislative chambers." Then in 1905, governors across the Midwest suddenly let loose denunciations of corporate bribery, lobbying, campaign contributions, and free passes. Nebraska's John H. Mickey was typical in attacking "the onslaught of private and corporation lobbyists who seek to accomplish pernicious ends by the exercise of undue influence." Missouri's Joseph W. Folk advised that "all franchises, rights and privileges secured by bribery should be declared null and void." By 1906, 1907, and 1908, such observations and recommendations were common to the governors of every region. In 1907 alone, no less than nineteen state executives called for the regulation of lobbying, while a similar number advised the abolition of free passes.

What is the meaning of this awakening to something that Americans had, in a sense, known all along? Should we accept the originality of the "discovery" that monied interests endangered free government or lay stress instead on the familiar elements the charge contained? It had, after all, been a part of American political thought since the eighteenth century and had been powerfully repeated, in one form or another, by major and minor figures throughout the nineteenth century. According to Richard Hofstadter, "there was nothing new in the awareness of these things." In fact, however, there was much that was new. First, many of the details of politico-business corruption had never been publicly revealed before. No one had ever probed the subject as thoroughly as journalists and legislative investigators were not doing, and, moreover, some of the practices they uncovered had only recently come into being. Large-scale corporation campaign contributions, for instance, were a product of the 1880s and 1890s. Highly organized legislative lobbying operations by competing interest groups represented an even more recent development. In his systematic study of American legislative practices, published in 1907, Paul S. Reinsch devoted a lengthy chapter to describing how business interests had de-

veloped a new and "far more efficient system of dealing with legislatures than [the old methods of] haphazard corruption."

Even more startling than the new practices themselves was the
fresh meaning they acquired from the nationwide character of the patterns that were now disclosed. The point is not simply that more
people than ever before became aware of politico-business corruption
but that the perception of such a national pattern itself created new
political understandings. Lincoln Steffens's autobiography is brilliant
on this point. As Steffens acknowledged, much of the corruption he
observed in his series on the "shame" of the cities had already come
to light locally before he reported it to a national audience. What he
did was take the facts in city after city, apply imagination to their tran-
scription, and form a new truth by showing the same process at work
everywhere. Here was a solution to the problem the Adams brothers
had encountered in writing *Chapters of Erie:* how to report shocking
corruption without making it seem too astounding to be representative. The solution was breadth of coverage. Instead of looking at only
two businessmen, study dozens; explore city after city and state after
state and report the facts to a people who were vaguely aware of corruption in their own home towns but had never before seen that a single
process was at work across the country. This concept of a "process" of
corruption was central to the new understanding. Uncovered through
systematic journalistic research and probing legislative investigations,
corruption was now seen to be the result of concrete historical developments. It could not just be dismissed as the product of misbehavior
by "bad" men (although that kind of rhetoric continued too) but had
to be regarded as an outcome of identifiable economic and political
forces. In particular, corruption resulted from an outmoded policy of
indiscriminate distribution, which could not safely withstand an onslaught of demands from private corporations that were larger than the
government itself.

Thus in its systematic character, as well as in its particular details,
the corruption that Americans discovered in 1905 and 1906 was different from the kind their eighteenth- and nineteenth-century forebears
had known. Compared to the eighteenth-century republican understanding, the progressive concept of corruption regarded the monied
interests not as tools of a designing administration but as independent
agents. If any branch of government was in alliance with them, it was
probably the legislature. In a curious way, however, the old republican
view that commerce inherently threatened the people's virtue still persisted, now informed by a new understanding of the actual process at
work. Compared to Andrew Jackson, the progressives saw big corporations not as monsters but as products of social and industrial development. And their activist remedies differed entirely from his negativis-

tic ones. But, like Jackson, those who now discovered corruption grasped that private interests could conflict with the public interest and that government benefits for some groups often hurt others. The recognition of these two things—both painfully at odds with the nineteenth century's conventional wisdom—had been at the root of the floundering over principles of political economy in the 1890s and early 1900s. Now, rather suddenly, the discovery that business corrupts politics suggested concrete answers to a people who were ready for new policies but had been uncertain how to get them or what exactly they should be.

Enacted in a burst of legislative activity immediately following the awakening of 1905 and 1906, the new policies brought to an end the paralysis that had gripped the polity and constituted a decisive break with nineteenth-century patterns of governance. Many states passed laws explicitly designed to curtail illicit business influence in politics. These included measures regulating legislative lobbying, prohibiting corporate campaign contributions, and outlawing the acceptance of free transportation passes by public officials. In 1903 and 1904, there had been almost no legislation on these three subjects; during 1905 and 1906, several states acted on each question; and, by 1907 and 1908, ten states passed lobbying laws, nineteen took steps to prevent corporate contributions, and fourteen acted on the question of passes (see Table 1). If these laws failed to wipe out corporation influence in politics, they at least curtailed important means through which businesses had exercised political power in the late nineteenth and early twentieth centuries. To be sure, other means were soon found, but the flood of state lawmaking on these subjects, together with the corresponding

TABLE 1
Selected Categories of State Legislation, 1903–08

Type of Legislation	1903–04	1905–06	1907–08	1903–08
Regulation of Lobbying	0	2	10	12
Prohibition of Corporate Campaign Contributions	0	3	19	22
Regulation or Prohibition of Free Railroad Passes for Public Officials	4	6	14	24
Mandatory Direct Primary	4	9	18	31
Regulation of Railroad Corporations by Commission	5	8	28	41
Totals	13	28	89	130

Note: Figures represent the number of states that passed legislation in the given category during the specified years.

attention they received from the federal government in these same years, shows how prevalent was the determination to abolish existing forms of politico-business corruption.

Closely associated with these three measures were two more important categories of legislation, often considered to represent the essence of progressivism in the states: mandatory direct primary laws and measures establishing or strengthening the regulation of utility and transportation corporations by commission. These types of legislation, too, reached a peak in the years just after 1905–06, when so many states had experienced a crisis disclosing the extent of politico-business corruption. Like the laws concerning lobbying, contributions, and passes, primary and regulatory measures were brought forth amidst intense public concern with business influence in politics and were presented by their advocates as remedies for that problem. Both types of laws had been talked about for years, but the disclosures of 1905–06 provided the catalyst for their enactment.

Even before 1905, the direct primary had already been adopted in some states. In Wisconsin, where it was approved in 1904, Robert M. La Follette had campaigned for direct nominations since the late 1890s on the grounds that they would "emancipate the legislature from all subserviency to the corporations." In his well-known speech, "The Menace of the Machine" (1897), La Follette explicitly offered the direct primary as "the remedy" for corporate control of politics. Now, after the awakening of 1905–06, that same argument inspired many states that had failed to act before to adopt mandatory direct primary laws (see Table 1). In New York, Charles Evans Hughes, who was elected governor in 1906 because of his role as chief counsel in the previous year's life insurance investigation, argued that the direct primary would curtail the power of the special interests. "Those interests," he declared, "are ever at work stealthily and persistently endeavoring to pervert the government to the service of their own ends. All that is worst in our public life finds its readiest means of access to power through the control of the nominating machinery of parties." In other states, too, in the years after 1905–06, the direct primary was urged and approved for the same reasons that La Follette and Hughes advanced it.

The creation of effective regulatory boards—progressivism's most distinctive governmental achievement—also followed upon the discovery of politico-business corruption. From 1905 to 1907 alone, fifteen new state railroad commissions were established, and at least as many existing boards were strengthened. Most of the new commissions were "strong" ones, having rate-setting powers and a wide range of administrative authority to supervise service, safety, and finance. In the years to come, many of them extended their jurisdiction to other public utilities, including gas, electricity, telephones, and telegraphs. Direct legislative supervision of business corporations was also significantly expanded in these years. Life insurance companies—whose corruption of the New York State government Hughes had dramatically disclosed—provide one example. "In 1907," as a result of Hughes's investigation and several others conducted in imitation of it, Morton Keller has reported, "forty-two state legislatures met; thirty considered life insurance legislation; twenty-nine passed laws. . . . By 1908 . . . [the basic] lines of twentieth century life insurance supervision were set, and thereafter only minor adjustments occurred." The federal regulatory machinery, too, was greatly strengthened at this time, most notably by the railroad, meat inspection, and food and drug acts of 1906.

The adoption of these measures marked the moment of transition from a structure of economic policy based largely on the allocation of resources and benefits to one in which regulation and administration played permanent and significant roles. Not confined for long to the transportation, utility, and insurance companies that formed its most immediate objects, regulatory policies soon were extended to other industries as well. Sometimes the legislative branch took responsibility for the ongoing tasks of supervision and administration, but more commonly they became the duty of independent boards and commissioners, staffed by experts and entrusted with significant powers of oversight and enforcement. Certainly, regulation was not previously unknown, nor did promoting commerce and industry now cease to be a governmental purpose. But the middle years of the first decade of the twentieth century unmistakably mark a turning point—that point when the direction shifted, when the weight of opinion changed, when the forces of localism and opposition to governmental authority that had sustained the distribution of privileges but opposed regulation and administration now lost the upper hand to the forces of centralization, bureaucratization, and government actions to recognize and adjust group differences. Besides economic regulation, other governmental policy areas, including health, education, taxation, correction, and the control of natural resources, increasingly came under the jurisdiction of independent boards and commissions. The establishment of these agencies and the expansion of their duties meant that American governance in the twentieth century was significantly different from what it had been in the nineteenth.

The developments of 1905–08 also changed the nature of political participation in the United States. Parties emerged from the years of turmoil altered and, on balance, less important vehicles of popular expression than they had been. The disclosures of politico-business wrongdoing disgraced the regular party organizations, and many voters showed their loss of faith by staying at home on election day or by casting split tickets. These trends had been in progress before 1905–06—encouraged by new election laws as well as by the crisis of confidence in traditional politics and government—but in several ways the discovery of corruption strengthened them. Some reigning party organizations were toppled by the disclosures, and the insurgents who came to power lacked the old bosses' experience and inclination when it came to rallying the electorate. And the legal prohibition of corporate campaign contributions now meant, moreover, that less money was available for pre-election entertainment, transportation to the polls, and bribes.

While the party organizations were thus weakened, they were also more firmly embedded in the legal machinery of elections than ever before. In many states the direct primary completed a series of new election laws (beginning with the Australian ballot in the late 1880s and early 1890s) that gave the parties official status as nominating bodies, regulated their practices, and converted them into durable, official bureaucracies. Less popular now but also more respectable, the party organizations surrendered to state regulation and relinquished much of their ability to express community opinion in return for legal guarantees that they alone would be permanently certified to place nominees on the official ballot.

Interest organizations took over much of the parties' old job of articulating popular demands and pressing them upon the government. More exclusive and single-minded than parties, the new organizations became regular elements of the polity. Their right to represent their members before the government's new boards and agencies received implicit recognition, and, indeed, the commissions in some cases became captives of the groups that were supposed to regulate. The result was a fairly drastic transformation of the rules of political participation: who could compete, the kinds of resources required, and the rewards of participation all changed. These developments were not brand new in the first years of the twentieth century, but, like the contemporaneous changes in government policy, they derived impressive, decisive confirmation from the political upheaval that occurred between 1905 and 1908.

Political and governmental changes thus followed upon the discovery that business corrupts politics. And Americans of the day explicitly linked the two developments: the reforms adopted in 1907–08 were to remedy the ills uncovered in 1905–06. But these chronological and rhetorical connections between discovery and reform do not fully explain the relationship between them. Why, having paid relatively little heed to similar charges before, did people now take such strong actions in response to the disclosures? Why, moreover, did the perception of wrongdoing precipitate the particular pattern of responses that it did—namely, the triumph of bureaucracy and organization? Of most importance, what distinctive effects did the discovery of corruption have upon the final outcome of the crisis?

By 1905 a political explosion of some sort was likely, due to the accumulated frustrations people felt about the government's failure to deal with the problems of industrialization. So combustible were the elements present that another spark besides the discovery of politico-business corruption might well have ignited them. But the recognition of such corruption was an especially effective torch. Upon close analysis, its ignition of the volatile political mass is unsurprising. The accusations made in 1905–06 were serious, widespread, and full of damaging information; they explained the actual corrupt process behind a danger that Americans had historically worried about, if not always responded to with vigor; they linked in dark scandal the two main villains—party bosses and big businessmen—already on the American scene; they inherently discredited the existing structure of economic policy based on the distribution of privileges; and they dramatically suggested the necessity for new kinds of politics and government. That businessmen systematically corrupted politics was incendiary knowledge; given the circumstances of 1905, it could hardly have failed to set off an explosion.

The organizational results that followed, however, seem less inevitable. There were, after all, several other known ways of curtailing corruption besides expert regulation and administration. For one, there was the continued reliance on direct legislative action against the corruption of politics by businessmen. The lobbying, anti-free pass, and campaign-contribution measures of 1907–08 exemplified this approach. So did the extension of legislative controls over the offending corporations. Such measures were familiar, but obviously they were considered inadequate to the crisis at hand. A second approach, favored by Edward Alsworth Ross and later by Woodrow Wilson, was to hold business leaders personally responsible for their "sins" and to punish them accordingly. There were a few attempts to bring individuals to justice, but, because of the inadequacy of the criminal statutes, the skill of high-priced lawyers, and the public's lack of appetite for personal vendettas, few sinners were jailed. Finally, there were proposals for large structural solutions changing the political and economic environment so that the old corrupt practices became impossible. Some men, like Frederic C. Howe, still advocated the single tax and the abolition of all privileges granted by government. Many more believed in the municipal ownership of public utilities. Hundreds of thousands (to judge from election returns) favored socialist solutions, but most Americans did not. In their response to politico-business corruption, they went beyond existing legislative remedies and avoided the temptation to personalize all the blame, but they fell short of wanting socialism, short even of accepting the single tax.

Regulation and administration represented a fourth available approach. Well before the discoveries of 1905–06, groups who stood to benefit from governmental control of utility and transportation corporations had placed strong regulatory proposals on the political agendas of the states and the nation. In other policy areas, the proponents of an administrative approach had not advanced that far prior to 1905–06, but theirs was a large and growing movement, supported—as recent historians have shown—by many different groups for varied, often contradictory, reasons. The popular awakening to corruption increased the opportunity of these groups to obtain enactment of their measures. Where their proposals met the particular political needs of 1905–08, they succeeded most quickly. Regulation by commissions seemed to be an effective way to halt corruption by transferring the responsibility for business-government relations from party bosses and legislators to impartial experts. That approach also possessed the additional political advantages of appearing sane and moderate, of meeting consumer demands for government protection, and, above all, of being sufficiently malleable that a diversity of groups could be induced to anticipate favorable results from the new policies.

In consequence, the passions of 1905–06 added support to an existing movement toward regulation and administration, enormously speeded it up, shaped the timing and form of its victory, and probably made the organizational revolution more complete—certainly more sudden—than it otherwise would have been. These accomplishments alone must make the discovery of corruption pivotal in any adequate interpretation of progressivism. But the awakening did more than hurry along a movement that already possessed formidable political strength and would probably have triumphed eventually even without the events of 1905–06. By pushing the political process toward so quick a resolution of the long-standing crisis over industrialism, the passions of those years caused the outcome to be more conservative than it otherwise might have been. This is the ultimate irony of the discovery that business corrupts politics.

Muckraking accounts of politico-business evils suggest one reason for the discovery's conservative impact. Full of facts and revelations, these writings were also dangerously devoid of effective solutions. Charles E. Russell's *Lawless Wealth* (1908)—the title itself epitomizes the perceptions of 1905–06—illustrates the flaw. Published originally in *Everbody's Magazine* under the accusatory title, "Where Did You Get It, Gentlemen?," the book recounts numerous instances of riches obtained through the corruption of politics but, in its closing pages, merely suggests that citizens recognize the evils and be determined to stop them. This reliance on trying to change how people felt (to "shame" them, in Steffens's phrase) was characteristic of muckraking and of the exposures of 1905–06. One can admire the muckrakers' reporting, can even accept David P. Thelen's judgment that their writing "contained at least as deep a moral revulsion toward capitalism and profit as did more orthodox forms of Marxism," yet can still feel that

their proposed remedy was superficial. Because the perception of politico-business corruption carried no far-reaching solutions of its own or
genuine economic grievances, but only a desire to clean up politics and
government, the passions of 1905–06 were easily diverted to the support of other people's remedies, especially administrative answers.
Had the muckrakers and their local imitators penetrated more deeply
into the way that business operated and its real relationship to government, popular emotions might not have been so readily mobilized in
support of regulatory and administrative agencies that business interests could often dominate. At the very least, there might have been a
more determined effort to prevent the supervised corporations themselves from shaping the details of regulatory legislation. Thus, for all
of their radical implications, the passions of 1905–06 dulled the capacity of ordinary people to get reforms in their own interest.

The circumstances in which the discovery of corruption became a
political force also assist in explaining its conservatism. The passions
of 1905–06 were primarily expressed in state, rather than local or national, politics. Indeed, those passions often served to shift the focus
of reform from the cities to the state capitals. There—in Albany, or
Madison, or Sacramento—the remedies were worked out in relative
isolation from the local, insurgent forces that had in many cases originally called attention to the evils. Usually the policy consequences
were more favorable to large business interests than local solutions
would have been. State utility boards, for example, which had always
been considered more conservative in their policies than comparable
local commissions, now took the regulatory power away from cities
and foreclosed experimentation with such alternatives as municipal
ownership or popularly chosen regulatory boards. In gaining a statewide hearing for reform, the accusations of politico-business corruption actually increased the likelihood that conservative solutions
would be adopted.

Considering the intensity of the feelings aroused in 1905 and 1906
("the wrath of thousands of private citizens . . . is at white heat over
the disclosures," declared a Rochester newspaper) and the catalytic political role they played, the awakened opposition to corruption was
surprisingly short-lived. As early as 1907 and 1908, the years of the
most significant state legislative responses to the discovery, the messages of the governors began to exhibit a more stylized, less passionate
way of describing politico-business wrongdoing. Now the governors
emphasized remedies rather than abuses, and most seemed confident
that the remedies would work. Criticism of business influence in government continued to be a staple of political rhetoric throughout the
Progressive era, but it ceased to have the intensity it did in 1905–06. In
place of the burning attack on corruption, politicians offered advanced
progressive programs, including further regulation and election-law re-

forms. The deep concern with business corruption of politics and government thus waned. It had stirred people to consciousness of wrongdoing, crystallized their discontent with existing policies, and pointed toward concrete solutions for the ills of industrialism. But it had not sustained the more radical, antibusiness possibilities suggested by the discoveries of 1905–06.

Indeed, the passions of those years probably weakened the insurgent, democratic qualities of the ensuing political transformation and strengthened its bureaucratic aspects. This result was ironical, but its causes were not conspiratorial. They lay instead in the tendency—shared by the muckrakers and their audience—to accept remedies unequal to the problems at hand and in political circumstances that isolated insurgents from decision-making. Once the changes in policy were under way after 1906, those organized groups whose interests were most directly affected entered the fray, jockeyed for position, and heavily shaped the outcomes. We do not yet know enough about how this happened, but studies such as Stanley P. Caine's examination of railroad regulation in Wisconsin suggest how difficult it was to translate popular concern on an "issue" into the details of a law. It is hardly surprising that, as regulation and administration became accepted public functions, the affected interests exerted much more influence on policy than did those who cared most passionately about restoring clean government.

But the failure to pursue antibusiness policies does not mean the outcry against corruption was either insincere or irrelevant. Quite the contrary. It was sufficiently genuine and widespread to dominate the nation's public life in 1905 and 1906 and to play a decisive part in bringing about the transformation of American politics and government. Political changes do not, of course, embrace everything that is meant by progressivism. Nor was the discovery that business corrupts politics the only catalytic agent at work; certainly the rise of consumer discontent with utility and transportation corporations and the vigorous impetus toward new policies given by Theodore Roosevelt during his second term as president played complementary roles. But the awakening to corruption—as it was newly understood—provided an essential dynamic, pushing the states and the nation toward what many of its leading men and women considered progressive reform.

The organizational thesis sheds much light on the values and methods of those who succeeded in dominating the new types of politics and government but very little on the political circumstances in which they came forward. Robert H. Wiebe, in particular, has downplayed key aspects of the political context, including the outcry against corruption. Local uprisings against the alliance of bosses and businessmen, Wiebe has stated, "lay outside the mainstream of progressivism"; measures instituting the direct primary and curtailing the political influence of business were "old-fashioned reform." Yet those local crusades, by spreading the dynamic perception that business corrupts politics, created a popular demand for the regulatory and administrative measures that Wiebe has claimed are characteristic of true progressivism; and those "old-fashioned" laws were enacted amidst the same political furor that produced the stunningly rapid bureaucratic triumph whose significance for twentieth-century America Wiebe has explained so convincingly. What the organizational thesis mainly lacks is the sense that political action is open-ended and unpredictable. Consequences are often unexpected, outcomes surprising when matched against origins. While it is misleading, as Samuel P. Hays has said, to interpret progressivism solely on the basis of its anti-business ideology, it is equally misleading to fail to appreciate that reform gained decisive initial strength from ideas and feelings that were not able to sustain the movement in the end. The farsighted organizers from business and the professions thus gained the opportunity to complete a political transformation that had been begun by people who were momentarily shocked into action but who stopped far short of pursuing the full implications of their discovery.

☆7☆

The New Deal

REVOLUTIONARY OR
CONSERVATIVE?

Franklin Delano Roosevelt was perhaps the most controversial president ever to occupy the White House. For over twelve years he led the American people, first through the worst depression in their history and then through a war that encompassed virtually the entire globe. To his admirers he was an individual of heroic stature, a leader who firmly believed that it was possible to preserve free and democratic institutions by internal reforms without adopting authoritarian or totalitarian methods and overturning the basic structure of American society. To his enemies he was a misguided, even immoral, individual who mistakenly believed that he could save American democracy by taking the people down the road to the welfare state—a road that would eventually end in socialism and therefore the negation of individual freedom. Unlike some other presidents Roosevelt had the uncanny ability to arouse strong passions. He was a person who was either loved or hated; few remained neutral toward him or reacted blandly to his personality or accomplishments.

Why did Roosevelt arouse such strong passions? The answer to this ostensibly simple question is anything but simple. Certainly there was little in his background or his accomplishments prior to 1933 that would explain the controversial nature of his presidential tenure. Even those friends and associates who worked closely with Roosevelt during his dozen years in the White House were not always able to grasp his many-sided personality or understand why he acted as he did. Frances Perkins, his longtime secretary of labor, described him as "the most complicated human being I ever knew," a comment that was echoed by others such as Henry Morgenthau and Robert E. Sherwood.

The controversy that surrounded Roosevelt's years in the White House has almost been matched by the quantity and quality of books written about him by friends, associates, and enemies. Unlike other presidents whose careers were not chronicled until decades after their death, Roosevelt has already been the subject of literally hundreds of books and articles. Part of the reason for this situation undoubtedly lies in the fact that much of the source material left by Roosevelt[1] and his associates was opened up to scholars within a surprisingly short time after his death in 1945. But part of the reason surely lies in the fascination with the New Deal and the changes that American society underwent during the years from 1933 to 1945. However the Roosevelt years are interpreted it is difficult to avoid the conclusion that the United States was a very different nation in 1945 as compared with 1933.

It was the sheer magnitude of the New Deal innovations early in his presidential career that caused Roosevelt to become such a highly controversial figure. Although his victory in 1932 was relatively broad-based he soon alienated many businessmen as well as other powerful interest groups. As a result he came under increasingly harsh attacks as the 1930s progressed. Some accused him of subverting traditional American ideals of individualism and liberty by moving toward a welfare state that could end only in socialism and an omnipotent state. Such a staunch Democrat as Al Smith, for example, hotly argued during the presidential campaign of 1936 that Roosevelt was indeed taking the American people down the road to socialism. "It is all right with me if they [the Roosevelt administration] want to disguise themselves as Norman Thomas or Karl Marx, or Lenin, or any of the rest of that bunch," Smith shouted, "but what I won't stand for is allowing them to march under the banner of Jefferson, Jackson and Cleveland."[2]

The attack on Roosevelt's New Deal from the right was echoed also by the critics of the left. There were many who felt that the traditional American attachment to individualistic values had been rendered obsolete by the nation's industrial and technological advances. Rexford G. Tugwell, a professor of economics and one of the early New Deal "brain trusters," was one such critic. He was convinced that America's competitive economy had never worked well; to attempt to reform it with minor changes would prove hopelessly inadequate. What was required, Tugwell concluded, was thorough and effective governmental planning for all aspects of the economic system; only in this way could the economy be stabilized and future depressions avoided. Much to his disappointment the New Deal seemed too pragmatic. Roosevelt, he finally concluded, was either unwilling or unable

---

[1]It has been estimated that Roosevelt's personal papers occupy more than 9,000 cubic feet at the Hyde Park Library; this figure does not include the papers of other important New Deal officials.

[2]Quoted in William E. Leuchtenburg, *Franklin D. Roosevelt and the New Deal 1932–1940* (New York, 1963), p. 178.

to plan in a rational and systematic manner. To the left of men like Tugwell stood the socialist and communist groups in America. Their criticism was that the New Deal was too conservative; the only proper approach to the depression was a complete overhaul of America's social and economic system and the establishment of a socialist state.

Thus during the depression years the New Deal was attacked from many points of view. To some it was too radical; to others it was too conservative or reactionary. Still others viewed Roosevelt's policies as a series of pragmatic and expedient moves in response to specific events and deplored the fact that the president never seemed to give much thought to the overall dimensions of the crisis facing the American people. To be sure, many of these critics were reflecting to a large extent the passions and emotions of the age in which they were living. Faced with the problem of coming to grips with the greatest depression the country had ever known, they did not have the perspective nor the dispassionate attitude required to view the issues at stake in a detached or objective manner. Their criticisms, nevertheless, helped to establish the framework of reference with which later writers were to approach the New Deal. In brief, the question usually raised by contemporary commentators and later historians revolved around the role of the New Deal in American life. Was the New Deal simply an extension of the Progressive tradition or did it involve a radical departure from the mainstream of American history?

For historians reared in the tradition of the Progressive school there was little doubt about the basic nature of the New Deal. Viewing America's past in terms of a conflict between liberalism and conservatism and the people versus the vested interests, they saw the New Deal as simply another phase in the struggle against monopoly, privilege, and special interests. To them the New Deal was related to earlier reform movements, including Jeffersonian and Jacksonian Democracy, populism, and progressivism, all of which had represented the people in their continuing struggle to achieve a greater measure of political, economic, and social equality. While they often referred to the revolutionary character of the New Deal, their use of the term "revolutionary" did not necessarily imply a sharp break with the past. Louis Hacker, although not squarely in the Progressive tradition referred to the New Deal as the "Third American Revolution" in the mid-1940s. His description of the New Deal, however, was anything but revolutionary. Some of its policies, he wrote, were improvisations; some were descended from populism and progressivism; but always "there existed the thought that the responsibility of public authority for the welfare of the people was clear and that the intervention of the state was justifiable."[3] Hacker's last point, while by no means acceptable to

---

[3]Louis M. Hacker, The Shaping of the American Tradition (New York, 1947), pp. 1125–1126.

all Americans, was hardly novel; reformers and intellectuals had been urging government-sponsored reforms since the mid-nineteenth century.

To Henry Steele Commager, one of America's most distinguished historians, the relationship between the New Deal and earlier reform movements was obvious. Writing at the time of Roosevelt's death Commager explicitly denied the revolutionary character of the New Deal. What was simply a new deal of old cards appeared radical for two reasons: the rapidity with which the New Deal program was enacted into law; and the fact that the movement contrasted so sharply with the do-nothing attitude of the Harding-Coolidge-Hoover administrations. If the New Deal was compared with the Progressive era rather than the 1920s, Commager maintained, "the contrast would have been less striking than the similarities . . . [For] precedent for the major part of New Deal legislation was to be found in these earlier periods." The achievements of Roosevelt—the restoration of self-confidence, the reassertion of faith in democracy, and the rehabilitation of the nation's human and natural resources—all demonstrated the affinity of the New Deal to the earlier reform movements in American history.[4]

Perhaps the fullest and most eloquent argument favoring the idea that the New Deal was a continuation and extension of America's liberal past was advanced by the outstanding historian writing in the Progressive tradition, Arthur M. Schlesinger, Jr. A former professor at Harvard University, Schlesinger has been the most persuasive and brilliant historian writing within and in defense of America's liberal tradition. He was, of course, much more than a historian. A leading intellectual, important member of the Kennedy administration, and shrewd commentator on current affairs, Schlesinger has been an activist as well as a scholar. As a historian Schlesinger since the close of World War II has championed a modified brand of American liberalism whose roots, he believed, go far back into the nation's history. Thus his Pulitzer Prize-winning study, *The Age of Jackson* (1945), argued that Jacksonian Democracy was a liberal political movement based on a coalition of urban workers and other democratic groups in American society. Schlesinger attempted also to rebuild the intellectual foundations of the liberal ideology in his writings. In *The Vital Center* (1948) he incorporated Niebuhrian theology into the corpus of American liberalism so as to give the latter a more realistic and viable character. Taking cognizance of the reaction against liberal ideas since the 1940s, Schlesinger borrowed Reinhold Niebuhr's emphasis on original sin and reinterpreted the liberal ideology in order to purge that ideology of the charge that its utopian optimism had been unrealistic and its adher-

---

[4]Henry Steele Commager, "Twelve Years of Roosevelt," *American Mercury* 40 (April 1945):391–401.

ents had been incapable of meeting the challenge of totalitarianism since the 1930s.

All of American history, according to Schlesinger, was characterized by a cyclical movement which saw periods of liberal reform followed by alternate periods of conservative consolidation. In his eyes Jacksonian Democracy followed the decline of Jeffersonian Democracy, the Progressive era followed the age of the robber barons, and the New Deal came after the sterile conservatism of the 1920s. Indeed, Schlesinger argued, the New Frontier of John F. Kennedy and the Great Society of Lyndon B. Johnson were themselves reactions to the inaction of the Eisenhower years. The generative force behind this cycle was social conflict—conflict which arose from a constant accumulation of disquietude and discontent within American society. Schlesinger spelled out his thesis in a series of books and articles, one of which was *The Age of Roosevelt*, a multivolume study of the New Deal.[5]

In the first selection in this chapter, Schlesinger discusses the origins of the New Deal. To him the New Deal represented much more than a mere response to the depression. On the contrary, the New Deal was an integral part of the history of American liberalism; it was another phase of the liberal-conservative cycle in American history. By the 1920s, Schlesinger claimed, the nation had tired of the Progressive crusade. National disinterest in politics meant that power gravitated inevitably toward powerful economic interests, and government increasingly came under the control and influence of the business community. As a result of this shift in power there was a progressive alienation of various groups from American society, including the farmers, workers, minority ethnic groups, and disenchanted intellectuals. Even without a depression, Schlesinger suggested, the New Deal was bound to have happened in one form or another. What the depression did was to give the New Deal its particular character—a political movement responding to the immediate problem of an impending economic collapse. The New Deal, he concluded, rejected the dogmatic absolutes and the simplistic dichotomies posed in contemporary ideologies such as communism and fascism. To Schlesinger the New Deal was a practical, energetic, and pragmatic movement based on the assumption that a "managed and modified capitalist order achieved by piecemeal experiment could combine personal freedom and economic growth."

Schlesinger's approach to the New Deal was echoed by other historians. Frank Freidel, author of what appears to be the most definitive multivolume biography of Roosevelt, wrote in much the same historiographical tradition as that of Schlesinger. Freidel, however, posed the

---

[5]Schlesinger has to date published three volumes of this study: *The Crisis of the Old Order, 1919–1933* (Boston, 1957), *The Coming of the New Deal* (Boston, 1958), and *The Politics of Upheaval* (Boston, 1960).

discussion in quite different terms. To him the New Deal was basically the work of a number of persons who had grown to maturity during the Progressive era and who still shared the moral fervor of that period. Like Roosevelt they were conservative men whose primary goal was to save rather than to destroy the free enterprise system. These humanitarian reformers were willing to use the machinery and authority of government to improve the lot of the common man. Taken as a whole the New Deal was based on "American objectives and experience in the Progressive Era and during the first World War"[6] To put it another way Roosevelt's program was squarely within the American tradition; his goals were essentially to conserve the existing economic and social system by eliminating obvious defects rather than changing it by radical programs.

Historians such as Commager, Schlesinger, and Freidel were all favorably disposed to the New Deal because they identified themselves with the American liberal or Progressive tradition. This is not to imply that they were uncritical toward Roosevelt and the New Deal; in many instances they found much that was inadequate, wrong, or misleading about the goals, program, and administration of many New Deal experiments. Generally speaking, however, they wrote with approval of Roosevelt's pragmatism, his faith in American democracy, and his obvious distaste for totalitarian methods. The alternative to the New Deal, they hinted, might very well have been a dictatorship of the right or left if the nation had continued to drift along as it had under Hoover.

While such historians who identified themselves in the Progressive tradition were interpreting the New Deal in a favorable light, others, particularly those adhering to a conservative ideology, were writing in quite a different vein. Conceiving of individual freedom and competition in almost absolutist terms, they saw the New Deal as a violent departure from traditional American values. To them the New Deal was anything but a continuation of America's political tradition; it represented rather an outright rejection of everything that was good and desirable within that tradition. During the decade of the thirties, many critics, especially spokesmen of conservative social groups and

---

[6]Frank Freidel, *The New Deal in Historical Perspective* (2 ed., Washington, D.C., 1965), p. 6. To date Freidel has published four volumes of his study of Roosevelt: *Franklin D. Roosevelt: The Apprenticeship* (Boston, 1952), *The Ordeal* (Boston, 1954), *The Triumph* (Boston, 1956), and *Launching the New Deal* (Boston, 1973).

In a recent study of Hoover, Roosevelt, the "Brain Trust," and the origins of the New Deal, Elliot A. Rosen argued that Roosevelt's domestic and diplomatic objectives were shaped in 1932 by a small group of advisers who gave the domestic economy priority. "A better distribution of income, achievement of the social minima, and federal intervention where necessary for social and economic purposes became part of our permanent past. This has remained the legacy of Roosevelt and the Brain Trust." Elliot A. Rosen, *Hoover, Roosevelt, and the Brain Trust: From Depression to New Deal* (New York, 1977), p. 380.

businessmen, took this position on the New Deal. Former President Hoover, for example, sounded a note of warning in 1934 when he condemned the expansion of the federal government's role and the subsequent regimentation of American life. "It is a vast shift," he wrote, "from the American concept of human rights which even the government may not infringe to those social philosophies where men are wholly subjective to the state. It is a vast casualty to Liberty if it shall be continued."[7]

Hoover's hostility was matched by other writers like John T. Flynn, a former liberal who had become progressively disillusioned by America's liberal tradition. The author of several books on Roosevelt, Flynn's antagonism against the New Deal reached a peak in his *The Roosevelt Myth*. Specifically denying the achievements that liberal historians had credited to the New Deal, he argued that Roosevelt had substituted for the free enterprise system one that operated upon "permanent crises and an armament economy." In the process of implementing New Deal programs the vigor of state governments had been sapped, the authority of Congress had be eroded, and unprecedented power had been concentrated in the hands of the president. One result of Roosevelt's New Deal policies was the appearance of a staggering federal debt; "a debt that can never be paid and which can be taken off our shoulders only by a great and devastating inflation."[8]

The charge by conservative writers that the New Deal represented a break with the past, interestingly enough, was echoed by some Progressive historians. One of these was Richard Hofstadter who, although writing within a liberal framework, was among the severest critics of America's liberal tradition. American liberalism, Hofstadter argued, had failed because of its moralizing tendencies and its inability to come to grips with the fundamental issues of the day. In *The Age of Reform: From Bryan to F.D.R.*, he insisted that the New Deal could not under any circumstances be interpreted as a continuation of the liberal-Progressive tradition. The section in his book devoted to the New Deal was appropriately entitled "The New Departure."

To Hofstadter the New Deal was markedly different from any other indigenous American political movement. Past reform movements, Hofstadter noted, had generally operated under the assumption that their purpose was to clear the way for new enterprises and new men—to smash established privilege and monopoly and to provide all Americans with an equal opportunity in life. Within this context the national government was considered to be either negative in its nature or an obstacle in the way of success. Earlier reform movements had

---

[7]Herbert Hoover, *The Challenge to Liberty* (New York, 1934), p. 103.

[8]John T. Flynn, *The Roosevelt Myth* (rev. ed.; New York, 1956), pp. 414 and 445.

taken it for granted that American society was essentially healthy but one that needed further democratization to reach its full potential.

The New Deal, according to Hofstadter, was based on entirely different premises. Instead of viewing American society as healthy New Deal reformers saw it as a sick society in need of changes that could only be instituted through federal action. Thus the New Deal accepted the idea of federal responsibility for the relief of the unemployed, supported legislation for social security, unemployment insurance, wages and hours, and public housing, and did not fear massive expenditures that resulted in deficit spending. Many of the traditional aims of past reform movements—to restore government to the people and to destroy big business and monopolies—were simply bypassed or ignored by Roosevelt. Considering the nature and magnitude of New Deal programs, Hofstadter concluded, the movement had to be considered a new departure in American life. "The New Deal, and the thinking it engendered," wrote Hofstadter, "represented the triumph of economic emergency and human needs over inherited notions and inhibitions. . . . At the core of the New Deal, then, was not a philosophy (F.D.R. could identify himself philosophically only as a Christian and democrat), but an attitude, suitable for practical politicians, administrators, and technicians, but uncongenial to the moralism that the Progressives had for the most part shared with their opponents."[9]

The New Deal, Hofstadter pointed out with an ironic touch, represented a change of the usual ideological roles of American conservatives and reformers. The conservatives had traditionally prided themselves on their sense of realism, their distrust of abstract plans for remaking society, and their belief in the necessity for institutional continuity. Reformers, on the other hand, had invariably appealed to moral sentiments, denounced existing injustices, and aroused the indignation of the community. By the 1930s, however, the traditional roles of the two had become reversed. Reformers appealed not to moral abstractions, but to concrete grievances of specific groups—farmers without markets, unemployed men without bread, laborers seeking to organize in unions of their own choosing, and to those groups concerned with the soundness of banks, investment markets, and manufacturing enterprises. Conservatives were now in the position of moral critics—they denounced the New Deal precisely because of its violation of traditional rules, its abandonment of the nation's moral heritage, its departure from sound principles, and its imposition of a federal tyranny upon the American people.

Oddly enough Hofstadter was unhappy with the efforts of both conservatives and reformers. The reformers from the New Deal on,

---

[9]Richard Hofstadter, *The Age of Reform: From Bryan to F.D.R.* (New York, 1955), pp. 314 and 323.

according to him, had refused to think in terms of rational planning and remained content to respond in a pragmatic way to individual pressures and situations as they arose. The criticisms of the conservatives, on the other hand, were "hollow and cliché-ridden," the complaints of a class increasingly cut off from the world of reality. But all that Hofstadter could do—at least in his role as historian and contemporary critic—was to hope that a better understanding of America's past political tradition might help future politicians to formulate a more realistic philosophy.

A similar criticism was voiced by Rexford G. Tugwell, a Columbia University professor who had joined Roosevelt's administration in the early 1930s as a strong advocate of governmental economic planning. The old faith in a self-regulating market, he maintained, had never been justified; it was part of the American mythology of a free enterprise system. Distrustful of business and businessmen Tugwell felt that only the federal government was in a position to control the economy in such a way as to make it run smoothly and efficiently.

After leaving government service to return to the academic world, Tugwell set out to write a biography of Roosevelt, which was finally published in 1957, although parts had appeared in a series of long articles somewhat earlier. The picture Tugwell drew of Roosevelt and the New Deal was a friendly one, but one also marked with a sense of disappointment. According to Tugwell the productive capacity of the American economy by the late 1920s had far outrun purchasing power, thus giving rise to a fundamental maladjustment which resulted in the depression. The Republicans under Hoover initially denied that the economic situation was serious. Later they adopted halfway measures and encouraged private rather than public relief. When Roosevelt came to power he was faced with a grave emergency but one which gave him an unprecedented opportunity such as no other president had had. Although he was a master improviser and politician, Roosevelt never conceived of New Deal measures in terms of rational planning. Many of the New Deal innovations, indeed, resulted from careful balancing between the claims of various competing pressure groups. Roosevelt, Tugwell concluded, was a political pragmatist with a progressive bent. Despite his essential greatness he was unable or unwilling to seize the opportunity and institute far-reaching reform measures. Whether future historians would continue to look upon the New Deal in this manner, Tugwell admitted, was an open question.[10]

Both Hofstadter and Tugwell were critical of Roosevelt because of his political opportunism and his pragmatic approach to serious prob-

---

[10]Rexford G. Tugwell, "The New Deal in Retrospect," *Western Political Quarterly* 1 (December 1948):373–385. See also Tugwell's full length study of Roosevelt, *The Democratic Roosevelt* (New York, 1957).

lems. Implicit in their writings was the belief that the New Deal could not be interpreted as a part of America's liberal tradition. Oddly enough they were in agreement with later neoconservative historians who had also rejected the thesis that American history could be understood in terms of class and ideological conflict. In the eyes of these subsequent historians American history had been marked not by conflict and divisions, but by stability and unity. Domestic struggles in the United States, they maintained, were over means, never over ends. To look upon the politics of the 1930s as an expression of fundamental divisions among the American people, they concluded, was a mistake.

But if the New Deal did not reflect fundamental class and ideological divisions, what did it reflect? To Heinz Eulau, a political scientist at Stanford University writing in essentially a neoconservative vein, the New Deal defied ideological classification. It is true, he admitted, that many individuals associated with Roosevelt had their own particular blueprints for the reconstruction of American society. Taken as a whole, however, the New Deal had many sides, and for this reason was not the product of a cohesive and rational ideology. Nor did the New Deal articulate a faith in a better tomorrow; it did not call upon people to join a crusade to remake their society or to experiment with new and untried schemes. But if the New Deal was not an ideology, a faith, a crusade, an experiment, a revolt, or a utopia, what was it? To Eulau the answer to this question was clear. The New Deal, he suggested, was "both a symbol and evidence of the nation's political maturity"; it represented an effort to solve problems "through politics rather than through ideology or violence." In Eulau's eyes a mature politics involves adjustment, compromise, and integration. By this standard the New Deal symbolized a mature politics because it was seeking solutions to problems rather than imposing preconceived solutions on problems.[11]

By implication Eulau was agreeing with those neoconservative historians who rejected class and ideological interpretations of American history in favor of an approach that emphasized the stability of American institutions and the pragmatism of American culture. The distinguishing characteristic of American history, therefore, was a rejection of the unrealistic intellectual and ideological characteristics of European thought and the substitution in their place of common sense. To writers like Eulau the New Deal must be understood as part of the basic commonsense approach of most Americans and their rejection of the world of ideology. In this sense the New Deal was not comparable to earlier liberal movements; the New Deal was simply an attempt to cope with unique problems in a simple and sensible manner.

---

[11]Heinz Eulau, "Neither Ideology Nor Utopia: The New Deal in Retrospect," *Antioch Review* 19 (Winter 1959–1960): 523–537.

During the 1960s the stature of Franklin D. Roosevelt and the New Deal again began to change as younger scholars asked some searching questions. If the New Deal had modified and humanized American society, why did poverty and racism continue to exist? If the New Deal had truly reformed an unbridled capitalism and made it more responsive to the needs of people, why were so many different groups—blacks, Puerto Ricans, Mexican Americans, and middle-class youths—alienated from their society? If the New Deal had led to a change for the better in terms of America's role in world affairs, how had the nation become involved first in the Korean War and then in the Vietnam conflict? Given the tensions and crises of the 1960s it was perhaps inevitable that the historical image of the New Deal would once again change.

Perhaps the sharpest critique—though by no means the only one—came from the pens of historians identified with the New Left. Many of these scholars were committed to radical changes in the structure of American society and they saw history as a discipline that would illuminate the present by a searching examination of the past. We have "sought explicitly," wrote the editor of a book of essays representing in part New Left scholarship, "to make the past speak to the present, to ask questions that have a deep-rooted moral and political relevance. In moving occasionally beyond description and causal analysis to judge significance, we have, by necessity, moved beyond objective history in the realm of values."[12]

Given their own values and commitment to social change it was natural that radical historians would see the New Deal in an unfavorable light. In an essay discussing the place of the New Deal in American history, for example, Barton J. Bernstein argued that the liberal reforms of the 1930s had not transformed the American system; rather they conserved and protected corporate capitalism. Nor had the New Deal significantly redistributed power in any way, or granted any meaningful recognition to unorganized peoples. Even its bolder programs had not extended the beneficence of government beyond affluent groups or used the wealth of the few for the needs of the many. The New Deal followed essentially conservative goals, for it was intended to maintain the American system intact. "The New Deal," Bernstein concluded, "failed to solve the problem of depression, it failed to raise the impoverished, it failed to redistribute income, it failed to extend equality and generally countenanced racial discrimination and segregation. It failed generally to make business more responsible to the social welfare or to threaten business's pre-eminent political power. . . . In acting to protect the institution of private property

---

[12]Barton J. Bernstein, ed., *Towards a New Past: Dissenting Essays in American History* (New York, 1968), p. xiii.

and in advancing the interests of corporate capitalism, the New Deal assisted the middle and upper sectors of society. It protected them, sometimes, even at the cost of injuring the lower sectors. Seldom did it bestow much of substance upon the lower classes."[13]

From the vantage point of the political left, therefore, the New Deal was a failure. Committed to capitalism it could not offer the lower classes anything but rhetoric and psychological comfort. So wrote even Paul K. Conkin in a penetrating analysis of Roosevelt and the New Deal. Judging the New Deal more from the perspective of a social democrat rather than a partisan of the New Left, he expressed considerable admiration for Roosevelt's political astuteness and charismatic qualities. Yet Conkin denied that Roosevelt was even a pragmatist, for his thought was too shallow and superficial and concerned largely with immediate issues. "For the historian," noted Conkin in his critical but compassionate summation, "every judgment, every evaluation of the past has to be tinged with a pinch of compassion, a sense of the beauty and nobility present when honest hopes and humane ideals are frustrated. He sees that the thirties could have brought so much more, but also so much worse, than the New Deal. The limiting context has to be understood—the safeguards and impediments of our political system, Roosevelt's intellectual limitations, and most of all the appalling economic ignorance and philosophic immaturity of the American electorate. . . . The New Deal solved a few problems, ameliorated a few more, obscured many, and created new ones. This is about all our political system can generate, even in crisis."[14]

Much of the historiography of the New Deal, therefore, reflected to some degree personal ideological commitments. To Progressive scholars Roosevelt was a hero; to conservatives he was too radical; and to radicals he was too conservative, if not reactionary. Each group, of course, judged Roosevelt in terms of the direction they felt America *should* have taken.

In a major study of New Deal economic policy, however, Ellis W. Hawley approached the problem quite differently. Americans, he noted, shared a commitment to two value systems that were not wholly compatible. On the one hand they cherished liberty and freedom, which implied a competitive economic and social order. On the other hand they valued order, rationality, and collective organization, and associated large business units and economic organizations generally with abundance, progress, and a rising standard of living. Yet the latter value posed a potential threat to the former; monopoly negated, at least in theory, freedom and competition. Much of twentieth-cen-

---

[13]Barton J. Bernstein, "The New Deal: The Conservative Achievements of Liberal Reform," in *ibid.*, pp. 264 and 281–282.

[14]Paul K. Conkin, *The New Deal* (New York, 1967).

tury American history, Hawley observed, revolved around the search for a solution "that would preserve the industrial order, necessarily based upon a high degree of collective organization, and yet would preserve America's democratic heritage at the same time." New Deal economic policy mirrored this basic ambivalence; it vacillated between rational planning and antimonopoly, neither of which was completely compatible. Hawley's conclusion offered little support to any of the competing ideologies that underlay many of the historical interpretations of Roosevelt and the New Deal. "If the experiences of the nineteen thirties have any relevance at all," he wrote, "it is in illustrating the limitations of logical analysis, the pitfalls inherent in broad theoretical approaches, the difficulty of agreeing on policy goals, and the necessity of making due allowances for the intellectual heritage, current trends of opinion, and the realities of pressure-group politics."[15]

As the political passions of the 1930s subsided, historians tended to move toward a middle position. Albert U. Romasco argued that Roosevelt wanted to cooperate with the business community, thereby stimulating investment and recovery. If Roosevelt was hostile to the business community, he nevertheless confronted its members with a little stick and a big carrot. Similarly, Nancy Weiss exploded the myth that Roosevelt was overly concerned with the plight of black Americans during the Great Depression. On racial issues the New Deal offered little; Roosevelt was reluctant to support antilynching legislation for fear of alienating Southern Democrats. Insofar as economic issues were concerned, blacks benefited only because they were not excluded from those broad New Deal programs designed to assist the poor and the unemployed as a whole. Consequently, blacks embraced the Democratic party and abandoned the Republican party even though Roosevelt did not directly woo their support.[16]

More recently other historians have begun to ask quite different kinds of questions. Michael Bernstein, for example, insisted that the focus on the Great Depression and the New Deal was somewhat misplaced. In his eyes the performance of any economy depended on long-range secular factors. By the 1930s those sectors of the economy that in the past had provided the basis for growth—textiles, lumber, iron, and steel—were slumping and could not provide the foundations for growth. Paradoxically, the most dynamic sectors—appliances, chemicals, and processed foods—were as yet in their infancy and were therefore incapable of fueling recovery. Thus the problem of economic re-

---

[15]Ellis W. Hawley, *The New Deal and the Problem of Monopoly: A Study in Economic Ambivalence* (Princeton, 1966), p. 493.

[16]Albert U. Romasco, *The Politics of Recovery: Roosevelt's New Deal* (New York, 1983), and Nancy J. Weiss, *Farewell to the Party of Lincoln: Black Politics in the Age of FDR* (Princeton, 1983). See also Peter Fearon, *War, Prosperity and Depression: The U.S. Economy, 1917–1945* (Lawrence, Kansas, 1987).

covery was more complex and difficult than contemporaries or subsequent scholars assumed.[17]

Similarly, John A. Garraty emphasized the importance of a comparative dimension in evaluating the New Deal. In an analysis of the early years of Franklin D. Roosevelt and Adolf Hitler, reprinted as the second selection in this chapter, he suggested that the New Deal was by no means unique. To be sure, the New Deal functioned within and maintained a commitment to democratic and representative institutions. The Nazis, by way of contrast, deliberately destroyed democratic institutions and imprisoned or murdered dissidents or Jews who did not fit within their racial stereotype. Yet the economic policies adopted in the United States and Germany were not fundamentally dissimilar. Both combined direct relief for the indigent with public-works programs to create jobs; both created semimilitary programs for the young; both were receptive to corporatist solutions that sought to enlist capitalists and workers in an effort to eliminate competition and restore harmony and order; both adopted similar agricultural policies; and both rested in part upon the charismatic personalities of their leaders.[18]

Considering the many ways that historians have written about the New Deal, is it possible to come to any sort of definitive conclusions about its essential nature? Can Roosevelt and the New Deal be positioned precisely in terms of their place within the American political tradition? In dealing with this question it should be emphasized that many of the apparent differences among students writing about the New Deal are partly semantical in nature. When describing the operation of specific New Deal programs, for example, the differences of opinion between historians tend to narrow sharply. Thus what the WPA, NRA, and other federal agencies *did* is often not a subject of dispute. The issue that invariably leads to conflict is the *intent* of participants. The controversy involves not the relief activities of the 1930s, to cite one instance, but whether or not the concept of federal relief undermined the cherished American ideals of individualism and liberty.

The semantic difficulty may be seen in the various ways historians have used the word *pragmatic*. When Roosevelt was described as a "pragmatic leader," what did this mean? Actually the term was employed in at least three different ways. Edgar E. Robinson, for example, described Roosevelt's personal leadership as "pragmatic—an individual playing by ear." What Robinson meant by his characterization was that Roosevelt, in order to gain an immediate political advantage,

---

[17]Michael A. Bernstein, *The Great Depression: Delayed Recovery and Economic Change in America, 1929–1939* (New York, 1987).

[18]See also Garraty's book *The Great Depression* (New York, 1986).

never considered the long-range effects of his policies. "Roosevelt's failure," Robinson concluded, "lay in his unsuccessful attempt to justify the means or establish the ends he had in view." Underlying Robinson's thesis was the criticism that the New Deal resulted in an almost fatal concentration of power in the hands of the executive—a "power that could destroy the world or build it in the image of an entirely new scientific perspective."[19]

A second use of the term "pragmatic," as we have already seen in Tugwell's case, involved the criticism that Roosevelt never even understood the need for long-range economic planning. Roosevelt limited himself to immediate problems and tended to neglect more fundamental issues. Consequently, he never took advantage of the unparalleled opportunity for reform that arose out of the greatest single economic crisis that the American people had ever faced. While New Deal measures were important in giving status and material benefits to hitherto neglected groups in American society, these reforms fell far short of their real potential. This view of Roosevelt, which has been echoed by many writers, is based on the underlying assumption that New Deal pragmatism and rational governmental planning were incompatible.

The term "pragmatic" has been used in a third way to describe a mental attitude and frame of mind that rejected the dogmatic thinking of the 1930s and remained open and receptive to new ideas. William E. Leuchtenburg argued that the pragmatism of the New Deal seemed striking only because the period as a whole was characterized by rigid ideological thinking. The New Deal was pragmatic, Leuchtenburg maintained, "only in contrast to the rigidity of Hoover and of the Left." Moreover, the movement was pragmatic in the sense that reformers themselves remained skeptical about final utopias and ultimate solutions and were always open to experimentation. To Leuchtenburg the New Deal was more than a movement to experiment or to improvise; it was a movement led by individuals who were committed to the proposition that it was possible to make human life more tolerable, that depressions were by no means inevitable events, and that human affairs were not necessarily guided by inexorable deterministic laws.[20]

Because of the preoccupation with the New Deal as a national phenomenon, historians have generally not dealt with its actual impact on the lives of individuals. In a study of Boston during the 1930s, Charles H. Trout observed that the "New Deal's manifestations were treated piecemeal and were perceived by individuals and groups

---

[19]Edgar Eugene Robinson, *The Roosevelt Leadership 1933-1945* (Philadelphia, 1955), pp. 383, 397, and 408.

[20]William E. Leuchtenburg, *Franklin Delano Roosevelt and the New Deal 1932-1940* (New York, 1963), pp. 344–345.

according to their particular needs." Indeed, many federal programs involving social and economic change were resisted by Bostonians precisely because of the weight of tradition and history; the concept "of a national or even a municipal communality of interest was seldom grasped."[21] From a local perspective, therefore, the accomplishments of the New Deal were limited and more remote.

The problem of understanding and assessing the achievements of the New Deal and its place in American history, therefore, is one whose answer will largely be shaped by a series of prior assumptions about the nature of the American past and the nation's ideals in both the present and future. To those historians whose view is that America is founded upon an atomistic philosophy—that the nation's greatness arose from the achievements of talented and ambitious individuals and was not always related to the activities of government—the New Deal will always appear as a movement alien and hostile to traditional values. In this context the New Deal represents a new departure in American history that will end in a collectivistic and authoritarian government. On the other hand, to those scholars who adhere to a corporate philosophy—that society is more than a mere aggregate of private individuals and that a modern complex industrial economy requires a certain amount of public regulation as well as government-sponsored reform—the New Deal becomes a political movement inspired by proper ideals. Instead of representing an aberration in terms of the American political tradition, the New Deal was a movement consonant with previous struggles for justice and equality. To those historians who maintain that only a radical restructuring of American society can eliminate poverty, racism, war, and inequality, the New Deal appears as a palliative or sham designed to gloss over fundamental defects. Finally, from a comparative vantage point, the New Deal suggests that the American experience is not as unique as many believe.

The problem of judging the nature and accomplishments of the New Deal is, then, a difficult one, for it involves the entire fabric of the American past. Indeed, to avoid any broad judgments is in effect to render a judgment, albeit on an unconscious level. In the final analysis, therefore, historians will continue to grapple with the place of the New Deal in American life. Was the New Deal a continuation of America's liberal tradition or was it a repudiation of that tradition? Did the New Deal reflect an attempt by corporate capitalism to maintain its power intact by forging a partnership with the federal government, with the latter in a subordinate position? Or did the New Deal give a significant voice to minority groups that in the past had been powerless? Can the New Deal even be understood in ideological terms

---

[21]Charles H. Trout, *Boston, The Great Depression, and the New Deal* (New York, 1977), pp. 321–322.

or should it be viewed as a political movement characterized by an underlying pragmatism? Or were the alleged inconsistencies of the New Deal a reflection of the underlying commitment of Americans to the values of order and freedom, which in turn gave rise to ambivalent policies? These are only some of the broad questions that must be answered in order to assess the nature and significance of the New Deal.[22]

---

[22]For a penetrating analysis of some of the historical literature on the New Deal, see Alfred B. Rollins, Jr., "Was There Really a Man Named Roosevelt?," in *American History: Retrospect and Prospect*, George A. Billias and Gerald N. Grob, eds. (New York, 1971), pp. 232–270.

Arthur M. Schlesinger, Jr.

ARTHUR M. SCHLESINGER, JR. (1917–   ) is Albert Schweitzer Professor of the Humanities at the City University of New York. He was also a special assistant to President John F. Kennedy. Among his many published works are The Age of Jackson (1945), The Age of Roosevelt, 3 vols. (1957–1960), A Thousand Days: John F. Kennedy in the White House (1965), and Robert Kennedy and His Times (1978).

In the background of any historical episode lies all previous history. The strands which a historian may select as vital to an understanding of the particular episode will vary widely according to his interest, his temperament, his faith and his time. Each man must unravel the seamless web in his own way. I do not propose here any definitive assessment of the sources of the New Deal. I doubt whether a final assessment is possible. I want rather to call attention to certain possible sources which may not have figured extensively in the conventional accounts, including my own—to the relation of the New Deal to the ebb and flow of American national politics and then its relation to the international dilemma of free society in this century.

Such relationships are speculative; nonetheless, an attempt to see them may perhaps cast light on some of the less discussed impulses behind the New Deal itself. To begin—and in order to make a sharp issue—let me ask this question: Would there have been a New Deal if there had been no depression? Without a depression, would we have had nothing but a placid continuation, so long as prosperity itself continued, of the New Era of the twenties?

I would answer that there would very likely have been some sort of New Deal in the thirties even without the depression. I think perhaps our contemporary thinking has come too unreflectively to assume depression as the necessary preliminary for any era of reform. Students of American history know better. The fight against depression was, to be sure, the heart of the New Deal, but it has not been the central issue of traditional American reform: it was not the heart of Jeffersonian Democracy nor of Jacksonian Democracy nor of the antislavery movement nor of the Progressive movement.

What preceded these other epochs of reform was an accumulation

---

Arthur M. Schlesinger, Jr., "Sources of the New Deal: Reflections on the Temper of a Time," Columbia University Forum 2 (Fall 1959): 4–12. Copyright © 1959 by Columbia University. Reprinted from The Columbia University Forum by permission.

of disquietudes and discontents in American society, often noneconomic in character, and producing a general susceptibility to appeals
for change—this and the existence within society of able men or
groups who felt themselves cramped by the status quo and who were
capable of exploiting mounting dissatisfaction to advance policies and
purposes of their own. This combination of outsiders striving for status
and power and a people wearying of the existing leadership and the
existing ideals has been the real archetype of American reform.

The official order in the twenties presented perhaps the nearest we
ever came in our history to the identification of the national interest
with the interests, values, and goals of a specific class—in this case, of
course, the American business community. During the generation before Harding, the political leaders who had commanded the loyalties
and the energies of the American people—Theodore Roosevelt and
Woodrow Wilson—expressed strains in American life distinct from
and often opposed to the dominant values of business. They represented a fusion of patrician and intellectual attitudes which saw in
public policy an outlet for creative energy—in Lippmann's phrase, they
stood for mastery as against drift. In the service of this conception,
they led the people into great national efforts of various sorts, culmi-
nating in the convulsive and terrible experience of war. Two decades
of this—two decades under the glittering eyes of such leaders as [Theo-
dore] Roosevelt and Wilson, Bryan and La Follette—left the nation in
a state of exhaustion.

By 1920 the nation was tired of public crisis. It was tired of discipline and sacrifice. It was tired of abstract and intangible objectives. It
could gird itself no longer for heroic moral or intellectual effort. Its
instinct for idealism was spent. "It is only once in a generation," Wilson himself had said, "that a people can be lifted above material things.
That is why conservative government is in the saddle two-thirds of the
time." And the junior official to whom he made this remark, the young
Assistant Secretary of the Navy, also noted soon after his unsuccessful
try for the vice-presidency in 1920, "Every war brings after it a period
of materialism and conservatism; people tire quickly of ideals and we
are now repeating history." John W. Davis, the Democratic candidate
in 1924, said a few years later. "The people usually know what they
want at a particular time. . . . In 1924 when I was a candidate what
they wanted was repose."

A nation fatigued with ideals and longing for repose was ready for
"normalcy." As popular attention receded from public policy, as values
and aspirations became private again, people stopped caring about politics, which meant that political power inevitably gravitated to society's powerful economic interests—the government of the exhausted
nation quite naturally fell to the businessmen. And for nearly a decade

the business government reigned over a prosperous and expanding country.

Yet, for all the material contentment of the twenties, the decade was also marked by mounting spiritual and psychological discontent. One could detect abundant and multiplying symptoms of what Josiah Royce, after Hegel, used to call a self-estranged social order. The official creed began to encounter growing skepticism, and even opposition and ridicule, in the community at large. Able and ambitious groups, denied what they considered fitting recognition or opportunity, began to turn against the Establishment.

If the economic crash of 1929 astonished the experts, a spiritual crash was diagnosed well in advance. "By 1927," reported Scott Fitzgerald, "a widespread neurosis began to be evident, faintly signaled, like a nervous beating of the feet, by the popularity of crossword puzzles." In the same year Walter Lippmann pointed more soberly to the growing discrepancy between the nominal political issues of the day and the actual emotions of the people. If politics took up these real issues, Lippmann said, it would revolutionize the existing party system. "It is not surprising, then, that our political leaders are greatly occupied in dampening down interest, in obscuring issues, and in attempting to distract attention from the realities of American life."

What was wrong with the New Era was not (as yet) evidence of incompetence or stupidity in public policy. Rather, there was a profound discontent with the monopoly of power and prestige by a single class and the resulting indifference of the national government to deeper tensions. Those excluded from the magic circle suffered boredom, resentment, irritation and eventually indignation over what seemed the intolerable pretensions and irrelevances of their masters. Now it is the gravest error to underrate the power of boredom as a factor in social change. Our political scientists have pointed out convincingly how the human tendency toward inertia sets limits on liberalism; I wish they would spend equal time showing how the human capacity for boredom sets limits on conservatism. The dominant official society—the Establishment—of the twenties was an exceedingly boring one, neither bright nor witty nor picturesque nor even handsome, and this prodded the human impulse to redress the balance by kicking up heels in back streets.

All this encouraged the defection of specific groups from a social order which ignored their needs and snubbed their ambitions. Within the business community itself there were dissident individuals, especially in the underdeveloped areas of the country, who considered that opportunities for local growth were unduly restrained by Wall Street's control of the money market. The farmers felt themselves shut out from the prevailing prosperity. Elements in the labor movement resented their evident second-class citizenship. Members of foreign nationality groups, especially the newer immigration and its children, chafed under the prevalent assumption that the real America was Anglo-Saxon, Protestant, middle class, and white. In time some of the younger people of the nation began to grow restless before the ideals held out to them; while others, in accepting these ideals, acquired a smug mediocrity which even depressed some of their elders.

Gravest among the symptoms was the defection of the intellectuals: writers, educators, newspapermen, editors—those who manned the machinery of opinion and who transmitted ideas. The fact of their particular estrangement and discontent guaranteed the articulation, and thus, to a degree, the coordination of the larger unrest. The intellectuals put the ruling class in its place by substituting for its own admiring picture of itself a set of disrespectful images, which an increasing number of people found delightful and persuasive; the insiders, who had before been seen in the reverent terms of Bruce Barton and the *American Magazine*, were now to be seen less reverently through the eyes of H. L. Mencken and Sinclair Lewis. Satire liberated people from the illusion of business infallibility and opened their minds to other visions of American possibility. The next function of the intellectuals was precisely to explore and substantiate those other visions. They did so with zest and ingenuity; and the result was that, beneath the official crust, the twenties billowed with agitation, criticism and hope. Dewey affirmed man's capability for social intervention and management; Beard argued that intelligent national planning was the irresistible next phase in history; Parrington insisted that Jeffersonian idealism had a sound basis in the American past, and indeed, expressed a truer Americanism than did materialism. Together the satirists and the prophets drew a new portrait of America—both of the American present and of the American promise—and the increasingly visible discrepancy between what was and what might be in America armed the spreading discontent.

The well of idealism was rising again; energies were being replenished, batteries recharged. Outsiders were preparing to hammer on the gates of the citadel. The 1928 election, in which an Irish Catholic challenged Yankee Protestant supremacy, illustrated the gathering revolt against the Establishment. And, though Hoover won the election, Samuel Lubell has pointed out that "Smith split not only the Solid South, but the Republican North as well." Smith carried counties which had long been traditionally Republican; he smashed the Republican hold on the cities; he mobilized the new immigrants. In losing, he polled nearly as many votes as Calvin Coolidge had polled in winning four years before. He stood for the vital new tendencies of politics; and it is likely that the prolongation of these tendencies would have assured a national Democratic victory, without a depression, in 1932 or certainly by 1936. And such a Democratic victory would surely have meant the discharge into public life of able and ambitious people denied preference under a business administration—much the same sort of people, indeed, who eventually came to power with the New Deal; and it would have meant new opportunities for groups that had seen the door slammed in their faces in the Twenties—labor, the farmers, the ethnic minorities, the intellectuals.

The suspicion that a political overturn was due even without a depression is fortified, I think, by the calculations of my father in his essay of some years back "The Tides of National Politics." In this essay he proposed that liberal and conservative periods in our national life succeeded themselves at intervals of about fifteen or sixteen years; this alternation takes place, he wrote, without any apparent correlation with economic circumstances or, indeed, with anything else, except the ebb and flow of national political psychology. By this argument, a liberal epoch was due in America around 1934 or 1935, depression or no.

In short, the New Deal was, among other things, an expression of what would seem—to use a currently unfashionable concept—an inherent cyclical rhythm in American politics. The depression did not cause the cycle: What the depression did was to increase its intensity and deepen its impact by superimposing on the normal cycle the peculiar and unprecedented urgencies arising from economic despair. One might even argue—though I do not think I would—that the depression coming at another stage in the cycle would not necessarily have produced a New Deal. It is certainly true, as I said, that depressions did not induce epochs of reform in 1873 or in 1893. I think myself, however, that the magnitude of the shock made a political recoil almost certain after 1929. Still, the fact that this recoil took a liberal rather than a reactionary turn may well be due to the accident that the economic shock coincided with a liberal turn in the political cycle.

In any event, the fact remains that the historical New Deal, whether or nor something like it might have come along anyway, was after all brought into being by the depression. It assumed its particular character as it sought to respond to the challenge of economic collapse. And, in confronting this challenge, it was confronting a good deal more than merely an American problem. Mass unemployment touched the very roots of free institutions everywhere. "This problem of unemployment," as Winston Churchill said in England in 1930, "is the most torturing that can be presented to civilized society." The problem was more than torturing; it was something civilized society had to solve if it were to survive. And the issue presented with particular urgency was whether representative democracy could ever deal effectively with it.

Churchill, in the same Romanes lecture at Oxford in 1930, questioned whether it could: Democratic governments, he said, drifted along the lines of least resistance, took short views, smoothed their path with platitudes, and paid their way with sops and doles. Parliaments, he suggested, could deal with political problems, but not with economic. "One may even be pardoned," Churchill said, "for doubting whether institutions based on adult suffrage could possibly arrive at the right decisions upon the intricate propositions of modern business and finance." These were delicate problems requiring specialist treatment. "You cannot cure cancer by a majority. What is wanted is a remedy."

The drift of discussion in the United States as well as in Britain in the early thirties revealed an increasingly dour sense of existing alternatives; on the one hand, it seemed, was parliamentary democracy with economic chaos; on the other, economic authoritarianism with political tyranny. Even more dour was the sense that history had already made the choice—that the democratic impulse was drained of vitality, that liberalism was spent as a means of organizing human action. Consider a selection of statements from American writers at the time, and their mortuary resonance:

> The rejection of democracy is nowadays regarded as evidence of superior wisdom. (Ralph Barton Perry)
>
> The moral and intellectual bankruptcy of liberalism in our time needs no demonstration. It is as obvious as rain and as taken for granted. (Nathaniel Peffer)
>
> To attempt a defense of democracy these days is a little like defending paganism in 313 or the divine right of kings in 1793. It is taken for granted that democracy is bad and that it is dying. (George Boas)
>
> 'Liberalism is dead.' So many people who seem to agree upon nothing else have agreed to accept these three sweeping words. (Joseph Wood Krutch)
>
> Modern Western civilization is a failure. That theory is now generally accepted. (Louise Maunsell Fields)
>
> Why is it that democracy has fallen so rapidly from the high prestige which it had at the Armistice . . . Why is it that in America itself—in the very temple and citadel of democracy—self-government has been held up to every ridicule, and many observers count it already dead? (Will Durant)

Only the most venerable among us can remember the creeping fear of a quarter of a century ago that the free system itself had run out of energy, that we had reached, in a phrase Reinhold Niebuhr used as a part of the title of a book in 1934, the "end of an era." What this pessimism implied for the realm of public policy was that democracy had exhausted its intellectual and moral resources, its bag of tricks was played out, and salvation now lay in moving over to a system of total control.

In affirming that there was no alternative between laissez-faire and tyranny, the pessimists were endorsing a passionate conviction held both by the proponents of individualism and the proponents of collectivism. Ogden Mills spoke with precision for American conservatives: "We can have a free country or a socialistic one. We cannot have both. Our economic system cannot be half free and half socialistic. . . . There is no middle ground between governing and being governed, between absolute sovereignty and liberty, between tyranny and freedom." Herbert Hoover was equally vehement: "Even partial regimentation cannot be made to work and still maintain live democratic institutions." In such sentiments, Hoover and Mills would have commanded the enthusiastic assent of Stalin and Mussolini. The critical question was whether a middle way was possible—a mixed system which might give the state more power than conservatives would like, enough power, indeed, to assure economic and social security, but still not too much as to create dictatorship. To this question the Hoovers, no less than the Stalins and Mussolinis, had long since returned categorical answers. They all agreed on this, if on nothing else: no.

As I have said, economic planning was not just an American problem. Great Britain, for example, was confronting mass unemployment and economic stagnation; moreover, she had had since 1929 a Labor government. In a sense, it would have been hard to select a better place to test the possibilities of a tranquil advance from laissez-faire capitalism to a managed society. Here was a Labor leadership, sustained by a faith in the "inevitability of gradualness," ruling a nation committed by tradition and instinct to the acceptance of empirical change. How did the British Labor government visualize its problem and opportunity?

The central figures in the Labor government of 1929 were Ramsay MacDonald, now prime minister for the second time, and Philip Snowden, his sharp and dominating chancellor of the exchequer. Both were classic Socialists who saw in the nationalization of basic industry the answer to all economic riddles. Yet in the existing political situation, with a slim Labor majority, nationalization was out of the question. With socialism excluded, MacDonald and Snowden—indeed, nearly all the Labor party leaders—could see no alternative to all-out socialism but nearly all-out laissez-faire. A capitalist order had to be operated on capitalist principles. The economic policy of the Labor government was thus consecrated as faithfully as that of Herbert Hoover's Republican administration in the United States to the balanced budget and the gold standard—and, far more faithfully than American Republicanism, to free trade.

Socialism across the Channel was hardly more resourceful. As the German Social Democrat Fritz Naphtali put it in 1930, "I don't believe that we can do very much, nor anything very decisive, from the point of view of economic policy, to overcome the crisis until it has run its course." In this spirit of impotence, the democratic Socialists of Europe (until Léon Blum came to power some years later) denied the possibility of a middle way and concluded that, short of full socialization, they had no alternative but to accept the logic of laissez-faire.

The assumption that there were two absolutely distinct economic orders, socialism and capitalism, expressed, of course, an unconscious Platonism—a conviction that the true reality lay in the theoretical essences of which any working economy, with its compromises and confusions, could only be an imperfect copy. If in the realm of essences socialism and capitalism were separate phenomena based on separate principles, then they must be kept rigorously apart on earth. Nor was this use of Platonism—this curious belief that the abstraction was somehow more real than the reality, which Whitehead so well called the "fallacy of misplaced concreteness"—confined to doctrinaire capitalists and doctrinaire socialists. The eminent Liberal economist Sir William Beveridge, director of the London School of Economics, braintruster for the Lloyd George welfare reforms before the First World War, spoke for enlightened economic opinion when he identified the "inescapable fatal danger" confronting pubic policy in the depression as "the danger of mixing freedom and control. We have to decide either to let production be guided by the free play of prices or to plan it socialistically from beginning to end. . . . Control and freedom do not mix." Beveridge, encountering Donald Richberg in Washington in the glowing days of 1933, asked a bit patronizingly whether Richberg really believed that there was "a half-way between Wall Street and Moscow." As for Britain, "there is not much that anyone can do now to help us," Beveridge said. "We must plan to avoid another crisis later. We shall not by conscious effort escape this one."

So dogma denied the possibility of a managed capitalism. But could dogma hold out in Britain against the urgencies of depression? Some Englishmen dissented from the either/or philosophy. In the general election of 1929, for example, John Maynard Keynes and Hubert Henderson had provided the Liberal party with the rudiments of an expansionist policy, based on national spending and public works. As unemployment increased in 1930, so too did the pressure for positive government action. That year Sir Oswald Mosley, a member of the Labor government, proposed to a cabinet committee on unemployment an active program of government spending, accompanied by controls over banking, industry and foreign trade. But he could make no impression on the capitalist orthodoxy of the Socialist leaders; Snowden rejected the Mosley memorandum. Another minister suggested leaving the gold standard; Snowden covered him with scorn. To the party conference of 1930, MacDonald said, "I appeal to you to go back to your Socialist faith. Do not mix that up with pettifogging patching,

either of a Poor Law kind or Relief Work kind." In other words, socialism meant all or—in this case—nothing!

As economic pressure increased, more and more had to be sacrificed to the balancing of the budget; and the implacable retrenchment
meant more governmental economy, reduction in salaries, reduction
in normal public works, until in time, the frenzy for economy
threatened the social services and especially the system of unemployment payments on which many British workers relied to keep alive.
The summer crisis of 1931, after the failure of *Kreditanstalt*, weakened
the pound; and to Snowden and the Labor government nothing now
seemed more essential than staying on the gold standard. To keep Britain on gold required American loans; American loans would not be
forthcoming unless satisfactory evidence existed of a determination to
balance the budget; and the evidence most likely to satisfy J. P. Morgan
and Company, which was arranging the American credit, was a cut in
unemployment benefits.

In August 1931, MacDonald and Snowden confronted the cabinet
with this dismal logic. Arthur Henderson made it clear that the whole
cabinet absolutely accepted Snowden's economic theory: "We ought to
do everything in our power to balance the Budget." But MacDonald's
proposal for a cut in the dole seemed downright wrong; the Labor government fell. MacDonald soon returned to office as head of a National
government. The new government, slightly more adventurous than its
predecessors, took Britain off gold in a few weeks. Sidney Webb, Labor's senior intellectual, provided the Labor government its obituary:
"no one ever told *us* we could do that!"

The Labor government having immobilized itself by its intellectual conviction that there was no room for maneuver, no middle way,
now succeeded through its collapse in documenting its major premise.
Then the experience of 1931 displayed the Right was too hardboiled
ever to acquiesce in even the most gradual democratic change. "The
attempt to give a social bias to capitalism, while leaving it master of
the house," wrote R. H. Tawney, "appears to have failed."

If piecemeal reforms were beyond the power of the Labor government, as they were beyond the desire of a Tory government, then the
only hope lay in the rapid achievement of full socialism; the only way
socialism could be achieved seemed to be through ruthlessness on the
Left as great as that on the Right. Such reasoning was responsible for
the lust for catastrophic change that suffused the British Left and infected a part of the American Left in the early thirties. No one drew
more facile and sweeping conclusions than Harold Laski. The fate of
the MacDonald government, Laski wrote, was "tantamount to an insistence that if socialists wish to secure a state built upon the principles of their faith, they can only do so by revolutionary means."

From this perspective Laski and those like him quite naturally looked with derision on the advocate of the middle way. In December 1934, for the perhaps somewhat baffled readers of *Redbook* magazine, Laski debated with Maynard Keynes whether America could spend its way to recovery. Public spending, Laski said with horror, would lead to inflation or heavy taxation or waste; it would mean, he solemnly wrote, "an unbalanced budget with the disturbance of confidence (an essential condition of recovery) which this implies": it would bequeath a "bill of staggering dimensions" to future generations. "Government spending as anything more than a temporary and limited expedient," he concluded, "will necessarily do harm in a capitalist society." This was, of course, not only the argument of Ramsay MacDonald but of Herbert Hoover; Laski's novelty was to use it to defend, not a balanced budget and the gold standard, but—socialist revolution.

One way or another, the British Left began to vote against liberal democracy. Sir Oswald Mosley, who had championed the most constructive economic program considered within the MacDonald government, indicated the new direction when, with John Strachey and others, he founded the authoritarian-minded New Party in 1931. Mosley's excesses soon led him toward fascism and discredit; but plenty of others were reaching similar conclusions about the impossibility of reform under capitalism. Sidney and Beatrice Webb abandoned Fabianism for the mirage of a new civilization in the Soviet Union. All peaceful roads to progress seemed blocked. After a visit with Roosevelt in Washington, Cripps wrote, "My whole impression is of an honest anxious man faced by an impossible task—humanizing capitalism and making it work." "The one thing that is not inevitable now," said Cripps, "is gradualness."

Both Right and Left—Hoover and Stalin, John W. Davis and Mussolini, Ogden Mills and Stafford Cripps—thus rejected the notion of a socially directed and managed capitalism, of a mixed economy, of something in between classical free enterprise and classical socialism. And the either/or demonstration commanded considerable respect in the United States—self-evidently on the American Right; and to some degree on the American Left. So Laski had made clear in *Democracy in Crisis* that the American ruling class would be as tough and hopeless as any other:

> What evidence is there, among the class which controls the destiny of America, of a will to make the necessary concessions? Is not the execution of Sacco and Vanzetti, the long indefensible imprisonment of Mooney, the grim history of American strikes, the root of the answer to that question?

In 1932 both Right and Left thus stood with fierce intransigence on the solid ground of dogma. In so doing, they were challenging an essential part of the American liberal tradition. When Professor Rexford G. Tugwell of the Columbia University economics department, on leave in Washington, revisited his campus in 1933, he rashly bragged of the New Deal's freedom from "blind doctrine," and the *Columbia Spectator*, then edited by a brilliant young undergraduate named James Wechsler, seized on this boast as the fatal weakness of Tugwell's argument and of the whole New Deal. "This is the crux of the problem," the *Spectator* said; "the blind stumbling in the most chaotic fashion—experimenting from day to day—without any anchor except a few idealistic phrases—is worthless. It is merely political pragmatism."

Merely political pragmatism—to ideologists, whether of Right or Left, this seemed conclusive evidence of intellectual bankruptcy. As the conservatives had said that any attempt to modify the capitalist system must mean socialism, so the radicals now said that any attempt to maintain the capitalist system must mean fascism. "Roosevelt's policies can be welded into a consistent whole," wrote I. F. Stone, "only on the basis of one hypothesis . . . that Mr. Roosevelt intends to move toward fascism." "The essential logic of the New Deal," wrote Max Lerner, "is increasingly the naked fist of the capitalist state."

Convinced of the fragility of the system, the radicals saw themselves as the forerunners of apocalypse. "American commercial agriculture is doomed," wrote Louis Hacker; capitalism was doomed, too, and the party system, and the traditional American way of life. In 1934 Sidney Hook, James Burnham, Louis Budenz, V. F. Calverton, James Rorty and others addressed "An Open Letter to American Intellectuals." "We cannot by some clever Rooseveltian trick," the letter warned,

> evade the unfolding of basic economic and political developments under capitalism. . . . Let us not deceive ourselves that we shall not have to face here also the choice between reaction, on the one hand, and a truly scientific economy under a genuine workers' democracy on the other.

In 1935 the *New Republic* stated with magisterial simplicity the argument of the radicals against the New Dealers, of New York against Washington, of the Marxists against the pragmatists.

> Either the nation must put up with the confusions and miseries of an essentially unregulated capitalism, or it must prepare to supersede capitalism with socialism. There is no longer a feasible middle course.

Both radicalism and conservatism thus ended in the domain of either/or. The contradictions of actuality which so stimulated the pragmatists of Washington, only violated the properties and offended the illusions of the ideologists. While they all saw themselves as hardheaded realists, in fact they were Platonists, preferring essence to existence and considering abstractions the only reality.

The great central source of the New Deal, in my judgment, lay precisely in the instinctive response of practical, energetic and compassionate people to those dogmatic absolutes. This passion to sacrifice reality to doctrine presented a profound challenge to the pragmatic nerve. Many Americans, refusing to be intimidated by abstractions or to be overawed by ideology, responded by doing things. The whole point of the New Deal lay in its belief in activism, its faith in gradualness, its rejection of catastrophism, its indifference to ideology, its conviction that a managed and modified capitalist order achieved by piecemeal experiment could combine personal freedom and economic growth. "In a world in which revolutions just now are coming easily," said Adolf Berle, "the New Deal chose the more difficult course of moderation and rebuilding." "The course that the new Administration did take," said Harold Ickes, "was the hardest course. It conformed to no theory, but it did fit into the American system—a system of taking action step by step, a system of regulation only to meet concrete needs, a system of courageous recognition of change." Tugwell, rejecting laissez-faire and communism, spoke of the "third course."

Roosevelt himself, of course, was the liberal pragmatist *par excellence*. His aim was to steer between the extremes of chaos and tyranny by moving always, in his phrase, "slightly to the left of center," "Unrestrained individualism," he wrote, had proved a failure; yet "any paternalistic system which tries to provide for security for everyone from above only calls for an impossible task and a regimentation utterly uncongenial to the spirit of our people." He constantly repeated Macaulay's injunction to reform if you wished to preserve.

Roosevelt had no illusions about revolution. Mussolini and Stalin seemed to him, in his phrase, "not mere distant relatives" but "blood brothers." When Emil Ludwig asked him about his "political motive," he replied, "My desire is to obviate revolution . . . I work in a contrary sense to Rome and Moscow." He said during the 1932 campaign:

> Say that civilization is a tree which, as it grows, continually produces rot and dead wood. The radical says: "Cut it down." The conservative says: "Don't touch it." The liberal compromises: "Let's prune, so that we lose neither the old trunk nor the new branches." This campaign is waged to teach the country to march upon its appointed course, the way of change, in an orderly march, avoiding alike the revolution of radicalism and the revolution of conservatism.

I think it would be a mistake to underestimate the extent to which this pragmatic attitude was itself a major source of New Deal vitality. The exaltation of the middle way seems banal and obvious enough today. Yet the tyranny of dogma was such in the early years of the Great Depression that infatuation with ideology blocked and smothered the instinctive efforts of free men to work their own salvation. In a world intoxicated with abstractions, Roosevelt and the New Dealers stood almost alone in a stubborn faith in rational experiment, in trial and error. No one understood this more keenly than the great English critic of absolutes; Keynes, in an open letter to Roosevelt at the end of 1933, stated the hopes generated by the New Deal with precision and eloquence. "You have made yourself," Keynes told Roosevelt,

> the trustee for those in every country who seek to mend the evils of our condition by reasoned experiment within the framework of the existing social system. If you fail, rational choice will be gravely prejudiced throughout the world, leaving orthodoxy and revolution to fight it out. But, if you succeed, new and bolder methods will be tried everywhere, and we may date the first chapter of a new economic era from your accession to office.

The question remains: Why did the New Deal itself have the pragmatic commitment? Why, under the impact of depression, was it not overborne by dogma as were most other governments and leaders in the world? The answer to this lies, I suspect, in the point I proposed earlier—in the suggestion that the New Deal represented, not just a response to depression, but also a response to pent-up frustration and needs in American society—frustrations and needs which would have operated had there been no depression at all. The periodic demand for forward motion in American politics, the periodic breakthrough of new leadership—these were already in the works before the depression. Depression, therefore, instead of catching a nation wholly unprepared, merely accelerated tendencies toward change already visible in the national community. The response to depression, in short, was controlled and tempered by the values of traditional American experimentalism, rather than those of rigid ideology. The New Deal was thus able to approach the agony of mass unemployment and depression in the pragmatic spirit, in the spirit which guaranteed the survival rather than the extinction of freedom, in the spirit which in time rekindled hope across the world that free men could manage their own economic destiny.

John A. Garraty

JOHN A. GARRATY (1920–   ) *is professor of history at Colum-bia University. He is the author of many articles and books, including* Right-Hand Man: The Life of George W. Perkins *(1960),* Unemploy-ment in History: Economic Thought and Public Policy *(1978), and* The Great Depression *(1986).*

The Great Depression of the 1930s was a unique phenomenon in that it happened simultaneously over almost the entire globe. It was experienced directly, not merely through its repercussions, by the people of nearly every nation and social class. Neither of the so-called world wars of this century was so pervasive, and while many distinct combinations of past events, such as the French Revolution, may be said to have had global results, these usually have been felt only over extended periods of time, long after the "event" itself has ended. The depression therefore presents a remarkable opportunity for historians interested in comparative study and analysis. It provides a kind of inde-pendent variable; when we look at how different nations or groups of people responded to the Great Depression, we can be sure, at least in a sense, that we are examining one single "thing," the existence of which was universally recognized at the time. Contemporaries dis-agreed among themselves about the causes of the depression (to say nothing of their disagreements about how it might be ended), but that there *was* a world-wide depression and that their own depression was related directly to those of their fellows, few denied.

In this article I shall compare the response to the depression in the United States and Germany during the period from 1933 to about 1936 or 1937—that is, during the early years of the regimes of Franklin Roo-sevelt and Adolf Hitler. The choice is neither capricious nor perverse. I hope to demonstrate that Nazi and New Deal antidepression policies displayed striking similarities. Since the two systems, seen in their totality, were fundamentally different, these similarities tell us a great deal about the depression and the way people reacted to it.

The differences between nazism and the New Deal scarcely need enumeration; within the context of Western industrial society two more antithetical systems would be hard to imagine. The Nazis de-

John A. Garraty, "The New Deal, National Socialism, and the Great Depression," *Ameri-can Historical Review* 78 (October 1973):907–944. Reprinted by permission of John A. Garraty.

stroyed democratic institutions. They imprisoned and murdered dissidents, even those, such as the Jews, who simply did not fit their image of a proper German. The New Dealers, whatever their limitations, threw no one in jail for his political beliefs and actually widened the influence of underprivileged elements in the society. Furthermore the historical experience, the traditions, and the social structure of the two nations could hardly have been more unlike. The Great War and its aftermath affected them in almost diametrically opposite ways. All the major economic groups in the two countries—farmers, industrialists, factory workers, and so on—confronted the problems of the depression with sets of expectations and values that differed greatly.

But these were the industrial nations most profoundly affected by the Great Depression, measured by such criteria as the percentage decline of output, or by the degree of unemployment. When Hitler and Roosevelt came to power both nations were in desperate straits; Hitler and Roosevelt followed leaders who had spectacularly failed to inspire public confidence in their policies. Both the severity of the depression and the sense of despair and crisis that existed in Germany and America in early 1933 set the stage for what followed.

I have focused on the early New Deal and Nazi years because at that time the new governments were primarily concerned with economic problems resulting from the depression. Hitler's expansionist ambitions no doubt existed from the beginning, but it was not until after the adoption of the Four Year plan in 1936 that he turned the German economy toward large-scale preparation for war. Similarly, although his motive was clearly defensive, after 1937 Roosevelt also began to be influenced by military considerations.

Needless to say, by considering the similarities in American and German experiences during the depression, I do not mean to suggest that the New Deal was a form of fascism or still less that nazism was anything but an unmitigated disaster. I slight the basic differences between the New Deal and Nazi experiments here partly because they are well known but also because the differences did not affect economic policy as much as might be expected. The worst horrors of nazism were unrelated to Nazi efforts to overcome the depression. Hitler's destruction of German democracy and his ruthless persecution of Jews had little impact on the economy as a whole. Discharging a Jew and giving his job to an "Aryan" did not reduce unemployment. The seizure of Jewish property merely transferred wealth within the country; it did not create new wealth. Moreover, actions undertaken by New Dealers and Nazis for different reasons often produced similar results. My argument concentrates on policies and their effects, not on the motives of the policy makers.

Finally, the fact that countless Germans were deluded by Nazi rhetoric (or that large but lesser numbers were repelled by the system) does not mean that nothing the Nazis did helped anyone but themselves and their sympathizers. Moral abhorrence should no more blind us to the success of some Nazi policies than should admiration of the objectives of the New Deal to its failures. As the English economic historian C. W. Guillebaud warned in *The Social Policy of Nazi Germany*, written in the midst of the Battle of Britain, "Modern Germany is a highly complex phenomenon, with much that is good and bad in it, and nothing is achieved except distortion and absence of reality by any attempt to reduce it to a simple picture of a vast population deluded and oppressed by a small number brutal gangsters."

Consider first how the two governments dealt with poverty and mass unemployment. Both combined direct relief for the indigent with public-works programs to create jobs. The Americans stressed the former, the Germans the latter, with the result that while acute suffering was greatly reduced in both nations, unemployment declined much more rapidly in Germany. Congress appropriated $3.3 billion for public works in 1933, but Roosevelt, unconvinced that public works would stimulate the economy and fearful of waste and corruption, did not push the program. Briefly, during the winter of 1933–34, he allowed Harry Hopkins to develop his Civil Works Administration, which found jobs for over four million people, but in the spring the program was closed down to save money. Only in 1935 did federal public works become important. Then, under Hopkin's Works Progress Administration and Harold L. Ickes's Public Works Administration, countless roads, schools, bridges, dams, and public buildings were constructed. The Germans, on the other hand, immediately launched an all-out assault on unemployment. Expanding upon policies initiated under Franz von Papen and Kurt von Schleicher, they stimulated private industry through subsidies and tax rebates, encouraged consumer spending by such means as marriage loans, and plunged into the massive public-works program that produced the autobahns, and housing, railroad, and navigation projects. If some New Deal projects seemed to critics wasteful and unnecessary, so did the Nazi penchant for gigantic stadiums and other public buildings, as described in Albert Speer's memoirs. The American boondoggle had its parallel in what the Germans called *Pyramidenbau*, pyramid-building.

It is fashionable, and not of course inaccurate, to note the military aspect of German public-works policies, although in fact relatively little was spent on rearmament before 1935. It is less fashionable, but no less accurate, to point out that the aircraft carriers *Yorktown* and *Enterprise*, four cruisers, many lesser warships, as well as over one hundred army planes and some fifty military airports (including Scott Field in Illinois, the new Air Force headquarters) were built with Public Works Administration money—more than $824 million of it. There was, furthermore, little difference in appearance or intent between the

Nazi work camps and those set up in America under the Civilian Conservation Corps. Unlike the public-works programs, these camps did not employ many industrial workers who had lost their jobs, nor were they expected to have much of a stimulating effect on private business. Both employed enrollees at forestry and similar projects to improve the countryside and were essentially designed to keep young men out of the labor market. Roosevelt described work camps as a means for getting youth "off the city street corners," Hitler as a way of keeping them from "rotting helplessly in the streets." In both countries much was made of the beneficial social results of mixing thousands of young people from different walks of life in the camps and of the generally enthusiastic response of youth to the camp experience.

Furthermore, both were organized on semimilitary lines with the subsidiary purposes of improving the physical fitness of potential soldiers and stimulating public commitment to national service in the emergency. Putting the army in control of hundreds of thousands of young civilians roused considerable concern in the United States. This concern proved to be unfounded; indeed, the army undertook the task with great reluctance and performed it with admirable restraint. It is also difficult to imagine how so large a program could have been inaugurated in so short a time in any other way. The CCC program nevertheless served paramilitary and patriotic functions not essential to its announced purpose. Corpsmen were required to stand "in a position of alertness" while speaking to superiors and to address them as "Sir." Camp commanders possessed mild but distinctly military powers to discipline their men, including the right to issue dishonorable discharges. Morning and evening flag-raising ceremonies were held as "a mark," the civilian director of the CCC, Robert Fechner, explained, "of patriotism, of good citizenship and of appreciation by these young men of the thoughtful care being given them by their government." Army authorities soon concluded that six months' CCC service was worth a year's conventional military training, and Secretary of War George Dern claimed that running the camps provided the army with the best practical experience in handling men it had ever had. Summing up the military contribution of the CCC, John A. Salmond, the most sympathetic historian of the agency, wrote:

> To a country engaged in a bloody war, it had provided the sinews of a military force. It had given young officers valuable training in command techniques, and the nearly three million young men who had passed through the camps had received experience of military life upon which the Army was well able to build.

New Deal and Nazi attempts to stimulate industrial recovery also resembled each other in a number of ways. There was at the start much jockeying for position between small producers and large, between manufacturers and merchants, between inflationists and deflationists, between planners, free enterprisers, and advocates of regulated competition. In Germany the great financiers and the leaders of the cartelized industries, most of them bitterly opposed to democratic institutions, demanded an authoritarian solution that would eliminate the influence of organized labor and increase their own control over the economy, whereas small operators, shopkeepers, and craftsmen wanted to reduce the power of bankers and to destroy not only the unions but also the industrial monopolies and chain stores. The former sought to manipulate the Nazis, the latter comprised, in the main, the Nazis enthusiastic supporters, but Hitler and the party felt and responded to pressures from both camps. In the United States most big business interests had no open quarrel with the existing order, but by 1933 many were calling for suspension of the antitrust laws in order to end the erosion of profits by competitive price cutting. Other interests wanted to strengthen the antitrust laws, still others favored various inflationary schemes, still others some attempt at national economic planning. All clamored for the attention of the new administration.

The ideas of these groups were contradictory, and neither Roosevelt nor Hitler tried very hard to resolve the differences. Roosevelt's method was to suggest that the contestants lock themselves in a room until they could work out a compromise. But Hitler, who freely admitted to being an economic naïf, was no more forceful. "I had to let the Party experiment," he later recalled in discussing the evolution of his industrial recovery program. "I had to give the people something to do. They all wanted to help. . . . Well, let them have a crack at it."

Out of the resulting confusion emerged two varieties of corporatism, a conservative, essentially archaic concept of social and economic organization that was supposed to steer a course between socialism and capitalist plutocracy. Corporatist theory argued that capitalists and workers (organized in industry-wide units) should join together to bring order and profit to each industry by eliminating competition and wasteful squabbling between labor and management. These associations should be supervised by the government in order to protect the public against monopolistic exploitation. In 1933 corporatism was already being experimented with by the Portuguese dictator Antonio de Oliveira Salazar and more tentatively by Benito Mussolini. It also had roots in American and German experience. The American trade association movement of the 1920s reflected basic corporatist ideas (with the important exception that industrialists were opposed to government representation in their councils). When the depression undermined the capacity of these "voluntary" associations to force individual companies to honor the associations' decisions, some trade association leaders became willing to accept government policing as a necessary evil. Among others, Gerard Swope of the General

Electric Company attracted considerable attention in 1931 with his Swope Plan for a nationwide network of compulsory trade associations supervised by the Federal Trade Commission. President Herbert Hoover, who had been among the most ardent supporters of trade associations, denounced the Swope Plan as both a threat to industrial efficiency and "the most gigantic proposal of monopoly ever made." He considered all such compulsory schemes fascistic. But a number of early New Dealers—Hugh Johnson, Donald Richberg, and Lewis Douglas among others—found corporatism appealing. In Germany the concept of government-sponsored cartels that regulated output and prices had a long tradition, but the existence of powerful trade unions precluded the possibility of a truly corporative organization before 1933. Hitler's success changed that swiftly. Nazi ideologues such as Gottfried Feder combined with big industrialists like Fritz Thyssen and leaders of small business interests like Dr. Heinrich Meusch to push the corporative approach. The works of one of the leading theorists of corporatism, Professor Othmar Spann of the University of Vienna, were widely discussed in Germany in 1933, and the Nazis established a complex system of "estates" governing all branches of industry.

In America the process went not nearly so far, but the system of self-governing industrial codes established under the National Recovery Administration was obviously in the same pattern. Production controls, limitation of entry, and price and wage manipulation were common characteristics of government policy in both countries. So were the two governments' justifications of drastic and possibly illegal or unconstitutional changes in the way the economy functioned on the ground that a "national emergency" existed, and the enormous propaganda campaigns they mounted to win public support. . . .

The success or failure of American and German efforts to stimulate industrial recovery is a separate question not central to my argument here. What is central to the argument is this: both were marked by vacillation, confusion, and contradictions, by infighting within the administering bureaucracies, by an absence of any consistently held theory about either the causes of the depression or how to end it. Both also subordinated economic to political goals. The "primacy of politics" in Nazi Germany is a commonplace, its most glaring expression occurring in 1936 when shortages of raw materials and foreign exchange led Hitler to choose between guns and butter. He chose, of course, guns. The problem could be solved by an act of will, he insisted; it was the task of the economy to supply the military needs of the state—so be it! When Schacht, his chief economic adviser, urged a more balanced use of available resources, the Führer fired him. Such ruthless subordination of economic interests to the state did not occur in the United States, although when military considerations began to dominate American policy after 1939 Roosevelt was also prepared to substitute guns for butter. I need only mention his famous announcement that he was replacing "Dr. New Deal" with "Dr. Win the War" as his prime consultant.

But conventional "politics"—the accommodation of political leaders to the pressures of interest groups—affected economic policy in both nations. Beset by business interests seeking aid, by trust busters eager to break up the corporate giants, by planners brimming with schemes to rationalize the economy, the Roosevelt administration survived in a state of constant flux, making concessions to all views, acting in contradictory and at times self-defeating ways. "The New Dealers," writes Ellis W. Hawley, "failed to arrive at any real consensus about the origins and nature of economic concentration." Nor did they follow any consistent policy in the fight against the industrial depression. And Roosevelt's inconsistency, as Hawley also notes, "was the safest method of retaining political power, . . . a political asset rather than a liability." The Nazis, as I have shown, also permitted pressures from various economic interests to influence policy. They did so partly because even a totalitarian dictatorship could profit from the active cooperation of powerful economic groups and partly because the Nazi party had no fixed economic beliefs. Roosevelt responded to pressure groups, Hitler for a time suffered them to exist—a most vital distinction—but the practical result was the same. Put differently, Hitler had a clear political objective—it was actually an obsession—but he was almost as flexible about specific economic policies as Roosevelt. "As regards economic questions," he boasted in 1936, "our theory is very simple. We have no theory at all." . . .

New Deal and Nazi methods of dealing with the agricultural depression also had much in common. Both sought to organize commercial agriculture in order to increase farm income, under the New Deal Agricultural Adjustment Act through supposedly democratic county committees to control production, in Germany through the centralized Estate for Agriculture. The purpose was to raise agricultural prices and thus farm income through a system of subsidies, paid for in each instance by processing taxes that fell ultimately on consumers. Both governments also made agricultural credit cheaper and more readily available and protected farmers against loss of their land through foreclosures. . . .

There remains the question of leadership, that is, of the personal roles of Roosevelt and Hitler in their nations' campaigns against the Great Depression. To overemphasize Roosevelt and Hitler as individuals would be to approach the problem simplistically, but certain parallels merit examination. It cannot be proved that neither would have achieved national leadership without the depression, but the depression surely contributed to the success of each. Yet on the surface they seem most improbable leaders of the two countries at that particular time. In an economic crisis of unprecedented severity, neither had a well-thought-out plan. Both lacked deep knowledge of or even much interest in economics.

It is no less than paradoxical that the American electorate, provincial in outlook, admiring of self-made men and physical prowess, and scornful of "aristocrats," should, at a time when millions were existing on the edge of starvation, chose for president a man who lived on inherited wealth, who came from the top of the upper crust, who had been educated in the swankest private schools, who had a broad cosmopolitan outlook, and (to descend to a lesser but not politically unimportant level) who was a cripple. But no more a paradox than that a country whose citizens were supposed to have an exaggerated respect for hard work, for education and high culture and family lineage, and who had a reputation for orderliness and social discipline should follow the lead of a highschool dropout, a lazy ne'er-do-well, a low-born Austrian who could not even speak good German, the head of a rowdy movement openly committed to disorder and violence. Equally strange, Roosevelt and Hitler appealed most strongly to their social and economic opposites: Roosevelt to industrial workers, to farmers, to the unemployed and the rejected; Hitler to hard-working shopkeepers and peasants, and, eventually, to industrialists, great landowners, and the military.

It may of course be true that these seeming contradictions are of no significance. Probably any Democrat would have defeated Hoover in 1932, and although Hitler became chancellor in a technically legal way, his subsequent seizure of total power was accomplished without the consent, if not necessarily without the approval, of a majority of the German people. Yet the personal impact of Roosevelt and Hitler on the two societies in the depths of the Great Depression was very large. Their policies aside, both exerted enormous psychological influence upon the citizenry. Roosevelt's patrician concern for mass suffering, his charm, his calm confidence, his gaiety, even his cavalier approach to the grave problems of the day had, according to countless witnesses, an immediate and lasting effect upon the American people. Hitler's resentment of the rich and well born, however psychotic in origin, appealed powerfully to millions of Germans. His ruthless, terrifying determination, always teetering on the edge of hysteria, combined with the aura of encapsulated remoteness that he projected to paralyze those who opposed him, to reduce most of his close associates to sycophancy, and to inspire awe among masses of ordinary Germans. Both the euphoria of the Hundred Days and the nationalistic fervor that swept Germany in the early months of 1933 made millions almost incapable of thought, let alone of judgment. Bills swept through Congress ill drafted and scarcely debated, basic rights were abolished in Germany without even an attempt at resistance, and both were possible largely because of the personalities of the two leaders.

Much of this was probably spontaneous, but not all. Roosevelt and Hitler employed the latest technologies to dramatize themselves and to influence public opinion. Roosevelt's flight to Chicago to accept the Democratic nomination and Hitler's whirlwind tours testify to their swift grasp of the psychological as well as the practical value of air travel to politicians. And no greater masters of the radio ever lived—Roosevelt with his low-keyed, fatherly, intimate fireside chats, Hitler with his shrill harangues beneath the massed swastikas at Nuremberg. Both were terrible administrators in the formal sense but virtuosos at handling subordinates. Their governments were marked by confusion, overlapping jurisdictions, and factional conflicts, yet somehow they transformed these inadequacies into political assets—symbols not of weakness or inefficiency but of energy and zeal in a time of grave emergency.

Both also made brilliant use of the crisis psychology of 1933, emphasizing the suffering of the times rather than attempting to disguise or minimize it. "The misery of our people is horrible," Hitler said in his first radio address after becoming chancellor. "To the hungry unemployed millions of industrial workers is added the impoverishment of the whole middle class and the artisans. If this decay also finally finishes off the German farmers we will face a catastrophe of incalculable size." Roosevelt's personal style was more reassuring than alarmist, but he also stressed the seriousness of the situation and the urgent need for decisive action: "Action, and action now," as he put it in his inaugural.

Both the Roosevelt and Hitler governments tried to influence public opinion in new and forceful ways. Roosevelt did not create a propaganda machine even remotely comparable to Goebbels's, but under the New Deal the government undertook efforts unprecedented in peacetime to sell its policies to the public. The NRA slogan "We Do Our Part" served the same function as the Nazis' incessantly repeated *Gemeinnutz geht vor Eigennutz*. With Roosevelt's approval, General Hugh Johnson, head of the NRA and designer of its Blue Eagle symbol, organized a massive campaign to rally support for the NRA. "Those who are not with us are against us," Johnson orated, "and the way to show that you are a part of this great army of the New Deal is to insist on this symbol of solidarity." Johnson denounced "chiselers" and "slackers"; his office plastered the land with billboard displays; distributed posters, lapel buttons, and stickers; dispatched volunteer speakers across the country; and published *Helpful Hints* and *Pointed Paragraphs* to provide them with The Word. Roosevelt himself, in a fireside chat, compared the Blue Eagle to a "bright badge" worn by soldiers in night attacks to help separate friend from foe. Placed beside the awesome Nazi displays at Nuremberg, even the ten-hour, 250,000-person NRA parade up Fifth Avenue in September 1933 may seem insignificant, but it and other NRA parades and hoopla were designed to serve the same functions: rousing patriotic feelings and creating in the public mind the impression of so extensive a support for government policies as to make disagreement appear close to treason. As Johnson himself explained, the purpose was to "put the enforcement of this law into the hands of the *whole* people."

Another example of New Deal propaganda is provided by the efforts of the Resettlement Administration and the Farm Security Administration under Rexford Tugwell. Because Pare Lorenz's government-sponsored films, *The Plow That Broke the Plains* (1936) and *The River* (1938), and the still photographs of Dorothea Lange, Walker Evans, Margaret Bourke-White, Gordon Parks, and others were esthetic achievements of the highest order, we tend to forget that they were a form of official advertising designed to explain and defend the New Deal approach to rural social and economic problems. They differed from Leni Riefenstahl's *Triumph of the Will* (also a cinematic masterpiece) and the annual volumes of photographs celebrating National Socialism chiefly in style—"soft" rather than "hard" sell—and point of view.

The New Deal efforts at mass persuasion were unparalleled among democracies in peacetime—nothing comparable was attempted in France or Great Britain before the outbreak of war in 1939. They reflect the attitude of the Roosevelt government, shared by Hitler's, that the economic emergency demanded a common effort above and beyond politics. The crisis justified the casting aside of precedent, the nationalistic mobilization of society, and the removal of traditional restraints on the power of the state, as in war, and it required personal leadership more forceful than that necessary in normal times. That all these attitudes were typical of Hitler goes without saying, but Roosevelt held them too. Consider this passage in his first inaugural:

> I assume unhesitatingly the leadership of this great army of our people. . . . Our true destiny is not to be administered unto but to minister to ourselves. . . . In the event that Congress shall fail . . . I shall ask the Congress for the one remaining instrument to meet the crisis—broad executive power to wage a war against the emergency, as great as the power that would be given to me if we were in fact invaded by a foreign foe.

Roosevelt was neither a totalitarian nor a dictator, real or potential, but his tactics and his rhetoric made it possible for anti-New Dealers and outright fascists to argue that he was both. Many of the accusations of conservatives and Communists in the United States were politically motivated, as were, of course, Nazi comments on the president. But during the first years of the New Deal the German press praised him and the New Deal to the skies. Before Hitler came to power he was, although impressed by Henry Ford's automobiles and the racially oriented American immigration laws, basically contemptuous of the United States, which he considered an overly materialistic nation dominated by Jews, "millionaires, beauty queens, stupid [phonograph] records, and Hollywood." Nevertheless, he and his party were impressed by New Deal depression policies. "Mr. Roosevelt . . . marches straight to his objectives over Congress, lobbies, and the bureaucracy," Hitler told Anne O'Hare McCormick of the New York Times in July 1933. In July 1934 the Völkischer Beobachter described Roosevelt as "absolute lord and master" of the nation, his position "not entirely dissimilar" to a dictator's. Roosevelt's books, Looking Forward (1933) and On Our Way (1934) were translated into German and enthusiastically reviewed, the critics being quick to draw attention to parallels in New Deal and National Socialist experiences. . . .

So far as the depression is concerned, Roosevelt and Hitler, the one essentially benign, the other malevolent, justified far-reaching constitutional changes as being necessary to the improvement of economic conditions in a grave emergency but used change also as a device for mobilizing the psychic energies of the people. Yet both their administrations were plagued by infighting and confusion, partly because of genuine conflicts of interest and philosophy within the two diverse societies, but partly because of ignorance. No one really knew how to end the depression or even how best to serve the different interests the governments presumed to represent. Time after time major American and German policies produced results neither anticipated nor desired, some of them—the effect of New Deal farm policy on share croppers and of its public housing policy on racial segregation, and that of Nazi rearmament on urban concentration, for example—directly contrary to the leaders' intentions.

Hitler papered over confusion, doubts, and rivalries with the Führerprinzip, unquestioning obedience to the leader, who was presumed to know what was best. Roosevelt, on the other hand, made a virtue of flexibility and experimentation. Both, however, masterfully disguised the inadequacies and internal disagreements in their entourages and to a remarkable extent succeeded in convincing ordinary citizens of their own personal wisdom and dedication.

The differences in the degree and intensity with which psychological pressures were applied by Nazis and New Dealers were so great as to become differences in kind—leaving aside the brute Nazi suppression not merely of those who resisted or disagreed, but of all who did not fit the insane Hitlerian conception of the proper order of things. The two movements nevertheless reacted to the Great Depression in similar ways, distinct from those of other industrial nations. Of the two the Nazis were the more successful in curing the economic ills of the 1930s. They reduced unemployment and stimulated industrial

production faster than the Americans did and, considering their resources, handled their monetary and trade problems more successfully,
certainly more imaginatively. This was partly because the Nazis employed deficit financing on a larger scale and partly because their totalitarian system better lent itself to the mobilization of society, both by
force and by persuasion. By 1936 the depression was substantially over
in Germany, far from finished in the United States. However, neither
regime solved the problem of maintaining prosperity without war. The
German leaders wanted war and used the economy to make war possible. One result was "prosperity": full employment, increased output,
hectic economic expansion. The Americans lacked this motivation,
but when war was forced upon them they took the same approach and
achieved the same result.

☆ 8 ☆

The Coming of World War II

AVOIDABLE OR INEVITABLE?

During the Great Depression of the 1930s the American people and their leaders remained preoccupied for much of the period with a myriad of domestic concerns. Concentrating on solving the problems of unemployment, underproduction, agricultural distress, and an economy that seemed to be on the verge of collapse, most individuals gave relatively little thought to events on the international scene. With a few notable exceptions the aim of Americans was to solve their internal problems; foreign relations were important only to the extent that they threatened to involve the nation in another world holocaust similar to the one that began in 1914 and ended tragically four years later. Indeed, the desire to remain isolated from developments on the international scene was so pervasive that between 1934 and 1937 the Congress enacted and the president signed a series of acts designed precisely to prevent a repetition of the events from 1914 to 1917 that eventually ended in America's participation in World War I.

The outbreak of World War II in Europe in 1939 proved to be an important turning point in the development of American foreign policy. Domestic concerns such as the Great Depression and mass unemployment receded into the background as the fear of war swept over the country. Unlike Woodrow Wilson, Roosevelt refused to ask his countrymen to remain neutral in thought as well as action. "This nation," he told the American people in a fireside chat in September 1939, "will remain a neutral nation, but I cannot ask that every American remain neutral in thought as well." From the very beginning of hostilities Roosevelt's hope was to offer as much military aid to the Allies as he could without going to war. Upon presidential urging Congress repealed the arms embargo that was then in effect because the two-year cash-and-carry clause of the Neutrality Act of 1937 had expired. The fall of France in the spring of 1940 intensified Roosevelt's desire to rebuild America's military forces and to give England all aid short of war. In 1941 the program of military aid to the Allied cause was expanded considerably by the Lend-Lease Act that was passed in March. By the summer of that year the United States was involved in an undeclared naval war with Germany as American naval forces assumed the responsibility of protecting shipping in the western half of the North Atlantic. The most dramatic gesture of American sympathy for the British cause came in August of 1941 when Roosevelt and Churchill met off the coast of Newfoundland and agreed to a joint statement on mutual war aims. Known as the Atlantic Charter the document not only spelled out the hopes of the two leaders for a better world, but referred specifically to "the final destruction of the Nazi tyranny" as a war aim.

The situation in Asia was equally explosive. Beginning in 1937 Japan renewed her attack upon the Nationalist regime of Chiang Kai-shek. The United States, having long been committed to the preservation of the territorial integrity and independence of China, found itself facing a diplomatic crisis. Nazi victories in Europe had the effect of stimulating Japanese ambitions even further; after the fall of France Japan occupied northern Indochina and signified its desire to establish a "coprosperity sphere" throughout eastern Asia—a euphemism for Japanese hegemony.

Roosevelt responded slowly to these developments in Asia. First, the American government adopted various forms of economic pressure. After Japan occupied southern Indochina in July of 1941 Roosevelt took the decisive step of imposing all-inclusive economic sanctions. At this point Japan faced the choice of curtailing its ambitions, particularly in China, or breaking the restrictions by resorting to armed conflict. During the remainder of the year Japan and the United States remained on a collision course that finally culminated in the fateful attack on Pearl Harbor on December 7, 1941.

Throughout the course of World War II, few Americans expressed any doubts over the issue of war guilt or their own involvement. Faced by totalitarian regimes in Germany, Italy, and Japan—regimes committed to the goal of regional or world domination—the United States, most felt, had no choice but to defend itself and become the champion of the free world. Roosevelt tried his best to avoid war and the use of American troops overseas, but the march of events seemed to destroy his hopes. The Japanese attack on Pearl Harbor settled the issue of going to war in a conclusive manner. From that point on America committed its industrial and military might against the forces of aggression. Such was the position taken by most contemporary scholars and writers who dealt with American diplomacy from 1937 to 1941.

The first criticisms concerning America's foreign policies in the years prior to 1941 came toward the end of World War II. Not until after the war was over, however, did the revisionists—as those critical of Roosevelt came to be known—spell out their case in great detail. The reaction against Roosevelt's policies after 1945 was not a totally unexpected or surprising development. After each of America's past wars, a debate had taken place over the question of whether the nation ought to have become involved in overt hostilities. More important in explaining the criticisms of Roosevelt's diplomacy, however, was the widespread disillusionment in the United States with the results of World War II. America had gone to war in 1941 to destroy the forces of totalitarianism and then found itself faced with an even greater menace—the Soviet Union. Germany was divided, half of Europe lay under Russian domination, and the United States and the Soviet Union entered upon a period of tense diplomatic relations in the postwar era that quickly became known as the Cold War. When the Soviet Union developed an atomic bomb of its own in 1949, the United States felt its physical security threatened for the first time since 1783. America's wartime allies, Britain and France, could no longer be considered first-rate powers, and the British Commonwealth was facing a severe crisis as a result of the rise of Asian and African nationalism. In the Far East the situation looked equally bleak: the destruction of Japanese power left a vacuum that was quickly filled by the Chinese Communist regime; India, gaining its independence, was weak; and Korea was left divided. At home the coming of the Cold War posed problems of internal security as some persons feared that the nation was being threatened by subversives and Communists. The result was a period of repression in the early 1950s that seriously impaired the civil rights that American citizens had traditionally enjoyed under the Constitution. All of these developments raised some doubts over the wisdom of America's participation in World War II.

Many of the major critics of Roosevelt's foreign policies, interestingly enough, had taken an isolationist position as regards America's foreign policy in the 1930s, and some even had been associated with the school of revisionist writers who opposed America's entry into World War I. Harry Elmer Barnes, the father of World War I revisionism, consistently opposed Roosevelt's diplomatic policies and addressed meetings of the America First Committee—an isolationist organization of the 1930s and early 1940s. Charles A. Beard spoke out against any American entanglements in the 1930s and testified before the Senate Foreign Relations Committee in opposition to the idea of a lend-lease program. And Charles C. Tansill, who published the leading study in the 1930s critical of Wilson's foreign policies between 1914 and 1917, also played a key role in attacking New Deal diplomacy.

One of the first scholarly attempts to discredit Roosevelt's diplomacy came in 1946 and 1948 when Charles A. Beard published *American Foreign Policy, 1932–1940*, and *President Roosevelt and the Coming of the War, 1941*, respectively. Beard's works, receiving a good deal of attention because of the eminent reputation of their author, were quickly followed by a series of other books. Although the positions they took varied markedly, all the revisionists were in basic agreement on certain fundamental points. Moreover, most of them had nothing but contempt for historians who refused to accept their anti-Roosevelt thesis. Harry Elmer Barnes, for example, characterized those who disagreed with him as "court historians," thereby implying that they had sacrificed their scholarly integrity to gain favor in government circles.

The revisionist hypothesis was based on a number of assumptions. First, the revisionists denied that the Axis powers had threatened America's vital interests. Germany had no plans to attack the Western Hemisphere, they claimed, and the Japanese were concerned only about Asia. Roosevelt's charge that the American people were being directly threatened from abroad, therefore, had little or no substance. Second, Roosevelt's foreign policy was one that he knew would inevitably lead to war in Europe and Asia. Indeed, some revisionists went so far as to suggest that Roosevelt deliberately misled the American people by telling them that he was working for peace while, in reality, he was laying the foundation for war. His famous speech in Boston during the presidential campaign of 1940 in which he promised that American boys would not fight on foreign soil was simply one example of his cupidity. Finally, the revisionists emphasized that the long-term results of America's involvement in World War II were largely negative—if not disastrous; the United States, by upsetting the European balance of power and creating a power vacuum, made possible the emergence of the Soviet Union—a nation that presented a far more serious threat to American security than did Nazi Germany.

Many, though not all, of the revisionists looked upon Roosevelt as a leader who deliberately misled and lied to the American people. In his critical study of New Deal diplomacy Charles A. Beard made this point quite explicit. Roosevelt, Beard wrote, kept reassuring the American people that he was doing everything he could to avoid war and maintain a neutral position. Yet every action that he took belied his statements. He gave military aid and assistance to Britain, first through the destroyer-base exchange, then through the lend-lease program, and finally by ordering American naval vessels to escort convoys. All of these steps were undertaken consciously; they were not forced upon a reluctant or unwilling president by events beyond his control. Roosevelt, claimed Beard, acted on the assumption that he was wiser than the American people and consequently did not feel that he had to tell them the truth. The American people, Beard concluded, were faced with the fact "that the President of the United States possesses limitless authority publicly to misrepresent and secretly to control foreign policy, foreign affairs, and the war power."[1] Beard's thesis was echoed by other revisionists. As William Henry Chamberlain put it in 1953, "One is left, therefore, with the inescapable conclusion that the promises to 'keep America out of foreign wars' were a deliberate hoax on the American people, perpetrated for the purpose of insuring Roosevelt's re-election and thereby enabling him to proceed with his plan of gradually edging the United States into war."[2]

Although the revisionists were critical of Roosevelt's European diplomacy they usually reserved their heaviest ammunition for his Far Eastern policy. Indeed, most of the criticism of Roosevelt centered around his dealings with Japan in the period from 1937 to 1941. Reduced to its simplest form the revisionist indictment boiled down to the fact that Roosevelt deliberately provoked the Japanese into attacking Pearl Harbor. At that point the president was able to take the American people into a war that he secretly wanted but had not desired to ask for publicly.

Such a thesis, of course, rested on the assumption that the Japanese leaders wanted peace—but that Roosevelt's maneuverings had forced them into an untenable position that could be resolved only by war. Although not all revisionists argued along precisely the same lines, their general arguments were remarkably similar. They maintained that Japan's desire for peace was sincere and that she wished to end her four-year-old war in China. Facing a crucial shortage of oil and other resources the Japanese hoped to end the conflict on the Asiatic mainland in order to assure themselves continued access to those materials that were indispensable to the economic well-being of the nation. To achieve these objectives the Japanese leaders did everything within their power to arrive at a satisfactory *modus vivendi* with the United States.

President Roosevelt, according to the revisionists, was not interested in peace; he wanted war. Instead of dealing with Japan on the basis of justice and equity he pursued a policy that he knew would ultimately provoke Japanese retaliation. During 1941 the United States increased its economic pressure upon Japan by curtailing the shipments of oil and other raw materials. At the same time the United States refused to agree to any concessions to Japan regarding China. By

---

[1]Charles A. Beard, *President Roosevelt and the Coming of the War, 1941: A Study in Appearances and Realities* (New Haven, 1948), p. 598.

[2]William Henry Chamberlain, "The Bankruptcy of a Policy," in *Perpetual War for Perpetual Peace*, Harry Elmer Barnes, ed. (Caldwell, Idaho, 1953), p. 491.

mid-1941 all Japanese assets in the United States had been frozen, and in August Roosevelt sent a strong warning to Japan to abandon her expansionist policies. All of these moves, the revisionists claimed, were deliberately designed to provoke Japan into some form of retaliation.

The final step, said the revisionist writers, was taken in late November 1941 when Secretary of State Cordell Hull submitted a ten-point proposal to Japan. This document demanded that Japan pull out of China and Indochina. To the revisionists the document represented an American "ultimatum" and not one that could serve as the basis for diplomatic discussions. The perfidy of American leaders became even clearer in the days preceding the attack on Pearl Harbor. Sometime earlier the United States had broken Japan's secret code. Roosevelt and his advisers, therefore, knew that Japan really desired peace, but that she was ready to take military action if the American government persisted in its unyielding course. High American officials, including the president, even knew that a Japanese attack on the military and naval installations at Pearl Harbor was imminent. According to the revisionists the desire of the Roosevelt administration for war was so strong that government officials did not inform the military commanders in Hawaii of the possibility of an attack. In the end, then, Roosevelt's harsh policies provoked the Japanese into an attack on the unprepared military at Pearl Harbor, and gave him the declaration of war that he had so ardently desired. To achieve his goal, some revisionists maintained, Roosevelt knowingly sacrificed American lives as well as a large part of the American fleet at Pearl Harbor. As Harry Elmer Barnes wrote in *Perpetual War for Perpetual Peace*—a volume in which a number of leading revisionists spelled out their case—"The net result of revisionist scholarship applied to Pearl Harbor boils down essentially to this: In order to promote Roosevelt's political ambitions and his mendacious foreign policy some three thousand American boys were quite needlessly butchered. Of course, they were only a drop in the bucket compared to those who were ultimately slain in the war that resulted, which was as needless, in terms of vital American interests, as the surprise attack on Pearl Harbor."[3]

For the most part American historians have rejected this revisionist hypothesis. They have done so largely on the grounds that it rests upon a simplistic conspiracy theory of history. Human beings, they claim, are complex creatures who have complex motives. To argue that Franklin D. Roosevelt knew the precise results of his policies would be

---

[3]*Ibid.*, p. 651. By far the most detailed revisionist interpretation of the events leading up to Pearl Harbor is Charles C. Tansill, *Back Door to War: Roosevelt Foreign Policy, 1933–1941* (Chicago, 1952). Other revisionist accounts include George Morgenstern, *Pearl Harbor: The Story of the Secret War* (New York, 1947); William H. Chamberlain, *America's Second Crusade* (Chicago, 1950); and Robert A. Theobald, *The Final Secret of Pearl Harbor: The Washington Contribution to the Japanese Attack* (New York, 1954).

to credit him with an omniscience that no human being could possibly possess. As a leading nonrevisionist historian pointed out, it is one thing to charge that the Roosevelt administration misunderstood Japan's intentions and underestimated its military strength; it is quite another matter to conclude that the tragic disaster of December 7, 1941, was a matter of calculated diplomatic planning by a scheming American president.[4]

As the passions over American involvement in World War II subsided, the revisionist argument was restated in a sharply modified form. In a balanced and less conspiratorial mode, Paul W. Schroeder questioned the wisdom of the "hard" line toward Japan in the crucial months preceding Pearl Harbor. Until mid-1941, he argued, American planners sought two reasonable and rather limited objectives: splitting the three Axis powers, and stopping Japan's advance in Asia. With these goals within reach, the United States then added a third: the liberation of China. The last objective, however, was not limited, nor could it be attained short of war. Because of its misguided sympathy toward China, the American government drove Japan back into the arms of the Axis powers and made inevitable an armed confrontation between the two nations. American policymakers, Schroeder concluded, were not evil men determined to bring about war; they were instead individuals blinded by a sense of their own moral righteousness and thus had abandoned the pragmatism required of all human beings if differences between nations are not always to end in war.[5]

Schroeder's thesis, in many respects, had already been anticipated by others. George F. Kennan, the former ambassador to Russia, State Department official, and historian, for example, argued in 1951 that the United States erred grievously in the twentieth century when it committed itself to the Open Door and the preservation of the territorial and administrative integrity of China. Although a nation-state, Kennan wrote, China had many attributes which failed to coincide with the European national state that had evolved in the eighteenth and nineteenth centuries. Consequently the Open Door policy was difficult to implement because it rested on the fallacious assumption that China was no different from other states. More important, Kennan insisted, the United States continuously "hacked away, year after year, decade after decade, at the positions of the other powers on the mainland of Asia, and above all the Japanese, in the unshakable belief that, if our principles were commendable, their consequences could not be other than happy and acceptable. But rarely could we be lured into a discussion of the real quantities involved: of such problems as Japan's

---

[4]Robert H. Ferrell, "Pearl Harbor and the Revisionists,": *Historian* 17 (Spring 1955):233.

[5]Paul W. Schroeder, *The Axis Alliance and Japanese-American Relations, 1941* (Ithaca, 1958).

expanding population, or the weaknesses of government in China, or the ways in which the ambitions of other powers could be practicably countered. Remember that this struck a particularly sensitive nerve in the case of countries whose interests on the Asiatic mainland were far more important to them than our interests there were to us. . . . There was always a feeling, both among the Japanese and among the British, that we were inclined to be spend-thrift with their diplomatic assets in China for the very reason that our own stake in China meant so much less to us than theirs did to them."[6] The result, he concluded, was that the United States never exploited the possibility of arriving at a mutually satisfactory compromise with Japan. Like Schroeder, however, Kennan vehemently denied that the failure to reach a meaningful compromise was a deliberate choice of evil and scheming leaders.

The majority of writers dealing with America's diplomacy in the years prior to Pearl Harbor, however, took an exactly opposite point of view from the revisionists. The internationalist or interventionist school—to differentiate it from the revisionist school—based its arguments upon an entirely different set of assumptions. Writers of the internationalist school began with the proposition that the Axis powers had, in fact, posed a very serious threat to America's security and national interests. By the summer of 1940 the Nazis had conquered most of western and central Europe and Britain seemed to be on the verge of surrender. When Hitler invaded the Soviet Union in June 1941 a German victory appeared to be a certainty. The danger, according to the internationalist school, was that America might have to face the victorious Axis powers alone. German and Italian campaigns in North Africa created a fear that control of that continent might provide a springboard for an attack upon the Western Hemisphere. Axis successes in Europe, meanwhile, had stimulated the Japanese to increase their aggressive moves in Asia on the theory that the Allies were too preoccupied in the West to divert any forces to the Far East.

Roosevelt, according to the internationalist school, believed that Germany represented the greatest threat to America's security. It was in the national interest, therefore, to follow a policy designed to bring about a German defeat. Thus Roosevelt embarked upon a program of extending to England all aid short of war in the belief that such a policy might prevent a Nazi victory and contribute to the eventual downfall of Germany. Although renouncing impartial neutrality, Roosevelt hoped that aid to England would permit his nation to protect its security without committing American troops to a foreign conflict. The

---

[6]George F. Kennan, *American Diplomacy 1900–1950* (Chicago, 1951), p. 48.

undeclared naval war in the North Atlantic against Germany represented the limit of America's involvement.

Roosevelt's primary interest lay in Europe—the internationalist
interpretation continued—and his Far Eastern policy was designed to
avert any showdown with Japan. The steps that he took in 1940 and
1941 were intended to check Japan by all means short of war. The embargo on oil and other resources, the freezing of Japanese assets in the
United States, the aid to China, and the massing of the American fleet
in the Pacific were aimed at deterring, not provoking, the Japanese.
America's objective was to seek a peaceful settlement with Japan, but
a settlement that would uphold American security and principles, protect China, and honor the British, French, and Dutch interests in the
Far East. Japan's expansionist ambitions, however, proved to be too
great, and Roosevelt came to realize that an armed conflict between
the two nations was inevitable. According to the internationalist
school of writers his policy at this point became one of stalling for
time in order to permit an American military buildup.

Although the internationalist school by no means approved of all
of Roosevelt's diplomatic policies, they believed that the fundamental
causes for America's involvement in the war lay outside the United
States and in the trend of world events over which this country had
little, if any, control. Most of them were convinced that Roosevelt had
sought the goal of peace with great sincerity. In fact, many argued that
his desire for peace led him to overestimate the opposition to his internationalist policies, which he could have pursued even more vigorously than he did.

Almost all of the historians in the internationalist school violently
rejected the revisionist point of view—particularly the insinuation
that Roosevelt had plotted to provoke the Japanese assault on Pearl
Harbor. While many admitted that there might have been some blundering in both Washington and Hawaii, there was general agreement
that the attack came as a genuine surprise. In Washington neither civilian nor military authorities had interpreted the decoded Japanese
messages correctly; virtually everyone assumed that the Japanese were
moving to attack British and Dutch installations in the southwest Pacific. Although it was true that the army and navy commanders in
Hawaii were not given all of the information gained from breaking the
Japanese code, most internationalist historians believed that the military officials on the spot would have interpreted the messages in the
same light as their superiors in Washington. Even if they had been
able to divine Japanese intentions correctly, there is some doubt as to
whether a military disaster could have been avoided; the American
fleet was extremely vulnerable to air attack and there were insufficient
landbased planes to ward off a Japanese raid. In retrospect, then, the

internationalist historians looked upon Pearl Harbor as a tragic disaster that grew out of faulty military and diplomatic planning rather than part of a presidential conspiracy.[7]

The first selection in this chapter is by Dexter Perkins, one of the deans of American diplomatic history, and represents the views of internationalist scholars while vigorously attacking the revisionist school. To Perkins historical revisionism at the close of a military conflict seems to be a common occurrence among Americans. In part this response stems from the letdown or disillusionment that results from a failure to secure all of the goals for which the war was fought; it is related also to the inevitable reaction against the strong executive leadership that characterizes most wartime administrations. Whatever the reasons for its rise, Perkins defines such revisionism as "history by hypothesis"; it suggests that the world would have been a better place had the United States remained aloof from any involvement in World War II. Perkins goes on to argue that a victorious Germany would have been a very serious menace to America. Nor did Roosevelt deceive the American people, according to Perkins. The president was basically in accord with public opinion, for even the Republican party nominated Wendell Willkie in 1940 and took an internationalist position on foreign affairs. Although Roosevelt may have been devious in his public statements from time to time he accurately reflected the mood and thinking of his fellow countrymen. In the final analysis Perkins ends up with a favorable, though by no means uncritical, appraisal of Roosevelt's foreign policy prior to the war.

Other internationalist scholars have also argued strongly against the revisionist thesis that Roosevelt deliberately exposed the American fleet at Pearl Harbor in order to provoke a Japanese attack. Herbert Feis, for example, insisted that Japan was bent on dominating Asia, thus threatening America's interests in that part of the world. Had the United States not placed an embargo on trade with Japan it would have been in the strange position of having undertaken preparations for war while at the same time strengthening the opponent it might meet in battle. Feis denied that there was conclusive evidence that Prince Konoye's offer to meet with Roosevelt in the autumn of 1941 might have averted a conflict. He rejected also the thesis that Secretary of State Cordell Hull's note of November 26, 1941, was in any sense an ultimatum. The basic cause of the war, concluded Feis, was Japan's insistence on becoming the dominant power in the Far East. Short of a complete surrender on America's part, the chances of avoiding war by means of diplomatic negotiations had always been remote.[8]

---

[7]See especially Roberta Wohlstetter, *Pearl Harbor: Warning and Decision* (Stanford, 1962).

[8]Herbert Feis, "War Came at Pearl Harbor: Suspicions Considered," *Yale Review* 45 (Spring 1956):378–390.

It should be emphasized that there are many points of disagreement among individual historians of the internationalist school even though all of them rejected the revisionist hypothesis. The differences between internationalist historians frequently reflected the same divisions that existed among Roosevelt's advisers prior to December 7, 1941. For example, Secretary of State Cordell Hull was generally cautious in his approach; he favored limiting overt action to steps short of war. Secretary of War Henry L. Stimson, on the other hand, believed that the policy of all aid short of war would not result in the defeat of the Axis powers, and that America would have to intervene sooner or later. Indeed, Stimson believed that the American people would have supported Roosevelt in a declaration of war even before Pearl Harbor. Similarly some internationalist historians, including Herbert Feis and Basil Rauch, were sympathetic to Hull and Roosevelt, while others, notably William L. Langer and S. Everett Gleason, argued that Roosevelt overestimated isolationist opposition to his policies and that the president actually lagged behind public opinion on the desirability of taking strong measures against the Axis powers.[9]

Beginning in the late 1950s, however, the internationalist school began to come under sharp attack from scholars who saw a close relationship between foreign and domestic policy; with the former growing out of the latter. These scholars took a quite different approach to the problem of war causation; rather than focusing on the immediate events that led to Pearl Harbor they studied the long-range trends in American foreign policy and provided an alternative framework for understanding our entry into World War II. Perhaps the most influential scholar in this regard was William Appleman Williams, who offered in a series of important books a view of American diplomacy that was sharply at variance with his internationalist contemporaries.

The Williams thesis, in its simplest form, was that American foreign policy since the late nineteenth century reflected a particular ideology known as Open Door imperialism. A reflection of American capitalism, this policy was based on the premise that foreign markets were indispensable for domestic prosperity and tranquility. By the 1890s, therefore, the United States had moved to acquire overseas possessions, strategically situated so as to facilitate trade and provide naval bases but involving few of the usual responsibilities associated

---

[9]Herbert Feis, *The Road to Pearl Harbor: The Coming of War Between the United States and Japan* (Princeton, 1950); Basil Rauch, *Roosevelt: From Munich to Pearl Harbor* (New York, 1950); William L. Langer and S. Everett Gleason, *The Challenge to Isolation, 1937–1940* (New York, 1952), and *The Undeclared War, 1940–1941* (New York, 1953). Other internationalist works include Donald F. Drummond, *The Passing of American Neutrality* (Ann Arbor, 1955); Robert A. Divine, *The Reluctant Belligerent: American Entry into World War II* (New York, 1965); and John E. Wiltz, *From Isolation to War, 1931–1941* (New York, 1968).

with an extensive overseas empire. The Open Door policy, argued Williams, was designed to win victories without wars; "it was derived from the proposition that America's overwhelming economic power would cast the economy and the politics of the poorer, weaker, underdeveloped countries in a pro-American mold."[10] Ultimately the ideology of the Open Door would lead the United States into a more and more militant opposition to any economic system—socialist, communist, totalitarian—that might diminish its overseas trade.

Williams's thesis led directly to a new interpretation of the diplomacy of the 1930s and the coming of World War II. The New Deal, according to Williams, was intended to define and institutionalize the roles, functions, and responsibilities of three important segments of industrial society—capital, labor, government—and to do so in harmony with the principles of capitalism. In foreign policy the New Deal continued to seek the overseas markets on which American prosperity supposedly rested; even Secretary of State Cordell Hull's reciprocal trade program was intended to control foreign sources of raw materials while simultaneously providing for the selling of American surpluses abroad. The result was strengthening of free trade imperialism, which in turn led to a rising distrust of the United States by nations increasingly fearful of domination by American capitalism. When Japan began to move south into China in 1937 and Germany became more active in Latin America, Roosevelt and his advisers moved toward an activistic and interventionist foreign policy because of the threat to our economic interests throughout the world. During World War II America's economic leaders also became enthusiastic converts to the mission to reform the world. This crusading zeal, in conjunction with Open Door imperialism, was in large measure responsible for the advent of the Cold War and the disastrous course that involved the nation in two wars in the 1950s and 1960s.[11]

More recently there has been a tendency among historians to avoid extreme interpretations of the events that led to American entry into World War II. Between 1939 and 1941, according to Robert Dallek, Roosevelt attempted to balance the nation's antiwar sentiment with the contradictory impulse to assure a Nazi defeat. Initially he attempted to fuse both by providing the Allies with military aid. Even

---

[10]William Appleman Williams, *The Tragedy of American Diplomacy* (rev. ed., New York, 1962), p. 49. See also Williams's *The Roots of the Modern American Empire* (New York, 1969).

[11]A detailed study of New Deal diplomacy in the Williams tradition is Lloyd C. Gardner's *Economic Aspects of New Deal Diplomacy* (Madison, Wis., 1964). See also Walter LaFeber, *America, Russia, and the Cold War 1945–1966* (New York, 1967); Lloyd C. Gardner, *Architects of Illusion: Men and Ideas in American Foreign Policy 1941–1949* (Chicago, 1970); and Gabriel Kolko's *The Politics of War: The World and United States Foreign Policy 1943–1945* (New York, 1968), and *The Roots of American Foreign Policy* (Boston, 1969).

when Roosevelt concluded in the spring of 1941 that American involvement in the conflict was all but inevitable, according to Dallek, "he refused to force an unpalatable choice upon the nation by announcing for war." Nor did the United States provoke an attack by Japan. Roosevelt's anti-Fascist commitment made it impossible for him to discriminate between Germany and Japan; "both had to be opposed at the same time." The attack on Pearl Harbor on December 7, 1941, was an unforeseen surprise. "Seeing the fleet in Hawaii as a deterrent rather than a target, lulled by the belief that the Japanese lacked the capability to strike at Pearl Harbor and by the information or 'noise' ... indicating that an attack might come at any one of a number of points," Dallek noted, "Roosevelt, like the rest of the nation, failed to anticipate the Pearl Harbor attack. Later contentions to the contrary had less to do with the actuality of Roosevelt's actions than with the isolationists' efforts to justify the idea that the country had never in fact been vulnerable to attack." David Reynolds demonstrated that the relationship between Great Britain and the United States between 1937 and 1941 was not altogether smooth. The British were not always certain about America's reliability, and feared its economic expansionist tendencies. Americans, on the other hand, were suspicious of their British brethren and disliked its imperial system. Ultimately a common culture and language, plus fear of Nazi Germany, proved decisive, and in the end the American hope of remaining neutral was frustrated by the Japanese attack on Pearl Harbor. Similarly, Waldo Heinrichs avoided sweeping generalizations and emphasized that operational limitations and Roosevelt's caution went hand in hand.[12]

In the second selection in this chapter Jonathan Utley has fused the Open Door interpretation with an emphasis on the role of organizational and bureaucratic conflicts. America's faith in a liberal commercial world order and Japan's effort to establish its hegemony in Asia assured Japanese-American tension. A rigid anti-Japanese mind set in Washington, combined with Secretary of State Cordell Hull's insistence upon a comprehensive settlement, rendered traditional diplomacy ineffectual. Added to an already difficult situation was a foreign-policy bureaucracy whose members often pursued their own agendas, thus moving the United States closer toward economic sanctions that neither Roosevelt nor Hull favored. The result was a form of chaos that eventually led to armed conflict.

To evaluate in a fair and objective manner the events leading up to Pearl Harbor, then, is not a simple task for scholars. The complexity

---

[12]Robert Dallek, *Franklin D. Roosevelt and American Foreign Policy, 1932–1945* (New York, 1979), pp. 530–532; David Reynolds, *The Creation of the Anglo-American Alliance 1939–41: A Study in Competitive Cooperation* (Chapel Hill, 1982); Waldo Heinrichs, *Threshold of War: Franklin D. Roosevelt and America's Entry into World War II* (New York, 1988).

of this historical problem arises from many reasons: the tangled web of interrelated events in the period before December 1941, which makes it difficult, if not impossible, to separate causes and to point to any particular one as "definitive"; the fact that some of the goals for which America went to war were not achieved by the end of the conflict; and the problem of ascertaining the precise motives of the national leaders and various interest groups of the period. Historical judgment, furthermore, rests to a considerable degree upon the starting assumptions held by various scholars; different historians approach the problem with a different set of starting assumptions and hence reach conflicting conclusions.

In contrasting the revisionist with the international school of historians, several differences are clearly discernible. First, both deal in a very different way with the issue of whether or not the Axis powers represented an immediate threat to American security. The revisionists maintained that there was no evidence that Hitler hoped to move into the Western Hemisphere. Even if he had the revisionists held that the best policy would have been for America to have waited until Germany and Russia had destroyed each other; such a policy would have avoided the power vacuum that developed in Europe in the postwar period that enabled the Soviet Union to expand without checks. In the Far East America also made a mistake by pushing Japan into the war by an inflexible policy and a refusal to offer any reasonable compromises. The internationalists, on the other hand, believed that a victorious Germany posed a serious threat to American security, especially if one considers the military prowess and scientific potential of the Third Reich. Given Hitler's past behavior there was no reason to assume that his ambitions would have been satisfied after conquering England and the Soviet Union. Insofar as the Far East was concerned the internationalists took the view that Japan's unwillingness to abandon its imperialist policy was the prime cause of the war. Scholars within the Williams tradition tended to see the diplomacy of the 1930s as an outgrowth of American economic expansionism; they paid relatively little attention to the Axis powers and to the question whether or not American security was, in fact, threatened by developments in Europe and the Far East.[13]

A second issue that scholars dealt with was the motivation behind Roosevelt's foreign policy. Did Roosevelt deceive the American people by telling them that his policy would lead to peace when in reality he

---

[13]Cf. Alton Frye, *Nazi Germany and the American Hemisphere, 1933–1941* (New Haven, 1967); James V. Compton, *The Swastika and the Eagle: Hitler, the United States, and the Origins of World War II* (Boston, 1967); Bruce M. Russett, *No Clear and Present Danger:A Skeptical View of the United States Entry into World War II* (New York, 1972); and Thomas A. Bailey and Paul B. Ryan, *Hitler vs. Roosevelt: The Undeclared Naval War* (New York, 1979).

wanted war? To this question the revisionists answered in the affirmative and the internationalists in the negative. The Williams school, on the other hand, tended to occupy a middle position, if only because this question was not central to its analysis. All schools had a serious problem on this score, however, because the issue revolved about the motivation and intentions of one man. How can the historian gauge the motives of any individual, particularly when so few human beings ever record their innermost convictions or are completely honest with themselves?

In many respects the most important difference separating the various schools was their judgment concerning the results of the war. To the revisionists the outcome of the war offered dramatic evidence of the blundering and evil policy followed by Roosevelt and his advisers. The United States, after all, had gone to war to destroy the menace of totalitarianism. Instead, it was confronted after 1945 with the Soviet Union, a supposedly far greater menace than Nazi Germany. On the continent Russia controlled all of eastern and a good part of central Europe; in the Far East the destruction of Japanese power created a situation that ultimately led to a Communist victory in China. The internationalist school, by way of comparison, readily admitted that the results of the war were anything but desirable, but its adherents also argued that these results did not necessarily make Hitler the lesser of two evils. Moreover, history suggests a tragic view of human destiny, for each problem solved more arise in its place. To expect a final solution to all problems is to be unrealistic. While Roosevelt may have miscalculated in some of his policies, he did not do so knowingly or deliberately; his mistakes were due to the limitations that characterize all human beings. The Williams school saw in World War II the origins and beginnings of the Cold War, for during that time America's economic imperialism was fused with a messianic sense; the result was a crusade against any system not modeled after the example of the United States.

In general, then, the differing interpretations of America's entry into World War II reflect the personal faith of historians in the particular policy they are advocating. The internationalist school believed that the United States, as a world power, could neither neglect its responsibilities nor ignore events in other parts of the world. The world is far too small a place for the provincial isolationism that characterized American diplomacy in the early years of the republic. Consequently, they believed that Roosevelt was on the right track even though some of his specific moves may have been inappropriate. The revisionists, on the other hand, argued that America's national interests could have been best served by remaining aloof from conflicts that did not immediately threaten the nation. Roosevelt, therefore, made a grievous error when he committed his nation—against the will of its people—to a world conflict. The American people, these revisionists concluded, paid a stiff price for that mistake. Those in the tradition of Williams argue by way of contrast that only a basic transformation in America's foreign policy (and hence domestic policies) can bring peace and an atmosphere conducive to meaningful social change. Consequently, with some exceptions, they see American diplomacy in the 1930s as a fateful error.

Which one of these schools is correct? Were the revisionists justified in their claim that the United States should have stayed out of World War II? Were they right in attributing evil and invidious motives to Roosevelt and his advisers? Or were internationalist historians right in arguing that World War II involved vital American interests and that Roosevelt was simply trying to safeguard these interests even though it meant that the nation might eventually enter the war? Or were Williams and his followers correct in attributing war to Open Door imperialism? These are some of the basic issues confronting the student who is attempting to understand the background and events that led up to Pearl Harbor.

Dexter Perkins

DEXTER PERKINS (1889–1984) *was emeritus professor of history at the University of Rochester. He was the author of many books on various phases of American diplomatic history, including three volumes on the Monroe Doctrine.*

Revisionism may be defined as an after-the-event interpretation of American participation in war, with the accent on the errors and blunders that provoked the struggle and on the folly of the whole enterprise. If we accept this definition, we shall certainly agree that there has been plenty of revisionism in the course of our history. The War of 1812 has sometimes been judged to have been futile and sometimes described as a war of intended conquest. The Mexican War has come in for harsh treatment as a war of unnecessary aggression. James G. Randall, one of the foremost students of the Civil War period, suggests that a less passionate view of the sectional problem might have made the conflict avoidable. Again and again it has been stated by reputable historians that William McKinley might have prevented the war of 1898 had he stressed in his message to Congress the very large concessions that had been made by Spain. The First World War was brilliantly represented by Walter Millis as the product of a blundering diplomacy and of economic pressures not entirely creditable. And since 1945 we have had a crop of historians, headed by so eminent a member of his historical generation as Charles A. Beard, attempting to show that the maddest folly of all was our entry into the conflict that ended less than a decade ago. Clearly, revisionism is an American habit; though, in saying this, I do not mean to imply that it is unknown in other lands.

The roots of the revisionist tendency are worth speculating about. Such a point of view, I take it, is particularly apt to find expression in a country where peace is highly treasured and where the glorification of war is relatively uncommon. Just as many Americans easily put away the hates and resentment of war at the end of the struggle and display a tendency towards reconciliation with the vanquished, so they tend to forget the passions that animated them and drove them into the conflict, and to view what at the time seemed reasonable and natural as something that with a little more forbearance or wisdom could have been avoided. And there are other factors that reinforce this

"Was Roosevelt Wrong?," *Virginia Quarterly Review* 30 (Summer 1954):355–372. Reprinted with permission of the *Virginia Quarterly Review* and Dexter Perkins.

point of view. Wars are apt to end in disillusionment. After the glorious hopes of the years 1917 and 1918 came the clash of national selfishness at Versailles, and a distraught and threatened world. In 1945 the defeat of Hitler and Japan was soon seen to have left grave problems ahead. In the East, the American defense of China and the hopes of a strong democratic nation in the Orient ended in the victory of the Chinese Reds. And in Europe, though the peril from the ambitions of Hitler was exorcized, the United States found itself face to face with a new totalitarianism, far-ranging in its ambitions like the old. In such a situation it was natural to forget the menace that had been defeated, and to ask whether there might not have been a better solution to the problems that ended with the capitulation ceremonies at Rheims and on the deck of the *Missouri.*

After every large-scale war, moreover, there is a reaction against that strong executive leadership which is almost inevitably associated with periods of crisis in the life of the nation. This was true in 1920; and it was true after 1945. During the conflict the personality of Mr. Roosevelt loomed large, and almost immune from attack. But under the surface there was hostility, and this was to take the form of criticism of his war policies. Sometimes this criticism came, as in the case of Frederic R. Sanborn in his "Design for War," from one who had a strong animus against the New Deal, and who approached the record of the administration in the field of foreign policy with this animus. Sometimes, on the other hand, as in the case of Charles A. Beard, it came from one who regarded the Roosevelt diplomacy as jeopardizing and perhaps wrecking far-reaching programs of internal reform. In these two cases, and in virtually every other, strong emotions entered into the account. It has been a satisfaction to the revisionists to tear down the President; and there has always been—and it was inevitable that there should be—a reading public to fall in with this point of view, either from personal dislike of Roosevelt or from partisan feeling.

Revisionism, then, has roots in the very nature of the case. But, if we analyze it coolly, what shall we think of it? This is the question I propose to examine in this essay.

It seems to me fair to say at the outset that it is impossible to avoid the conclusion that revisionism is essentially history by hypothesis. It suggests—indeed in some instances it almost claims—that the world would have been a better place, or that any rate the present position of the United States would have been happier, if this country had not intervened in the Second World War. Such a proposition can be put forward, but it cannot be established like a theorem in geometry. We cannot go back to 1939 or 1941 and reenact the events of those stirring and tumultuous years. In a sense, we are bound by the past.

Nonetheless, it seems worthwhile, even though we are in the realm of speculation rather than scientific history, to state the revisionist point of view. First, with regard to Germany the point of view is advanced that the United States was in no essential danger from Adolf Hitler, that he demonstrated no very great interest in the American continents, that he desired until almost the day of Pearl Harbor to keep out of trouble with the United States, that there is no reliable evidence that he meditated an assault upon the New World. It is possible for the revisionist to go further. The ambitions of Hitler, it would be maintained, would have been checked and contained within limits by the presence of the great totalitarian state to the East. The two colossi would act each as a restraint on the other. It needed not the intervention of the American government to preserve the safety of the New World. As to Asia, the argument runs somewhat differently. Less emphasis is placed on the question of national security and more on a certain interpretation of national interest. The United States, we are told, had only a meager interest in China; its trade and investments there were insignificant, and were likely to remain so. They were distinctly inferior to our trade and investments in Japan. The shift in the balance of the Far East that might come about through a Japanese victory over Great Britain was no real concern of the United States. As to the Philippines, they might have been left alone had we stayed out of the war, or conversely, they were not worth the sacrifice involved in maintaining our connection with them. Such are the assumptions, implied, if not always expressed, in the revisionist view of the problem of the Orient.

Now some of the assertions in this rationale are unchallengeable. It is true that Hitler desired to avoid a clash with the United States until just before Pearl Harbor. It is true that the economic interests of the United States in China were inferior to our interests in Japan. These are facts, and must be accepted as facts. But there still remain a good many questions about the revisionist assumptions. For example, was there in 1940 and 1941 no danger of the destruction of British naval power, and would that destruction have had no unhappy consequences for the United States? Granted that the documents show great reluctance on the part of the Führer to challenge the United States, would this reluctance have outlasted the fall of Great Britain? Granted that the Kremlin might have exercised a restraining influence on the Germans, is it certain that the two powers might not have come to an understanding as they did in 1939, and had at other periods in the past? Just how comfortable a world would it have been if the psychopathic leader of Germany had emerged from the Second World War astride a large part of the Continent, with the resources of German science at his command? There are questions, too, that can be asked about the Orient. Did the United States have no responsibility for the Philippines, and would the islands have been safe for long if the Japanese had dominated the Far East? Could the United States divest itself of all concern for China, abandoning a policy of nearly forty years duration and a deep-seated American tradition? Was the destruction of British power in this part of the world a matter of no concern to this country? Could the defeat of Britain in the East be separated from the fate of Britain in the world at large? These are extremely large questions, and it is a bold man who will brush them aside as inconsequential or trivial, or who will reply to them with complete dogmatism. Indeed, it is because they raise so many problems cutting to the root of our feelings, as well as our opinions, that they arouse so much controversy. Nor is there any likelihood that we can ever arrive at a complete consensus with regard to them.

We must, I think, seek a somewhat narrower frame of reference if we are to answer the revisionists with facts, and not with speculations. One of the ways to answer them, and one particularly worth pursuing with regard to the war in Europe, is to analyze the policy of the Roosevelt administration in its relation to public sentiment.

Foreign policy, in the last analysis, depends, not upon some logical formula, but upon the opinion of the nation. No account of American diplomacy in 1940 and 1941 can pretend to authority which does not take into account the tides of sentiment which must always influence, and perhaps control, the course of government. It is not to be maintained that a president has no freedom of action whatsoever; he can, I think, accelerate or retard a popular trend. But he does not act independently of it; the whole history of American diplomacy attests the close relationship between the point of view of the masses and executive action. A peacefully minded president like McKinley was driven to war with Spain; a president who set great store by increasing the physical power of the nation, like Theodore Roosevelt, was limited and confined in his action; and Franklin Roosevelt himself, when, in the quarantine speech of October 1937, he sought to rouse the American people against aggression, was compelled to admit failure, and to trim his sails to the popular breeze. These things are of the essence; to fail to observe them is to fail to interpret the past in the true historical spirit.

Let us apply these conceptions to the period of 1939 to 1941. It will hardly be denied that from the very beginning of the war public sentiment was definitely against Germany. Indeed, even before the invasion of Poland, the public opinion polls show a strong partiality for the democratic nations. As early as January 1939, when asked the question [of] whether we should do everything possible to help England and France in case of war, 69 percent of the persons polled answered in the affirmative, and the same question in October produced a percentage of 62 percent on the same side. No doubt this sentiment did not extend to the point of actual participation in the war, but it furnished a firm foundation for the action of the President in calling Congress in special

session, and in asking of it the repeal of the arms embargo on shipments of war in the interest of the Allies. The measure to this effect
was introduced in the Congress towards the end of September; and it
was thoroughly debated. There are several things to be said in connection with its passage. The first is that after its introduction there was
a consistent majority of around 60 percent in the polls in favor of passage. The second is that, though there was a strong partisan flavor to
the debate, the defections when they came were more numerous on
the Republican than on the Democratic side. It is true that, without
the leadership of the President, the repeal could not have been enacted.
But also it did not fly in the face of public sentiment (so far as that can
be measured), but on the contrary reflected it.

With the fall of France there took place a deep and significant development in public opinion. This change the revisionists usually do
not mention. They prefer to treat of American policy as if it were
formed in a vacuum without regard to the moving forces that have so
much to do with the final decisions. Yet the evidences are ample that
in June of 1940 the American people were deeply moved. Take, for
example, the action of the Republican nominating convention. There
were several outstanding professional politicians in the running in
1940, Senator Taft, Senator Vandenberg, Thomas E. Dewey. Each one
of these men represented a policy of caution so far as Europe was concerned. Yet what did the convention do? It turned to a relative unknown figure, to a novice in politics who had, however, more than
once declared himself as advocating extensive assistance to the democracies. The choice of Wendell Willkie as the Republican candidate for
the presidency is a fact the importance of which cannot be denied. It
is worthwhile calling attention to other like phenomena. One of these
is the overwhelming majorities by which the Congress appropriated
largely increased sums for the armed forces, not only for the navy but
for the army and the air force as well. Perhaps the American people,
or the representatives of the American people, ought not to have been
perturbed at what was happening in Europe. But the fact is that they
were perturbed. They were perturbed in a big way. And the votes in
the legislative halls demonstrate that fact.

Or take another example. The movement for a conscription law in
time of peace developed rapidly after June of 1940. It developed with
very little assistance from the White House. It cut across party lines.
And it resulted in a legislative enactment which reflected the excitement of the public mind. How can we interpret the measure otherwise? Was there not a substantial body of opinion in the United States
that feared a Germany victory?

Another important factor to be noted is the formation in June of
1940 of the Committee to Defend America by Aiding the Allies. It is
highly significant that this movement arose at all. It is doubly signifi-

cant that it found a leader in a Kansan Republican such as William Allen White. It is trebly significant that, once initiated, it spread like wildfire, and that by September there were more than 650 chapters in the United States. And it is also to be noted that in New York there soon came into being a more advanced group, the so-called Century Group, which advocated war if necessary to check the aggressions of Germany.

And it is further to be observed that out of the Committee to Defend America came an agitation for what was eventually to be the bases-destroyer deal of September 2, 1940. This deal, by the way, was approved by 62 percent of the persons polled on August 17, 1940, two weeks before it was actually consummated.

Let us go further. The next important step forward in American policy was the lend-lease enactment of the winter of 1941. This measure, it would appear from the polls, was based on a very distinct evolution of public sentiment. In July of 1940, 59 percent of the persons polled preferred to keep out rather than to help England at the risk of war, and 36 percent took the contrary view. In October the percentages were exactly reversed: they were 36 to 59. By January of 1941, 68 percent of those interviewed thought it more important to assist Great Britain than to keep out of war. And the lend-lease enactment, when presented to the Congress, passed the Lower House by the impressive vote of 317 to 71 and the Senate by 60 to 31. As in the legislation of 1939, though the vote again had a partisan flavor, there were more defections from the Republicans in favor of the measure than of Democrats against it. And there is something more to be added to the account in this instance. By the winter of 1941 the America Firsters had appeared upon the scene. A counterpropaganda was now being organized against the administration. Yet this new group, despite its vigorous efforts, failed signally to rally majority opinion. And Senator Taft, who represented the most thoughtful opposition to the administration, himself proposed a measure of assistance to Great Britain.

I shall treat a little later of the various measures requiring no legislative sanction which the President took in the course of the year 1941. But it is important to observe that throughout the period there was a strong public sentiment that believed that it was more important to defeat Germany than to keep out of war. This view was held, according to the polls, by 62 percent of those interrogated in May of 1941 and by 68 percent in December of 1941. As early as April 1941, 68 percent of the pollees believed it important to enter the war if British defeat was certain.

We should next examine the legislation of the fall of 1941. By this time the Congress was ready to authorize the arming of American merchant ships, and this by a heavy vote. The measure was passed by 259 to 138 in the House and the Senate amended it and passed it by 50 to

37. Congress was ready, more reluctantly, to repeal those provisions of the neutrality acts which excluded American vessels from the so-called war zones. It was moving in the direction of fuller and fuller engagement against Hitler. We shall never know, of course, what the next step would have been had not that step been taken by Germany. It was the dictator of the Reich who declared war on the United States, not the American national legislature that declared war on the Führer and his minions. But in the period between 1939 and 1941 it seems safe to say that the foreign policy of the Roosevelt administration was in accord with the majority opinion accepted, and pursuing a course of action which majority opinion approved.

This circumstance is naturally either ignored or obscured in the revisionist literature. And what makes it easier to forget is the undeniable fact that Franklin Roosevelt was unhappily sometimes given to equivocation and shifty conversation. Very early, it is true, as early as the quarantine speech of October 1937, he sounded the alarm against the totalitarians. Very often he stated his conviction that their continued progress presented a threat to the United States. On occasion he took his courage in his hands as, when at Charlottesville in June of 1940, in an election year, he came out frankly in favor of aid to the democracies, or in the declaration of unlimited emergency in the address of May 27, 1941. There is little doubt that he deemed the defeat of Hitler more important than the avoidance of war (as did many other Americans, as we have seen). Yet he was often less than frank in his approach, and the emphasis he laid on his devotion to peace was often excessive. He shocked even his ardent admirer, Robert Sherwood, in the election of 1940. His presentation of the case for lend-lease does not at all times suggest candor; indeed, the very phrase seems a bit of cajolery. With regard to the question of convoy, in the spring of 1941, he was clever and, though verbally correct, hardly wholly open in his approach to the problem. In the famous episode of the *Greer* (an attack by a German submarine on a vessel which was reporting its position to a British destroyer), he misrepresented the facts, or spoke without full knowledge of them. All this it is only right to admit. Yet we must not exaggerate the importance of these considerations. The country knew where it was going with regard to Germany. It accepted lend-lease as desirable. Of the patrolling of the ocean lanes which followed, the President spoke candidly in the speech of May 27, 1941. There was nothing clandestine about the occupation of Greenland or Iceland. The pattern in the fall of 1941 would most probably not have been much altered if Roosevelt had been more scrupulous with regard to the *Greer*. In the last analysis we come back to the essential fact that Roosevelt represented and expressed in action the mood of the country with regard to Germany.

The question is, I believe, more difficult when we come to examine American policy towards Japan. We can say with some assurance that the denunciation of the treaty of commerce of 1911, undertaken by the administration in July of 1939 as an indication of American displeasure with Japanese policy, was distinctly well received. Indeed, if the State Department had not acted, the legislature might have. We can also that in August of 1939 there was an overwhelming feeling against sending war materials to Nippon. When in September of 1940, an embargo on the export of scrap iron was imposed, 59 percent of the persons polled on this issue approved the step that had been taken. And in 1941 the number of persons who believed that some check should be put on Japan even at the risk of war rose from 51 percent to 70 percent between July and September, and stood at 69 percent at the time of Pearl Harbor.

But we have fewer indications of the direction of public sentiment in the action of Congress, and no actual votes on which to base our estimate of how the representatives of the American people felt with regard to the important problem of our course of action in the Orient. We must, I think, speak less confidently on this question of public opinion than in the case of Germany. We must turn rather to an analysis of the policy of the administration, and to revisionist criticism of that policy.

First of all, let us look at some of the uncontroverted facts. We know that there were militarist elements in Japan. We know that as early as 1934 Japan proclaimed its doctrine of a Greater East Asia in the famous Amau statement. We know that in the same year it upset the naval arrangements made at Washington and London. We know that it set up a special régime in North China in 1935. We know that it became involved in a war with China in 1937. This, of course, was only prelude. The outbreak of the European conflict in Europe, and the collapse of France, offered to the sponsors of further aggressive action a great opportunity. The occupation of northern Indochina followed. In the summer of 1940, the impetuous and aggressive Matsuoka came to the Foreign Office. On September 27, 1940, there was signed a tripartite pact with Japan, which bound Nippon to come to the assistance of the Axis powers if they were attacked by a power then at peace with them. In other words, the Tokyo government sought to confine and limit American policy. In April of 1941 came a neutrality pact with Russia which freed the hands of the Japanese militarists for a policy of advance towards the South. In July came the occupation of the rest of Indochina. The occupation of *northern* Indochina made some sense from the point of view of blocking the supply route to the Chinese Nationalists. The occupation of *southern* Indochina made no sense, except as the prelude to further acts of aggression. And in due course the aggression came.

Admittedly, this is only one side of the story. The question to be examined is, did these acts take place partly as a result of American provocation? Was it possible for a wider and more prudent diplomacy to have avoided the rift that occurred in December 1941? Revisionist criticism of our Oriental policy has been expressed in a variety of ways. In its most extreme form, it suggests that the President and his advisers actually plotted war with Japan. In its less extreme form, it directs its shafts at a variety of actions, of which I shall examine the most important. They are the conversations with the British as to the defense of the Far East, the commitments made to China, the severance of commercial relations, the failure to accept the proposals of Prince Konoye for direct conversations with the President, and the breakdown of the *modus vivendi* proposal of November 1941. I shall examine each of these briefly, but let us first turn to the accusation that American policy was directed towards producing and not avoiding an armed conflict in the Orient.

It seems quite impossible to accept this view on the basis of the documentation. During the greater part of 1940 and 1941, it was certainly not the objective of the Roosevelt administration to bring about a clash in the Far East. On the contrary such a clash was regarded as likely to produce the greatest embarrassment in connection with the program of aid to Britain. The military and naval advisers of the President were opposed to it, and said so again and again. Even on the eve of Pearl Harbor this was the case. In addition, Secretary Hull was opposed to it. Ever the apostle of caution, he made his point of view quite clear almost up to the end. And as for the President, it is worth pointing out that on the occasion of the Japanese occupation of southern Indochina he came forward with a proposal for the neutralization of that territory in the interests of peace, and that in August he frankly stated it to be his purpose to "baby the Japanese along." That he feared Japanese aggression is likely, almost certain; that he desired it is something that cannot be proved.

But let us look at the various specific actions which have awakened criticism on the part of the revisionists. In the first place I cannot see that staff conversations with the British were open to any objections whatsoever. If the object of the Roosevelt administration was to limit Japanese aggression in the Far East, then it seems wholly rational to take precautions against such aggression and surely it could reasonably be expected that such precautions would serve as a deterrent rather than as an incitement to action. It is, in my judgment, rather distorted thinking that regards such action as provocation. This is precisely the point of view of the Kremlin today with regard to the North Atlantic Treaty and the European defense pact, or, to take another example, very like the contention of the Germans when they invaded Belgium in 1914. Because the British had engaged in military conversations with the Belgians looking to the possible violation of the neutrality treaty of 1939, it was claimed by apologists for Germany that the violation of neutrality was defensible. Where is the possible justification for such reasoning?

There is more to be said with regard to the breaking off, by the United States, of commercial and financial relations with Japan on the heels of the Japanese occupation of southern Indochina in the summer of 1941. Undoubtedly this created an extraordinarily difficult situation for the government in Tokyo. Undoubtedly the cutting off of the oil supply from the United States gave great additional force to the arguments of the militarists. Undoubtedly, in the absence of a far-reaching diplomatic arrangement, it presented a strong reason for "bursting out" of the circle, and going to war. If the administration put faith in this measure of economic coercion as a substitute for physical resistance, its faith was to turn out to be groundless. For myself, I have for a long time believed that economic coercion against a strong and determined power is more likely to produce war than to prevent it. But there are circumstances that ought to be mentioned in favor of the action of the administration. It is to be emphasized that the severance of commercial and financial relations resulted not in a breach of the negotiations with Japan but in a resumption of those negotiations. It is to be remembered that Prince Konoye's proposal for a personal conference with the President came after and not before the President's action. American policy by no means put an end to the efforts of those substantial elements in Japan who feared a clash with this country and who were laboring to prevent it. It must be pointed out, also, that the alternative was by no means a pleasant one. At a time when we were deeply engaged in the Atlantic, when we were being more and more deeply committed with regard to the war in Europe, when our domestic supply of oil might have to be substantially curtailed, the continuation of our exports to the Far East to assist Japan in possible projects of aggression was a very difficult policy to follow. It may even be that it would have proven to be totally impracticable from a political point of view.

We come in the third place to the efforts of Premier Konoye to establish direct contact with President Roosevelt. It is well known that Ambassador Grew believed at that time, and that he has more than once stated since, that a good deal was to be hoped from such a meeting. And it is by no means clear why, if the objective were the postponement of a crisis, the experiment should not have been tried. Secretary Hull brought to this problem, as it seems to me, a rigidity of mind which may properly be criticized. In insisting on a previous definition of the issues before the meeting was held, he was instrumental in preventing it. While we cannot know what the result of such a meeting would have been, we are entitled, I think, to wish that it had been held. All the more is this true since it would appear likely that Prince Konoye was sincere in the effort which he made to avoid war.

But there is another side to the matter. We cannot be absolutely sure of Konoye's good faith. We can be still less sure of the willingness of the Tokyo militarists to support him in the far-reaching concessions that would have been necessary. And in the final analysis we cannot be sure of the ability of the American government to make concessions on its own part.

And here we come, as it seems to me, to the crux of the matter. It was the American policy in China that created an impassable barrier in our negotiations with Japan. It is necessary to examine that policy. From one angle of vision the patience of the American government in dealing with the China incident seems quite remarkable. There was a good deal to complain of from 1935 onward, certainly from 1937 onward, if one were to think in terms of sympathy for an aggressed people and in terms of the traditional policy of the United States with regard to this populous nation. The Roosevelt administration moved very slowly in its opposition to Japan. It made its first loan to Chiang Kaishek in the fall of 1938. It denounced the commercial treaty of 1911 with Nippon only in the summer of 1939. And it embarked upon a policy of really substantial aid to China only contemporaneously with the signing of the tripartite pact in the fall of 1940. Its increasing assistance to Chiang is intelligible on the ground that to keep the Japanese bogged down in China was one means of checking or preventing their aggressive action elsewhere.

The fact remains, however, that it was the Chinese question which was the great and central stumbling block in the long negotiations that took place in 1941. Though the Japanese had entered into an alliance with the Axis powers, it seems not unlikely that, in 1941, as the issue of peace or war defined itself more clearly, they would have been willing to construe away their obligations under that alliance had they been able to come to terms with the United States on the Chinese problem. But by 1941 the American government was so far committed to the cause of Chiang that it really had very little freedom of maneuver. The various Japanese proposals for a settlement of the China incident would have involved a betrayal of the Chinese Nationalist leader. The proposal for a coalition government, a government of the Nationalists and the puppet régime of Wang Ching-wei, could hardly have been accepted. The proposal that America put pressure on Chiang to negotiate, and cut off aid to him if he refused, was by this time equally impracticable. And the question of the withdrawal of the Japanese troops in China presented insuperable difficulties. True it is that in October of 1941 the idea of a total withdrawal seems to have been presented to Mr. Welles by Mr. Wakasugi, Admiral Nomura's associate in the negotiations. But the idea was emphatically rejected by the militarists in Tokyo, and perhaps there was never a time when they would have agreed to any proposal that at the same time would have been acceptable to Chungking. The American government had been brought, by its policy of association with the Chinese Nationalists, to the point where understanding with Japan was practically impossible.

This fact is dramatically illustrated by the negotiations over the *modus vivendi* in November 1941. At this time, as is well known, proposals were brought forward for the maintenance of the status quo, and a gradual restoration of more normal relations through the lifting of the commercial restrictions, and through the withdrawal of the Japanese from southern Indochina. At first it seemed as if there were a possibility of working out some such proposal. But the Chinese objected most violently, and Secretary Hull dropped the idea. In the face of Chinese pressure, and of the possible popular indignation which such a policy of concession might produce, and acting either under the orders or at least with the assent of the President, he backed down. We must not exaggerate the importance of this. There is no certainty that the *modus vivendi* would have been acceptable to Tokyo, and, judging by the Japanese proposals of November 20, there is indeed some reason to think otherwise. But the fact remains that our close association with Chiang was a fundamental factor in making the breach with Japan irreparable. And it seems fair to say in addition that our hopes with regard to Nationalist China were at all times, in 1941 as later, very far removed from political reality.

Let us not, however, jump to absolute conclusions with regard to questions that, in the nature of the case, ought not to be a matter of dogmatic judgment. If there was a party in Japan, and a substantial one, which feared war with the United States and earnestly sought for accommodation, there was also a party which regarded the course of events in Europe as a heaven-sent opportunity for national self-aggrandizement. That this party might in any case have prevailed, whatever the character of American policy, does not seem by any means unlikely. It is significant that in July of 1941 the fall of Matsuoka brought no change in policy in the Far East, and that the so-called moderate, Admiral Toyoda, gave the orders for the crucial and revealing occupation of southern Indochina in the summer of 1941.

Let us not forget, either, that after all it was the Japanese who struck. The ruthless act of aggression at Pearl Harbor was no necessary consequence of the breakdown of negotiations with the United States. If new oil supplies were needed, they were, of course, to be secured by an attack on the Dutch East Indies, not by an attack on Hawaii. Though there were strategic arguments for including America in any warlike move, there were strong political reasons for not doing so. No greater miscalculation has perhaps ever been made than that made by the militarists at Tokyo in December 1941. By their own act, they unified American opinion and made their own defeat inevitable. It will always remain doubtful when the decisive involvement would have come for the United States had the bombs not dropped on Pearl Harbor on the seventh of December of 1941.

What, in conclusion, shall we say of revisionist history? There is a sense in which it is stimulating to the historian, and useful to historical science, to have the presuppositions, the conventional presuppositions, of the so-called orthodox interpreters of our foreign policy, subjected to criticism. There is surely some reason to believe that the candid examination of the views of these critics will, in the long run, result in a more accurate and a more objective view of the great events of the prewar years and in a better balanced judgment of President Roosevelt himself.

But there is another side of the question which, of course, must be recognized. It is fair to say that virtually all revisionist history (like some orthodox history) is written with a *parti pris*. It is hardly possible to speak of it as dictated by a pure and disinterested search for truth. It is, on the contrary, shot through with passion and prejudice nonetheless. It also rests upon hypotheses which, in the nature of the case, cannot be demonstrated, and assumptions that will, it is fair to say, never be generally, or perhaps even widely, accepted. As to its practical effects, there are no signs that the isolationism of the present era has important political effects, so far as foreign policy is concerned. Conceivably, it provides some reinforcement for partisan Republicanism. But even here it seems considerably less effective than the unscrupulous campaign of Senator McCarthy and his colleagues to represent the previous administration as one saturated with Communists. The urgency of present issues may make revisionism less of a force in our time than it was two decades ago. As to this, we shall have to see what the future unfolds.

Jonathan G. Utley

JONATHAN G. UTLEY (1942–   ) *is professor of history at the University of Tennessee. He is the author of* Going to War with Japan 1937–1941 *(1985).*

No one during the fall of 1941 wanted war with Japan. Navy preferred to concentrate on the Atlantic. Army said it needed a few more months before it would be ready in the Philippines. Hull had made the search for peace his primary concern for months. Roosevelt could see nothing to be gained by a war with Japan. Hawks such as Acheson, Ickes, and Morgenthau argued that their strong policies would avoid war, not provoke one. Even Hornbeck said the same thing, though he probably would not have been displeased by a Japanese-American war.

The problem confronting the Roosevelt administration was the method to follow to avoid war. Was it best to resume negotiations with Nomura, even though they had produced so little in May and June, or should the United States give Japan an ultimatum that one more step would mean war? Should Hull and Nomura conduct the negotiations or should Roosevelt and Prime Minister Konoye Fumimaro meet in a summit to cut through bureaucratic red tape and find grounds for an agreement? Should the diplomatic goal be a comprehensive agreement or just a limited, temporary one designed to postpone war? And what price would the United States be willing to pay to buy peace? The answers to those questions would determine whether the United States was going to plod along on a path that would end in war or have the energy and imagination to gamble on achieving a peace.

The freeze of Japanese assets had not signaled the end of diplomacy. Neither Roosevelt nor Hull was optimistic about achieving a diplomatic settlement, but Hull was prepared to make an effort. When the secretary returned to his office on August 4, he began preparations for reopening his talks with Nomura, suspended since June 21.

Meanwhile, Roosevelt was meeting secretly in Newfoundland with Churchill, who was trying to move the United States away from talk and toward confrontation with Japan. The British worried that the sanctions the United States had recently initiated—to which Britain fully subscribed—would spark a Japanese attack on Britain's Asian possessions while the United States would sit by and do nothing. To prevent this Churchill and the British delegation urged Roosevelt to warn Japan that if it attacked a third power (i.e., Britain) Roosevelt would ask Congress for authority "to give aid to such a power" (i.e., declare war). Though Roosevelt dismissed such talk out of hand, Churchill did persuade him to accept a less militant ultimatum, warning Japan that any further expansion would compel the United States to take "any and all steps of whatsoever character it deems necessary in its own security notwithstanding the possibility that such further steps on its part may result in conflict between the two countries." Hull refused to accept this ultimatum. He rewrote it to leave out any reference to conflict and linked it with a more positive document proposing reopening the talks with Nomura. When Roosevelt returned to Washington on August 17, Hull easily persuaded him to substitute the weaker language for that agreed on with Churchill.

Once again Hull managed to scuttle action that would provoke a confrontation with Japan. But as soon as he persuaded the president to abandon the British ultimatum, Nomura proposed something that threatened to snatch the entire question of Japanese-American relations out of Hull's hands.

The Japanese had grown very apprehensive about the future course of Japanese-American relations. The freeze and resulting end of trade caused great concern in Tokyo, as some Americans had predicted it would. Army leaders, who were always strongly anti-American, had become restless, while Navy leaders, who were usually more circumspect, recognized that time was running out. Prime Minister Konoye decided it was no longer possible to achieve a settlement with the United States through the painstaking discussions conducted by Ambassador Nomura and Secretary Hull. It would be necessary to break the diplomatic deadlock by a face-to-face meeting with Roosevelt. The idea of a conference with Konoye appealed to Roosevelt. Having just returned from the Atlantic Conference, where he and Churchill had fashioned the Atlantic Charter to guide the democracies through the coming struggle against the dictatorships, Roosevelt would have been less than human if he had not wondered whether something equally dramatic might come from a Pacific conference. More important, personal diplomacy appealed to the president, who had immense confidence in his ability to charm statesmen, even a prince of the royal house of Japan. If what was needed to assure peace in the Pacific was for the leaders to journey to Alaska or Hawaii to have a meeting of minds, Roosevelt was prepared, even eager, to go.

Everything that made the leaders' conference appealing to Roosevelt made it appalling to Hull. From the moment he heard it proposed he opposed it, and not always for reasons of state.

Hull considered Japanese-American relations his peculiar domain and would have resented Roosevelt usurping him even under the best of circumstances. But the leaders' conference proposal came on the heels of the (to Hull) unsatisfactory Atlantic Conference, where Roosevelt had excluded his secretary of state and proceeded to deviate from the careful policy Hull had prescribed. If the president could do that much damage in the Atlantic Conference talking to a virtual ally, he could do much more in a Pacific conference with a virtual enemy. After four years of struggling to keep control of foreign policy, Hull would not yield it to Roosevelt without a fight.

Beyond an understandable desire to protect his bureaucratic "turf," Hull had substantive reasons for objecting to the Roosevelt-Konoye meeting. A fundamental agreement with Japan was not possible, he believed, and the meeting would only produce a general agreement on vague principles that the Japanese would interpret differently from the Americans. The Chinese might feel betrayed and make a deal with Japan, Hull worried. If that happened, Japan could move some of its one million troops out of China against the British, the Dutch, or even the Americans. As we shall see below, such a development would have been disastrous to the efforts in the western Pacific of the army and the navy.

Hull's assumption that the conference could not succeed in fashioning a settlement rested upon the deeply held suspicion of Japan that permeated all levels in official Washington. This suspicion prompted Hull and company to interpret every Japanese position in the least charitable way. The Konoye government agreed to accept the principles of a liberal commercial order throughout the Southwest Pacific, but remained silent about China; Hull saw it not as a welcome first step but as a Japanese demand to establish its New Order in East Asia. Tokyo provided informal assurances that it would not invoke the Tripartite Pact against the United States; instead of welcoming them and urging still stronger ones Hull insisted that such assurances meant nothing and only a full renunciation would do. Recognizing that the terms of Japanese-Chinese agreement would only block any agreement with the United States, Konoye omitted that issue from the talks; Hull saw the maneuver not as a sincere effort to find something on which the two countries could agree but as a trick, and insisted that the disposition of China was central to any peace in the Pacific. Hull did not doubt that Konoye could carry out an agreement along the lines he had specified—he doubted that Konoye could carry out an agreement along the lines *Hull* specified.

From Tokyo, Grew bombarded the department with cables urging support for the Roosevelt-Konoye meeting and voicing optimism. But his advice did no good. After it was all over—after diplomacy had failed, the war had begun, Grew had been interned and then repatriated—he wondered why Konoye was not given more encouragement. "Could this have been due merely to the quibbling over formulas? Was the transcendent importance to our country of preserving peace to depend on the utterly futile effort to find mutually satisfactory formulas?"

Grew was correct. Locked into his search for a comprehensive peace, Hull would not consent to a futile attempt to find a solution through summitry. But Hull did not call it "quibbling over formulas," nor did he see it as a choice between peace and war. These two men looked at the situation differently because they began with different perspectives. Grew thought Konoye sincere—Hull "knew" he was not. . . .

By November, Cordell Hull's approach to Japanese-American relations no longer suited the national interest. The Tojo government refused to withdraw from China. Hull refused any agreement with Japan that did not include total withdrawal from China (except, of course, Manchuria.) Unless Japan could get an agreement it would strike south toward the Indies (the critical source for oil in any war with the Western powers). American forces in the Philippines would be able to stop that Japanese drive, but only after a few more months of preparations and only if China continued to tie down one million Japanese troops.

If Hull persisted in his search for a comprehensive peace while continuing to impose economic sanctions, there would be a war for which the United States was not prepared. On the other hand, if he offered Japan a settlement in China that did not involve total withdrawal it would be a serious blow to Chinese morale and might cause the collapse of Chinese resistance. That would only increase Japan's ability to move against the Philippines and thus undercut the entire American military strategy for the South Pacific. The only hope was to shift the diplomatic effort from a search for a lasting, comprehensive agreement to the negotiation of a temporary agreement that would buy a little time. Hull had to stop trying to find a just and lasting peace and start trying simply to avoid war.

Just about everyone except Cordell Hull understood what had to be done. The Japanese government, Roosevelt, and some Japan officers in the State Department all proposed abandoning the search for a comprehensive agreement in favor of negotiating a temporary agreement, what the diplomats called a modus vivendi (from the Latin, a way of living). Such an agreement was not intended to resolve Japanese-American tensions, only buy time.

Japanese leaders suspected that Hull and Roosevelt were trying to drag out the talks in order to further deplete Japanese resources before the inevitable war began. But the emperor's insistence on searching for a peaceful solution to Japanese-American differences compelled the Tojo government to make one more effort. First it would try plan A—reach an accord on the vexing issues of southern expansion, the Tripartite Pact, and Japanese troops in China. If that did not work (and no one expected it would), Nomura could offer plan B, a modus vivendi that specified that the United States would sell Japan some oil.

No sooner had Roosevelt (through the medium of MAGIC) read of Japan's interest in postponing a war than he outlined his own plan, a six-month agreement with no movement of armaments on either side, during which Japan and China would discuss peace. Stimson objected because the freeze on armaments would prevent the improvement of American defenses in the Philippines, which was Army's primary purpose in postponing a clash with Japan. Rather than come up with a

revised plan, Roosevelt did nothing. Hull showed no interest in it, so the American government waited for the Japanese to make their offer.
. . .

The triumph of bureaucratic rigidity over boldness occurred on the morning of November 26, when Cordell Hull gave up on diplomacy and decided to "kick the whole thing over." Rather than presenting the anemic modus vivendi, the secretary gave Nomura and special envoy Kurusu a robust statement of the extreme American position.

Since it was the final document handed to the Japanese, the November 26 statement has received attention it does not deserve. It was not a diplomatic document, not even an ultimatum. It was a statement for the record, which Hull knew could never be the basis for continued negotiations. When Nomura and Kurusu protested the harsh terms Hull showed no intention to negotiate. To Kurusu's question whether the United States was interested in a modus vivendi, the secretary replied simply that he had done his best in the way of exploration. Lamely placing the blame on the agitated state of public opinion, Hull gave the Japanese diplomats no hope. In fact, Hull placed so little importance on the November 26 statement that when the British ambassador came by the next day Hull called it simply something general and could not lay his hands on a copy to show him.

In respect to war or peace, Hull's decision on November 26 made no difference. The bureaucracy had so restricted the proposed modus vivendi that it stood no chance of being accepted in Tokyo. What the November 26 note illustrates is that after nearly four years and five months of trying to bring peace to the Pacific, Hull had given up. As he told Stimson the next day, "I have washed my hands of it and it is now in the hands of you and Knox—the Army and the Navy."

To understand why Hull finally gave up and accepted war with Japan we must examine the mood within the Washington foreign policy establishment throughout November, and Hull's reaction to the events of November 23–25 in particular.

A strong sense of fatalism surrounded everything Hull did in November. At a cabinet meeting early that month the talk was of war with Japan and rallying public opinion, not avoiding war. State Department officials had given up any hope of a settlement with Japan and talked only of buying some time. The only hope of postponing war was the proposed modus vivendi. On November 22, Hull called in the representatives of Britain, China, Australia, and the Netherlands. For two and a half hours he explained how he hoped to strengthen the hands of the moderates in Japan by presenting the now much-modified White/FE proposal. But to do that he needed time, and that meant offering Japan a modus vivendi, a three-month agreement by which Japan would withdraw its fifty thousand troops from southern Indochina and limit its troops in northern Indochina to twenty-five thousand. In return, Japan would receive some modest amounts of oil. Hull did not think there was more than one chance in three that the Japanese would accept the American proposal, but if they did it would postpone war and give the American military the time it desperately needed.

While the diplomats consulted their governments, Hull learned that time had almost run out. MAGIC revealed that Japan had set November 29 as the absolute deadline: "After that things are automatically going to happen." Roosevelt warned: "We must all be prepared for real trouble, possibly soon." So it was under the press of time that Hull called back the British, Australian, Dutch, and Chinese representatives on November 25 to see what their governments thought of his proposal. The Chinese ambassador objected to Japan leaving twenty-five thousand troops in Indochina under the proposed agreement. Of the Western powers, only the Dutch representative had received instructions from his government. Hull was bitterly disappointed. He lectured those present on the value of postponing a war. Although Asia was more important to their countries than to the United States, he complained, they expected his government to take the lead in militarily defending the entire area. Sounding like a hurt child, Hull reported: "I was not sure that I would present it to the Japanese Ambassador without knowing anything about the views and attitude of their Governments. The meeting broke up in this fashion."

The next day the news was no better. The British responded with an ambiguous statement that offered to support the United States whatever it decided to do yet raised some questions about the wisdom of leaving Japanese troops in Indochina. Most disappointing was the Chinese government, which strongly objected to the modus vivendi and warned that should it be imposed, there could be dire consequences in China. . . .

Given a half-century of American refusal to defend China from Japanese incursion, it is ironic that it was the issue of China that in the final hours of negotiations stood as an insurmountable obstacle between Japan and the United States. To understand why, we must not look to the sanctity of treaties or the burden of the clean record that had characterized American relations with China for decades. China loomed large in Hull's thinking during the final days of peace because the Roosevelt administration had put itself in a position where its diplomatic goals exceeded its military means, thus forcing it to depend too much upon China.

We might trace the origins of this problem to the Five Power Treaty of 1922, to the absence of naval building during the 1930s, to the fall of France and the British retreat from Asia in 1940, or to the more recent gap between a war plan that stressed the Atlantic and Europe and foreign policy that defined the East Indies and Singapore as vital. Whatever the reasons, by 1941 the United States needed China as much as China needed the United States, or more. Only if China continued to engage a million Japanese troops could American and British forces in the South Seas hope to contain the Imperial Japanese army and navy. It was the reality of American weakness that placed Hull in such a difficult position. He was not thinking about sanctity of treaties when, on November 26, he made a decision that, in effect, chose war with Japan rather than the collapse of China.

In retrospect, Hull probably made the wrong decision on November 26. China was not going to collapse if Hull offered the modus vivendi to Japan. Presidential assurances and shipment of military supplies would have kept up Chinese morale and left open a chance, a slim chance, to avoid war. Hull's decision was the result of emotional, physical, and mental exhaustion. In human terms it was understandable. But to dwell on it is to give it a significance it does not deserve. By November 26, Cordell Hull was a man in the middle of an ocean wondering what straw he should grasp. The important question is how he got there.

The Japanese-American conflict grew out of two mutually exclusive views of world order. Japan, seeing itself as a poor nation surrounded by richer and more powerful nations, sought to gain security through the establishment of a New Order. By dominating the political and economic life of East Asia, then Greater East Asia, and ultimately Greater East Asia and the South Seas, Japanese leaders hoped to assure safe access to the markets and raw materials vital to Japan's role as a great nation. American leaders could agree that a secure source of raw materials and markets was essential for all nations, but they flatly rejected Japan's autarchic approach. Americans favored the liberal commercial world order, characterized by free trade and free investment. If Germany succeeded in establishing its autarchic order over Europe and Japan over Asia, the world would be set back 750 years, or so Roosevelt and Hull believed. The United States would never accept Japan's New Order in Greater East Asia and the South Seas. It was learning to live with Japan in China, but expansion farther south was intolerable.

Since each nation equated its own system with national survival it is tempting to conclude that this was a conflict not susceptible to peaceful resolution and that it could be resolved only on the field of battle. Yet neither side wanted to fight the other. Japanese leaders looked upon the massive economic and military resources of the United States and concluded that almost anything would be better than a war with such a great power. American leaders, while not respecting the Japanese, saw America's real interests in Europe and wished to avoid war in Asia. This mutual desire for peace meant an opportunity for diplomacy.

The purpose of diplomacy is to find a way for nations with conflicting interests to resolve their differences other than on the battlefield, and if not to resolve those differences at least to learn to coexist with them. By this criterion, American foreign policy managers failed. During a period of more than four years they were unable to guide either American or Japanese policy in a direction that would avoid war.

Where did American leaders go wrong? Or phrased more discreetly, how might they have acted differently?

To begin with Cordell Hull and his staff approached Japan with strongly held preconceptions. They could not see Japan, they could not understand what Japan was saying, they could not believe that any Japanese leader was both sincere and capable of delivering on promises. This negative view of Japan and the Japanese led Hull and company to make many tactical errors. When, as early as 1938, Grew warned that the Japanese people would never turn on the military and that sanctions would only unite the nation, Washington ignored his advice. When Grew and Foreign Minister Nomura negotiated the first tentative steps toward an understanding in December 1939, Hull turned a cold shoulder. When Ballantine noted in the summer of 1941 that Japan had legitimate complaints about its treatment at the hands of the Western powers, his advice caused not even a ripple within State. It fell to someone from the Treasury Department, Harry Dexter White, to draft a plan that recognized Japan's legitimate economic needs and proposed to meet them. And when the State Department was finished with that proposal it offered Japan nothing and demanded much.

Though Hull turned a deaf ear to the voices of conciliation in the administration, he also refused to heed those who called for confrontation. As Ickes, Maxwell, Stimson, Knox, Morgenthau, Leahy, Davis, and even the president discovered, when Hull set his mind to something he was a formidable opponent. Though he won the vast majority of his battles with the hawks of the Roosevelt administration, neither Hull nor the president managed to maintain control over the constantly growing and increasingly complex foreign policy bureaucracy. By losing control over the execution of policy, they lost control over the direction the nation moved.

None of the bureaucratic sleights of hand that proliferated during 1940 and 1941 was critical. But the cumulative effect of these little actions moved the United States further toward economic sanctions than Hull or Roosevelt intended. As a result, Japan felt increasingly encircled, and responded by expanding into the resource-rich areas of Southeast Asia. When it moved into southern Indochina in July 1941, and Dean Acheson transformed Roosevelt's financial freeze into sweeping economic sanctions, the damage to American foreign policy was irreparable. This is not to say that without Acheson's machinations there would have been no war. But in the summer of 1941 time was the critical factor. If a confrontation with Japan could have been put off to the spring of 1942 it might have been avoided indefinitely, because by then American military power would have been much greater and German victory in Europe less certain. Acheson and the others who moved the nation toward economic warfare denied the United States that time.

As the two nations inched their way along the road to Pearl Harbor, Hull committed his most serious tactical error. He tried to establish a lasting peace with Japan through the negotiation of a comprehensive agreement. To the secretary, peace was not merely the absence of war but the maintenance of fair, decent, and equal relations between nations. But to achieve a diplomatic agreement that would bring about a change of that magnitude was beyond Hull's grasp. In 1938 and 1939 that did not seem to make much difference because the United States could afford to wait for Japan to see the futility of its chosen path of conquest. Hull and Roosevelt saw a war coming in Europe, but they did not foresee the collapse of France with the resulting disruption of the world balance of power. That event, more than any other, out-moded the policy of waiting for Japan to undergo a regeneration of spirit before reaching an agreement. That was the time when Hull should have set aside his search for a comprehensive peace and begun working on a limited understanding, something to avoid war. If he could not bring himself to do this in June 1940, then he should have done so in October, after Japan moved closer to the Axis and into Indochina. An even better opportunity to shift the focus came with the Hull-Nomura talks in the spring of 1941. Or if Hull was waiting for a position of strength to seek a compromise, he had it in August when the freeze was imposed and the talks reopened. In September 1941, when Hull learned that the freeze had cut off Japan's access to oil, the secretary had all the incentive he needed to change his diplomatic objective.

Through all these events Hull tenaciously held to his goal of a sweeping agreement with Japan on fundamentals. This policy was not inspired by a slavish devotion to the sanctity of treaties or a sentimental attachment to China—it was the result of Hull's belief that anything less would be a futile appeasement of Japan. The fact that it was pragmatic, however, did not make it wise.

If the secretary had so little faith in temporary agreements as to shun becoming involved in them, then Roosevelt should have intervened to change the focus of Japanese-American talks. But the president never did so, and permitted his secretary of state to lead the nation along a diplomatic path that could only end in tragedy.

Roosevelt's failure of leadership might be explained by any of a number of factors. He too was deeply suspicious of Japanese intentions. He was also preoccupied with the pressing matters of Europe and did not have the time to devote to Asian affairs. Moreover, to take charge of the negotiations with Japan meant taking them away from

Hull, who jealously guarded his territory. Beyond all these reasons, the problem of Japanese-American relations was clearly a diplomatic question, and Roosevelt was not comfortable with the intricacies of diplomacy. He enjoyed meeting with Churchill and would have enjoyed meeting with Konoye. He liked to think in terms of a quarantine, naval blockades, and simple economic sanctions. The stuff of which the negotiations with Japan were made did not suit him.

A variety of factors brought Cordell Hull to that point on the morning of November 26, 1941 when he gave up on diplomacy and accepted war. The American faith in the liberal commercial world order and Japan's attempt to establish a New Order in Asia at the point of a gun assured Japanese-American tension. In responding to this tension, the Roosevelt administration failed to employ diplomatic efforts that were consistent with American national interest. The rigidly anti-Japanese Washington mind-set and Cordell Hull's fixation with a comprehensive settlement made diplomacy ineffectual. Even had Hull and Roosevelt been more sensitive to Japan's concerns and more flexible in their diplomatic negotiations, they still faced the problem of a bureaucracy that was out of control. The president and the secretary of state had a policy, but so did Morgenthau, Ickes, Stimson, Knox, Acheson, Grew, Welles, Hornbeck, Maxwell, Yost, Green, Leahy, Stark, and the rest. As a result, the course Roosevelt and Hull charted was not the one that the nation followed. Perhaps stronger control over the bureaucracy would have made no difference, but the chaos that characterized the execution of American policy left no chance for success.

☆ 9 ☆

America
and the Cold War

CONTAINMENT OR COUNTERREVOLUTION?

After World War II the American people faced a succession of external and internal challenges for which they had few historical precedents. By 1945 the United States had emerged as the strongest nation on earth. Having triumphed over the forces of Nazi and fascist totalitarianism American citizens looked forward with confidence and optimism to the promise of a bright future. Such hopes and expectations were soon dashed. Within two years after the fighting ended the United States found itself confronting the Soviet Union, its former ally. Instead of peace the American people were plunged headlong into an era of "Cold War"—a series of crises that required economic and military mobilization even in the absence of actual hostilities.

Two developments during the war established the context within which the Cold War would be waged. One was the toppling of five major nations from the ranks of first-rate powers. America's enemies—Germany, Japan, and Italy—were defeated. Her friends—Britain and France—spent so much blood and treasure that they found it impossible to regain their prewar military and economic importance. This situation left only two superpowers—the United States and the Soviet Union. The second development was the technological revolution in warfare. With the exploding of the atomic bomb in 1945, and the capability of destroying mankind, diplomacy entered upon a new age. These two considerations led one historian to liken the relations between the United States and Russia to a scorpion and tarantula together in a bottle, each tragically committed to trying to outdo the other.[1]

---

[1]Louis Halle, *The Cold War as History* (New York, 1967), p. xiii.

Most historians, but by no means all, agreed that World War II created the setting for the Soviet-American confrontation. Although ideological differences existed between the two great powers prior to that time the war produced suspicion, distrust, and a gap in understanding that became increasingly difficult to bridge. The Cold War, most scholars and laymen concluded, arose from two seemingly incompatible conceptions of the ideal shape of the postwar world order. The American point of view pictured the Soviet Union as a ruthless power, driven by its communist ideology, bent upon global revolution and domination, and headed by leaders like Stalin who embarked upon an aggressive policy of expansion with the ultimate aim of destroying the free world. From Russia's perspective, however, America represented the main threat to peace. The Soviet view was that the United States emerged from the war militantly committed to the idea of a capitalist world order. America, as an imperalist power, sought to encircle the Soviet Union with hostile capitalist countries, to isolate Russia from the rest of the world, and to destroy communist regimes wherever they existed. Thus the free world and communist camp each viewed the other side as being dedicated to its destruction.

American scholars disagreed, however, when they came to evaluate the causes of the Cold War and to pass judgment on the roles of the two adversaries. Since 1945 American historians, when inquiring into the origins of the Cold War, divided into three schools: the orthodox, or traditional school; the revisionists; and the realists. Although the arguments of each school changed somewhat with the passing of time and appearance of new developments, they established the framework of the important historiographical debate that took place.

The first to appear was the orthodox school, which came into being during the immediate postwar years. At the time most of the American people, and the vast majority of scholars, were inclined to accept the official explanation of events set forth by the Truman administration in justifying its foreign policy. According to the orthodox interpretation Soviet aggression and expansionist desires were primarily responsible for the coming of the Cold War.

The orthodox or traditional interpretation reflected closely the official view of the American and British governments at the time. Winston Churchill, speaking at Fulton, Missouri, in the spring of 1946, set forth the basic outline of this interpretation. An "iron curtain," said Churchill, had been lowered across Eastern Europe by the Soviets. No one knew for sure what secret plans for expansion were being hatched behind the iron curtain. The British leader viewed not only the Soviet Union, but communist ideology, communist parties, and "fifth column" activities as a growing peril to what he called "Christian civilization." President Truman in 1947 echoed similar sentiments when announcing his now-famous Truman Doctrine. Although the United

States had made every effort to bring about a peaceful world, he said, the Soviet Union had used "indirect aggression" in Eastern Europe, "extreme pressure" in the Middle East, and had intervened in the internal affairs of many countries through "Communist parties directed from Moscow." Because of the Truman Doctrine many scholars of the traditionalist school held that the Cold War had officially commenced in 1947.

The orthodox interpretation was presented in scholarly books and journals in the late 1940s and early 1950s by historians like Herbert Feis and policymakers such as George F. Kennan. These men, too, held that the Cold War had been brought about mainly because of Soviet actions. Motivated by the traditional desires for greater security, power, and larger spheres of influence, they said, the Soviet Union resorted to an expansionist foreign policy. Coupled with these age-old drives was the new ideological zeal of communism which made the Soviets ambitious to foment revolution and conquest in behalf of their cause. Scholars sometimes disagreed about the primary motivation of the Soviets; some favored the importance of ideology as an explanation, while others believed the main focus should be placed on Russia's traditional policy of imperialism and pursuit of national interest. But they all tended to agree that no matter what the motivation might be, Soviet objectives were expansionist in scope. The orthodox view also argued that the Soviet Union violated its agreements with the Western powers, including the Yalta accords as they concerned the political future of Eastern Europe and, to a lesser extent, the role of China in the postwar world.

America's foreign policy, according to the orthodox interpretation, was in marked contrast to that of the Soviet Union. The United States, at first, held high hopes for a peaceful postwar world. The actions of its leaders were predicated on the principles of collective security, and they looked to the newborn United Nations for the solution to any future conflicts. Faced with Soviet aggressive moves, however, America was reluctantly forced to change its views and foreign policy. To prevent the Soviet Union from spreading its influence over large parts of the world, the United States finally felt compelled to embark upon a policy of "containment." Without this containment policy, argued many, the Soviet Union would probably have become the master of all Europe—instead of dominating only Eastern Europe.

Many of the arguments of the orthodox position were set forth in an article published by George F. Kennan under a pseudonym, "Mr. X," in 1947. Kennan, an American diplomat, provided many of the insights upon which the foreign policy of the Truman administration was based. In his piece Kennan suggested, among other things, an American containment policy to check Russia's expansionist tendencies.

Kennan subsequently claimed, however, that he was not thinking primarily in terms of containment along military lines.[2]

The orthodox version, despite challenges, remains the dominant school of thought on the origins of the Cold War. Many of its proponents, however, differ widely in their interpretations. They all place differing emphases upon such crucial matters as the role of ideology, the inevitability of the conflict, the presumed unintentional provocation of the West, and the like. Although it may seem arbitrary to lump them together, they may be identified as "orthodox" because they generally found that responsibility for the Cold War rested to a major degree with the Soviet Union.[3] Even this categorization remains tenuous, however, because men like Kennan and Feis have changed their minds and shifted their views with the passage of time. Moreover, there are significant differences even among orthodox historians. John Lewis Gaddis, for example, insisted that neither the Soviet Union nor the United States was solely responsible for the Cold War. Yet he also noted that major responsibility rested with Stalin, who had greater opportunity to adjust to American foreign policy than Truman to Soviet policy.[4]

The roots of the revisionist interpretation, like that of the orthodox thesis, also originated in the statements from public figures as well as scholars. From the outset of the Cold War the official explanation of events had not gone unchallenged. Henry Wallace, former vice-president, had raised a powerful voice which questioned the soundness of President Truman's analysis of the international situation during the immediate postwar years. Running as a presidential candidate of a minority party in 1948 Wallace sought to be more sympathetic toward the Russians. But his relatively poor showing revealed how little public support there was for this position.

Walter Lippmann, one of the nation's leading intellectuals and a scholarly journalist, likewise refused to place the blame for international tensions exclusively on the Soviet Union. It was Lippmann who popularized the term "Cold War" by using it in the title of a book he

---

[2][George F. Kennan], "The Sources of Soviet Conduct," *Foreign Affairs* 25 (July 1947): 566–582.

[3]For a few examples of the orthodox interpretation see Herbert Feis's three books, *The Road to Pearl Harbor* (Princeton, 1950), *The China Tangle* (Princeton, 1953), and *Roosevelt-Churchill-Stalin* (Princeton, 1957); William H. McNeill, *America, Britain, and Russia: Their Cooperation and Conflict, 1941–1946* (London, 1953); Norman Graebner, *Cold War Diplomacy:American Foreign Policy 1945–1960* (Princeton, 1962); and André Fontaine, *History of the Cold War from the October Revolution to the Korean War, 1917–1950*, 2 vols. (New York, 1968).

[4]John Lewis Gaddis, *The United States and the Origins of the Cold War. 1941–1947* (New York, 1972). See also George G. Herring, Jr., *Aid to Russia, 1941–1946: Strategy, Diplomacy, the Origins of the Cold War* (New York, 1973).

published in 1947.[5] In his work he argued that America's statesmen expended their energies assaulting Russia's vital interests in Eastern Europe. By doing so they had furnished the Soviet Union with the reasons for rationalizing an iron rule behind the iron curtain. They also gave the Russians grounds to suspect what the Soviets had been conditioned to believe: that a capitalist coalition was being organized to destroy them. As a result of Lippmann's writings, in part, revisionist-minded historians began with one underlying assumption contrary to that of the orthodox interpretation: they were skeptical about accepting the claim that the Soviet Union was primarily or solely responsible for precipitating the Cold War.

Over the years the revisionist approach to the origins of the Cold War gradually came to represent not merely a challenge but an antithetical position to the orthodox thesis. Many revisionists came to the conclusion that the United States and its policies—rather than Russia and communism—had brought about the Cold War. The conflict had been precipitated by Western—and especially American—moves which threatened the Soviets and compelled them to react defensively. This the Russians had done by resorting to strict control over those areas that had fallen under their influence during World War II.

It is difficult to generalize about the revisionists because of the diversity of approaches in this school of scholars. Each historian stressed different aspects of the Cold War, offered different arguments, and professed to see different motives behind the acts of the principal protagonists. Most revisionists, nevertheless, tended to agree that Russia was weak, not strong, after 1945 because of the ravages of war. Beginning with this premise they then argued that the Soviet Union was neither willing nor able to pursue an aggressive policy after the war ended. Indeed, some revisionists maintained that while the Russians feared America's technological superiority and military power, they still viewed the United States as the main potential source of assistance to enable them to recover from the disastrous effects of the war. Other revisionists stressed that under Stalin the Soviet Union consistently pursued only cautious, defensive, and limited goals of foreign policy despite the rhetoric of ideological bravado. Thus the worldwide policy of aggression which the traditionalists believed they had detected in Russia's behavior seemed to the revisionists to be entirely out of character and beyond the means of the Soviet leaders.

During the 1950s and 1960s many differing shades of revisionism appeared among American historians. Some scholars approached the problem by attempting to evaluate the degree to which the United

---

[5]Walter Lippmann, *The Cold War* (New York, 1947). Lippmann's book was a collection of newspaper articles written to counter Kennan's interpretation of the motivation behind Soviet policy.

States had been responsible for precipitating the Cold War. In tackling this issue these writers sought to explain and justify Soviet actions since the war. Others analyzed American objectives in such a way as to show that these goals had been the basis for the postwar split. Some radical revisionists, especially those associated with the New Left, went even further: they viewed the United States as having been an aggressive power in the world not only during World War II, but throughout the entire twentieth century.

When revisionist-minded historians came to the matter of America's motivation they were likewise in disagreement and offered different explanations. Some claimed that the Western powers in general, and the Truman administration in particular, tried to deny the Soviet Union its due in the matter of the Yalta agreements: the West, they said, had sought to reinterpret the meaning of these accords, and refused to recognize what Roosevelt and Churchill had been compelled by circumstances to concede at Yalta. Other historians argued that the United States—imbued with the missionary zeal of a latent "manifest destiny"—had hoped to reshape the world to suit its exaggerated attachment to the democratic principles of representative government. Still other scholars stressed the theme of economic expansion—postulating that America's postwar foreign policy represented a drive to capture world markets and to establish this country's economic and political influence all over the globe. Certain historians concluded that the United States used its early monopoly of nuclear weapons and economic strength to browbeat other nation-states and to force them to submit to Washington's leadership. As proof of this position they pointed out that the Truman administration had refused major economic assistance to the Soviet Union, and that the Marshall Plan had been designed in such a way as to preclude Soviet participation in it.

Despite the complexities with the revisionist school it is possible to distinguish two main groups in this category—the moderate revisionists and those associated with the New Left, who were more extreme. Although the revisionist scholars disagreed about the degree of responsibility they assigned to the United States in bringing on the Cold War, they all held America, in large part, accountable for the conflict because of her aggressive and menacing policy toward Russia.

One example of the moderate revisionist position was Denna F. Fleming's two-volume study entitled *The Cold War and its Origins 1917–1960*, published in 1961. Fleming focused upon President Truman as the crucial figure in the coming of the Cold War. Within weeks after Roosevelt died, Fleming wrote, Truman dramatically reversed the course of America's foreign policy. Roosevelt had been dedicated to a Wilsonian "internationalism," and, recognizing that the Soviet Union would be the key to any new league of nations in the postwar period, had done his utmost to maintain good relations with Russia. But Truman adopted a tough policy toward the Russians as soon as he assumed the presidency. In April 1945 he ordered the Soviets to change their policy in Poland or else America would withdraw certain promised economic aid. Contrary to the orthodox version, which generally dated the beginning of the Cold War in 1947 with the Truman doctrine, Fleming believed it began in 1945.

Fleming's thesis that America provoked the Cold War was amplified by the picture he presented of the postwar era. The United States was invariably portrayed as taking the initiative in relations between the two powers. Russia, on the other hand, was usually depicted as reacting to events in a defensive way. Fleming's interpretation differed greatly from the orthodox version which had pictured the Soviets as the ruthless aggressor, but his findings were suspect because they were not based on solid documentation.[6]

Writing in the same revisionist tradition was Gar Alperovitz. In *Atomic Diplomacy: Hiroshima and Potsdam*, published in the mid-1960s, Alperovitz held that President Truman had helped to start the Cold War in 1945 by dropping the atomic bomb. Alperovitz added a new viewpoint to the debate by arguing that Truman resorted to "atomic diplomacy." With the United States possessing a monopoly of atomic weapons at the time Truman adopted a hard line toward the Soviets—one which was aimed at forcing Soviet Russia's acquiescence in America's postwar plans. In short, Truman fell back upon the modern equivalent of saber-rattling to play power politics and to drive Russia out of East Europe by a show of force.

Like most of the moderate revisionists, however, Alperovitz did not heap all the blame for beginning the Cold War on the United States. The Russians by their actions also helped to poison the postwar atmosphere, he said. "The cold war cannot be understood simply as an American response to a Soviet challenge," he wrote, "but rather as an insidious interaction of mutual suspicions, blame for which must be shared by all." Nevertheless the thrust of Alperovitz's work clearly placed responsibility for the beginnings of the Cold War on American shoulders.[7]

Most New Left historians were bitter in their condemnation of the orthodox interpretation. In large part this was so because of their own ideological commitments; they were highly critical about the very nature of American society as a whole, and hence unsympathetic with the aims of the United States abroad. Moreover, where the more moderate revisionists tended to picture Roosevelt or Truman as men of unlimited vision who fumbled their way to disaster in the postwar

---

[6]Denna F. Fleming, *The Cold War and Its Origins, 1917–1960*, 2 vols. (New York, 1961).

[7]Gar Alperovitz, *Atomic Diplomacy: Hiroshima and Potsdam* (New York, 1965).

period, some New Left scholars were inclined to view developments against a much broader background. They wrote within a context that stretched far beyond the immediate postwar years: such New Left scholars held that America's foreign policy in the 1940s, 1950s, and 1960s was simply an extension of a trend that had been under way since the Spanish-American War at the turn of the century.

The most significant assault on the orthodox position came from William Appleman Williams in his books *The Tragedy of American Diplomacy* and *The Contours of American History*, published in the late 1950s and 1960s. Although Williams never regarded himself as a member of the New Left, his writings were seized upon and extended by other radical historians. What Williams did was to provide a provocative hypothesis to explain America's diplomacy throughout our entire history. America's foreign policy was expansionist from our very beginnings, he declared. Writing from a neo-Beardian point of view Williams went all the way back to the 1760s. He showed that even before gaining its independence America had adopted a course to achieve economic self-sufficiency within the British Empire by applying English mercantilist principles in the New World environment. Once independence had been won the United States was committed to the idea of an independent American empire to enable the growing new nation to have markets for its products. Until the 1890s that empire lay mostly to the west on the American continent, but once the frontier was gone the search for markets led to overseas expansion. Despite the controversy between imperialists and anti-imperialists around the turn of the century, both groups agreed that economic expansion overseas was vital to the nation's prosperity and future. The debate was over means rather than ends. Imperialists felt that physical acquisition of traditional colonies was necessary; anti-imperialists, on the other hand, believed that America's economic expansion throughout the world could be achieved without the expense of maintaining a colonial empire.

The Open Door policy, according to Williams, resolved the dilemma and ultimately became the basis for America's future foreign policy. America's Open Door policy represented an effort to achieve all the advantages of economic expansion without the disadvantages of maintaining a colonial empire. It called for an open door for trade with all foreign countries on a most-favored-nation principle—a principle that had a long tradition in American diplomacy stretching back to 1776. Although formulated originally to apply to China the policy was expanded geographically to cover the entire globe and economically to include American investments as well as trade.[8]

---

[8]William A. Williams, *The Tragedy of American Diplomacy* (2d ed.; New York, 1962) and *The Contours of American History* (Cleveland, 1961).

Williams, operating from this premise, saw the Cold War within a different context than the orthodox school of historians. To him the postwar period represented nothing more than the extension of the Open Door policy as America, seeking markets for its goods and money, hoped to penetrate into Eastern Europe and other parts of the globe. Thus America was primarily responsible for the Cold War, for in seeking to extend economic influence it took whatever steps were necessary to maintain or put into power governments that would do business with the United States. Counterrevolution to make the world safe for American capitalism, not containment, was the major motive behind the postwar policies of the United States.[9]

One of Williams's followers, Walter LaFeber (who in 1963 had published an important study of the origins of American expansionism in the late nineteenth century), developed and expanded this view in a monograph that appeared in 1967. LaFeber was critical of both the United States and the Soviet Union for failing to maintain peace. Focusing upon the internal reasons behind the formulation of foreign policy in the two countries, he concluded that domestic developments played a large part in determining those foreign policies that finally emerged. In the United States domestic events—presidential campaigns, economic recessions, the era of repression identified with Senator Joseph McCarthy of Wisconsin, and the struggle for power by various factions within the government—contributed as much to the making of America's foreign policy as did external events. Within Russia itself the same was true: the machinations of Stalin and Khrushchev, problems with the Soviet economy, and power struggles within the communist party laid the basis for most foreign policy changes. In terms of economic penetration LaFeber found that the United States and the Soviet Union showed equal interest in exploiting foreign markets wherever possible. Both nations, he concluded, created their postwar policies with an eye to maintaining freedom of action in those areas they considered vital to their economic and strategic interests.

Conflicting aims arising from domestic concerns, LaFeber said, led to a continuing rivalry between the two giant powers as they confronted one another over two decades in many parts of the globe. America's foreign policy was based on the assumption that the nations's political, economic, and psychological needs at home dictated those commitments undertaken abroad. During the first phase of the struggle—1945 to 1953—those commitments were Europe-oriented, and even the Korean War was fought, in part, to preserve America's image as the main bulwark in the West against the communist monolith. But after the mid-1950s both America and Russia shifted their

---

[9]Christopher Lasch, "The Cold War, Revisited and Re-Visioned," *New York Times*, January 14, 1968.

focus from Europe to the newly emerging nations all over the world, and the Cold War entered its second phase. The Vietnam War, according to LaFeber, represented a "failure" in America's foreign policy because it sought to answer the political and economic global changes posed by the newly emerging nations with military solutions. There was continuity in America's policy, concluded LaFeber, because the American people had decided to accept the responsibility of answering challenges of such a global nature as far back as 1947 with the Truman Doctrine. In a similar vein Lloyd C. Gardner, a student of Williams's at the University of Wisconsin, emphasized the commitment of American leaders to a liberal world order based on the Open Door policy. Haunted by fears of depression these leaders strove to create a world economy conducive to American capitalism and prosperity. "Responsibility for the *way* in which the Cold War developed, at least," Gardner concluded, "belongs more to the United States."[10]

Gardner's work in particular influenced a number of revisionist and New Left scholars. Athan Theoharis, for example, accepted Gardner's contention that the United States was largely responsible for the way in which the Cold War developed. Theoharis insisted that a wide variety of options were available to American policymakers in 1945; nothing compelled the adoption of policies that led to the Cold War. During World War II, for example, Roosevelt followed a diplomatic policy that was strikingly vacillating and ambivalent. At Yalta, on the other hand, he pursued a conciliatory path based upon the acceptance of Soviet postwar influence and the need to arrive at an accommodation that would avert disharmony and conflict. His death, however, altered the diplomatic setting by introducing an element of uncertainty. More importantly it brought Harry S. Truman to the White House, an individual who was more rigidly anti-Soviet. Truman's accession to the presidency, according to Theoharis, provided the opening wedge for policy advisers whose recommendations were ignored at Yalta. The result was that the opportunities for détente provided at Yalta were effectively subverted under Truman, and the stage was set for years of conflict and confrontation.[11]

While neither Williams, LaFeber, nor Gardner necessarily included themselves as members of the New Left, it was clear that their respective studies could easily serve as a point of departure for radical scholars. In 1968 Gabriel Kolko, whose earlier study of the origins of political capitalism from 1900 to 1917 had heralded the advent of the

---

[10]Walter LaFeber, *America, Russia, and the Cold War, 1945–1966* (New York, 1967), and Lloyd C. Gardner, *Architects of Illusion: Men and Ideas in American Foreign Policy, 1941–1949* (Chicago, 1970). See also Thomas G. Paterson, *Soviet-American Confrontation: Postwar Reconstruction and the Origins of the Cold War* (Baltimore, 1973).

[11]Athan Theoharis, "Roosevelt and Truman on Yalta: The Origins of the Cold War," *Political Science Quarterly* 87 (June 1972):210–241.

New Left school of historiography, brought out a detailed study of the origins of the Cold War that picked up where Williams and LaFeber had left off. Kolko dealt with America's foreign policy within a much narrower chronological framework; he covered only the years from 1943 to 1945. But Kolko felt that the policies forged in that crucial period were the key to the long-range plans of the United States in the postwar era. His *The Politics of War* represented an attempt to document in detail and to extend the general themes introduced by Williams. Kolko advanced the thesis that the United States had acted not only to win the war in these two years, but to erect the structure for peacetime politics in the postwar world. To Kolko America's objectives were twofold: to use its military power to defeat the enemy, and to employ its political and economic power to gain leverage for extending America's influence throughout the world. Thus Kolko, like Williams, viewed the United States as a counterrevolutionary force bent on restoring the old order in Europe and making the world safe for American capitalism.[12]

Kolko's assumptions regarding America's postwar policies were typical of many of the New Left scholars. He assumed, first of all, that the United States, not Russia, represented the greatest threat to international stability; that America was mainly responsible for bringing on the Cold War. Second, that the United States was dedicated to worldwide counterrevolution: to a policy of employing its military and economic power to extend its influence throughout the world because American capitalism was dependent upon ever-expanding foreign markets for survival. And third, that the origins of the Cold War lay not solely within World War II but stretched back to World War I and beyond.

Significantly the revisionist view of Cold War diplomacy—both moderate and extremist—developed mainly in the 1960s. This decade was a period of deepening disillusionment among American intellectuals over the nation's foreign policy. Disenchanted by America's intervention in Cuba and Santo Domingo and the escalating involvement in Vietnam, many intellectuals had begun to question whether the United States had not taken too seriously the responsibilities of world leadership; it had involved itself unnecessarily in the internal affairs of other nations where it had no business. Moreover they feared that this country was so conditioned to fighting totalitarianism that American leaders tended to see enemies where none existed. It is not too much to suggest that this reaction among intellectuals helped to shape

---

[12]Gabriel Kolko, *The Politics of War: The World and United States Foreign Policy, 1943–1945* (New York, 1968). See also Joyce and Gabriel Kolko, *The Limits of Power: The World and United States Foreign Policy, 1945–1954* (New York, 1972).

the unsympathetic view that the revisionists had taken toward America's foreign policy.

To some scholars neither the orthodox nor the revisionist explanations were adequate. Joseph R. Starobin, a former communist who broke with the American Communist Party in the 1950s, insisted that historians had ignored a key element in the origins of the Cold War, namely, the contradictions within the communist movement itself. During and after World War II, the Soviet Union attempted to overcome the diversity within a system of states and parties in which earlier political and ideological premises had become obsolete. For Stalin, therefore, the Cold War was a struggle involving Russia's internal objectives and the subordination of an international movement. Viewed in this light the struggle between the Soviet Union and the United States was brought about by an internal crisis within the former. Starobin's article is presented as the first selection in this chapter.

If the orthodox and revisionist interpretations represented antithetical views about the origins of the Cold War the realist school has become, in some ways, a middle-of-the-road position. The realists, unlike the revisionists who followed them, were less likely to dismiss containment because it represented in their eyes a necessary response to Soviet expansionism. On the other hand they were critical of the orthodox scholars because of the excessive moralism and legalism in the traditional interpretation. The realists were more prone to view foreign relations in terms of *realpolitik* from which the school derived its name, and to place more emphasis upon power politics and conflicting national interests. Historians of the realist school were less concerned with determining the degree of moral responsibility for the Cold War and focused their attention instead on the pragmatic political problems facing the policymakers.

Like the other two schools of scholars the realists could trace their origins back to the late 1940s and early 1950s. Their writings began as a response, in part, to the strong criticisms of Roosevelt's role in the developing East-West impasse. These criticisms held that America's supposed weakness in the postwar period had resulted either from Roosevelt's misunderstanding of Soviet intentions or from his failure to foresee the incompatibility of Soviet and American goals. In the eyes of his critics Roosevelt was responsible for the subsequent subjugation of Eastern Europe. But the realists argued that Roosevelt, in fact, was faced with a *fait accompli* in Eastern Europe with powerful Russian armies occupying that area, and that the diplomatic options open to him were severely limited as a result.

Generally speaking the realists held that the blame for the Cold War belonged either to both sides or, more accurately, to neither. Indeed, neither the United States nor the Soviet Union had wanted to precipitate a conflict. Both had hoped that cooperation among the allies would continue—but on their own terms, of course. Each country had sought limited objectives but had expected the other to accept them as such. To be specific the Soviet Union was motivated by fear and acted in the interests of its security rather than out of any expansionist ambitions. However, whenever one side made a move in pursuit of its limited objectives the other side perceived the act as a threat to its existence and, in reacting accordingly, triggered a countermeasure which led to increasing escalation. As a result small and otherwise manageable foreign crises had led inevitably to a widening conflict, which gradually assumed global proportions. In short, the realists found that both sides in pursuing their interests had sought limited goals, but the spiraling effect of such measures had inadvertently precipitated the Cold War.

The realist school tended also to view the Cold War as a traditional power conflict rather than a clash of ideologies. To many of these historians the Cold War was comparable to some of the previous struggles that had taken place to prevent a single power from dominating Europe's east-central regions. Other scholars saw the conflict within the context of the age-old battle over the European balance of power.

When viewing the situation in postwar Europe members of the realist school took a hard look at political realities rather than indulging in speculations about diplomatic possibilities. While stressing Soviet determination to create in Eastern Europe satellite states that would enhance Russia's security, the realists also emphasized how vulnerable the countries in that part of Europe were to outside pressures because their own social, political, and economic systems had proven incapable of solving the problems of their people. These societies were ripe for revolution, the realists concluded, and an easy prey to the indigenous communist movements that existed and were Moscow-directed. The countries of Western Europe, they argued, were not susceptible to the same pressures; their social, economic, and political institutions, though weakened by the war, were still viable. Hence the realists concluded that the fear expressed in the orthodox interpretation—that Soviet influence might extend across Europe to reach the English Channel—was not only exaggerated but revealed a misunderstanding of the nature of the conflict.

The realists usually disagreed with the moderate revisionists who, like Alperovitz, claimed that the United States had used its monopoly of atomic weapons to force other nation-states into submission. On the other hand they accepted the thesis that in employing nuclear weapons against Japan the American government was motivated not only by a desire to conclude the Pacific war, but by the hope of doing so before the Soviet Union could enter that theater of war. America, they wrote, feared that Moscow might attempt to do in the Far East, what it appeared to be doing in Eastern Europe. Thus the presence of nuclear weapons in American hands was believed by the realists to have had a psychological effect upon both the atomic "haves" and "have-nots" during the initial phases of the Cold War.

The realists likewise disagreed with those revisionists associated with the New Left. They challenged the assumptions, ideological considerations, and political misconceptions upon which they felt the New Left historians based their arguments. In his review of Kolko's *The Politics of War*, Hans J. Morgenthau (one of the leading realist scholars) charged that Kolko was reflecting the mood of his own generation in attributing blame for the origins of the Cold War. That mood, Morgenthau noted,

> . . . *reacts negatively to the simple and simplistic equation, obligatory during the war and postwar periods, of American interests and policies with democratic virtue and wisdom, and those of their enemies with totalitarian folly and vice. As the orthodox historiography of the Second World War and the Cold War expressed and justified that ideological juxtaposition, so the revisionism of Professor Kolko expresses and justifies the new mood of ideological sobriety. However, given the moralism behind American political thinking regardless of its content, revisionism tends to be as moralistic in its critique of American foreign policy as orthodoxy is in defending it. While the moralistic approach remains, the moral labels have been reversed: what once was right is now wrong, and vice versa. Yet as historic truth may emerge from the dialectic of opposite extremes, qualified and tempered by charity and understanding, so sound political judgment requires both the recognition of extreme positions as inevitable and of their possible transcendence through a morality which is as alien to the moralism of our political folklore as Thucydidean justice is to the compensatory justice of opposing historical schools.*[13]

Morgenthau's own writings represented one of the best examples of the realist point of view. In them he was critical of what he called the legalistic-moralistic tradition which presumably prevented American statesmen from perceiving foreign policy in terms of national power and national interest in the past. His *In Defense of the National Interest: A Critical Examination of American Foreign Policy*, published in 1951, claimed that America's foreign policies since 1776 had been much too utopian in outlook. Only in the years since World War II, he suggested, had Americans become more realistic and formulated their policy on the basis of power politics and national interest.[14]

---

[13]Hans J. Morgenthau, "Historical Justice and the Cold War," *New York Review of Books*, July 10, 1969.

[14]Hans J. Morgenthau, *In Defense of the National Interest: A Critical Examination of American Foreign Policy* (New York, 1951). In this same regard it should be noted that George Kennan has come much closer to the realist school by arguing in his memoirs that the Truman administration pursued the wrong priorities in Europe by concentrating on a policy of *military* containment. George F. Kennan, *Memoirs, 1925–1950* (Boston, 1967).

Nevertheless American policymakers had misunderstood Soviet foreign policy; they failed to see the essential continuity in the expansionist objectives sought by the czars and later by the communists and focused instead on the new goals supposedly arising out of a revolutionary ideology. Thus Morgenthau criticized the orthodox interpretation by suggesting that the United States had contributed to the coming of the Cold War by its long-standing tendency to view its relationship to the rest of the world in rather unrealistic terms.

Another member of the realist school, Louis Halle, took a somewhat different approach. In *The Cold War as History*, published in the mid-1960s, Halle was more interested in stressing the tragic nature of the conflict. He suggested that neither side was really to blame for the Cold War. Misconceptions on both sides had led to the rise of ideological myths—myths which often had little relation to existing social realities. The West, led by the United States, was governed by the myth of a monolithic conspiracy among communists the world over to drive for global domination, initially under the leadership of the Soviet Union. The communists, on their part—Lenin and his associates in 1917–1918 and Mao Tse-tung a generation later in 1949–1950—were under the spell of another myth. Their world view pictured a globe divided between capitalist-imperialists on the one hand and exploited peasants and proletariat on the other. Each of these two communist leaders in his own time had believed that the historical moment had come when the oppressed lower classes were about to rise up in revolution, to overthrow their upper-class masters, and to establish a utopian society of the brotherhood of man along lines predicted by Karl Marx. It was the belief in such myths which drove the free world and the communist camp to embark upon what each side considered to be a struggle for survival.

Historical interpretations, of course, often run in cycles. Just as the revisionists challenged their more orthodox predecessors, so too did they come under scrutiny as the disillusionment of the 1960s and early 1970s gave way to new moods. Their implicit acceptance of American hegemony, moreover, seemed less tenable after the Arab-Israeli war of 1973, when an oil embargo and a subsequent quadrupling of oil prices demonstrated the vulnerability of the United States as well as its inability to use power without restraint. Some of the attacks on the revisionists were frontal in nature. In an analysis of the works of seven leading revisionist historians, Robert J. Maddox accused them of distorting facts to prove their thesis. "Stated briefly," he noted in his introduction, "the most striking characteristic of revisionist historiography has been the extent to which New Left authors have revised the evidence itself. And if the component parts of historical interpretations are demonstrably false, what can be said about the interpretations? They may yet be valid, but in the works examined they are often irrelevant to the data used to support them. Until this fact is recognized, there can be no realistic assessment of which elements of revisionism can justifiably be incorporated into new syntheses and which must be disregarded altogether." Similarly Robert W. Tucker insisted that New Left revisionism was based on a simple-minded explanatory mechanism that related all policy decisions to the imperatives of a capitalist economy. Charles S. Maier, on the other hand, was critical of virtually all scholars who had written on the origins of the Cold War. "Spokesmen for each side," he noted in 1970, "present the reader with a total explanatory system that accounts for all phenomena, eliminates the possibility of disproof, and thus transcends the usual process of historical reasoning. More than in most historical controversies, the questions about what happened are transformed into concealed debate about the nature of freedom and duress, exploitation and hegemony. As a result much Cold War historiography has become a confrontation manqué—debatable philosophy taught by dismaying example."[15]

More recently there has been a tendency for historians to avoid extremes. In a study of the decision to use the atomic bomb Martin Sherwin explicitly rejected Gar Alperovitz's contention that the use of the bomb was largely directed at influencing Soviet postwar policy. Sherwin insisted that the decision to use the bomb was laid earlier during Franklin Delano Roosevelt's presidency. Although he conceded that the development of the bomb was predicated on the belief that it would be a diplomatic asset in the postwar era, Sherwin nevertheless insisted that Truman used the bomb to win the war against Japan and not to stop the Soviet Union from entering the war in the Far East. On the other hand Truman hoped that Stalin would recognize American power and adopt a more conciliatory policy. Robert L. Messer, by way of contrast, characterized Truman's foreign policy as inconsistent and somewhat confused. The atomic bomb was used primarily to win the war in the Pacific. The weapon, however, had a subsidiary purpose: to pressure the Russians to make the Yalta agreement a reality. When this failed Truman switched tactics by proposing international control of nuclear weapons. The vagaries of American policy, Messer argued, led to a hard Soviet line, and eventually to the American policy of containment.[16]

Even scholars with a revisionist orientation have muted their ex-

---

[15]Robert J. Maddox, *The New Left and the Origins of the Cold War* (Princeton, 1973), pp. 10–11; Robert W. Tucker, *The Radical Left and American Foreign Policy* (Baltimore, 1971); Charles A. Maier, "Revisionism and the Interpretation of Cold War Origins," *Perspectives in American History* 4 (1970):311–347.

[16]Martin J. Sherwin, *A World Destroyed: The Atomic Bomb and the Grand Alliance* (New York 1975); Robert L. Messer, *The End of an Alliance: James F. Byrnes, Roosevelt, Truman, and the Origins of the Cold War* (Chapel Hill, 1982). See also Gregg F. Herken, *The Winning Weapon: The Atomic Bomb in the Cold War* (New York, 1981).

planations of the origins of the Cold War. In 1977 Daniel Yergin observed that wartime and postwar American diplomacy reflected two competing perceptions of the Soviet Union. The first, which he named the Riga axioms, was based on an image of the Soviet Union "as a world revolutionary state, denying the possibilities of coexistence, committed to unrelenting ideological warfare, powered by a messianic drive for world mastery." The second, the Yalta axioms, downplayed ideology and instead saw the Soviet Union as "behaving like a traditional Great Power within the international system, rather than trying to overthrow it." The first remained the dominant element in American foreign policy until the Nazi invasion of Russia in 1941, when Roosevelt decided to aid the beleaguered Soviets. During the war the Yalta axioms replaced the Riga axioms. At the end of the conflict the latter regained its predominance and it was within this framework that Truman formulated his hard-line policy toward the Soviet Union. Although conceding the brutality of Stalin's regime Yergin nevertheless insisted that the "U.S.S.R. behaved as a traditional Great Power, intent upon aggrandizing itself along the lines of historic Russian goals," and that American leaders who accepted the Riga axioms "misinterpreted both the range and degree of the Soviet challenge and the character of Soviet objectives and so downplayed the possibilities for diplomacy and accommodation."[17]

More recently the passion that was characteristic of the debate dealing with responsibility for inaugurating the Cold War has begun to diminish. Changes within the Soviet Union—the collapse of the Soviet empire, reduced role of the CPSU (Communist Party of the Soviet Union), and the appearance of more democratic tendencies—as well as changes in Eastern Europe, such as the destruction of the Berlin Wall, reunification of Germany, and revolutions in the former satellite states, have contributed to a fundamental re-evaluation of American diplomacy. As the contours of the international order change in as yet undetermined ways, the need to justify (or condemn) a militant and activist foreign policy by fixing blame for the advent of the Cold War may undoubtedly diminish still further. Moreover, the internal changes in the Soviet Union could conceivably open to scholars documents that would illuminate the archival sources of that nation's foreign policies after 1945.

Indeed, during the 1980s it was apparent that the heated exchanges and debates about the origins of the Cold War were already diminishing in intensity. In a paper published in 1983, John Lewis Gaddis suggested that the term "postrevisionism" most accurately described recent historiographical trends. Although susceptible of various inter-

---

[17]Daniel Yergin, *Shattered Peace: The Origins of the Cold War and the National Security State* (Boston, 1977), pp. 11–12.

pretations, postrevisionism rejected both the New Left and orthodox points of view, but incorporated elements from both and was based on examination of hitherto unpublished archival sources. American foreign policy employed economic means to serve political ends; policy did not embody a Leninist model in which internal contradictions forced capitalist societies to search for foreign markets. Moreover, American diplomacy was hardly as monolithic as either orthodox or New Left historians suggested. Nor was fear of the Soviet Union exclusively American; other nations shared these perceptions.[18] Gaddis's analysis of recent historiographical trends is presented as the second selection in this chapter.

The passions engendered by the Cold War, however, have not entirely disappeared. In a rereading of the historical literature dealing with American diplomacy since 1945, Edward Pessen charged that the indictment of the Soviet threat by American leaders "was either groundless, absurd, false, or known by those making the charges to be false." Questions that should have been asked about America's Cold War policy "went largely unasked." Indeed, Pessen, a historian of nineteenth-century American history never identified with the New Left, went beyond even the most extreme condemnations of American diplomacy. "The most rigid relativism," he concluded, "cannot deny that our government's flagrant lies, plans to incinerate much of the world, secret wars, and arbitrary assassinations are unworthy actions."[19]

In reviewing the various schools of thought, students should decide for themselves the fundamental questions raised regarding America's role in world affairs since the 1940s.[20] Did the Cold War commence with World War II, or did it stretch back in time to World War I? Did the move of the Soviet Union into Eastern Europe represent the

---

[18]See especially Terry H. Anderson, *The United States, Great Britain, and the Cold War, 1944–1947* (Columbus, Mo., 1981); Robert M. Hathaway, *Ambiguous Partnership: Britain and America, 1944–1947* (New York, 1981); Robin Edmonds, *Setting the Mould: The United States and Britain, 1945–1950* (New York, 1986); James L. Gormley, *The Collapse of the Grand Alliance, 1945–1948* (Baton Rouge, 1987); Herbert B. Ryan, *The Vision of Anglo-America: The US-UK Alliance and the Emerging Cold War. 1943–1946* (New York, 1987).

[19]Edward Pessen, "Appraising American Cold War Policy by Its Means of Implementation," *Reviews in American History* 18 (December 1990):453–465.

[20]See the fascinating debate in Lloyd C. Gardner, Arthur M. Schlesinger, Jr., and Hans J. Morgenthau, *The Origins of the Cold War* (Waltham, Mass., 1970), as well as the responses to John Lewis Gaddis's article "The Emerging Post-Revisionist Synthesis on the Origins of the Cold War" by Gardner, Lawrence S. Kaplan, Warren F. Kimball, and Bruce R. Kuniholm in *Diplomatic History* 7 (Summer 1983):191–204. In recent years historians have also begun to study the Cold War in Asia. See Robert J. McMahon, *Colonialism and Cold War: The United States and the Struggle for Indonesian Independence* (Ithaca, 1981), and Robert M. Blum, *Drawing the Line: The Origins of the American Containment Policy in East Asia* (New York, 1982).

realization of a centuries-old Russian dream of a sphere influence in that region? Was it an effort by the Kremlin to extend the influence of communism in the immediate postwar period? Or did it represent a Soviet determination to ensure that the massive casualties sustained during the Nazi invasion would never again be repeated? Had the course of American diplomacy since the Spanish-American War been committed to the defense of a global status quo in an attempt to find the everexpanding foreign markets supposedly necessary for the survival of American capitalism? Or could the roots of the Cold War crisis be traced back to the mid-1940s, when Russian military forces occupied Eastern Europe? Were America's moves dictated by a containment policy aimed at checking what was believed to be a Soviet plan for spreading communism throughout the world? Or was the United States bent upon a conservative counterrevolution that would maintain the world economic and political order in a condition conducive to the purposes of American capitalism? In answering such questions students will deal not only with the Cold War but with the very nature of American society.

Joseph R. Starobin

JOSEPH R. STAROBIN (1913–1976) was for many years a promi-
nent member of the American Communist Party. He broke with the
party in 1954, although never renouncing his commitment to Marx-
ism. In his later career he was professor of political science at the
University of Toronto. Among his publications were Paris to Peking
(1955) and American Communism in Crisis, 1943–1957 *(1972).*

It is surely a suggestive irony that just at the point when younger
American historians had made serious intellectual headway with their
reinterpretation of the Cold War, fixing historical responsibility in
terms of the mistakes, delusions, and imperatives of U.S. policy, the
Soviet Union astonished friends and foes by overwhelming Czechoslovakia and turning its clock of history backwards. If the Cold War has
not revived, small thanks are due the Soviet leaders. Their extraordinary nervousness, their maneuvers to propitiate both the outgoing and
incoming American administrations, indicate very plainly how much
they have feared political retaliation; this in itself is a comment on
where responsibility for the Cold War today should rest. That Prague
should have been the vortex in 1968 as it was in 1948 of critical problems within communism is uncanny, but on deeper examination it
may not be fortuitous.

After all, the least credible explanation of Moscow's desperate attempt to resolve the crisis within its own system of states and parties
is the one which pictures Czechoslovakia as the helpless Pauline at
the crossroads of Europe, about to be dishonored by West German *re-*
vanchards, with agents of the CIA grinning in the background, suddenly saved by the stalwart defenders of socialist honor and morality.
Today this type of argument is reserved within the Communist world
for its most backward members—that is, for the Soviet public and the
fringes of the most insignificant and expendable Communist parties.
Yet arguments of this kind had wide currency a generation ago. New
Left historians would have us believe that Stalin was simply reacting
to external challenge. In their view, the Cold War might not have set
in if small-minded American politicians had not been determined to
reverse bad bargains, if congenital imperialists had not been mesmer-

Joseph R. Starobin, "Origins of the Cold War: The Communist Dimension," *Foreign Affairs* 47 (July 1969):681–696. Reprinted by permission from *Foreign Affairs.* Copyright 1969 by Council on Foreign Relations, Inc.

ized by the monopoly of atomic weapons which statesmen and scientists knew to be temporary. Since all this is so plainly a half-truth when juxtaposed to events of today, then clearly the half-truth of yesteryear will hardly explain the whole of the Cold War.

Sophisticated Communists, both East and West, are asking why Czechoslovakia, which escaped the upheavals in Poland and Hungary of 1956 after a decade of Stalinist pressure, then experienced such a mounting crisis in the subsequent decade of relative détente and peaceful competition. How is it that twenty years after Communist rule had been secured in February 1948 basic verities are now placed in question—whether centralized planning may not be counterproductive, whether a one-party régime can really articulate the needs of a politically evolved people, whether the inner relations of such an unequal alliance as that administered by the Soviet Union are not so inherently antagonistic as to become explosive? Indeed, why did the rebirth of Czechoslovak political life in the first half of 1968—viewed with hope and excitement by Western Communists—raise such menacing ghosts from the past and such fearful question marks for the future that supposedly sober-minded men in Moscow took fright?

Twice within a dozen years the unmanageability of the Communist world has been revealed. The crisis which shattered the Sino-Soviet alliance after manifesting itself first in Eastern Europe now rebounds at the supposed strong-point of Czechoslovakia. And it has done so both in conditions of intense external pressure and times of relatively peaceful engagement. Perhaps it is here, in the dimension of communism as a contradictory and intractable system, that one may find the missing element in the discussions thus far on the origins of the Cold War.

II

That world history would someday polarize around two great nations, America and Russia, was a de Tocquevillean insight with which Communists were familiar a long time ago. Stalin gave it what seemed like a very clear definition back in 1927 during a talk with an American labor delegation. He envisaged that a socialist center would arise "binding to itself the countries gravitating toward socialism" and would engage the surviving capitalist center in "a struggle between them for the possession of the world economy." The fate of both would be decided by the outcome of this struggle. What appeared at first glance as a sweeping projection was, however, profoundly ambiguous on close examination. Stalin did not spell out how the countries "gravitating to socialism" would get there. Good Communists believed this could come about only by the formulas of the October Revolution; yet even Lenin, in 1922, had lamented that perhaps a "big mistake" was being made in imposing Russian precepts on foreign Communists. Nor did Stalin elucidate how new nations recruited to socialism would order their relations with Russia as the hub of the socialist center. Presumably "proletarian internationalism" would replace the domination of the weak by the strong which was, in their view, the hallmark of capitalism. Yet even by 1927 the Russification of the international movement had brought catastrophic results—in Germany and China.

Stalin did not, moreover, meet the fundamental intellectual challenge of whether "the struggle for the possession of the world economy" necessarily had to be military in character. On this crucial point, everything could be found in the Leninist grabbag. "Peaceful coexistence" is there, but so is the expectation of "frightful collisions" between the first workers' state and its opponents; the caution that socialism had to be secured in one country first is to be found along with pledges that once socialism was strong enough in Russia, it would raise up revolts in the strongholds of capitalism.

The one possibility which Leninism did not anticipate was a stalemate between rival systems, precluding a "final conflict." The notion was not even entertained that an equilibrium between contending forces might set in, that the subsequent evolution of both contenders under the impact of this equilibrium could alter their distinguishing characteristics and therefore outmode the original Leninist theorems.

Out of such doctrinal ambiguities the Second World War created policy choices affecting most of humanity. The Soviet Union and the international Communist movement found themselves allied with democratic-capitalist states among whom public power had grown drastically in an effort to overcome the Great Depression; the welfare state was expanded by the very demands of warfare while democracy was in fact enhanced. Keynes had made a serious rebuttal to Marx. Would capitalism in the West collapse in a repetition of the crisis of the 1930s after withstanding the test of war? Or had the war itself changed something vital within the workings of capitalism? Moreover, the first global war in history led to the end of colonialism and hence a new relation of metropolitan states to subject peoples. Would the former necessarily collapse because, in Lenin's analysis, they had depended so heavily on colonies? Or might they undergo transformations—short of socialism—to make them viable? Would the countries of the underdeveloped world make socialism the indispensable form of their modernization or might they, dialectically enough, find a new relation with capitalism?

Thus, the war brought on to the world stage a powerful Russia on whose survival a rival system's survival also depended. Simultaneously America came to center stage with a greatly expanded economy no longer limited by laissez-faire economics and inwardly altered

by technological change created by the war. America was indispensable to Russia as an ally but formidable as a rival in a sense far deeper
than its outward power. This wartime relationship was unexpected,
and it challenged ideology and practice on all sides.

Something very particular happened with communism, considered
as a most uneven system of a single state and a variety of parties. The
fortunes of war, thanks perhaps to Churchill's postponement of the
second front, brought the soviet armies beyond their own borders
where they had to be welcomed by the West if only because their help
was also being solicited on the plains of Manchuria once Hitler was
defeated. Yet at the moment of Russia's greatest need and harshest difficulties, the Communist movements *least* helpful to her were those
of Eastern Europe; in the one country outside of Russia where a decade
before the Communists had been a real power—namely, in Germany—
the party lay shattered. No anti-Hitler force of any practical significance emerged. On the East European landscape there were only two
exceptions. In Yugoslavia a handful of veterans of Comintern intrigue
and the hard school of the International Brigades in Spain had succeeded in establishing their power—prior to the arrival of Soviet forces
in the Danubian basin. In Czechoslovakia, a Communist movement
of a very different sort—that is, with a legal and parliamentary tradition—was joined by Slovak guerrillas. Both came to terms with the
leadership of the government-in-exile, which both Moscow and the
West recognized. A long-term cooperation of diverse social forces was
implied.

On the other hand, the Communist movements underwent a spectacular resurrection in a wide arc from Greece through Italy, France,
the Low Countries and Scandinavia, while in widely separated corners
of Asia they also flourished—in Northwest China, in the peninsula of
Indochina, in the Philippines and Malaya. All of them were successful
to the degree that they identified with the defense of their nationhood
and either subordinated social issues or subsumed them in national
ones; where this proved too complicated, as in India, long-term disabil-
ities resulted. But all these movements grew at a distance from the
Soviet armies; their postwar fate could not depend on physical contact.
Even parties at the periphery of world politics showed striking
changes. They entered cabinets in Cuba and Chile, emerged from prewar disasters with great dynamism in Brazil, became legal in Canada
and stood a chance of legitimizing their considerable influence in Britain and the United States. In these latter countries, they could hope to
achieve "citizenship" only by ceasing to be propagandist groups reflecting Soviet prestige, and only as they grappled with the specific
peculiarities of their societies in rapid change.

Yet for all this success, and perhaps because of it, communism
faced the gravest problems. The peculiarity of the moment lay in the

fact that some definition of Russia's relation with the West was essential to assure the most rapid conclusion of the war in Europe, and this had to precede a common strategy in Asia. Hence Moscow was obliged to define relations with the Communist parties. Simultaneously these movements—of such unequal potential and geographical relation to Russia—had to make a fresh judgment of their strategies in view of those changes within capitalism which challenged their own doctrine. Perhaps the most ambitious attempt to do this came in May 1943 with the dissolution of the Communist International.

Stalin, who had sworn at Lenin's bier to guard this "general staff of the world revolution" like the apple of his eye, was now abandoning it; and in so doing he signaled to Churchill and Roosevelt that he would project the postwar Soviet interest in essentially Russian terms. This decision was consistent with the fact that the Russian Communists had not been able to rely on ideology or internationalism in mobilizing their own peoples for the enormous sacrifices of the war. They had been forced to appeal to the Russian love of soil and the solace of the Orthodox faith. "They are not fighting for us," Stalin had once mused to Ambassador Harriman. "They are fighting for Mother Russia."

All of this would not, of course, make Russia easier to deal with. And in studying the details in the monumental accounts of Herbert Feis or W. H. McNeill, one is struck by Stalin's political opportunism and the enormous part which is played in his calculations by the need to exact material resources from friend and foe. Throughout 1944, Stalin dealt with anyone who would cease fighting, or mobilize men and matériel for the Soviet armies, safeguard their lines and pledge reparations; and everyone was suitable to Moscow in terms of these objectives—agrarians and monarchists in the Axis satellites, veteran Communist haters in Finland, a Social Democratic old-timer in Austria, Dr. Beneš in Prague or Comrade Tito in the Yugoslav mountains. Had the putsch against Hitler succeeded in July 1944, Stalin was prepared, by his committee of Nazi generals rounded up at Stalingrad, to bargain.

His only real complication arose over Poland. Here the Soviets had the tactical advantage that a generation earlier the victors at Versailles had been willing to establish the Curzon Line as Russia's western frontier. Churchill and Roosevelt were now obliged not only to ratify this line but to impose it on the intractable London Poles. Moscow's own dilemma lay in the fact that the pro-Soviet Poles, exiled in the U.S.S.R., had little political substance; they had one thing in common with their counterparts in London—lack of standing inside Poland. The Polish Communists had been decimated in the great purges and the Polish officer corps had been wiped out in the Katyn murders. Perhaps it was the need to shift the balance in his favor that led Stalin to such extraordinary measures as letting the "Home Army" be wiped

out at the banks of the Vistula or continuing to murder Polish Socialists as they came to Moscow as guests. The earlier hope of some pres-
tigious figure who would bridge the gap between Poles and yet be satisfactory to all the great powers had faded with the death in an airplane
accident of General Wladislaw Sikorski.

But it is questionable whether the Soviet use of vestigial figures of
Comintern experience should be viewed, as of 1944, in terms of "com-
munization." Everything we know of the Kremlin at that time denies
this. In the remarkable account by Milovan Djilas in his "Conversations with Stalin," the Kremlin was far from being a citadel of revolution, as this young Montenegrin idealist expected (like so many in
Moscow for the first time, before and after him). The Kremlin was really a sort of Muscovite camping-ground such as the great Russian
painter Repin might have portrayed. Crafty and boorish men, suspicious of all foreigners and of each other, contemptuous of Communists
who were non-Russian but expecting their obedience, were crowded
around the maps of Europe as around some Cossack camp fire, calculating how much they could extract from Churchill and Roosevelt, to
whom they felt profoundly inferior.

Thus, when Ulbricht and Rakosi, Anna Pauker, and even Dmitroff
were being prepared to return to the homelands where they had previously failed, Stalin advised them not to spoil their second chance by
their chronic leftism and adventurism.[1] They did not go back as revolutionaries. For all of Moscow's hopes that they root themselves in native soil, they were intended to be the guarantors of control, to stabilize this backyard of Europe and mobilize its resources on Russia's
behalf. The troubles with the Yugoslavs began for the very reason that
as revolutionaries they would not let themselves be used.

Was Stalin already building a bloc? To be sure he was. But he also
knew that the onetime *cordon sanitaire* was a veritable swamp of historic and intractable rivalries and economic backwardness, even
though wealthier in immediate resources than the U.S.S.R. itself. Hoping to transform this bloc, Stalin also entertained most seriously the
idea of a long-term relationship with America and Britain based on
some common policy toward Germany that would make its much
greater resources available to Russia. Thus, when Churchill came to
Moscow in September 1944 to work out a spheres-of-influence agreement, demanding 50:50 and 75:25 ratios in the political control of

---

[1]Herbert Feis is the source for the famous and revealing anecdote that when Stalin
said farewell to Dr. Beneš, after signing a mutual assistance pact, he urged Beneš to help
make Klement Gottwald, the Communist leader now became premier, "more worldly
and less provincial"—an amazing piece of arrogance. Having themselves helped emascu-
late their foreign friends, the Russians now taunted them and hoped that perhaps the
bourgeois world might take men of them. *Churchill, Roosevelt, Stalin* (Princeton:
Princeton University Press, 1957), p. 569.

areas already liberated by the Soviet armies, Stalin agreed by the stroke of a pen. He did so without comment. He contemptuously left it to Churchill to decide whether the piece of paper should be retained by him or destroyed. The cobbler's son from Gori, the onetime seminary student, was giving a descendant of the Marlboroughs a lesson in Realpolitik.

But as he disposed of Greeks and interposed with Yugoslavs (without asking their consent) the Soviet dictator demanded no quid pro quo in Western Europe where the ultimate world balance could be determined, and where Communist movements had powerfully revived, guided by intimates of Stalin—Togliatti and Thorez—whose work he respected. Molotov is on record as inquiring about the disposition of Italian colonies, but not about the operations of the American Military Government in Italy in which Russian participation was passive. At the moment when the French Communists were debating whether to turn in their arms, Moscow recognized the Gaullist régime and invited it to sign a treaty with what de Gaulle was to call "chère et puissante Russie." Churchill's assault on Belgian and Greek Communists was reproved, in private. But no Soviet leverage was employed to help them, and the Greek Communists were advised to strike the best bargain they could to avert civil war. Only much later, when assistance was useless to them, did the Soviets reluctantly help the Greeks, though their hapless plight was useful for Cold War propaganda. Even as late as February 1945, at Yalta, Stalin pledged to renew his pact with Chiang Kai-shek in return for special treaty control of Dairen and the Manchurian railways. Half a year later, the Soviet armies ransacked the industrial installations that were by right Chinese. In central Asia they dickered with warlords, advising them against joining the Chinese communists. Stalin shied away from the governance of Japan, asking and getting its northern islands instead. All this was accompanied by rather snide references by Molotov to Mao Tse-tung's "margarine Communists." American liberals and roving ambassadors may have been more naïve but they were also less offensive in believing the Chinese Communists to be "agrarian reformers."

III

How then did the Communist parties respond to the Comintern's dissolution? Its final document had some curious and pregnant phrases, alluding to "the fundamental differences in the historical development of the separate countries of the world"—differences, it was now discovered, which had "become apparent even before the war"; Communists were now told most authoritatively that they were "never advocates of the outmoded organizational forms." This suggests that a great watershed had been reached. The implicit self-criticism was bound to encourage those Western Communists for whom the "popular front" of the 1930s and the experience of the Spanish Republic were not defensive deceptions but major experiments in skirting the limits of Leninism. The Chinese Communists, as the specialized literature shows, saw in the disappearance of the Communist International a ratification of their own "New Democracy," in which the peasantry and the "national bourgeoisie" had been credited with revolutionary potentials for which no precedent existed in the Russian experience.

The most interesting instance of how new systems of ideas and new organizational forms were bursting the Leninist integument came in the minor party of a major country—among the American Communists. Their leader, Earl Browder, concluded that peaceful coexistence had become obligatory; he saw such coexistence as a whole historical stage in which the contradictions between antagonistic social systems would have to work themselves out—short of war; it is curious that he ruled out war as too dangerous to both sides *before* the advent of the atomic bomb. To give this very novel view some inner logic, Browder postulated a new type of state power, intermediate between capitalism and socialism, which, he thought, would prevail between the Atlantic and the Oder-Neisse Line. Thus he anticipated the "people's democracy" concept which was to have wide currency in the next few years only to be brusquely rejected by the end of 1948, when the Cold War demanded rationales of another kind.

To what extent Browder had sanction in Moscow, or only *thought* he had, or whether this sanction was even intended to be more than temporary are all fascinating matters; but for our discussion what seems more important is the fact that Browder revealed the incoherence of communism and tried to overcome it. Perhaps America was not as backward as European communists traditionally assumed. The more advanced country was simply showing a mirror to the less advanced of the problems of their own future, to borrow an image from Marx.

One may put this dilemma in very specific terms. In 1944–1945, a quasi-revolutionary situation prevailed in key areas of Western Europe and East Asia. The Communist parties had become mass movements. They were no longer Leninist vanguards but had significant military experience. The old order had been discredited and few charismatic rivals existed. One of two options could be taken, each of them having its own logic. If the Communists seized power they might be able to hold it, as in Yugoslavia, with great good luck. But as the Greek experience was to show, the success of a prolonged civil war would involve the rupture of the Anglo-Soviet-American coalition; and the war with Hitler was by no means over, while the Pacific war appeared only begun. To pursue this option meant to oblige the Soviet Union to assist revolutions at a distance from its own armies at a moment of its own greatest weakness and when it seriously entertained the possibility of a long-range postwar relationship with the West. Alternatively, the U.S.S.R. would be obliged to disavow its own ideological and political allies in an even more explicit way than the dissolution of the Comintern suggested. Stalin's entire diplomacy warned against revolution now. So did his opinion, in a speech of November 6, 1944, that whatever disagreements existed among the great powers could be overcome; he had said flatly that "no accidental, transitory motive but vitally important long-term interests lie at the basis of the alliance of our country, Great Britain and the United States."

On the other hand, to reject the revolutionary path meant for the Western parties (if not for the Chinese and Vietnamese) forgoing an opportunity that might not return; for a generation this choice caused intense misgivings and internal battles within these parties. To take part in the wholehearted reconstruction of their societies on a less-than-socialist basis would have involved a revision of fundamental Leninist postulates, a fresh look at capitalism, and presumably a redefinition of their relations with the Soviet Union. Having taken such a sharply Russocentric course, could Stalin give his imprimatur to the embryonic polycentrism of that time? The U.S.S.R. was in the paradoxical position of trying to be a great power with a shattered economic base, and of trying to lead a world movement whose interests were quite distinct from those of Russia, both in practice and in ideas. The ambiguities inherent in communism, in Stalin's projections of 1927, had come home to roost.

IV

If one tries, then, to make intellectual sense and order out of the bewildering events between early 1945 and mid-1947, the least satisfactory themes are the ones which have been so popular and have dominated the discussion of the origins of the Cold War. The revisionist historians are so hung up on the notion that a meticulous rediscovery of America will reveal the clues to the Cold War that they ignore the dimensions of communism altogether. They have little experience with communism (and perhaps they are better off for it) but they have yet to show the scholarship required to explore it. To say this is not to deny the value of reappraising American policy, especially since so many of today's follies have roots in the past. Communists, anti-Communists, and ex-Communists have all had troubles with the imperatives of coexistence. But this is quite different from explaining the

Cold War on one-sided grounds and succumbing to the elementary fallacy of *post hoc, propter hoc.*

On the other hand, the most sophisticated and persuasive rebuttal to the younger historians—that by Arthur Schlesinger, Jr.[2]—suffered from the limitations of his own major premise: the assumption that communism was a monolithic movement which disintegrated only as the Cold War was vigorously prosecuted. Certainly the monolith functioned in a pell-mell fashion after 1948, but one wonders whether its explosive decomposition in the late fifties, continuing to the events in Czechoslovakia, can be comprehended without realizing that all the elements of crisis within it were already present in its immediate postwar years. It was the futile attempts by Stalin and the Communists who everywhere followed him (even if hesitantly and in bewilderment) to stifle the nascent polycentrism and to curtail the inchoate attempts to adjust to new realities which constitute communism's own responsibility for the Cold War. Herein also is the key to communism's own disasters.

Thus, the events of 1946 and 1947 were in fact incoherent and contradictory, and for that very reason offer an important clue to the origins of the Cold War. For example, Earl Browder was roundly denounced by the French Communist leader, Jacques Duclos, in an article written early in 1945 (with data that was available only in Moscow), on the grounds that the very concept of peaceful coexistence and Europe's reconstruction on a bourgeois-democratic basis was heresy; yet the curious thing is that most of the Communist parties continued to operate on Browder's assumptions—including the party led by Duclos. Such a state of affairs suggests that the Duclos article was not the tocsin of the Cold War but one of the elements of communism's incoherence. By the close of 1946, only the Yugoslavs—and William Z. Foster, who had ousted Browder in the United States—were convinced that even the "temporary stabilization" of capitalism was unlikely. This concept was of course an echo from the 1920s. "Relative and temporary stabilization" was Stalin's own justification in the late 1920s for "turning inward" and seeking a truce in external affairs. Ruling out this concept in the 1940s, Foster went even further than Tito in raising the alarm over an ever-more-imminent danger of an American attack on the Soviet Union. It is not generally known that when Browder's successor visited Europe in March 1947 he was amazed to find that few Communist leaders agreed with his views, and one of those who disagreed most sharply was Jacques Duclos.

In studying the French Communists of that period one finds unusual emphasis on the need for a policy of "confident collaboration"

---

[2]Arthur M. Schlesinger, Jr., "Origins of the Cold War," *Foreign Affairs* 46 (October 1967):22–52.

with "all of the Allied nations, without exception," and a declaration by Duclos that "we are not among those who confuse the necessity and fertility of struggle with the spirit of adventurism. That is why—mark me well—we ask of a specific historic period what it can give and only what it can give . . . but we do not ask more, for we want to push ahead and not end up in abortive and disappointing failures."

In this same year of 1946, it is sometimes forgotten that the Chinese Communists negotiated seriously for a long-term coalition with Chiang Kai-shek. They did so under the aegis of General George Marshall, which suggests that their own antagonism to "American imperialism" had its limits; their view that the United States was necessarily hostile to a unified China with a large Communist component was a later development. During the recent Great Proletarian Cultural Revolution, Chinese historians blamed this coalition strategy on the now-disgraced Liu Shao Chi, alleging that he was under the influence of "Browder, Togliatti, Thorez and other renegades to the proletariat." But the official Chinese Communist documents show that at the time Mao Tse-tung took credit for it and was himself viewed as a "revisionist"—by the Indian Communists, for example. In those same months, Ho Chi Minh led a coalition delegation to Paris, trying to work out the terms for remaining within the French Union; it is a curious but revealing detail that Ho had the previous winter dissolved his own creation, the Communist Party of Indochina, in favor of an Association of Marxist Studies, without, however, receiving a rebuke from Jacques Duclos.

Throughout 1946, almost every Communist leader in the West voiced the view that peaceful roads to socialism were not only desirable but were—because of objective changes in the world—now the theoretically admissible. If in Eastern Europe this popularity of the "people's democracy" can be explained in terms of Stalin's attempt to stabilize a chaotic region of direct interest to Russia, in Western Europe it was part of a serious effort to implement the nonrevolutionary option which the Communists had chosen, and for which they needed a consistent justification.

Nor were the Soviet leaders immune to what was happening within communism. Stalin himself can be cited in contradictory assertions which also stimulated the diversity within the Communist world as well as baffling some of its members. Early in February 1946 Stalin declared that wars could not be abolished so long as imperialism prevailed; this came in his election campaign speech which is viewed by Sovietologists as another tocsin of the Cold War. Yet throughout 1946 Stalin gave interviews to British and American newsmen, and held a long discussion with Harold Stassen that spring, in which the key theme was the viability of peaceful coexistence. In September 1946 Stalin declared that the ruling circles of both Britain and the

United States were *not* in fact oriented toward war—a view which Communists from China to Italy hailed, although it baffled Tito and William Z. Foster. Stalin also told a British Labor delegation headed by Harold Laski that socialism might well come to Britain by parliamentary means, with the monarchy remaining as a genuine institution. Earlier in the year, in a polemic with a certain Professor Razin on the significance of the doctrines of Clausewitz, Stalin is quoted as believing "it is impossible to move forward and advance science without subjecting outdated propositions and the judgments of well-known authorities to critical analysis. This applies . . . also to the classics of Marxism." Significantly, this exchange was published a full year later—in February 1947—on the eve of Cold War decisions which made such thinking heretical throughout the Communist movement.

Yet in 1946 Soviet diplomacy was in fact moving "with all deliberate speed" toward settlements of a partial kind with the West—as regards the peace treaties, the evacuation of northern Persia and other matters. Browder was cordially received in Moscow in May after his expulsion from the American party—a rather unprecedented detail in the annals of communism. The deposed Communist leader was heard out by Molotov, at the latter's request, and was given a post which enabled him to work energetically for the next two years in behalf of the proposition that Stalin wanted an American-Soviet settlement.

All students of this period have paused on the famous Varga controversy. The title of the book which the foremost Soviet economist, Eugen Varga, published in November 1946 (it was completed the year before) in itself suggests what was bothering Russian leaders, namely: *Changes in the Economy of Capitalism Resulting from the Second World War.* Within six months, Varga was under severe attack, which he resisted for the following two years. Major issues lay at the heart of the controversy. When might a crisis of overproduction be expected in the United States? How severe would it be? And to what extent would rearmament or a program for rebuilding Western Europe affect capitalism's inherent propensity for crisis, which was, of course, taken for granted. Another question was whether the new role of governmental power, so greatly enhanced by the war, might not have a bearing both on the onset of the crisis and the terrain of Communist activities. Varga did forecast an early crisis, after a brief postwar boom. In so doing, he surely misled Stalin into one of his most fundamental Cold War miscalculations. But Varga also clung to the view that something important had changed within classical capitalism; he insisted that "the question of greater or smaller participation in the management of the state will be the main content" of the political struggle in the West, and he deduced that people's democracy was in fact a transitional form between the two systems, replacing the "either-or" notions of classical Leninism. There was a plaintive protest in Varga's answer to his critics (one of whom was Vosnessensky, who would shortly disappear because of mysterious heresies of his own). "It is not a matter of enumerating all the facts so that they inevitably lead to the former conclusions of Marxism-Leninism," Varga argued, "but to use the Marxism-Leninist method in studying these facts. The world changes and the content of our work must change also."

V

In what sense, then, did all these crosscurrents determine Stalin's decision for Cold War? It would seem that the matter turned on the incompatibility between immediate Soviet objectives and the real interests of the Communist parties—or more exactly, in the particularly Stalinist answer to these incompatibilities. The Russians, it will be remembered, had set out to achieve rapid and ambitious reconstruction including, of course, the acquisition of nuclear weapons. They were most concerned with reparations. When it became plain that little help would come by loans or trade with the West (they had used up what was still in the pipelines after the abrupt cessation of lend-lease in mid-1945 and were not getting a response to their $6 billion request to Washington), they needed either the resources of Germany beyond what they could extract from their own Eastern Zone, or a desperate milking of their friends and former foes in Eastern Europe. At home, moreover, they could not rely on the ultrachauvinist themes which had served them during the war; rejecting liberalization of Soviet society, they tightened the screws and fell back on the doctrine of the primacy of the Soviet party, the purity of its doctrine and the universal validity of that doctrine. Consistent with these objectives, the Soviet leaders wanted to erase all sympathy for America which until then was widespread in the Soviet Union.[3]

These objectives, taken together, ran counter to all the tendencies among the foreign Communist parties. Both the revolutionary ambitions of the Yugoslavs, their jealous quest for autonomy as well as the emphasis on peaceful non-Soviet roads to socialism—that is, the "revisionist" themes so urgently needed by the parties in the West—could be countenanced by Moscow only if it were prepared to accept diversity within international communism. This very diversity (which they had themselves half entertained) now became an obstacle. The Stalinist premise that what was good for Russia was good for all other Com-

---

[3]This task was assigned to the late Ilya Ehrenburg following his 1947 visit to the States, when he deliberately oversimplified everything American with the crudest methods. The pattern for this had been set late in 1946 by Andrei Zhdanov.

munists (a notion which he himself considered abandoning) was now reaffirmed.

The origins of the Cold War lie deeper, however, than any analysis of Russia's own interest. Nor can they be understood only in terms of an attempt to prevent economic recovery and political stability in Western Europe. The Cold War's origins must be found in a dimension larger than the requirements of Soviet internal mobilization or the thrust of its foreign policy; they lie in the attempt to overcome the incipient diversity within a system of states and parties, among whom the changes produced by the war had outmoded earlier ideological and political premises. The conditions for the transformation of a monolithic movement had matured and ripened. The sources of the Cold War lie in communism's unsuccessful attempt to adjust to this reality, followed by its own abortion of this attempt. For Stalin the Cold War was a vast tug-of-war with the West, whereby not only internal objectives could be realized but the international movement subordinated; its constituent parts went along—bewildered but believing—on the assumption that in doing so, they would survive and prosper. The price of the Stalinist course was to be fearsome indeed; and by 1956 the Soviet leaders were to admit that the Cold War had damaged the U.S.S.R. more than the West, that a stalemate of systems had to be acknowledged, and ineluctable conclusions had to be drawn. Thus, the Cold War arose from the failure of a movement to master its inner difficulties and choose its alternatives.

The analysis could be continued to the turning-point of mid-1947—the Marshall Plan decision and Stalin's riposte, for example, in humiliating his Czechoslovak and Polish partners, who thought in terms of what might be good for them, and indirectly for the Soviet Union. Such an analysis would take us through the near insurrections of late 1947 in France and Italy, adventurist upheavals in Asia, the Berlin blockade and the coup in Prague in 1948. But this involves another subject—how the Cold War was fought. It was indeed fought by both sides. But to say this cannot obscure the crisis within communism, where its origins lie. The record would show how recklessly entire Communist movements were expended and to what a dangerous brink the Soviet Union itself was brought. In 1956, Khruschev was to lament these miscalculations but he did so with such a *desinvolture* as to leave a memory bank of disasters and skeletons that still rattle in communism's closets. Was the Cold War but a test of strength between systems? Or has it not also been the process whereby communism disclosed such an intellectual and political bankruptcy that a dozen years after Khruschev's revelations, the issues still agonize—as in Czechoslovakia—all the states and parties involved? A world movement claiming to comprehend history and accepting the responsibility for "making history" still grapples with the alternatives opened by the

Second World War. It has yet to face what it has tried to avoid at such a heavy cost to coexistence—namely, understanding itself.

John Lewis Gaddis

JOHN LEWIS GADDIS (1941–   ) *is distinguished professor of history at Ohio University. He has written widely on American diplomacy, and his books include* The United States and the Origin of the Cold War, 1941–1947 *(1972),* Strategies of Containment *(1982), and* The Long Peace *(1987).*

It is no secret that there was once a certain amount of disagreement among American historians about the origins of the Cold War. A decade ago this subject was capable of eliciting torrents of impassioned prose, of inducing normally placid professors to behave like gladiators at scholarly meetings, of provoking calls for the suppression of unpopular points of view, threats of lawsuits, and most shocking of all, the checking of footnotes. Today, in contrast, the field is very much quieter, its occupants are much more polite to one another, and talk of consensus is heard throughout the land. It may be that we are all getting older and have not the stomach for combat any longer. But I prefer to think that what is happening is the emergence of a genuine synthesis of previously antagonistic viewpoints, based upon an impressive amount of new research. . . .

Despite this volume of work, and despite the array of newly declassified sources upon which most of it is based, the recent literature on Cold War origins has not attracted the same attention New Left historiography was receiving in the late 1960s and early 1970s. In part, this is because the revisionism of that period coincided with the growth of public opposition to the Vietnam War; no comparable contemporary issue has drawn the interest of nonspecialists to the more recent literature. In part, as well, one must acknowledge that much of the new writing is sober stuff: it lacks the pungency of the earlier revisionist accounts; its conclusions, most of the time, are less than spectacular. Nevertheless, the new literature is making some fundamental changes

John Lewis Gaddis, "The Emerging Post-Revisionist Synthesis on the Origins of the Cold War," *Diplomatic History* 7 (Summer 1983):171–191. Copyright 1983 by Scholarly Resources Inc. Reprinted by permission of Scholarly Resources Inc.

in our understanding of the early Cold War, to such an extent that it is now generally acknowledged that we have reached a third stage, beyond both orthodoxy and revisionism, in the historiography of that period.

Various labels have been proposed to characterize this new school—"neoorthodoxy," "eclecticism," "postrevisionism"—the latter term seems to have caught on more than the others and is the one that will be used here. In the best assessment of it we have had to date, J. Samuel Walker describes postrevisionism as a "new consensus" which "draws from both traditional and revisionist interpretations to present a more balanced explanation of the beginning of the cold war." What follows is an attempt to examine some of the elements of that consensus, to indicate where they differ from both orthodox and revisionist accounts, and to suggest some of the implications they may pose for future research.

As its name implies, the postrevisionist literature on Cold War origins cannot be understood apart from the "revisionism" that preceded it. A useful starting point, therefore, might [be] a brief review of the fundamental propositions of New Left historiography, with a view to clarifying how postrevisionism differs from them. It should be emphasized at the outset that the New Left perspective on the origins of the Cold War was never monolithic. No one revisionist would have accepted all lines of argument associated with that school of thought; differences among New Left scholars at times rivaled in intensity those with more "orthodox" colleagues. Nevertheless, and allowing for these differences, there would appear to have been four interlocking propositions upon which the New Left view rested:

1) That postwar American foreign policy approximated the classical Leninist model of imperialism—that is, that an unwillingness or inability to redistribute wealth at home produced an aggressive search for markets and investment opportunities overseas, without which, it was thought, the capitalist system in the United States could not survive.

2) That this internally motivated drive for empire left little room for accommodating the legitimate security interests of the Soviet Union, thereby ensuring the breakdown of wartime cooperation.

3) That the United States imposed its empire on a mostly unwilling world, recruiting it into military alliances, forcing it into positions of economic dependency, maintaining its imperial authority against growing opposition by means that included bribery, intimidation, and covert intervention.

4) That all of this took place against the will of the people of the United States, who were tricked by cynical but skillful leaders into supporting this policy of imperialism through the propagation of the

myth that monolithic communism threatened the survival of the nation.

With regard to the first assertion—that postwar American foreign policy fits the Leninist model of imperialism—postrevisionists have pointed out several problems:

1) If we can accept the testimony, both public and private, of the policymakers themselves, there is little evidence that they saw a crisis of capitalism as the most pressing issue facing the country at the end of World War II. There was concern about a postwar depression, to be sure, but that concern was only one aspect of a more general preoccupation with what was now coming to be called "national security." As Michael Sherry and Daniel Yergin have pointed out, the experience of war had sensitized American leaders to the possibilities of future external threats even before the Soviet Union had emerged as the most obvious postwar adversary. This sense of vulnerability reflected not so much fears of an economic collapse at home as it did a new awareness of the global balance of power and the effect recent developments in the technology of warfare might have on it. Although it does not totally dismiss concerns about the future of the domestic economy, this emphasis on national security does assign them a considerably lower priority than was characteristic of most New Left accounts.

2) Even if the fate of capitalism had been primary in the minds of American leaders at the time, the policies they actually followed did less than one might think to advance it. The concept of multilateralism, upon which postwar economic security was thought to rest, quickly took a back seat to containment, which to a considerable extent involved preserving rather than breaking down regional economic blocs. It also is becoming clear that the United States made no systematic effort to suppress socialism within its sphere of influence, despite the fact that one might have expected a militantly capitalist nation to promote free enterprise wherever possible. We are coming to understand as well that domestic economic interests themselves were not monolithic and hardly could have provided precise guidance to policymakers had they been inclined to give primacy to them.

3) All of which is not to say that the United States was bashful about using the very considerable economic power that it did possess. Here, postrevisionists generally have accepted revisionist arguments that the United States did in fact employ Lend Lease, prospects of reparations shipments from Germany, postwar credits, and Marshall Plan aid to achieve certain political objectives. But that is just the point: economic instruments were used to serve political ends, not the other way around as the Leninist model of imperialism would seem to imply. American economic strength was a potent weapon that could be used—and indeed, in the early days of the Cold War, was the primary

weapon used—to help redress the political-military balance of power. But that is very different from saying that U.S. political-military power was used to stave off what was seen as an otherwise inevitable collapse of the capitalist order.

The second major proposition upon which the New Left account of the origins of the Cold War rested was that the American drive for world empire, motivated primarily by the requirements of capitalism, left no room for accommodating the legitimate security interests of the Soviet Union and therefore made the Cold War unavoidable. The main point to note about this argument is that it was based upon faith, not research. However great their energies in mining the American archives, not one of the New Left revisionists was a Soviet specialist; few, if any, knew Russian. They simply assumed a willingness to coop- erate on the part of Stalin's Russia that was frustrated by American intransigence. Soviet specialists in the United States and elsewhere were skeptical of this argument, but few of them had mastered the American archives, so their efforts to refute the revisionists were not very convincing.

We now have, though, a comprehensive account of Soviet policy regarding the origins of the Cold War, written not only from American and British records but also from the admittedly fragmentary Soviet and East European sources that are available. This is Vojtech Mastny's *Russia's Road to the Cold War,* and in it he makes several points that deserve attention:

1) Stalin at no point was willing to entrust Soviet postwar security primarily to a policy of cooperation with the West. Rather, he was de- termined from the start to seek security by unilateral means.

2) The Soviet leader was never clear in his own mind as to the limits of his country's security needs. Not content with imposing boundary changes at the expense of his Western neighbors, he insisted as well on surrounding himself with subservient states, giving no clear indication as to where this policy of building spheres of influence would stop.

3) The failure of the West was not a failure to accommodate Stalin, Mastny argues; here he appears to share the view of Geir Lundestad that the United States probably facilitated more than it resisted the expansion of Soviet control over Eastern Europe. The West's failure, rather, was its passivity. For only the West could have defined the lim- its of Stalin's ambition; Stalin himself was incapable of doing so. Had the West acted more firmly at an earlier point, the Cold War would not necessarily have been more intense; just the reverse, for as Adam Ulam has suggested, Stalin tended to show reason and restraint when opposed, irrationality and excess when given a free hand.

4) Mastny concludes then—and his analysis has now been rein- forced by William Taubman's recent treatment of the same subject and

by several other more specialized works as well—that the primary cause of the Cold War was Stalin's own ill-defined ambition, his determination to seek security in such a way as to leave little or none for other actors in the international arena. A secondary cause was the West's failure to act soon enough to stop him.

This is a striking and powerful new interpretation. Admittedly, it is based on less in the way of source material than one would like to have—until the Russians institute their own version of a Freedom of Information Act, anything written in the West on Soviet policy must be. But this is an interpretation future students of the Cold War are going to have to take seriously. It should, at the very least, go far toward correcting the curious American habit of writing about the Cold War as if only the United States had a major role in bringing it about.

The third New Left argument was that the United States imposed its empire on unwilling clients, forcing them into military alliances and into positions of economic dependency against their will. This, too, was an argument derived more from intuition than research: familiarity with the concerns of third parties in the Cold War was no more a strong point of revisionist literature than was consideration of the Soviet Union's role in that conflict. Postrevisionist scholarship, to some extent, has corrected that deficiency by giving attention to the domestic background of decisions that caused countries in Western Europe, the Mediterranean, and the Near East to align themselves with the United States after World War II. . . .

What these postrevisionist arguments seem to show, then, is that the United States was not alone in perceiving the Soviet Union as a threat after World War II. Other countries shared this impression and sought to bring in the United States to redress the balance. It remains to be seen whether this same pattern will hold up in parts of the world that have not yet been studied in the same detail as Britain, Scandinavia, or the Near East—or whether these generalizations can be projected forward into the 1950s, when the American presence became far more overbearing than it was in the late 1940s. Revisionists might legitimately ask, as well, who was doing the inviting in each of these cases—the governing elite, or the "masses"? Still, enough work has been done to make it clear that the revisionist view of an American empire imposed upon unwilling subjects is in some need of revision itself.

The fourth argument made by the New Left was that the policy of containment evolved against the will of the American people, who had to be tricked into supporting imperialism by the government, using the imaginary threat of an international Communist monolith. Postrevisionists have not dealt extensively with the interaction between domestic influences and foreign policy, although the logic of their analysis, which stresses the extent to which Soviet policies alarmed other countries, would seem to suggest that policymakers would not have had to work very hard to convince the public to support containment. Indeed, some postrevisionists have suggested that public and congressional opinion moved in this direction before the policymakers did. Other postrevisionists have stressed the capacity of policymakers to shape public opinion in predetermined directions. The two viewpoints may not be as contradictory as they might seem: it is possible that policymakers sought to move public opinion in anti-Soviet directions at a time when it was shifting in that direction of its own accord. Still, this is one area where postrevisionists remain divided.

Furnishing the means to support a "get tough" policy was something else again. Here revisionist charges that the government found it necessary to manipulate public opinion have found support among postrevisionists, whether one is looking at the effort to sell aid to Greece and Turkey, the Marshall Plan, the Military Assistance Program, or, had the Korean War not intervened, the massive increases in the defense budget called for in NSC-68. Perhaps the explanation for this campaign is consistent with what we know to be true of human nature—people find it easy to view with alarm, but more difficult to accept without some persuasion the sacrifices necessary to do something about it.

Two variations of this argument about administrations manipulating public opinion should be mentioned here. One is the assertion that something like a "military-industrial complex" came to dominate the making of foreign policy during the early Cold War years. It is true that World War II had brought about close cooperation between defense contractors and the government. It is true, as Yergin has pointed out, that expenditures for research and development in the military sphere increased impressively during the early Cold War period. But, significantly, overall military spending did not. The era of budgetary plenty for the military did not come until the Korean War had legitimized the conclusions of NSC-68. Prior to that time, defense spending was kept under such tight control that the Joint Chiefs of Staff despaired of meeting the obligations to which political leaders had committed them. There was, as well, as Lawrence S. Kaplan has pointed out, a curious passivity among military leaders of that day, who seemed content to leave key decisions, even on significant military matters, up to civilians in the State Department. This is hardly the pattern one would expect if a military-industrial complex had been operating at that time.

Another argument relating to internal developments and foreign policy has to do with the origins of McCarthyism. It has been strongly suggested by several New Left scholars that that phenomenon was a logical outgrowth of the Truman administration's efforts to remove suspected disloyal elements from the government, beginning in 1947.

Truman, according to this interpretation, created a climate of suspicion without which McCarthyism could not have flourished. Postrevisionists make no particular effort to defend the president's loyalty program, which clearly had its excesses, but, as Richard Fried has pointed out, the habit of red-baiting did predate, by a considerable extent, implementation of those procedures. Similarly, Alonzo Hamby has suggested that McCarthyism might have developed sooner than it did had the administration not initiated those investigations. The trend now seems to be toward exculpating Truman and his advisers from any direct responsibility for the rise of McCarthyism and toward viewing that development much as it was seen originally—as a combination of hysteria bred by the shocks of the Cold War, together with the efforts of certain highly placed Republicans to find an issue with which to assault the Democrats.

More work clearly needs to be done on this whole matter of the relationship between public opinion and foreign policy, but it would seem that enough has been done to call into question the revisionist view of cynical national administrations imposing their cold-blooded geopolitical visions upon an unsuspecting public.

One might well ask, at this stage, just how postrevisionism differs from traditional accounts of the origins of the Cold War written before New Left revisionism came into fashion. What is new, after all, about the view that American officials worried more about the Soviet Union than about the fate of capitalism in designing the policy of containment, about the assertion that Soviet expansionism was the primary cause of the Cold War, about the argument that American allies welcomed the expansion of U.S. influence as a counterweight to the Russians, about the charge that the government responded to as well as manipulated public opinion? Were not all of these things said years ago?

The answer is yes, but they were said more on the basis of political conviction or personal experience than systematic archival research. What the postrevisionists have done is to confirm, on the basis of the documents, several of the key arguments of the old orthodox position, and that in itself is a significant development. But postrevisionism should not be thought of as simply orthodoxy plus archives. On several major points, revisionism has had a significant impact on postrevisionist historiography. This coincidence of viewpoints between the revisionists and their successors needs to be emphasized, if only to make the point that postrevisionism is something new, not merely a return to old arguments.

1) Postrevisionist accounts pay full attention to the use by the United States of economic instruments to achieve political ends. This dimension of American diplomacy was given short shrift in orthodox accounts; it was as if to mention economics was to call into question

the aura of innocence and naiveté that somehow was supposed to distinguish Washington's policies from those of other countries. The revisionists have made it emphatically clear that when it came to the use of economic power, the United Sates was neither naive nor innocent. It was, as Truman once said, the "economic giant" of the world, and most postrevisionists now accept that it was determined to make thorough use of this unique strength to promote specific political ends.

2) Postrevisionism tends to stress the absence of any ideological blueprint for world revolution in Stalin's mind; this is another point at which revisionism and postrevisionism are closer to each other than to orthodoxy. Stalin is now seen as a cagey but insecure opportunist, taking advantage of such tactical openings as arose to expand Soviet influence, but without any long-term strategy for or even very much interest in promoting the spread of communism beyond the Soviet sphere.

3) Postrevisionist analyses differ from their orthodox predecessors in confirming revisionist assertions that the government, from time to time, did exaggerate external dangers for the purpose of achieving certain internal goals. Attempts to manage public and congressional opinion were not wholly products of a later generation.

4) But the aspect of New Left historiography that postrevisionists are likely to find most useful—and the point upon which their work will depart most noticeably from orthodox accounts—is the argument that there was in fact an American "empire." I should like to develop this line of thought at greater length because it not only illustrates the most important line of continuity between revisionist and postrevisionist scholarship; it also provides some interesting opportunities for future research.

One curiosity of New Left scholarship on the Cold War is that although it assumed the existence of an American empire, it made no effort to compare that empire with those that have existed at other times and in other places. And yet, Washington's experience in projecting first its interests and then its power on a global scale does bear a striking resemblance to the experiences of other great imperial powers in history; from these resemblances, it would seem, revealing comparative insights might be derived.

For example, the New Left seemed to find it difficult to understand how an empire could arise for what its leaders perceived to be defensive reasons. Surely, they insisted, there must have been sinister forces—for which read economic forces, because they always seem more sinister than others—operating behind the scenes. Policymakers either refused to acknowledge them or were unaware of their existence.

But the history of other empires suggests that they can as often arise from perceptions of external as well as from internal insecurity: it is one of the characteristics of great powers that they often do offensive things for defensive reasons. Empires can arise at the invitation of those seeking security as well as by the impositions of those who would deny it. They can develop as unexpected responses to unforeseen circumstances as well as by crafty and farsighted design. They can vary considerably in the extent to which they tolerate diversity within their boundaries.

What the postrevisionists are showing, it would seem, is that the American empire fits more closely the model of defensive rather than offensive expansion, of invitation rather than imposition, of improvisation rather than careful planning. That it was an empire, subject to patterns of development and decay that have affected other empires in the past, can hardly be denied. That it expanded more rapidly and more widely than its Soviet counterpart must be admitted, though that is not too surprising given the facts of geography and the extent of American power in the postwar era. But, as Lundestad has pointed out, this was expansion with limitations; it was an empire operated, at least initially, along defensive lines, and with some sense of restraint.

One can argue at length about the reasons for this restraint: did it reflect the basic decency and good will of the American people, or did the Americans hold back simply because they lacked the manpower and the expertise to remake other societies in their image? Answering this question should provide broad opportunities for future research, as will the question, discussed earlier, of how and by whom the Americans were invited to expand their influence in the first place. It seems beyond argument, though, that there was an American empire, and that a surprising number of governments around the world wanted to be associated with it, given the alternative.

The "imperial" framework of analysis also should prove useful in explaining what happened to Washington's Cold War policies later on. As had been the case with other empires in history, distinctions began to be lost between vital and peripheral interests, between threatening and nonthreatening adversaries; the result was overcommitment and, as a consequence, the exposure of vulnerable flanks. Local insurgencies arose, calling forth disproportionate but ineffectual responses; these in turn exhausted patience at home. It is all an old story, played out many times before. "Your empire is now like a tyranny," Thucydides has Pericles telling the Athenians in the year 430 B.C.; "it may have been wrong to take it; it is certainly dangerous to let it go." But it is precisely an awareness of these earlier analogies that has been missing from accounts of the American imperial experience in the Cold War, and that could provide those accounts with a degree of depth and resonance they have so far lacked.

There would be another advantage as well to using this "imperial" analogue: it should enable us better to understand, make comparisons with, and even to some extent anticipate the policies of the Soviet Union. Few today would deny that Moscow's foreign policy is showing some of the same imperial tendencies that influenced Washington's approach to the world during much of the Cold War. Crane Brinton suggested long ago that revolutions go through certain predictable stages of development. If, as seems likely, imperialisms go through similar phases of growth, maturity, and decline, whatever the ideological complexion of the nations in which they are rooted—and here one must depart from the Leninist view of imperialism as particular to capitalism—then the study of imperialisms might not only generate useful insights about Soviet policy in the Cold War; it also might provide the basis as well for a less alarmist official view of the "present danger." For if the American experience, and the experience of other imperialisms in the past, is any guide, then the Russian flirtation with that doctrine will bring Moscow neither profit nor power, nor the security it no doubt seeks by expanding its influence with so little regard for the security of others.

We owe a considerable debt to the New Left for forcing us to think about the Cold War in these "imperial" terms. To the extent that we can move beyond revisionism's dependence on the inadequate Leninist explanation of imperialism, and beyond the parochialism that sees only the American experience as relevant, then we may in fact be approaching a basis upon which the long sought-after synthesis of orthodox and revisionist viewpoints can be constructed.

Apart from this "imperial" paradigm, there are several other points that postrevisionist scholarship might profitably address in the future:

1) We need more work on Washington's perception of the adversary in the Cold War. For how long, and on what basis, did the United States see international communism as a monolith? How early, and with what results, did strategies exist for exploiting differences within that movement? The archives offer tantalizing evidence that, despite their rhetoric, American officials never really regarded communism as a unified force directed from Moscow; and that, in both the Truman and Eisenhower administrations, efforts were being made behind the scenes to take advantage of the differences that existed within it. We will need more research, though, before we can gauge the extent and success of these maneuvers—or why both administrations felt obliged to portray international communism in public as more unified than they knew it to be.

2) We need more work on the American perception of the balance of power during the early Cold War years. One of the fundamental arguments of the revisionist school was that, because the power of the United States far outstripped that of the Soviet Union, it therefore bore a greater share of the responsibility for the way in which the Cold War developed. But that was a retrospective judgment, not one made by

policymakers at the time. Recent research strongly suggests that American officials did not see themselves as enjoying a clear predominance of power over the Soviet Union in the late 1940s. Soviet conventional forces were obviously superior to those of the West throughout this period, and the pioneering work of David A. Rosenberg has now confirmed, in a striking way, the small size and limited capabilities of the American atomic arsenal during the first five years of the Cold War. These liabilities, combined with the Truman administration's self-imposed budgetary ceilings through the middle of 1950, raise questions as to how expansive Washington's perception of its own power actually was.

3) We need more sophisticated work than we have had so far on the role of bureaucracies and those who inhabit them. The view that was fashionable in the early 1970s—that "where you stand depends on where you sit"—becomes less and less adequate the more one looks into such matters. How was it, for example, that the State Department had to convince the Defense Department in 1950 that it would be a good idea to triple the defense budget? How is it, as Richard K. Betts has shown, that civilian officials generally have been more willing to use force than their military counterparts (except for Chiefs of Naval Operations)? We clearly need organizational histories grounded not only in the records of the agency in question but also in the larger context within which they operated; histories sensitive not only to organizational procedures and prejudices but also to the ability of distinctive personalities from time to time to transcend them.

4) We need more work on the internal determinants of foreign policy. The whole field of domestic politics in relation to diplomacy has been curiously neglected in our narrower preoccupation with whether administrations manipulated the public, or the other way around. The role of Congress in foreign affairs has been treated only superficially in this period. Little work has been done on the role of domestic interest groups, whether academic, economic, ethnic, or religious. The idea of corporatism, that has proven so fruitful a framework for analysis of the 1920s and the 1950s, needs to be tested out for the late 1940s as well. The relationship between culture and diplomacy, it has been suggested, may provide revealing insights. In short, postrevisionism has only begun to scratch the surface in dealing with the domestic setting of foreign policy—much more needs to be done.

5) We need more comparative history. For too long American students of the Cold War—orthodox and revisionist—have followed the false doctrine of "exceptionalism"—the belief that the American experience in the Cold War bears little resemblance to what has happened at other times and in other places. Postrevisionism has made a start toward breaking down that parochialism with regional comparative studies like those of Kuniholm and Lundestad, but we will need more

of them before sharp conclusions about the nature of the American empire will begin to emerge. We could benefit from comparative historical studies across time; two provocative examples of what can be done are Richard Smoke's study of how deterrence worked before the advent of nuclear weapons and Michael Mandelbaum's examination of international politics both before and after Hiroshima. We could use as well comparative biographical studies, especially of the second-level career diplomats whose influence was so pervasive in the period with which we are dealing: Hugh DeSantis, in his study of the State Department's early Soviet specialists, has provided not only an excellent model to follow in this regard, but also a valuable antidote to a recent susceptibility within the profession to interpretive pigeonholes named for Russian cities.

6) We need to begin to consider, more than we have, the impact of U.S. policies on foreign societies. The American empire, like other empires in history, brought about profound changes in countries that came into contact with it. What the American "proconsuls" did in occupied Germany and Japan are only the most obvious examples: Americans were also on the scene, and attempting in one way or another to change the status quo, in places as diverse as Iran, India, Indonesia, Italy, and Iceland. Whether for good or ill is a question we should begin to wrestle with, just as we have had to consider it for other empires stretching back from Britain's to Rome's. A start has been made by works as varied as Lundestad's on Scandinavia, Kuniholm's on the Near East, Lawrence Wittner's on Greece, Robert McMahon's on Indonesia, Bruce Cumings's on Korea, and Michael Grow's on Paraguay, but much remains to be done. Despite detailed work on specific aspects of occupation policies in Germany and Japan, we still have no comprehensive assessments of how those policies related to the overall context of postwar foreign policy. It is remarkable that we still have no full accounts based on archival research of postwar U.S. relations with France, Italy, and Spain, and the whole of Africa and Latin America. Nor has the "special relationship" with the Philippines received the attention it deserves. It is even more surprising that post-revisionist historians have almost totally neglected the debate over "dependency theory" that has been under way for some years now among Third World area specialists.

7) We need more work on the nature of international systems. What are the elements that make for stability and instability in international relations? What are the constituents of power? To political scientists these are old, if unsolved, problems, but historians of the Cold War are only beginning to grapple with them. Were we to give more attention to this area, we might make progress toward unraveling such mysteries as why the post-World War II international order, which no one designed, has proven more durable than its much more

carefully structured World War I counterpart; why, contrary to most expectations, a divided Germany has proven to be a less disruptive force in European politics than a unified Germany was; why the Cold War, at one level a period of unprecedented tension, has at another level turned out to be a period of unusual order and stability.

8) Finally, we might give more thought than we do to the impact of what we write on the making of history itself. Historians like to think they have the luxury of the last word, but that is not really true. What we write will affect historical consciousness in the future, and that in turn can and probably will affect history itself in ways that are impossible to foresee. That prospect imposes on us an obligation to get our history as straight as we can in the beginning—to avoid the temptation to turn history into an instrument of politics, whether of the right or the left. Revisionism in one form or another always will be with us, and that is no bad thing, because the writing of history would be much less interesting without it. But our revisionism should be the kind that reflects new ideas and new sources, not the kind that simply responds, as if by reflex, to the changing ideological fashions of the day.

The field of early Cold War studies is a good bit quieter, perhaps more prosaic, but certainly no less active than it was at the height of our controversies over this subject a decade ago. It is also more mature: we have at last begun, so to speak, to "put away childish things." Possibly we required a certain dimming of the public spotlight in order to accomplish this—in an age when fewer people outside the profession care much one way or another about the origins of the Cold War, the temptation either to pontificate or provoke is thereby diminished. It may be as well that the progression we have seen from truculent orthodoxy through militant revisionism to what some critics regard as the "toothless" stage—postrevisionism—is the way history usually gets written in any event, regardless of the topic. By this logic there may be predictable stages of historical interpretation, just as Walt Rostow once suggested there were stages of economic growth. Whether we have reached the necessary "take-off point" for genuine synthesis is difficult to say: one of the more interesting issues in the profession right now is what constitutes a synthesis in the first place, with believers in multicausal explanations contending against those who demand sweeping integrative frameworks. What is clear, though, is that the field remains a fruitful one, that those who toil in it are doing promising work that ought to be more widely known, but that—as has been said more than once in this article—there is still a lot that remains to be done.

☆ 10 ☆

The Rise of the National Security State

LIBERTY OR SECURITY?

"The price of liberty is eternal vigilance," wrote an American clergyman in the nineteenth century. In one sense this statement could refer to the tension that has always existed within a democratic state between protecting the liberties of the citizen while at the same time allowing the nation-state to take the necessary measures to defend itself. The age-old dilemma of reconciling liberty and security did not hit home with full force in the United States until after 1945. With the development of nuclear weapons that threatened instant annihilation, the appearance of long-range bombers and intercontinental ballistic missiles, and America's rise to the status of a superpower with worldwide responsibilities, what was called the "age of free security" for the United States came to an end. The tension that had traditionally existed between protecting the liberty of the individual on the one hand and ensuring the security of the state on the other entered upon a new era.[1]

To protect the liberty of the individual, institutional mechanisms had been created by the founding fathers to limit the powers of government such as the Bill of Rights, constitutional guarantees, and the like. Yet to survive in a modern world that resembled an armed camp the United States had increasingly moved toward a greater concentration of governmental power and in the direction of a national security state.

---

[1] The term "age of free security" was coined by historian C. Vann Woodward in his article entitled "The Age of Reinterpretation," *American Historical Review* 66 (1966):1–19. Woodward essentially divided American history into two periods: the period before 1945 being the "age of free security" when the oceans flanking America and weak neighbors to the north and south on the North American continent protected this country from attack; and the post-1945 period when long-range bombers, intercontinental ballistic missiles, and atomic and nuclear bombs exposed the United States to attack and possible annihilation.

These conflicting aims raised a crucial question: Should the liberty of the individual or the security of the state be given the higher priority?

The rise of the "state within a state"—a national security state within the American government—was part of the price the United States had to pay for its rise to world power. During the eighteenth and nineteenth centuries, when America was less important on the world scene, it had been possible to think in terms of clear-cut periods of war and peace. But with the coming of the twentieth century, the emergence of the United States as a world power, and the loss of geographical security, the lines between war and peace became blurred. Conditions normally associated with war extended into peacetime; security measures exercised in wartime became peacetime preoccupations. The concept of a national security state came into being to place the country on a continual wartime footing. Most scholars today would agree that since the close of World War II the United States has been in a virtual wartime posture compared to the prewar era.

The concept of a national security state consisted of a unified triad of three elements—*attitudes, policies,* and *institutions*—aimed at keeping the country in a condition of permanent war preparedness. The attitudes arose from the two major considerations in America's foreign policy since World War II: the idea of containing communism, and the new doctrine of national security designed for an age of missiles and nuclear weapons. The policies included containment, confrontation, and intervention—the methods used by American leaders to try and make the world safe for the United States. The institutions included government bureaucracies—such as the F.B.I., C.I.A., and National Security Council—that served to keep the country in a constant state of readiness.

The term "national security state" was first used by Daniel Yergin in 1977.[2] But the antecedents for all three elements could be traced back to World War I. With respect to the attitudes the strong anti-communist stand of the United States had its origins in the sharp American reaction to the Russian Revolution of 1917. America's foreign policy emphasizing more internationalism may be said to date from Woodrow Wilson's motto that World War I was waged to "make the world safe for democracy." Insofar as institutions were concerned the use of the F.B.I. against domestic radicals during World War I and the "red scare" of 1919–1920 marked the beginnings of a national police force within the United States.

Those who disagreed about the relative merits of the national security state—and they included historians, political scientists, scholars of international law as well as policymakers—may be said to fall into two broad groups: "idealists" and "realists."

---

[2]Daniel Yergin, *Shattered Peace* (Boston, 1977), pp. 5–6.

The idealists were those who placed the greatest emphasis on liberty, both at home and abroad. At home they were interested more in protecting the civil liberties of individual citizens, and believed this goal to be as important a priority as the security of the state. As regards events abroad the idealists were convinced that it was necessary to maintain freedom round the world to secure America's own freedom. Hence they urged that the United States should play an activist role in maintaining a liberal world order.

The realists took an opposite point of view. At home they were concerned more with the security of the state and less with the liberties of the individual. On the international scene they were interested more in maintaining a structure of world peace along American lines. They were even willing, during the times of the Nixon-Kissinger détente, to often undertake a policy of *realpolitik* and to enter into a virtual complicity with the Soviet Union in order to maintain a status quo.

The lines between the two groups were not always clear, however, because each recognized that the position of the other had some validity. Idealists realized that the threats from totalitarian countries were real, not imagined; even the most wild-eyed libertarians recognized that all liberties would be lost if the state could not secure and defend itself. By the same token realists who demanded tight security measures realized the irony involved in attacking at times the very liberties they were hoping to protect. It should be noted, moreover, that some individuals who were idealists in the early days of the Cold War changed their minds at a later date and became realists. Conversely, certain realists reversed themselves and became idealists. Thus scholarly writings on this issue could not easily be confined to strict categories.

The term "idealist" presents other difficulties of definition, for it is impossible to eliminate confusion when using this slippery word. In this chapter the word *idealist* will be used in several ways. First, it will be employed to denote those who have presented an interpretation of diplomatic events that differs from the standard Cold War accounts. Second, the term will be used to categorize those persons who believed it was possible to construct a world order along the lines of liberalism. "Liberalism" in this chapter will be understood to mean a mixture of moderate government and a welfare capitalist economy.

The term "realist" presents a similar problem in definition. In this chapter *realist* will be used within a certain context. It will be employed to identify those who accepted the orthodox Cold War interpretation of diplomatic history. These persons supported the containment policy followed by the United States since World War II, and they adhered, generally speaking, to a hard line against the Soviet Union. In terms of domestic policies the realists tended to agree with security measures taken by various administrations—even when such measures were at the expense of civil liberties.

Daniel Yergin, a historian, represented best the idealist point of view in his *Shattered Peace*. In this work Yergin traced the origins of the national security state to Wilsonianism and the ideology of liberal internationalism that lay at the heart of America's foreign policy. Wilson threw the weight of the United States into the politics of the international system, and into the issue at the center of that system: the balance of power in Europe. What Wilson sought, said Yergin, was to project American values into world politics—the values of a liberal society united in a broad Lockean consensus.

The United States hoped to work within the old international system, but only in order to reform and change it. The Wilsonian program aimed to create a middle way between revolution and reaction. It contained a bundle of policies: support for the idea of representative government; democratic liberties and human rights; nonrecognition of revolutionary change; national self-determination; a league of nations; the end to formal empires; the reduction of armaments; a belief in and use of an enlightened public opinion; and the maintenance of a liberal capitalist world economy. Although economic objectives were an important part of the program they represented only one element of the overall scheme. According to Yergin America saw itself as a disinterested, innocent power—one whose own aims were thought to express the yearnings of all people, and whose responsibilities were bound to become inescapable, inevitable, and worldwide.

The Soviet leaders, on the other hand, shared none of these Wilsonian values, Yergin argued. They were concerned primarily with power as it was traditionally conceived in the international system. During the 1920s and 1930s they began to plan for a sphere of influence in the countries on their European borders. While they were doing so a great debate developed among American policymakers regarding Soviet motives. Was that sphere of influence all that Russia wanted, or was it only the first step on the road to worldwide revolution?

Behind this debate lay two questions that confronted American planners who had to shape policy toward the Soviet Union. What was the connection between Marxist-Leninist ideology and Soviet foreign policy? Marxist-Leninist ideology calls for Marxist-Leninists to be conscious agents of revolution. Were the Soviet leaders fomentors of revolution to make the world over in a Communist image? The second question arose out of the brutal horrors of Stalinism—the campaign of terror inside the Soviet Union during the 1920s and 1930s that took an estimated 20 million lives. Did harsh totalitarian practices at home necessarily bring about a foreign policy that was totalitarian in intent abroad? A foreign policy, in other words, committed to the use of force and one dedicated to endless expansion in the pursuit of world domination?

American policymakers struggled from World War I through the mid-1940s to think through these questions and to arrive at an appropriate foreign policy. Two interpretations competed for primacy in this process, according to Yergin. At the heart of the first interpretation was the image of the Soviet Union as a world revolutionary state—one that denied any possibility of coexistence, was committed to unrelenting ideological warfare, and was powered by a messianic drive for world mastery. The second downplayed the role of ideology and the foreign policy consequences of totalitarian domestic practices. It saw the Soviet Union instead behaving like a traditional great power within the international system, rather than trying to overthrow that system.

In the years following World War II, Yergin concluded, the first interpretation became dominant. It provided a foundation for the anti-communist consensus that was to prevail. With this view in mind, any serious attempts at diplomacy were unthinkable. American policy planners felt they could not deal diplomatically with a revolutionary, messianic, predatory power like Russia. The only possible course of action was confrontation and eventually a policy of containment.

Thus Yergin suggested that America's foreign policy planners had misinterpreted the Soviet challenge and Soviet objectives. In doing so they downplayed the possibilities for diplomacy or accommodation of any kind. They formulated a new doctrine of national security premised on the belief that Russia posed an immediate threat to America. This doctrine presupposed an interpretation of America's security needs that was expansionist in its purpose in order that the United States might protect itself. The new doctrine, according to Yergin, marked a major redefinition of America's relation to the rest of the world from the end of World War II to the 1970s. It caused American leaders to pursue a global, crusading foreign policy. The first selection for this chapter is from Yergin's book.

Other idealist historians suggested interpretations of the policies that flowed from the attitudes suggested by Yergin. Melvyn Leffler took issue with the realist historians in an article he published in the *American Historical Review* in 1984. Leffler's research differed from that of Yergin in several important respects. He concentrated mainly on the work of military planners instead of civilian policymakers. His sources were different because he had available to him recently declassified Pentagon material. And his focus in terms of time was different: he was interested only in World War II and the postwar period. As a result he came to a number of different conclusions regarding America's policies.

Leffler located the origins of the Cold War at an earlier date than many realist historians. Most realists believed that the overt Cold War began around 1947 with the formulation of the containment policy enunciated in the Truman Doctrine. Leffler pointed out, however, that American military men had already begun developing plans for a defense-in-depth in 1944–1945 involving a series of far-flung overseas bases to protect America's security. Two world wars had taught military planners one important lesson in geopolitics, said Leffler. Any power or combination of powers seeking to dominate the Eurasian land mass was to be regarded as hostile by the United States. Since Russia represented the only major power possessing such a capability, America's policies toward the Soviet Union became unnecessarily provocative, according to Leffler.[3]

Turning to the institutions of the national security state Richard Barnet, an idealist political scientist, discussed the professional elite who helped to devise national defense policies. In *Roots of War*, published in 1971, Barnet postulated the presence of a group within the government that he called "national security managers." Serving as advisers to American presidents these men had come to power as the result of an organizational revolution during World War II. This revolution has raised the entire federal bureaucracy to a new position of authority over American society, and within that bureaucracy national security institutions had emerged as the most dominant.

The national security managers were drawn primarily from law and banking, and Barnet's thesis held that they symbolized the triumph of the military-industrial complex over the government. They placed the country on a permanent war economy, and reshaped the idea of America's national interest. Barnet believed that this national security establishment was strongly influenced in its predilection for expansion by its close connections with the American business community. The national security managers, concluded Barnet, were amoral, ruthless and had a penchant for violence as well as a fascination with the lethal technology of the day.[4]

The institutions of the national security state in one respect presented scholars with a paradox: to defend freedom and the democratic way of life, institutions such as the F.B.I. and C.I.A. sometimes violated the very liberties they had been created to protect. One characteristic of a classic police state was the formation of independent state bureaucracies such as a secret police. Although the United States was

---

[3]Melvyn Leffler, "The American Conception of National Security and the Beginnings of the Cold War, 1945–1948," and "Comments," *American Historical Review* 89 (1984):346–390. Leffler also suggested that the national security approach might be employed to study the history of American foreign policy in the eighteenth and nineteenth centuries. See *Journal of American History* 77 (1990):143–152.

[4]Another book critical of the professional elite in policy-making was I. M. Destler, Leslie Gelb, and Anthony Lake, *Our Own Worst Enemy* (New York, 1984).

far from a police state, the F.B.I. and C.I.A. frequently violated the First Amendment, search-and-seizure constitutional rights, and other civil liberties in the course of their operations.

Such violations had a history stretching back to World War I, according to Frank Donner, an idealist lawyer-historian. In *Age of Surveillance*, published in 1980, Donner noted that the federalization of domestic intelligence operations took place during World War I and the Russian Revolution. During the war and the famed "red scare" of 1919–1920 that followed, the F.B.I. carried out massive assaults against domestic radicals. In the 1930s the Bureau continued to conduct large-scale illegal investigations against political dissidents—almost invariably against left-wingers.

The creation of the C.I.A. in 1947 expanded this political intelligence network. The mission of the C.I.A. was to gather secret information or intelligence for security purposes throughout the world. In 1950, under memorandum NSC-68, it was recommended that the United States employ the same kind of Cold War intelligence methods that the Soviets were using against this country. This recommendation was applied with a vengeance. The C.I.A., F.B.I., and other security agencies rapidly developed into a national police force—one that was fenced off by tight security and operated with little or no oversight by Congress.

In the years that followed, spying on ordinary citizens by such agencies became a common occurrence, Donner noted. The Watergate crisis of the early 1970s revealed that both the C.I.A. and the F.B.I. had engaged in illegal wiretapping and other clandestine operations that violated civil liberties. The C.I.A. it was discovered had for years violated its charter, which specifically forbade it from carrying on operations within the United States. During the Vietnam War it had regularly conducted illegal operations against antiwar protesters and other groups of political dissidents. At the same time it came to light that the F.B.I. had gathered for over three decades political information on journalists, political opponents of sitting presidents, and critics of national policy and had delivered such information to the White House.

The substantial scholarly literature that developed on the subject showed the lengths to which the United States government was willing to go in assaulting the constitutional rights and civil liberties of citizens in the interests of national security during the Cold War. Every branch of government was involved, including presidents from both major parties, congresses both liberal and conservative, the F.B.I. and C.I.A., the House Un-American Activities Committee, the Office of Management and Budget, the United States Information Agency, and government agencies on the state and local level as well. The rights of individual citizens and various social groups were abridged through executive orders, congressional hearings, and administrative decrees. Time and again the Constitution was brushed aside and persons branded as subversives or their loyalty questioned, sometimes on the basis of spurious and dated allegations.

Stanley Kutler's *The American Inquisition* (1982) presented some in-depth case studies during the 1940s and 1950s that showed official political oppression on an unprecedented scale. The government challenged the loyalty of thousands of its employees and others, resorted to illegal surveillance, vindictiveness, and harassment of individuals, and charged or prosecuted for treason prominent persons like Ezra Pound and "Tokyo Rose." What Kutler was particularly interested in was the whole process of legal repression: the interaction between law and politics, the exercise of public and private power alike, and the covert as well as overt operations of power. Those exercising such powers—the power holders in various bureaucracies—subverted the law at times to achieve their ends. But ironically enough, he concluded, there were limits to repression and the abuse of norms: these same power holders as guardians and executors of law ultimately found themselves bound to follow the rule of law and were restrained by that self-same doctrine. The second selection in this chapter is from Kutler's book.

One authority on the Cold War, Athan Theoharis, who wrote, edited, and co-edited a series of books in the 1970s and 1980s, was much harsher in his judgment regarding political repression. Theoharis began with *Seeds of Repression* in 1971 which argued that the McCarthyism of the 1950s derived its effectiveness from two sources. The first was the changed political climate which intensified following the death of President Roosevelt when the American leaders adopted policies making the United States responsible for originating the Cold War. They pictured the Soviet Union as a threat to the creation of a global system of stability, peace, and prosperity that America was proposing. The second source was President Truman's rigid anti-Soviet rhetoric which took on the fervor of a crusade against communism, stressing America's innocence, Soviet depravity, and the necessity for confronting the Soviet threat abroad and possible subversive communist dangers on the domestic front. Thus, Theoharis located the origins of McCarthyism, not in Senator Joseph A. McCarthy himself (which had been the conventional view), but within the Cold War which created the context for this political movement, and in President Truman's rhetoric and flawed leadership which helped to create the climate that eventually led to McCarthyism.

Theoharis followed up his earlier work with *The Specter* (1974), a book he co-edited with Robert Griffith, who had authored a prize-winning book on McCarthy and the Senate. This volume of collected essays by different authors delved more deeply into the subject. Some scholars examined groups traditionally identified with McCarthyism—Catholics, conservatives, and businessmen. Others studied liberal groups—the American Civil Liberties Union, Americans for Democratic Action, and the C.I.O.—which had not been examined as part of the repressive politics of the period. Finally, an effort was made to assess McCarthy's impact on internal security legislation, and his pre-1950 use of the anti-communist issue.[5]

Beginning in the early 1970s, Theoharis began to shift his focus to the role of the F.B.I. His research was helped by a number of developments: the passage of the Freedom of Information Act in 1966; the revelations in 1971 that the F.B.I. had conducted surveillance of anti-war protestors during the Vietnam era; J. Edgar Hoover's death in 1972; the Watergate Affair and subsequent exposés of the Bureau's actions in the episode. Perhaps the most decisive event was the formation in 1975–76 of the Church Committee in Congress, with which Theoharis worked, that made public the Bureau's role. The result was *Spying on Americans* (1978) which described and analyzed in detail the history of F.B.I. break-ins, wiretappings, politically-motivated investigations, and preventive detention programs from 1936 to 1978. His conclusion was that by the 1970s the nation faced a serious constitutional crisis. Laws had been violated with impunity, responsible executive officials had failed to fulfill their assigned oversight roles, and Congress had been virtually excluded from its proper legislative and oversight responsibilities.[6]

One of Theoharis's students, Kenneth O'Reilly, showed in his *Racial Matters* (1989) how the F.B.I. kept secret files on black Americans from 1960 to 1972 as the Bureau waged war along racial lines. Hoover viewed black people as inferior and subordinate all his life, and became convinced there were communist influences behind the civil rights movement of the 1960s and 1970s. To him all black America, not only Martin Luther King, Jr., whom he harassed, presented a threat to internal peace and stability. Black urban communities were placed under surveillance, black leaders persecuted, and the Counterintelligence Program of harassment the Bureau had initiated against the Communist and Social Workers Parties and the Ku Klux Klan was extended to include blacks. It made no difference whether Democrats or Republicans were in control of the White House: the Kennedy, Johnson, and Nixon administrations all solicited F.B.I. intelligence and permitted illegal surveillance and disruption of black activities.[7]

———————

[5]For works on McCarthy and McCarthyism, see Robert Griffin, *Politics of Fear* (Lexington, Ky., 1970) and David Oshinsky, *A Conspiracy So Immense* (New York, 1983).

[6]For additional work by Theoharis on the F.B.I.'s investigative and political role during the Cold War years, see the volume of collected essays he edited, *Beyond the Hiss Case* (Philadelphia, 1982).

[7]For the harassment of King by the Bureau, see David Garrow, *The FBI and Martin Luther King, Jr.* (New York, 1981). For a wide-ranging study of the F.B.I., House committee on Un-American Activities, and fear of communist menace by the federal government from 1919 through the election of Ronald Reagan, see Kenneth O'Reilly, *Hoover and Un-Americans* (Philadelphia, 1983).

The outstanding scholar presenting the realist point of view was Samuel P. Huntington, a Harvard University political scientist. In *The Soldier and the State,* published in 1957, Huntington discussed the idea of a "garrison state." He derived this concept from Harold Laswell, a political scientist who predicted that in the post-World War II period both the United States and the Soviet Union might evolve into garrison states because of a prolonged Cold War era. The garrison state idea possessed many characteristics of the national security state. Within a garrison state a military oligarchy would take charge, Laswell said, because of the overwhelming need for military security. Democratic institutions would be either abolished or become purely ceremonial, since military institutions and democratic institutions would prove incompatible within such a society. The garrison state differed markedly, moreover, from both a capitalist and a socialist state in an economic sense. In the former the ultimate aim of production and natural resources would be for military purposes, while in a capitalist or socialist state the aim of production was use of goods and services by the citizenry.

Huntington explored the implications of the garrison state idea in his book and concluded that the relations between the military and civilian segments of American society had undergone a profound revolution since World War II. Before the war the main question had been: What pattern of civil-military relations was most compatible with America's liberal democratic values? After the war this question had been succeeded by what Huntington considered a more important issue: What pattern of civil-military relations would best maintain the security of the United States? The threat of the Soviet Union, claimed Huntington, had made security and sheer survival the main objective of American policy. In this new age the soldier, not the civilian, was destined to play the more important role; security not liberty was to be the ultimate aim of American society.

The thesis of Huntington's book was that under these circumstances America had to abandon its traditional attitude of suspicion toward the military. Heretofore legislators who dealt with military affairs had been concerned primarily with protecting America's liberal democratic heritage from creeping militarism. According to Huntington, however, liberalism as a philosophy did not permit the nation to think in realistic terms about war and military institutions. In the new age, when security would be America's primary goal, there had to be a more realistic attitude—one that accepted the military more readily and at the same time reduced the high expectations of liberty by American liberals.

Huntington pursued this theme but broadened his focus in subsequent books. In a work entitled *The Crisis of Democracy,* which he coauthored in 1975, Huntington's essay took up the relationship of the military to the state within the context of a much larger problem. That problem was implicit in the question: "Who governs America?" When providing answers to this question Huntington did so with the new age of the national security state in mind. There were two possible answers. Should elites make public policy and rule America—with "elites" being defined as those men whom Barnet termed "national security managers" as well as members of the private establishment made up of important businessmen, banks, law firms, foundations, and the national media? Or should public policy be made through public opinion, mass democracy, and the rule of the people through their elected officials—the president and the Congress? By asking the question "Who governs?," Huntington, by implication, was raising an even more profound historical question. Had the ideology and institutions spawned by the Cold War changed the character of traditional American democracy? Had the nature of American democracy changed from the "great republic" envisioned by the founding fathers in which the people were sovereign into a remote, impenetrable national security state controlled by elites?[8]

When answering the question "Who governs?," Huntington reviewed in his book some of the dynamic changes that had occurred in the United States during the 1960s and early 1970s. The 1960s, he noted, was "a decade of dramatic surge and the reassertion of democratic egalitarianism." This democratic surge manifested itself in a variety of ways. First, there was the increased political participation in electioneering campaigns. Second, there was greater citizen participation in protest movements, demonstrations, marches, and in organizations devoted to causes such as preserving peace and improving the environment. Finally, there was a markedly higher level of self-consciousness among blacks, Indians, Chicanos, white ethnic groups, college students, and women.[9]

This democratic surge, among other things, had resulted in what Huntington called "an excess of democracy." Al Smith had once remarked that "the only cure for the evils of democracy was more democracy." But Huntington concluded that more democracy would simply create more problems. His prescription for America was less democracy: What the country needed in the new age of national security, said Huntington, was fewer democratic demands. In short, liberty was to be sacrificed in the interests of security.[10]

Huntington pushed the implications of his realist thesis in yet another book, *American Politics: The Politics of Disharmony,* pub-

---

[8]Michael Crozier, Samuel Huntington, and Joji Watanuki, *The Crisis of Democracy* (New York, 1975), pp. 59–118.

[9]*Ibid.,* 60.

[10]*Ibid.,* 113.

lished in 1981. In this work Huntington explored the tension between the ideal and the real within the political system. He defined as the ideal an American creed made up of a set of beliefs in liberty, individualism, equality, and distrust of authority. The real was comprised of the actual political institutions with their inevitable restraints on freedom. The tension between the two created a persistent gap between the promise of American ideals and the performance of America's political institutions—between what ought to be and what is. Throughout their history as a nation Americans were united by the American creed, said Huntington. At the same time these ideals were perennially frustrated by those institutions and hierarchies required to carry out the functions of governing a democratic society. The clash between the two—American ideals and institutions—resulted in an enduring tension.

Americans, according to Huntington's analysis, tried to adjust to this tension in four ways: by moralistic reform; by cynicism; by complacency; and by hypocrisy. In *American Politics* Huntington was primarily concerned with moralistic reform. Every sixty to seventy years the American people attempted to close the gap between ideals and institutions with outbursts of reform that Huntington termed periods of "creedal passion." The four major reform periods—the American Revolution, Jacksonian period, Progressive movement, and the political rebellion of the 1960s and early 1970s—reflected in his eyes attempts to make political institutions conform more closely to the American creed. Despite some limited successes each of these periods inevitably resulted in a reversion to complacency, cynicism, and hypocrisy. Huntington's analysis provided a cyclical explanation of why America had experienced both so much consensus and so much conflict throughout its history.

Huntington's writings in his various books were aimed at justifying a society far less liberal than the one Americans had experienced throughout their history. Such a society was necessary, he felt, given the needs of America's security in the post-World War II world. He developed the concept of "objective civilian control" in *The Soldier and the State* to justify setting the military apart from the demands of a liberal society, and suggested the scaling down of traditional civilian safeguards in future civil-military relations.[11] In *American Politics* he criticized as "creedal passion" American actions taken in defense of this country's liberal ideology during the 1960s and early 1970s. Huntington, for example, decried the American "crusades" against the activities of the F.B.I. and C.I.A., excessive defense spending, the use of military force abroad, the military-industrial complex, and the so-called "imperial presidency." Such actions in his view threatened to

---

[11]Samuel P. Huntington, *The Soldier and the State* (New York, 1957), pp. 80–97.

expose, weaken, dismantle, or abolish the very institutions that provided security for America's liberal society against foreign threats.[12] To sum up, Huntington's works provided the clearest exposition of the realist position on the national security state, and advanced the strongest arguments for placing security ahead of liberty.

Unlike Huntington other realists revealed a greater anxiety about the need for a national security state along with the protection of liberty. Hans Morgenthau, a pronounced realist, was one of America's most distinguished scholars of international relations. Although he did not deal directly with the idea of a national security state in his *The Purpose of American Politics*, published in 1960, many of the issues he took up had a bearing on this matter. Morgenthau in his other books had been critical of America's foreign policy from 1776 to World War II as being too utopian, and he suggested that only since 1945 had Americans become realistic and framed their foreign policy in accordance with international power politics and along the lines of national interest.

In *The Purpose of American Politics* Morgenthau raised the question of whether America had lost its national purpose in the twentieth century. From its beginnings, he said, the United States had sought the establishment of equality in freedom in order to present an example to the rest of the world. The depression of the 1930s had brought reforms and a reaffirmation of that principle at home. Americans then moved outward in a manner consistent with its national purpose by fighting Hitler, and, after 1947, in opposing the spread of communism. But from 1947 to 1960 everything had gone wrong according to Morgenthau. The sense of national purpose declined: America failed to keep China in the American camp and accepted a stalemate in Korea; McCarthyism was embraced in the 1950s; the spread of communism was not checked; government was paralyzed by three developments (executive-legislative divisions, a governance-by-committee approach, and too great a reliance on public opinion polls); private interests outweighed public interests; and objective standards of excellence were replaced by the notion that what the majority wanted should prevail. The only hope, as Morgenthau saw it, was a move to recapture the sense of national purpose through reforms at home and through the export abroad of the American concept of equality-in-freedom. To Morgenthau the restoration of the sense of national purpose was a precondition for America's survival.

To remedy the situation Morgenthau proposed a greater degree of authoritarianism. A strong president, he felt, would help lead America back to the correct path. The National Security Council, which formu-

---

[12]Samuel P. Huntington, *American Politics: The Promise of Disharmony* (Cambridge, Mass., 1981), p. 238.

lated public policy on the most momentous matters of state affecting security, he believed, should be influenced less by the "government-by-committee" attitude that prevailed in Washington circles. And from his viewpoint there should be "less abdication of government before the specter of public opinion."[13] Although Morgenthau's argument was sophisticated and subtle he was clearly prepared to check excessive liberties in favor of more security.

George Kennan, the policymaker and diplomat, was close to the realist position but showed even more ambivalence on this issue. Like Morgenthau he had been critical of America's foreign policy in the early twentieth century because it was based too much on moral grounds and not enough on realism. Although he had helped frame America's containment policy, Kennan argued in the first volume of his *Memoirs*, published in 1967, that the Truman administration had pursued the wrong priorities in Europe by concentrating on a policy of military containment rather than one which balanced political and military considerations.

As concerns other features of the national security state, Kennan in his second volume published in 1972 described with distaste the events during the McCarthy era when the civil liberties of his colleagues in the State Department were violated in the presumed interests of national security. The excesses of McCarthyism alarmed Kennan. Although he approved of strong measures for purposes of protecting national security, he recognized the dangers of going too far. The greatest threat to America was, he pointed out:

> . . . a danger that something may occur in our minds and souls which will make us no longer like the persons by whose efforts this republic was founded and held together, but rather like the representatives of that very power we are trying to combat: intolerant, secretive, suspicious, cruel and terrified of internal dissension. . . . The worst thing the Communists could do to us, and the thing we have most to fear from their activities, is that we should become like them.[14]

The fourth and final scholar who represented the realist position, though with serious qualifications, was John L. Gaddis, who published *Strategies of Containment* in 1981. Gaddis provided an analysis of how America's policy of containment had unfolded over time. It originated with George Kennan's recommendations in 1947, he said, and then was articulated more fully in NSC-68—the secret memorandum framed by the National Security Council in 1950. This memorandum—one of the key documents of the Cold War—viewed the world as being divided between America and Russia. Soviet foreign policy

---

[13]Hans Morgenthau, *The Purpose of American Politics* (New York, 1960), p. 267.

[14]George F. Kennan, *Memoirs*, 2 vols. (Boston, 1967–1972), II:200. Emphasis added.

was seen as dedicated to two goals: the preservation of Russia's power and ideology, and the extension of Soviet power by the absorption of new satellite states and the weakening of any other competing system of power in the world. To contain such a threat it was proposed that the United States assume unilaterally the defense of the free world. The argument advanced for this policy was that it was no longer possible to distinguish between America's national security and global security. Gaddis then followed the strategies based on this containment policy through Eisenhower's "New Look," the Kennedy-Johnson "flexible response," the Vietnam War, and the Nixon-Kissinger period of détente.

Gaddis believed, however, that the United States had vacillated between two foreign policies personified by the two men mostly responsible for framing the containment policy. Paul Nitze, an arms control expert, held that the United States should respond to each and every Soviet threat—regardless of the cost. George Kennan, then head of the Policy Planning Staff, suggested instead a strategy of selective responses. His strategy called for making a distinction between tolerable and intolerable threats, America's vital and peripheral interests, and bearable and unbearable costs. Oscillating between these two views resulted in disastrous consequences, according to Gaddis. America failed to achieve a national consensus, to develop a coherent approach to foreign policy, or to enhance its authority throughout the world. Gaddis, by taking a more skeptical view of the orthodox interpretation of the Cold War advanced by other realist scholars, might therefore be more fairly categorized as an idealistic realist on the issue of the national security state.

With the ending of the Cold War in the late 1980s, America faced a crossroads: what should the country do about the national security state that had been built up over the period of almost half a century? With the Cold War over, should the United States reverse the process that had increasingly placed national security concerns above individual liberties? Or should the country maintain its guard high against prospective enemies in the future? Had the modern nature of warfare changed the situation so that the United States would have to be saddled with a perpetual national security state? Or was it possible to think in terms of a new world order that might enable the traditional rights of citizens to be restored to the status enjoyed in pre-Cold War years? In answering such questions, students will be determining not only the future course of America but their own destiny in the years ahead.

Daniel Yergin

DANIEL YERGIN (1947–   ) *has taught at the Kennedy School of Government at Harvard University, and is currently president of the Cambridge Energy Research Association. He is the author of several books, including* Shattered Peace *(1977),* Global Insecurity *(1982), and* The Prize: The Epic Quest for Oil, Money, and Power *(1991).*

By 1945 the world had been refashioned by death, destruction, and social upheaval. Germany and Japan, two of the most powerful nations, had been defeated and occupied, and the aging European empires were on the way to distintegration. With the defeat or decline of most of the European states, the old international system collapsed, leaving just two powers dominant, the United States and the Soviet Union. Many basic questions had no clear answers in 1945, and even as Stalin spoke in September of that year, the victor states were already busy assessing each other across the devastated lands and the wreckage of states, anxiously calculating possible gains and losses.

The victors never did find the tie that would hold them together. The Grand Alliance gave way to a global antagonism between two hostile coalitions, one led by the United States and the other by the Soviet Union—those two countries standing opposed to each other as nation-states, as ideologies, and as economic and political systems. After 1945 the two superpowers were able to approximate a state of general mobilization without general war being the consequence.

The confrontation brought about fundamental changes in American life, a permanent military readiness in what passed for peacetime. "We are in a period now I think of the formulation of a mood," Dean Acheson told a group of American policymakers at the end of 1947. "The country is getting serious. It is getting impressed by the fact that the business of dealing with the Russians is a long, long job. People don't say any more why doesn't Mr. Truman get together with Uncle Joe Stalin and fix it up. That used to be a common idea. There is less and less talk even among silly people about dropping bombs on Moscow. They now see it as a long, long pull, and that it can only be done by the United States getting itself together, determining that we cannot maintain a counter-balance to the communistic power without strengthening all those other parts of the world which belong in the

---

system with us. That takes money, imagination, American skill and American technical help and many, many years." Confident that the public was coming to accept this view, Acheson added, "We are going to understand that our functions in the world will require all of the power and all the thought and all the calmness we have at our disposal."

Acheson spoke about the "United States getting itself together." By this, he meant that the country had to become organized for perpetual confrontation and for war. The unified pattern of attitudes, policies, and institutions by which this task was to be effected comprise what I call America's "national security state." It became, in fact, a "state within a state." The attitudes were derived from the two commanding ideas of American postwar foreign policy—anticommunism and a new doctrine of national security. The policies included containment, confrontation, and intervention, the methods by which U.S. leaders have sought to make the world safe for America. The institutions include those government bureaucracies and private organizations that serve in permanent war preparedness. These developments have helped to increase dramatically the power of the Executive branch of the U.S. government, particularly the presidency. For the national security state required, as Charles Bohlen put it in 1948, "a confidence in the Executive where you give human nature in effect a very large blank check."

And so the Second World War was succeeded not by the peace that Yalta had promised, but by a new conflict, the Cold War, an armed truce, precarious and dangerous—and still today, the central and defining fact of international life. . . .

This is not a book for those who want a simple story, a morality play, a confirmation of prejudices, or a rationalization for or against present-day policies. It is my hope that the narrative that follows will enable us to penetrate the myths and the polemics so that we might learn how and why the confrontation between the United States and the Soviet Union came about—not as people have chosen to remember it, but as it really happened.

One of the great diplomatic sports between East and West in the latter part of the 1940s was what might be called "onus-shifting"— each side trying to make a record and place blame on the other for the division of Europe and the Cold War itself. In this sense, much of the subsequent writing about the Cold War, both "orthodox" and "revisionist," has been a continuation of the Cold War by other means. The impulse to apportion blame is understandable simply from the magnitude of the circumstance. But the very name "Cold War" has provided an important additional reason, for historians spend much time tracking responsibilities for the outbreak of wars. The Cold War, however, was something other than a war. If one imagines that this phenomenon had instead become conventionally known as the "global antagonism," as it might have, then it becomes instantly clear how difficult it is to assign guilt in a meaningful way. For how do you blame a single man—whether Stalin, Churchill, or Truman—for so complicated a phenomenon, involving events in so many different countries and at so many different levels. Of course, it was hard to resist the impulse during the years when the antagonism was as its sharpest, but perhaps the passage of time has liberated us from the need to apportion blame in the course of explanation.

For the fundamental source of the Cold War, we must turn to the interests and positions of nation-states, which are the basic unit in international politics. As the historian F. H. Hinsley has observed, "In an international system the independent state is unable to abandon its primary concern with advancing the interests of that society in competition with other states, if also by collaboration with them." This imperative applies as much to states that draw their inspiration and legitimacy from Marx as to those based on Locke or divine right. The four-century-old state system that was centered in Europe, and which had been weakened in the First World War, collapsed in the course of the Second. A new system would have to emerge. There was much uncertainty about the shape it would take, and about the two countries that were sure to dominate it. One of them, the United States, had been little involved in the old system; the other, the Union of Soviet Socialist Republics, had been mostly excluded from it in the years between the two world wars. The U.S.A. and the U.S.S.R. had little in the way of common traditions, no common political vocabulary, precious few links. They looked upon themselves as rival models for the rest of mankind. They shared little except distrust.

In a system of independent states, all nations live rather dangerously. Therefore, the reduction of dangers becomes a nation's objective in international politics. A country will take actions and pursue policies that it considers defensive, but which appear ominous, if not threatening, to rivals. And so a dialectic of confrontation develops.

But why did the Cold War confrontation take the shape it did? Here we must look closely at the diplomacy of the postwar period. For it is central to my argument that diplomacy *did* matter. There has been too much of a tendency to assume that all that happened was of a single piece, foreordained and determined. But how world leaders perceived their interests and acted on those perceptions counted for a very great deal.

The Soviet outlook was not the only significant ideological factor involved in the development of the global antagonism. There was also the American ideology—the ideas and outlook that U.S. leaders brought to international affairs, their *world set.* The understanding American leaders had of events and possibilities controlled their own actions and reactions in the dialectic of confrontation.

We shall pay close attention to three key elements in their world set—Wilsonianism, an interpretation of Soviet objectives, and the new doctrine of national security.

Wilsonianism, an ideology of liberal internationalism, has been at the heart of twentieth-century American foreign policy. It is a powerful vision of how the world might be organized, and of America's role in it. Woodrow Wilson was its most articulate proponent in the years 1917–19, when the United States threw its full weight into the politics of the international system and into the issue at the center of that system—the balance of power in Europe. Wilson sought to project American values into world politics, the values of a liberal society united in a broad Lockean consensus.

Wilson, like many other American leaders then and now, thought that the often brutal anarchy of the international system and the balance of power could be superseded by a juridical international community, committed to due process and common values. The United States would work within the old system only in order to reform it. The Wilsonian program, meant to produce a middle way between reaction and revolution, included national self-determination, representative government, a league of nations, an end to formal empires, nonrecognition of revolutionary change, democratic liberties and human rights, reduction of armaments, a belief in an "enlightened public opinion," and an open-door world economy. The economic objectives were an important element, but only part of the picture. The United States saw itself as a disinterested, innocent power, whose own desires and aims were thought to express the yearnings of all people, and whose responsibilities were to become inescapable and worldwide.

But, almost immediately after the First World War, a disillusioned American polity put aside the pursuit of the program, though not its values. Europe slid into political and economic chaos, and then again into war. The men guiding U.S. policy in the 1940s had witnessed events in their own lifetimes that provided a compelling impetus for once again trying to make Woodrow Wilson's enterprise work. They saw the Great Depression as a very close call for their own kind of liberal capitalist society. The rise of the dictatorships and the experience of two world wars made their quest for a different kind of world order even more urgent. They wanted to fulfill the Wilsonian vision so that, as Secretary of State Cordell Hull told Congress in 1943, "there will no longer be a need for spheres of influence, for alliances, for balance of power, or any other of the special arrangements through which, in the unhappy past, the nations strove to safeguard their security or to promote their interests." These men thought the best of all worlds was a world without nazism, communism, and colonialism. This desire was not cynical. They feared that a world laden with reaction or revolution would be a world dangerous for American society, a rapacious world soon to be embroiled again in war. And autocracy of any kind offended their deepest democratic instincts.

The unhappy past was much with American leaders. "I cannot tell you how much I appreciate your very comforting letter recalling the obstacles of 1919," James Byrnes, who became Secretary of State in 1945, wrote to a friend in December of that year, shortly before flying to Moscow to continue the arid attempts to make a postwar settlement with the Russians. "As I read your letter I recalled the hurdles we had to overcome after World War I. . . . It is remarkable how history repeats itself."

But, as it sought to remove conflict and anarchy from international relations, Wilsonianism was truly seeking to abolish the very substance of world politics—balance of power, spheres of influence, power politics. These are the ineluctable features of an international system composed of sovereign nations. It is paradoxical, but in order to achieve his goals, a Wilsonian must be a renegade Wilsonian, like Franklin Roosevelt, facing the world as it is, not as one would wish it to be, using traditional means to achieve Wilsonian ends.

The Soviet leaders, on the other hand, shared none of the Wilsonian values. Though they spoke in the language of Marxism-Leninism, they were primarily concerned with power as traditionally conceived in the international system. They were carving a sphere of influence, a glacis, out of bordering countries. As they did so, a great debate developed within the American policy elite over how to evaluate Soviet intentions and capabilities. Was that sphere all Russia wanted or was it only a first step on a road to world revolution?

Underlying the debate were two related questions that have always confronted those in the West who have to shape policies toward the Soviet Union. They are the same two questions we face today.

The first was raised by the October 1917 Revolution itself. What is the connection between Marxist-Leninist ideology and Soviet foreign policy? The ideology proclaims that communism will inevitably inherit the entire world from capitalism, and calls upon Marxist-Leninists to be the conscious agents of the revolution. But the men who have ruled the Soviet Union were not and are not merely ideologues with many idle hours to dream about tomorrow's utopia. For the most part, they must concern themselves with today, with governing a powerful state that has pressing interests to protect, dangers to avoid, tasks to accomplish, and problems to solve. "There is no revolutionary movement in the West," said Stalin during the debates over the Brest-Litovsk treaty in 1918. "There are no facts, there is only a possibility, and with possibilities we cannot reckon."

The second question was brutally posed by the horrors of Stalinism, in particular by collectivization and the Great Terror of the 1930s. Does a totalitarian practice at home necessarily produce a foreign policy that is totalitarian in intent, committed to overturning the international system and to endless expansion in pursuit of world dominance? The policies of Adolf Hitler seemed to confirm that a powerful relationship did exist between such domestic practice and international behavior.

The changes wrought by the Second World War gave urgent and highest priority to these questions. What was the American response to be? Within the ensuing debate, there were two sets of generalizations, two interpretations that competed for hegemony in the American policy elite in the middle 1940s. At the heart of the first set was an image of the Soviet Union as a world revolutionary state, denying the possibilities of coexistence, committed to unrelenting ideological warfare, powered by a messianic drive for world mastery. The second set downplayed the role of ideology and the foreign policy consequences of authoritarian domestic practices, and instead saw the Soviet Union behaving like a traditional Great Power within the international system, rather than trying to overthrow it. The first set I call, for shorthand, the Riga axioms; the second, the Yalta axioms.*

The Riga axioms triumphed in American policy circles in the postwar years and provided a foundation for the anticommunist consensus. Charles Bohlen summarized this outlook when he wrote to former Secretary of State Edward Stettinius in 1949. "I am quite convinced myself, and I think all of those who have been working specifically on the problems of relations with the Soviet Union are in agreement," said Bohlen, "that the reasons for the state of tension that exists in the world today between the Soviet Union and the non-Soviet world are to be found in the character and nature of the Soviet state, the doctrines to which it faithfully adheres, and not in such matters as the shutting off of Lend-Lease and the question of a loan."

With a view of this sort, the effort to make a diplomatic settlement became irrelevant, even dangerous, for the Cold War confrontation was thought to be almost genetically preordained in the revolutionary, messianic, predatory character of the Soviet Union.

Though not so named, the Riga and Yalta axioms still today provide the points of reference for the continuing debate about how to organize U.S. relations with the Soviet Union. The Riga axioms help form the outlook of the Cold War. The Yalta axioms underlie détente.

Neither set of axioms had a monopoly on the truth. Both empha-

---

*To my knowledge no one ever before referred to these two interpretative structures as the Riga and Yalta axioms. My reasons for doing so will become clear as the narrative unfolds.

sized some aspects of reality, and obscured others. No decent human being, whatever his political values, can be anything but appalled by the monstrous horrors of the Stalinist regime. As Solzhenitsyn has written, the prison camps stretched across the Soviet Union like a great archipelago. As many as twenty million people may have died because of Stalin's tyranny. So awful is the legacy that the Soviet leadership today, a quarter century after the dictator's death, still cannot acknowledge what Khrushchev called Stalin's "crimes." To do so would be to undermine the very legitimacy of the Soviet system.

The terror merely abated during the time of the Grand Alliance. Of her experiences during the war years, Nadezhda Mandelstam, the widow of the poet Osip Mandelstam, writes: "By this time I had talked with many people who had returned from the camps (and most of them were sent back to them in the second half of the forties)." She asks, "What manner of people were they, those who first decreed and then carried out this mass destruction of their own kind?" There is no good answer. But she pleads, "No one should lightly dismiss our experience, as complacent foreigners do, cherishing the hope that with them—who are so clever and cultured—things will be different."

For my part, I do not want to suggest that Stalin's character, intentions, or methods were, by any means, benign or kindly. But in the international arena, Stalin's politics were not those of a single-minded world revolutionist. The truth is that the Soviet Union's foreign policy was often clumsy and brutal, sometimes confused, but usually cautious and pragmatic. The U.S.S.R. behaved as a traditional Great Power, intent upon aggrandizing itself along the lines of historic Russian goals, favoring spheres of influence, secret treaties, Great Power consortiums, and the other methods and mores from the "old diplomacy." Moreover, if the Soviet Union had harbored ambitions of unlimited expansion, it was hardly in a position to pursue them. Unlike the United States, whose gross national product had actually doubled during the war, it was a ruined, ravaged country in 1945.

American leaders who accepted the Riga axioms misinterpreted both the range and degree of the Soviet challenge and the character of Soviet objectives and so downplayed the possibilities for diplomacy and accommodation. It was the new doctrine of "national security" that led them to believe that the U.S.S.R. presented an *immediate military* threat to the United States. That doctrine, an expansive interpretation of American security needs, represented a major redefinition of America's relation to the rest of the world.

If American interests were in jeopardy everywhere in the world, the exercise of Soviet power anywhere outside Russian borders appeared ominous. Any form of compromise was therefore regarded as appeasement, already once tried and once failed.

The doctrine of national security also permitted America's postwar leaders to harmonize the conflicting demands of Wilsonianism and realpolitik—to be democratic idealists and pragmatic realists at the same time. So emboldened, American leaders pursued a global, often crusading, foreign policy, convinced that it was made urgent by something more earthy than the missionary impulse of Woodrow Wilson.

History is shaped by the time in which it is written. This work was researched and executed during the latter years of the Vietnam War and the period of what might be called tentative détente. Consequently, two separate questions have informed my inquiry. First, I wanted to determine, if I could, the origins of the ideologies, policies, and institutions that played a major role in the U.S. intervention in Indochina. That is, what gave rise to the national security state? Of course, if would be simplistic to say that the ideology, policies, and institutions that are the subject of this book in themselves *caused* the Vietnam War. Nor do I mean to suggest that the United States alone is "guilty" of possessing a national security state or that, somehow, the national security state is a creature of capitalism. As embedded as the national security state may be in our political and economic system, a national security state is even more firmly entrenched in the Soviet Union, beyond the reach of question. Indeed, the U.S.S.R. might be called a "total security state." . . .

And so, equipped with the requisite budgets, the national security state grew as an awesome collage of money, institutions, ideology, interests, commitments, capabilities, and firepower. The 1977 peacetime defense budget of the United States was over $104 billion. The national security state has long since acquired a life of its own. It has helped to create a powerful presidency, and has turned legions of "private" companies into permanent clients of the Defense Department. Of course, the national security state does not exist apart from other realities. It has grown, in part, dialectically with the "total security state" of the Soviet Union.

This book has narrated the rise of America's national security state, and the origins of the Cold War and the postwar international system. Today, more than three decades after its inception, the international order wrought by the Cold War is breaking down. Economic issues have become matters of high politics, cutting across political alignments. The respective unities of the Eastern and Western blocs have been reduced, and new power centers are making their influence felt. In the communist world, the schism with Yugoslavia was followed by the much more significant split with China. A third schism between the Soviet Union and the Western communist parties may be imminent. The monopoly over military force by the two superpowers has also been reduced by the proliferation of conventional weapons and of nuclear capabilities.

The American commitment to Vietnam resulted from the postwar world set of U.S. leaders. The Riga axioms and the doctrine of national security made Indochina appear a crucial arena in what was perceived as a struggle to frustrate the "fundamental design" of communism. The consequences of that intervention have taught us that "fundamental designs" may be illusory and that global implications may be secondary to local issues. The Vietnam experience has thus created new checks on both intervention and the imperial presidency, and has also raised central questions about the entire world view.

The marked weakening of the anticommunist consensus in the United States has, on the American side, helped to make possible a new kind of relationship with the Soviet Union—tentative détente. This does not mean an end to the competition between the two superpowers. But it does mean a somewhat more explicit agreement on the rules of competition; a certain number of cooperative projects, of which arms control, based on the purported acceptance of parity, is the most important; increasing communication and contacts on many levels; and a reduction in the state of permanent alarm on both sides. In practice, it means a return to the Yalta axioms as the basic mode of dealing with the Soviet world, and perhaps a vindication for Franklin Roosevelt and his aims and methods in those fateful negotiations with Stalin and Churchill during the winter of 1945 in the ballroom of the Czar's summer palace. Détente is not possible with a world revolutionary state, but it is with a more conventional imperialistic and somewhat cautious nation, interested as much in protecting what it has as in extending its influence. With a country of this sort, the United States can uneasily coexist.

Make no mistake. A reduction in tension does not mean that the worthy Wilsonian vision of a harmonious international order is at hand. In dealing with the Soviet Union, in trying to analyze its objectives and capabilities, we continue to tread, as George Kennan wrote in his diary in 1950, "in the unfirm substance of the imponderables." The global antagonism between the Soviet Union and the United States does remain the single most important and dangerous element in international politics. The balance of terror is now measured in megatons so large that no human being can comprehend the horrors that an atomic war would bring. It continues to be a balance between the United States and the Soviet Union—each one's missiles remain targeted on the other.

So the Cold War is still very much with us, as are the ever-perplexing questions about the Soviet Union's role in international politics and about the means, meaning, and measure of American security. There are no final answers, only the spectacle of men and women moved by ambitions and opportunities, beset by fears and dangers, struggling to find transient certainties midst the onrush of events. We cannot therefore regard the story of the shattered peace as merely a fascinating and tragic history. It is, in truth, still the story of the origins of our own time.

Stanley I. Kutler

STANLEY I. KUTLER (1934–   ) *is E. Gordon Fox Professor of American Institutions, Law and History at the University of Wisconsin in Madison. He is the author of many articles and books, including* Judicial Power and Reconstruction *(1968),* The American Inquisition *(1983), and* The Wars of Watergate *(1990).*

Liberty is a constant, familiar theme in American history, yet the counterpoint of official repression is part of the reality. All governments, including our own, have limits to their tolerance as they seek to repress or punish foes, real or imagined. Their action serves to satisfy political needs and reinforce their power. Consequently, a regime will seek to punish those who directly challenge its security or symbolically threaten it. The victim may be a person or group directly challenging the stability of the regime, or he may be simply a scapegoat selected to serve a higher purpose or explain a failure of the regime.

Political demands invariably distort any equation of law to justice. In the United States, within the framework of constitutionalism, the government legitimately claims authority to defend itself against direct assaults on its integrity and security. But when power holders use the system repressively to pursue their own political and social goals, they risk—and often do—violence to the constitutional recognition of political diversity and due process.

Political repression reflects the particular attitudes and will of power holders, often supported by popular consent. Liberty is never absolute. Government may legitimately restrict individual liberty in pursuit of social stability and for the protection of some interests essential to humane society. Law and public policy are designed to restrain the potentially disruptive tendencies of personal passions and pursuits. Yet law presupposes a system of equal protection and equal restraint, with a known, readily observed content of policy. Government certainly may punish citizens who offer aid and comfort to its enemies during wartime; it may require passports for travel abroad; it may deport aliens who violate their lawful obligations; it may extract a measure of loyalty (other than partisan) from its employees; and it may even punish the expressions of opinions designed to raise a substantive evil the government may prohibit. But when such policies are implemented in a vindictive, capricious, haphazard, secret, or illegal manner by legislators, administrators, or judges largely to serve the purposes of power holders, then official action becomes repression and violates whatever legitimacy or high purpose may have been intended. There is nothing inevitable about the process. The operation of a legal system is largely a story of rendered choices. The system is not some vast, impersonal *deus ex machina;* instead it operates through discretionary judgments reflecting political and personal needs of power holders. Yet in the American system, the machinery is so vast and complex that it is difficult to manipulate—as long as the process is in open view—and its various parts can negate and check abuses in other parts.

The formula for political repression follows a classic pattern, reflecting a wider state of affairs. Internal stress and external threats, sometimes in combination, heighten tensions in a society and stimulate demands for conformity. Such developments have periodically plagued the United States. The controversy over the Alien and Sedition Acts in the 1790s, the conflicts between slaveholders and advocates of abolition in the pre-Civil War years, the confrontation between capital and labor in the late nineteenth and early twentieth centuries, the Red Scare of the World War I era, and, in our own time, Cold War concerns for loyalty and national security have generated bitter, divisive uses of official power. We can view these experiences optimistically as contributions to the evolution of liberty; yet they also left permanent scars, both for the victims and for society.

The essays in this book depict events largely dictated by the loyalty and security demands of the post–World War II period. The Cold War of the late 1940s and 1950s evoked official repression on an unprecedented scale. The outline of that repression is familiar, as well as its expression through a variety of laws, legislative inquiries, executive orders and policies, judicial opinions, and surveillance. Sometimes the repression operated within the law, sometimes not. The focus usually is on broad, often abstract concerns, such as anti-Communism, loyalty, and security. Our understanding of how and why events and incidents occurred largely involves the consideration of vague trends and movements. Curiously, this often results in a simplistic, overarching interpretation, such as notions of conspiracy or a paranoid style, or, on a more personal level, the cynical opportunism of Senator Joseph McCarthy or the ineptness of President Harry Truman.

While I have acknowledged the traditionally understood causes, incidents, and references in this study of political repression in the Cold War period, I have sought to portray this history through the prism of in-depth case studies. The essays do not necessarily fit the mold of the Great Political Trial, such as those of Socrates, Thomas More, Galileo, Warren Hastings, Alfred Dreyfus, or Stalin's purge trials, where prominent but isolated persons confront the massed resources of the state in often contrived show trials, laden with symbolic and ulterior purposes. My essays seek to illustrate the whole process of legal repression—a process that involves the interaction between law and politics, public and private power alike, and the covert, as well as the overt, operations of power. These essays, although focusing on individuals or particular groups of persons, nevertheless project a symbolic and larger meaning for the incidents.

I am, of course, interested in the individual versus the government. While the actions and motives of the persecuted are relatively easy to discover, the "government" is another matter altogether. We often use the term in a focused way when in fact we are dealing with a vague, inchoate, amorphous apparatus—and an entity that has its own inherent conflicts and contradictions.

In the American process, power is fragmented; the sources of authority are divided, so that power is in a measure both independent and countervailing. The system, while certainly capable of abuse, lacks the terror of a Stalinist scheme where the only check on power was a dictator's self-restraint. In short, there *is* a Rule of Law, whatever its periodic lapses. Certainly the American institutional device of separation of powers is not foolproof. That system requires some continuing conflict and tension to function properly, to check and balance rampaging power. Indeed, Justice Louis Brandeis praised the separation-of-powers design, for he believed it produced "inevitable friction," thereby limiting power "to save the people from autocracy." The most prominent periods of anti-libertarian drives—the late 1790s and the Red Scare periods following each of the two world wars in our century—largely witnessed concerted, coordinated activities by the executive, legislative, and judicial branches, with melancholy, often tragic results.

Governmental functions in the post–World War II period are particularly complicated. The scale of governmental activities in the twentieth century stimulated the rise of the administrative state, with a subsequent growth and sprawl of governmental agencies, with their own drives, biases, and interests. Modern Presidents have expended enormous energies prodding or combating the independent, often self-fulfilling will of what in formal organization are their departments.

The fact is that the various agencies—bureaucracies, as we may call them for convenience—are also power holders. The situation is not so new. A century ago, the sociologist William Graham Sumner suggested that "the State" is not just the known and accredited high officials, but rather often is "some obscure clerk, hidden in the recesses of a Government bureau, into whose power the chance has fallen for the moment to pull one of the stops which control the Government function."

My essays offer some attention to the activities of such power holders, who often operated with their own agendas reflecting their parochial interests. Operating backstage, as it were, this supporting cast of relatively anonymous players constituted another important source of authority and sometimes even another check on the powers of others. The process of checking bureaucratic power, however, is not as neat and overt as, for example, a presidential veto or a judicial ruling. Bureaucracies perform their tasks largely hidden from public view. Furthermore, their jurisdictions and duties overlap. The FBI, for example, may be restrained or uninterested in a particular case, but that same case may stimulate determined drives from a Senate subcommittee staff or concerned sections in the State, Defense, or Justice departments. The consequence is delay, as each separate entity demands deference and its own accounting. . . .

Some of the persons discussed in these essays are familiar, others less so. Their stories are intrinsically interesting, but more importantly, I am interested in who did what to whom in the name of the law and what happened to the victims. I have sought to explain how the political demands of the state, often coupled with the drives and interests of bureaucracies, distorted the relationship between law and justice. I have tried to locate the role of political interests both in and out of government, and the operation of discretionary power to repress persons and groups regarded as threatening and dangerous. . . .

The Cold War years were grim, bleak times for American liberty as the threat of international Communism produced repression unprecedented in scale, intensity, and duration. The menace from abroad heightened concerns for potential domestic subversion. Even before the dream of peace was shattered in the late 1940's, the combination of external and internal forces had activated governmental repression. The depression years had increased the allure of extremist solutions (from both the left and the right), and the Nazi-Soviet Pact of 1939 heightened the worst fears of totalitarian threats to the United States. The rapprochement with Communism during World War II proved tenuous, of course. The Soviet spy revelations in Canada, the subjugation of Eastern Europe, the Czechoslovakian coup, and the Communist takeover in China reinforced long-standing convictions of Soviet aggressiveness and hostility. Beyond that, the sensational disclosures that the Soviets had recruited ostensibly loyal Americans as spies spurred political and popular demands of repression.

Anti-Communism long had been a staple of American political religion, at least since the Bolshevik Revolution. Periodically, anti-Communism took on the fervor of a crusade, ruthlessly trampling those who did not march in lockstep. After 1945, the government sanctioned that religion with official acts that included prosecuting the American Communist Party, imposing vague, capricious loyalty standards for government employees, conducting arbitrary, at times extra-legal persecution of alleged subversives, compiling and loosely disseminating personnel files filled with spurious, dated allegations, and publicly castigating those who expressed views that deviated from officially sanctioned or politically popular versions of events.

There was some basis for the fears of the times, but the record of official reaction betrays a cavalier disregard for liberty and due process. The ready use of nameless, faceless informers, the promiscuous use of surveillance, the arbitrary standards of administration, and the challenges to private beliefs and associations cast a dark shadow over all attempts to maintain security. Anti-Communist ideology, to be sure, animated much of this behavior; but ideological drives were all too often colored by self-serving political ambitions and the whims of strategically placed power holders. Those choices reflected personal animus and aggrandizement, rather than committed ideological goals. J. Edgar Hoover, for one, certainly was a prominent, articulate anti-Communist. Yet that ideology generally was subservient to his personal, territorial concerns. Ideology, it appears, was for public consumption and after-the-fact justification.

We will never fully tally the incidence of official wrongdoing and attempts at repression. In employee loyalty proceedings, for example, there are thousands of cases which offer little more than ambiguous statistical evidence of action, and they include innumerable cases in which the government never was challenged or which never required action, as persons quietly resigned, rather than run a process which appeared rigged, potentially embarrassing, and certainly terribly expensive. Moreover, we will never fully explore and comprehend the hundreds of incidents in which persons were investigated and interrogated by federal and state legislative committees, the callous unrestrained deportations of undesirable aliens, the mischievous results of alleged counter-intelligence activities by the FBI and police agencies, the stifling of dissent in professions and unions, the chilling intimidation of critics of official policies, and even the use of extralegal tactics to aid and abet desired political aims. What we know, however, offers a distressing record of abuse and portrays a legal system that at times mocked its very purpose and being.

It is instructive to note that these terrible wrongs were done with a terrifying consent and encouragement of the society. Fear and intolerance pervaded the citizenry as well as officialdom, and official initiatives worked in tandem with social demands. The premium on unquestioning, uncritical loyalty, the search for scapegoats, and the pressure for conformity gathered momentum from below as well as above. Unity was confused with uniformity. Curiously, only the more sober, more restrained spirit that is reflected in our institutions rather than in ourselves established limits and ended the American Inquisition.

Law was subverted and repressed in the name of law. The ill-defined discretion inherent in large claims to act against subversion, as well as the multiplicity and dispersal of sources of authority, inevitably impaired the integrity and the sanctity of law. Whim and caprice often animated the exercise of discretion; inertia or conflict marked the determination of jurisdiction between competing authorities. The procedural results, consequently, abused the sanctity of personal liberties and rights and, at times, perverted legal norms. To a point, the legal system tolerated the accompanying distortion; yet the very autonomy of the law thwarted any total inversion of the system. There *were* limits to repression and abuse of the norms, as the guardians and executors of law ultimately found themselves bound to the Rule of Law.

The English historian E. P. Thompson, arbitrating the myopic claims of nationalistic celebrants of an ever-progressing society and legal system, and of those Marxists who see the legal system as an oppressive weapon in the hands of the ruling class, has argued that the law eventually develops autonomy. Law has its own ideology, within the context of which specific rules may stand in particular relationship to general social norms. "It may," Thompson contends, "be seen simply in terms of its own logic, rules, and procedures—that is, simply *as law*." And, he reminds us, "it is not possible to conceive of any complex society with law."

Rulers make law, and among other things, that law legitimates their power and authority. But there is a two-way street here. Law reinforces the regime's will, but the rules are for rulers and ruled alike. The effectiveness of the law's ideology requires an impartial and just application of the law, otherwise "it will mask nothing, legitimize nothing, contribute nothing to any class's hegemony." Law, Thompson observes, must in some measure be independent from manipulation and seem to be just. Yet "it cannot seem to be so without upholding its own logic and criteria of equity; indeed, on occasion, by actually *being* just." Power holders, in short, must to some extent respect the Rule of Law that they impose; if they do not, they are reduced to the exercise of arbitrary, extralegal power, which usually offers only momentary security and authority. If law is to maintain its hegemony and supremacy, then power holders sometimes have to risk losing their immediate goals. Law is not irrelevant; it is not, as Thompson rightly concludes, humbug.

But the reality is that power holders *do* sometimes subvert the law and cynically manipulate it to their own ends. Does this not then justify a certain contempt, a justification of rejection, for any notion of the Rule of Law? What "legitimacy" cloaked the endless, grinding persecution of Harry Bridges, the vengeful disbarment of Abraham Isserman, the cynical prosecution of Owen Lattimore, the vindictive indictment of John William Powell, or the petty harassment of Rockwell Kent?

Law was subverted, to be sure; yet *that* law also trumped its own excesses. The house of law has many mansions. Such division, unfortunately, occasionally threatens the vitality of the Rule of Law. If, however, the latter is to be enforced by the regime, and if the Rule of Law is to maintain its supremacy, then ultimately its autonomy and ideology must be allowed to prevail.

All is not entirely well that ends well, of course, as the pain and costs for the victims of injustice are indelible. But eventual justice and vindication are important, whether it be at the bar of law, as for Bridges, Isserman, Lattimore, Powell, or Kent, or ultimately at the bar of history, as for Iva d'Aquino or Beatrice Braude. For then we reinforce, reaffirm, and enrich the Rule of Law as we discover and acknowledge the law's manipulation—even when the victim can only receive an apology or a historical footnote. The "victories" over repression and the subversion of the law—however long in coming and however painful to the victims and society—reflect the power holders' submission to the Rule of Law. The Rule of Law must be judged by its mistakes, of course; but it also is entitled to be judged by its whole record. For the United States in the Cold War era, it was the worst of times; however redeemed, it sadly was not the best of times. There was a large cast of villains and victims; still it was not "Darkness at Noon." It was not a closed system. We have a society that permits the individual to resist under the Rule of Law and to use it to rectify the violations of the norms of that system.

In *ancien régime* France, Cardinal Richelieu argued that for reasons of state "urgent conjecture" must sometimes take the place of assured truth. But wherever law ends, tyranny begins, as John Locke wrote in his great apologia for constitutionalism. While we certainly have had our Richelieus, the Lockean faith in the Rule of Law has prevailed. It is indeed a fragile, precarious perch, yet the alternative is unthinkable. Plainly, to paraphrase Lincoln, a rapacious, partial government will not always respect liberty. The sheep and the wolf invariably will be at odds over the nature and extent of liberty. The Rule of Law is their only shepherd.

☆ 11 ☆

The 1980s

AMERICAN WATERSHED?

The United States may well have crossed an historic watershed in the decade of the 1980s. In foreign affairs, the Cold War came to a close with dramatic consequences. The collapse of the Soviet empire, the demise of communist ideology in many parts of the globe, and the downturn in the arms race marked the end of the Cold War era. The astounding events of the European revolutions in 1989 made obsolete many assumptions that had shaped America's foreign policy for the 45 years since the end of World War II. The United States appeared to be entering a new phase of its history—one in which the conduct of its foreign policy would no longer be seen through East-West lenses.

In domestic affairs, American society seemed to be facing changes of similar magnitude. The United States, once the financial capital of the world, found itself hardpressed to meet its obligations, and the country went from the world's largest creditor to the world's largest debtor nation. The national debt and trade deficits, which had not been major problems before, suddenly ballooned. At the same time, a triad of President Ronald Reagan's economic policies—tax reduction, defense spending expansion, and a strong dollar—resulted in a significant redistribution of wealth within American society. Money began trickling up rather than down. Tax reform beginning in the 1980s meant the richest 1 percent of the population had income tax rates slashed by 25 percent, and by the end of the decade they were earning more of the nation's overall income than the poorest 40 percent. The rising inequality in income and redistribution of wealth brought about a serious economic imbalance among American citizens.

Such cataclysmic changes precipitated two major debates in academic circles, public discourse, and the media. The first focused on the question of America's status as a world power. Was the United States a country in the process of decline, as some critics claimed? Or was it reviving, and in the midst of a renewal? The second concerned the domestic realm of America's wealth and income. Had there been a significant shift of wealth from the poor and middle classes to the rich? Was poverty growing and the middle class shrinking, as certain authors argued? If such changes were taking place, what were the implications for America's future?

There were two opposing schools of thought regarding America's future as a world leader: one labeled the "declinists," and the other the "revivalists." Briefly put, the declinists saw America sagging beneath the burdens of empire, economically losing its competitive edge to other countries, and socially suffering from a series of domestic crises. The revivalists presented a different picture. They viewed the United States as the greatest power on earth—one capable of maintaining its leadership in world affairs, meeting economic challenges from competing countries, and coping adequately with domestic problems.

The outstanding proponent of the declinist point of view was Paul Kennedy, the Yale professor, whose 1988 book *The Rise and Fall of the Great Powers* precipitated the debate. Kennedy argued that the United States was following the pattern of mighty empires of the past. Great powers came into being by building a prosperous economic base upon which they could construct gigantic military forces which, in turn, enabled them to rise, take advantage of other nations, and build huge empires. Inevitably such economic power led to what Kennedy called "imperial overstretch." The more powerful a nation became, the more it expanded; the more territory it had to protect, the more it spent on defense. At the same time, the more likely it was to neglect the flourishing economic base that had given it power in the first place. Ironically, the more it overextended its empire, the more its power diminished.

The costs of maintaining military power eventually proved fatal. No great power over the past 500 years had remained in the forefront for long. Weakened relative to other nations, a great power fell, usually militarily, to another unencumbered by the costs of empire. Kennedy cited Spain, England, France, and Holland as examples of imperial overstretch. The United States, claimed Kennedy, was now suffering the same symptom. America's *relative* economic decline was caused primarily by overspending for military purposes, and by trying to maintain commitments abroad that it could no longer afford.

Kennedy's book analyzed America's situation in detail, and noted parallels between the United States in the 1980s and Britain around 1900, when that country had been a world leader. In both countries, the elites had participated in debates about ways of reversing what were seen as a growing lack of economic competitiveness with other nations. In Britain all political parties had been concerned about slipping from world leadership as a result of the decline in commercial expertise, levels of education, and standard of living among those not well-off. Kennedy warned there would be similar implications for America's grand strategy if its industrial base continued to shrink. For example, he wondered what the effect would be if the decline of blue collar jobs in certain key industries continued, and the trend remained of replacing millions of relatively highly paid jobs in manufacturing with poorly paid jobs in the service sector.

Kennedy was particularly concerned with the relationship between slow economic growth and high defense spending. Although the United States was currently devoting about 7 percent of its gross national product to defense—as compared to the 10 percent under Eisenhower and 9 percent under Kennedy—the country nevertheless was at a disadvantage compared to Japan and Germany. Both these countries concentrated more of their income in civilian investments, and placed more research and development funds in commercial enterprises. The Pentagon drained off many of America's scientists and engineers, while in other countries such personnel devoted themselves to producing better goods for peacetime purposes. It seemed inevitable, Kennedy wrote, that America's share of world manufacturing would steadily decline. It also seemed likely that its economic growth rates would be slower than those countries dedicated more to producing for the marketplace.

In answering the question of whether the United States could preserve its present position of world leadership, Kennedy was inclined to answer "No." Historically, no one society could remain permanently ahead of all others for many reasons: different patterns of economic growth rates; technological advances; and new military developments. The United States had already declined from a high of more than 40 percent of the world's wealth after 1945, when it emerged unscathed from the war. Much of that decline had been masked, however, by America's great military capabilities and its success in internationalizing American capitalism and culture.

Kennedy concluded that since the United States was in an era of *relative* decline, the country should cut back on its military spending and reduce its global commitments. The task of American statesmen over the next few decades would be to recognize the broad trends under way and to make policies in keeping with America's newfound status. Failure to adjust to the new world order in the making would create a serious threat to the true interest of the United States. The first selection in this chapter is from an article by Kennedy based on his book.

Thomas J. McCormick, another declinist, took a different position in his *America's Half-Century* (1989)—a revisionist study of United States foreign policy during the 45 years the Cold War lasted. A disciple of William Appleman Williams, McCormick believed like his mentor that domestic considerations drove America's foreign policy which, in turn, were related to the international political economy.

Viewed from a long-range perspective and a leftist orientation, McCormick provided a theoretical interpretation by setting America's role within a world-system analysis. Assuming that foreign policy was an extension and reflection of domestic considerations, he analyzed the motives of American leaders. McCormick argued that they had deliberately seized upon the opportunity created by World War II to establish American global dominance and capitalist hegemony. Believing they possessed almost limitless power in the postwar period, they set out to create a "free world" to replace the old economic order that had collapsed. The free world would constitute an integrated global economy in which goods and services, capital and consumer values, people and ideas would flow freely across international boundaries.

McCormick held that America's economic and moral power had been used to help rebuild Europe and the Far East as favorable markets for United States dollars, goods, and services. Until the late stages of the Vietnam War, American hegemony—that is, global supremacy— proved to be the driving force in world affairs. The urge for hegemony was accompanied by a massive military buildup as America assumed the role of global policeman. The results proved to be counterproductive. Between 1968 and 1976, the age of hegemony wound down: military spending and overseas investment designed to shore up America's steadily weakening position only accelerated its decline.

Assuming that the United States had already declined, McCormick raised the question of whether Americans would accept the loss of world dominance. Henry Kissinger voiced his answer in 1988: "[W]e have neither the resources nor the stomach for [hegemony]. The only question is how much we have to suffer before we realize this." Thus for scholars like Kennedy and McCormick, America's decline was linked to social policy and the role the United States should play in the future in world affairs.[1]

The arguments of Kennedy and certain members of the declinist school were summarized and then countered by revivalist Samuel P. Huntington, a Harvard professor, in a lengthy article.[2] The declinists, Huntington said, tended to paint a rather impressionistic picture of America's economic decline. They arbitrarily mixed references to economic trends such as economic growth and productivity with educational data on Scholastic Aptitude Test scores, trade and budget deficits, international capital flows, and savings and investment rates.

Declinists pointed first to mounting deficits in trade and the national debt. The United States as a result of these and other factors had gone from being a creditor nation in the 1970s to a debtor status to the

---

[1]Thomas J. McCormick, *America's Half-Century* (Baltimore, 1989), p. 243.

[2]Samuel P. Huntington, "The U.S.—Decline or Renewal," *Foreign Affairs* 67 (Winter 1988–89):76–96.

tune of $400 billion by 1987. Assets owned by foreigners in the United States doubled roughly between 1982 and 1986 to $1.3 trillion. One major cause for these changes was the mounting national debt which had been $50 to $75 billion in the Ford and Carter administrations but reached as high as $221 billion under Reagan in the fiscal year of 1986. The declinists demonstrated how such deficits had weakened America's economy. To finance these debts, the United States was forced to borrow heavily. But the massive influx of foreign funds had not gone into investments; they were used primarily for private consumption and government spending for defense. America was living in a style it could not afford with an "eat, drink and be merry" psychology. Kennedy, for example, warned that the only historical precedent where a great power had increased indebtedness to such a degree during peacetime had been France in the late 1780s. The results had been disastrous: the ensuing financial crisis had contributed to the coming of the French Revolution.[3]

Huntington's rebuttal was that the deficits stemmed not from long-term weaknesses of the American economy but specifically from Reagan's economic programs. The crisis produced by one set of policies, he claimed, could be reversed almost as quickly by another set of policies. A drop in the budget deficit, in fact, had already begun before Reagan left office, partly from policies adopted by foreign governments as well as from the workings of the international economy. The deficit of 1988 was only about one-half of what it had been in 1983 as a percentage of the gross national product (3.1 percent as compared to 6.3 percent). The trade deficit had also decreased temporarily with the expansion of American exports in 1988.[4]

But both the deficits and processes for curing them had imposed significant costs on America's economy. Huntington agreed with the declinists that trade and budget deficits resulted mainly from the Reagan spending spree. One effect was that a larger portion of America's gross national product would have to be paid to foreigners for debt service. America's standard of living in the future, Huntington conceded, would be lower than it might otherwise have been.

One of Kennedy's main arguments had been that America's share of the world's manufacturing output had decreased. Huntington agreed that the declinists were correct if one went back to the decade after World War II. The United States had provided about 40 to 45 percent of the gross world product in the late 1940s and early 1950s because of the wartime destruction in other countries. But reducing of that imbalance was a major goal of American policy as a result of the Marshall Plan and other programs. Between 1970 and 1987, America's share of

[3]*Ibid.*, 78–79.
[4]*Ibid.*, 80.

the gross world product had varied between 22 and 25 percent and it had fluctuated only within a relatively narrow range during those 17 years.[5]

America's economic efficiency and growth was likewise pictured as declining. Between 1965 and 1980, it was true, the United States ranked 15th out of the 19 industrialized market economies in terms of economic growth. But in the 1980s, America's economic performance improved markedly; between 1980 and 1986 the United States ranked third out of the 19 economies. In this same connection, economists were fond of comparing Japan's rapid economic growth with America's decline. According to Huntington, however, the American and Japanese economies grew at almost the same rate in the years from 1983 to 1987, with the United States leading in three of those years. In all of those years, America's growth had exceeded that of another rival, the European Community.[6]

Other phenomena cited by the declinists were what Huntington called systemic failures. These factors involved the sustained inability of American society to function either at levels of comparable societies or at standards necessary to maintain this country's leadership role in the world. The most heavily emphasized systemic weakness concerned low savings and investment rates; Americans clearly saved less than most other peoples, and averaged only about 6 percent of personal income during the 1960s and 1970s. These rates compared unfavorably with those of the Germans and Japanese who saved 14 percent and 20 percent respectively. Similar patterns existed with respect to investment capital. Between 1965 and 1984, America's gross fixed capital formation varied between 17 percent and 19.8 percent of the gross national product. These figures compared unfavorably with those of Japan which varied between 27 and 35 percent for the same period. Poor performance in savings and investment in the long run would result in systemic weaknesses, Huntington agreed. But he claimed these factors had not noticeably affected America's economic growth as yet.[7]

Kennedy's main contention that decline resulted from imperialism and militarism seemed to have few arguments to support it, according to Huntington. Analyzing Kennedy's historical examples, such as Britain, Huntington estimated that the burden of empire reached dangerous levels only when it amounted to 10 percent or more of a society's gross national product. America had reached that level only in the 1950s under Eisenhower. The declinist's thesis seemed more clearly applicable to the Soviet Union, Huntington said. The Soviets spent an

---

[5]*Ibid.*, 82.
[6]*Ibid.*, 82–83.
[7]*Ibid.*, 85.

estimated 17 to 18 percent for military purposes—though Huntington conceded that accurate statistics from Russia were hard to come by.[8]

Declinists pointed to external expansion more than internal stagnation as the principal cause for the decline of great powers for the most part. Such an argument ran counter to the tradition of political thought going back to Plato and Aristotle that focused instead on the internal ability of a society to renew itself. According to the modern formulations of this view, a society declined when bureaucratic stagnation, monopoly, castes, hierarchy, social rigidity, and organizational breakdowns made innovation and adaptation difficult or impossible.

Huntington discussed certain features of American society that showed it to be flexible and capable of constantly renewing itself. One was the continuing inward flow of ambitious immigrants throughout American history. They kept refilling pools of cheap labor, entrepreneurial skills, and intellectual talents. A second was the individual mobility, both horizontal and vertical, which enabled American workers to shift from one job to another, to move up and down the income scale, and to relocate from one region to another. A third was the competition characteristic of the capitalist system, and the tradition of opposition to both public and private monopolies. The United States, for example, had led the way in institutionalizing antitrust and antimonopoly practices in business. Government bureaucracy, in America, moreover, was weaker and more divided internally than the bureaucracies in most other countries. State-owned enterprises rather than private enterprises were the rule in other countries. Finally, American universities, which ranked as the best in the world, also helped to make renewal possible by their research activities.

These features were accompanied by three considerations which, according to Huntington, belied the declinists' arguments and assured America's dominant position for the foreseeable future. In contrast to those countries dependent upon a single source of power (Soviet military might, Japanese manufacturing, or Saudi Arabian oil), the United States was extraordinarily broad-based in terms of the major elements required for national power. Being multidimensional in such sources— population, geographical size, natural resources, economic development, social cohesion, political stability, military strength, ideological appeal, diplomatic alliances, education, and technological development—America was capable of sustaining reverses in one category while maintaining its overall influence in the others.

A second consideration was America's geographical and structural position. The United States benefited from being geographically distant from most major areas of world conflict, from espousing an economic and political philosophy that was anti-statist in nature (and

---

[8]*Ibid.*, 86

hence less likely to prove threatening to other peoples) and from being involved in a historically uniquely diversified network of alliances. These and other factors inevitably placed the United States in a leadership role in international disputes whether it wished to lead or not.

Finally, no hegemonic power, with one possible exception, seemed likely to emerge in the coming century to replace the United States. Japan—the choice of many declinists as a challenger—had neither the size, natural resources, military strength, diplomatic affiliations, nor, most important of all, the ideological appeal to emerge as a superpower, according to Huntington. The most probable challenge could come from a united European Community. This region possessed many positive features—population, resources, economic wealth, technology, and actual as well as potential military strength. It might emerge as the preeminent power in the twenty-first century, though this outcome was by no means a certainty.[9]

Other revivalists took a different point of view from that of Huntington. Henry R. Nau in *The Myth of America's Decline* (1990)—an economic history of the United States from the 1940s to the late 1980s—agreed there had been some degree of economic decline. For two decades after 1947, he noted, America had experienced unprecedented prosperity as a result of three conditions: stable domestic prices, reduced trade barriers, and limited government interference in the workings of the market. But after 1967 new ideas and policies had emerged, and global growth stalled. Fiscal and monetary policies of the United States and foreign governments intervened to undermine existing favorable conditions. From 1967 to 1980 there was instability as a result of the Vietnam War, high inflation, and disruption of the international economic order by policies that intervened in the marketplace. The Reagan presidency after 1980, according to Nau, restored free market policies, encouraged laissez faire at home and abroad, and reinvigorated the national purpose. These policies ushered in a new era of low inflation and revived global prosperity. Nau, who served in the Reagan administration until 1983, was a confirmed free market advocate; he was convinced that such policies followed in the future could achieve a long-term economic recovery.

Nau did not believe in Kennedy's idea of imperial overstretch; he felt that reducing America's presence abroad was both dangerous and misconceived. Like many other conservatives, Nau countered claims of economic decline by arguing that the American way of life had triumphed and was spreading around the globe. The United States led less because of its resources or dominance over international institutions, Nau held, and more because of its political stability, sense of national purpose, and its free market policies. America would either

---

[9]*Ibid.*, 93.

lead by its democratic example and market policies, Nau warned, or it would be forced to follow the purposes and policies of other nations.[10]

Joseph Nye in *Bound to Lead* (1990), like many revivalists, took the position that the United States was destined to hold a predominant position well into the future. Although he did not believe that America was as influential after World War II as other scholars claimed, neither did he see the United States declining. Nye argued that power as a determinant, though more diffused because the world had become more interdependent, was still traditional in form. Military power, in which the United States was dominant, remained the crucial factor. In terms of other sources of power—the influence of ideas, flow of finances, mass communications, and dominance of multinational corporations—the United States still enjoyed a clear advantage in most instances.[11]

No other nation-state was capable of the special roles and functions that the United States performed, Nye concluded. The Soviet Union possessed large military forces but its domestic structure was shaky. Japan, although impressive in economic terms, was unable to play a world role because of its insularity. For these and other reasons, Nye did not believe the United States should adopt a policy of strategic entrenchment. Nye's book was more cautious, based strongly on statistical evidence, and less inclined to be partisan than Nau's.[12]

Richard Rosecrance in *America's Economic Resurgence* (1990) was much more ambivalent about America's future than either Nau or Nye. In his previous writings, Rosecrance appeared to be in the declinist camp. He edited a book in 1976 entitled *America as an Ordinary Country* whose very title conveyed his view of the United States as a superpower. In 1986 he published *The Rise of a Trading State* whose thesis was that while the Soviet Union and the United States engaged in a ruinous arms race, the world watched the rise of Japan, Taiwan, and other commercially oriented societies. In *America's Economic Resurgence*, Rosecrance admitted the United States had declined over the past decades economically, technologically, and commercially. He feared that continuance of this relative decline would result in a second class status for America, and in ultimate dependence on Japan.

But most of Rosecrance's book was devoted to what he called "the preconditions of resurgence" which could reverse the disastrous trends already underway. The preconditions included the now-familiar proposals: reduction of the federal debt; diversion of funds from military

---

[10]Henry R. Nau, *The Myth of America's Decline* (New York, 1990), Introduction.

[11]For a comprehensive review article analyzing Nye and Nau and related works, see Paul Kennedy, "*Fin-de-Siecle* America," *New York Review of Books*, June 28, 1990, 33–34 and 37–40.

[12]*Ibid.*, 35–40.

to domestic needs; increase of national savings; expansion of investment in research and development; raising of educational levels; and
changing the tendency of American businessmen and financiers to
chase short-term profits at the expense of long-term market needs. Although these negative trends had been in place for some time, Rosecrance argued that the psychological effect of some financial shock
(such as a Tokyo stock market crash) might galvanize American leaders into adopting badly needed reforms. Such a crisis could have a salu-
tary effect by forcing America to take the road to resurgence.[13]

The declinist-revivalist debate was probably destined to continue
for some time, particularly as the United States faced new challenges
like the war with Iraq. It should be noted, however, that some, but not
all, of the scholars taking part in the debate were operating under certain unspoken assumptions that were bound to affect their conclusions. Many believed in the idea of American exceptionalism: they assumed a greater independent economic role for America in the global
economy than the growing international interdependence allowed.
They believed also that the United States would inevitably have complete control over its own destiny, an assumption belied by past history. Others based their analyses on the assumption that economic liberalism would be the world norm. They failed to take into account
the thinking and actions of communist and socialist regimes operating
under different premises. They also overlooked certain recent global
developments such as the internationalization of elements of the
working class throughout the world. With the spread of industrialization in the Pacific rim, for example, millions of rural peasants had been
transformed into an urban proletariat producing for an international
market. The consequences of this great change remain unknown. The
same was true in other parts of the world where workers left their own
countries to labor as "guest workers" in other nations. Finally, scholars
like Kennedy, who emphasized economic factors as the most important moving forces in historical causation, neglected other important
considerations—such as religion—and ignored the resurgent fundamentalism sweeping parts of the world like the Middle East.[14]

---

[13]*Ibid.*, 34–35.

[14]This discussion of the declinist-revivalist debate by no means accounts for all of
the important works written on the subject. See, for example, the writings of the follow-
ing authors in the declinist school: David P. Calleo, *Beyond American Hegemony* (New
York, 1987); Walter R. Mead, *Mortal Splendor* (Boston, 1987); and Mancur Olson, *The
Rise and Decline of Nations* (New Haven, 1982). For the revivalist side see George
Gilder, *Wealth and Poverty* (New York, 1981); Ben Wattenberg, *First Universal Nation*
(New York, 1991); and Paul C. Roberts, *Supply-Side Revolution* (Cambridge, 1984).

This discussion, moreover, does not take into account world historians who did not
address the issue of decline vs. revival directly: William H. McNeill, *Rise of the West*
(Birmingham, rev. ed., 1989); Theo H. Von Laue, *World Revolution of Westernization*
(New York, 1987); and Leften S. Stavrianos, *Global Rift* (New York, 1981).

Turning from the declinist-revivalist debate, America seemed also to undergo significant domestic changes during the decade of the 1980s that may have long-term consequences. One of the most important was the change in the distribution of national income. Whether measured by individuals, families, or households, income and wealth in the United States shifted in favor of the very rich and away from the very poor. This was true whether one compared the top fifth of the population to the bottom fifth, or examined individual earnings, family income, or household earnings. The income gap between the richest and poorest families, for example, was wider in the mid-1980s, according to the Census Bureau, than at any time since the Bureau began keeping statistics in 1946.[15]

The rich got richer largely as the result of the Reagan tax program. When completed in 1986, this program dramatically shifted the tax burden from corporations to individuals by $120 billion over one five-year period. One study found that the share of the national income going to the wealthiest 1 percent rose from 8.1 percent in 1981 to 14.7 percent in 1986. Between 1981 and 1989, the net worth of the 400 richest Americans on one list nearly tripled. The gap in income between corporate executives and ordinary factory workers, for example, widened dramatically. In 1980 corporate chief executive officers made roughly 40 times the income of average factory workers; by 1989 the executive officers were making 93 times as much.[16]

The poor, on the other hand, got poorer and there were more of them. The bottom fifth of American families in 1985 received only 4.7 percent of total family income—their lowest share in 25 years. Between 1980 and 1984 alone, the richest fifth of American families gained more than $25 billion in income while the poorest lost $6 billion. In 1988 one newspaper reported that there were 9 million working American adults whose wages were not enough to lift them and their families above the federal poverty level.[17]

The middle class, at the same time, seemed to be shrinking and suffering. If defined in terms of family income of $20,000 to $50,000, the percentage of families in this range dropped from 53 percent in 1973 to fewer than 48 percent in 1984. Moreover, an income at that level no longer guaranteed one of the presumed prerequisites of middle-class status—home ownership. In 1984 a family required an annual income of approximately $37,000 to afford a median-priced home, but in the same year the median family income was $26,167—almost $11,000 short of the necessary amount. For the first time in the post–

---

[15]Barbara Ehrenreich, *Fear of Falling* (New York, 1989), p. 202.

[16]Kevin Phillips, "Reagan's America, A Capital Offense," *New York Times Magazine*, June 17, 1990, 26.

[17]Ehrenreich, *Fear of Falling*, p. 203.

World War II period, a middle-level income no longer assured what Americans had come to think of as a middle-class lifestyle.[18]

In this same connection, the Census Bureau in 1991 published a revealing breakdown of the annual income within the United States for the year 1989. It showed that between 1969 and 1989 the median income per household had remained almost the same—$28,334 and $28,906—measured in constant dollars. This figure could be viewed as an actual decline because more households needed two earners to reach the slightly higher sum by 1989. Andrew Hacker, a political scientist, estimated that it took at least $40,000 to live in a reasonably comfortable style in 1989, but only one-third of American households had reached that level. Of course, not all those below that figure could be considered "poor." Those in the bottom two-thirds ranged from people in dire poverty all the way up to families struggling to get along on $35,000 a year.[19]

Even more revealing was the explosion in numbers of those in the higher income levels, as shown by Internal Revenue Service statistics published in 1990. Between 1968 and 1988, those declaring adjusted gross income of 1 million dollars or more increased from 1,122 persons to 65,303. Indeed, in a single two-year period—1985 to 1987—the number doubled; and in a single year—1987 to 1988—the growth was almost that great. These figures revealed, once again, that the income gap within the United States widened during the 1980s. There were far more American millionaires owning greater wealth than ever before in American history.[20]

One persistent American myth, however, has been that of the United States as a classless society. The myth of classlessness has existed since colonial times, continuing evidence to the contrary notwithstanding. Although mobility studies show the majority of those born at the bottom of the social scale tend to remain there, enough upward social mobility took place to lend credence to the myth. There is, moreover, the problem of how to define classes—whether in economic terms by income, political terms by voting patterns, social terms by lifestyle, or in psychological terms by the self-perception of a given class, or the perception of one class of another. Many in the

---

[18]*Ibid.*, 205. It is true that different studies produced different answers regarding whether people were moving downward or upward from the middle class. Two studies by economists showed those leaving the middle-income range in the late 1970s and early 1980s were heading downward and falling out of the middle class. A recent Bureau of Labor Statistics study covering middle-class shrinkage between 1969 and 1986, however, claimed that the decline in the middle class was the result of families moving to the upper class, not the lower.

[19]Andrew Hacker, "Class Dismissed," *New York Review of Book*, March 7, 1991, 44–46.

[20]*Ibid.*

American working class, for example, view themselves as middle class rather than proletarian. For these and other reasons, many Americans deny the existence of a class system in the United States.[21]

Scholars were somewhat more successful in dealing with the problem of the perception of class in social, political and economic terms, however. Barbara Ehrenreich, a social critic, claimed in her *Fear of Falling* (1989), that this economic polarization was the result of conscious efforts by the Reagan administration. The president's tax overhaul sharply reduced the corporate share of total obligations and thereby increased the percent of wealth controlled by the very rich. At the same time, the Reagan administration reduced the social programs designed to help those down-and-out. Spending cuts for the poor, combined with the tax cuts for the rich, she concluded, resulted in a government-induced upward redistribution of wealth.

Not only was the middle class shrinking, according to Ehrenreich, but the blue collar working class was also being weakened. Business interests, which formed the greatest strength of the political New Right, deliberately set about to shake themselves loose from the burdens of high-priced American labor. Beginning in the 1970s, corporation executives "out-sourced" their manufacturing jobs to work forces located in third world countries, where workers were willing to work for lower wages and were more easily intimidated. Simultaneously some executives shifted their capital resources from traditional manufacturing to financial speculation; they indulged in corporate mergers, corporate take-overs, and leveraged buy-outs. Such policies resulted in outmoded methods of production, technological decay in plant equipment, and a gradual process of "deindustrialization" in America. More importantly from the point of view of the blue collar working class, such policies led to reduced wages, lowered standards of living, and unemployment. Between 1979 and 1984, 11.5 million workers lost their jobs because of plant shutdowns or relocations. Of that number, only 60 percent found new jobs, and nearly half of these paid less than the jobs lost. More than half of the 9 million jobs created between 1981 and 1986, for example, paid less than $7,000 a year.[22]

The lives of blue collar workers, Ehrenreich pointed out, were disrupted in many other ways. As America's "rust belt" grew and factories shut their doors, entire communities went into decline. With so-called smoke-stack industries disappearing to other countries, more jobs in the service sector became available. But most of them—in fast-

---

[21]A recent work claimed that class lines represented a central reality in American life, but argued that powerful forces, such as the media, have duped the public into accepting the myth of classlessness. See Benjamin DeMott, *The Imperial Middle* (New York, 1991).

[22]*Ibid.*, 207.

food establishments, banks, filling stations, supermarkets, and hotels—were low-paying, non-unionized, and offered few or no fringe
benefits. Many, moreover, paid only the standard minimum wage.
Throughout the 1980s, the minimum wage was kept at a low level,
paying only $3.35 an hour—or $6,900 a year. This figure was $4,000
less than what the federal government defined as the poverty level for
a family of four.

What Ehrenreich was interested in, however, were the social effects of economic polarization. She traced the growing self-consciousness of what she called the "professional middle class"—a class defined abstractly more in terms of education and its educational capital
rather than the ownership of economic capital or property. Comprising
only about 20 percent of the population, this class of white collar professionals—ranging from school teachers and social workers to lawyers, middle class managers in business, media and advertising people
as well as intellectuals—wielded great power over American culture.
The way this class viewed itself and its relations to other classes was
of the utmost importance. In the 1950s this professional class had been
liberal in its outlook and believed in the achievement of an egalitarian
society. But it retreated from liberalism, and its mood of generosity
and optimism in the 1950s changed to a meaner, more selfish outlook
by the 1980s. Fearful of falling from its privileged status, the professional middle class became much less liberal, turned to the right politically, and altered its views of the working class.

The journey of professionals to the right resulted from a series of
"discoveries" or myths about itself and other classes. In the early
1960s this class "discovered" the poor, and in keeping with the negative reference group theory identified them as living in a "culture of
poverty." This "discovery" was nothing more than a psychological projection onto the lower classes of the uneasiness and guilt the professionals themselves were experiencing about their unrestrained consumption.

The next "discovery" of the professionals was about their own
children. Since many professionals had achieved their status through
discipline and by deferring gratification to continue their education,
they were shocked to find that their children as protesters and members of the youthful counterculture were unwilling to make such sacrifices. Failing to perpetuate themselves in many instances, they became
an insecure elite and pressed their progeny hard, though often unsuccessfully, to achieve.

At the same time the professionals "rediscovered" the poor, and
viewed them in a different light during the late 1960s and early 1970s.
Now the poor were seen as anti-democratic, bigoted, and racist—a
stereotype that suited the mood of the professionals who were seeking
legitimization for their own growing conservative impulses. Ironically,

the working class in these years was in fact engaged in the greatest wave of labor militancy since the end of World War II.

In the late 1970s and 1980s, the most significant "discovery" was made not only by, but about, the professional middle class. First of all, professionals began to recognize themselves as a beleaguered and insecure elite. But, more importantly, the New Right attacked professional middle class liberals as elitists, denouncing the social programs they had supported as self-serving, opportunistic, and decadent. The New Right accused professionals of "permissiveness"—permissiveness toward the generation of the spoiled young, toward the poor, and toward the social programs that supposedly had unleashed a swarm of ills on America from crime and obscenity to sexual abandon. By using permissiveness as a rhetorical weapon, the New Right caused middle class liberals to retreat from their former leadership role and to adopt a more conservative, selfish, and defensive stance in the 1980s. The New Right, by attacking middle-class liberal beliefs, Ehrenreich concluded, succeeded in placing the Democrats on the defensive, electing Presidents Reagan and Bush, and implementing antilabor and antipoverty policies.

Robert Reich had a different explanation for the class changes in American society before and during the 1980s. In *The Next American Frontier* (1983), Reich, a declinist, argued that America was fast becoming a second rate nation because it had failed to make necessary changes to accommodate the new economic world order: one in which human capital, not financial capital, was the core of corporate endeavor. America had a choice: either it could adapt itself to the new economic realities by altering its organizations, or it could maintain the status quo and continue its decline. A "flexible-system firm" which depended on human skills in the manufacture of technology-based, precision-tailored products was the hope of the future. Recent developments in the changing world economy—the resurgence of Europe and Japan, the rise of third world industrialization, and the emergence of a world trade system—had placed America in jeopardy. These changes had left American workers facing unemployment and dead-end jobs as well as decreases in real wages. America's labor force, Reich concluded, was not involved in the growing segments of the world economy and its fortunes were declining accordingly.

Reich's book *The Work of Nations* (1991) carried this theme further to indicate why the gap between rich and poor was widening in America. He linked differences in income to levels of education, and divided the universe of jobs into three categories: symbolic analysts, routine producers, and in-person servers. Symbolic analysts were those who knew how to conceptualize problems and solutions and could manipulate symbols—data, words, and oral and visual representations. They included, among others, corporate executives, engineers, consultants, lawyers, investment bankers and top-flight entertainers. A rising new elite, they were in great demand and doing well because their work and value were linked to the emerging economic world order.

The new segregation taking place in American society was not racial but economic in nature, according to Reich. As the federal government relinquished more responsibility to the states, only the wealthiest cities and towns could afford to train and educate future symbolic analysts in those complex skills required for such work. As a result, symbolic analysts were retreating into residential and work enclaves that segregated them from much of the rest of American society.

The fortunes of the other two groups were declining because the standard of living was dependent on the value contributed to the new global economy, and they had less to offer. Routine producers—factory workers, their supervisors, and middle-level managers—did less well because they were hurt by direct competition from low-priced workers abroad. Their future was bleak also because jobs of this kind were becoming increasingly scarce as more highly automated factories came into being.

In-person servers—such as auto mechanics, store clerks, secretaries, nurses, and taxi drivers—were also suffering. Although they were sheltered from global competition, they faced increased competition for their jobs at home from displaced and unemployed routine producers. At the same time, many of their jobs were being automated and they were rendered obsolete.

Reich argued that Americans should develop skills that would tie into the world economy more. They should invest in education, training, and the nation's infrastructure to become more competitive and viable. Only in this way, Reich wrote, could Americans create a more just society with a more equitable distribution of income and wealth.

Kevin P. Phillips, an analyst, considered the possible political consequences of the continued imbalance in the distribution of income of America. He predicted a populist revolt by voters in the 1990s in reaction to the dire developments of the 1980s. His credentials for making such a forecast were sound. In 1969 he had anticipated in his book, *The Emerging Majority*, the Republican resurgence that dominated much of American politics over the next 20 years.

In his *The Politics of Rich and Poor*, published in 1991, Phillips placed the Reagan decade within a historical context. Not since the Gilded Age of the 1880s and the Roaring Twenties had the rich gained so much. Both these periods were followed by political countermovements—William Jennings Bryan's populism and Franklin D. Roosevelt's New Deal. Predicating his analysis on the tradition of cyclical historians like Arthur Schlesinger, Jr., who predicted alternating periods of reaction and reform, Phillips prophesied a Democratic resurgence in the 1990s.

The gluttony and greed of the rich in America, Phillips said, would spark this populist revolt. While the top one-half of 1 percent of Americans rolled in money, a disproportionate share of the poor—foreclosed farmers, laid-off steel workers, women (especially in single-parent households), blacks, Hispanics and some young Americans—lost ground during the 1980s. One study—using an index of inflation-adjusted income for families with children headed by an adult over 30—showed that they suffered losses of roughly one-quarter of their income between 1973 and 1986. At the bottom of the economic scale were the homeless, roaming the streets begging, sleeping on sidewalk grates for warmth, and making many American cities resemble Calcutta.[23]

The Republican part, according to Phillips, was identified historically with the policies that had caused such conditions in the 1880s, 1920s, and 1980s. In all three periods, America had witnessed conservative politics, a reduced role of government, admiration for businessmen, corporate restructuring, tax reduction, rising inequalities in wealth, and a build-up in debt and speculation. But the analogy broke down when the three eras were compared. During the two previous eras, America had been on the rise economically. In the 1980s the country was consuming, rearranging, and borrowing more than it had built. Some of America's wealth had already been redistributed, Phillips pointed out, to foreign investors who purchased securities based on the United States national debt.

Phillips conceded that few had raised questions about the concentration of wealth and economic inequities during the 1980s. Even when faced with the largest financial fiasco in American history—a savings and loan bailout that could cost up to one-half a trillion dollars—taxpayers had not risen in protest. But in the decade of the 1990s, he predicted, a different chapter would be written in the annals of American wealth and power. The second selection in this chapter is an article by Phillips based on his book.

Other authors were more interested in the effects that the economic imbalance had upon both labor and industry. Two economists, Bennett Harrison and Barry Bluestone wrote *The Deindustrialization of America* (1982), which showed how American corporations had begun restructuring industry as far back as the mid-1960s. Responding to the cry for more profits, corporate executives adopted policies that caused a gradual process of deindustrialization.

In a second book, *The Great U-Turn* (1988), the same authors analyzed the effects of these changes upon American workers and their families from World War II to 1987. During the immediate postwar period, America's remarkable economic growth had resulted in rising earnings, greater equality in family incomes, and the movement of

---

[23]See Carol L.M. Caton, *Homeless in America* (New York, 1990).

many workers into the middle class. Inflation rather than employment appeared to be the major threat to economic stability. Workers at the time responded to the decline in purchasing power with a series of strikes that won substantial wage increases as well as cost-of-living adjustments.

But during the mid-1960s, there occurred what Harrison and Bluestone called the "Great U-Turn." This change constituted a terrible trend for labor: lower wages, stagnant family incomes, and greater inequalities in wealth distribution. Most important of all, the middle class shrank as declining wages caused workers to fall from their former status.

American corporations undertook two forms of restructuring, both of which hurt labor badly. First, employers launched a fierce initiative against labor costs in almost every industry. Wages were cut and wage concessions demanded as the price for continued employment. Managerial control was reasserted through wage freezes or reductions. A two-tiered wage structure was instituted in which recently hired workers were paid on a much lower scale than those with seniority. Full-time workers were replaced by part-time employees who were offered few or no fringe benefits. Services were purchased outside the firm, further weakening labor's control of the workplace. Anti-union policies were adopted, including public-relations drives to discredit unions, and psychological methods were used to divide and demoralize the work force.

The second step in corporate restructuring, financial in nature, likewise hurt labor's cause. Corporate executives acquired other companies to make profits instead of improving manufacturing, indulged in stock manipulations, and speculated in commodity futures. Many executives emphasized short-term profits at the expense of long-term benefits from investment in plant and equipment or research and development. Some multinational corporations deliberately engaged in global diversification simply to cut labor costs.

Focusing on the 1980s and the so-called Reagan recovery, Harrison and Bluestone noted the costs to the country's future. The recovery set records in the formation of new debts: about $1.3 trillion by the federal government; perhaps $400 billion by private consumers; and record amounts by businessmen. Contrary to what administration supply-siders had predicted, the results of the recovery proved counterproductive. Instead of increasing savings as a result of tax cuts, both the private and public sectors were spending savings at an alarming rate. Rates of investment in productive capital lagged well behind trends noted in earlier economic upturns. Finally, the productivity gains of the Reagan recovery ranked last among the expansions that took place during the post–World War II period. The authors concluded that Reagan's debt-financed recovery failed to rebuild the future foundation for any long-term economic growth with equality.

There were, nevertheless, dissenting writers in the face of this overwhelming evidence who viewed the 1980s in a more positive light. Benjamin J. Wattenberg, a member of a conservative think tank, the American Enterprise Institute, published *The First Universal Nation* in 1991 which countered claims made by these critics. For one thing, Wattenberg argued that the shrinkage of the middle class occurred because of upward mobility, not because people dropped down to a lower economic class. Wattenberg concluded also that there was less poverty in America than pictured in many studies. Critics were using Census Bureau statistics, he insisted, which failed to include non-cash items for poor families, such as food stamps, rent supplements, Medicaid, and Medicare. Disparities in wealth within the United States were likewise skewed because they did not account for income from social security and private pension plans. Wattenberg, who had written books on the decades of the 1960s and 1970s based on decennial census data, painted a much different picture of the 1980s than the critics.[24]

Time alone will tell whether the 1980s was a watershed—a decade divided and set apart from others in this century. In foreign affairs students living through the 1990s will look back and decide whether the declinists were wrong and reflected only a passing millennium-ending mood, or if the United States was indeed in the midst of a deep and permanent decline. They will judge whether the Cold War commanded a new phase in American history unlike anything experienced in the past 45 years, or if the world resembled much that had gone on before. In domestic affairs they will evaluate the Reagan legacy to determine if it aroused national discontent about the problems people saw about them—homelessness, poverty, and physical deterioration—or if Reagan will continue to be a popular president in the public mind. Finally, students will be able to see whether or not Phillips' prediction about a Republican backlash will come true. No matter what the future may hold, the question of whether the 1980s was a watershed will continue to intrigue students and historians alike for years to come.

---

[24]Benjamin J. Wattenberg, *The First Universal Nation* (New York, 1991), pp. 119–142.

Paul Kennedy

PAUL KENNEDY (1945–   ) *is Dilworth Professor of History at Yale University. He has written many books, including* The Rise and Fall of British Naval Mastery *(1976),* The Realities Behind Diplomacy *(1981),* The Rise and Fall of the Great Powers *(1987), and* African Capitalism *(1988).*

The Erosion of U.S. Grand Strategy

In February of 1941, when Henry Luce's *Life* magazine announced that this was the "American century," the claim accorded well with the economic realities of power. Even before the United States entered the Second World War, it produced about a third of the world's manufactures, which was more than twice the production of Nazi Germany and almost ten times that of Japan. By 1945, with the Fascist states defeated and America's wartime allies economically exhausted, the U.S. share of world manufacturing output was closer to half—a proportion never before or since attained by a single nation. More than any of the great world empires—Rome, Imperial Spain, or Victorian Britain—the United States appeared destined to dominate international politics for decades, if not centuries, to come.

In such circumstances it seemed to American decision-makers natural (if occasionally awkward) to extend U.S. military protection to those countries pleading for help in the turbulent years after 1945. First came involvement in Greece and Turkey; and then, from 1949 onward, the extraordinarily wide-ranging commitment to NATO; the special relationship with Israel and, often contrarily, with Saudi Arabia, Jordan, Egypt, and lesser Arab states; and obligations to the partners in such regional defense organizations as SEATO, CENTO, and ANZUS. Closer to home, there was the Rio Pact and the special hemispheric defense arrangements with Canada. By early 1970, as Ronald Steel has pointed out, the United States "had more than 1,000,000 soldiers in 30 countries, was a member of 4 regional defense alliances and an active participant in a fifth, had mutual defense treaties with 42 nations, was a member of 53 international organizations, and was furnishing military or economic aid to nearly 100 nations across the face of the globe."

Although the end of the Vietnam War significantly reduced the number of American troops overseas, the global array of U.S. obligations that remained would have astonished the Founding Fathers.

Yet while America's commitments steadily increased after 1945, its share of world manufacturing and of world gross national product began to decline, at first rather slowly, and then with increasing speed. In one sense, it could be argued, such a decline is irrelevant: this country is nowadays far richer, absolutely, than it was in 1945 or 1950, and most of its citizens are much better off *in absolute terms.* In another sense, however, the shrinking of America's share of world production is alarming because of the implications for American grand strategy—which is measured not by military forces alone but by their integration with all those other elements (economic, social, political, and diplomatic) that contribute toward a successful long-termed national policy.

The gradual erosion of the economic foundations of America's power has been of several kinds. In the first place, there is the country's industrial decline relative to overall world production, not only in older manufactures, such as textiles, iron and steel, shipbuilding, and basic chemicals, but also—though it is harder to judge the final outcome at this stage of industrial-technological combat—in robotics, aerospace technology, automobiles, machine tools, and computers. Both areas pose immense problems: in traditional and basic manufacturing the gap in wage scales between the United States and newly industrializing countries is probably such that no efficiency measures will close it; but to lose out in the competition in future technologies, if that indeed should occur, would be even more disastrous.

The second, and in many ways less expected, sector of decline is agriculture. Only a decade ago experts were predicting a frightening global imbalance between food requirements and farming output. But the scenarios of famine and disaster stimulated two powerful responses: the first was a tremendous investment in American farming from the 1970s onward, fueled by the prospect of ever larger overseas food sales; the second was a large-scale investigation, funded by the West, into scientific means of increasing Third World crop outputs. These have been so successful as to turn growing numbers of Third World countries into food exporters, and thus competitors of the United States. At the same time, the European Economic Community has become a major producer of agricultural surpluses, owing to its price-support system. In consequence, experts now refer to a "world awash in food," and this state of affairs in turn has led to sharp declines in agricultural prices and in American food exports—and has driven many farmers out of business.

Like mid-Victorian Britons, Americans after 1945 favored free trade and open competition, not just because they held that global commerce and prosperity would be advanced in the process but also because they knew that they were most likely to benefit from a lack of protectionism. Forty years later, with that confidence ebbing, there is a predictable shift of opinion in favor of protecting the domestic market and the domestic producer. And, just as in Edwardian Britain, defenders of the existing system point out that higher tariffs not only might make domestic products *less* competitive internationally but also might have other undesirable repercussions—a global tariff war, blows against American exports, the undermining of the currencies of certain newly industrializing countries, and an economic crisis like that of the 1930s.

Along with these difficulties affecting American manufacturing and agriculture has come great turbulence in the nation's finances. The uncompetitiveness of U.S. industrial products abroad and the declining sales of agricultural exports have together produced staggering deficits in visible trade—$160 billion in the twelve months ending with April of 1986—but what is more alarming is that such a gap can no longer be covered by American earnings on "invisibles," which are the traditional recourse of a mature economy. On the contrary, the United States has been able to pay its way in the world only by importing ever larger amounts of capital. This has, of course, transformed it from the world's largest creditor to the world's largest debtor nation in the space of a few years.

Compounding this problem—in the view of many critics, causing this problem—have been the budgetary policies of the U.S. government itself.

Federal Deficit, Debt, and Interest (in billions)

	Deficit	Debt	Interest on Debt
1980	$59.6	$914.3	$52.5
1983	$195.4	$1,381.9	$87.8
1985	$202.8	$1,823.1	$129.0

A continuation of this trend, alarmed voices have pointed out, would push the U.S. national debt to around $13 *trillion* by the year 2000 (fourteen times the debt in 1980) and the interest payments on the debt to $1.5 *trillion* (twenty-nine times the 1980 payments). In fact a lowering of interest rates could make those estimates too high, but the overall trend is still very unhealthy. Even if federal deficits could be reduced to a "mere" $100 billion annually, the compounding of national debt and interest payments by the early twenty-first century would still cause unprecedented sums of money to be diverted in that direction. The only historical examples that come to mind of Great Powers so increasing their indebtedness *in peacetime* are France in the

1780s, where the fiscal crisis finally led to revolution, and Russia early in this century.

Indeed, it is difficult to imagine how the American economy could have got by without the inflow of foreign funds in the early 1980s, even if that had the awkward consequence of inflating the dollar and thereby further hurting U.S. agricultural and manufacturing exports. But, one wonders, what might happen if those funds are pulled out of the dollar, causing its value to drop precipitously?

Some say that alarmist voices are exaggerating the gravity of what is happening to the U.S. economy and failing to note the "naturalness" of most of these developments. For example, the midwestern farm belt would be much less badly off if so many farmers had not bought land at inflated prices and excessive interest rates in the late 1970s. The move from manufacturing into services is understandable, and is occurring in all advanced countries. And U.S. manufacturing *output* has been rising in absolute terms, even if employment (especially blue-collar employment) in manufacturing has been falling—but that too is a "natural" trend, as the world increasingly moves from material-based to knowledge-based production. Similarly, there is nothing wrong in the metamorphosis of American financial institutions into world financial institutions, with bases in Tokyo and London as well as New York, to handle (and profit from) the heavy flow of capital; that can only increase the nation's earnings from services. Even the large annual federal deficits and the mounting national debt are sometimes described as being not very serious, after allowance is made for inflation; and there exists in some quarters a belief that the economy will "grow its way out" of these deficits, or that government measures will close the gap, whether by increasing taxes or cutting spending or both. A too hasty attempt to slash the deficit, it is pointed out, could well trigger a major recession.

The positive signs of growth in the American economy are said to be even more reassuring. Because of the boom in the service sector, the United States has been creating jobs over the past decade faster than it has done at any time in its peacetime history—and certainly a lot faster than Western Europe has been. America's far greater degree of labor mobility eases such transformations in the job market. Furthermore, the enormous American commitment to high technology—not just in California and New England but also in Virginia, Arizona, and many other places—promises ever greater production, and thus national wealth (as well as ensuring a strategic edge over the Soviet Union). Indeed, it is precisely because of the opportunities existing in the American economy that the nation continues to attract millions of immigrants and to generate thousands of new entrepreneurs, and the capital that pours into the country can be tapped for further investment, especially in research and development. Finally, if long-term shifts in the global terms of trade are, as economists suspect, leading to steadily lower prices for foodstuffs and raw materials, that ought to benefit an economy that still imports enormous amounts of oil, metal ores, and so on (even if it hurts particular American interests, such as farmers and oilmen).

Many of these points may be valid. Since the American economy is so large and diverse, some sectors and regions are likely to be growing while others are in decline—and to characterize the whole with generalizations about "crisis" or "boom" is therefore inappropriate. Given the decline in the price of raw materials, the ebbing of the dollar's unsustainably high exchange value since early 1985, the reduction that has occurred in interest rates, and the impact of all three trends on inflation and on business confidence, it is not surprising that some professional economists are optimistic about the future.

Nevertheless, from the viewpoint of American grand strategy, and of the economic foundation necessary to an effective long-term strategy, the picture is much less rosy. In the first place, America's capacity to carry the burden of military liabilities that it has assumed since 1945 is obviously less than it was several decades ago, when its shares of global manufacturing and GNP were much larger, its agriculture was secure, its balance of payments was far healthier, the government budget was in balance, and it was not in debt to the rest of the world. From that larger viewpoint there is something in the analogy that is made by certain political scientists between America's position today and that of previous "declining hegemons." Here again it is instructive to note the uncanny similarity between the growing mood of anxiety in thoughtful circles in the United States today and that which pervaded all political parties in Edwardian Britain and led to what has been termed the national efficiency movement—a broad-based debate among the nation's decision-making, business, and educational elites over ways to reverse a growing uncompetitiveness with other advanced societies. In terms of commercial expertise, levels of training and education, efficiency of production, and standards of income and (among the less well off) living, health, and housing, the number-one power of 1900 seemed to be losing its superiority, with dire implications for its long-term *strategic* position. Hence the calls for "renewal" and "reorganization" came as much from the right as from the left. Such campaigns usually do lead to reforms here and there, but their very existence is, ironically, a confirmation of decline. When a Great Power is strong and unchallenged, it will be much less likely to debate its capacity to meet its obligations than when it is relatively weaker.

In particular, there could be serious implications for American grand strategy if the U.S. industrial base continues to shrink. If there were ever in the future to be a large-scale war that remained conventional (because of the belligerents' fear of triggering a nuclear holocaust), one must wonder, would America's productive capacities be adequate after years of decline in certain key industries, the erosion of blue-collar employment, and so on? One is reminded of the warning cry of the British nationalist economist Professor W.A.S. Hewins in 1904 about the impact of British industrial decay upon that country's power:

> *Suppose an industry which is threatened [by foreign competition] is one which lies at the very root of your system of National defense, where are you then? You could not get on without an iron industry, a great Engineering trade, because in modern warfare you would not have the means of producing, and maintaining in a state of efficiency, your fleets and armies.*

It is hard to imagine that the decline in American industrial capacity could be so severe: America's manufacturing base is simply much broader than Edwardian Britain's was and—an important point—the so-called defense-related industries not only have been sustained by Pentagon procurement but also have taken part in the shift from materials-intensive to knowledge-intensive (high-tech) manufacturing, which over the long term will also reduce the West's reliance on critical raw materials. Even so, the expatriation from the United States of, say, semiconductor assembly, the erosion of the American shipping and shipbuilding industry, and the closing down of so many American mines and oil fields represent trends that cannot but be damaging in the event of another long, Great Power, coalition war. If, moreover, historical precedents have any validity at all, the most critical constraint upon any surge in wartime production will be the number of skilled craftsmen—which causes one to wonder about the huge long-term decline in American blue-collar employment, including the employment of skilled craftsmen.

A problem quite different but equally important for sustaining a proper grand strategy concerns the impact of slow economic growth on the American social-political consensus. To a degree that amazes most Europeans, the United States in the twentieth century has managed to avoid overt "class" politics. This, one imagines, is a result of America's unique history. Many of its immigrants had fled from socially rigid circumstances elsewhere; the sheer size of the country had long allowed those who were disillusioned with their economic position to escape to the West, and also made the organization of labor much more difficult than in, say, France or Britain; and those same geographic dimensions, and the entrepreneurial opportunities within them, encouraged the development of a largely unreconstructed form of laissez-faire capitalism that has dominated the political culture of the nation (despite occasional counterattacks from the left). In consequence, the earnings gap between rich and poor is significantly larger in the United States than in any other advanced industrial society, and state expenditures on social services claim a lower share of GNP than in comparable countries except Japan, whose family-based support system for the poor and the aged appears much stronger.

This lack of class politics despite obvious socio-economic disparities had been possible because the nation's overall growth since the 1930s has offered the prospect of individual betterment to a majority of the population, and, disturbingly, because the poorest third of American society has not been mobilized to vote regularly. But given the different birthrates of whites on the one hand and blacks and Hispanics on the other, given the changing composition of the flow of immigrants into the United States, given also the economic metamorphosis that is leading to the loss of millions of relatively high-paying jobs in manufacturing, and the creation of millions of poorly paid jobs in services, it may be unwise to assume that the prevailing norms of the American political economy (such as low government social expenditures and low taxes on the rich) would be maintained if the nation entered a period of sustained economic difficulty caused by a plunging dollar and slow growth. An American polity that responds to external challenges by increasing defense expenditures, and reacts to the budgetary crisis by cutting existing social expenditures, runs the risk of provoking an eventual political backlash. There are no easy answers in dealing with the constant three-way tension between defense, consumption, and investment as national priorities.

Imperial Overstretch

This brings us, inevitably, to the delicate relationship between slow economic growth and high defense spending. The debate over the economics of defense spending is a heated one and—bearing in mind the size and variety of the American economy, the stimulus that can come from large government contracts, and the technological spin-offs from weapons research—the evidence does not point simply in one direction. But what is significant for our purposes is the comparative dimension. Although (as is often pointed out) defense expenditures amounted to ten percent of GNP under President Eisenhower and nine percent under President Kennedy, America's shares of global production and wealth were at that time around twice what they are today, and, more particularly, the American economy was not then facing challenges to either its traditional or its high-technology manufactures. The United States now devotes about seven percent of its GNP to defense spending, while its major economic rivals, especially Japan, allocate a far smaller proportion. If this situation continues, then America's rivals will have more funds free for civilian investment. If the United States continues to direct a huge proportion of its research and development activities toward military-related production while the Japanese and West Germans concentrate on commercial research and development, and if the Pentagon drains off the ablest of the country's scientists and engineers from the design and production of goods for the world market, while similar personnel in other countries are bringing out better consumer products, then it seems inevitable that the American share of world manufacturing will decline steadily, and likely that American economic growth rates will be slower than those of countries dedicated to the marketplace and less eager to channel resources into defense.

It is almost superfluous to say that these tendencies place the United States on the horns of a most acute, if long-term, dilemma. Simply because it is *the* global superpower, with military commitments far more extensive than those of a regional power like Japan or West Germany, it requires much larger defense forces. . . . Whose economy will decline *fastest*, relative to the economies of such expanding states as Japan, China, and so forth? A small investment in armaments may leave a globally overstretched power like the United States feeling vulnerable everywhere, but a very heavy investment in them, while bringing greater security in the short term, may so erode the commercial competitiveness of the American economy that the nation will be less secure in the long term.

Here, too, the historical precedents are not encouraging. Past experience shows that even as the relative economic strength of number-one countries has ebbed, the growing foreign challenges to their position have compelled them to allocate more and more of their resources to the military sector, which in turn has squeezed out productive investment and, over time, led to a downward spiral of slower growth, heavier taxes, deepening domestic splits over spending priorities, and a weakening capacity to bear the burdens of defense. If this, indeed, is the pattern of history, one is tempted to paraphrase Shaw's deadly serious quip and say: "Rome fell. Babylon fell. Scarsdale's turn will come."

How is one to interpret what is going on? And what, if anything, can be done about these problems? Far too many of the remarks made in political speeches suggest that while politicians worry more than they did about the nation's economic future, they tend to believe that the problems have quick and simple-minded solutions. For example, some call for tariffs—but they fail to address the charge that whenever industry and agriculture are protected, they become less productive. Others urge "competitiveness"—but they fail to explain how, say, American textile workers are to compete with textile workers earning only a twentieth of American wages. Still others put the blame for the decline of American efficiency on the government, which they say takes too much of the national income—but they fail to explain how the Swiss and the Germans, with their far higher tax rates, remain competitive on the world market. There are those who want to increase defense spending to meet perceived threats overseas—but they rarely concede that such a policy would further unbalance the economy. And there are those who want to reduce defense spending—but they rarely suggest which commitments (Israel? Korea? Egypt? Europe?) should go, in order to balance means and ends.

Above all, there is rarely any sense of the long-term context in which this American dilemma must be seen, or of the blindingly obvious point that the problem is not new. The study of world history might be the most useful endeavor for today's decision-makers. Such study would free politicians from the ethnocentric and temporal blinkers that so often restrict vision, allowing them to perceive some of the larger facts about international affairs.

The first of these is that the relative strengths of the leading nations have never remained constant, because the uneven rates of growth of different societies and technological and organizational breakthroughs bring greater advantage to one society than to another. For example, the coming of the long-range-gunned sailing ship and the rise of Atlantic trade after 1500 were not uniformly beneficial to the states of Europe—they benefited some much more than others. In the same way, the later development of steam power, and of the coal and metal resources upon which it relied, drastically increased the relative power of certain nations. Once their productive capacity was enhanced, countries would normally find it easier to sustain the burdens of spending heavily on armaments in peacetime, and of maintaining and supplying large armies and fleets in wartime. It sounds crudely mercantilistic to express it this way, but wealth is usually needed to underpin military power, and military power is usually needed to acquire and protect wealth. If, however, too large a proportion of a state's resources is diverted from the creation of wealth and allocated instead to military purposes, that is likely to lead to a weakening of national power over the long term. And if a state overextends itself strategically, by, say, conquering extensive territories or waging costly wars, it runs the risk that the benefits ultimately gained from external expansion may be outweighed by the great expense—a problem that becomes acute if the nation concerned has entered a period of relative economic decline. The history of the rise and fall of the leading countries since the advance of Western Europe in the sixteenth century— that is, of nations such as Spain, the Netherlands, France, Great Britain, and, currently, the United States—shows a significant correlation over the long term between productive and revenue-raising capacity on the one hand and military strength on the other.

Of course, both wealth *and* power are always relative. Three hundred years ago the German mercantilistic writer Philip von Hornigk observed that "whether a nation be today mighty and rich or not depends not on the abundance or security of its power or riches, but principally on whether its neighbors possess more or less of it."

The Netherlands in the mid-eighteenth century was richer in absolute terms than it had been a hundred years earlier, but by that stage it was much less of a Great Power, because neighbors like France and Britain had more power and riches. The France of 1914 was, absolutely, more powerful than the one of 1850—but that was little consolation when France was being eclipsed by a much stronger Germany. Britain has far greater wealth today than it had in its mid-Victorian prime, and its armed forces possess far more powerful weapons, but its share of world product has shrunk from about 25 percent to about three percent. If a nation has "more of it" than its contemporaries, things are fine; if not, there are problems.

This does not mean, however, that a nation's relative economic and military power will rise and fall in parallel. Most of the historical examples suggest that the trajectory of a state's military-territorial influence lags noticeably behind the trajectory of its relative economic strength. The reason for this is not difficult to grasp. An economically expanding power—Britain in the 1860s, the United States in the 1890s, Japan today—may well choose to become rich rather than to spend heavily on armaments. A half century later priorities may well have altered. The earlier economic expansion has brought with it overseas obligations: dependence on foreign markets and raw materials, military alliances, perhaps bases and colonies. Other, rival powers are now expanding economically at a faster rate, and wish in their turn to extend their influence abroad. The world has become a more competitive place, and the country's market shares are being eroded. Pessimistic observers talk of decline; patriotic statesmen call for "renewal."

In these more troubled circumstances the Great Power is likely to spend much more on defense than it did two generations earlier and yet still find the world to be less secure—simply because other powers have grown faster, and are becoming stronger. Imperial Spain spent much more money on its army in the troubled 1630s and 1640s than it had in the 1580s, when the Castilian economy was healthier. Britain's defense expenditures were far greater in 1910 than they were, say, at the time of Palmerston's death, in 1865, when the British economy was at its relative peak; but did any Britons at the later date feel more secure? The same problem appears to confront both the United States and the Soviet Union today. Great Powers in relative decline instinctively respond by spending more on security, thereby diverting potential resources from investment and compounding their long-term dilemma.

After the Second World War the position of the United States and the USSR as powers in a class by themselves appeared to be reinforced by the advent of nuclear weapons and delivery systems. The strategic and diplomatic landscape was now entirely different from that of 1900, let alone 1800. And yet the process of rise and fall among Great Powers had not ceased. Militarily, the United States and the USSR stayed in the forefront as the 1960s gave way to the 1970s and 1980s. . . . Over the same few decades, however, the global productive balances have been changing faster than ever before. The Third World's share of total manufacturing output and GNP, which was depressed to an all-time low in the decade after 1945, has steadily expanded. Europe has recovered from its wartime batterings and, in the form of the EEC, become the world's largest trading unit. The People's Republic of China is leaping forward at an impressive rate. Japan's postwar economic growth has been so phenomenal that, according to some measures, Japan recently overtook the Soviet Union in total GNP. Meanwhile, growth rates in both the United States and the USSR have become more sluggish, and those countries' shares of global production and wealth have shrunk dramatically since the 1960s. . . .

Although the United States is at present still pre-eminent economically and perhaps even militarily, it cannot avoid the two great tests that challenge the longevity of every major power that occupies the number-one position in world affairs. First, in the military-strategic realm, can it preserve a reasonable balance between the nation's perceived defense commitments and the means it possesses to maintain those commitments? And second, as an intimately related question, can it preserve the technological and economic bases of its power from relative erosion in the face of the ever-shifting patterns of global production? This test of American abilities will be the greater because America, like Imperial Spain around 1600 or the British Empire around 1900, bears a heavy burden of strategic commitments, made decades earlier, when the nation's political, economic, and military capacity to influence world affairs seemed so much more assured. The United States now runs the risk, so familiar to historians of the rise and fall of Great Powers, of what might be called "imperial overstretch": that is to say, decision-makers in Washington must face the awkward and enduring fact that the total of the United States's global interests and obligations is nowadays far too large for the country to be able to defend them all simultaneously.

To be sure, it is hardly likely that the United States would be called upon to defend all of its overseas interests simultaneously and unilaterally, unaided by the NATO members in Western Europe, Israel in the Middle East, or Japan, Australia, and possibly China in the Pacific. Nor are all the regional trends unfavorable to the United States with respect to defense. For example, while aggression by the unpredictable North Korean regime is always possible, it would hardly be welcomed by Beijing—furthermore, South Korea has grown to have more than twice the population and four times the GNP of the North. . . .

Despite such consolations, the fundamental grand-strategic problem remains: the United States today has roughly the same enormous array of military obligations across the globe that it had a quarter century ago, when its shares of world GNP, manufacturing production, military spending, and armed-forces personnel were much larger than they are now. In 1985, forty years after America's triumph in the Second World War and more than a decade after its pull-out from Vietnam, 526,000 members of the U.S. armed forces were abroad (including 64,000 afloat). That total is substantially more than the overseas deployments in peacetime of the military and naval forces of the British Empire at the height of its power. Nevertheless, in the opinion of the Joint Chiefs of Staff, and of many civilian experts, it is simply not enough. Despite a near-trebling of the American defense budget since the late 1970s, the numerical size of the armed forces on active duty has increased by just five percent. As the British and the French military found in their time, a nation with extensive overseas obligations will always have a more difficult manpower problem than a state that keeps its armed forces solely for home defense, and a politically liberal and economically laissez-faire society sensitive to the unpopularity of conscription will have a greater problem than most.

Managing Relative Decline

Ultimately, the only answer to whether the United States can preserve its position is *no*—for it simply has not been given to any one society to remain permanently ahead of all the others, freezing the patterns of different growth rates, technological advance, and military development that have existed since time immemorial. But historical precedents do not imply that the United States is destined to shrink to the relative obscurity of former leading powers like Spain and the Netherlands, or to disintegrate like the Roman and Austro-Hungarian empires; it is too large to do the former, and probably too homogeneous to do the latter. Even the British analogy, much favored in the current political-science literature, is not a good one if it ignores the differences in scale. The geographic size, population, and natural resources of Great Britain suggest that it ought to possess roughly three or four percent of the world's wealth and power, all other things being equal. But precisely because all other things are never equal, a peculiar set of historical and technological circumstances permitted Great Britain to possess, say, 25 percent of the world's wealth and power in its prime. Since those favorable circumstances have disappeared, all that it has been doing is returning to its more "natural" size. In the same way, it

may be argued, the geographic extent, population, and natural resources of the United States suggest that it ought to possess 16 or 18
percent of the world's wealth and power. But because of historical and
technological circumstances favorable to it, that share rose to 40 percent or more by 1945, and what we are witnessing today is the ebbing
away from that extraordinarily high figure to a more natural share.
That decline is being masked by the country's enormous military capability at present, and also by its success in internationalizing American
capitalism and culture. Yet even when it has declined to the position
of occupying no more than its natural share of the world's wealth and
power, a long time into the future, the United States will still be a very
significant power in a multipolar world, simply because of its size.

The task facing American statesmen over the next decades, therefore, is to recognize that broad trends are under way, and that there is
a need to manage affairs so that the relative erosion of America's position takes place slowly and smoothly, unaided by policies that bring
short-term advantage but long-term disadvantage. Among the realities
that statesmen, from the President down, must be alert to are these:
that technological and therefore socio-economic change is occurring in
the world faster than it has ever before; that the international community is much more politically and culturally diverse than has been assumed, and is defiant of simplistic remedies offered by either Washington or Moscow for its problems; that the economic and productive
power balances are no longer tilted as favorably in America's direction
as they were in 1945. Even in the military realm there are signs of a
certain redistribution of the balances, away from a bipolar and toward
a multipolar system, in which American economic and military
strength is likely to remain greater than that of any other individual
country but will cease to be as disproportionate as it was in the decades
immediately after the Second World War. In all the discussions about
the erosion of American leadership it needs to be repeated again and
again that the decline is relative, not absolute, and is therefore perfectly natural, and that a serious threat to the real interests of the
United States can come only from a failure to adjust sensibly to the
new world order.

Just how well can the American system adjust to a state of relative
decline? Already, a growing awareness of the gap between U.S. obligations and U.S. power has led to questions by gloomier critics about the
overall political culture in which Washington decision-makers have to
operate. It has been suggested with increasing frequency that a country
needing to reformulate its grand strategy in the light of the larger, un-
controllable changes taking place in world affairs may be ill served
by an electoral system that seems to paralyze foreign-policy decision-
making every two years. Foreign policy may be undercut by the extraordinary pressures applied by lobbyists, political-action commit-

tees, and other interest groups, all of whom, by definition, are prejudiced in favor of this or that policy change, and by the simplification of
vital but complex international and strategic issues, inherent to mass
media whose time and space for such things are limited and whose
raison d'être is chiefly to make money and only secondarily to inform.
It may also be undercut by the still powerful escapist urges in the
American social culture, which are perhaps understandable in terms of
the nation's frontier past but hinder its coming to terms with today's
complex, integrated world and with other cultures and ideologies. Finally, the country may not always be helped by the division of decision-making powers that was deliberately created when it was geographically and strategically isolated from the rest of the world, two
centuries ago, and had time to find a consensus on the few issues that
actually concerned foreign policy. This division may be less service-
able now that the United States is a global superpower, often called
upon to make swift decisions vis-à-vis countries that enjoy far fewer
constraints. No one of these obstacles prevents the execution of a coherent, long-term American grand strategy. However, their cumulative
effect is to make it difficult to carry out policy changes that seem to
hurt special interests and occur in an election year. It may therefore
be here, in the cultural and political realms, that the evolution of an
overall American policy to meet the twenty-first century will be subjected to the greatest test.

Nevertheless, given the considerable array of strengths still possessed by the United States, it ought not in theory to be beyond the
talents of successive Administrations to orchestrate this readjustment
so as, in Walter Lippmann's classic phrase, to bring "into balance . . .
the nation's commitments and the nation's power." Although there is
no single state obviously preparing to take over America's global burdens, in the way that the United States assumed Britain's role in the
1940s, the country has fewer problems than had Imperial Spain, be-
sieged by enemies on all fronts, or the Netherlands, squeezed between
France and England, or the British Empire, facing numerous chal-
lengers. The tests before the United States as it heads toward the
twenty-first century are certainly daunting, perhaps especially in the
economic sphere; but the nation's resources remain considerable, *if*
they can be properly utilized and *if* there is a judicious recognition of
both the limitations and the opportunities of American power.

Kevin P. Phillips

KEVIN P. PHILLIPS (1940–   ) *is president of American Political Research Corporation. He is a television commentator, newspaper writer, and author of* The Emerging Republican Majority *(1969),* Post-Conservative America *(1982), and* The Politics of Rich and Poor *(1990).*

The 1980's were the triumph of upper America—an ostentatious celebration of wealth, the political ascendancy of the rich and the glorification of capitalism, free markets and finance. Not only did the concentration of wealth quietly intensify, but the sums involved took a megaleap. The definition of who's rich—and who's no longer rich— changed as radically during the Reagan era as it did during the great nouveaux riches eras of the late 19th century and the 1920s, periods whose excesses preceded the great reformist upheavals of the Progressive era and the New Deal.

But while money, greed and luxury became the stuff of popular culture, few people asked why such great wealth had concentrated at the top and whether this was the result of public policy. Political leaders, even those who professed to care about the armies of homeless sleeping on grates and other sad evidence of a polarized economy, had little to say about the Republican Party's historical role: to revitalize capitalism but also to tilt power, Government largess, more wealth and income toward the richest portion of the population.

The public, however, understood and worried about this Republican bias, if we can trust late 80's opinion polls; nevertheless, the Democrats largely shunned the issue in the '88 election, a reluctance their predecessors also displayed during Republican booms of the Gilded Age of the late 19th century and the Roaring Twenties.

As the decade ended, too many stretch limousines in Manhattan, too many yacht jams off Newport Beach and too many fur coats in Aspen foreshadowed a significant shift of mood. Only for so long would strungout $35,000-a-year families enjoy magazine articles about the hundred most successful businessmen in Dallas, or television shows about greed and glitz. Class structures may be weak in the United States, but populist sentiments run high. The political pendulum has swung in the past, and may be ready to swing again.

Indeed, money politics—be it avarice of financiers or the question of who will pay for the binges of the 80's—is shaping up as a prime theme for the 1990's. As we shall see, there is a historical cycle to such shifts: Whenever Republicans are in power long enough to transform economic policy from a middle-class orientation to capitalist over-drive, the rich get so far ahead that a popular reaction inevitably fol-lows, with the Democrats usually tagging along, rather than leading.

But this time, the nature of the reaction against excess is likely to be different. The previous gilded ages occurred when America was on the economic rise in the world. The 1980's, on the other hand, turned into an era of paper entrepreneurialism, reflecting a nation consuming, rearranging and borrowing more than it built. For the next generation of populists who would like to rearrange American wealth, the bad news is that a large amount of it has already been redistributed—to Japan, West Germany and to the other countries that took Reagan-era I.O.U.'s and credit slips.

Society matrons, Wall Street arbitrageurs, Palm Beach real-estate agents and other money-conscious Americans picking up USA Today on May 22, 1987, must have been at first bewildered and then amused by the top story. In describing a Harris survey of the attitudes of upper-bracket citizens, the article summed up the typical respondent as "rich. Very. He's part of the thinnest economic upper crust: households with incomes of more than $100,000 a year."

A surprising number of 1980's polls and commentaries contributed to this naïve perception—that "rich" somehow started at $50,000 or $100,000 a year, and that gradations above that were somehow less important. The truth is that the critical concentration of wealth in the United States was developing a higher levels—decamillionaires, centimillionaires, half-billionaires and billionaires. Garden-variety American millionaires had become so common that there were about 1.5 million of them by 1989.

In fact, even many families with what seemed like good incomes— $50,000 a year, say, in Wichita, Kan., or $90,000 a year in New York City (almost enough to qualify as "rich," according to USA Today)— found it hard to make ends meet because of the combined burden of Federal income and Social Security taxes, plus the soaring costs of state taxes, housing, health care and children's education. What few under-stood was that real economic status and leisure-class purchasing power had moved higher up the ladder, to groups whose emergence and rela-tive affluence Middle America could scarcely comprehend.

No parallel upsurge of riches had been seen since the late 19th century, the era of the Vanderbilts, Morgans and Rockefellers. It was the truly wealthy, more than anyone else, who flourished under Rea-gan. Calculations in a Brookings Institution study found that the share of national income going to the wealthiest 1 percent rose from 8.1 percent in 1981 to 14.7 percent in 1986. Between 1981 and 1989, the net worth of the Forbes 400 richest Americans nearly tripled. At the same time, the division between them and the rest of the country became a yawning gap. In 1980, corporate chief executive officers, for example, made roughly 40 times the income of average factory workers. By 1989, C.E.O.'s were making *93 times as much.*

Finance alone built few billion-dollar fortunes in the 1980's relative to service industries like real estate and communications, but it is hard to overstate Wall Street's role during the decade, partly because Federal monetary and fiscal policies favored financial assets and because deregulation promoted new debt techniques and corporate restructuring.

Selling stock to retail clients, investment management firms or mutual funds paid well; repackaging, remortgaging or dismantling a Fortune 500 company paid magnificently. In 1981, analysts estimate, the financial community's dozen biggest earners made $5 million to $20 million a year. In 1988, despite the stock-market collapse the October before, the dozen top earners made $50 million to $200 million.

The redistribution of American wealth raised questions not just about polarization, but also about trivialization. Less and less wealth was going to people who produced something. Services were ascendant—from fast food to legal advice, investment vehicles to data bases. It is one thing for new technologies to reduce demand for obsolescent professions, enabling society to concentrate more resources in emerging sectors like health and leisure. But the distortion lies in the disproportionate rewards to society's economic, legal and cultural manipulators—from lawyers and financial advisers to advertising executives, merchandisers, media magnates and entertainers.

A related boom and distortion occurred in nonfinancial assets—art and homes, in particular. Art and antiques appreciated fourfold in the Reagan era, to the principal benefit of the richest 200,000 or 300,000 families. Similar if lesser explosions in art prices took place in the Gilded Age and in the 1920's. While the top one-half of 1 percent of Americans rolled in money, the luxuries they craved—from Picassos and 18th-century English furniture to Malibu beach houses—soared in markets virtually auxiliary to those in finance.

Meanwhile, everyone knew there was pain in society's lower ranks, from laid-off steelworkers to foreclosed farmers. A disproportionate number of female, black, Hispanic and young Americans lost ground in the 1980's despite the progress of upscale minorities in each category. According to one study, for example, the inflation-adjusted income for families with children headed by an adult under 30 collapsed by roughly one-fourth between 1973 and 1984.

Even on an overall basis, median family and household incomes showed only small inflation-adjusted gains between 1980 and 1988. Middle America was quietly hurting too.

While corporate presidents and chairmen feasted in the 1980's, as many as 1.5 million midlevel management jobs are estimated to have been lost during those years. Blue-collar America paid a larger price, but suburbia, where fathers rushed to catch the 8:10 train to the city, was counting its casualties, too. "Middle managers have become insecure," observed Peter F. Drucker in September 1988, "and they feel unbelievably hurt. They feel like slaves on an auction block."

American transitions of the magnitude of the capitalist blowout of the 1980's have usually coincided with a whole new range of national economic attitudes. Evolving government policies—from tax cuts to high interest rates—seem distinct, but they are actually linked.

Whether in the late 19th century, the 1920's or the 1980's, the country has witnessed conservative politics, a reduced role for government, entrepreneurialism and admiration of business, corporate restructuring and mergers, tax reduction, declining inflation, pain in states that rely on commodities like oil and wheat, rising inequality and concentration of wealth, and a buildup of debt and speculation. The scope of these trends has been impressive—and so has their repetition, though the two periods of the 20th century have involved increasingly more paper manipulation and less of the raw vigor typical of the late 19th-century railroad and factory expansion.

Federal policy from 1981 to 1988 enormously affected investment, speculation and the creation and distribution of wealth and income, just as in the past.

The reduction or elimination of Federal income taxes was a goal in previous capitalist heydays. But it was a personal preoccupation for Ronald Reagan, whose antipathy toward income taxes dated back to his high-earning Hollywood days when a top tax bracket of 91 percent in the 40's made it foolish to work beyond a certain point. Under him, the top personal tax bracket would drop from 70 percent to 28 percent in only seven years. For the first time since the era of Franklin D. Roosevelt, tax policy was fundamentally rearranging its class loyalties.

Reaganite theorists reminded the country that the Harding-Coolidge income-tax cuts—from a top rate of 73 percent in 1920 to 25 percent in 1925—helped create the boom of the 20's. Back then, just as in the 80's, the prime beneficiaries were the top 5 percent of Americans, people who rode the cutting edge of the new technology of autos, radios and the like, emerging service industries, including new practices like advertising and consumer finance, a booming stock market and unprecedented real-estate development. Disposable income soared for the rich, and with it, conspicuous consumption and financial speculation. After the 1929 crash and the advent of the New Deal, tax rates rose again; the top rate reached 79 percent by 1936 and 91 percent right after the war. In 1964, the rate fell in two stages, to 77 percent and then to 70 percent.

Under Reagan, Federal budget policy, like tax changes, became a factor in the realignment of wealth, especially after the 1981–82 recession sent the deficit soaring. The slack was made up by money borrowed at home and abroad at high cost. The first effect lay in who received more Government funds. Republican constituencies—military producers and installations, agribusiness, bondholders and the elderly—clearly benefited, while decreases in social programs hurt Democratic interests and constituencies: the poor, big cities, housing, education. Equally to the point, the huge payments of high-interest charges on the growing national debt enriched the wealthy, who bought the bonds that kept Government afloat.

Prosperous individuals and financial institutions were beneficiaries of Government policies in other ways. Starting in the Carter years, Congress began to deregulate the financial industry; but the leap came in the early 1980's, when deposit and loan interest ceilings were removed. To attract deposits, financial institutions raised their interest rates, which rose and even exceeded record postwar levels. The small saver profited, but the much larger gain, predictably, went to the wealthy. (The benefits of high interest were intensified of course, by the declining maximum tax rate on dividend and interest income. The explosion of after-tax unearned income for the top 1 percent of Americans was just that—an explosion.)

The savings and loan crisis now weighing on American taxpayers also had roots in deregulation. Before 1982, savings and loan associations were required to place almost all their loans in home mortgages, a relatively safe and stable class of assets. But in 1982, after soaring interest rates turned millions of low-interest mortgages into undesirable assets, a new law allowed savings and loans to invest their funds more freely—100 percent in commercial real-estate ventures if they so desired. Like banks in the 1920's, many thrifts proceeded to gamble with their deposits, and by 1988 many had lost. Gamblers and speculators enriched themselves even as they stuck other Americans with the tab.

Reagan's permissiveness toward mergers, antitrust enforcement and new forms of speculative finance was likewise typical of Republican go-go conservatism. Unnerving parallels were made between the Wall Street raiders of the 1980's—Ivan Boesky and T. Boone Pickens—and the takeover pools of the 1920's, when high-powered operators would combine to "boom" a particular stock. For a small group of Americans at the top, the pickings were enormous.

An egregious misperception of late 20th-century politics is to associate only Democrats with extremes of public debt. Before 1933, conservatives—Federalists, Whigs and Republicans alike—sponsored Government indebtedness and used high-interest payments to redistribute wealth upward.

In addition, Republican eras were noted for a huge expansion of private debt. In the 1920's, individual, consumer and corporate debt kept setting record levels, aided by new techniques like installment purchases and margin debt for purchasing securities. In the kindred 80's, total private and public debt grew from $4.2 trillion to more than $10 trillion. And just as they had 60 years earlier, new varieties of debt became an art form.

Government fiscal strategists were equally loose. In part to avoid the deficit-reduction mandates of the Gramm-Rudman-Hollings Act, they allowed Federal credit programs, including student and housing loans, to balloon from $300 billion in 1984 to $500 billion in 1989.

In contrast to previous capitalist blowouts, the fast-and-loose Federal debt strategies of the 80's did not simply rearrange assets within the country but served to transfer large amounts of the nation's wealth overseas as well. America's share of global wealth expanded in the Gilded Age and again in the 1920's. The late 1980's, however, marked a significant downward movement: one calculation, by the Japanese newspaper Nihon Keizai Shimbun, had Japan overtaking the United States with estimated comparative assets of $43.7 trillion in 1987 for Japan versus $36.2 trillion for the United States.

The United States was losing relative purchasing power on a grand scale. There might be more wealthy Americans than ever before, but foreigners commanded greater resources. On the 1989 Forbes list of world's billionaires, the top 12, with the exception of one American, were all foreigners—from Japan, Europe, Canada and South Korea. Dollar millionaires, once the envy of the world, were becoming an outdated elite.

This shift partly reflected the ebb of America's postwar preeminence. Yet the same Reagan policies that moved riches internally also accelerated the shift of world wealth, beginning with the budget deficits of the early 1980's but intensifying after the ensuring devaluation of the dollar from 1985 to 1988.

If the devalued dollar made the Japanese, French and Germans relatively richer, it also increased their purchasing power in the United States, turning the country into a bargain basement for overseas buyers. This is the explanation for the surging foreign acquisition of properties, from Fortune 500 companies to Rockefeller Center in Manhattan and a large share of the office buildings in downtown Los Angeles.

The dollar's decline also pushed per capita gross national product and comparative wages in the United States below those of a number of Western European nations. The economist Lester C. Thurow summed up the predicament: "When it comes to wealth, we can argue about domestic purchasing power. But, in terms of international purchasing power, the United States is now only the ninth wealthiest country in the world in terms of per capita G.N.P. We have been surpassed by Austria, Switzerland, the Netherlands, West Germany, Denmark, Sweden, Norway and Japan."

Not everyone looked askance at foreign wealth and investment. American cities and states welcomed it. From the textile towns of South Carolina to the rolling hills of Ohio, foreigners were helping declining regions to reverse their fate. Yet as Warren Buffett, the investor, said: "We are much like a wealthy family that annually sells acreage so that it can sustain a life style unwarranted by its current output. Until the plantation is gone, it's all pleasure and no pain. In the end, however, the family will have traded the life of an owner for the life of a tenant farmer."

Nowhere was Japanese investment more obvious than in Hawaii, where real estate moguls from Tokyo pronounced the property they were grabbing up "almost free." An economist at a Hawaiian bank warned that the state was "a kind of test lab for what's facing the whole country." Indeed, in 1988, broader foreign ambitions were apparent. The author Daniel Burstein quoted Masaaki Kurokawa, then head of Japan's Nomura Securities International, who raised with American dinner guests the possibility of turning California into a joint U.S.-Japanese economic community.

Public concern over America's international weakness had been a factor in Ronald Reagan's election back in 1980. Voters had wanted a more aggressive leader than Jimmy Carter. For various reasons, the great things promised were not delivered. Reagan could re-create a sense of military prowess with his attacks on Grenada and Libya. But in the global economy he took a country that had been the world's biggest creditor in 1980 and turned it into the world's largest debtor. Despite opinion polls documenting public concern about this erosion, surprisingly little was made of the issue in the 1988 Presidential campaign, possibly because the Democrats could not develop a coherent domestic and international alternative.

Much of the new emphasis in the 1980's on tax reduction and the aggressive accumulation of wealth reflected the Republican Party's long record of support for unabashed capitalism. It was no fluke that three important Republican supremacies coincided with and helped generate the Gilded Age, the Roaring Twenties and the Reagan-Bush years.

Part of the reason survival-of-the-fittest periods are so relentless, however, rests on the performance of the Democrats as history's second most enthusiastic capitalist party. They do not interfere with capi-

talist momentum, but wait for excesses and the inevitable popular reaction.

In the United States, elections arguably play a more important cultural and economic role than in other lands. Because we lack a hereditary aristocracy or Establishment, our leadership elites and the alignment of wealth are more the product of political cycles than they are
elsewhere. Capitalism is maneuvered more easily in the United States,
pushed in new regional and sectoral directions. As a result, the genius
of American politics—failing only in the Civil War—has been to manage through ballot boxes the problems that less fluid societies resolve
with barricades and with party structures geared to class warfare.

Because we are a mobile society, Americans tolerate one of the
largest disparities in the industrial world between top and bottom incomes, as people from the middle move to the top, and vice versa.
Opportunity has counted more than equality.

But if circulating elites are a reality, electoral politics is an important traffic controller. From the time of Thomas Jefferson, the nation
has undulated in 28- to 36-year waves as each watershed election puts
a new dominant region, culture, ideology or economic interest (or combination) into the White House, changing the country's direction. But
after a decade or two, the new forces lose touch with the public, excessively empower their own elites and become a target for a new round
of populist reform. Only the United States among major nations reveals such recurrent electoral behavior over two centuries.

The Republicans rode such a wave into office in 1968, as a middle-
class, anti-elite correction, successfully squelching the social permissiveness and disorder of the 60's. Significantly, each Republican coalition—from Lincoln's to Nixon's—began by emphasizing national
themes and unity symbols, while subordinating commercial and financial interests.

But it is the second stage—dynamic capitalism, market economics
and the concentration of wealth—that the Republican Party is all
about. When Republicans are in power long enough, they ultimately
find themselves embracing limited government, less regulation of
business, reduced taxation, disinflation and high real interest rates.
During America's first two centuries, these policies shaped the three
periods that would incubate the biggest growth of American millionaires (or, by the 1980's, billionaires). History suggests that it takes a
decade or more for the Republican Party to shift from broad middle
class nationalism into capitalist overdrive, and the lapse of 12 years
between the first Nixon inauguration in 1969 and the first Reagan inauguration repeats this transformation.

Nixon, like the previous Republican nationalist Presidents Abraham Lincoln and William McKinley, was altogether middle class, as

was his "new majority" Republicanism. He had no interest in unbridled capitalism during his 1969–74 Presidency.

In fact, many of the new adherents recruited for the Republican coalition in 1968 and 1972 were wooed with the party's populist attacks on inflation, big government, social engineering and the Liberal Establishment. Many Republican voters of that era embraced outsider and anti-elite values, and like similar participants in previous Republican national coalitions, they would become uneasy in the 1980's as Reagan or Bush Republicanism embraced Beverly Hills or Yale culture and the economics of leveraged buyouts, not of Main Street.

Besides this uneasiness, reflected in opinion polls, a second sign that a conservative cycle is moving toward its climax has been the extent to which Democratic politics has been cooperative: when wealth is in fashion, Democrats go along. The solitary Democratic President of the Gilded Age, Grover Cleveland, was a conservative with close Wall Street connections. In the 20's, the Democratic Presidential nominees in both 1920 (James Cox, an Ohio publisher) and 1924 (John W. Davis, a corporate lawyer) were in the Cleveland mold. Alfred E. Smith, who ran in 1928, would eventually oppose Roosevelt and the New Deal. In the 20's, Congressional Democrats competed with Republicans to cut upper-bracket and corporate taxes.

Fifty years later, Jimmy Carter, the only Democratic President to interrupt the long Republican hegemony after 1968, was accused by the historian Arthur M. Schlesinger Jr. of an "eccentric effort to carry the Democratic Party back to Grover Cleveland." Despite his support for substantial new Federal regulation, Carter clearly deviated from his party's larger post-New Deal norm. He built foundations that would become conservative architecture under Reagan: economic deregulation; capital gains tax reduction and the tight-money policies of the Federal Reserve. (The Feds chairman, Paul A. Volcker, was a Carter appointee) Congressional Democrats even echoed their policies of the 1920's by colluding in the bipartisan tax-bracket changes of 1981 and 1986.

Thus, the Democrats could hardly criticize Reagan's tax reductions. For the most part, they laid little groundwork for an election-year critique in 1988, leaving the issue to Jesse Jackson, whose appeal was limited by his race and third-world rhetoric, and to noncandidates like Mario M. Cuomo. Michael S. Dukakis was obviously uncomfortable with populist politics. Though several consultants and economists urged him to pick up the theme of economic inequality, Dukakis made competence, not ideology, his initial campaign issue. Only in late October, with his campaign crumbling, did the Democratic candidate reluctantly convert to a more traditional party line. It came too late.

Republican strategists could hardly believe their luck. Said Lee Atwater, Bush's campaign manager, after the election: "The way to win a Presidential race against the Republicans is to develop the class-war-fare issue, as Dukakis did at the end—to divide up the haves and have-nots and to try to reinvigorate the New Deal coalition and to attack."

On the surface, this was a missed Democratic opportunity. But the lesson of history is that the party of Cleveland, Carter and Dukakis has rarely rushed its anti-elite corrective role. There would be no rush again in 1988—nor, indeed, in 1989.

Early in his presidency, George Bush replaced the Coolidge portrait hung by Ronald Reagan in the White House with one of Theodore Roosevelt, reflecting Bush's belief in T. R.'s commitment to conservation, patrician reform and somewhat greater regulatory involvement.

Yet there has not been too much evidence of a kinder, gentler America beyond softer, more conciliatory rhetoric. The budget remained unkind to any major expansion of domestic programs, and Bush's main tax objective was a reduction in the capital gains rate, a shift that critics said would continue to concentrate benefits among the top 1 percent of Americans.

By spring 1990, Washington politicians confronted the most serious debt- and credit-related problems since the bank failures, collapsed stock prices, farm foreclosures and European war debt defaults of the Great Depression. From the savings and loan associations bailout to junk bonds, from soaring bankruptcies and shaky real-estate markets to Japanese influence in the bond market, Federal policy makers were forced to realize that a crucial task—and peril—of the 1990's would involve cleaning up after the previous decade's credit-card parties and speculative distortions.

In May, the facade of successful deficit reduction crumbled as Administration officials confessed that bailing out insolvent savings and loans could cost as much as a half-trillion dollars. It became clear that taxes would have to rise. In California, where the anti-tax revolt began more than a decade ago, the approval by the state's voters earlier this month of an increase in the gasoline tax was seen by many as a sign of public willingness to come to grips with the fiscal deficiencies of the 1980s.

Even some Democrats who previously collaborated with Republican economics have begun to argue that the rich who had made so much money in the 80's should bear a larger share of the new burdens of the 90's. A number of Republicans share this disquiet. The Senate minority leader, Bob Dole of Russell, Kan., insisted in late 1989 that if the White House wanted to cut capital-gains taxes for the prosperous, it should also raise the minimum wage for the poor. Last month, the House Republican leader, Robert H. Michel of Peoria, Ill., was reported to favor an increase in the tax rate for the top 1 percent of Americans, from 28 percent to 33 percent. The second-ranking Republican leader in the House, Newt Gingrich of Georgia, suggested in April that conservatives, too, had to develop some ideas for economic redistribution.

Meanwhile, opinion poll after opinion poll has shown lopsided voter support for raising the income-tax rate for people making more than $80,000, $100,000 or $200,000. The 1990's seem ready to reflect a new anti-Wall Street, anticorporate and antigreed outlook set forth in books (and coming movies) like "Bonfire of the Vanities," "Liar's Poker" and "Barbarians at the Gate."

Nor was the changing mood apparent only in the United States. Kindred psychologies and political analyses could also be seen in other countries like Britain, Japan and Canada, where 1980's financial and real-estate booms likewise concentrated wealth in the hands of the very rich and increased economic inequity. A headline last month in the Financial Times of London could have been written in the United States: "The Rich Get Nervous."

Whether the populist reactions that followed past boom periods recur in the 90's no one can know. But there could be no doubt that the last decade ended as it had begun: with a rising imperative for a new political and economic philosophy, and growing odds that the 1990's will be a very different chapter than the 1980's in the annals of American wealth and power.

INDEX